OIL SHALE AND TAR SANDS TECHNOLOGY

3

OIL SHALE
AND TAR SANDS
TECHNOLOGY
Recent Developments

2 1

M.W. Ranney

6 **NOYES DATA CORPORATION**

5 Park Ridge, New Jersey, U.S.A.

7 1979

Sole distribution in the UK by:
Gothard House Publications
Gothard House
Henley-on-Thames, Oxon
RG9 1AJ   Tel. 049 12 3602

Published in the United States of America by
Noyes Data Corporation
Noyes Building, Park Ridge, New Jersey 07656

Library of Congress Cataloging in Publication Data

Ranney, Maurice William, 1934-
Oil shale and tar sands technology.

(Energy technology review ; no. 49) (Chemical
technology review ; no. 137)
Includes index.
1. Liquid fuels--Patents. 2. Shale oils--
Patents. 3. Oil-shales--Patents. 4. Oil sands--
Patents. I. Title. II. Series. III. Series:
Chemical technology review ; no. 137)
TP343.R334   665'.5   79-16122
ISBN 0-8155-0769-0

FOREWORD

The detailed, descriptive information in this book is based on U.S. patents, issued since March 1975, that deal with the technology of oil shale and tar sands. This title contains all recent advances since our previous title *Oil from Shale and Tar Sands* published in 1975. This new book also contains an introductory overview of the subject.

This book serves a double purpose in that it supplies detailed technical information and can be used as a guide to the U.S. patent literature in this field. By indicating all the information that is significant, and eliminating legal jargon and juristic phraseology, this book presents an advanced, commercially oriented review of recent advances in the technology of oil shale and tar sands.

The U.S. patent literature is the largest and most comprehensive collection of technical information in the world. There is more practical, commercial, timely process information assembled here than is available from any other source. The technical information obtained from a patent is extremely reliable and comprehensive; sufficient information must be included to avoid rejection for "insufficient disclosure." These patents include practically all of those issued on the subject in the United States during the period under review; there has been no bias in the selection of patents for inclusion.

The patent literature covers a substantial amount of information not available in the journal literature. The patent literature is a prime source of basic commercially useful information. This information is overlooked by those who rely primarily on the periodical journal literature. It is realized that there is a lag between a patent application on a new process development and the granting of a patent, but it is felt that this may roughly parallel or even anticipate the lag in putting that development into commercial practice.

Many of these patents are being utilized commercially. Whether used or not, they offer opportunities for technological transfer. Also, a major purpose of this book is to describe the number of technical possibilities available, which may open up profitable areas of research and development. The information contained in this book will allow you to establish a sound background before launching into research in this field.

Advanced composition and production methods developed by Noyes Data are employed to bring these durably bound books to you in a minimum of time. Special techniques are used to close the gap between "manuscript" and "completed book." Industrial technology is progressing so rapidly that time-honored, conventional typesetting, binding and shipping methods are no longer suitable. We have by-passed the delays in the conventional book publishing cycle and provide the user with an effective and convenient means of reviewing up-to-date information in depth.

The table of contents is organized in such a way as to serve as a subject index. Other indexes by company, inventor and patent number help in providing easy access to the information contained in this book.

15 Reasons Why the U.S. Patent Office Literature Is Important to You —

1. The U.S. patent literature is the largest and most comprehensive collection of technical information in the world. There is more practical commercial process information assembled here than is available from any other source.

2. The technical information obtained from the patent literature is extremely comprehensive; sufficient information must be included to avoid rejection for "insufficient disclosure."

3. The patent literature is a prime source of basic commercially utilizable information. This information is overlooked by those who rely primarily on the periodical journal literature.

4. An important feature of the patent literature is that it can serve to avoid duplication of research and development.

5. Patents, unlike periodical literature, are bound by definition to contain new information, data and ideas.

6. It can serve as a source of new ideas in a different but related field, and may be outside the patent protection offered the original invention.

7. Since claims are narrowly defined, much valuable information is included that may be outside the legal protection afforded by the claims.

8. Patents discuss the difficulties associated with previous research, development or production techniques, and offer a specific method of overcoming problems. This gives clues to current process information that has not been published in periodicals or books.

9. Can aid in process design by providing a selection of alternate techniques. A powerful research and engineering tool.

10. Obtain licenses — many U.S. chemical patents have not been developed commercially.

11. Patents provide an excellent starting point for the next investigator.

12. Frequently, innovations derived from research are first disclosed in the patent literature, prior to coverage in the periodical literature.

13. Patents offer a most valuable method of keeping abreast of latest technologies, serving an individual's own "current awareness" program.

14. Copies of U.S. patents are easily obtained from the U.S. Patent Office at 50¢ a copy.

15. It is a creative source of ideas for those with imagination.

CONTENTS AND SUBJECT INDEX

INTRODUCTION AND OVERVIEW

OIL SHALE

Information in this section is based on *Energy Analysis and Oil Shale Reserves* (NTIS N78-31584/3WE) by D.F. Hemming of the Energy Research Group, The Open University, Milton Keynes, England; and *Ground Disposal of Oil Shale Wastes: A Review with an Indexed Annotated Bibliography Through 1976,* prepared for the U.S. Department of Energy, under DOE Contract EY-76-C-06-1830, by R.C. Routson and R.M. Bean of Battelle Pacific Northwest Laboratories.

Introduction

Oil shales are widely distributed throughout the world with known deposits in every continent. Shales have been used in the past as a source of fuel in many parts of the world including Scotland, Sweden, France, South Africa, Australia, U.S.S.R., Brazil, and the United States.

The oil shale industry in the United States was an important part of the U.S. economy prior to the discovery of crude oil in 1859 when it virtually disappeared with the availability of vast supplies of cheap domestic fuel. Interest in shale revived in the 1920s as domestic reserves of crude oil began to decline, but discoveries of large quantities of oil in Texas again set aside the hopes of an embryonic oil shale industry. More recently, cheap supplies of oil from the Middle East have supplemented the United States' domestic supplies as requirements for liquid fuels have increased and domestic production has fallen.

It remains to be seen if the desire for energy self-sufficiency will again swing the balance in favor of the development of the western oil shales. At present, oil shale is exploited in only two countries—the U.S.S.R. where it is fed directly into a power station for electricity generation, and in China where oil production has been estimated at about 40,000 bpd.

1

Description of Oil Shale

Oil shale is not a shale nor does it contain oil. Oil shales are geologically classified as marlstones because of a large percentage of carbonates. Synthetic crude oil (syncrude) is produced only after addition of heat (retorting) and prerefining the retort product. Average mineral composition of oil shales averaging 85 liters/metric ton (l/MT) is given in Table 1.1. These shales are composed of about 86% mineral matter and 14% organic matter. Organic matter that occurs in oil shale is a resinous solid, not an oily liquid.

Table 1.1

Estimated Mineral Composition	Percent
Carbonates, principally dolomite	48
Feldspar	21
Quartz	13
Clay, principally illite	13
Analcite	4
Pyrite	1
Total	100

Source: DOE EY-76-C-06-1830

Table 1.2 gives the chemical composition of the organic matter. The organic matter in oil shale is composed of bitumen, about 10%, and kerogen, about 90%. Bitumen is a heteroatomic polymer soluble in many organic solvents. Kerogen is a heteroatomic polymer having a molecular weight of greater than 3,000 and is insoluble in most organic solvents. The kerogen subunits are cross-linked to one another by oxygen and sulfur giving kerogen a continuous three dimensional molecular structure throughout an oil shale formation. The minerals are scattered throughout the kerogen network. Kerogen and bitumen are thermally unstable and, with the application of heat (250°C or greater), thermally decompose to form gaseous and liquid products that can be refined to syncrude.

Table 1.2

Ultimate Composition	Percent
Carbon	81
Hydrogen	10
Nitrogen	2
Sulfur	1
Oxygen	6
Total	100

Source: DOE EY-76-C-06-1830

Location and Estimated Potential Reserves

Figure 1.1 gives the location of known oil shale deposits in the U.S.; however, only the Green River Formation is considered to contain deposits of present commercial interest (Figure 1.1 and Figure 1.2). Areas shown in Figure 1.2 represent approximately 11 million acres. The federal government has title to approximately 80% of this land. Although oil shale resource estimates vary widely, it is indeed a large resource even by the most conservative estimates and is of a similar magnitude to the world's known petroleum reserves.

Figure 1.1: Oil Shale Deposits of the United States

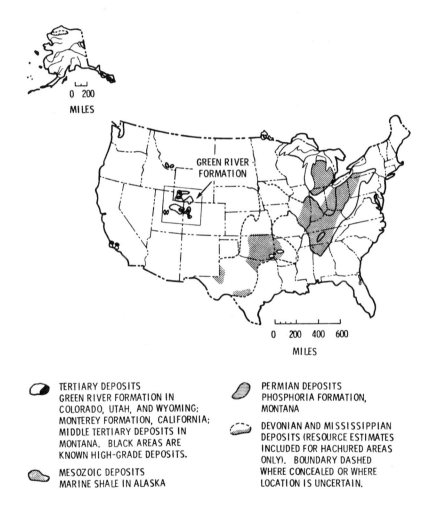

TERTIARY DEPOSITS
GREEN RIVER FORMATION IN
COLORADO, UTAH, AND WYOMING;
MONTEREY FORMATION, CALIFORNIA;
MIDDLE TERTIARY DEPOSITS IN
MONTANA. BLACK AREAS ARE
KNOWN HIGH-GRADE DEPOSITS.

MESOZOIC DEPOSITS
MARINE SHALE IN ALASKA

PERMIAN DEPOSITS
PHOSPHORIA FORMATION,
MONTANA

DEVONIAN AND MISSISSIPPIAN
DEPOSITS (RESOURCE ESTIMATES
INCLUDED FOR HACHURED AREAS
ONLY). BOUNDARY DASHED
WHERE CONCEALED OR WHERE
LOCATION IS UNCERTAIN.

Source: Modified by Battelle (DOE EY-76-C-06-1830) from D.C. Duncan and
V.E. Swanson, "Organic-Rich Shale of the United States and World
Land Areas," U.S. Geological Survey Circular No. 523, 1965.

Several surveys have been published outlining the extent of the resource base for oil shales, but an accurate appraisal cannot be made because of the lack of definitive data from most nations of the world. Exploration for shales has not been as intensive as it has been for the more conveniently utilized fuels such as crude oil, natural gas and coal.

Figure 1.2: Oil Shale Deposits in the Green River Formation of Colorado, Utah, and Wyoming

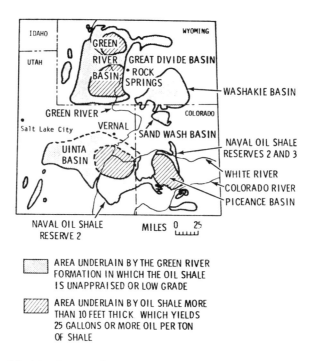

Source: Modified by Battelle (DOE EY-76-C-06-1830) from D.C. Duncan and V.E. Swanson, "Organic-Rich Shale of the United States and World Land Areas," U.S. Geological Survey Circular No. 523, 1965.

Despite the uncertainty and incompleteness of much of the data (much of Asia, Africa and South America has not been explored for shales and estimates there were judged to be conservative), it is clear that the vast majority of known oil shale resources are found in the United States, 75 to 80% of the estimated recoverable oil resources, with other major deposits in China (about 11% of estimated world reserves) and Canada (about 7% of estimated world reserves).

A compilation of global oil shale resources is further hampered by a lack of common terminology for reporting assay values (units used include U.S. gallons/short ton, liters/tonne, m^3/tonne, weight-percent oil, volume-percent oil), by different groupings of resources according to grade and by different assessments as to the minimum grade and seam thickness of shale which represents a recoverable resource. Although there has not been an exhaustive search for shales throughout the world, Table 1.3 represents an assembly of the current estimates of global resource of oil shale (in place).

Table 1.3: Shale Oil Resources (In Place) of the World

Grade of Shale (U.S. gal/ton)	Order of Magnitude of Total Resource (10^9 bbl)			Known Resources, Marginal or Submarginal Recovery (10^9 bbl)			Known Resources, Recoverable (10^9 bbl)
	5–10	10–25	25–100	5–10	10–25	25–100	10–100
Africa	450,000	80,000	4,000	—	—	90	10
Asia	590,000	110,000	5,500	?	14	70	20
Oceania	100,000	20,000	1,000	?	1	—	—
Europe	140,000	26,000	1,400	?	6	40	30
North America	260,000	50,000	3,000	2,200	1,600	520	80
South America	210,000	40,000	2,000	?	750	—	50
Total	1,750,000	325,000	17,000	2,200	2,400	720	190

Table 1.4: Shale Oil Resources (In Place) of the United States

Grade of Shale (U.S. gal/short ton)	Order of Magnitude of Total Resource (10^9 bbl)			Known Resources, Marginal, Submarginal and Recoverable (x 10^9 bbl)		
	5–10	10–25	25–100	5–10	10–25	25–100
Green River Formation						
Piceance Creek Basin (Colorado)	—	—	—	200*	800,* 900**	500,* 560**
Washakie and Green River Basins (Wyoming)	—	—	—	300*	400,* 400**	30,* 50**
Uinta Basin (Utah)	—	2,800	1,200	1,500*	230,* 360**	90,* 130**
Total	4,000	2,800	1,200	2,000*	1,430,* 1,660**	620,* 740**
					1,460	600
Devonian and Mississippian Shale (Central and Eastern U.S.A.)	2,000	1,000	?	200	200	0
Marine Shale (Alaska)	large	200	250	—	—	—
Other deposits	134,000	22,250	500	?	—	—
Total	140,000–260,000	26,000–50,000	2,000–3,000	2,200	1,600–1,900	600–740

*"Synthetic Fuels Data Handbook," Cameron Engineers, Denver Colorado, 1975.

**Matveyev, "Oil Shales Outside the Soviet Union," *Deposits of Fossil Fuels*, Vol 4, G.K. Hall and Co., Boston, MA, 1974.

Source: D.C. Duncan and V.E. Swanson, "Organic Rich Shale of the United States and World Land Areas," U.S. Geological Survey Circular No. 523, 1965. (NTIS N78-31584/3WE.)

Table 1.4 gives a summary of recent estimates of oil shale resources of the United States. The data given in Tables 1.3 and 1.4 represent estimates of resources in place. Known resources refer only to those that have been evaluated. In addition to evaluated deposits, the order of magnitude estimate of the total resource includes possible extensions of known resources and geologically based estimates of undiscovered and unappraised resources.

Of the estimated known resources of shale in place, only a fraction is recoverable using existing technology (regardless of cost) and these are usually termed "recoverable reserves." This is partly due to the fact that much rich shale is very deeply buried and large tonnages occur in very thin seams which cannot be recovered by current mining methods.

Secondly, the methods suggested for mining oil shale do not recover the whole deposit—room-and-pillar mining may recover 60 to 70% of the resource (the remainder being left as roof support for the mine), whereas surface mining may recover as much as 90% of a deposit although good reclamation practices may limit recovery to about 75%.

Thus, mining restraints may mean that less than 50% of the resource can be recovered. Table 1.5 gives an estimate of the effect of different recovery technologies on the recoverable reserves of the Green River formation. Of the recoverable reserves defined above, even less will be commercially exploitable—under 1974 economic conditions it has been suggested that shales assaying less than 25 gallons/ton could probably not have been processed economically.

Table 1.5: The Effect of Technology on Recoverable Reserves of Oil in the Green River Formation

Technology	Grade of Shale (U.S. gal/short ton)	Recoverable Reserves (x 10^9 bbl)
Underground room and pillar mining	$\geqslant$35	20
With surface retorting	$\geqslant$30	54
Open pit mining	$\geqslant$25	380
With surface retorting	$\geqslant$20	760
Conventional in situ (after mining plus explosives)	$\geqslant$20	300
Nuclear in situ	$\geqslant$20	200

Source: S. Rattien and D. Eaton, "Oil Shale: The Prospects and Problems of an Emerging Energy Industry," *Annual Review of Energy*, V1, 1976, Annual Reviews, Inc., Palo Alto, CA. (NTIS N78-31584/3WE.)

Although considerable data has been assembled on the richness of shales (particularly in the United States), many other factors such as depth (overburden ratio), seam thickness and geographical features affect the recovery of oil from shales and these have not been documented. Thus, one can only make a fairly tentative estimate of the potential quantities of oil which could be recovered from oil shales.

Perhaps a greater appreciation of the magnitude of the oil shale resource can be gained from the technique of distorting the world map to proportion a country's size according to the relative amount of each fossil fuel resource available in that country (Figures 1.3, 1.4, 1.5 and 1.6). From Figure 1.3 it can be seen that the U.S. has only about 5% of the world's known recoverable crude oil.

Figure 1.3: Known World Reserves of Recoverable Crude Oil

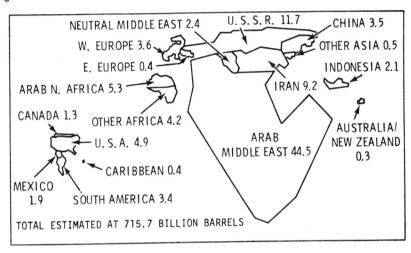

Source: P.A. Petzrick, "Oil Shale—An Ace in the Hole for National Security," *Shale Country,* 1(10):18-20, 1975. (DOE EY-76-C-06-1830.)

Figure 1.4: Known World Reserves of Recoverable Coal Supplies

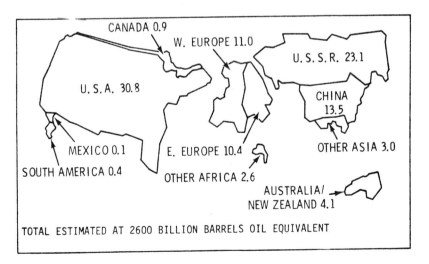

Source: P.A. Petzrick, "Oil Shale—An Ace in the Hole for National Security," *Shale Country,* 1(10):18-20, 1975. (DOE EY-76-C-06-1830.)

Figure 1.5: Known World Reserves of Recoverable Oil Shale

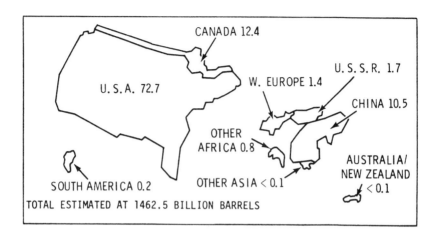

Source: P.A. Petzrick, "Oil Shale—An Ace in the Hole for National Security,"
         Shale Country, 1(10):18-20, 1975. (DOE EY-76-C-06-1830.)

Figure 1.6: Known World Reserves of Recoverable Fossil Fuels

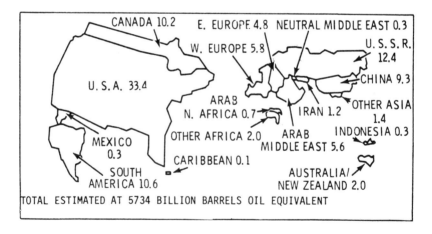

Source: P.A. Petzrick, "Oil Shale—An Ace in the Hole for National Security,"
         Shale Country, 1(10):18-20, 1975. (DOE EY-76-C-06-1830.)

In contrast the U.S. presently uses about 33% of the world energy. To augment
the present U.S. petroleum supplies, large quantities of crude are imported, with
an attendant loss of control in times of national emergency. Figure 1.4 shows
that the U.S. is indeed rich in coal resources. However, coal is an inherently
dirty energy source and is not presently suitable as an automotive fuel, although

research is now underway in coal liquefaction. Figure 1.5 shows that the U.S. is also rich in shale oil resources, having almost three-fourths of the world's known reserves. Additionally, shale oil can be refined to an automotive fuel. Figure 1.6 demonstrates that, including coal and shale oil, the U.S. has about 33% of the world's total fossil fuel or almost the same percentage of world energy that the U.S. uses. This strongly suggests, therefore, that the U.S. can obtain energy independence, but only if industry efficiently uses the vast coal and oil shale resources.

Extraction Processes

Oil shale processes can be divided into two general categories; those in which the shale oil is produced by pyrolysis in the shale formation (in situ), and those in which the shale is mined, and the oil extracted from the mined shale in aboveground retorts (ex situ).

In in situ processing, the shale is fractured by either explosive or hydrostatic pressure. A portion of the shale organic material then is burned to obtain heat for retorting. An external fuel such as natural gas may be used to start and control the burning. The retorted shale oil is extracted by pumping in a manner similar to the extraction of crude petroleum.

In situ processes may ultimately have certain advantages over ex situ processes including: avoidance of mining costs; no solid waste disposal; lower water requirements; and amenability to low grade shales. Disadvantages include: difficulty of controlling combustion; high drilling costs; low recovery efficiencies; difficulty of establishing the required porosity; and possible contamination of aquifers.

Much shale occurs within the zone saturated and since spent shale is known to contain large amounts of soluble sodium and calcium salts, in situ processing would pollute the groundwater directly with such waste. In addition, large volumes of groundwater may be contaminated by soluble organic material or radioactive material if nuclear explosives are used for rubbling.

Some of the major objections to pure in situ recovery of shale oil are overcome by modified in situ recovery where a portion of shale is mined and retorted aboveground. This creates the needed pore space to assure adequate recovery of the in situ oil.

Ex situ oil shale recovery processes (aboveground retorting) are simple in principle, but more complicated in application. These processes consist of mining the shale, grinding it to the size needed, heating the shale in a retort at high temperatures to convert the kerogen and bitumen to volatile organic products, collecting the volatiles in a condenser, and prerefining the product to produce a syncrude which can be refined in a manner similar to crude oil in existing refineries. The disposal of waste effluents includes: mining wastes; spent shale; off-gases; process waters; cooling waters; and prerefinery wastes.

Mining: Underground and open pit mining techniques will require an estimated 1.4×10^6 ton/day of oil shale to operate the smallest economical plant (10^5 bpd). A mine of this size will be larger than any mine presently operating in the U.S.

Open pit mining is economically attractive for some surface and near surface oil shales since nearly 100% of the oil shale can be recovered compared to a maximum of 50 to 70% for underground mines. Surface disturbance and its resulting environmental impact are the primary obstacles. Because of large overburdens, a combination of open pit and underground methods may ultimately be used in certain cases.

Underground mining will probably be accomplished by the room-and-pillar method. This method consists of removing a portion of the shale from large underground rooms, leaving the remainder of the shale in place to act as pillars to support the roof. It is estimated that 30 to 50% of the shale will be left unmined by this technique.

Completed mines of high grade shales will be likely candidates for further modified in situ mining. These mines will provide ready access for the placement of rubbling charges and will obviate the porosity problems found in conventional in situ experiments. However, room-and-pillar mines will generally be deep which will make recovery of any in situ produced shale oil difficult. Both open pit and underground methods will require the disposal of extensive volumes of highly saline groundwater during mining operations in certain locations.

Retorting: Although several categories of aboveground retorting have been proposed, only two classes of processes are under active consideration. These are the direct heating (DH) and indirect heating (IH) processes. In the DH process, hot gases resulting from the combustion of a portion of the carbonaceous material in the shale within the retort (about 435°C), are circulated through the oil shale.

In the IH process, heat is transferred to the shale by contact with externally heated hot recyclable solids (265°C). DH retorts handle mine-run shale requiring little grinding. Fines tend to plug DH retorts and thus briquetting is required. The efficient burning of residual carbon in the DH process results in a low carbon spent shale, reducing the potential for release of organic pollutants to the environment upon disposal. DH processes also tend to be mechanically simple compared to IH processes.

Product Properties and Prerefining Operations: Although product properties vary with type of retorting process, all shale oils tend to be heavy viscous liquids with high pour points. Compared to crude petroleums, the pour point, viscosity, and nitrogen content are all significantly higher for shale oils. The high pour point oils are unsuitable for transportation by pipeline or tanker without additional heating.

Sulfur and nitrogen compounds present tend to poison heavy metal catalysts used in refining processes; thus, retorting complexes will likely have prerefining facilities on site to reduce product viscosity and remove sulfur and nitrogen prior to pipeline transport.

A proposed complex could include holding tanks for retort product storage, a distillation column, a delayed coker, a hydrocracker for nitrogen removal, a Claus reactor for sulfur recovery, a steam reformer for hydrogen generation and product cleanup facilities. A partially refined low sulfur, low nitrogen premium syncrude will be the resulting product, while sulfur, ammonia and coke would be by-products which would have additional commercial value.

Environmental Aspects

Essentially all of the anticipated liquid and solid oil shale wastes have been proposed for ground disposal. Thus, the potential wastes, liquid and solid, which may be disposed of to the ground, are equivalent to a list of all wastes produced. These are discussed under the following headings: (1) mining wastes; (2) retort residual wastes; and (3) prerefining wastes. In situ and modified in situ wastes are expected to be qualitatively similar to the aboveground retorting wastes; however, the amounts will undoubtedly be different from aboveground operations.

Mining Wastes: Overburdens from open-pit mining and mine dewatering from both open-pit and room-and-pillar mining could produce large volumes of waste. A single mine could produce 3½ billion m^3 of overburden plus 39 billion m^3 of low grade unusable shale. In the center of Piceance Basin, open-pit mines are contemplated even though the overburden in some areas has been estimated at more than 300 m.

The ratio of overburden to extractable ore (stripping ratio) is an important factor in the economics of mining operations. For oil shale, the economical stripping ratio is 1:2, although it may be as high as 1:1 for coal mining. Assuming a volume expansion of 25% during removal, a ratio of 1:2 represents approximately 3.0 barrels of overburden per barrel of shale oil. Primary disposal problems with overburden are associated with the potential leaching of solubles and erosion of stockpiled overburden during the temporary storage following mining, and revegetation following closure of open-pit mines.

The large volumes of shale occurring in the saturated zone may be dewatered before mining. Unfortunately, some of the deeper groundwater is saline and cannot be disposed of to surface waters without treatment. Total dissolved solid concentrations of nearly 17,000 mg/l have been reported and are not uncommon. Discharge to saline deep well aquifers may be an acceptable disposal method for the most highly saline waste.

Retort Residuals: Aboveground retorting will produce spent shale, retort process water, and retort off-gas scrubbing residuals. Of these, spent shale would appear to constitute the largest disposal problem.

Spent Shale—The quantity of spent shale produced by a 10^6 bpd, mature industry has been estimated at 1 to 1.8 million MT/day. This quantity of shale is sufficient to cover 2.5 sq km to a depth of 75 cm. In comparison to the volumes of shale oil produced, it represents approximately 5 to 6 barrels of spent shale per barrel of shale oil. Disposal of such quantities of spent shale is a prodigious task.

Anticipated disposal problem areas include: disposal location; aboveground spent shale stabilization; and mitigation of effects of spent shale leachates. The original mining location is a natural consideration for spent shale disposal. However, spent shale volume is 10 to 25% greater than its original unmined volume depending on the process used. The volume increase occurs primarily because of an increase in pore space from the production of fine particles during the mining and grinding processes. Porosities of unmined oil shales are small (less than 5 to 10%) compared to porosities of spent shale. Depending on the amount of compaction, spent shales may have porosities of up to 40%. Thus, even if the original mines could be completely filled with spent shale, a considerable portion must be disposed of by other means.

However, the possible simultaneous operations of a dawsonite and nahcolite industry may open up additional volumes of underground mines for the subsurface solid waste disposal. Some oil shale may be mined from the saturated zone and methods for efficiently replacing the spent shale in these mines are not available.

Furthermore, nominal quantities of Na, Ca, and Mg oxides, which are soluble in water, may be produced by the partial conversion of carbonates and other minerals at the high retorting temperatures of the shale oil extraction processes. Thus, disposal of spent shales in locations close to existing water tables could present a potential source of groundwater pollution by dissolution of these metal oxides.

Emplacement of spent shale in canyons near retorting operations is suggested as a supplement or alternative to mine-filling strategies. Serious problems may be generated by surface disposal because stabilized, spent shale is subject to water and wind erosion. Compaction of shale and establishment of vegetative cover will be required to minimize the erosion of surface disposed spent shale. Control reservoirs, retaining dams, and water interception systems will be needed to collect runoff from possible summer flash floods and accumulated snow melt.

To establish sufficient vegetation on spent shale and leach soluble salts from the shale, addition of fertilizer (N and probably P) and irrigation water will be required. It has been estimated that up to 1.2 m of water is required to adequately leach spent shale to obtain a suitable plant growth medium. Covering the shale with a layer of soil has been suggested. To assume downward movement of water (to avoid salt transport from the spent shale to the soil) both initial leaching of the spent shale and possibly continued additions of supplemental irrigation water may be required.

Of the two process types, the DH type would appear to minimize environmental problems associated with ground disposal. Leachate composition is a function of shale composition and the retorting process. In the DH processes, virtually all of the carbon residue is burned, minimizing related potential problems such as complexing of trace elements and solubilization of potential carcinogens; however, the DH processes result in the greatest quantity of readily soluble salts.

Retort Wastes — Large quantities of water are removed from the oil shale during retorting (up to 1.5% of the raw shale by weight). Although this waste may contain some inorganic salts, the component most likely to limit its disposal is the soluble and particulate organic matter. Little has been reported on the properties of organics in the retort wastewater. The pyrolytic retorting processes can produce a variety of polynuclear aromatic hydrocarbons (PAHs), some of which are known carcinogens.

In addition, shale oil contains much higher concentrations of polar heterocyclic components (particularly N compounds) than do crude oils. The nitrogen content of whole shale oils usually varies between 1 and 2% by weight, depending on the source and the process used.

Oil derived from gas-combustion retorting has been reported to contain 1.46% N, oils produced by conventional retorting contained between 1.27 and 1.59% N, and in situ methodology yielded nitrogen contents of 1.36 to 1.84%. As much as 20% of the compounds in shale oil naphthas contained nitrogen, with 96% of these classified as basic, probably consisting largely of pyridine-type compounds. 16 pyridine-type and 11 phenolic compounds were identified in shale oil naphtha as well as pyrroles and benzonitriles. There was also evidence of carbonyl, phenolic, and carboxylic compounds in a shale oil heavy gas oil containing about 3.5% total nitrogen (2% basic nitrogen).

The environmental significance of the presence of large concentrations of polar and heterocyclic components in shale oil is twofold. As with almost any mixture of organic compounds, a number of compound types are potentially toxic and/or carcinogenic, and the polar characteristics increase their solubility and accommodation in water systems. Retort waste is amenable to treatment by charcoal sorption with eventual destruction of its organic compounds by heating, thus preventing adverse environmental effects.

Off-Gas Scrubber Wastes — Off-gases from aboveground retorts may be expected to contain environmentally deleterious compounds, but limited data appear in the literature on either the quantities or general composition of these gases. Liquid scrubber treatments of these off-gases may be candidates for ground disposal. Information pertaining to the environmental consequences of this waste disposal is not available.

Prerefinery Wastes: Wastes from the prerefinery distillation, coking, hydrogen steam reforming, hydrogenation, and Claus kiln processes will be similar to the wastes produced by these processes in the petroleum industry. For a 50,000 bpd IH plant, it was estimated that spent catalyst wastes would average about 708 MT/yr. Additional estimated wastes include approximately 425 MT/yr of diatomaceous earth, 425 MT/yr of deactivated carbon, 860 MT/yr of caustic wash, 300,000 MT/yr of coke, and 95 MT/yr of extracted As. It has been proposed that all of the above wastes be mixed into and disposed with spent shale (20 million MT/yr).

Assessment of the Ultimate Recoverable Reserves of Oil Available from Oil Shale

In exploiting oil shales only a proportion of the resources can be physically recovered for reasons of accessibility and practical mining techniques. This factor is usually indicated by distinguishing between resources in place and recoverable reserves. Here it will be assumed that 50% of resources in place could be recovered by a combination of underground and surface mining. (It has been suggested that perhaps only 15 to 20% of the mineable shale reserves could be recovered by open-pit methods.)

In discussing recoverable reserves, the energy required to extract and process shales and deliver oil is never considered and in some cases this can be a significant proportion of the energy potentially obtainable. Calculations have been made of the energy requirements for producing synthetic crude oil from shales in a hypothetical facility (since none exists at present) based on underground mining and surface retorting. The effects of the grade of shale processed, retorting efficiency, transport distances, and efficiency of electricity generation on calculated energy requirements have also been investigated. It was found that no net energy (i.e., energy recovered as products less energy required for processing) was produced from shales assaying from 5 to 10 gallons/ton—the exact "point of futility" depending primarily on retorting efficiency and to a lesser extent transport distances and other factors.

An analysis of one in situ process indicated that a similar lower limit also applies to in situ processing of shales. The analysis also showed that even for the richest shales processed in surface retorts, the energy requirement always exceeded 10% of the output and as shale grade decreased, this proportion increased.

At present it is not possible to calculate definitive energy requirements since operating data is not available for a commercial scale plant and it will in any case be site specific (depending on transport distances, spent shale disposal arrangements, etc); however, it is clear that retorting efficiency (within the limits examined) is a crucial parameter in processing lean shales and at present one can only guess as to the efficiency which would be obtained in a full scale retort.

It is not possible to determine a definitive economic grade limit for oil shales in isolation, since it would depend (in theory, in a free market situation) on the comparative cost of the alternative which at present is crude oil flowing either under gas pressure or pumped to the surface, but in the future may be oil recovered from conventional oil wells by tertiary methods (steam, polymer injection, etc) or synthetic oil from coal or tar sands.

However, this is obviously an oversimplification since the "price" of oil from the Middle East is patently not related to the cost of production and it is this price which determines the economics of syncrude production. However, in North America it may not be unreasonable to assume a minimum cost strategy for an alternative supply of oil to imported oil for a time when crude oil is all but exhausted.

If it is assumed that 15 gallons/ton is the economic cut-off grade, then estimates can be made of the economically recoverable reserves of oil available from shales. Again, because of the aggregated nature of resource estimates and in lieu of more detailed information, it will be assumed that shales of grades 15 to 25 gallons/ton (having an average grade of 20 gallons/ton) account for 50% of the resources specified in the range from 10 to 25 gallons/ton.

Of the estimated total resources of shale in place perhaps only 3 to 4% is economically recoverable and, of the known resources, about 15% of resources in place may be economically recoverable. However, these small fractions of recoverable shale resources represent a vast potential source of oil. From "known" deposits in the United States, it is estimated that 650×10^9 barrels of oil may be available—a quantity of the order of the known reserves of crude oil in the world.

Despite considerations about energy efficiency and economics, it seems certain that other factors will play an important part in determining the future of oil shale exploitation. In particular, a plant producing 50,000 barrels syncrude per day will require about 170,000 bpd of water or about 8,000 acre feet per year of which 45% is for setting and compaction of spent shale, 25% for prerefining and 30% for mining, crushing and retorting and over a 20 year lifetime will produce (from rich shales) over 400 million tons of spent shale of which only a maximum of 3% could be used for other products.

Since the vast majority of U.S. recoverable reserves of oil from shale occurs in the arid states of Colorado, Utah and Wyoming where much of the available water is required for agricultural and other purposes, water requirements seem likely to impose severe restrictions on the size of oil shale industry which could be supported in the Green River area.

Upper limits of production on the order of a million barrels of oil per day have been suggested, but this may be increased by providing water storage or by using saline water from artesian wells. The constraints imposed by the disposal of spent shale in an environmentally acceptable way will depend on the ingenuity of the industry in solving this problem and the legal requirements with which it is forced to comply. (The in situ processing of shales has not been considered in the above assessment of reserves largely because of the lack of information concerning its possible implementation. At present there are a number of unanswered questions about possible oil recoveries, minimum grades which could be processed profitably, methods of fracturing the shale underground, etc. In situ processing has an obvious attraction in that the problem of waste disposal is avoided, but its practical application has yet to be demonstrated.)

Status of Oil Shale Commercialization

Considering the recent dramatic increases in world price of crude oil, why does the U.S. continue to have no commercial oil shale industry? The answer is complex, but can be related to four factors: (1) high initial capital investments; (2) possible instability of world crude oil prices; (3) lack of clearly defined federal oil shale development policy; and (4) environmental considerations.

The proposed oil shale industry will be capital intensive, requiring an enormous initial investment which must be spread over the lifetime of the plant for the venture to be economically attractive. Estimates of $0.5-3 \times 10^9$ per 50,000 bpd aboveground plants seem to be reasonable.

These large capital investments must be made in the face of uncertain world crude oil prices which are not determined on a competitive basis, but are set arbitrarily by a cartel of oil-producing nations. It is cheaper to drill for crude oil than to produce syncrude from oil shale. Crude oil can be produced at a profit for less than a dollar per barrel in the Middle East. Thus, the oil cartel can lower prices at will to make an oil shale operation unprofitable. To overcome this obstacle it was concluded that it would be possible to establish an oil shale industry if the federal government would do one or more of the following:

(1)   make low interest federal loans to private industry;
(2)   establish an independent federal agency to exploit federally owned oil shale deposits;
(3)   establish a clearly defined national oil shale policy;

(4)   give tax credits to encourage private development; or

(5)   give grants or guarantee a fixed price per barrel through contract provisions.

Strong environmental concerns have also added to the potential oil shale industry's problem. There are environmental uncertainties related to the disposal of spent shale and other residuals, restoration and revegetation of disturbed land, water supply, and air quality. These have been discussed in more detail in a previous section.

CANADIAN TAR SANDS

The information in this section is excerpted from "Tar Sands: A New Fuels Industry Takes Shape," by T.H. Maugh II, *Science,* Vol. 199, February 17, 1978 (copyright 1978 by the American Association for the Advancement of Science).

Background

The huge tar sands deposits of northeastern Alberta [Canada] are covered by as much as 6 m of muskeg, a semifloating mass of partially decayed vegetation. In summer, land vehicles are swallowed up by the morass. In winter, the muskeg freezes so solidly that the earth beneath is virtually inaccessible. To reach the tar sands, it is necessary to begin draining water from the muskeg at least 2 years before any digging is planned; the remaining vegetation must then be removed while it is frozen. Despite these difficulties, muskeg removal is one of the simpler problems which confront companies that attempt to exploit tar sands. The more severe problems include the inhospitable weather and the exceptional difficulties of handling the tar sands.

These problems have delayed exploitation of tar sands, but they have certainly not halted it. One by one, these problems have been overcome until, today, tar sands are the most promising near term alternative source of fossil fuels. One company has been mining tar sands and extracting oil from them for 10 years, the last 2 years at a profit.

A second, much larger plant is now about 95% complete, and a third plant and a possible fourth are on the drawing board. More than 20 companies, furthermore, have operated pilot projects for in situ recovery of oil from the tar sands. About 16 of these pilot projects are still in operation and one commercial facility may be under construction within 2 years.

The greatest immediate beneficiary of this activity will be Canada, where most of the work is taking place. Canada has the largest confirmed deposits of tar sands in the world—the equivalent of more than 900 billion barrels of oil, not counting some large, unexplored deposits in the Northwest Territories.

By the 1990s, production of oil from tar sands could approach 1 million barrels per day (bpd), or nearly a third of Canada's domestic requirements. Little or none of this oil will reach the United States, but the experience gained in Canada will have application here and elsewhere. The United States has the equivalent of more than 30 billion barrels of oil embedded in tar sands, 90% of it in Utah. The equivalent of some 200 billion barrels of oil is known to lie in tar sands along the north bank of the Orinoco River in Venezuela, and some geologists speculate that there may be as much as 2 trillion barrels. Smaller deposits are scattered throughout the world, and it is thought that a substantial deposit exists in the Soviet Union.

Description and Properties

Tar sands, also known as oil sands and heavy oil, are a mixture of 84 to 88% sand and mineral-rich clays, 4% water, and 8 to 12% bitumen. Bitumen is a dense, sticky, semisolid that is about 83% carbon. At room temperature, it does not flow and is heavier than water; at higher temperatures, it flows freely and floats on water.

Tar sands can be divided roughly into three categories, depending on their viscosity. The viscosity, in turn, depends primarily on reservoir temperature. Tar sands near Lloydminster in Alberta are about 300 times as viscous as conventional petroleum; part of the bitumen there can be pumped directly from the ground. Deposits in the Peace River and Cold Lake regions are about 1,000 times more viscous than those at Lloydminster, and must be heated substantially before they are mobile enough to pump. Deposits near the surface in the Athabasca and Wabasca regions are another ten times more viscous and can be mined in open pits.

Near-Surface Deposits

An important feature of the deposits in Athabasca and Wabasca is that the bitumen is separated from the sand by a thin film of water that surrounds each grain of sand. The bitumen will thus separate readily from the sand in hot water. In the absence of this film, separation of bitumen from the rock is much harder.

Federal and provincial governments in Canada and private companies have attempted to exploit the tar sands since the 1880s. The basic flotation technique for separating bitumen from sand was developed in the 1920s by Karl Clark of the Scientific and Industrial Research Council of Alberta and Sidney Ells of the Ottawa Department of Mines. The economics of mining and processing the sands, however, prevented any commercial development until recently.

The pioneer in development and application of tar sands technology is unquestionably Great Canadian Oil Sands Ltd. (GCOS), which is 96% owned by the Sun Company Inc. of Philadelphia. In 1964 GCOS began construction of an extraction facility on a 1,600 hectare site about 30 kilometers north of Ft. McMurray, Alberta, and in 1968 began commercial production. The plant now produces an average of about 50,000 bpd of synthetic crude oil.

By far the greatest expense and difficulty lie in mining and handling the tar sands. For each 50,000 barrels of oil produced, approximately 33,000 cubic meters of overburden must be removed, and about 100,000 tons of tar sand must be mined and disposed of. The tar sands are more difficult to handle than any other substance that has been mined on a large scale.

In summer, the tar sand can be mined with a bucket wheel without prior preparation of the deposit, but the sands are highly abrasive. During the first summer of mining, the 120 teeth of the bucket wheel—each of which then weighed about 46 kg—would wear out in 4 to 8 hours of digging; replacements had to be flown in from throughout the world. Blades on bulldozers and scrapers would last for only about 40% of their expected life.

The tar sands also stick tenaciously to everything they touch. They thus clog the cooling systems and external controls of vehicles, stick to conveyer belts and accumulate at transfer points on the belts, and create general havoc with machinery. The bitumen, furthermore, slowly dissolves natural rubber in tires, conveyer belts, and other machinery.

In winter, when temperatures drop to -50°C, an undisturbed deposit of frozen tar sands resembles carborundum. The teeth of a bucket wheel digging in a frozen deposit glow red. The steel plates, 0.6 cm thick, from which the buckets are made would frequently be ripped apart, and the teeth torn from their sockets. Other equipment failures also become more frequent.

The problem of winter mining was largely overcome by dynamiting the tar sands in the summer so they cannot freeze as solidly. The teeth on the bucket wheels were redesigned to minimize friction and improved alloys are now used. Different rubber formulations were developed for tires and conveyer belts, and vehicle maintenance schedules were refined and rigorously adhered to. Similar refinements were developed throughout the complex. These refinements are now being licensed to other tar sands operations.

Once the tar sands reach the extraction plant—a process that now involves transporting them more than 11 km by conveyer belts—the process is relatively straightforward. The tar sand is first mixed with alkaline water at about 80°C in a rotating drum. The resulting slurry is dumped into separation cells where the sand and clay settle out and bitumen floats to the surface. The bitumen is then coked, a process in which large, nonvolatile organic molecules are broken down into products that can be distilled; by-product coke from this process is used to fuel the facility's electric generating station, and gases are used for the manufacture of hydrogen.

Distillation of the products from the coking produces naphtha, kerosene, and gas oil, each of which is treated with hydrogen to remove sulfur. Aromatic and olefin components are also removed, gasified, and used as fuel for the power plant. The three distillates are then blended into a synthetic crude oil that is shipped by pipeline to Edmonton, about 400 km to the south. GCOS recovers 92 to 93% of the bitumen in place.

The first beneficiary of GCOS's problem-solving experience will be Syncrude Ltd., which is now building a 129,000 bpd plant about 7 km north of the GCOS site. Syncrude is a consortium of three companies (Imperial Oil Ltd., Gulf Oil Canada Ltd., and Canada-Cities Service Ltd.), the Canadian government, and the governments of Alberta and Ontario. The three governments purchased 30% of the project when one of the original partners dropped out because of escalating costs.

Syncrude has licensed much of the proprietary technology developed by GCOS, so initial operations there should proceed much more smoothly. Among the important lessons learned from the GCOS project was the necessity of having duplicate systems so that the entire facility will not be shut down if one sub-system fails. The plant is expected to begin production this spring, and Syn-crude estimates the cost of producing oil at about $9.50 per barrel. [The in-stallation actually came on-stream in September, 1978. Figure 1.7 illustrates the Syncrude process.]

Figure 1.7: Synthetic Crude Oil from Tar Sands

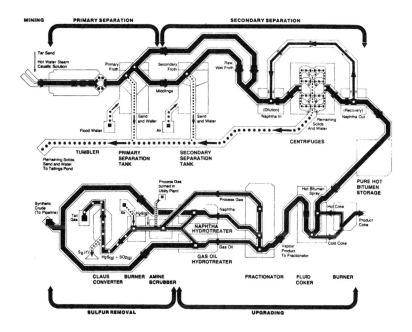

Source: *Science*, February 17, 1978

The overall scale of the project is staggering. Mining will be performed by four draglines, each of which has a 60 m³ bucket on the end of a 110 m boom. Electricity for the draglines and for the rest of the project is provided by a coke-fired 260 MW generating plant, large enough to light a city of 300,000. The total area to be mined is about 2,800 hectares, and the tailings pond for dis-posal of clean sand occupies an area of 3,000 hectares, making it one of the largest lakes in the area. Considering the isolated location, there have been few other projects like it.

In Situ Processing

Despite the bright prospects for these surface projects, less than 10% of the tar sands in Canada lie within 50 m of the surface, which is generally considered to be the maximum depth at which open-pit mining is viable. The vast majority of of the resources will thus have to be exploited with in situ technology. The in situ processes required for tar sands are somewhat simpler than those required for oil shale, for example, but they are still sufficiently difficult that a great deal of experimental work is required. Private companies have already invested more than $150 million for pilot projects during the last two decades and, in conjunction with the Alberta Oil Sands Technology and Research Authority (AOSTRA), are expected to invest an additional $250 million during the next 10 years. There are 16 pilot projects at which work is being performed; the nature of the technology being used at each of these depends on the character of the tar sands themselves.

The first deep tar sands that will be exploited are at Cold Lake, where reserves are estimated at about 160 billion barrels. The greatest experience at Cold Lake has been obtained by Imperial Oil, which has operated a series of pilot projects there since 1964 at a cost of more than $40 million. The most recent project is producing about 5,000 bpd of bitumen by steam stimulation, or what is known colloquially as the "huff and puff" process. Steam at 350°C and a pressure of 2,000 psi is injected into the 500 m deep formation through a pattern of wells for 4 to 6 weeks (huff). Bitumen can them be pumped from the wells for as long as 6 months (puff).

The primary goals of the pilot projects have been to find the best ways to bring the steam into intimate contact with the bitumen and to determine the optimum configuration and spacing for the wells. Imperial has applied to the Alberta government for permission to build an in situ facility that would produce as much as 160,000 bpd. The cost of the project will probably exceed $4 billion. Fully half that total is for facilities to upgrade the bitumen to a synthetic crude oil that can be used in existing refineries. If approval for the project is obtained in 1979, construction would begin in 1981 and production in 1985.

The project will involve drilling about 10,000 wells over a period of 20 years or longer. There will be from 2,000 to 2,500 wells in operation at any one time, and each is expected to produce for 5 to 8 years. Energy to produce the steam will require burning either about 5 million tons of coal each year or about 25,000 bpd of bitumen. Despite the large capital investment, the cost of producing the oil is expected to be less than that at Syncrude.

Other companies are also conducting pilot operations at Cold Lake. Norcen Energy Resources Ltd. is using much the same process as Imperial. Murphy Oil Ltd. is also using steam stimulation, but is injecting the steam continuously. AOSTRA, BP Canada Ltd., Hudson's Bay Oil and Gas Ltd., and PanCanadian Petroleum Ltd. are jointly studying a combination method employing steam injection and in situ combustion. This approach is considered desirable because the production rate of each well should be higher than it is with steam injection alone.

Another well-developed approach is known as COFCAW, for combination of forward combustion and water-flood. This process has been developed by Amoco Canada Petroleum Ltd. at a cost of more than $20 million. In its simplest form, four wells are drilled at the corners of a square, and a fifth is drilled at the center. Combustion of the bitumen is initiated at the center well as air is injected at a pressure high enough to fracture the tar sand zone.

After fracturing is achieved, the pressure is reduced, and air and water are injected. The water helps to spread the heat evenly and forces the liquid bitumen toward the four production wells. Amoco, AOSTRA, and Pacific Petroleums Ltd. have recently begun production of 1,000 bpd at a pilot facility in the Athabasca tar sands.

The $69 million program is expected to produce more than 1 million barrels of bitumen by its completion in 1984 and to demonstrate whether commercial production is feasible. The COFCAW process is expected to recover at least half the bitumen in place under the 10 hectare test tract, consuming 4 to 5% of the bitumen while doing so.

AOSTRA is sponsoring studies of four other major approaches to in situ technology. In the first, Shell is studying cyclic pressurization and depressurization of tar sand deposits near the Peace River with steam. These sands are unusual in that there is an underlying zone saturated with water; this zone will provide a path for the steam as it moves between wells. Extension of the approach to other sites, however, will require development of methods to connect the wells underground. One way to do this is with hydraulic fracturing, which will be studied in the Athabasca deposits by Numac Oil and Gas Ltd.

A proprietary steam heating technique for shallow deposits is being studied by In-Situ Research and Engineering Ltd. High pressure steam cannot be used in such deposits because it would disrupt the overburden. AOSTRA and others are exploring a modified in situ process, based on Soviet experience, in which steam is injected through wells emanating from a tunnel drilled through the deposit horizontally.

In an independent project, electrical resistance heating of deposits at intermediate depths is being studied by Petro-Canada Exploration Ltd., Canada-Cities Service, and Imperial. The passage of alternating current through the sands would raise the temperature enough so that oil could be flushed out with steam. The potential advantage of this process is that no fracturing should be required. At least one of these techniques, says John H. Nicholls of AOSTRA, should be suitable for any tar sand deposit in Canada.

In the United States, there has been little interest in tar sands because it was thought that the country had deposits equivalent to only about 1 billion barrels of oil. Only recently has it become clear that the deposits total 30 times that amount, at least. Much of the work in the United States has been done by L.C. Marchant and his colleagues at the Department of Energy's Laramie Energy Research Center. They are now conducting their second in situ combustion experiment near Vernal, Utah. The Utah tar sands do not have a film of water between the bitumen and the sand, so separation of the two is more difficult.

The Laramie investigators' first experiment used reverse combustion, in which a fire is ignited in one well and air injected into a second well to draw the fire to it. Unfortunately, the tar sands at Vernal are more heterogeneous than the samples that were used for laboratory simulation of the process. The fire channeled through the deposit in a narrow band of high porosity and did not heat the deposit effectively.

The second experiment, which began in late August [1977], used reverse combustion followed by forward combustion. Marchant says this approach will require less air injection and should be easier to control. This experiment has proceeded much more smoothly.

At the approximate midpoint of the experiment, the Laramie investigators had recovered about 20% of the bitumen in place and expect to recover about 50% while consuming about 10%. They are presently planning a third experiment to study steam-heating. The Department of Energy is also exploring ways to achieve a greater amount of cooperation with Canadian investigators.

The Future

In situ recovery of tar sands thus looks promising, but there are several major hurdles that must be overcome. The most important of these is probably capital investment. Whereas in situ recovery of oil shale is expected to be substantially cheaper than surface extraction, this is not the case for tar sands, as is readily seen by a comparison of the costs of the projects. The Syncrude and Imperial projects will require a capital investment of $20,000 to $24,000 per daily barrel of oil produced.

In Saudi Arabia, in contrast, the comparable cost [for crude oil] is about $325. The companies thus feel, justifiably, that they need some guarantees to keep the price floor from being pulled out from under them. Most companies feel that the absolute minimum requirement that must be met to justify this large investment is to allow oil from the projects to be sold at the prevailing world price.

Some executives feel that even more could be done to provide incentives. The government of Alberta will receive a royalty of 50% of the profits on all oil produced in the province since it owns the land on which the tar sands are located. Several oil companies argue that a reduction in this royalty, combined with some federal tax credits, could make a large number of projects commercially viable. But, perhaps the most important thing, according to Russ Powell of Imperial, is that the government establish prices and regulations and stick to them. That kind of stability is needed before the companies will feel confident enough to put up their money.

Environmental Concerns

Environmental problems are not particularly severe. Canadian tar sands contain 4 to 6% sulfur, but most of this is removed during processing. Emissions of sulfur dioxide at GCOS have generally been within government guidelines. The Alberta government has given Syncrude permission to emit 287 long tons of sulfur dioxide per day, but Save Tomorrow, Oppose Pollution (STOP), an Edmonton-based environmental group, says that the company could reduce the emissions to 40 long tons per day by installation of about $35 million worth of equipment. STOP contends that the frequent temperature inversions in winter could trap dangerous quantities of sulfur dioxide.

Perhaps a more substantive problem are the tailings ponds. STOP contends that these ponds contain substantial quantities of organic chemicals and metals and that the surface is coated with a thin film of bitumen. The group argues that spillover or leakage of these materials into the Athabasca River could cause a severe pollution problem. Syncrude's pond, furthermore, is on a major flyway for migratory waterfowl, and the bitumen is quite toxic to the fowl. Syncrude contends that there is little danger of leakage from the ponds and that there are not toxic levels of pollutants in them anyway. The company concedes the problem with waterfowl and is trying to devise some way to keep them away from the ponds.

Another potential problem is pollution of underground aquifers during in situ extraction, but this does not seem to be insurmountable. There may eventually be a shortage of water for processing the bitumen, but AOSTRA is already sponsoring research on ways to reuse water produced from the sands. Even the effects of an influx of population into the mining area seem to be controllable.

Counterbalancing these potential problems is the industry's greatest asset—the eagerness of the Canadian government to spawn production of alternative fossil fuels. Despite arguments that more tax and royalty breaks should be provided, all levels of government have clearly been supportive of development efforts—even to the point of purchasing a part interest in Syncrude when no other partner could be found. It seems likely that this type of accommodation will continue in the future, and that the extraction of oil from tar sands has a very good chance of developing into a full-fledged industry.

U.S. TAR SANDS

The material in this section is based on *The Economic Potential of Domestic Tar Sands* by V.A. Kuuskraa and S. Chalton of Lewin and Associates, Inc. and T.M. Doscher of the University of Southern California, prepared by the U.S. Department of Energy under DOE Contract 9014-018-021-22004.

Background

Like many oil-producing countries, the United States contains considerable deposits of tar sands—heavy petroleum (bitumen) that will not flow into a wellbore without stimulation. The size of these deposits has been estimated at 24 to 30 billion barrels of resource in place. (See Table 1.6.)

The State of Utah contains by far the largest portion, 23.4 to 29.5 billion barrels or 98% of the domestically measured deposits. Within Utah, five major deposits account for 21 to 27 billion barrels. These are: Tar Sand Triangle, P.R. Spring, Sunnyside, Asphalt Ridge, and Hill Creek. Given that these five major Utah deposits account for about 90% of the total measured domestic tar sands resource, it appears reasonable to expect that an analysis of these five deposits will substantially reflect the national tar sand potential.

Much effort has been focused on these deposits and ways of unlocking their potential as an energy source. This includes basic research appraisal work by the Utah Geological and Mineral Survey; resource appraisal, data collection, and pilot testing by the Laramie Energy Research and Development Center (LERC); basic research on extraction/separation by the College of Mines and Minerals Industries, University of Utah and resource definition efforts by several domestic industrial firms. The analysis in this section draws from these important efforts.

Table 1.6: Deposits of Bitumen-Bearing Rocks in the U.S. with Resources over
1,000,000 Barrels*

State and Name of Deposit	Estimated Resources (millions of barrels)
California:	
Edna	141.4–166.4
South Casmalia	46.4
North Casmalia	40.0
Sisquoc	26.0–50.0
Santa Cruz	10.0
McKittrick	4.8–9.0
Point Arena	1.2
Total	269.8–323.0
Kentucky:	
Kyrock Area	18.4
David-Dismal Area	7.5–11.3
Bee Spring Area	7.6
Total	33.5–37.3
New Mexico:	
Santa Rosa	57.2
Texas:	
Uvalde	124.1–140.7
Utah:	
Tar Sand Triangle**	12,504.0–16,004.0
P.R. Spring**	4,000.0–4,500.0
Sunnyside**	3,500.0–4,000.0
Circle Cliffs	1,000.0–1,300.0
Asphalt Ridge**	1,000.0–1,200.0
Hill Creek**	300.0–1,160.0
San Rafael Swell	385.0–470.0
Raven Ridge	125.0–150.0
Argyle Canyon	100.0–125.0
Asphalt Ridge, Northwest	100.0–125.0
Whiterocks	65.0–125.0
Cottonwood-Jacks Canyon	80.0–100.0
Wickiup	60.0–75.0
Minnie Maud Creek	30.0–50.0
Rimrock	30.0–35.0
Willow Creek	20.0–25.0
Parlette	12.0–15.0
White Canyon	12.0–15.0
Littlewater Hills	10.0–12.0
Lake Fork	6.5–10.0
Nine Mile Canyon	5.0–10.0
Chapita Wells	7.5–8.0
Ten Mile Wash	1.5–6.0
Tabiona	1.3–4.6
Thistle	2.2–2.5
Spring Branch	1.5–2.0
Cow Wash	1.0–1.2
Total	23,369.5–29,530.0

*Prepared by the Laramie Energy Research Center
**Deposits analyzed in the report

Source: DOE 9014-018-021-22004

Purpose of the Analysis

The purpose of the analysis was sixfold, namely to:

(1) Establish the size and nature of the resource base, concentrating on the major deposits.

(2) Identify the technically recoverable portion of the resource.

(3) Prepare a net energy analysis for three of the in situ thermal technologies (steam drive, reverse combustion and forward combustion), to ensure that, within the boundary of a local project, the energy output is greater than the energy input.

(4) Appraise the economic feasibility of recovering the tar sands using in situ thermal and surface mining technology.

(5) Estimate the target size of the potentially recoverable resource.

(6) Identify the technology performance needed to realize the tar sands recovery target.

Given the considerable uncertainties and unknowns still surrounding the nature of the deposit and the technology required to economically recover it, no steps were taken in this study to: assess the probability of success in reaching the estimated target, establish production rates for the near-term, between now and 1990 or assess the environmental and institutional concerns that might constrain the recovery of the tar sand resource.

Review of Major Findings

The significant findings from this analysis of the domestic tar sands are organized around six major topics: size and nature of the deposit; technical recovery potential; net energy and economic feasibility; recovery estimates; key resource and technological uncertainties; and a proposed research and development agenda.

Magnitude of Utah Deposits: Past efforts on size estimations of the tar sand deposits were often based on surface geology, chiefly outcrops and areal reconnaissance. This analysis relied on data from subsurface cores, taken by the Laramie Energy Research Center and various private firms. The two approaches lead to similar estimates for the overall resource size as shown below:

Deposit	Estimated Area (miles²)	.... Estimated Size .... Previously* ... (billion barrels)	Currently**	Core Samples Used ....for Estimate .... Full Data	Partial Data
Tar Sand Triangle	230	12.5-16.0	14	7	26
P.R. Spring	270	4.0-4.5	6	17	28
Sunnyside	90	3.5-4.0	5	13	2
Asphalt Ridge	25	1.0-1.2	<1	9	–
Hill Creek	125	0.3-1.2	2	3	–

*Based on surface geology.
**Based on core data.

However, the core data show that the deposits are geologically less favorable than originally assessed from outcrop samples. The P.R. Spring, Asphalt Ridge and the Hill Creek deposits consist of a series of lean, thin and noncontinuous pay zones. It appears the Sunnyside deposit contains numerous vertical fractures impeding volumetric sweep conformance between adjoining areas. The essential geologic and reservoir properties of the Tar Sand Triangle are inadequately defined.

Mining Potential: Using a minimum required oil content of 8% and overburden to net pay ratios of 0.4 for Tar Sand Triangle, P.R. Spring, Sunnyside, and Hill Creek and a ratio of 1.0 for Asphalt Ridge (the 8% minimum required oil content and the 0.4 and 1.0 overburden to net pay ratios were established by the LERC study staff), the Utah tar sand deposits do not appear to provide a large mining potential. The size of this potential is estimated below.

Deposit	Size/Nature of the Mining Potential
Tar Sand Triangle	None identified from core data; outcrops near Hatch Canyon (southwest) and oil seeps in the northeast indicate some localized potential
P.R. Spring	None identified from core data
Sunnyside	None identified from core data; mining activity may be feasible on the western edge but given current core data it is not possible to estimate the mining potential of this section
Asphalt Ridge	100 to 200 million barrels; although the oil content falls slightly below the 8% by weight standard, this is somewhat mitigated by an overburden to net pay ratio of less than 1.0
Hill Creek	None identified from core data

Further resource definition, particularly in the northeast section of the Tar Sand Triangle and the western edge of the Sunnyside deposit, could increase this potential. For the present, the deposits would only justify small scale (e.g., 10,000 bpd) upgrading facilities.

In Situ Thermal Recovery Potential: Approximately one-half of the tar sand in place may be technically amenable for in situ thermal recovery using existing technology. Much more geologic and reservoir data would be required to fully ascertain the technical feasibility of using in situ thermal (steam drive, combustion) technology on these deposits. Given this lack of data, only one technical criterion was applied—that the deposits have sufficient overburden to contain the high pressure steam or air that would be injected, set at 350 feet.

Using this standard, the technically feasible sections of these deposits are shown on the following page. However, based on discussions with industry persons knowledgeable of these deposits, the two areas with the largest technical potential, Tar Sand Triangle and Sunnyside, contain several technically unfavorable characteristics, including vertical fractures, thief (air) zones, poor continuity, and thin/crossbedded pay zones.

Deposit	Total Size	Technically Feasible Segment for In Situ Thermal Recovery
	. . . .(billion barrels).	
Tar Sand Triangle	14	12
P.R. Spring	6	negligible
Sunnyside	5	3
Asphalt Ridge	<1	0.4
Hill Creek	2	negligible

Feasibility analyses indicate that 8 billion barrels of the resource could be economically feasible for in situ thermal recovery under advanced technology conditions. A net energy and economic analysis was conducted to identify the economic potential of using surface mining and/or in situ thermal technology as a means of recovering the domestic tar sand deposits. The results are shown below. Other technical criteria beyond the net energy/economic criteria would include adequate continuity of pay and sufficient oil content to support the required level of combustion.

Deposit	Technically Feasible	Economically Feasible
	. . . .(billion barrels).	
Tar Sand Triangle	12	6
P.R. Spring	negligible	none
Sunnyside	3	2
Asphalt Ridge	0.4	none
Hill Creek	negligible	none

Adequate potential exists to justify further resource definition and technological development for in situ thermal recovery.

Net Recovery: Assuming a 50% gross recovery factor and deducting the energy consumed, approximately 2 billion barrels could be the net recovery target for the domestic tar sands, under advanced technology conditions.

Given considerable uncertainties regarding the resulting sweep efficiencies of steam drive or forward combustion in the domestic tar sands, a factor of 50% of the resource in place was used for estimating gross recovery. [The use of reverse combustion as the primary recovery mechanism was considered to be inapplicable for the tar sands (based on technical guidance provided by the ERDA regional panels on thermal recovery).] This 50% factor is derived from an aggregate of steam drive recovery experienced within the heavy oils of California and from personal communications with certain of the industry practitioners considering application of forward wet combustion on tar sands.

Considerable energy is expended as part of the recovery process, for generating steam or for compressing air. Thus, the energy used must be deducted from the energy produced to obtain the net additions of recovered oil. (It could be possible to burn coal to generate steam or compress air. This would provide additional liquid fuels, although no overall increase in domestically available Btu.) Overall about one-half of the recovered energy would be consumed as part of in situ thermal recovery. Applying the 50% gross recovery factor and subtracting the energy consumed leads to the recoveries listed on the next page, for the two economically feasible deposits.

Deposit	In Place Resource	Economically Feasible Resource	Gross Recovery	Net Recovery
	. . . .(billion barrels).			
Tar Sand Triangle	14	6	3	1.5
Sunnyside	5	2	1	0.5

Future Needs: Several technical and resource definition questions will need to be answered before any portion of the 2 billion barrel target for the tar sands can be classified as a potential domestic energy reserve. Even with the substantial advances made in thermal recovery in the past ten years, these key questions will need to be answered before the domestic tar sands can be commercially exploited.

How can adequate rates of steam and air injectivity be obtained in these low permeability deposits?

How can the thermal efficiency of the in situ recovery technologies be improved?

How can the high sweep efficiencies required for ensuring adequate project economics be obtained?

How can continuity best be established between the injection and production wells?

How can air and steam utilization best be confined to the target pay?

In addition, the resource needs to be better defined and understood, not so much as to its overall size, but more in terms of its specific applicability for in situ thermal recovery. This involves a better definition of the continuity of the pay, the nature of any naturally occurring fractures, the competency of the overburden, and the oil saturation.

Assuming the domestic tar sand resource is judged to have sufficient merit, several key research tasks would need to be undertaken. Unlocking the potential of the domestic tar sands appears a more technically difficult and a less favorable undertaking than anticipated from initial outcrop samples. Considerable advances would be required in the in situ thermal technologies for achieving the performance conditions set forth in the recovery equations used in the net energy and economic analysis, including:

Lowering the thermal input requirements for reducing the viscosity of the bitumen—it may be that the use of solvent, or other viscosity reducing materials (such as carbon dioxide) when used jointly with steam, could substantially reduce the input heat requirement for obtaining adequate rates of flow.

Improving the displacement efficiency—it may be that the addition of surfactants or caustics would materially reduce the amount of bitumen left trapped after steam flooding and also serve to reduce thermal requirements.

Using water as a scavenger of heat in an in situ combustion project—the major wet combustion (COFCAW) project by AMOCO in the Canadian Tar Sands could provide important technical information in this area.

Placing horizontal fractures within the target for enhancing injectivity and oil flow—adequate rates of steam and air injection will be essential for realizing any reasonable levels of thermal efficiency.

Beyond these four tasks, numerous laboratory research tasks are required, particularly for: determining the temperature-viscosity relationships of the more favorable deposits, especially at temperatures higher than being currently tested; establishing the final residual oil saturations after steam flooding or combustion; and testing the actual versus theoretical thermal efficiencies of the various deposits.

Finally, it may be that an entirely new recovery process, employing a combination of mining and thermal recovery, may prove to be the most likely technique for unlocking significant quantities of oil from the domestic tar sands. If sufficient vertically continuous sections can be identified and this process becomes better defined from experience in oil recovery from shale, it would be timely to perform similar technical/economic appraisal prior to launching major field testing of the approach.

Summary

This analysis of the domestic tar sand resources and the technologies currently available for recovering them indicates:

Much of the resource is lean and scattered, having too little overburden for an in situ thermal process and too much overburden for surface mining.

From available core data only a small portion (100 to 200 million barrels) would be recoverable under current surface mining technology; this currently identified amount is sufficient only for small scale separation/upgrading facilities of about 10,000 bpd.

Assuming that the in situ thermal recovery technologies can be made to perform as well as stipulated in the analysis, and the economics remain favorable (requiring considerable advances over the current state of thermal recovery technologies), the target may be on the order of 2 billion barrels of recoverable oil.

Substantial portions of the deposits are only sketchily defined, particularly the geologic and reservoir data essential for appraising technical performance. Should the geology prove to be less favorable, the target could fall below 1 billion barrels, conversely if found more favorable, the target could reach 3 billion barrels or more.

OIL SHALE RETORTING

Several processes have been proposed and conceived for the production of oil and gas from oil shale, differing one from the other chiefly in the method and means employed to promote the oil shale pyrolysis and extraction of its products. Besides the characteristics of each oil shale, the yields, operating costs, product quality and therefore the profitability of the oil shale industry will depend on: the process and/or operating methods employed to generate and transfer heat to the oil shale; the fuel utilized; the operating temperatures and many other operating procedures and details. The commonly known processing methods can be classified in two principal groups:

(a) External-Combustion Processes, in which the oil shale pyrolysis is promoted by transfer of the sensible heat of a material-solid in some cases (as TOSCO Process, of The Oil Shale Corp., that utilizes ceramic balls as heat carrier) or recycle gas, in other cases — the gaseous or solid material which serves as heat carrier being heated separately from the oil shale to be processed and recycled or recirculated through the bed of oil shale and a heater, in which the heat carrier is reheated after it has given heat to the oil shale, promoting its pyrolysis;

(b) Internal-Combustion Processes where combustion of the residual carbon and hydrogen from the spent shale of the pyrolysis is carried out in the same processing vessel where pyrolysis takes place by injecting air and recycle gas into the processing vessel; or by the combustion of the shale gas with air, the shale gas product being partially recycled into the process vessel, generating the heat required for the pyrolysis and promoting internal heat exchange through the different zones of the oil shale moving bed by direct counter-current contact between the gas and oil shale.

The liquid products are condensed and separated from the gaseous flow. As some examples of this group one can name the process of Union Oil Company and the Bureau of Mines Gas-Combustion Process.

30

Among others there can also be still cited the processes in use in Estonia, U.S.S.R., of the external-combustion type, with indirect heating of crude oil shale, wherein the pyrolysis heat source is the combustion gases, from the air combustion of the spent shale of the pyrolysis process and where the combustion gases do not make direct contact with the oil shale being subjected to pyrolysis, heating the oil shale through the vessel walls to prevent dilution of the products of pyrolysis by the combustion gas.

This Estonian process is used for the richer oil shale with average oil content 20% or of higher grade. Oil shale of low grade, about 7% oil content, is used in that country as solid fuel in fluidized bed combustion process for electrical power generation. Another alternative that is being studied is the so-called in situ retorting whereby oil shale is heated where it occurs in nature, in its own deposit and this is further described in Chapter 2.

GAS COMBUSTION

Retorting-Gasification with Recycle Gas Stream

According to a process described by *R.F. Deering; U.S. Patent 4,010,092; March 1, 1977; assigned to Union Oil Company of California* spent, coke-containing shale derived from a gas-heated eduction zone is passed through a combustion-gasification zone countercurrently to an upflowing mixture of steam and oxygen-containing gas to effect partial combustion of the coke on the spent shale, the resulting heat of combustion being used to effect concurrent endothermic gasification reactions of steam with unburned coke.

The resulting net production of hot, steam- and hydrogen-containing water gas is then mixed with hot recycle gas derived from the shale eduction zone, the resulting mixture forming the heat carrier required for the gas-heated eduction zone. A recycle portion of the steam-rich water gas from the combustion-gasification zone is continuously withdrawn, passed through a steam generator to effect simultaneous cooling and steam enrichment thereof, and then recycled to the bottom of the gasification reactor. In this manner, a substantial portion of the necessary gaseous heat-carrying capacity is provided in the combustion-gasification zone without losing the heat of vaporization of the steam in the recycle portion of water gas.

A significant aspect of the process is that even though the recycled water gas contains hydrogen, and must pass through the combustion-gasification zone in which hydrogen-burning temperatures prevail, the overall yield of hydrogen is not significantly affected.

Referring to Figure 2.1, raw crushed oil shale is fed at 2 into hopper 4 of shale feeder 6 from which it is pumped upwardly into retort 8. The details of shale feeder 6 are described in more detail in U.S. Patent 3,361,644. The shale feed rate will, of course, vary considerably depending upon the size of the retort and the desired holding time. The raw shale passes upwardly through retort 8, traversing a lower preheating zone and an upper pyrolysis zone. Temperatures in the lower portion of the retort are sufficiently low to condense product oil vapors from the superjacent pyrolysis zone.

Figure 2.1: Oil Shale Retorting–Gasification

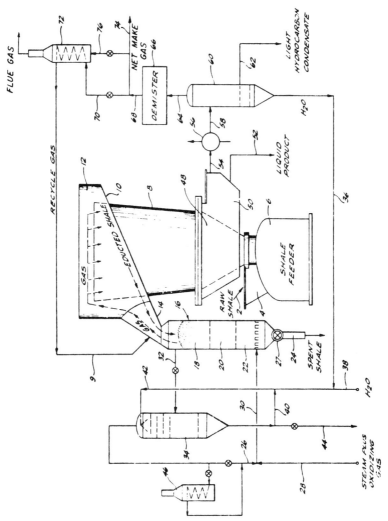

As the shale progresses upwardly through the retort its temperature is gradually increased to eduction levels by countercurrently flowing eduction gases comprising a preheated recycle portion of retort make-gas from line **9**, and the net make of water gas from gasifier **16**. Eduction temperatures are conventional, usually in excess of about 600°F, and preferably between about 700° and about 1000°F. Essentially all of the oil will have been educted from the shale by the time it reaches a temperature of about 900°F. Gas temperatures above about 1300°F in the eduction zone should not be exceeded since they result in excessive shale oil cracking.

Other retorting conditions include shale residence times in excess of about 10 minutes, usually about 30 minutes to 1 hour, sufficient to educt the desired amount of oil at the selected retort temperatures. Shale feed rates usually exceed about 100, and are preferably between about 400 and about 1,000 lb/hr/ft^2 cross sectional area in the retort. These values refer to average cross sectional areas in the tapered retort. Pressure in the retort may be either subatmospheric, atmospheric or superatmospheric. Retorting pressures normally exceed about 0.5 and are preferably about 5 to 400 psig. Heating gas temperatures and flow rates must be sufficient to heat the crushed shale to pyrolysis temperatures.

Heat transfer rates depend in large part on the heating gas flow rate, temperature and heat capacity. Flow rates of at least about 3,000, generally at least about 8,000 and preferably between about 10,000 and 40,000 scf of total heating gas per ton of raw shale are employed. The temperature differential between the heating gas and solids at the top of the pyrolysis zone is usually between 10° and 100°F. Excessive temperature differentials, e.g., in excess of about 400°F, should be avoided.

The retorted oil shale overflowing the top of the retort **8** falls onto the inclined peripheral floor **10** of shroud **12**, which is affixed in fluid-tight fashion to the outer wall of the retort. The retorted shale then gravitates down floor **12** through chute **14** into the top of vertical gasifier **16**, in which is maintained a spent shale preheating zone **18**, a combustion-gasification zone **20** and an ash cooling zone **22**. The retorted shale is essentially oil-free and will contain at least about 2%, usually between 3 and about 5%, and preferably at least 3% by weight of carbon as coke.

In shroud **12**, chute **14** and preheating zone **18**, the retorted shale will ordinarily be at a temperature below about 1100°F. These transition zones are also essentially oxygen-free, and accordingly the retort recycle gas can be introduced into any one or more of such zones. Downflowing spent shale in gasifier **16** is first preheated by direct heat exchange with the upflowing gas stream in preheating zone **18**, and is then gasified in combustion-gasification zone **20** by countercurrent contact with steam and oxygen. Peak temperatures in zone **20** should be sufficiently high to react at least about 20% of the coke with steam to give hydrogen and carbon oxides. Some degree of gasification can be obtained at temperatures as low as 1000°F.

However, peak temperatures above 1100°F, preferably between about 1200° and 1800°F are usually required to obtain feasible gasification rates. Extreme temperatures, e.g., on the order of 2000°F, should be avoided to minimize carbonate decomposition and shale ash fusion, commonly referred to as clinkering. Reaction times should be on the order of at least about 5 minutes, preferably at least about 20 minutes. In cooling zone **22** the shale ash temperature is normally reduced to about 200° to 500°F. The inlet temperature of the steam-oxygen mixture admitted to cooling zone **22** via line **30** will ordinarily range between about 150° and 1000°F, preferably about 200° to 500°F. Spent shale ash is discharged from gasifier **16** via ash outlet **24** controlled by solids flow controller **27**, which may be a star feeder or a vane feeder or the like, and operates to control the solids level in gasifier **16**. A mixture of makeup steam and air or oxygen is brought in via line **28**, and admixed with steam-enriched gasifier recycle gas from line **26**. The resulting mixture is then passed into the bottom of cooling zone **22** via line **30**.

Oxygen addition rates are between about 25 and 250 lb, and preferably between about 50 and 150 lb per ton of raw shale. The amount to be used depends primarily upon the coke content of the retorted shale. For spent shale containing, e.g., 4 to 5 weight percent of coke, it is normally desirable to provide sufficient oxygen to convert (theoretically) about 30 to 50% of the carbon content of the coke to CO_2. This provides the necessary heat to give substantially complete gasification of the remaining coke.

Steam addition to the combustion-gasification zone, including recycled steam, may range between about 200 and 1,000, preferably between 250 and 800 lb per ton of raw shale if oxygen is used as the oxidizing gas. If air is used as the oxidizing gas, about 20 to 50% less steam is needed since the nitrogen in the air supplies part of the heat-carrying capacity. The water-gas product emerging from the top of preheating zone **18** is normally at a temperature of about 800° to 1100°F, and is composed primarily of water vapor, carbon dioxide, and hydrogen (and nitrogen if air was used as the oxidizing gas).

Stable operation of gasifier **16** requires more gaseous heat carrying capacity in the gases entering via line **30** than would be supplied merely by the chemically required oxygen and steam. If additional gaseous heat carrier is not supplied, the combustion in zone **20** (in which peak temperatures prevail) will descend into cooling zone **22**, and conversely if too much gaseous heat carrier is employed peak temperatures will rise into preheating zone **18** and combustion may eventually be extinguished. Since steam is as noted an advantageous heat carrier, an excess thereof is employed, sufficient to render the heat carrying capacity of the total gas steam approximately equal to the heat carrying capacity of the downflowing solids.

In the past the entire water-gas product from the gasifier, with its excess water vapor, was passed first through retort **8** in order to utilize its useful sensible heat content for eduction purposes and then, in admixture with retort make gases, was passed through an air cooler to condense out light hydrocarbons and water and thereby recover a useful total make gas. In this system, all the heat of vaporization of the water vapor from the gasifier was lost since water vapor would either be condensed out at temperatures below 212°F, or leave the system at its low dew-point concentration in the retort off-gases. Consequently, it was necessary to revaporize all water needed for each pass through the gasifier.

It has now been discovered however that a substantial proportion of this heat loss can be avoided by operating the gasifier with an internal recycle of water gas. In Figure 2.1, this recycle water gas stream which normally amounts to about 20 to 50 volume percent of the total gas effluent from the gasifier, is withdrawn via line 32 and passed into steam generator 34, in which steam is generated with concomitant cooling of the recycle gas. At the same time, fines are scrubbed from the recycle gas. Water is supplied to steam generator 34 via condensate water recycle line 36, makeup water line 38, and internal recycle line 40, all of which feed into the top of steam generator 34 via line 42.

In steam generator 34, liquid water cascades downwardly, countercurrently to the rising recycle gas from line 32 whereby simultaneous steam generation, recycle gas cooling and scrubbing take place. The steam-enriched recycle gas is then withdrawn overhead via line 26 as previously described. Excess liquid water accumulating in steam generator 34 is in part recycled internally via lines 40 and 42, and is in part withdrawn to blowdown via line 44 to remove dissolved and suspended solids from the system. Auxiliary gasifier recycle gas heater 46 is provided for startup purposes to assist in establishing the desired temperature profile in gasifier 16. After startup, heater 46 is either bypassed or turned down to low firing, as needed.

In shale retort 8, eduction gases and product oil flow downwardly into the cooler, condensing portion thereof, and then into slotted, frusto-conical product disengagement zone 48, from which product oil and vapors flow into product collection tank 50. Liquid product is withdrawn therefrom via line 52, and vapor effluent is withdrawn via line 54 at a temperature of, e.g., 200° to 300°F. To recover light hydrocarbons therefrom, the vapor effluent is passed through an air cooler 56, and then via line 58 at a temperature of, e.g., 100° to 150°F into separator 60. Condensed water is recovered therefrom and recycled via line 36 as previously described, while the light hydrocarbon condensate is withdrawn via line 62.

Overhead product gas from separator 60, comprising mainly carbon oxides, hydrogen, light hydrocarbons and steam (and nitrogen if air was used as the oxizing gas), as well as some suspended shale oil mist, is taken overhead via line 64 and passed through a demisting unit 66, which may comprise a conventional circulating oil scrubber. The demisted gas from demister 66 is withdrawn via line 68, and disposed of according to two principal alternatives.

According to the first alternative, it is assumed that the oxidizing gas used in gasifier 16 was air, in which case the off-gas in line 66 has a low heating value, useful primarily as fuel gas and as a heat carrier for the retorting zone. For the latter purpose, a recycle portion is passed via line 70 through fired heater 72 and then recycled via line 9 as previously described. Another portion of the off-gas in line 68 is withdrawn as net make gas via line 74, and may be utilized as fuel gas in another gasification-retorting unit which is being operated with an oxygen gasification zone to produce a hydrogen-rich off-gas having higher than mere heating value. Another portion of the make-gas in line 74 is withdrawn via line 76 for use as fuel in heater 72.

If oxygen, or a gas rich in oxygen (containing, e.g., more than about 50% oxygen) was used in gasifier 16, the resulting off-gas in line 66 is much richer in hydrogen, and accordingly the portion not recycled via line 70 is preferably withdrawn via line 74, and the heating requirement for preheater 72 is supplied by gases derived from other sources. The nominal concentration of hydrogen in the net make-gas derived from a pure oxygen gasifier-retorting combination usually ranges between about 15 and 40 volume percent. It also contains about 30 to

70% CO_2, 2 to 6% light hydrocarbons having up to about 8 carbon atoms and minor amounts, e.g., less than 5%, of H_2S, and carbon monoxide.

In the air gasification-retorting systems, the volume of gas recycled via line 9 to the retort should be at least about 2,000 and preferably between about 5,000 and 25,000 scf per ton of raw shale feed. In oxygen gasification-retorting systems, the required retort recycle gas rates are normally about 10 to 30% less than that required for the air gasifier-retorting systems.

Retort recycle gas is employed in order to increase the volume and heat capacity of the gases entering the retorting zone. By this procedure the same amount of heat can be conducted to the retorting zone at a lower temperature thereby minimizing over-cracking and affording more versatile temperature control in the pyrolysis and shale preheating zone.

Introduction of the retort recycle stream to an essentially oxygen-free zone downstream of the combustion-gasification zone results in additional advantages. Firstly, the hydrocarbons in the recycle gas do not interfere with the combustion and gasification of coke on retorted shale in the gasifier. The water vapor partial pressure in the combustion-gasification zone is correspondingly higher resulting in higher hydrogen production rates and yields.

Example: In this example, two operations are compared, in one of which cryogenic oxygen is utilized in the gasifier and in the other of which air is used. Both cases are compared on the basis of a retorting unit to which 5,000 tons per stream day of 34 gallons per ton (Fischer Assay) crushed shale is fed to a retort similar to that illustrated in Figure 2.1, operating at a pressure of 10 psig. The principal operating conditions and results are as follows.

	Oxygen Gasifier	Air Gasifier
Temperatures, °F		
Raw shale	60	60
Eduction maximum (solids)	950	950
Eduction gas maximum	1000	1000
Gasification maximum	1500	1500
Ash from gasification cooling zones	300	300
Inlet gases to gasification zones	250	250
Gas rates per ton of raw shale*		
Recycled from gasification zone, lb	234	117
Generated in steam generator, lb	100	100
Extraneous makeup, lb	300	100
Oxidizing gas to gasification zones, lb	95	500
Retort recycle gas to retorting zones, scf	10,650	12,770
Gasifier make-gas to retorting zones, scf	13,930	13,930
Gasifier off-gas recycled to gasification zones, scf	6,710	7,886
Approximate residence times, hr		
Shale at 800°–1000°F eduction	0.50	0.50
Spent shale at 1000°–1500°F gasification	0.30	0.30
Product yields		
Full range shale oil, bpd	3,845	3,845
Net product gas, MM scfd	35.7	59.5

*Steam to gasification zones.

Composition of the raw retort product gases and retort recycle gases are:

	Oxygen Gasifier (vol %)	Air Gasifier (vol %)
H_2	25.2	15.1
H_2S	0.9	0.6
CO_2	54.7	32.8
CO	2.8	1.7
C_{1-6} hydrocarbons	6.0	3.5
H_2O	10.4	10.4
N_2	nil	35.9

If the respective retort recycle gases in the above example were recycled through the combustion-gasification zones, only a small fraction of the residual coke on the retorted shale fed to the gasifier would be gasified and the yield of hydrogen would be too low to provide an economical source thereof. By virtue of the above gas recycle maintained in the respective gasification zones, a heat saving of about 370,000 Btu per ton of raw shale is obtained in the oxygen gasification case, and about 415,000 Btu per ton in the air gasification case.

R.F. Deering; U.S. Patent 4,043,897; August 23, 1977; assigned to Union Oil Company of California describes a process for educing shale oil having a low arsenic content and for producing hydrogen from oil shale in high yields. It comprises passing shale upwardly through a gas-heated pyrolysis zone to educe oil therefrom, and then passing the spent, coke-laden shale downwardly through a gasification-combustion zone to produce hydrogen-rich heating gas and/or substantially pure hydrogen for use in catalytic refining of the educed shale oil.

Air or oxygen is introduced to the gasification-combustion zone to burn part of the residual coke, thereby heating the spent shale up to gasification temperatures. Steam is injected concurrently with the oxidizing gas in order to gasify unburned coke via the water-gas reaction. Improved hydrogen yields and purity and more effective shale retorting are achieved by recycling hot product gas for eduction into admixture with the gasifier product between the gasification and pyrolysis zones, and eliminating recycle to the gasification-combustion zone.

Multiple Level Fuel Injection

A process described by *J.B Jones, Jr. and A.A. Reeves; U.S. Patent 4,042,485; August 16, 1977* involves a direct retorting method in which combustion in the kiln produces the heat necessary for the pyrolysis for the oil shale. In this process, a generally nonoxygenous gas (usually produced by the pyrolysis) is passed at a low temperature into the bottom of the shale bed so as to cool the hot retorted shale and simultaneously heat the gas as it passes up the column of the shale. A carefully controlled quantity of oxygen-containing gas is then introduced into two mid-locations of the bed to provide a high rate oxidation process, termed combustion, in the kiln and to produce sufficient heat for retorting the oil shale.

The resultant gases and shale oil mist pass from the pyrolysis upwardly through the incoming raw shale, and are disengaged from the shale and passed out to a shale oil recovery system. With properly controlled parameters, the operational efficiency of the process, on an extended production run, approaches 100%

recovery of shale oil and low Btu gas, based on the Fischer Assay Method of testing the oil shale. Such a method is also used for determining the physical qualities and/or quantities of shale oil and gaseous products of the pyrolysis as well as other compositions. In general, the shale is sized to consist of between +½ to 2¾ inches, the quantity of the injected air into the kiln is above about 5,000 scf/ton of shale and the amount of nonoxygenous gas is above about 15,000 scf/ton, producing some 20,000 to 25,000 scf/ton shale.

Cyclone Separators and Absorption Column

M.W. Putman; U.S. Patent 4,075,083; February 21, 1978 describes a retorting process which involves the steps of passing the solid hydrocarbonaceous material in particulate form downwardly in a continuous, substantially vertical column successively through a preheating zone, a distillation zone, a combustion zone, and a residue cooling zone. The solid residue is removed in a cool condition at the bottom of the column while the distillation and combustion products, including a gas relatively lean in combustibles are removed from the top of the column also in a relatively cool condition (110° to 130°F).

The gas stream and distillation products from the top of the column are passed through a gas blower and two mist separators to recover the liquid mist droplets in the stream. The mist-free stream then enters the bottom of an oil absorber column and flows up through the column countercurrent to a cool suitable absorption fluid such as kerosene. The purpose of the absorber is to recover the lower boiling hydrocarbons in the gas stream which were not condensed in the retort. The low-boiling hydrocarbons are recovered by the desorber. The desorbed kerosene is recycled to the top of the absorber and the low-boiling hydrocarbons recovered are added to the oil product.

A portion of the gas now free of volatile hydrocarbons is vented from the system. Although this gas has a low heat content, it is combustible in a special burner and must either be burned under a steam boiler to generate power or be flared to the air to avoid pollution of the atmosphere. The balance of the gas now free of almost all volatile hydrocarbons is mixed with the correct amount of air and the mixture is admitted to the bottom of the retort column and the mixture of air and relatively noncombustible gases passes upwardly through the downwardly moving residue from the combustion zone, thus cooling the hot residue and itself becoming heated.

No combustion can take place in this section of the column because the retorted shale is essentially free of carbonaceous residue and the gas is too lean in combustibles to ignite below the ignition temperatures of the gases present. Since no combustion can take place in this portion of the column, sensible heat is merely exchanged in countercurrent fashion between the upwardly rising gas and the downwardly moving combustion zone residue in this zone of the retort.

The ascending oxygen-containing gas stream meets descending retorted shale; the carbonaceous residue always present in the retorted shale combines with the oxygen and a combustion zone is established. A portion of the combustible gases in the ascending gas stream is also burned. There is great flexibility available with respect to the location of the combustion zone. It is only necessary to increase the rate of withdrawing the retorted shale to lower the combustion zone and vice versa. The rate is normally maintained such that the top temperature is in the 110° to 130°F range and the spent shale temperature is between 200° and 250°F.

The hot gases produced in the combustion zone pass upwardly through the column of shale and quickly give up their heat to the downwardly moving material, thereby establishing a relatively narrow zone of distillation immediately above the combustion zone. The gaseous products of distillation and combustion, still relatively hot, pass upwardly through the column in contact with the downwardly moving raw carbonaceous material, whereby the combustion and distillation products rapidly become cooled and the hydrocarbonaceous solids become heated.

The principles of the process are applicable to any sort of retorting process where the carbonaceous solid and the gas flow countercurrent to each other and where the gas stream is withdrawn from the shale bed at a sufficiently low temperature so that substantially all, or the major portion of the vapor content of the gas stream undergoes condensation before leaving the shale bed. However, this process teaches that it would be necessary to pass the cool gas through an absorber-desorber system to recover the gasoline range hydrocarbons present as a vapor in the cool gas stream.

Moving Bed Reactor

E. DaCosta Barcellos; U.S. Patent 4,060,479; November 29, 1977 describes a process for obtaining oil, gas, sulfur and other products from shale. The process comprises drying, pyrolysis, gasification, combustion and cooling of pyrobituminous shale or similar rocks in a single passage of the shale continuously in a moving bed, the charge and discharge of the shale being intermittent and the maximum temperature of the bed being maintained in a range of about 1050° to 1200°C (1900° to 2200°F) or higher. The shale is essentially completely freed from the organic matter, fixed carbon and sulfur, resulting in a clean solid residue which can be disposed of without harming the ecology.

Figure 2.2, which serves as a flowsheet, schematically illustrates the process. Shown therein is vessel **1** preferably insulated to prevent heat loss and complementary parts and accessories: charge buckets **7**, charge bin **2**, oil shale feeder duct **6**, upper valve **8** of the charge bin, bottom valve **9** of charge bin, discharge mechanism **5**, auxiliary discharge bin **4**, discharge bin **3**, upper valve **10** of discharge bin, bottom valve **11** of discharge bin, gas collectors **12**, charge bin exhaustor device **13** and discharge bin exhaustor device **14**, purge device **33** of charge bin **2** and similar purge device **15** for discharge bin **3**, tube for moving bed internal thermocouple bundles **16** and gas injector **17**.

Accordingly, as shown in the flowsheet, the process operates as follows: crude raw shale to be processed, having been mined, crushed, classified in adequate particle size range and homogenized by a suitable method of mixing, is charged into the charge buckets **7** by suitable transportation and charging equipment, staying therein until the proper moment for its introduction into the charge bin **2**. The oil shale processing is continuous, although the charge of raw oil shale and discharge of spent shale are intermittent.

When the charge bin **2** gets emptied, which is detected by a device just below the charge bin bottom valve **9**, the upper valve **8** of the charge bin being closed and the bottom valve **9** open, the bottom valve is then closed and the preparation

Figure 2.2: Moving Bed Reactor

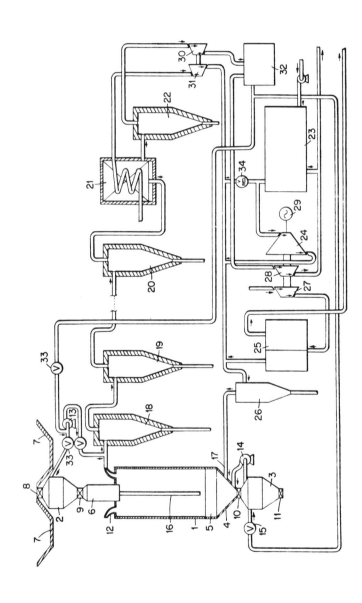

Source: U.S. Patent 4,060,479

of the next charge bin 2 for the charge takes place as later described. Once the bin 2 is prepared to receive a new charge of oil shale, a pair of buckets 7, each having half the capacity of charge bin 2, is operated to completely fill the bin.

Next, the upper valve 8 is closed and the air contained in bin 2 is purged by means of an appropriate operation of suitable devices provided for this purpose. After the air (that has penetrated into the bin) has been expelled or reduced to the practical minimum, the upper valve 8 is closed and the charge bin 2 is pressurized, equalizing its internal pressure with the internal pressure of the vessel 1 by introducing a pressurized purge gas into the charge bin 2. Next the charge bin bottom valve 9 is opened and the charging operation is completed.

The volume of feeder duct 6 of the vessel is compatible with the processing mass flow rate and the time period needed for the operation of charging the charge bin 2 (including the complete preparation of the charge bin 2 to be put in communication with the process vessel 1 interior by the feeder duct 6) in order to assure an essentially continuous oil shale supply to the moving bed. Once the charging operation of the charge bin 2 is completed, the cycle is repeated with the discharge and recharge of the charge bin 2.

The charging operation, in resume, consists in the chronological sequence: closing of the charge bin bottom valve 9; recovery of the gases therein contained; opening of the charge bin upper valve 8; filling the charge bin with the oil shale from the buckets 7; removal of the air that has been trapped with the oil shale, on the closing of the charge bin upper valve 8; repressurization of the charge bin with a gas from the process; and, finally, opening of the charge bin bottom valve 9. The bulk oil shale held in the charge bin 2, after completion of the charging of the charge bin operation, flows by gravity through the feeder duct 6 to the top of the moving bed contained in the vessel 1 where the coarse oil shale spreads along a conical surface area in accordance with the angle of repose of bulk oil shale.

Alternatively, the oil shale is spread, by means of a mechanical antisegregation device, along an essentially horizontal area at the top of the moving bed. The bulk oil shale introduced in a continuous way to the top of the moving bed contained in the vessel 1 flows downward by gravity action, traversing, slowly the entire height of the vessel, wherein the oil shale is subjected to the processing action and the resultant spent shale (the solid residue of the process, essentially a calcined material) is collected in the auxiliary discharge bin 4.

The rate of flow of the spent shale (and so the process rate of flow) is controlled by means of a discharge mechanism 5 which proportionates a controlled and essentially uniform discharging rate along the bottom vessel cross section, so that all the particles of oil shale have essentially the same residence time along the moving bed, flowing essentially at the same velocity downward. It is also important to avoid channeling, i.e., preferential gas flow through holes or channels inside the moving bed, that would provoke or involve bad gas flow distribution through the moving bed, with loss of process efficiency.

The spent shale of this process is the raw oil shale after it has been essentially exhausted of organic matter, fixed carbon and sulfur. The oil shale processing occurs in its descending flow through the vessel 1, in various simultaneous, successive and continuous stages: in the upper bed occurs the drying of oil shale moisture and heating to the level of temperature needed for the oil shale kerogen pyrolysis. Heating is provided by heat exchange through direct contact with the ascending gases which percolate countercurrently through the moving bed. The gases are composed of steam, admitted in the auxiliary discharge bin **4** below the discharge mechanism **5** and of the gases and vapor generated successively by pyrolysis, gasification and combustion of the oil shale.

After drying the oil shale is subjected to progressive heating until it reaches the zone corresponding to the pyrolysis temperature range [320° to 700°C (the pyrolysis zone)] wherein takes place the pyrolysis of the kerogen of the oil shale, the pyrolysis being characterized by the transformation of the kerogen into, essentially: oil, gases and water vapor that evolve from the oil shale and are incorporated in the ascending gaseous stream. Just below the pyrolysis zone, without a clear boundary, the continuous heating or pyrolysis spent shale causes it to attain, in the subsequent gasifying zone, a temperature range of about 760°C up to the maximum bed temperature.

In the gasifying zone there takes place essentially the known water-gas reaction, consisting in the combination of the water vapor with the residual carbon of pyrolysis spent shale, resulting in the formation of H_2, CO and CO_2, and the formation of H_2S derived from the residual sulfur of the pyrolysis spent shale.

Just below the gasifying zone the gasified spent shale enters the combustion zone (also without a clear limit between the combustion and gasification zones) wherein its temperature rises to the moving bed maximum temperature (maximum process temperature) by the effect of the heat generated by the combustion of the fuel matter remaining in the gasified spent shale, i.e, essentially carbon, sulfur and hydrogen, the combustion consisting of the combination of C, H, S with the oxygen injected below the moving bed mixed with steam. The combustion is the source of heat required for the process.

Below the combustion zone there takes place the cooling of the spent shale (calcined shale) by heat exchange in direct contact with the ascending gaseous mixture, the mixture consisting essentially of water vapor (steam) and oxygen, the mixture being injected below the moving bed. The spent shale is cooled to the lowest feasible temperature; the spent shale discharge temperature is controlled at around 120° through 150°C, just above the inlet temperature of the steam-oxygen mixture, which is of the order of 105° through 135°C.

From the discharge mechanism **5**, installed in the bottom of the process vessel **1**, the spent shale falls into the auxiliary discharge bin **4** integral with vessel **1**, and duly tight against gas leakage from and to the outside. The discharge bin upper valve **10**, situated between the auxiliary discharge bin **4** and the discharge bin **3**, being open and the discharge bin bottom valve **11** being shut, the spent shale continuously falls from the auxiliary bin into the discharge bin. Once the discharge bin **3** is completely filled, which is detected by a suitable device, the discharge operation and preparation of the discharge bin for refilling is started.

The discharge and preparation of the discharge bin **3** for the refilling operation consists in an operation similar to the feeding and preparing operation of the charge bin **2** for each new feed of the charge bin. In brief, the discharge operation, preferably performed automatically by means of suitable control devices is carried out in the following operational sequence: after the level of spent shale at the highest level settled is detected by the above-mentioned suitable device as being just below the discharge bin upper valve **10**, the valve is shut off. The discharge bin upper valve **10** is constructed to completely seal the discharge bin against gas leakage from and to the discharge bin **3** during the spent shale discharge operation.

Next the discharge bin **3** is depressurized in order to avoid or lessen loss of the gaseous mixture of oxygen and steam contained therein by the exhaustion, through the discharge bin exhausting device **14**, of the gaseous mixture, this mixture being readmitted into the process vessel **1** through the auxiliary discharge bin **4**. At the same time as exhaustion of the oxygen-steam mixture is effected, a purge gas is injected into the bottom of the discharge bin so that the purge gas displaces the oxygen-steam mixture. The purpose of this purge operation is to avoid loss of oxygen and steam.

The gas flow occurs in the following manner: steam is generated in a conventional boiler **23** at high pressure and a superheat temperature suitable for driving steam turbine **24** that moves gas compressor **27, 28** and electric power generator **29**. Also, in the desulfurization of oil shale gas plant **21**, there is produced steam of medium superheat temperature and pressure, which is first utilized to drive turbine **31** that moves gas compressor **30**. From the turbines steam is withdrawn at saturation temperature or near that, at low pressure, about 1.5 to 3 atm abs, and is collected in a process steam pipeline to which is connected the line of oxygen that is separated in the oxygen separation plant **25**.

The mixture of the oxygen and process steam is homogenized by a suitable device that can be a cyclone **26** and the mixture is injected into the auxiliary discharge bin **4** connected to the process vessel **1** and constituting an integral part thereof. The injection of the gaseous mixture is done through a device designed to provide an essentially perfect gas distribution all along the bottom of the discharge mechanism **5** through which the mixture reaches the shale moving bed.

In addition to the amounts of steam withdrawn from the turbines, a complementary amount of steam, quantity sufficient for the process temperature control, is withdrawn directly from the boiler **23**, through a pressure reduction valve **34**. Inside the vessel, in an upward flow through the moving bed, the oxygen-steam mixture brings about the chemical and physical phenomena reactions, heat exchange and removal of liquid and gaseous products of the process already mentioned in the above description of the oil shale flow and processing.

The gases, vapors and mist of liquid products delivered in the process, mixed with the steam admitted through the bottom of the moving bed are collected by suitable gas collectors **12** fabricated and arranged to provide good gas distribution of gas flow through the moving bed, ideally equal along all the cross sections of the moving bed to assure the uniform and efficient processing of all the bulk shale.

The measurement of moving bed temperatures at several suitable points can be effected by means of thermocouple bundles held in alloy steel tubes **16** arranged vertically, inserted within the moving bed and tightly sealed against process gas infiltration. The number and arrangement or location of the thermocouple points are such as to provide suitable process control. With the purpose of protecting the wires of the thermocouples, an inert atmosphere is provided and maintained inside the thermocouple bundle tubes by means of suitable devices.

The liquids recovery system operates as follows: the gaseous mixture, with oil mist, collected in each one of the gas collectors **12**, flowing through appropriate piping, reaches a primary cyclone-condenser **18** wherein it is cooled and partially condensed. The liquid products, essentially oil and water effluent from each one of the cyclone-condensers, are collected in tight containers, through the drain of the corresponding cyclone. From the oil and water containers, where these products are separated by difference of densities, into two well-defined phases, each one of the liquid products is separately pumped to a suitable destination.

The gaseous flow not condensed in the primary condenser-cyclones **18** goes through a series of other condenser-cyclones **19, 20** that constitute, with the primary condenser-cyclones, the liquid recovery system. In passing successively through the condenser-cyclones, the gases are submitted to gradual cooling and at each cooling stage successively lighter oil fractions and decreasing amounts of water are condensed. The gradual cooling can be continued down to temperatures as low as about $10°$ to $0°C$, in order to attain maximum condensation of water and light fractions of oil under economically favorable conditions.

The product gas effluent of the last condenser-cyclone **20** of the liquid recovery system flows to the gas treatment process unit **21**, wherein elementary sulfur recovery takes place by means of the known Claus Process Reaction and separation of the sulfur from the gas by a cyclone-condenser **22** and the components of the desulfurized gas are further separated in the degree of refinement suitable for the utilization to which the desulfurized gas and components are destined. The treatment of the product raw gas effluent of the above-described system of liquid recovery can be effected by many known methods.

Oil-Depleted Shale

According to a process developed by *T.E. Ban; U.S. Patent 4,039,427; August 2, 1977; assigned to McDowell-Wellman Engineering Company* oil-depleted material containing uncombusted carbon and hydrocarbons is used as a combustible heat source to educe oil from oil-bearing material. The oil-bearing material is charged on a traveling grate to form a burden, and the remaining carbon and hydrocarbons in the bed of oil-depleted material are combusted to raise the temperature of the bed to above about $1000°F$.

A reducing atmosphere is passed through the oil-depleted and combusted bed to raise the temperature of the reducing atmosphere. The heated reducing atmosphere is then passed through the oil-bearing material to raise the temperature of the oil-bearing material to at least about $800°F$, to thereby educe oil from the oil-bearing material.

According to one preferred aspect of the process, the oil-bearing material is layered on a sealed, circular traveling grate to form the burden. On a separate grate, oil-depleted material recycled from the discharge station of the circular traveling grate and having uncombusted carbon and hydrocarbons contained therein is combusted to raise the temperature to between about $1000°$ and $1700°F$. The oil-depleted combusted material is then layered onto the burden of oil-bearing material. Adjacent the discharge zone for the oil-depleted, uncombusted material and for the oil-depleted, combusted material, a reducing atmosphere is updrafted through those materials to raise the temperature of the reducing atmosphere. The reducing atmosphere is then downdrafted through the layers to further raise its temperature to between about 1000° and 1700°F.

As the heated reducing atmosphere passes through the oil-bearing material, the temperature of the oil-bearing material is raised to above about 800°F. This temperature educes oil from the material and the oil is separated and collected. At the discharge station, the combusted oil-depleted material is sliced from the uncombusted oil-depleted material and is sent to a waste area. The uncombusted oil-depleted material is recycled to the combustion grate by way of a mineral reclamation station if the material contains such valuable minerals.

Continuous Monitoring of Density and Specific Gravity

A process described by *A.A. Reeves; U.S. Patent 4,090,945; May 23, 1978; assigned to Paraho Corporation* involves providing a continuous and real time readout of such important kiln feed properties as raw and retorted shale bulk density, raw oil shale richness, as well as shale specific gravity. The continuous determination of the various data of the raw shale provides means for an accurate and continuous adjustment of the retorting to meet the process requirements of the varying properties of the raw shale. The continuous determination of the bulk density of the retorted shale is especially responsive to the degree of carbonate decomposition and, therefore, reflects a temperature history of the oil shale processing in the retort.

The process provides a combination of density and weight measurements to infer the specific gravity of granular solids. The combination of weight and volumetric measurements are used to determine continuously the bulk density of the granular solids. The process furthermore involves detection of solids fractions in differential movement in large kilns. It provides for the use of an eccentric plug feeder rotating over a large retarder plate to distribute granular solids uniformly over a large area without segregation.

An important feature of the combination of the eccentric feeder and the annular bin is the distributing and mixing action of the eccentric plug feeder. The radial movement of the feeder on the horizontal extent of the retarder plate moves all solids over the edges, so that material falling from the conveyor belt becomes uniformly distributed over a large cross section with minimum particle size segregation. For example, if the retarder plate is 20 ft in diameter, a 40 ft diameter kiln could be accommodated with a low vertical height for the feed mechanism.

The feed mechanism of the retarder plate and the annular bin provides an excellent position for the introduction of purge gas. The purge gas seals the top of the kiln to prevent the loss of product and toxic gases out through the feed mechanism.

EXTERNAL HEAT PYROLYSIS

Control of Gas Flow Parameters

A process described by *J.B. Jones, Jr., and A.A. Reeves; U.S. Patent 4,116,810; September 26, 1978; assigned to Paraho Corporation* involves the indirect retorting method in which an externally heated gas provides the heat necessary for the pyrolysis for the oil shale. In this process, a generally nonoxygenous gas (produced by the pyrolysis) is passed at a low temperature into the bottom of the shale bed. The gas cools the hot retorted shale as it passes up the column of the shale. A carefully controlled quantity of a hot, nonoxygenous gas is then introduced into at least one location in the shale bed, generally near the middle point of the kiln, to provide a sufficient temperature of the shale for a pyrolysis of the organic carbonaceous material in the oil shale.

The resulting gases and shale oil mist pass upwardly through the raw shale feed into the bed, and when disengaged from the shale, it is passed out to a shale oil recovery system. With properly controlled parameters, the operational efficiency of the process, on an extended production run, approaches a 100% recovery of shale oil based on the Fischer Assay Method of testing of oil shale. The shale oil, gaseous products of the pyrolysis, and other compositions may, likewise, be assayed by the testing method.

In general, the shale is sized to between +½ to 2¾ inches, the quantity of the injected hot gas into the kiln is about 9,000 to 11,500 scf/ton of shale and the amount of cooled, nonoxygenous gas is about 9,000 scf/ton introduced into the bottom of the shale bed.

The schematic flow diagram of Figure 2.3 shows a general equipment arrangement used for the indirect mode retorting and includes the use of a vertical kiln **10**, shown schematically in cross section. Normally the vessel will be provided with thermocouple probes extending downwardly for monitoring the temperature of various portions of the shale bed.

Figure 2.3: Indirect Heat Pyrolysis

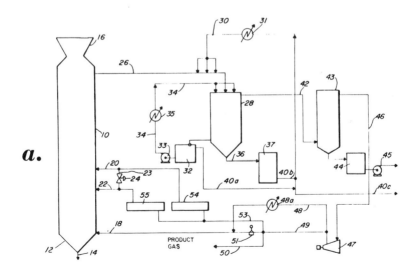

(continued)

Figure 2.3: (continued)

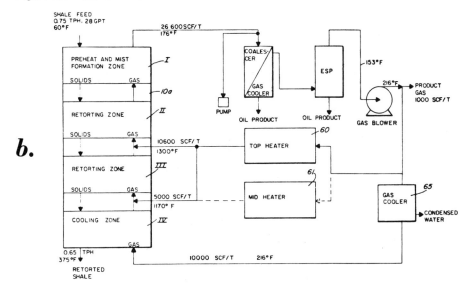

b.

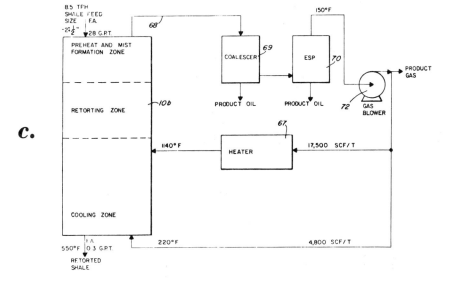

c.

(a) Schematic view of a flow diagram for the retorting of oil shale in a single vertical column

(b) Schematic flow diagram using a double injection of heated gas into a single column of oil shale with the general parameters of the material flows and temperature ranges

(c) Schematic flow diagram of a modified form of the process illustrating the parameters of the flows and temperature ranges of the mode

Source: U.S. Patent 4,116,810

This is typically a circular vessel, lined with refractory and having a metal skin for containing the refractory and protecting it from injury. The refractory need not be resistant to high heat, but should have high insulating material to minimize heat losses.

Such a kiln is provided with a grate mechanism in the bottom just above the conical bottom head **12**, such grates being well known in the prior art. A very suitable grate is described in U.S. Patent 3,401,922. The retorted shale passes through the grate and out locks, not shown, in the outlet line **14**. Such locks are well known in the art and they may be rotary locks, valved locks or the like. Raw shale is introduced by a feed mechanism into the top **16**. The shale is generally fed through locks, which are also common in the art, such as rotary feed lock means or the like.

Gas for cooling the retorted shale is introduced into the bottom of the kiln **10** through a line **18**; an explanation of the cooling gas is given below. The gas for cooling may be introduced by distribution means across the bottom of the column of shale through various means. One effective means is shown in U.S. Patent 3,777,940. Heated gas is introduced into the kiln in one or two levels or locations in the shale bed by means of lines **20** and **22**. The injection device may be such as described in U.S. Patents 3,432,348 and 3,589,661.

The distributors should provide uniform contacting of the particulate solids in the bed with the incoming gas. For large shaft vessels it should be noted that a substantial problem exists in the introduction of gas, and the two patents illustrate effective means for injecting gas into large diameter vessels to provide a uniform flow of the gas across the cross-sectional extent of the vessel. A bypass line **23** provided with a valve **24** provides means for cross-flows of the gas in the lines **20** and **22**, if desired. Ordinarily the bypass is closed. Off-gas is removed from the kiln by means of line **26** which also includes products of retorting including gases, condensable gases, oil mist or vapor and the like, explained below.

The off-gas, containing the products of the retorting, is passed through a coalescer **28**, which is initially provided with a spray of coalescing oil from line **30** injected into line **26** immediately ahead of the coalescer. The coalescing oil through line **30** is at a lower temperature, by a heat exchanger **31**, than the material coming from the kiln and, therefore, a substantial quantity of the oil mist is coalesced and recovered in the coalescer **28**. To further aid the action of the coalescer, some of the oil from the coalescer **28** is collected in a sump **32** and is passed by means of pump **33** to a line **34**, through a wash oil heat exchanger **35** into the coalescer. This helps to lower and maintain the temperature of the materials in the coalescer.

Recovered oil from the coalescer **28** passes through line **36** into a sump **37** and subsequently out through a product oil line **40b**. Oil from sump **32** passes out line **40a**, joining oil from line **40b** in product line **40c**. A spray oil cooler **31** mounted in the line **30** from the product sump **37** provides means for lowering and maintaining the temperature of the spray oil injected into the line **26**. The gaseous component not coalesced in the coalescer **28** passes out line **42** into an electrostatic precipitator **43** where the residual oil, shale dust, or any other solids left in the gas are precipitated. With an adequate coalescer the amount of liquid recovered in the electrostatic precipitator should normally be less than about 50%. The liquid from the electrostatic precipitator passes into a sump **44** and subsequently out through line **45**, along with the product of line **40c** to tankage or use.

The clean gas from the electrostatic precipitator passes out line **46** through a blower **47**. The out line splits the stream into a line **48** passing through a heat exchanger **48a** and a line **49**. The line **49** is also split and terminates at one end through a product gas line **50**. Line **49** also feeds cool gas to line **18**, being controlled by a valve **51**. The gas, not passing out through the product line **50**, flows through a line **53** which is split into two parts. One part goes into a heater **54**, and the other part goes into a second heater **55**, which respectively feeds lines **20** and **22**, entering the kiln.

The schematic flow diagram of Figure 2.3a essentially provides basis for the diagram of Figure 2.3b, which shows the rates of the various streams along with their temperatures for a 2½ ft kiln. In this indirect mode using an 8½ ft inside diameter kiln, providing a shale bed of 24 to 26 ft, shale is fed into the kiln **10a** at a rate of 11 tons per hour at about 60°F. In one test (No. 3) a 2½ ft inside diameter kiln was used, with a shale rate of about 0.75 ton per hour. The nominal assay of this shale feed is about 28 gal/ton of shale containing about 2.5% of water. This shale has a size consist shown in the table below, which is nominally ⅜ to 2 inches. The table is the screen analysis of the shale of the three tests.

Table 1

Shale Size	Test 1	Test 2	Test 3
	. . . . (weight percent).		
2.00 inches	0	0	0
1.50 inches	20.0	25.0	10.7
1.05 inches	37.5	34.4	29.0
0.742 inch	22.3	23.2	25.7
0.525 inch	16.0	13.9	18.0
0.371 inch	1.4	1.3	2.6
0.263 inch	1.4	0.7	3.3
0.185 inch	0.4	0.4	2.6
0.093 inch	0.6	0.5	4.8
Pan	0.4	1.0	2.6
Loss	0.0	0.2	0.5

This shale passes through the preheat and mist formation zone, I, Figure 2.3b, into the first or upper retorting zone, II, then into a lower retorting zone, III, and finally through a cooling zone, IV, and it is discharged from the kiln at about 375°F. The quantity of the retorted shale in the 8½ ft diameter kiln is about 9.5 tons per hour with the difference between the retorted shale quantity and the raw shale quantity being withdrawn from the kiln in the form of liquid and gas products.

The off-gas, which includes recycle gas as well as the products of the retorting gas and liquid, amounts to about 22,500 scf/ton at about 200°F. This passes through the coalescer which recovers about 14 gal/ton of the oil which is formed as a mist in the retorting. The gas leaving the coalescer passes into the electrostatic precipitator (ESP) which recovers an additional 14 gal/ton of oil. The gas from the ESP passes into a gas blower which provides about 733 scf/ton product gas at 220°F; a typical gas analysis is shown in the table below.

Table 2

	Test 1	Test 2	Test 3
	. . . . (mol percent)		
H_2	14.1	17.06	35.0
N_2	0.5	0.37	0.7
O_2	0.1	0.0	0.1
CO	2.0	1.64	7.4
CH_4	10.5	17.34	11.8
CO_2	14.7	11.19	11.7
C_2H_4	2.5	6.41	0.8
C_2H_6	2.7	4.91	0.6
C_3 fraction	2.2	4.19	0.5
C_4 fraction	0.9	1.57	0.4
C_5 fraction	0.3	0.79	−
H_2S	1.9	3.34	1.0
H_2O	45.3	29.90	30.0
Oil	0.3	0.50	−
NH_3	2.0	0.79	−
Total	100.0	100.0	100.0
Specific gravity	0.80	0.78	0.59

The remainder of the gas passes a line which is split; one part of 12,750 scf/ton passes into the two heaters **60** and **61**, while 9,000 scf/ton at 142°F, after passing a gas cooler **65**, is injected into the bottom of the kiln. In the cooling of the gas which enters the cooler at 220°F and is exhausted at 142°F, about 4.9 gallons per ton of water is condensed. The gas is split into approximately two equal parts and one-half of each passes through each heater into different levels in the kiln. Thus, about 6,375 scf/ton at about 1200°F are introduced into the two retorting zones.

In a specific set of tests a single heater (Figure 2.3c) was used to introduce gas into the 8½ ft i.d. kiln, and the schematic flow diagram of the same indicated about 8.5 tons per hour of raw, crushed shale, with a size consist of ½ to 2 inches, at a Fischer Assay of 28 gallons per ton, is passed into the kiln **10b** and retorted shale is withdrawn from the kiln from about 550°F. In this configuration, about 17,500 scf/ton of gas is passed through the heater **67** and is introduced into the bed at about 1140°F. About 4,800 scf/ton of gas at 220°F is passed into the bottom of the kiln to provide cooling for the retorted shale, and to recover some of the sensible heat of the shale for introducing into the retorting zone.

The off-gases withdrawn through line **68**, in the range of 225° to 305°F pass through the coalescer **69** and the ESP **70**, and the final clean gas at about 150°F is passed into the blower **72** for producing the product gas and the cooling gas. It is noted that in passing through the blower, the gas is heated from 150° to 220°F.

In following the flow diagram of Figure 2.3c, the following Tables 3 and 4 show the results of two extended runs in the 8½ ft i.d. kiln. Another run was made in the 2½ ft i.d. kiln. Table 3 sets up the particular length of the test, the rates and quantities of the materials into and out of the kiln. The tests are arranged to show the total amount of recycle gas passed into the kiln at 21,101, 24,276 and 32,625 scf/ton. Even though the operating conditions were different for these three tests, the recovered oil in each test was 90 to 92 volume percent based on the Fischer Assay. Additional hydrocarbon is recovered in the product gas, which makes the high yield.

Table 3

	Test 1 100 Hours	Test 2 16 Hours	Test 3 8 Hours
Rates and quantities			
Recycle, scf/ton			
Top	18,100	12,544	17,650
Middle	0	0	4,885
Bottom	6,176	8,557	10,080
Total	24,276	21,101	32,615
Raw shale, tons/hr	7.9	12.3	0.75
Raw shale properties			
Moisture content, wt %	1.27	0.84	0.39
Fischer Assay, gal/ton	27.7	26.1	30.4
Fischer Assay, wt % oil	10.55	9.94	11.6
Fischer Assay, wt % water	1.86	1.88	1.2
Fischer Assay, wt % gas + loss	1.91	1.78	2.1
Mineral CO_2, wt %	17.27	17.65	17.39
Ignition loss, wt %	33.23	33.25	33.68
Carbon, wt %	17.10	17.44	18.03
Hydrogen, wt %	1.77	1.83	1.93
Nitrogen, wt %	0.49	0.48	0.53
Nominal part size, in x 2	0.50	0.50	0.50
Temperatures, °F			
Product oil out	161	189	153
Retorted shale out	499	396	375
Raw shale in	47	50	70
Product and recycle gas	216	205	216
Off-gas	296	322	176
Top heater	1193	1242	1300
Mid heater	—	—	1170
Top dist inlet	1141	1198	1290
Mid dist inlet	—	—	1160
Bottom dist inlet	216	150	216
Yields			
Oil collected, gal/ton	25.5	24.2	27.4
Oil collected, FA vol %	92	92	90
Product gas, scf/ton	1,552	950	1,040
Retorted shale, wt % RS	84	85	86
Liquid water, lb/ton	17.5	37.8	5.0
Material recovery, wt %	98	99	98
Miscellaneous			
Retort dp inch H_2O/ft bed	0.62	0.82	0.88
Carbonate decomposition, wt %	10	5	5
Retort bed height, ft in	24'0"	24'0"	24'4"
Throughput, lb/hr/ft^2	573	463	305

Table 4

	Test 1	Test 2	Test 3
Product oil properties			
Gravity, deg API	20.3	21.0	22.8
Viscosity, SUS 130°	110.3	85.4	92.2

(continued)

Table 4 (continued)

	Test 1	Test 2	Test 3
Viscosity, SUS 210°	53.0	49.1	44.8
Ramsbottom carbon, wt %	2.31	1.52	2.03
Water content, vol %	6.84	2.77	0.1
Solids, BS, wt %	1.47	1.27	0.1
Carbon, wt %	84.36	85.15	84.53
Hydrogen, wt %	11.41	11.42	11.55
Nitrogen, wt %	1.92	1.99	1.72
Retorted shale properties			
Fischer Assay, gal/ton	0.3	0.6	0.1
Mineral CO_2, wt %	18.63	19.82	19.14
Organic carbon, wt %	2.71	3.14	2.53
Fischer Assay, wt % oil	0.13	0.25	0.0
Fischer Assay, wt % water	0.34	0.63	0.2
Fischer Assay, wt % gas + loss	0.15	0.49	0.1
Ignition loss, wt %	21.29	23.17	22.35
Carbon, wt %	7.78	8.55	7.78
Hydrogen, wt %	0.21	0.34	0.22
Nitrogen, wt %	0.27	0.31	0.30
Retort heat requirements			
Heater duty, MBtu/ton	498	410	670
lb Shale per lb hot gas	1.81	2.66	1.97

The properties of the retorted shale are shown in Table 4, and it can be seen that the shale was completely retorted since only 0.1 to 0.6 gallon per ton was left in the retorted shale. Thermal efficiency of the retort is reflected in the low heater duty in the tests in the larger retort and the high shale-to-hot-gas weight ratio.

A related process described by *A.A. Reeves; U.S. Patent 4,066,529; January 3, 1978; assigned to Paraho Corporation* involves a method of designing the gas flow parameters of a vertical shaft oil shale retorting vessel. The process requires determining the proportion of gas introduced in the bottom of the vessel and into intermediate levels in the vessel to provide for lateral distribution of gas across the vessel cross section, providing mixing with the uprising gas, and determining the limiting velocity of the gas through each nozzle.

The total quantity of gas necessary for oil shale treatment in the vessel may be determined and the proportion to be injected into each level is then determined based on the velocity relation of the orifice velocity and its feeder manifold gas velocity. A limitation is placed on the velocity of gas issuing from an orifice by the nature of the solid being treated, usually physical tests of gas velocity impinging the solid.

Multiple Stage Retorting

In accordance with a process described by *H.C. Reed; U.S. Patent 4,092,237; May 30, 1978; assigned to Kerr-McGee Corporation* oil shale is introduced into a lock which discharges into a closed, vertical, stationary kiln fitted with mechanisms which cause the particulate oil shale to move continuously downwardly in a controlled, uniform plug-type flow. The shale is heated by a counterflow of hot, nonoxidizing gases to the temperature required to pyrolyze the kerogen.

The gaseous fraction of the kerogen joins the counterflowing gases for removal from the top of the kiln. The hot particulate shale containing the carbonaceous fraction of the kerogen moves downwardly through a second lock into a conveyance connected to the top of a second similar kiln wherein the carbonaceous residue is reacted with gaseous water and oxygen in a cocurrent manner to supply heat to the decarbonized shale and to produce carbon oxides and hydrogen.

The heat in the decarbonized shale is then partially removed by a counterflow of a nonoxidizing recycle gas which joins with the carbon oxides and hydrogen to supply heat for retorting in the first kiln. The cooled decarbonized shale passes out of the second kiln through a lock onto a conveyor for disposal.

Referring to Figure 2.4, a Section One comprising a crushing and screening zone **10** is provided to crush the mined oil shale into a coarse (+½ to 3 inches) and a fine (–½ inch) particulate fraction and separate the same. The coarse particulate shale fraction thereafter enters a Section Two via a line **12** comprising a feed mechanism of any type known in the art and is distributed by a solids distributor **14**.

Figure 2.4: Oil Shale Retorting Process

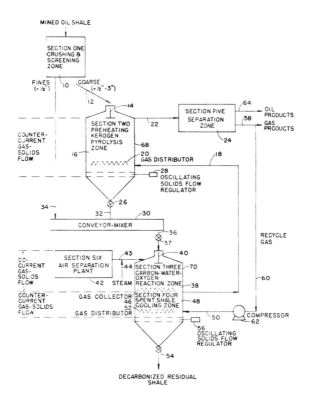

Source: U.S. Patent 4,092,237

Section Two comprises a shale preheating-kerogen pyrolysis zone **16** comprising a vertical refractory lined kiln **68** in which the coarse particulate shale is contained in a downwardly continuously moving bed. The kerogen contained in the coarse particulate shale is removed by pyrolysis reaching a maximum temperature of about 900°F within the zone **16** and leaves a solid, nondistillable carbonaceous residue on the shale. The net heat required for the pyrolysis is supplied through a line **18** comprising a counterflow of hot nonoxidizing combined gases generated in a Section Three and a Section Four. The hot nonoxidizing combined gases entering via line **18** are distributed within zone **16** by a gas distributor **20** to rise within the downwardly moving particulate shale bed and comingle with the gaseous pyrolysis products and flow through a line **22** into a Section Five comprising a separation zone **24** after being cooled to about 200°F by the incoming cold particulate oil shale.

Thereafter, the pyrolyzed coarse particulate shale on which the solid, nondistillable carbonaceous residue remains exits kiln **68** through a lock **26** controlled by an oscillating solids flow regulator **28** to enter a conveyor-mixer **30** via a line **32**. The pyrolyzed shale then is mixed with a raw fine particulate oil shale from Section One which enters via a line **34** and flows by a line **36** through a lock **37** to enter Section Three, a second vertical, refractory-lined kiln **70**.

Section Three comprises a carbon-water-oxygen reaction zone **38** comprising the upper portion of the second vertical, refractory-lined kiln **70**. The pyrolyzed shale and raw oil shale particles entering Section Three are distributed by a solids distributor **40** within kiln **70** and oxygen and steam in predetermined and controlled amounts are supplied from (1) a Section Six (an air separation plant **42**) through a line **43** and (2) a steam line **44** to react with the downward flow of shale particles.

The amount of raw oil shale, oxygen and steam added is determined by the hydrocarbons needed to supply the net heat required to operate the system and the water gas required to refine the oil produced in Section Five. The hot combustion gases and gases due to the decomposition of minerals, water gases resulting from the reaction of oxygen and steam with the carbon and hydrocarbons in the mixed shales, flow cocurrently downward with the spent shale to a gas collector **46** to combine with hot upward flowing recycle gas from Section Four. The combined gases comprising hot recycle gas, combustion gas, mineral carbonate decomposition gas and water gas withdrawn by gas collector **46** flows by line **18** to Section Two to provide the necessary heat for retorting the shale therein and results in a more selective distillation occurring and higher quality products being produced.

Section Four comprises a spent shale cooling zone **48** comprising the lower portion of the second kiln **70** below the gas collector in which a stream of recycle nonoxidizing gas from Section Five entering via a line **50** is distributed by a gas distributor **52** to flow countercurrently to the combined downward flow of hot decarbonized residual shale from Section Three. The recycle gas cools the decarbonized residual shale and carries the heat back to Section Two together with the gases generated in Section Three. Thereafter, the decarbonized residual shale flows downwardly and out of a lock **54** controlled by an oscillating flow regulator **56**. A uniform, plug flow of the particulate shale in both kilns is due to gravity assisted by oscillating flow regulators.

Section Five comprises a separation zone **24** wherein the gaseous products of Section Two, comprising gases, mists and liquids are separated into a gas products stream and a liquid or oil products stream. A portion of the gas product stream exiting by a line **58** is recycled to Section Four via a line **60** and a compressor **62**. The remainder, plus liquid hydrocarbons in a line **64**, flows to an adjacent refinery, where suitable methods beyond the scope of this process are used to produce commercial fuels, or to storage. Section Six is an air separation plant **42** which supplies the gaseous oxygen for Section Three.

Sloping Retort Chamber

According to a process developed by *H. Brown; U.S. Patent 4,094,769; June 13, 1978; assigned to Mineral Concentrates & Chemical Company, Inc.* controlled amounts of raw oil shale are delivered into an upper inlet of a downwardly sloping retort chamber that is constructed as readily portable.

The raw oil shale is first moved in a direction countercurrent to gravity flow and crushed in the retort chamber by means of a rotating member that also serves to retain the oil shale in the retort chamber until a satisfactory recovery is completed. The crushed oil shale is confined to a relatively thin, downwardly moving layer in contact with a heated, inner, annular wall surface and moves by gravity flow between the inlet and a lower outlet to produce oil product vapors that rise to an upper portion of the retort chamber. The moving layer of the oil shale becomes spent as it passes through the retort chamber and finally is selectively discharged through the lower outlet.

The oil product vapors are removed from the retort chamber into a condensing tube in which the vapors are condensed to a liquid form. The oil products are removed from the condenser by weight or are further refined in the adjacent refinery.

Reduced Residence Time in Cross-Flow Device

J.H. Knight; U.S. Patent 4,058,905; November 22, 1977; assigned to The Superior Oil Company describes a method for improved operation of a cross-flow device for heating and/or cooling a moving bed of solids by reducing residence time and eliminating gas leakage between adjacent heating and cooling zones. A bed of solid particles is formed on a grate for movement through heating and cooling zones or chambers. As the bed of particles is moved through the heating and cooling zones, cross flows of hot or cool gas are passed through the bed normal to the direction of bed movement.

The use of downdraft gas flow in each zone of the cross-flow device permits the same pressure profile to be produced in each zone, and a zero pressure differential between zones from top to bottom of the bed. Thus active grate space between adjacent zones is reduced, and greater efficiency obtained. In addition, when heating of the solids is followed by cooling, the passage through the bed of the heating and cooling gas streams in the same direction permits heating of the lowermost particles in the bed after these particles have passed into the cooling zone of the device.

Referring to Figure 2.5a, the solids bed is formed and moved successively through a heating zone and a cooling zone. The traveling grate moves continuously

Figure 2.5: Traveling Grate Retort Process

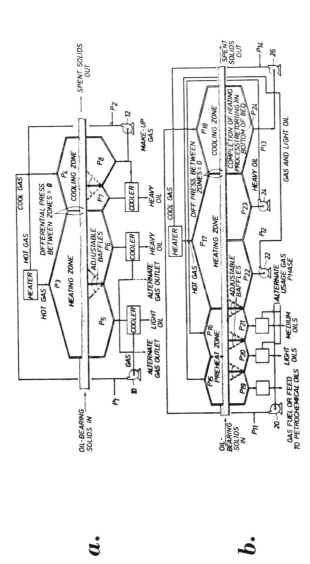

a.

b.

(a)   Schematic sectioned elevation of a traveling grate oil shale retort

(b)   Alternative form of the retort of Figure 2.5a, including a preheat zone immediately
      upstream of the heating zone

Source: U.S. Patent 4,058,905

through the zones at a predetermined rate that, in combination with the length of the respective zones, determines the residence time for the solids in each of the zones. Blowers **10, 12** are provided to produce the desired cross flows of hot and cool gas through the bed. The gas pressures at the outlets of the blowers **10, 12** are designated by references P_1 and P_2, respectively. The gas pressures in the heating and cooling zone hoods above the traveling solids bed are designated by P_3 and P_4, respectively. The gas pressures in the various windboxes immediately below the traveling solids bed are designated by P_5, P_6, P_7, and P_8 as shown.

In the process, the usual interzone seal that would normally be required along the grate path between the heating and cooling zones of the illustrated apparatus is no longer required. This is accomplished by maintaining the hood pressures P_3, P_4 just above the bed at values approximately equal to one another, and by maintaining the windbox pressures P_5, P_6, P_7, and P_8 just below the bed at values approximately equal to one another, so that the differential pressure along the path of the bed and between the respective zones is substantially zero. Of course, it will be appreciated that this condition need be maintained only at the interzone interface, and that variations may occur to a greater or lesser extent without significant degradation of the various processes to which this method is applied.

In the example of Figure 2.5b, the bed is moved horizontally through the first chamber or zone designated the preheat zone. In this zone the mined oil shale solids are preheated in preparation for retorting. Preheating is accomplished by a downwardly directed flow of heated gas, which conventionally may be obtained from the gas outlet from the spent shale cooling zone. The outlet gas from the preheat zone may be reused or vented as desired. Blowers **20, 22, 24,** and **26** supply the desired gas flows through the preheat, heating, and cooling zones.

The hood, or inlet side, pressures P_{15}, P_{16}, P_{17}, and P_{18} are maintained at values approximately equal to one another and the windbox, or outlet side, pressures P_{19}, P_{20}, P_{21}, P_{22}, P_{23}, and P_{24} are maintained at values approximately equal to one another and lower than the hood pressures. In this manner, the differential pressures between the respective zones along the path of the bed is substantially zero and no significant interzone gas leakage occurs.

Movement of the grate carries the bed into a high-temperature heating or retorting zone which is supplied with hot gas at a temperature of about 1000° to 1500°F. In the embodiment of Figures 2.5a and 2.5b, the gas is heated by an external heater. Of course, other means for heating the incoming retorting gas may be used. The hot retorting gas is directed downwardly through the bed, normal to the direction of movement of the bed. As the bed moves through the heating zone, the oil shale particles at the gas inlet side of the bed are contacted by the hot gas and heated. As these uppermost particles are heated, the gas is cooled, reducing the driving force for heat transfer to the lower particles. As the solids move through the heating zone, hotter particles are initially presented to the incoming hot gas and the heat of the gas therefore provides an increasing driving force to heat the lower particles in the bed.

In conventional oil shale retorting operations, the oil shale remains in the heating or retort zone of the apparatus until all of the solids have been brought to the desired retorting temperature, and maintained at that temperature for the desired retorting time. This controls the rate of bed movement through any given retort for a fixed hot gas inlet temperature. This minimum residence time of a particle in the bed is based on two important factors, the time required for the hot gas to reach the bottom of the bed, plus the time required to heat the entire particle, from surface to center core, to the desired temperature for recovery of hydrocarbons.

It will be understood that a greater heating time is required for larger particles and, since the upper layer of the bed is exposed to higher temperatures for longer times than the remainder of the bed, the segregation of particle sizes in the bed to place the smallest particles at the bottom and the largest at the top will improve the overall thermal efficiency of the operation. However, the difficulty and expense of so segregating the particles by size usually is not justified by the savings achieved.

At the initial stage of retorting, in the preheat or heating zone, the bed reaches a temperature sufficient for some light oil product to be educed from the oil shale solids. The higher temperature to which the bed is heated as the grate advances through the heating zone results in progressively heavier oil products being educed from the solids. A plurality of varying oil products may be collected in the manner illustrated as the bed passes through the respective preheat and/or heating zones. Product collection is into a corresponding plurality of containers, or divided collection means in the respective windboxes, from which the products are passed to respective cooler-condenser systems where the gas and oil products are separated and the liquids condensed.

In this process, directed to the retorting of oil shale, the solids in the bed are moved from the heating zone into the cooling zone before the solids at the bottom of the bed have reached the desired retorting temperature. The hot, spent shale particles entering the cooling zone at the top of the bed provide sensible heat to the incoming cool gas. This sensible heat is transferred to the gas and carried down through the bed to bring the shale particles at the bottom of the bed to the desired temperature. Only after the upper shale particles have been cooled by the incoming gas will the lower particles be exposed to the cool gas, which will occur only after the particles have moved some distance into the cooling zone.

Thus the final heating of the lower portion of the bed takes place at the same time and in the same location along the solids path as does the initial cooling of the upper portion of the bed. The heavy oil product from the shale in this area of the device is then collected in a manner similar to that described above for the product educed in the preheat and heating zones.

Pyrolysis Vessel and Spent Shale Burner

According to a process described by *R.N. Hall; U.S. Patent 3,976,558; August 24, 1976* a finely divided heat carrier, such as catalytic cracking catalyst, is circulated between a pyrolysis vessel and a spent shale burner. Both the pyrolysis vessel and the burner are operated as fluid beds, with special apparatus used for maintaining fluidity of the pyrolysis bed and for achieving efficient burning and shale ash separation in the combustion bed. A portion of the shale ash is used for direct heat transfer to preheat the raw shale prior to pyrolysis, thus cooling this portion of the shale ash and facilitating disposal.

A slip stream of the lighter fraction of the pyrolysis vapor is recycled to the pyrolysis zone to permit controlled fluidization and to accomplish improved heat transfer. To prevent attrition of the heat carrier, the heat carrier is separated from the larger spent shale particles prior to entering the spent shale burner, with the larger spent shale particles, free of heat carrier, being pulverized separately and injected into the fluid bed burner.

Crushed raw shale from source **1**, nominally ¼ inch or less in particle size is introduced through line **2** into the bottom of first-stage preheater **3**, which is a concurrent, direct contact heat exchanger, with the raw shale particles being entrained in hot dust-free vapor for a short period of time. The dust-free vapor is air which has been heated by indirect heat exchange with hot shale ash to around 1000°F. The air would be introduced into the bottom of first-stage preheater **3** via line **4**. The raw shale will thus be heated to approximately 250°F and the air would be cooled to around 350°F. The gas velocity during preheating would be approximately 10% greater than the drop-out velocity for ¼-inch shale particles at the preheater exit, i.e., a velocity of approximately 75 fps.

Figure 2.6: Pyrolysis of Oil Shale

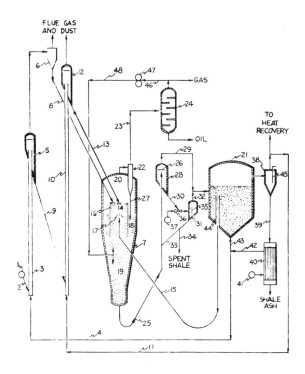

Source: U.S. Patent 3,976,558

The shale and warm air would exit the top of first-stage preheater **3** into shale fines elutriator **5**. Elutriation would be accomplished in a vessel having a cross-sectional area such that shale particles greater in size than around 100 mesh would drop out. The –100 mesh shale particles, which amount to 5% of the total shale quantity, and which depend to a great extent upon the method of crushing, would be entrained and pass through shale fines cyclone 6 and the fine shale particles removed will flow via line 8 directly to pyrolyzer 7. The warm air and a small amount of raw shale dust will exit shale fines cyclone 6 to be processed in dust removal facilities before venting to the atmosphere.

The warm raw shale particles larger in size than 100 mesh (+100 mesh) will flow through line 9 to the bottom of second-stage preheater 10, which is also a concurrent, direct-contact heat exchanger, similar in design to first-stage preheater 3. Hot flue gas and entrained shale ash from shale ash cyclone 38 at around 1350°F will be injected via line 11 into the bottom of second-stage preheater 10. The entrained shale ash is a finely divided material consisting of particles predominantly less than 200 mesh in size. The warm flue gas, warm ash and +100 mesh preheated raw shale will exit into shale ash elutriator 12. Elutriation will be accomplished in a vessel having a cross-sectional area whereby the +100 mesh raw shale particles will drop out and the finely divided shale ash will be entrained overhead. The exit warm flue gas and warm shale ash from shale ash elutriator 12 will flow through dust removal facilities before venting to the atmosphere.

The +100 mesh raw shale particles will flow through line 13 to pyrolyzer 7. More than two stages of preheat can be used for greater heat efficiency if desired with series units of similar design. The +100 mesh shale can be preheated to around 600°F before any substantial pyrolysis will occur, for which condition the flue gas and shale ash would be cooled to approximately 700°F.

Heating a material such as oil shale with a solid heat carrier in a fluid bed is somewhat difficult due to the wide particle size range of the shale, coupled with the fact that the shale disintegrates to some extent upon pyrolysis. For example, if the shale and the heat carrier are introduced at the top of the bed, then those particles having a slightly higher settling velocity than the vapor velocity will accumulate in the upper part of the fluid bed and will tend to choke the flow of solids.

The foregoing problem of fines accumulation in the pyrolysis fluid bed can be essentially eliminated by the technique as described in this paragraph. Main pyrolysis zone 14 would be provided inside of pyrolyzer 7, created by hollow cylinder 16, open at the top and bottom. The –100 mesh raw shale from shale fines cyclone 6 at around 250°F would be introduced through line 8 slightly below the bed level of pyrolysis zone 14. A shorter period of time would be required to pyrolyze the –100 mesh particles than for the +100 mesh fraction since the smaller particles would be heated more rapidly to pyrolyzing temperature. The +100 mesh raw shale which has been preheated to around 600°F, would be introduced via line 13 from shale ash elutriator 12 a short distance below the fluid bed level of pyrolysis zone 14.

The hot heat carrier at around 1400°F would be introduced via heat carrier lift line 15 into the upper part of pyrolysis zone 14. A device, such as conical baffle 17, would deflect the heat carrier to prevent jetting action and to provide distribution. As the shale is pyrolyzed, the spent shale fines would be carried upward by elutriating action and would overflow the upper rim of hollow cylinder 16 into dormant annulus zone 18.

The flow of spent shale fines would combine with the circulating heat carrier and larger spent shale particles in accumulator zone **19**. Pyrolysis zone **14** would be designed to have a residence time of approximately 2 minutes, sufficient to achieve pyrolysis of the ¼-inch particles. Disengaging zone **20** above pyrolysis zone **14** would have a larger cross-sectional area than pyrolysis zone **14** to permit the larger spent shale particles which have been entrained with the pyrolysis vapor to drop out and fall into annulus zone **18**.

The heat carrier at around 1400°F would be transported from combustor **21** into pyrolyzer **7** by means of lift line **15**, which would be of similar design to a conventional fluid catalytic cracker lift line. The flow rate of the circulating heat carrier would be controlled to maintain the temperature of pyrolysis around 875° to 900°F, at which temperature maximum oil yield will be obtained. This temperature control would be similar to that used in conventional fluid catalytic cracking technology. Pyrolysis vapors would exit from the top of pyrolyzer **7** and pass through pyrolysis vapor cyclone **22** via line **23** to fractionator condenser **24**, where the vapors would be partially condensed and separated into oil and gas.

Further processing would be required to remove the hydrogen sulfide and carbon dioxide from the gas, and the oil would have to be catalytically hydrotreated to remove the sulfur and nitrogen to produce a premium synthetic crude oil. A slip stream of gas taken overhead from fractionator **24** via line **46** would be compressed by device **47** and recycled via line **48** to pyrolyzer **7** to permit controlled fluidization and improved heat transfer in pyrolysis zone **14**. A small portion of this recycle gas stream would also be injected into the lower part of pyrolyzer **7** to prevent the formation of stagnant areas in accumulator zone **19**, and thus eliminate rat-holing through this zone.

Warm heat carrier and spent shale would exit from the bottom of pyrolyzer **7** via lift line **25**. Spent shale from pyrolysis vapor cyclone **22** would flow through seal leg **27**, discharging below the level of the spent shale in annulus zone **18**. The heat for pyrolysis would be obtained by burning off the carbon on the spent shale. Calculations show that oil shale containing as low as 25 gal/ton can be pyrolyzed using only that heat available from the carbon on the spent shale. Rather than inject the mixture of heat carrier and spent shale directly into combustor **21**, the heat carrier, together with smaller spent shale particles, would be entrained overhead from heat carrier elutriator **28** and then fed to combustor **21** via line **29**.

Deflector baffle **26** would prevent jetting larger spent shale particles out the top of heat carrier elutriator **28**. The larger spent shale particles would exit from the bottom of heat carrier elutriator **28** and then feed through line **30** into the throat of venturi **36**, with high-pressure stream or air from source **37** being used to eject the particles and jet them against wear-resistant plate **35** in pulverizer **31**. The smaller spent shale particles would be entrained overhead from pulverizer **31** via line **32** and transported into combustor **21**. The larger spent shale particles are recycled back to heat carrier elutriator **28** via line **33**. To prevent an accumulation of large spent shale particles in the system, a small amount of spent shale would be withdrawn via line **34**.

By such a feed preparation technique as described above, attrition of the heat carrier would be avoided, the energy required for pulverizing the spent shale would be low, the wear rate during impacting would be minimal, the amount of shale ash recycled with the heat carrier would be small, the carbon burn-off rate on the spent shale would be greatly accelerated and the fluidization during spent shale burning would be facilitated. The carbon on the spent shale and on the heat carrier would be burned off at a temperature of around 1400°F in combustor **21**. The temperature can be controlled by introduction of air in excess of that required for combustion.

The shale ash thus formed by spent shale combustion is very friable and decrepitates to produce a material which consists predominantly of –200 mesh particles. Essentially all of the shale ash will be elutriated from combustor **21** with hot flue gas and flow through shale ash cyclone **38**. The solids stream of hot shale ash from shale ash cyclone **38** will flow through line **39** to air preheater **40**. The hot heat carrier at around 1400°F will exit combustor **21** through standpipe **44** and be transported to pyrolyzer **7** through lift line **15**. Based on the operating conditions as herein described, the circulation rate of heat carrier to raw oil shale will be approximately one to one.

Compressor air from source **41** will be heated to around 1000°F in air preheater **40** by indirect heat exchange with the solids stream of hot shale ash from shale ash cyclone **38**. The solids stream of cooled shale ash, which exits air preheater **40** at approximately 300°F, will be sent to disposal. The hot air will exit air preheater **40** via line **42** and the flow will be divided to provide combustion air to combustor **21** through line **43** and hot air for first-stage preheater **3** via line **4**.

Hot ash cyclone **38** will be provided with interrupter baffle **45** to control the desired amount of finely divided, hot shale ash particles to be entrained into the hot flue gas. By the method as defined herein, the shale ash will be intentionally introduced into the hot flue gas to supply a portion of the heat for second-stage preheater **10**. The velocity of the gas to preheater **10** is essentially a fixed rate, and since it is undesirable to change the spent shale combustion temperature, then the temperature to which the raw shale is heated in preheater **10** can be controlled by positioning interrupter baffle **45** to vary the amount of shale ash entrained into the flue gas.

The finely divided shale ash, thus cooled to around 700°F during raw shale preheat, is removed from the +100 mesh raw shale as previously described. The efficient use of the hot shale ash fines for supplying direct heat to the process is made possible by removal of the raw shale fines by shale fines elutriator **5** prior to being contacted with hot ash, whereby the loss of raw shale into the ash is prevented.

Pyrolyzer **7** will be operated at around 5 psig and combustor **21** at approximately 10 psig, with the pressure balance being accomplished by controlling the density of the solids-gas mixture in the spent shale and heat carrier lift lines. Excess heat will be produced by the described process when oil shale richer than around 25 gal/ton is processed. This excess heat can be recovered by such a technique as the generation of steam in a waste heat boiler, utilizing the excess flue gas and entrained hot ash which would be produced from hot ash cyclone **38**.

Relationship of Oil Assay and Rock Pressure

According to a process described by *R.F. Deering, R.O. Dhondt and T.A. Seesee;*

U.S. Patent 4,025,416; May 24, 1977; assigned to Union Oil Company of California it has been found that there is a relationship which exists between the oil assay of the fresh shale and the rock pressure which will bring about agglomeration in the 750° to 850°F zone. Shales having a high oil assay, above about 35 gal/ton, will agglomerate and impede gas flow at solids pressures above about 3 psi bearing upon the 750° to 850°F zone. Shales of lower assay can withstand considerably higher solids pressures without agglomeration. It has been found that the level of the 750° to 850°F temperature interval in the retort can be controlled in response to oil assay of the raw shale so as to render the rock pressure bearing upon that interval insufficient to bring about significant agglomeration, in either solids-upflow or -downflow retorting.

The overall objective is to provide sufficient total heat input into the retort to obtain the desired solids temperature at the solids outlet end of the retort (900°F or higher) without heating the solids to the 750° to 850°F range at a level in the retort where the rock pressure is high enough to cause agglomeration. This objective is achieved by selecting the right combination of recycle gas rate and temperature. At the same total heat input, the position of the critical 750° to 850°F zone can be raised or lowered in the retort by proper correlation of recycle gas rate and temperature. The combination of high temperatures and low recycle gas rates will elevate the critical zone sufficiently to avoid agglomerating pressures for any oil shale of up to about 60 gal/ton Fischer Assay.

However, it is usually undesirable to maintain high recycle gas temperatures unless a high assay shale is being retorted, for preheating the recycle gas to above about 1050°F tends to cause thermal cracking of hydrocarbons in the recycle gas, and more rapid coking of the recycle gas heater. When shales of lower oil assay are being retorted, it is therefore preferable to reduce the recycle gas temperature and increase the flow rate thereof. This lowers the level of the 750° to 850°F zone. However, the recycle gas rate should not be too high or the shale will reach the critical 750° to 850°F temperature range at a level where solids pressures are too high and agglomeration can occur.

High oil yields and high throughput rates can be obtained without agglomeration in a solids upflow retort when feeding shales of 30 to 35 gal/ton Fischer Assay by adjusting the recycle gas rate and recycle gas inlet temperature to obtain a temperature profile which approaches a uniform slope when the temperature is plotted against bed height. When richer shales are fed to the retort, to the point where agglomeration and plugging begin to occur, such agglomeration and plugging can be avoided by decreasing the recycle gas flow rate and increasing the gas inlet temperature so as to obtain a higher rate of solids temperature increase per unit change in bed height near the top of the retort as compared to the rate of temperature increase per unit change in bed height in the bottom half of the retort.

From the foregoing, it will be apparent that there is a critical intermediate temperature interval of about 750° to 850°F in the shale bed. Further, the horizontal level of this intermediate temperature zone can be shifted upwardly or downwardly in the shale bed by suitably correlating eduction gas temperature and flow rate. Also, the middle of the intermediate temperature zone, i.e., the 800°F level, should not be below a critical level at which shale agglomeration at any point within the zone becomes significant, the critical level being directly related to the oil assay of the shale being fed to the retort.

Resorting to this relationship, the critical level can be defined as that level at which the rock pressure bearing thereon in pounds per square inch is about $[120,000/(FA)^3] + 0.5$, where FA is the Fischer Assay of the shale, in gallons per ton. Preferably however, the 800°F level of the intermediate temperature zone is no lower in the bed than the level at which the rock pressure is $[100,000/(FA)^3] + 0.5$ psi.

However, in order to minimize thermal cracking of hydrocarbons in the recycle gas preheater, as well as over-cracking in the upper high-temperature portion of the shale bed, the top of the intermediate zone, i.e., the 850°F level, should preferably be at least about 1 ft below the top of the shale bed in a solids-upflow retort. (It should be noted that the foregoing formulations based on rock pressure cannot be accurately and conveniently expressed in terms of bed depth; the former is not a simple linear function of the latter.)

Thus, one aspect of the process involves the retorting of shale feeds which may vary substantially, e.g., by at least 5 gal/ton, in oil assay from time to time. In such cases, the intermediate temperature zone will be maintained at a relatively low level in the shale bed when the shale feed assays relatively lean in oil, and at a higher level when the feed assays relatively rich in oil, the lower level and the the higher level each preferably being at least about 1 ft below the top of the bed, but sufficiently high therein to substantially prevent agglomeration of shale particles.

Misting of Reactor Recycle Gas

S. Ueta and O.C. Ivo; U.S. Patent 3,887,453; June 3, 1975; assigned to Petroleo Brasileiro S.A.-Petrobras, Brazil describes an operating system with means for substantially increasing the extraction of mineral oil and other derivatives from shale. A technique is employed such that a mist is formed by the carrier recycling gases for carrying with it the largest possible amount of extracted material.

The system consists of a vertical cylindrical retort with tapered ends, through the upper end of which the shale is fed in pieces for downward flow moving countercurrent with the heated gases. Thereafter the shale is discharged through the bottom of the reactor. The recycling gases, heated outside the retort, are introduced through the bottom of the reactor, moving countercurrent with the descending shale, and leave the retort by a side pipe at the top in the form of a mist saturated with extracted material and carrying the partially condensed pyrolysis products. The importance of the process of pyrolysis resides in that it is unnecessary, and indeed deleterious, to use water for cooling the discharged shale, after extraction, in the bottom of the retort.

Another aspect is that the recycling gases coming from the retort in the form of a mist pass through a filtration, separation and condensation system before being heated. Equally important is the introduction of recycling the extraction gases at such a temperature and rate that a mist is permitted to form, this being important for the good performance of the process. The recycled extraction gas will pass through the bed upwardly, countercurrent with the shale, at a rate not less than 0.2 to 2.0 m/sec. The mist formed should leave with 5% minimum and 25% maximum of condensed material with respect to the pyrolysis products, and at a temperature ranging from 121° to 177°C.

Desulfurization of Flue Gas

R.F. Deering; U.S. Patent 4,069,132; January 17, 1978; assigned to Union Oil Company of California describes a method for retorting oil shale whereby full utilization of the heat energy available in the retorted shale and maximum desulfurization of the flue gas released to the atmosphere are simultaneously effected. Basically, the process comprises passing a crushed shale feed upwardly through preheating and retorting zones in a retort vessel wherein eduction of shale oil and product gases is achieved by direct heat exchange with a preheated, recycled portion of the product gases passed countercurrently to the shale feed, and then passing the retorted shale downwardly through combustion and cooling zones.

Complete combustion of coke on the retorted shale in the combustion zone not only results in full utilization of the potential heat energy stored within the retorted shale, but also in the production of gaseous sulfur components (mostly SO_2) that chemically react with the alkaline components of the shale. Concurrent flow of gas and retorted shale in the combustion zone at temperatures between 900° and 1670°F permits the reaction between the SO_2 and the alkaline components of the shale to proceed essentially to completion, thus desulfurizing the flue gas produced in the combustion zone.

Reduction of Particulate Content in Gas Stream

J.W. Unverferth; U.S. Patent 4,069,133; January 17, 1978; assigned to Chevron Research Company describes a process and apparatus for reducing the particulate content in a gaseous stream containing entrained particulate matter and condensable hydrocarbons wherein the stream is obtained from the retorting of hydrocarbon-containing solids, particularly from retorted shale.

A gaseous effluent containing condensable hydrocarbons and entrained solid particulate matter is produced during the retorting of hydrocarbon-containing solids and is discharged from a retorting vessel through a conduit containing a rotating elongate spiral-shaped element on which a portion of the particulate matter and condensable hydrocarbons form a semisolid mass. The rotating spiral collects and conveys the semisolid mass back into the retorting vessel for further processing thereby reducing the solid particulate content of the condensable hydrocarbon product.

Referring to Figure 2.7a, hydrocarbon-containing solids are transported from storage hopper **1** and introduced into gasification vessel **2**, by any suitable means, e.g., by using a star feeder or an auger-like conveyor. In the gasification vessel, the solid is gasified or retorted by heating the solids to an elevated temperature typically in the range 800° to 1100°F or higher for shale. After a sufficient residence time in the gasification vessel, spent shale or other residual ungasified solids are removed from the vessel via line **4** by any suitable means, e.g., by gravity or use of an auger-like conveyor.

As the hydrocarbon-containing solids are gasified, a substantially vaporous hydrocarbon stream containing condensable hydrocarbons is formed and removed from the vessel via conduit **6**. Generally, the gasification of the solid will produce sufficient pressure to force the gases out of the vessel; however, a stripping gas or other reactive gases may be forced through the vessel to entrain and transport the gaseous and any liquid hydrocarbons formed in the vessel.

Particulate matter is entrained in the effluent stream. This particulate matter generally comprises finely divided portions of the hydrocarbon-containing solids and can vary widely in size from 0.001 to 0.1 inch and more commonly 0.001 to 0.01 inch in diameter. The quantity and size of the entrained particulate matter will of course depend on numerous factors such as the amount of fines introduced into or formed in the vessel and the velocity of the effluent stream. As the effluent stream passes through conduit 6 at least a portion of the condensable hydrocarbons and the entrained particulate matter coalesces forming a semi-solid mass. This coalescence of hydrocarbons and particulate matter can result from condensation of a portion of the hydrocarbons in the conduit, or can result from coalescence of a portion of the particulate matter and entrained liquid hydrocarbon droplets formed in the vessel.

Rotatably positioned in outlet conduit 6 is a spiral-shaped element 9, connected by shaft 11 to a means for rotation, such as electric motor 10. The spiral-shaped element is rotated in a direction such that the thrust of the element forces the semi-solid mass of accumulated solids back into the vessel.

The rotating spiral-shaped element serves many important functions. First, it has been found that the particulate matter entrained in the effluent stream serves as nuclei for coalescence and condensation of a portion of the hydrocarbons. The rotation of the spiral impedes the flow of material through the conduit and increases the contacting of the entrained solid particulate matter and the condensed hydrocarbons resulting in the coalescence of particulate matter and condensed hydrocarbons and the formation of a semi-solid mass. Secondly, the rotating spiral prevents the clogging of the conduit by constantly conveying the accumulated semi-solid mass back into the gasification vessel.

Figure 2.7: Retorting Process

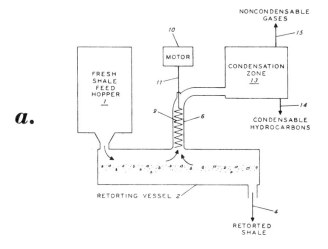

(continued)

Figure 2.7: (continued)

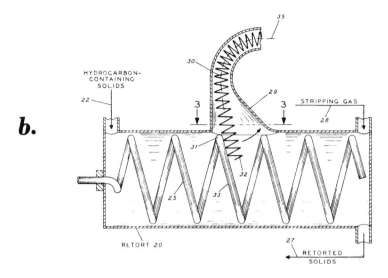

b.

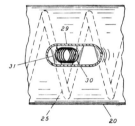

c.

(a)   Process using a spiral-shaped conveying element inserted in
      the gaseous discharge conduit of a retorting vessel

(b)   Another preferred embodiment of the process

(c)   Cross section of a portion of the apparatus shown
      in Figure 2.7b

Source: U.S. Patent 4,069,133

Thirdly, the spiral significantly increases the quality of the product condensed
hydrocarbons by substantially reducing the particulate content in the oil.
Fourthly, the spiral serves the important purpose of increasing the yield of condensed hydrocarbons by forcing the accumulated semi-solid mass back into the
retorting vessel for further processing and eventual recovery of the hydrocarbon
content of the semi-solid mass.

After passing through conduit **6**, the effluent stream passes into condensation
zone **13**, wherein the stream is separated into condensable hydrocarbon fraction
14 and a noncondensable fraction **15**.

The spiral-shaped element can have various shapes. What is essential is that the spiral impedes the flow of solids through the conduit and simultaneously collects and conveys the accumulated semisolid mass back into the vessel. Preferably, the spiral is rotated at a speed sufficient to transport the semisolid mass back into the vessel at a velocity of 0.1 to 0.5 fps. Preferably, it comprises a hollow-core, flexible, helical-shaped element with a uniform diameter. Less preferred is a screw-like conveyor comprising a solid shaft with a spiral flange attached, shaped to force the accumulated mass back into the retort. Preferably the spiral-shaped element does not contain a rigid shaft, but consists of an elongated flexible spiral. The spiral can be made of any suitable material, but preferably it is made of metal which best withstands the high temperatures of the effluent gases, and also has the desired flexibility as described in reference to Figure 2.7b.

Figure 2.7b illustrates a preferred example of the process and apparatus. In this embodiment a helical-shaped conveyor is used in a retorting vessel to transport solids through the retorting vessel and a spiral-shaped element is rotatably positioned in the vaporous discharge conduit of the retort. The spiral extends sufficiently far into the vessel to contact one coil of the helical-shaped conveyor.

Hydrocarbon-containing solids and a solid heat transfer material heated to an elevated temperature are fed into the retort **20** via inlet **22**. In this preferred case, both solids are conveyed from one end of the retort to the other end via an elongate spiral or helical-shaped conveyor **25** rotatably positioned in the vessel and connected to conventional rotational driving means not shown. The retorted solids are removed from the retort by conventional means via line **27**. A stripping gas is fed into the end of the retort via line **28**.

The spiral **30** comprises a flexible elongate, coiled spring-like element which is rotatably positioned in conduit **29** and extends sufficiently far into the vessel to make contact with at least one coil of conveyor **25**. As conveyor **25** rotates, the end of the spiral **32** bends away from the end of the conveyor as shown by the arrow. As the spiral **30** clears the top edge **31** of the coil, the spiral springs back making contact with the next coil on the conveyor or the wall of the conduit. The end of the conduit is enlarged as shown to provide for this bending of the spiral.

Figure 2.7c is a cross-sectional top view of the outlet conduit **29** on line **3-3** as marked in Figure 2.7b. Other shapes for conduit **29** can readily be designed by any person skilled in the art, to provide for the bending of the end of the spiral. For example, conduit **29** can be shaped so that as conveyor **25** rotates the spiral bends and moves around the side-edge **33** of the coil rather than the top-edge **31**.

The contact of the spiral with conveyor **25** serves an important purpose. After a period of time a deposit may build up on the spiral which is not removed by the rotary action of the helix. The contact of the end-portion **32** of the spiral with conveyor **25** results in a constant bending of the end section of the spiral which tends to break off any solid deposits. The solid deposits then drop back into the retort or are conveyed back into the retort by the rotating spiral.

Although the contact of the spiral with the conveyor **25** effectively prevents build-up of solids on the end of the sprial, deposits may still tend to accumulate on other portions of the spiral, thus reducing its efficiency. This problem, however, can be solved by shaping the conduit such that the spiral has a longitudinal bend to it such that a line passing through the center of the spiral forms an arcuate path as shown, e.g., by line **35** in Figure 2.7b. Preferably the outlet conduit has such a continuous bend for the entire length of the spiral. With this bend in the conduit, the rotation of the spiral also causes the spiral to be constantly flexing which tends to break off any carbonaceous deposits from the spiral.

Thus, with the flexing of the end of the spiral due to the contact with conveyor in the retort coupled with the flexing of the spiral due to the rotation of the spiral through the bend in the conduit, the spiral can continue to serve its purpose in essentially continuous operation with a minimum build-up of solids.

Vapor Phase Water Process

A process described by *V.D. Allred; U.S. Patent 3,960,702; June 1, 1976; assigned to Marathon Oil Company* employs vapor phase water as a dual heat transfer agent/chemical reactant in the pyrolysis of oil shale to produce hydrocarbons. Pressure, temperature and superficial gas velocity are maintained within the specified ranges in order to achieve maximum efficiency in the recovery of hydrocarbons. In the process, oil shale is retorted using vapor phase water at about 850° to 950°F, at a superficial gas velocity of about 20 fpm and at a pressure in the range of from about 1 to 150 psia.

Hydrostatic Sealing Technique

D.C. Jennings and R.O. Dhondt; U.S. Patent 4,004,982; January 25, 1977; and G.D. Cheadle and R.O. Dhondt; U.S. Patent 4,003,797; January 18, 1977; both assigned to Union Oil Company of California have found that in a continuous, solids-upflow, gas-downflow shale retorting process carried out at superatmospheric pressures, hydrostatic sealing means can be provided at the shale inlet and retorted shale outlet ends of the retort, thereby avoiding the need for mechanical sealing means, lock vessels, etc.

The raw shale is fed into the retort through a standing reservoir of product oil, or preferably a light fraction thereof, and the retorted shale is discharged from the retort through a water quenching zone and seal, in the lower portion of which is maintained a sufficient hydrostatic head of water to prevent the discharge of retort gases. Steam generated in the quench zone, containing some entrained hydrocarbonaceous matter, is treated in a multistage cooling and condensing manner for gas cleanup and for recovery of heat and an oil-free water condensate for recycle to the water sealing and quench zones.

R.F. Deering; U.S. Patent 4,083,770; April 11, 1978; assigned to Union Oil Company of California has discovered that in gas-solids contacting processes involving the transfer of granular solids from a high-temperature, nonoxidizing treating zone through an enclosed conduit to a combustion zone, the transfer of gases between the treating zone and the combustion zone is prevented by using a special steam sealing technique which avoids the use of mechanical sealing means and differential pressure controllers.

Steam is injected into the system between the two contacting zones, and by the use of flow rate controllers and a pressure controller, a portion of such steam is forced at all times to flow through the combustion zone, while another portion is withdrawn from the transfer conduit in admixture with a portion of net off-gas from the treating zone. The control system is particularly adapted for use in oil shale retorting, wherein coke on the retorted shale is burned in a combustion zone.

EXTERNAL HEAT PYROLYSIS AND PARTICULATE HEAT SOURCE

Staged Heating

According to a process described by *E.W. Knell and N.W. Green; U.S. Patent 4,071,432; January 31, 1978; assigned to Occidental Petroleum Corporation* carbonaceous material is contacted with a particulate source of heat in a pyrolysis reaction zone maintained at a temperature greater than about 600°F to yield as products of pyrolysis pyrolytic vapors and a carbon-containing solid residue. The carbon-containing solid residue is separated from the pyrolytic vapors and then preheated in a heating zone with hot gases, preferably by direct contact with the hot gases to allow complete heat transfer from the hot gas to the carbon-containing residue. The preheated carbon-containing solid residue is then separated from at least the bulk of the hot gases.

Next, a portion of the preheated carbon-containing solid residue is at least partially oxidized in a combustion zone in the presence of an oxygen-containing gas, thereby yielding gaseous combustion products of the carbon-containing solid residue including carbon monoxide and forming the particulate source of heat. The particulate source of heat is then separated form the gaseous combustion products of the carbon-containing solid residue and passed to the pyrolysis reaction zone to provide at least a portion of the heat required for pyrolysis of the carbonaceous material.

The gaseous combustion products of the carbon-containing solid residue are combined in the heating zone with a sufficient amount of oxygen to completely oxidize the carbon monoxide in the gaseous combustion products to form the hot gases for preheating the carbon-containing solid residue in the heating zone. At least a stoichiometric amount of oxygen in an oxygen-containing gas is used to oxidize the gaseous combustion products of the carbon-containing solid residue so that all the carbon monoxide in this stream is oxidized to carbon dioxide. Any excess oxygen reacts with carbon-containing solid residue in the heating zone to form the particulate source of heat.

Preferably the carbon-containing solid residue and the gaseous combustion products are combined, and then this combined stream is combined with the oxygen in the heating zone. This sequence of combining the three streams minimizes exposure of the carbon-containing solid residue to high temperatures and thereby helps prevent carbon monoxide formation in the heating zone.

The heating zone preferably is maintained at a temperature less than 1800°F and less than the temperature in the combustion zone to minimize carbon monoxide formation where excess oxygen is used to oxidize the gaseous combustion products of the carbon-containing solid residue. The combustion zone is maintained at a temperature consonant with the temperature desired in the pyrolysis reaction zone, and depending upon the weight ratio of the particulate source of heat to carbonaceous material in the pyrolysis reaction zone, from about 100° to 500°F higher than the temperature in the pyrolysis reaction zone. It is preferred that when separating preheated carbon-containing solid residue from the hot gas present in the heating zone, a portion of the hot gas stream be withdrawn with the preheated carbon-containing solid residue.

Preferably, the step of preheating the carbon-containing solid residue and the step of separating the preheated carbon-containing solid residue from the hot gas stream occur simultaneously in a cyclone heating-separation zone to minimize production of carbon monoxide and to reduce operating and capital costs. The step of partially oxidizing preheated carbon-containing solid residue and the step of separating particulate source of heat from gaseous combustion products occur simultaneously in a cyclone combustion separation zone. This reduces capital and operating costs of the process.

In order to minimize production of carbon monoxide in the cyclone combustion-separation zone, it is preferred that the residence time of solids in the separation zone be less than about 5 seconds, and more preferably, less than about 3 seconds. The process is an effective and efficient method for preparing a particulate source of heat for pyrolysis of a carbonaceous material because the gaseous combustion products of the carbon-containing solid residue of the carbonaceous material are substantially completely oxidized to form an oxidized, hot gas stream for preheating the carbon-containing solid residue. Thus, almost all of the potential heating value of the carbon atoms oxidized is utilized by this process.

Also, high temperatures can be maintained in the pyrolysis reaction zone without fear that this will result in thermal inefficiency due to increased carbon monoxide production during the oxidation of the carbon-containing solid residue. Furthermore, the amount of fines lost from the system can be minimized by operating the cyclone separation for the preheated carbon-containing solid residue such that a portion of the hot gas is withdrawn along with the preheated carbon-containing solid residue. This minimizes loss of the valuable carbon-containing solid residue from the process.

Multiple Retort Zones and Controlled Oxidation

According to a process described by *J.H. Knight, L.A. St.Cyr and O.L. Wilson; U.S. Patent 4,082,645; April 4, 1978; assigned to The Superior Oil Company* substantially all of the carbonaceous residue in spent shale may be effectively oxidized, without the undesirable results of combustion, by means of a sustained, controllable process at temperatures as low as 800°F. This controlled oxidation reaction takes place during the retort operation itself, thus eliminating the need for any subsequent processing of the shale or shale ash, other than to recover noncarbonaceous mineral values. Further, the process utilizes the exothermic oxidation reaction as a primary source of the heat necessary to initially raise the shale bed to oil-educing temperatures and break down the higher molecular weight hydrocarbons for easier recovery.

The process may be characterized broadly as an improvement in the so-called retort process for recovering energy values from oil shale. Previously heated reducing or inert gases are passed in cross-flow fashion through a moving, quiescent bed of crushed shale in a direction normal to the direction of travel of the bed. That portion of the shale bed facing the gas inlet and which is initially contacted by the hot gases is heated to oil-educing temperatures. The gases strip the oils from the shale particles, leaving a nonvaporizable carbonaceous residue in the spent shale.

According to this process, the hot gases are passed through the moving bed at a temperature and flow rate such that by the time a zone is created wherein only a portion of the layers of shale particles at the gas inlet side of the bed are heated to oil-educing temperatures, a temperature profile is established within the bed which is below those temperatures at which adverse chemical and physical reactions involving the spent shale would occur.

As the moving bed passes from the first retorting zone, and while the spent shale particles at the gas inlet side of the bed remain above oil-educing temperatures, the bed is transferred to a second zone wherein heat is produced and transferred to the deeper regions within the bed, in order to complete oil reduction from those regions, by means of a controlled oxidation of the carbonaceous residue in the spent shale regions of the bed. Oxygen-containing gases are directed through the bed in the same direction as the hot gases of the first zone.

The oxygen mass flow rate initially contacting the bed is preadjusted to take into account the existing temperature of the spent shale and produce a sustained combustion of the carbonaceous residue without raising the temperature of the bed above the established range. Thereafter, the oxygen flow rate is incrementally adjusted such that as the bed proceeds through the second zone, the carbonaceous residue in the remaining portions of the bed continues to be oxidized down to the gas outlet portion of the bed, while at the same time the established temperature profile of the bed is maintained.

Ultimately, the point will be reached when the bed will have been permeated with oxygen and substantially no further carbonaceous residue is available for oxidation and the accompanying generation of heat. Downstream from this point the bed will continue to cool as lower temperature cooling gases are downdrafted through it.

Fast Fluidized Bed Reactor

According to a process developed by *C.K. Choi; U.S. Patent 4,064,018; December 20, 1977; assigned to Occidental Petroleum Corporation* carbonaceous material contained in a carrier gas which is nondeleteriously reactive with respect to pyrolysis products is introduced to the base of an upwardly flowing fast fluidized bed. Simultaneously there is introduced to the base of the fast fluidized bed a particulate source of heat which contacts and pyrolyzes the carbonaceous material. The introduced quantity of particulate source of heat is sufficient to raise the carbonaceous material to a pyrolysis temperature of at least about 600°F. The pyrolysis of the carbonaceous material yields a particulate carbon-containing solid residue and a pyrolytic vapor containing hydrocarbons.

The fast fluidized bed is contained in a substantially vertically disposed open duct. The open duct is at least partially surrounded by a descending dense fluidized mass of particulate solids including particulate carbon-containing solid residue of pyrolysis and spent particulate source of heat. Simultaneously with the introduction of the carbonaceous material and particulate source of heat, a flow of solids from the dense fluidized mass is maintained upwardly along the inner surface of the duct to prevent contact of the carbonaceous material with the inner surface of the duct. Preferably, this flow of solids along the inner surface of the duct is maintained by discharging into the base of the duct upwardly along its inner surface a fluidizing gas which is nondeleteriously reactive with respect to pyrolysis products.

At least a portion of the spent particulate source of heat and particulate carbon-containing solid residue resulting from pyrolysis is discharged over the top edge of the duct to the descending dense fluidized mass of particulate solids around the outside of the duct. In addition, a stream containing a gaseous mixture of the carrier gas and pyrolytic vapor and entrained solids including particulate source of heat and carbon-containing solid residue is discharged from the upper portion of the duct and through an outlet above the fast fluidized bed. The gaseous mixture is separated from the entrained solids mixture, and the hydro-carbons are recovered from the gaseous mixture. The separated entrained solids mixture is cycled back to the pyrolysis reactor.

The dense fluidized mass is maintained along the outer surface of the duct by contacting spent particulate source of heat and carbon-containing solid residue discharged over the top edge of the duct with an ascending stream of a stripping gas which is nondeleteriously reactive with respect to pyrolysis products. This stripping gas also serves to strip hydrocarbons from the solids mixture in the dense fluidized bed, thereby increasing the yield of hydrocarbon product. Pref-erably the weight ratio of the fluidized solids mixture passing upwards along the inner surface of the duct to carbonaceous material introduced to the fast fluid-ized bed is above about 6 to prevent agglomeration on the reactor walls and less than about 40 for economy of operation.

In the process, pyrolysis occurs at a temperature from about $600°$ to $2000°F$. Short reaction times and low temperatures in the fast fluidized bed enhance for-mation of middle distillate hydrocarbons, i.e., hydrocarbons in the range of C_5 hydrocarbons to hydrocarbons having an end point of $950°F$. As a consequence, it is preferred to conduct pyrolysis at pyrolysis times of less than about 5 sec-onds, and more preferably from about 0.1 to 3 seconds, and at a temperature of from about $900°$ to $1400°F$. To achieve pyrolysis the solid particulate source of heat generally is introduced at a temperature from about $100°$ to $500°F$ higher than the pyrolysis temperature to be achieved. The weight ratio of the particu-late source of heat to the carbonaceous feed ranges from about 2 to 20:1.

Particles of the solid pyrolysis product and particulate source of heat not flu-idized in the fast fluidized bed are collected in a stripping zone. The stripping zone is below and communicates with the fast fluidized bed. In order to obtain improved yields hydrocarbons preferably are stripped from particles in the strip-ping zone with a stripping gas which is nondeleteriously reactive with respect to pyrolysis products. This stripping gas passes through the stripping zone, into the fast fluidized bed, and out through the outlet above the fast fluidized bed for recovery of the hydrocarbons recovered from the particles in the stripping zone.

Two streams of solids are removed from the stripping zone. A first stream of large chunks is removed from the bottom of the stripping zone. A second stream of smaller particles consisting of spent particulate source of heat and carbon-con-taining solid residue is withdrawn as product. A portion of this stream can be passed to a combustion zone where the carbon-containing solid residue is at least partially oxidized to form the particulate source of heat for feed to the fast fluidized bed. The apparatus employed to carry out the process is a pyrolysis reactor comprising a vertically oriented outer vessel. Inside the vessel and in spaced relationship therefrom is an open, substantially vertically disposed duct. Between the duct and the outer vessel is a substantially vertically disposed passageway.

Two solids inlets are provided at the base of the duct and in open communication therewith. These inlets are laterally spaced apart from the duct. Means are provided for introducing a particulate carbonaceous material to undergo pyrolysis to one of the two solids inlets and means are provided for introducing a particulate source of heat to pyrolyze the carbonaceous material to the other solids inlet. There is a gas inlet around and preferably surrounding the solids inlets. This gas inlet, which is in open communication with the base of the duct, receives a fluidizing gas which fluidizes a layer of particulate solids moving along the inner surface of the conduit. This layer of solids, which enters the duct at its base from the passageway between the duct and the outer vessel, prevents the carbonaceous material from contacting and agglomerating against the inner surface of the duct.

Means are provided for introducing a stripping gas to flow upwardly through the passageway to fluidize solids descending through the passageway between the duct and outer vessel towards the base of the duct to be fluidized therein by the fluidizing gas introduced to the fluidizing gas inlet. An outlet is provided above the duct for withdrawal of pyrolytic vapors from the outer vessel, and there is another outlet below the duct for withdrawal of carbon-containing solid residue. The outlet above the duct preferably is a vertically oriented hood which tapers inwardly away from the duct to minimize the residence time of the pyrolytic vapor in the reactor.

When it is desired to strip hydrocarbons from the particulate carbon-containing solids residue and carbonaceous material not fluidizable in the fast fluidized bed, a stripping chamber is provided below the duct as well as an inlet for passing a stripping gas through the stripping chamber. Outlet means are provided at the bottom of the stripping chamber for withdrawing large stripped solids from the stripping chamber. When carbon-containing solid residue is oxidized to provide heat for the pyrolysis reaction, means are provided for transferring solids withdrawn via the outlet below the duct to a combustion chamber where the carbon-containing solid residue is at least partially oxidized to form the particulate source of heat.

Means are provided for passing a source of oxygen into the combustion chamber and for transferring the particulate source of heat from the combustion chamber to a solids inlet at the base of the duct. The vapors removed from the outlet above the fast fluidized bed contain entrained solids. Means such as a cyclone are provided for separating the vapors from the entrained solids as well as connection means to transfer the vapors to the separation means and means for transferring the entrained solids from the separation means back to the passageway between the duct and the outer vessel.

In order to obtain immediate intimate contact between the source of heat and carbonaceous material as the carbonaceous material enters the duct, the inlet for the carbonaceous material preferably is a first tube and the inlet for the particulate source of heat is an annular region between the outer wall of the first tube and the inner wall of a second tube which surrounds and is coaxial with the first tube. Because a carbonaceous material and hot solid particles are injected into a fast fluidized bed where heat transfer and the pyrolysis reaction take place within a short period of time, increased yield of the middle-boiling hydrocarbons results. Because there is an internally circulating fluid bed containing particulate source of heat and carbon-containing solid residue along the inner surface of the duct surrounding the fast fluidized bed, carbonaceous material agglomeration on the duct is prevented.

Cyclone Reactor-Separator

According to a process described by *C.K. Choi; U.S. Patents 4,101,412; July 18, 1978; 4,070,250; January 24, 1978; and 4,105,502; August 8, 1978; all assigned to Occidental Petroleum Corporation* carbonaceous materials are rapidly pyrolyzed by feed of the carbonaceous material at a high velocity tangentially to a cyclone reactor-separator while introducing a high velocity stream of a particulate source of heat into the cyclone reactor-separator at an angle inclined to the path of travel of the carbonaceous material.

The cyclone reactor-separator induces separation of solids consisting of the particulate carbon-containing solid residue of pyrolysis and particulate heat source from a vapor stream which includes condensable and noncondensable hydrocarbon products of pyrolysis. The particulate source of heat and solid particulate carbon-containing residue of pyrolysis are transported to a cyclone burner and heated by partial combustion to a temperature suitable for feed to the cyclone reactor-separator. Rapid pyrolysis maximizes the yield of middle-boiling hydrocarbons and olefins.

With reference to Figures 2.8a and 2.8b, the carbonaceous material enters feedline **10** along with, if necessary, a carrier gas **12** and, if desired, steam, to a venturi mixer **14**.

Figure 2.8: Flash Pyrolysis Process

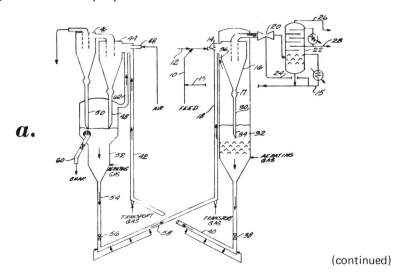

(continued)

Figure 2.8: (continued)

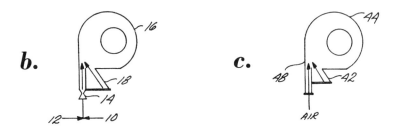

(a)   Process apparatus

(b)   Top view of the cyclone reactor separator

(c)   Top view of a cyclone burner

Source: U.S. Patent 4,101,412

If desired, the heavy hydrocarbons of pyrolysis may be combined with the feed and added by line **15**. The carrier gas, if employed, is nondeleteriously reactive with respect to the products of pyrolysis. By the term nondeleteriously reactive as applied to the carrier gas or gas stream, there is meant a gas essentially free of free oxygen, but which may contain constituents which react with the pyrolysis products to upgrade their value. To be avoided are constituents which by reaction degrade the pyrolysis products.

The gas can serve as a diluent to minimize pyrolysis contact time and in the case of solid carbonaceous materials as the transport gas. The carrier gas may, for instance, be the inert off-gas product of pyrolysis, steam which will react under suitable conditions with the char or coke formed from pyrolysis to yield by a water-gas shift reaction hydrogen which serves to react with and stabilize unsaturates in the products of pyrolysis or any desired inert gas or mixtures thereof.

With reference to Figure 2.8b, the carbonaceous feed and the carrier gas, if present, are injected as a stream into cyclone reactor separator **16** tangentially to the walls thereof.   Venturi **14** serves to intimately mix the carbonaceous feed with the carrier gas to enhance dilution of the feed to promote short reaction pyrolysis times. Simultaneously, there is introduced a particulate solid source of heat through line **18** at an angle inclined to the path of travel of the stream of carbonaceous material. The solid particulate source of heat is transported into the pyrolysis reactor by carrier gas which may be the same or different from the gas carrying the carbonaceous feed into the pyrolysis reactor, although it will be at a temperature approximately equal to the temperature of the particulate solid source of heat.

The hot particulate solids are supplied at a rate and at a temperature consonant with maintaining a temperature along the walls of the cyclone reactor-separator **16** suitable for pyrolysis. Pyrolysis will initiate at about 600°F below the softening temperature of the inorganic constituents of the particulate source of heat or the carbonaceous feed which would lead to slagging or fusion, preferably from 600° to about 2000°F. More typically, however, pyrolysis is conducted at a temperature from about 600° to about 1400°F, more preferably 900° to about 1400°F to maximize the yield of middle-boiling hydrocarbons and olefins. Higher temperatures may be employed with equal ease to facilitate, where desired, gasification reactions.

Depending upon pyrolysis temperature, normally from about 2 to about 20 lb of particulate solid source of heat are fed per pound of carbonaceous material entering reactor 16. The solids employed may be solids provided external to the process such as sand or the solid product resulting from pyrolysis of the carbonaceous material such as char or coke or in the instance of municipal solid waste, the glass-like inorganic residue resulting from the decarbonization of the solid residue of pyrolysis. The particulate source of heat is generally at a temperature from about 100° to 500°F or more above the desired pyrolysis temperature.

The amount of gas employed to transport the solid carbonaceous material and the particulate source of heat is sufficient to maintain transport of the materials and avoid plugging and normally in excess of that amount to dilute materials and minimize pyrolysis contact time. Normally, the solids content will range from about 0.1 to 10% by volume based on the total volume of the stream.

The particulate solid source of heat penetrates and enters the stream of carbonaceous material. This penetration initiates the rate of heat transfer from the particulate solid source of heat to the carbonaceous material, instantaneously causing pyrolysis which is a combination of vaporization and cracking reactions. As the vaporization and cracking reactions occur, condensable and noncondensable hydrocarbons are generated from the carbonaceous material with an attendant production of a carbon-containing solid residue such as coke or char. The carbon-containing solid residue and the particulate source of heat being the heaviest materials present are retained and pass spirally along the walls of the cyclone reactor-separator 16 and settle to reservoir 17 at the base.

The carrier gas as well as the pyrolytic vapors separate in the spiral vortex flow towards the center of the cyclone reactor-separator 16 and rapidly terminate the primary pyrolysis reactions due to the absence of solids. Effective pyrolysis contact time will be less than 3 seconds, preferably from about 0.1 to 1 second, and more preferably from 0.2 to about 0.6 second.

Pyrolysis contact time or contact time as referenced to pyrolysis, as used herein, means the time from which the carbonaceous material first contacts the particulate source of heat until the vaporized products separate from the particulate source of heat. A convenient measure of contact time is the average residence time of the carrier gas in the cyclone reactor-separator. The lower limit is that required to heat the carbonaceous material to the desired pyrolysis temperature. This is a function of particle size and concentration of solid particulate source of heat. For example, under average feed conditions, contact time to achieve about 1000°F is about 1.5 seconds for particles of about 250 μ in diameter and 0.5 second for particles of 75 μ in diameter.

The carrier gas along with the pyrolytic vapor exit reactor 16 and enter venturi mixer 20 where they are contacted with a quench fluid to reduce gas temperature at least below pyrolysis and cracking temperatures to prevent further cracking reactions from occurring. Preferably, the quench fluid reduces temperatures below the dew point of the condensable hydrocarbons.

Typically a portion of the condensed heavier hydrocarbons formed from the pyrolysis reactor employed as a quench fluid is fed to venturi by line 24. Immiscible quench oils may also be used and when used are separated from the products and recycled to venturi 20.

The quench effluent, normally a mixture of gas and liquids, is fed to fractionating tower 22. In fractionating tower 22 the carrier gas and lighter hydrocarbons are separated from the middle distillate hydrocarbons which are, in turn, separated from heavy hydrocarbons. Normally, the gaseous cut, containing about C_4 hydrocarbons and less, exit the top of fractionator 22 by line 26.

The cut of about C_5 hydrocarbons to those with an end point of about 950°F which constitutes gasoline, diesel and heating fuel components is separated as middle distillate hydrocarbon products in line 28. A portion may be cooled and recycled as reflux.

The heavy hydrocarbon residue exits the base of fractionator 22 and is cooled. One portion is recycled as reflux, another as quench and the balance, if not recovered, as a product returned to cyclone reactor-separator 16 to be pyrolyzed to extinction.

Because of short residence time and at pyrolysis temperatures below about 1400°F, the amount of C_4 hydrocarbons plus the carbon-containing solid residue of pyrolysis will be a minimum while the C_5 to 950°F end point fraction will be maximized. The C_4 and lower hydrocarbons will tend to be rich in olefins if hydrogen is not added to or generated in cyclone reactor-separator 16. The amount of C_4 or less hydrocarbons generated will increase with pyrolysis temperature and pyrolysis contact time.

The presence of hydrogen during pyrolysis whether internally generated or externally supplied is desired to enhance stabilization of the hydrocarbons formed, particularly the heavier hydrocarbons to prevent their polymerization to tars.

The particulate carbon-containing solid residue of pyrolysis and the particulate solid source of heat exit reservoir 17 and pass by line 30 and are collected in a fluidized stripper 32. A flow of a carrier gas which is also nondeleteriously reactive with respect to the products of pyrolysis enters the base of stripper 32 to maintain the solids in a mixed condition and in at least a semifluidized state.

Flap 34 on leg 30 prevents backflow of the aeration gas into the cyclone. Rather, the aeration gas is bypassed around cyclone reactor-separator 16 through conduit 36 for combination with the feed. The aeration gas serves to remove any of the hydrocarbon oils which result from pyrolysis from the surface of the particles and return them to the system for further pyrolysis.

The cooled particulate source of heat and carbon-containing solid residue of pyrolysis are passed through slide valve 38 and transported along angle riser 40 and vertical riser 42 to a combustion zone, preferably cyclone burner 44; the top view of cyclone burner **44** has been depicted in Figure 2.8c. The cyclone burner may be operated in conjunction with an identical cyclone burner **46** or simply a cyclone separator for fines. If other combustion apparatus is used, a cyclone separator is employed to separate flue gases from the particulate source of heat.

Combustion cyclone **44** operates in a manner substantially identical to cyclone reactor-separator **16**. The transport gas used to introduce the particles to cyclone burner **44** may be air or flue gas with the balance of the combustion air injected tangentially through line **48** of cyclone burner **44**. As shown in Figure 2.8c, the solids penetrate the air stream at an inclined angle and rapidly undergo oxidative combustion. The heavier particles rapidly pass through the air stream, such that effective combustion residence time is short, ranging from about 0.1 to 0.6 second.

As a consequence, even despite the fact that excess air is supplied, the effective residence time for combustion is short. As a result the amount of carbon dioxide generated will be maximized, as the faster carbon dioxide reaction rate is favored as compared to the slower carbon monoxide reaction rate. As a consequence, the amount of heat generated per unit of carbon consumed is maximized. In general, partial combustion will yield a flue gas having a CO_2 to CO ratio of about 2:1.

The gases and fine solids which elude recovery from cyclone **44** enter cyclone **46** where additional air may be added again using a cyclone as depicted in Figure 2.8c for short contact time combustion. Alternatively, a simple cyclone separator may be employed.

The high-temperature particulate source of heat collected in cyclones **44** and **46** pass by standpipes **48** and **50** to aerated surge hopper **52**. Surge hopper **52** is maintained at a temperature consonant with the operating temperature of the pyrolysis reactor **16** and generally from about 300° to 500°F above the pyrolysis temperature.

As required, the particulate source of heat is passed through standpipe **54**, slide valve **56**, angle riser **58** to vertical riser **18** for feed to cyclone reactor-separator **16**. Excess particles are withdrawn from surge hopper **52** through screen siphon tube **60** as product char.

The aeration gas employed in surge hopper **52** may be steam which becomes super-heated by contact with the contained particulate source of heat and forms hydrogen by a water gas shift reaction. This gas passes through pass line **62** for feed to cyclone **44** and cyclone **46** as part of the carrier gases. The use of the gas, however, is contingent on complete consumption of oxygen in cyclones **44** and **46** as the gas entering pyrolysis cyclone reactor **16** must be essentially free of oxygen.

The transfer gas in vertical riser **18** serves to accelerate the particulate source of heat to the velocity required for feed to cyclone reactor-separator **16**.

Pyrolysis with Cyclone Burner

N.W. Green, K. Duraiswamy and R.E. Lumpkin; U.S. Patent 4,102,773; July 25, 1978; and N.W. Green; K. Duraiswamy, R.E. Lumpkin, E.W. Knell, Z.I. Mirza and B.L. Winter; U.S. Patent 4,085,030; April 18, 1978; both assigned to Occidental Petroleum Corporation describe a continuous process for recovery of values contained in solid carbonaceous materials. In this process a particulate feed stream containing solid carbonaceous material particles of a size less than about 1,000 microns in diameter, and preferably less than about 250 microns in diameter in the case of an agglomerative coal, is provided.

The feed stream is subjected to flash pyrolysis by transporting the feed stream contained in a carrier gas which is substantially nondeleteriously reactive with respect to products of pyrolysis to a solids feed inlet of a descending flow pyrolysis reactor. The pyrolysis reactor contains a substantially vertically oriented pyrolysis zone operated at a temperature above about 600°F. In addition, a particulate source of heat is fed at a temperature above the pyrolysis temperature to a substantially vertically oriented chamber surrounding the upper portion of the pyrolysis reactor.

The inner peripheral wall of the chamber forms an overflow weir to the vertically oriented mixing region of the pyrolysis reactor. The particulate heat source is maintained in a fluidized state in the chamber by an aerating gas which also is substantially nondeleteriously reactive with respect to the products of pyrolysis. The particulate source of heat is discharged over the weir and downwardly into the mixing region at a rate sufficient to maintain the pyrolysis zone at the pyrolysis temperature.

The solid carbonaceous material feed stream and carrier gas are injected from the solids feed inlet into the mixing region to form a resultant turbulent mixture of the particulate source of heat, the carbonaceous material particles and the carrier gas. This resultant turbulent mixture is passed downwardly from the mixing zone to the pyrolysis zone of the pyrolysis reactor. In the pyrolysis zone the carbonaceous material feed is pyrolyzed to yield a pyrolysis product stream containing as solids, the particulate source of heat and a carbon containing solid residue of the carbonaceous material, and a vapor mixture of carrier gas and pyrolytic vapors comprising hydrocarbons. The pyrolysis product stream is then passed to a first separation zone such as one or more cyclone separators to separate at least the bulk of the solids from the vapor mixture.

The particulate source of heat is formed by transferring the separated particulate solids from the separation zone to at least one oxidation zone where a portion of the carbon in the solids is oxidized in the presence of an amount of free oxygen at least sufficient to raise the solids to a temperature sufficient for introduction to the pyrolysis zone. Preferably, oxidation occurs in two stages, the first involved during transport of the solids, and the second in a communicating oxidation stage. Of the total free oxygen fed, the amount of free oxygen introduced to the second stage is at least 50% of the molar amount of carbon monoxide entering the second stage.

The formed particulate source of heat and the gaseous combustion products of the solids are passed from the second oxidation stage to a second separation zone such as one or more cyclone separators. In the second separation zone the particulate source of heat is separated from the gaseous combustion products for feed to the chamber surrounding the upper portion of the pyrolysis reactor.

Preferably the second separation zone comprises at least two cyclone separation stages in series, where the bulk of the particulate source of heat is separated from the gaseous combustion products in a first cyclone separation stage. The remaining cyclone separation stages of the second separation zone serve to separate a fines fraction of the particulate source of heat from the gaseous combination products. These separated fines are not used for the particulate source of heat. By not using this fines fraction for the particulate source of heat, there is less chance of fines contaminating the hydrocarbon mixture passing overhead from the first separation zone.

It also is preferred that the second oxidation zone and the first cyclone separation stage of the second cyclone separation zone be the same vessel, i.e., a cyclone oxidation-separation zone. This minimizes formation of carbon monoxide by allowing quick removal of the formed particulate source of heat from its gaseous combustion products, thereby increasing the thermal efficiency of the process.

In the process, short reaction time and low temperatures in the pyrolysis reaction zone enhance formation of the middle distillate hydrocarbons, i.e., hydrocarbons in the range of C_5 hydrocarbons to hydrocarbons having an end point of 950°F. As a consequence, it is preferred to conduct pyrolysis so that the residence time of the carrier gas in the pyrolysis section of the pyrolysis reactor and the first separator is less than about 5 seconds, and more preferably from about 0.1 to about 3 seconds. It also is preferred that pyrolysis be conducted at a temperature from about 900° to 1400°F.

To achieve pyrolysis the solid particulate source of heat generally is introduced at a temperature from about 100° to about 500°F higher than the pyrolysis temperature to be achieved. The weight ratio of the particulate source of heat to the carbonaceous feed ranges from about 2 to about 20:1.

To provide turbulence to obtain rapid heat transfer from the particulate source of heat to the carbonaceous material, the turbulent mixture preferably has a solids content ranging from about 0.1 to about 10% by volume based upon the total volume of the stream.

The process has many advantages. Among these is improved process control because of a reservoir of the particulate source of heat behind the weir which dampens the effect of minor system upsets. Another advantage is that agglomerative materials can be processed readily because the turbulent flow in the mixing region can scour buildups of coal from the reactor walls. In addition, high yield of the valuable middle distillates can be obtained by operating the process under the preferred conditions.

Another advantage of the method is that high thermal efficiencies are achieved because carbon monoxide formed by free oxygen in the transport gas reacting with carbon in the carbon containing residue in the first oxidation stage is oxidized in the second oxidation stage.

This process also contemplates recovering hydrocarbon values from the vapor mixture. This is effected by progressively cooling the vapor mixture by directly contacting the vapor mixture with progressively cooler liquid coolant streams containing condensate of the vapor mixture.

Hot Recycle Shale

According to a process described by *A.A. Gregoli; U.S. Patent 3,972,801; August 3, 1976; assigned to Cities Service Research & Development Company* crushed oil shale is treated in a vertical retorting vessel, with fresh shale being mixed with hot recycle shale and the mixture being fed into the top of the vessel at a rate commensurate with the removal of hot spent shale from the bottom of the vessel. From top to bottom, the vessel is separated into distinct sections or zones, each having its own function and operating conditions. Broadly, these zones can be labeled top, intermediate and bottom zones, with fresh shale entering the top zone and spent shale exiting the bottom zone and with various phases of the process occurring in the intermediate zones.

These zones, while contiguous, are physically separated, one from the other, by horizontally inclined plates containing a plurality of vertically inclined pipes or tubes that allow the crushed or granular shale to move by gravity downwardly through the various zones. At the same time, the intermediate zones are equipped with horizontally inclined inlet and outlet conduits for the introduction and removal of various fluids. The pressures in these various zones can be super- or subatmospheric, as well as atmospheric, depending on the function of that particular zone.

One example of the process is described in general fashion by referring to Figure 2.9a. Crushed shale is delivered to fresh shale hopper 9, with the fresh feed going either to zone 1 or zone 3 of the vertical retorting vessel 34. Hot spent shale, typically recovered from the bottom of the retorting vessel 34, is also fed from spent shale disengager 12, to zone 1, called recycle hopper section. Here the hot spent shale, or recycle shale, can be mixed with fresh feed shale, cooling the hot spent shale and warming the fresh feed shale. It is emphasized that the residence time or time of contact between the hot and feed shales is short enough so that thermal decomposition of the feed shale is minimized and yet long enough to give some preheating of the feed shale.

The mixture travels downward to zone 2, the first low pressure zone, from which various gases, entrained dust and steam are removed through line 14. The mixture next enters zone 3, the upper purge section, wherein stripping steam, entering by line 15, is passed through the mixture of shale. In an alternate embodiment, fresh shale is introduced in zone 3 and mixed with the hot spent shale received from zone 2. It is recognized that any air, free or absorbed, entering with the fresh shale, will be substantially removed through zone 2. The steam flow exits from zone 3 partly through zone 2, removing a majority of air and trapped (or absorbed) gases from the shale mixture, and partly through zone 4, wherein the steam and reaction products are removed through line 16. The operating pressure in zone 3 is higher than the pressure in zone 2 or zone 4.

Zone 4, the reaction section, is where the majority of reactions occur (i.e., the thermal decomposition of the kerogen) that liberate the hydrocarbonaceous products from the feed shale and result in the formation of a carbonaceous resi-

Figure 2.9: Oil Shale Retort Process

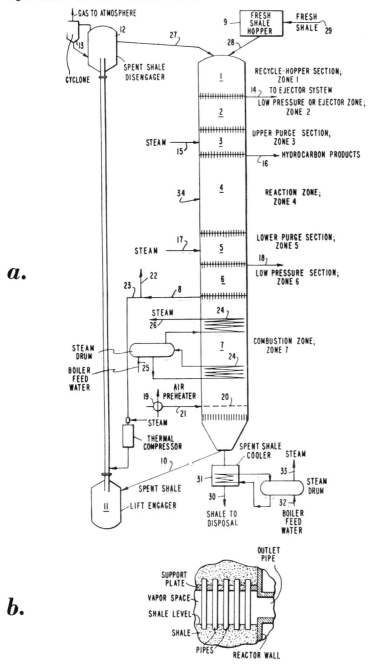

(a) Vertical section of the retorting vessel
(b) Detail of zone separation

Source: U.S. Patent 3,972,801

due on and in the shale particles. The volatilized gaseous products are separated and removed from the reaction section through line **16**.

The shale mixture, now substantially deleted of desirable hydrocarbonaceous products, enters zone **5**, the lower purge section. In this purge section, as in the upper purge section, steam is introduced through line **17** in order to segregate the desirable reaction products in zone **4** from any undesirable gaseous products in zone **6**, which is the lower ejection zone, in the same manner in which zone **3** segregates zone **2** from zone **4**. After undesirable gases are ejected from the shale mixture in zone **6** through line **18**, the shale enters zone **7**, the combustion zone wherein any residual carbonaceous material on the shale reacts with air introduced into the zone through line **21**, resulting in an exothermic reaction which raises the temperature of the shale mixture and produces various products of combustion, including inert nitrogen, oxides of carbon and unreacted oxygen. Although not shown in the drawing, the combustion zone can be further physically separated into subzones, with air introduced to one or more subzones for controlled combustion.

This zone furnishes the heat energy required in zone **4** to separate the desirable oil shale products from the shale feed. The temperature of the exiting spent shale is controlled by regulating the air rate, i.e., oxygen rate, entering zone **7**. Other controlling factors useful in maintaining the desired spent shale temperature include utilization of heat exchange coils **24** in one or more subzones and/or varying the spent shale residence time by changing the flow or movement rate of the descending solids. As noted, steam is made by introducing boiler feed water into exchanger coils located in zone **7**. The hot spent shale exits zone **7**, for further disposition. Those skilled in the art will recognize that the spent shale cooler **31**, located below zone **7**, is a heat exchanger by which at least some of the residual heat is recovered from the spent shale.

It is also recognized that the gaseous combustion products from zone **7** can be utilized to preheat the fresh shale and incoming air, such as in air preheater **19** and that further heat can be obtained from the waste gas stream by more complete combustion of, for example, the carbon monoxide component of the stream.

Since no outside fuel is used as a source of heat, essentially none of the desirable reaction products from the thermal decomposition of the shale is combusted to form heat, and no gaseous products of combustion are mixed with the desirable reaction products obtained in the reaction zone. It is well known in the art that typical retorting of the shale results in a deposit of coke-like material on the retorted shale. The controlled combustion of this carbonaceous material can and does furnish the heat necessary for the decomposition of kerogen. Thus, heat is transferred from the combustion zone **7** to the reaction zone **4**, without being accompanied by combustion gases. This step simplifies the ultimate purification of the reaction products from the reaction zone.

Another facet of this process is the low energy requirement relative to prior art versus combustion processes. The theoretical energy required to raise the shale to a retorting temperature of 900°F (482°C) from ambient is about 640,000 Btu/ton (178 g-cal/g). At retorting temperatures above about 1100°F (593°C), mineral carbonates begin to decompose. This decomposition not only absorbs a large amount of heat, approximately 1,300 Btu/lb (723 g-cal/g) of CO_2 liberated, but also dilutes the retort gas. The mineral CO_2 content of oil shale ranges from

300 to 400 lb/ton (150 to 200 g/kg), and thus additional energy requirements due to carbonate decomposition range from 400,000 to 500,000 Btu/ton (111 to 139 g-cal/g). Since the temperature of the process is well below the carbonate decomposition temperature, CO_2 will range from 0 to 20 lb/ton (0 to 10 g/kg) shale. This is well below the amount expected for other combustion type processes wherein CO_2 is 200 to 400 lb/ton (100 to 200 g/kg) shale. Furthermore, no CO_2 from combustion dilutes the retort products in the process, which is in contrast to combustion type processes. Thus, the noncombustion process requires the separation and disposal of much less CO_2 than does the combustion process or other shale processes.

As an example of this process, fresh shale assaying 30 gal/ton, (129 l per MT) by Fischer assay, is used as a basis for calculating inputs and outputs. For every ton (0.9 metric ton) of fresh shale, C_{3-} gas product is obtained in the amount of about 700 scf (19.8 m^3) (dry basis) having a heating value of approximately 775 Btu/scf (6,900 kg-cal/m^3). This is approximately 48 lb/ton (24 g/kg). A liquid C_{4+} product is obtained in the amount of about 31.7 gal/ton (132 l per MT), having about 0.8 weight percent S, 2 weight percent N and 24° API. This is approximately 240 lb/ton (120 g/kg).

The retorted shale (from zone 4) is approximately 1,712 pounds (777 kg), based on 1 ton (907 kg) of fresh shale, of which approximately 62 pounds of carbon per ton (31 g/kg) of fresh shale are burned off under controlled combustion, leaving approximately 1,650 pounds (750 kg) of hot spent shale discharged from zone 7 to the spent shale cooler per ton (907 kg) of fresh shale introduced. This amount of carbon is approximate and is based on the reaction of carbon being oxidized to CO_2, giving the equivalent heat required to raise the temperature of one ton (907 kg) of fresh shale from ambient to reactor temperature. A greater quantity of carbon will be burned if CO is an appreciable amount of the combustion gas.

Recycle shale, at an approximate temperature of about 1200°F (649°C), is withdrawn and used at about 5,600 pounds per ton (2.8 g/kg) of fresh shale. This amount of recycle shale can vary, depending on the amount of preheating done on the fresh shale.

The apparatus used for the abovedescribed process is typically a vertically oriented cylindrical retorting vessel, having the described zones placed in the proper order and physically separated, one from the other, as described. The physical dimensions of the vessel are naturally dependent upon the desired throughput. The L/D ratio for the retort is not critical but is typically in the range of about 8. Typical materials of construction are used, since the maximum operating temperature is about 1400°F (760°C). A 20 foot (6.1 m) diameter retort would have the capacity for producing 25,000 bpd (3,980 m^3/day) of shale oil. The relative sizes or proportions of the various zones, based on the total vessel size, are approximately 25 to 30% for the reaction section, 35 to 40% for the combustion zone, 5 to 10% for the recycle hopper zone and each of the first and second low pressure zones, and 10 to 15% for each of the purge zones.

More importantly, the reaction zone is sufficient in volume to maintain a fresh shale residence time of from about 2 to about 6 minutes.

Addition of Coal and Stripped Shale

T.G. Reed, Jr.; U.S. Patents 3,939,057; February 17, 1976 and 4,058,205; November 15, 1977 describes a process for producing a crude shale oil and a high Btu gas by retorting crushed oil shale admixed with a small quantity of crushed coal in an indirectly heated, horizontal, rotary calciner equipped with mechanical seals to contain the vapors produced and a condensing system to recover the oil vapors. The process includes introducing on a continuous basis crushed shale, which has been preheated to about 300°F, to the retort where it is further heated to 900°F and held at this temperature for about 15 minutes, from which the shale is continuously discharged into a hopper, sized to permit a residence time of about 15 minutes, during which time residual vapors are swept out with a small quantity of super heated steam.

The vapors from the retort and the soaking hopper are passed to a system of air cooled condensers where the shale oil and water are condensed and thus separated from the gas which is then suitable for compression and drying. The oil free shale, containing the char produced during retorting, is fed to a furnace where it is burned to produce the heat for retorting and preheating the shale. It is necessary to add the coal to provide additional heat since the char is insufficient in itself to provide all the heat required. Referring to Figure 2.10a, an indirectly fired retort 2 is provided for heating the crushed shale to the temperatures required for destructive distillation. This retort is a rotary calciner equipped with mechanical seals to prevent the product vapors from leaking to the atmosphere. Equipment of similar design is used to react gases with solids at elevated temperatures.

The temperature within the retort is maintained at 850° to 1050°F, preferably between 900° and 950°F. At temperatures below 850°F the decomposition of the kerogen is usually incomplete and at temperatures above 1050°F the mineral carbonates begin to decompose, a reaction which takes up large quantities of heat and which produces undesirable carbon dioxide which could reduce the value of the gas produced. The pressure in the retort is only a few inches of water and is the result of the vaporization of the organic material. The presence of light gases and water vapor assist in sweeping the vapors out of the retort.

The crushed shale is fed to the retort from a preheater 1, where the shale is continuously heated by directly contacting it with the hot gases from the heating chamber surrounding the retort. The temperature of these gases is moderated by cooling them in a waste heat boiler. The preheater consists of a rotary calciner in which the gases and the shale are fed cocurrently or preferably countercurrently. This calciner is of the same general design as that used for the commercial production of lime or Portland cement except that the low temperatures experienced in shale preheating do not require refractory lining of the steel tube. The temperature of the shale is controlled by regulating the quantity of gas fed. The temperature of the exiting shale must be maintained below the temperature where decomposition begins. This is normally 350°F but may vary somewhat with shale from different deposits.

If the temperature is allowed to exceed this temperature there will be a loss in yield since the gases from the preheater 1 are vented to the atmosphere and the organic material in the stack gas may exceed allowable limits.

Figure 2.10: Retort Process

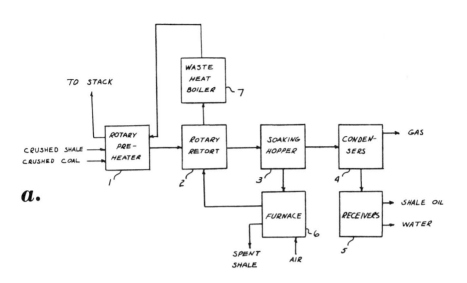

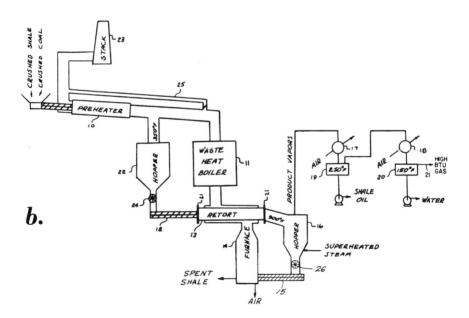

(a) Simplified block diagram illustrating the process
(b) Diagrammatic view illustrating the process of
Figure 2.10a in somewhat more detail

Source: U.S. Patent 4,058,205

The shale must be crushed sufficiently fine that the oil vapors can easily pass out of the particle. Also heat transfer is improved by using a small size. However, finely crushed shale tends to dust badly and can create serious separation problems downstream of the retort. Thus a balance must be achieved which may vary with different deposits. Typically, shale crushed to 90% <¼ inch will be satisfactory.

The product vapors and the shale are allowed to flow from the retort 2 into a hopper 3 which serves as a vapor solid separator and where the residual product vapors are allowed to escape from the shale and in fact are swept out by a small quantity of steam, which has been super heated to about 900°F, and which is introduced near the bottom of the hopper. This hopper is sized such that the residence of the shale is sufficient to permit substantially all the product vapors to be removed. The retention time required will vary somewhat with different grades of shale but will typically be about 15 to 20 minutes.

From the bottom of the hopper, the retorted shale containing the char is fed to a furnace 6 where it is burned to produce the heat required for retorting. The hot gases from the furnace pass first through the heating chamber of the retort 2, then through the waste heat boiler 7 and then through the preheater 1 and are then vented out a stack after such treatment as is necessary to meet air emission standards.

The product vapors including the shale oil, the light gases and moisture pass overhead from the hopper to a condenser system 4 where the liquids are recovered and separated from the light gases. The liquids, shale oil and water, pass from the condenser to receivers and decanter 5 where the water is removed. The shale oil product is ready for storage and shipment. The vapors passing overhead of the hopper 3 will contain various amounts of solids, these solids being fine particles of shale and these must be removed prior to shipment. The quantity of solid can vary from only a trace to several percent depending on a number of factors including size of crushed shale, design of the retort 2, operating conditions of the retort 2, and the design of the soaking hopper 3. A number of devices are available for removing these solids and the selection of the best for a given retorting plant will depend on the design of the major equipment for the plant.

The furnace should be of such a design that retention of the solids is sufficiently short that decomposition of the mineral carbonates does not occur to a substantial degree and that clinkers do not form. The furnaces used for firing high ash powdered coal such as those of the cyclone design should be suitable. Once again, solid carry out is a problem and precipitators or other types of equipment for solid removal from the stack gas may be necessary to prevent a fly ash pollution problem.

Typical high quality oil shale has a density of about 140 lb/ft^3 or about 14 ft^3/ton. This typical shale will yield per ton upon retorting about 26.7 gallons of oil with a gravity of 7.75 pounds per gallon, about 30 pounds of light gas with a gross heating value of about 300,000 Btu and 70 pounds of char with a heating value of about 500,000 Btu. The retorting requires that shale be heated to about 900°F for about 15 minutes. The heat required to raise the temperature of the shale to 900°F is about 275 Btu/lb or 550,000 Btu/ton.

It can be seen from the above information that if the heating process were 100% efficient that there would be almost enough heat produced from burning the char, 500,000 Btu/ton, to retort the shale which requires 550,000 Btu/ton. However, these heating processes are relatively inefficient and additional heat is required. In this process the additional heat is provided by adding relatively small quantities of coal to the raw shale.

The coal used will probably be a relatively high volatile type such as is found in the western states not far from the shale deposits. This coal, when heated to 900°F along with the shale undergoes a decomposition whereby about 25% of the coal is volatilized. The tar oil produced by this coking augments the oil from the shale.

In the preferred case, the heat efficiency of the combined retort and preheater system is about 35%. This means that the actual heat requirement is about 1,571,000 Btu/ton of shale. Since 500,000 Btu is available from the char, 1,071,000 Btu must come from the coal. A typical low temperature coke has a heating value of 11,700 Btu/lb. This means therefore, that 91.5 pounds of such coke must be burned per ton of shale. For a coal which is 25% volatilized in the retort, about 125 pounds of coal must be fed per ton of shale fed. The volatiles from the coal will increase the oil production by about 3.2 gallons per ton of shale. Obviously these quantities may vary somewhat depending on the type and quality of coal used.

Referring to Figure 2.10b, the process in more detail is as follows: crushed shale and crushed coal are fed continuously to a preheater **10** which is a horizontal rotary calciner where the mixture of shale and coal is contacted directly and countercurrently with hot stack gas thereby warming the feed to 300° to 350°F. The preheated feed is discharged into a hopper **22** and a gas is vented through a stack **23**. The preheated feed is picked up from the hopper by a conveyor **12** which continuously charges the retort **13**. The conveyor is of such a design that the product gas from the retort cannot escape through the feed system. This can be accomplished by using a rotary feeder **24** or other devices commonly used for similar purposes.

The retort **13** consists of an indirectly fired horizontal rotary calciner equipped with mechanical seals **21** to retain the product vapors and prevent their contamination with gases used as a source of heat. An excellent description of indirect heat calciners of this type is found in *Perry's Chemical Engineer's Handbook,* 4th Edition, McGraw-Hill, 1963, pages 20 to 28.

The product vapors and shale are discharged from the retort into a hopper **16** which serves several functions. It provides a means for separating the vapors from the solids, it provides residence time for the residual vapors to escape from the solids, and it provides storage of fuel for the furnace. A small quantity of steam, superheated to 900°F is injected near the bottom of the hopper **16** to assist in sweeping the product vapors out of the solids. The quantity of steam required will vary somewhat with the geometry of the hopper, but will be in the range of about 0.1 pound of steam per ton of shale to about 10 pounds per ton, preferably 2 to 4 pounds per ton.

The vapors from the overhead of the hopper **16** pass first to a high temperature condenser **17**, preferably using air as the cooling medium, where most of the shale oil is condensed. The outlet of this condenser must operate at temperatures above 212°F to avoid the condensation of water. The oil is collected in a receiver **19** from which it is pumped to storage. The gases which are uncondensed pass on to a low temperature condenser **18** where the water is condensed along with very small quantities of hydrocarbons. The temperature of the outlet of this condenser must be lower than 212°F in order to condense the water. The water is collected in a receiver **20** where the hydrocarbons are decanted and either collected or mixed with the shale oil from the high temperature receiver **19**.

Commercially available air cooled condensers generally consist of multiple parallel finned tubes mounted nearly horizontal with air forced over the tubes by a fan. The uncondensed gas which amounts to about 500 standard cubic feet per ton of shale is transferred to a compression and treatment unit which is beyond the scope of this process. However, it is important to note that since it was not diluted by the combustion gases, there is little or no nitrogen present and minor treatment can make this gas suitable for blending with natural gas. The steam generated in the waste heat boiler **11** can be used to drive the gas compressors.

The shale from the bottom of the hopper is conveyed using a mechanical conveyor **15** or other system of conveying to the furnace **14** where the char is burned. In the embodiment shown in Figure 2.10b, the steam injected into the hopper **16** serves as a gas seal preventing the loss of product. However, other sealing systems such as the rotary valve **26** could be employed.

The spent shale from the furnace **14** is allowed to cool and then is discarded. The hot gases from the furnace **14** are passed first through the heating chamber of the retort **13**, then through the waste heat boiler **11**, then through the preheater **10**, and lastly out the stack **23**. Some hot gas may bypass the preheater **10** through the bypass flue **25** by which means the preheated shale temperature is controlled.

Quenching Reactor Effluent Streams

S. Sack; U.S. Patent 4,097,360; June 27, 1978; assigned to Occidental Petroleum Corporation describes a process for recovery of values contained in a solid carbonaceous material which exhibits the following features: high thermal efficiency, high overall yield, and high yield of light hydrocarbon products.

This process comprises the steps of directly contacting in a quench zone at least a portion of a feed stream containing a solid carbonaceous material with a stream containing hot volatilized hydrocarbons resulting from the pyrolysis of the solid carbonaceous material. Because the volatilized hydrocarbons are hotter than the carbonaceous material the volatilized hydrocarbons are quenched and the feed stream is preheated. Following this a stream containing preheated solid carbonaceous material is withdrawn from the quench zone and subjected to pyrolysis in a pyrolysis zone maintained at a temperature higher than the temperature in the quench zone by the feed of a particulate solid source of heat.

The effluent pyrolysis product stream from the pyrolysis zone contains condensible and noncondensible volatilized hydrocarbons and a solids mixture of the carbon containing particulate solid residue and particulate source of heat. A volatilized hydrocarbon stream is separated in a separation zone from the solids mixture and at least a portion of this stream is passed to the quench zone to directly contact the carbonaceous material in the feed stream. Values are also recovered by withdrawing at least a portion of the particulate residue and noncondensible hydrocarbons as product and by condensing condensible hydrocarbons.

This process exhibits high overall yield and high thermal efficiency because the solid carbonaceous material is preheated prior to pyrolysis by the volatilized hydrocarbons. Thus the energy contained in the volatilized hydrocarbon stream is recovered and recycled back to the pyrolysis zone. This means that less of the solid residue of pyrolysis has to be oxidized to provide the heat required for the endothermic pyrolysis reaction.

In one version of this process, the quench zone is maintained at a temperature to condense a portion of the volatilized hydrocarbons in the quench zone to leave a residual uncondensed volatilized hydrocarbon stream. The condensed hydrocarbons are then recycled to the pyrolysis reaction zone to increase the yield of lighter noncondensible hydrocarbons by further thermal cracking.

This process is useful for such solid carbonaceous materials as oil shale, tar sands, agglomerative and nonagglomerative coals, and the organic fraction of solid waste.

SOLID HEAT TRANSFER PROCESSES

Segregation of Heat Carrier Flows

A process described by *J.E. Gwyn and S.C. Roberts; U.S. Patent 4,110,193; August 29, 1978; assigned to Shell Oil Company* is directed to a retorting procedure for subdivided solid materials, such as crushed oil shale, employing a particulate heat carrier in stage-wise heating and in heat recovery from the retorted particulate residue. According to the process, particulate heat carrier is passed downwardly at a substantially uniform rate through fluidized beds of the solid materials under the influence of gravitational force to effect the requisite sensible heat transfer, a primary feature of the process being the segregation of the heat carrier flows in order to minimize overall thermal stress on the heat carrier.

Moreover, it has been found that hydrocarbonaceous fluids can be recovered from subdivided, substantially nonvolatile carbonaceous solid material in a highly effective and energy efficient way by a retorting process employing sensible heat transfer from solid heat carrier to preheat the subdivided solid, retort the preheated solid and recover heat from the retorted solid in separate process zones, if the heat carrier flow is segregated in a critical manner and the sensible heat transfer is carried out in a particular fashion.

In this process, which is particularly applicable to mined and comminuted oil shale, the subdivided solid is contacted, sequentially, as a fluidized mass in a series of vertically-oriented process zones with particulate solid heat carrier in a manner such that the heat carrier falls or rains through the fluidized mass at a substantially uniform and nonaccelerating rate under the influence of gravitational force, said falling rate being controlled by heat carrier properties such as specific gravity and particle size and fluidized bed characteristics such as apparent bed density and fluidizing gas velocity. Tracing subdivided solid material flow through the process, the first or preheating stage and the last or heat recovery stage of the process, involving sensible heat transfer from or to a solid heat carrier, are carried out by fluidizing the solid material in an upward direction at a superficial fluidizing gas velocity at least equal to that known in the art as the "dilute-phase transition velocity," thereby obtaining a dilute-phase, fluidized mass in gas which is contacted countercurrently in the manner described with a particulate heat carrier.

In the first or preheating process stage, the subdivided solid material is heated to an elevated temperature below that required for retorting, while in the last or heat recovery stage, heat is recovered from the solid material, now in the form of a particulate solid carbonaceous material-containing residue after being subjected to an intermediate retorting stage. In the intermediate retorting stage of the process, the preheated subdivided solids in the form of a dense, well-mixed fluidized bed are contacted with particulate heat carrier in the manner described previously to obtain a vapor phase containing hydrocarbonaceous solids and a solid particulate phase comprising a solid carbonaceous material containing residue.

According to the process, the flow of particulate heat carrier is segregated in the process scheme such that one mass of heat carrier is utilized in both the preheating and heat recovery stages of the process whereby heat is recovered from the retorted solid material and utilized to preheat incoming solid material while a second mass of heat carrier, heated to high temperature in a separate carrier heating zone, is utilized exclusively for retorting of the subdivided solid material. Preferably, the particle size and specific gravity of the heat carrier is such that it may be pneumatically transported from one process zone to another as necessary in the overall process scheme.

By segregating the particulate heat carrier into two distinct masses and circulating each mass through separate and nonintersecting flow circuits in the process scheme, as described above, several distinct advantages are obtained. In the first place, thermal stresses on the total heat carrier charge to the process are minimized in that only a portion of the total charge is subject to the high temperatures required for heat transfer in the retorting step of the process and the heat carrier charge to the retorting step is not subject to the wide temperature variations of prior art processes since it is not utilized to preheat relatively cool incoming solid material.

Further, by segregating the heat carrier flow in the manner described, it is now possible to optimize the heat carrier properties for its particular application in the process by utilizing two different heat carriers, one for preheating and heat recovery and one for retorting. This advantage takes on special significance not only because of the potential economic savings involved in using cheaper, more conventional heat carriers in the preheating and heat recovery steps, but also because, as explained below, heat transfer is not a limiting process variable in the retorting phase of the process. Thus, the particle size of the heat carrier can be larger in the retorting heat carrier flow circuit for easier separation from the retorted solid but still small enough, if desired, to permit pneumatic transport. Finally, segregation of the heat carrier flow in the manner described optimizes recovery of thermal energy from the process since the heat content of both the retort zone-heat carrier and the heat recovery zone-heat carrier is conserved by return to the retort carrier heating zone and the preheating zone, respectively, while at the same time facilitating discharge of retorted solids at a desirably low temperature as a result of heat exchange in the heat recovery zone with heat carrier cooled to relatively low temperature in the preheating zone.

Further advantages accrue from the particular fashion in which sensible heat transfer is effected between particulate heat carrier and the subdivided solid material in the process sequence. According to the process, sensible heat transfer from or to the particulate heat carrier is effected by direct heat carrier contacting of the subdivided solid material as a dilute-phase fluidized mass in the preheating zone, and preferably the heat recovery zone, and as a well-mixed, dense phase fluidized mass in the retort zone.

The particular fluidized form of subdivided solid material selected for each process step derives from the finding that optimum process operation is obtained when heat transfer governs the preheating and heat recovery process steps and pyrolysis reaction rate governs the retorting step. Thus, by using a dilute-phase fluidization in the preheating and heat recovery zones, the rate and efficiency of heat transfer is maximized since the sensible heat transfer is countercurrent and the degree of subdivided solid material backmixing is inherently reduced by dilute-phase operation.

Again, since the pyrolysis reaction rate governs operation of the retort zone, a dense-phase fluidized bed can be utilized to obtain the longer residence times required for reaction without causing the retort vessel to be prohibitively large. Finally, the properties of the particulate heat carrier in each process flow circuit can be optimized on the basis of heat transfer and reaction rate criteria such that a small particle size, high heat capacity and surface area carrier can be employed to maximize heat transfer in the preheating and heat recovery stages, whereas a larger particle size carrier can be employed in the retorting zone to promote ease of separation from the retorted solids.

The complete process also includes various solids-gas and solids-solids separation and recovery steps associated with integrated and sequential operation of the preheating, retorting and heat recovery phase of the process as well as recovery of the desired hydrocarbonaceous fluid product of the process.

Accordingly, it is convenient to describe the process, in its most basic terms, as a retorting process for recovery of hydrocarbonaceous fluids from solid material, leaving upon retorting a solid carbonaceous material-containing residue, which comprises countercurrently contacting the solid material subdivided to a particle size fluidizable in gas in the form of a relatively cool, upwardly moving fluidized mass in a vertically-oriented preheating zone with a relatively hot first particulate heat carrier thereby transferring sensible heat from the heat carrier to the subdivided solid material and heating the solid material to an elevated temperature below that required for retorting, the subdivided solid material being fluidized in a manner to create a dilute-phase fluidized mass in the preheating zone and the particulate heat carrier being introduced at the upper portion of the preheating zone and having a particle size and density such that it falls through the dilute-phase fluidized mass at a substantially uniform rate and collects in the lower portion of the vertical preheating zone as a relatively cool first particulate heat carrier.

The bulk of the subdivided solid material is recovered at elevated temperature in the upper portion of the preheating zone and the recovered solid material is passed to a retorting zone.

The relatively cool first particulate heat carrier is recovered in the lower portion of the solid material preheating zone, and the recovered heat carrier is passed to a heat recovery zone.

The subdivided solid material is introduced at elevated temperature into a vertically-oriented retorting zone as a dense-phase, fluidized mass, and the fluidized mass is contacted with a second particulate heat carrier heated to a temperature above that required for retorting to transfer sensible heat from the heat carrier to the subdivided solid material to obtain a vapor phase containing hydrocarbonaceous fluids and a solid particulate phase comprising a solid carbonaceous material-containing residue, the second particulate heat carrier being preheated in a separate heating zone and introduced into the upper portion of the retorting zone wherein its particle size and density are such that it falls at a substantially uniform rate and collects in the lower portion of the vertical retorting zone along with a minor amount of entrained solid material and solid carbonaceous material-containing residue.

The hydrocarbonaceous fluids are recovered from the upper portion of the retorting zone. The second particulate heat carrier is separated in the lower portion of the retorting zone from solid carbonaceous material-containing residue and then passed to a carrier heating zone where the carrier's temperature is raised to a level about that required for retorting. The second particulate heat carrier is returned after heating to the upper portion of the retorting zone.

The solid carbonaceous material-containing residue is removed from the upper portion of the dense fluidized phase in the retorting zone and passed to a heat recovery zone.

The solid carbonaceous material-containing residue is introduced from the retorting zone into a heat recovery zone and countercurrently contacted with the relatively cool, first particulate heat carrier from the preheating zone to transfer sensible heat from the residue to the first particulate heat carrier and form a relatively cool particulate residue. The relatively hot first particulate heat carrier is returned to the preheating zone and the relatively cool particulate residue is recovered from the heat recovery zone.

In the preferred form of the process, the carbonaceous material-containing residue is fluidized in the heat recovery zone in a manner to create a dilute-phase fluidized mass in the heat recovery zone and the first particulate heat carrier is introduced in the upper portion of the heat recovery zone, the first particulate heat carrier having a particle size and density such that it falls through the dilute-fluidized mass at a substantially uniform rate and collects in the lower portion of the heat recovery zone; and the first particulate heat carrier in the lower portion of the heat recovery zone is recovered and passed to the solid material preheating zone where it supplies sensible heat for preheating the solid material containing non-volatile hydrocarbonaceous material.

Recovery of Heat Carriers

In an oil shale retorting process described by *G.A. Myers, Y.A.K. Abdul-Rahman and J.L. Skinner; U.S. Patent 4,118,309; October 3, 1978; assigned to Atlantic Richfield Company* hot heat-carrying spherically-shaped solids are cycled to a retort zone to mix with and retort crushed oil shale, thereby producing gas and oil products and a mixture of irregularly-shaped, laminar spent shale and spherically-shaped solids. The spherically-shaped solids are separated and recovered from the spent shale for recycle through the process.

In one stage of the separation procedure, a mixture of spent shale and spherically-shaped solids is fed to a continuously restored inclined surface whereon the spherically-shaped solids roll from the surface while the irregularly-shaped spent shale solids are separately removed from the inclined surface. Continuous restoration of the inclined surface is achieved through movement of the feed and the impingement area of the inclined surface relative to each other. The separation system may be used for separating other types of spherically-shaped solids which will roll from nonspherical, irregularly-shaped solids which do not roll.

Continuous Thermal Reactor Using Refractory Pebbles

A process described by *E. Koppelman and R.G. Murray; U.S. Patent 4,069,107; January 17, 1978* involves the use of a continuous pyrolysis reactor consisting of a reactor vessel of a generally upright configuration having a reaction chamber to which a feed inlet is connected at the upper portion thereof for introducing a particulated carbonaceous feed material. Preheated solid heat transfer media or pebbles are introduced into the upper portion of the reaction chamber through a distribution system in which a portion of the pebbles is substantially uniformly mixed with the carbonaceous feed material forming a downwardly moving columnar reaction mass and the balance of the pebbles is distributed in the form of a layer surrounding the reaction mass which is substantially devoid of any of the carbonaceous feed material.

The reaction chamber is provided with a gas inlet and a gas outlet for introducing a gas, such as steam, carbon dioxide and/or air, into the reaction chamber in a manner to pass transversely through the pebble layers and reaction mass to effect a sweeping of the gaseous pyrolysis decomposition products and volatile constituents formed which are withdrawn through a gas outlet disposed in transverse spaced relationship from the gas inlet. The layer of the pebbles adjacent to the gas inlet effects a preheating of the introduced gas, or a superheating of the steam introduced, as the case may be, to a desired temperature level, while the layer of pebbles adjacent to the gas outlet serves to further thermally decompose and gasify the volatilized gaseous constituents and serves as a depository for the carbonaceous substances produced, effecting an extraction thereof from the gaseous effluent before coming in contact with the structure and associated conduits defining the gas outlet.

The lower portion of the reaction chamber is provided with a separator for separating the pebbles and the carbonaceous char product or solid ash residue which, after further cooling, is discharged from the reactor. The separated pebbles are recirculated to a heater in which the pebbles are reheated in a manner so as to effect combustion and removal of the carbonaceous deposits thereon, whereafter they are returned to the upper portion of the reactor for reuse. In the operation of the reactor to produce an activated char, the immediate removal of the gaseous pyrolysis products formed prevents a redeposition thereof on the active sites of the carbonized product produced such that the carbonized product is characterized as being possessed of high adsorptive capacity, necessitating no further activation treatment.

In the process, a pyrolysis and/or gasification of particulated carbonaceous feed materials at an elevated temperature is effected by mixing the feed material with a preheated particulated heat transfer media in a stratified manner to form a reaction mass enclosed within a layer of heat transfer media, substantially devoid of any feed material, and through which a gas is passed transversely in a manner to sweep the volatiles and gaseous pyrolysis reaction components from the reaction mass employing the downstream layer of heat transfer media as a depository for tarry and carbonaceous residues produced which subsequently are removed during the recirculation and reheating of the heat transfer media.

In the specific adaptation of the process to production of activated carbon products, the purging gas is continuously passed through the reaction bed transversely to prevent any significant redeposition of the gaseous pyrolysis products formed on the active sites of the carbonaceous product, which is characterized as having a high adsorptive capacity without requiring any supplemental activation treatments.

Spouted-Bed Reactor

P.W. Tamm and C.W. Kuehler; U.S. Patent 4,125,453; November 14, 1978; assigned to Chevron Research Company describe a process for the retorting of shale in which the solids to be retorted are mixed with a solid heat-transfer material to provide the necessary heat for retorting. The shale is retorted in a spouted bed of the shale and heat-transfer solids.

The continuous process for retorting hydrocarbon-containing solids comprises directing a jet of gas substantially vertically up into a vessel containing subdivided solids, the solids comprising hydrocarbon-containing solids and heat-transfer solids, thereby forming a spouted bed of the solids in the vessel. The spouted-bed comprises as the minor volume of the bed a rapidly moving upward spout of the solids in dilute suspension in the gas, and as the major volume of the bed a downwardly, relatively slowly moving annular columnar loosely packed body of the solids.

Continuously introduced into the vessel are heat-transfer solids at an elevated temperature and hydrocarbon-containing solids, the solids being introduced into the vessel by entraining the solids in the jet of gas. Retorted solids and the heat-transfer solids from the vessel are continuously withdrawn from a lower portion of the body portion of the spouted bed; and vaporized hydrocarbons are continuously withdrawn from an upper portion of the vessel.

Preferably, the gas is maintained essentially free of oxygen and essentially all of the heat for the retorting process is supplied by the heat-transfer solids.

G.E. Langlois and P.W. Tamm; U.S. Patent 4,087,347; May 2, 1978; assigned to Chevron Research Company describe a process for the retorting of shale in which the solids to be retorted are mixed with a solid heat-transfer material to rapidly heat the hydrocarbon-containing solids to a high temperature. The shale and heat-transfer material are entrained in a high-velocity gaseous stream and conveyed upward in a vertical dilute phase lift pipe retorting vessel whereby the hydrocarbon-containing solids are rapidly heated to an elevated temperature vaporizing a minor portion of the hydrocarbons in the solid. The hydrocarbon-containing solids then pass into a disengaging zone wherein the gas and solids are separated. The partially retorted solids then pass into a gravitating bed retort and flow downward countercurrent to the flow of a stripping gas. The process is characterized by a high liquid yield and a minimum gas yield along with minimal amounts of volatile components being left in the retorted solids.

Flexible, Helical Shaped Conveyor

J.W. Unverferth; U.S. Patent 4,056,461; November 1, 1977; assigned to Chevron Research Company describes a process for the retorting of shale and other similar hydrocarbon-containing solids in which the solids to be retorted are mixed with a hot solid heat transfer material to rapidly heat the hydrocarbon-containing solids to a high temperature and conveyed through the retorting vessel by means of a flexible, generically helical shaped, elongated, hollow longitudinal core element. The shale and heat transfer material are conveyed concurrently through a first section of a cylindrical vessel while a stripping gas is introduced into a latter section of the vessel and flows countercurrent to the movement of the two solids. The stripping gas along with entrained fines, gaseous hydrocarbons, and liquid hydrocarbons in the form of a mist are removed from a middle section of the vessel while the retorted shale is removed from the end of the vessel.

The process has a high overall mechanical and thermal efficiency for a combination of reasons. First, the raw shale enters the system at an ambient temperature while the spent shale leaves the system at a low temperature. Second, all of the heat for the process can be substantially supplied by the residual carbonaceous matter left on the retorted shale. Thirdly, the shale is moved through the entire retorting vessel by a highly efficient and simple mechanical conveyor which may be driven by a single prime mover.

The process furthermore produces very high yields of high quality synthetic shale oil for several reasons. First, by having a rapid direct heating of the shale followed by rapid removal of the vaporized components, excessive cracking and other undesired side reactions are avoided. Secondly, by forcing a stripping gas through the third section of the retort, the more slowly volatilized hydrocarbons are also quickly transported out of the retort. Thirdly, by maintaining a relatively uniform temperature in the retort, one can easily vary the residence time of the solid to vaporize and recover essentially all of the hydrocarbons in the shale, even though the shale may vary greatly in size. Fourthly, by having a relatively uniform high retorting temperature in the retort, condensation of hydrocarbons in the retort is substantially prevented. Also, recycle of the oil wet solids from the particulate separation zone further increases the yield of condensable hydrocarbons.

Heated Gas and Depressurization

J.M. O'Ffill; U.S. Patent 4,088,562; May 9, 1978; assigned to Twenty Farms, Inc. describes a high efficiency process for treating oil shale which allows essentially complete recovery of the valuable hydrocarbon fraction of the shale, including light ends, without direct firing of the shale or use of other expensive processing steps. In the process, the oil shale is heated in a closed heating system using circulating, oxygen-free gases until the shale "break point," or temperature at which the hydrocarbons begin to vaporize from the shale, is reached; at this point the system is slowly depressurized and hydrocarbons are simultaneously released to a condensation stage for recovery and control of circulating fan horsepower. Steam may also be added to the circulating system to further purge hydrocarbons from the shale and provide additional control of fan horsepower.

A prime advantage of the method stems from the fact that a sidestream of hydrocarbons is drawn off from the recycle stream for condensation, thereby eliminating the costly (in terms of energy use) practice of cyclically passing the entire recycle stream through condenser means. Preferably, air which has been treated to remove the oxygen therefrom is used as the circulating heating gas, and such air is cyclically heated in an indirect manner and sequentially passed downwardly through a substantially stationary pile of ground oil shale.

OTHER RECOVERY PROCESSES

Simultaneous Heating and Classification

P.E. Prull; U.S. Patent 4,028,222; June 7, 1977 describes a method for extracting oil from shale having simultaneous heating and classification of the crushed oil shale particles according to size.

Referring to Figure 2.11, it may be seen that the process for extraction of oil from oil shale is generally indicated by the arrow **11** and includes the step of crushing the oil shale, as in a crusher, as schematically indicated at **12**. The process **11** further includes the step of classifying the crushed oil shale by particle size into at least two portions of differing range of particle sizes, as schematically indicated at **13**, where a classifying means is diagrammatically indicated. The crushed oil shale is also heated, as symbolically shown at **14**, to a temperature sufficient to release the oil and below the flash point of the oil released.

The crushed, classified and heated oil shale is then centrifuged, as indicated schematically at **16**, each portion being separately centrifuged at a centrifuge speed and for a time selected for the greatest efficiency of oil extraction per unit of driving energy applied to the centrifuge. As shown, the steps of classifying and of heating the crushed oil shale are carried out simultaneously by application of heat to the crushed oil shale as it passes through the classifying means **13**.

Preferably, the crushed oil shale is classified into four portions of differing range of particle size, the portion having the largest particle size being recrushed and reclassified. The three remaining portions are then subjected to the separate centrifuging. Ideally, the first of the portions, that having the smallest particle size, would be approximately that passing a $\frac{1}{4}$-inch mesh screen while the second of the portions would be that not passing a $\frac{1}{4}$-inch mesh screen but passing a $\frac{1}{2}$-inch mesh screen. The third portion would be that passing a $\frac{3}{4}$-inch mesh screen and not passing a $\frac{1}{2}$-inch mesh screen. The fourth portion, the one to be recrushed, would be that not passing a $\frac{3}{4}$-inch mesh screen.

Figure 2.11: Extraction of Oil from Oil Shale

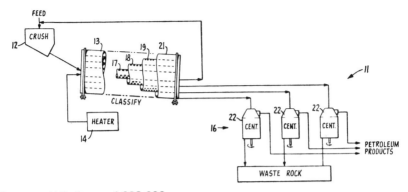

Source: U.S. Patent 4,028,222

Heat may be applied to the oil shale for extraction of the oil therefrom by dry heat, dry steam or wet steam, and may be carried out at or somewhat above atmospheric pressure. The upper limit of temperature would be the flash point of the extracted petroleum products, and the lower limit for practical extraction seems to be about 200°F. The choice of level of temperature, to which the crushed oil shale is heated, may also be optimized for the greatest effectiveness and efficiency of extraction per unit input energy.

The classification step may be carried out by a rotating trammel screen as schematically indicated at **13**. In such a screen, the material to be classified is fed axially into the center member of a series of rotating, concentric, perforated drums. The inner drum has perforations in its circumference, sized here to pass particles of average dimensions, ¾ inch and below. The next outer drum has perforations sized to particles of average dimension, ½ inch and below, and the third drum radially outward of the axis has perforations sized to pass particles of average dimension, ¼ inch and below. The outermost drum has no perforations.

In a manner well understood for trammel screen grading devices, the entire drum apparatus is slightly tilted from the horizontal so that the oil shale tumbles from the higher end toward the lower as the drum rotates. The material retained by each drum then exits separately at the low end to an appropriate conveyor. Heat may be applied to the interior of the trammel screen **13** by appropriate conduits conducting hot gases, dry or wet steam to the space within the drums **17, 18, 19** and **21** for release there.

The classified oil shale particles are then conveyed to a bank of centrifuges **22**, where each separate batch of particle sizes may be separately centrifuged for a longer or shorter time, at a higher or lower centrifuge rotation rate, according to the most energy-efficient program of extraction of the oil therefrom. The centrifuges **22** are preferably of the continuous-feed type. If needed, additional heat may be applied to any of the classified portions of crushed oil shale during the centrifuging step, but energy will be conserved by applying the heat only to that range of particle sizes requiring additional heat. The additional heat may be applied by any of the techniques discussed above in connection with heating in the classification step.

Horizontal Bed on Perforated Support Using Radiant Heat

K.L. Storrs; U.S. Patent 3,985,637; October 12, 1976 describes a process for the heat treatment of both liquid and solid substances to educe and recover useful products. The process comprises forming the substance to be treated into a elongate, substantially horizontal bed supported on a perforate support. A substantially closed space of substantially constant volume is maintained above the bed. An inert atmosphere, which will not support combustion of the substance making up the bed, is contained in the closed space in contact with the bed of material being treated.

The substance, i.e., bed of material, is heated to progressively increasing temperatures by means of a radiant heat source located at the top of the closed space. As the bed is heated, useful liquid products, usually decomposition products, form throughout the substance being treated and are removed by the force of gravity from the bottom side of the bed through the perforate support. The liquids, liquid droplets, and any gaseous material derived from the heat treatment of the substance are conducted away from the underside of the perforate support by suitable gravity-flow conduits leading downward to one or more collection chambers.

It has been found that improvements in yields of liquids educed from the substance being treated, can be obtained, together with greatly decreased heat consumption, by providing a closed space of substantially constant volume above the bed and maintaining a substantially static, inert atmosphere in the closed space. The inert atmosphere, which is in contact with the upper surface of the bed, is maintained in a substantially static condition by controlling a particular combination of process variables within specified critical ranges.

The substance being treated is formed into a substantially horizontal bed having a thickness of up to about 1 inch, preferably from about $\frac{1}{2}$ to 1 inch. The bed is heated to progressively increasing temperatures by the radiant heat source which is located up to about $1\frac{1}{2}$ inches above the upper surface of the bed, preferably from about $\frac{3}{8}$ to $1\frac{1}{2}$ inches above the upper surface of the bed; the temperatures being no greater than will progressively cause liquid products to form throughout the substance, while the atmosphere in the closed space above the bed is maintained in substantially static condition.

Preferably, the substance to be treated is formed into an elongate, substantially horizontal bed, and the bed is progressively passed through an elongate, closed space containing the radiant heat source. As the bed passes through the closed space, it progressively absorbs heat and its temperature progressively increases.

By maintaining the depth of the bed and the distance from the top of the bed to the heat source within specified values, the temperature of the bed can progressively be increased so that liquid eduction products form throughout the bed without releasing vapors or gases from the top of the bed. A static condition is thereby maintained in the closed space above the bed, and the liquid products so formed are removed by the force of gravity from the bottom of the bed through the perforate support. It has been found that when the thickness of the bed and/or the distance from the top of the bed to the heat source are increased beyond about 1½ inches respectively, vapors are released from the top of the bed. These vapors absorb radiant heat and are subjected to destructive cracking reactions which greatly diminish the yield of useful, liquid products from the process. The destructive cracking reactions further consume large quantities of heat, thus reducing the thermal efficiency of the process.

Various types of equipment may be employed in the process, the preferred being an elongate horizontal or near horizontal enclosure closed at the top and having discharge conduits positioned longitudinally along the bottom thereof. The enclosure is divided into an upper heating chamber and a lower collection chamber by a perforated plate or screen upon which the substance to be treated is supported. Radiant heating means are positioned along the top surface of the upper chamber to heat the substance on the perforated plate or screen. The apparatus preferably has means for continuously advancing the perforated plate or screen through the enclosure, and means for introducing the substance to be treated at one end and withdrawing the residue at the other end.

A variety of substances, both solid and liquid, may be treated in accordance with the process, the exact manner of handling being determined by the nature of the particular substance being treated, as can be appreciated by those skilled in the art. The knowledge requisite for determining the amount and rate of heat input to the heating zone and the rate of travel of the substance along the heating zone, is advantageously acquired by laboratory testing of the substances.

It has been found that liquid substances such as petroleum, tars, liquids derived from heat treatment of solid materials, and oils can be treated by supporting the liquid substances directly on a perforated plate or screen having apertures of such size that the liquid substances can be supported thereon. It has been found that the liquid decomposition products which are formed, will separate from the liquid substance being treated and will pass through the apertures of the screen or perforated plate by the force of gravity. The liquid being treated progressively becomes more viscous and finally exits from the heat treatment as a solid, semisolid, or very viscous liquid.

Microwave Energy

L. Hanson; U.S. Patent 4,065,361; December 27, 1977 describes a microwave apparatus for processing crushed oil shale to recover vaporized products. In Figure 2.12a the hopper **10** is designed to receive incoming crushed oil shale and is disposed in registry with the upper portion **12** of solids heat exchanger **13** (see Figure 2.12b).

The heat exchanger consists generally of a box **14** which is open at the top and bottom and is provided with a series of longitudinal and transverse heat exchanger tubes **15** and **16**.

Such tubes are set in apertures **17** and **18** and communicate with manifolds **19**, **20** and also **21**, **22**, as indicated. Conduits **23** and **24** are thus interconnected by this series of tubes **15** so that flow proceeds from arrow **25** to arrow **26**. Conduit **27** and conduit **28** are likewise disposed in communication by their respective manifolds **21** and **22** and a series of tubes **16** which interiorly communicate with the interior of the manifold structures at **21** and **22**. Accordingly, there is a gas flow path from arrow **29** and arrow **30**, to arrows **31** and **32**.

Figure 2.12: Processing of Oil Shale

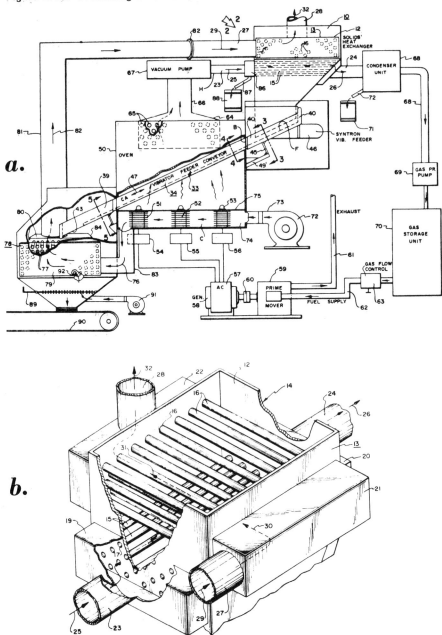

(continued)

Figure 2.12: (continued)

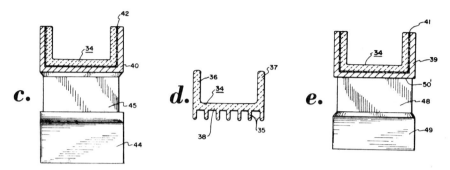

(a) Side elevation, shown partially cut-away and in schematic form, of a microwave system for treating oil shale.
(b) Enlarged perspective, partially broken away, of a heat exchanger utilized proximate the hopper structure of the system, and is taken along the arrow 2—2 in Figure 2.12a.
(c) Enlarged transverse section taken along line 3—3 in Figure 2.12a.
(d) Enlarged fragmentary section taken along line 4—4 in Figure 2.12a.
(e) Enlarged transverse section taken along line 5—5 in Figure 2.12a.

Source: U.S. Patent 4,065,361

In operation as to this portion of the structure, the series of tubes **16** and **15** in Figure 2.12b serve to retard the flow of feedstock appropriately for feeding the vibratory feeder conveyor **33** hereinafter described, and also permits a heat exchange to occur as between the tubes **15** and the tubes **16** relative to the incoming ore. Such heat is thus supplied by the hot gases proceeding through conduit **23** and conduit **27** in Figure 2.12a, see also Figure 2.12b. Accordingly, the solids heat exchanger **13** serves to preheat the ore prior to its descent onto the vibratory feeder conveyor **33**.

As to the latter, feeder conveyor **33** includes a conveyor trough member **34** that may be made of glass, pyrex, or clay material, or other ceramic material, see Figure 2.11d. All of such materials shall be considered "ceramic". The conveyor trough member preferably includes a series of fins or ribs **35** that extend in a direction reverse to the upstanding sides **36** and **37**. Accordingly, the fins or ribs depend from base **38** of the conveyor trough member **34**. These ribs or fins **35** will extend between the electromagnetically reflective steel frame **39** and **40** facing the oven and which seat the conveyor trough member **34** at asbestos liners **41** and **42**.

Relative to steel frame **39**, the same will be provided with an aperture or open end at **43** to accommodate the downward movement of ore dropped through after traversing the vibratory feeder conveyor **33**. Plate **44** includes a spring steel flange or web **45** that is attached to the steel frame **40** and is thin enough to permit an oscillatory movement as supplied by Syntron vibratory feeder **46** which is coupled and attached to the steel frame **40**. Accordingly, member **45** serves as a spring finger, in effect, which carries or oscillates back and forth the steel frame **40** and the vibratory feeder conveyor carried thereby.

The vibratory feeder conveyor can be reciprocated back and forth, in its angulated condition in the direction of arrow **47** so as to convey material from the upper righthand end of the feeder down to the aperture **43** in frame **39**.

In the latter regard the steel frame at **39** may likewise be carried by a flange type finger **48** which is supported by structure **49**. Finger **48** is constructed to oscillate back and forth at its upper edge **50'** to accommodate the vibratory movement of the feeder conveyor **33** as produced by electromagnetic vibrating unit **46**. Oven support structure **49'** mounts finger **45**.

In operation as to this part of the structure, ore passing through the heat exchanger above alights on the feed end **F** of the vibratory feeder conveyer **33** and particularly the conveyor trough member **34** thereof. The vibrations of the feeder conveyor **33**, in its angulated condition, produces a progressive downward travel of the ore so that the same can be heated during such transit through oven **50** before finally being exhausted from the conveyor at opening or port **43** at the lower left portion of Figure 2.12a.

A manner of heating such ore is provided by microwave energy emanating from magnetron tubes **51**, **52** and **53** which may be found in any conventional domestic microwave oven. Microwave power units **54**, **55** and **56** are strictly conventional and coupled to panel **57** of generator **58**. Generator **58** is driven by prime mover **59**, being coupled thereto by coupling shaft unit **60** of conventional form. The prime mover, being an internal combustion engine, gas turbine, or any other conventional prime mover, will include an exhaust stack **61** and also a fuel supply conduit **62** leading from gas flow control **63**. This may comprise a manual control for regulating gas fuel flow to the prime mover **59**. The prime mover may be any type of internal combustion engine or other means, generally receiving some type of gaseous or liquid fuel to produce power for converting such power to electrical energy at panel **57**.

In attending to a consideration of the oven **50**, it is seen that the manifold **64** receives gases generated in the oven since such gases will come into the manifold at the series of side perforations **65** of such oven. Perforations **65** preferably should not be larger than ⅛" in diameter, for proper oven-entrapment of microwave energy. Manifold **64** includes a stack **66** leading to vacuum pump unit **67**. The gases sent upwardly by the vacuum pump **67** are routed through conduit **23** and through conventional condenser unit **86** which may simply comprise a manifold communicating with the series of heat exhaust tubes **15** leading to conduit **24**.

Likewise important is the provision of a pair of heat exchangers, one proximate the hopper **10** at the input side of the equipment, and the other at **78**, at the spent shale area of the equipment. It is noted that the heat exchanger in both cases serves as a flow-retarding grate and also as a means whereby hot gases may be used to heat incoming ore prior to its deposit on the vibratory feeder conveyor used. If desired, an initial conventional unit at **86** having downspout **87** may be supplied for collecting and conveying initial droplets of oil into collector **88**.

Accordingly, what is provided is a microwave operated system wherein the apparatus employs a vibrating-type ceramic or glass conveyor, this for ensuring a continuous throughput of material through the microwave oven employed. Solids heat exchanger means are used at both the input and discharge ends relative to the ore so as to preheat incoming oil shale prior to its treatment on the vibratory feeder conveyor employed.

If desired, a reciprocating grate **89** may be employed to loosen the descending spent shale in the unit preparatory to dropping down onto endless conveyor **90** in Figure 2.12a, or truck, to be disposed of.

As seen at the lower lefthand portion of Figure 2.12a, the heat exchanger **78** is provided with opposite manifolds **79** and **80** interconnecting the heat exchanger tubes **77**. Heated air currents at **76** are routed through such tubes to conduit **81** leading through coupler **82** and conduit **27** to the tubes **16**, heat exchanger **10** and from there rise in exhaust stack **28**. Air blower **91** may be installed as shown, to add oxygen to the spent shale to further heat the same and to enter the manifold **79** at opening **92**.

Vacuum System

A process described by *J.L. Mercer and H.J. Togashi; U.S. Patent 4,052,293; October 4, 1977; assigned to Cryo-Maid Inc.* is predicated on the discovery that oil and other hydrocarbons in various hydrocarbonaceous solid materials (oil shale, tar sands, coal, lignite) can be recovered by a process of advancing discrete individual pieces of the hydrocarbonaceous solid material along a pathway in a substantially evacuated system, that is, where the pressure is no more than about 50 torr, while simultaneously supplying heat energy to advancing pieces of material to raise the temperature to within the indicated range from about 600° to no more than 900°F.

It has been found that at temperatures within this range, and below about 700°F, the oil and other hydrocarbons within the oil shale are liberated as a vapor within the evacuated system, without any appreciable pyrolytic conversion of the liberated substances. Thereafter, the vapors can be selectively condensed to recover the desired oil and like hydrocarbon fractions from the vapors with minimum energy requirements and generally higher yields. The "spent" shale which is not subjected to any appreciable pyrolytic decomposition, is likewise generally in its original state, and can be appropriately returned to its source without concern as to environmental hazards.

It has additionally been found that this process can be carried out in a very short period of time, ranging from 30 to 360 minutes. In fact, generally less than about 70 minutes is required to recover at least 50% of the oil present in oil shales and like hydrocarbonaceous solid materials. In a preferred procedure, the solid material is heated within the substantially evacuated system by means of radiant heat energy supplied by a black body source at a temperature within the range from about 900° to 1500°F, so as to achieve vaporization of oil and like hydrocarbons from the solid material at the relatively low temperatures indicated.

Apparatus for carrying out the foregoing processing is generally characterized by its simplicity and includes a housing, means to evacuate the housing, a pathway for advancing oil shale or like solid material through the housing, means to supply energy to the pieces of shale advancing within the housing, at least one condenser surface within the housing in proximity with the pathway, means to supply cooling medium to the condenser surface, means to remove oil and other hydrocarbons condensing on the condenser surface within the housing, and means to feed the oil shale material to the housing and to remove the spent shale therefrom while maintaining the desired low pressure and temperature conditions.

Molten Heat Transfer Material

V.H. Stout; U.S. Patent 3,977,960; August 31, 1976 describes a method and apparatus for the recovery of hydrocarbon products from a particulate composite. Crushed oil shale at ambient temperature, is conveyed into the system through an initial air sealing means, then to a first collection chamber. The first chamber may have apparatus to heat the crushed ore. Any products vaporized from the particulate composite are collected in the first collection chamber as the particulate composite is conveyed toward a second collection chamber.

The second collection chamber contains a liquid metal or salt which is maintained at a temperature above the vaporizing temperature of the vaporizable constituents of the particulate composite. The particulate composite is then conveyed from the second collection chamber as the vaporized parts are collected, and transmitted through an exit sealing means which prevents entry of air into the recovery chambers. The spent particulate composite is then preferably conveyed into a recovery apparatus for recovering any metal or salt and then discarded. The vaporized products may be recovered in any known manner.

Leaching and Roasting for Metals and Sulfur

T.K. Miöen; U.S. Patent 4,120,934; October 17, 1978; assigned to Boliden AB, Sweden describes a method for working up shale while recovering metals and sulfur. The method comprises crushing the shale and leaching and roasting the shale. The sulfur content is oxidized and converted into sulfuric acid, concentrated sulfur dioxide or sulfur. The leaching operation is effected with sulfuric acid. The leached metals are recovered in a manner known per se and the residual solution is passed to the roasting stage.

In Figure 2.13 there is shown a crushing stage 1 to which shale is passed via a line 2. The crushed shale is passed to a leaching tank 3 via a line 4. Sulfuric acid is passed to the tank 3 via a line 5 and water is passed to the tank via a line 6.

The solution formed during the leaching operation is passed to an extraction stage 8 through a line 7, in which stage uranium, molybdenum and possibly other metals present, such as aluminum and vanadium together with phosphorus, are recovered in a manner known per se. The residual solution is passed through a line 9 to a slurrying stage 10 and is there used to slurry leaching residue from the leaching tank 3, this leaching residue being passed to the slurrying stage 10 through a line 11. The arrow 12 indicates the removal of valuable elements separated in the extraction stage. The slurry is passed from the slurrying stage 10 to a roasting furnace 14 through a line 13. Conveniently, the roasting furnace 14 is in the form of a fluidized bed furnace to which oxygen and a fluidizing gas are charged separately or in mixture through a line 15. Roaster gases are removed from the roasting furnace 14 and are passed through a line 16 to a waste heat boiler 17, where steam is generated and thus energy is taken out through a line **18**. Condensed water is removed through a line **19** and is passed to the leaching stage **3** through a line **6** and to a sulfuric acid plant **21** through a line **20**. Roaster gases containing sulfur dioxide are also passed to the sulfuric acid plant, the gases optionally being passed to cleaning apparatus for the removal of dust, arsenic, mercury and like harmful substances through a line **22**.

Figure 2.13: Leaching and Roasting Process Schematic

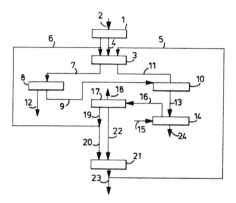

Source: U.S. Patent 4,120,934

Sulfuric acid is then passed from the plant **21** for external use through a line **23** and back to the leaching tank **3** through the line **5** for use in subsequent leaching operations. The roasted product is removed from the roasting furnace **14** through a line **24** and may then be subjected to further leaching operations for the removal of, for example, K, Na or Mg, whereafter the product is either deposited or further worked up.

Example 1: In a plant according to Figure 2.13 7,500 tons of shale were treated each day. The shale was of the Billingen type and contained, inter alia, 16% by weight C and 0.4% by weight S and was leached while adding approximately 450 tons of 97% by weight sulfuric acid and approximately 2,800 tons of water per day. The temperature of the water was approximately 90°C and the water was recovered from the gases obtained in the subsequent roasting stage, subsequent to the gases being cooled in the waste-heat boiler and their water content being condensed out in a cooling tower.

2,750 tons of leaching solution were used each day, from which solution uranium and molybdenum were recovered. The residual leaching solution was then passed to the roasting stage and used for slurrying 3,200 tons per day of moist leaching residue from the shale leaching stage. The resulting slurry was charged to a roasting furnace as were also a further 4,800 tons per day of leaching residue, this latter residue being charged to the furnace without previously being slurried.

Roasting was effected at a temperature of approximately 800°C while supplying air to the furnace in a manner such as to obtain complete combustion of the carbon content of the material. The gases obtained during the roasting operation contained approximately 45% by volume steam, of which approximately 5%

originated from the combustion of shale and the remainder from the combustion of the leaching solution slurry charged to the furnace. Subsequent to cooling the gases in a waste-heat boiler, the gases were passed to a cooling tower in which approximately 3,000 tons of water were obtained each day in the form of a condensate. Of this condensate approximately 2,800 tons were passed each day to the leaching stage and the remainder was passed to a plant for the manufacture of sulfuric acid in accordance with the contact method, as was also the gas, which was substantially free of water, this gas containing approximately 3.2% by volume SO_2.

Approximately 870 tons of 97% by weight sulfuric acid were produced from this gas each day, of which quantity approximately 450 tons were returned each day to the leaching stage.

A roasted product having a residual content of approximately 0.4% by weight S and less than 0.5% by weight C was also discharged from the roasting furnace, the product being deposited. Approximately 3,000 tons of steam were obtained each day from a steam plant connected to the roasting stage, the steam having a pressure of 4 MPa and a temperature of approximately 400°C. This steam was passed to a steam-turbine driven electric generator, with which electrical energy reaching to approximately 13,850 GJ at a power of approximately 160 MW was obtained each day. Of the total energy content of the shale, approximately 53,000 GJ, approximately 26% was recovered in the form of electric energy. The following sulfur balance was true for the roasting stage:

Sulfur Balance

	Tons S/Day
Input Quantities	
Leaching shale	450
Leaching solution (returned)	100
	550
Output Quantities	
Roaster gas containing 3.2% by volume SO_2	525
Roasted products containing 0.4% by weight S	25
	550

Energy Balance

	GJ/h	%
Input		
Shale 312 tons/h at 7.13 GJ/ton	2,225	100
Output		
Steam from waste-heat boiler	612	27.5
Steam from fluidized bed cooling	734	33.0
From Cooling Tower		
Condensate	293	13.2
Cooling water	105	4.7
Gases to H_2SO_4-plant	314	14.1
Roasted products (300°C)	62	2.8
Losses	105	4.7
	2,225	100

Example 2: The method described in Example 1 was supplemented with a step in which residual leaching solution, obtained after extracting uranium and molybdenum from the leaching solution, was neutralized. The residual solution was neutralized with lime, whereupon precipitates containing, inter alia, Al, V and P were formed. The neutralized leaching solution has a pH of 4.1 and was passed to the roasting stage, as with the method described in Example 1. In this way the sulfur dioxide content of the roaster gases was lowered to 2.3% by volume owning to the fact that sulfates were precipitated out during the neutralizing operation.

Reduction of Arsenic Content Prior to Retorting

According to a process described by *D.A. Young; U.S. Patent 4,127,469; November 28, 1978; assigned to Union Oil Company of California* crushed oil shale about to be retorted in a conventional oil shale retort is admixed with at least sufficient of a nickel component additive so that in the resulting mixture of oil shale and additive the proportion of added nickel, as the metal, is at least 5 ppm by weight. When the mixture is fed to a retort wherein kerogen in the oil shale is pyrolyzed in a retorting zone at temperatures above about 600°F to release shale oil vapors, the amount of vaporous arsenic also released in the retorting zone is reduced.

Thus, the concentration of arsenic that will be present in the produced shale oil is reduced, with the concentration of arsenic in the shale oil decreasing with increasing proportions of added nickel in the shale-additive mixture fed to the retort. The proportion of nickel additive in shale-additive mixtures is based on the weight of added nickel.

Example: Three 751-gram samples of oil shale obtained from the Green River formation in Colorado were crushed to less than ⅜" mean diameter granules. One sample was wetted with an ammoniacal solution of nickel carbonate (0.018 gram $NiCO_3 \cdot 2Ni(OH)_2 \cdot 4H_2O$ in 50 ml of 1.0 N NH_4OH) so that the shale-additive mixture contained 11 ppm by weight nickel (as nickel). A second sample was wetted with aqueous nickel nitrate (0.0438 gram $Ni(NO_3)_2 \cdot 6H_2O$ in 10 ml water) so that the shale-additive mixture contained 12 ppm by weight nickel (as nickel). The third sample was admixed with no additive.

The following experiment was then performed on each sample individually. The sample was supported as a 16-inch column in a 2-inch diameter, 5-foot long, stainless steel tube. A synthetic retort product gas, dehydrated to a water vapor dewpoint of 100°F, and consisting, on a dry basis, of 28.3 mol % H_2, 50.0 mol % CH_4, 2.3 mol % H_2S, 7.0 mol % CO, and 12.5 mol % CO_2, was then passed downwardly through the tube.

The tube itself was gradually pushed upwardly through a furnace maintained at about 1000°F such that any gradient of shale in the tube took 1 hour to heat up to 1000°F and was maintained at 1000°F for 1 hour. The educed shale oil vapors were condensed in a condenser situated external to the stainless steel tube, and the collected shale oil was analyzed for arsenic. These data and other data obtained in the three experiments are recorded in the following table.

	Test 1	Test 2	Test 3
Additive solution	None	$NiCO_3 \cdot 2Ni(OH)_2$	$Ni(NO_3)_2$
Added nickel in mixture, ppm by wt	0	11	12
Collected shale oil, g	67	67	84
Arsenic in collected shale oil after filtration, ppm by wt	13	7.1	8.6
Arsenic in collected shale oil after filtration and extraction in 2 N NH_4OH	8.2	6.1	5.2

Optical Sorting of Nahcolite

In a process described by *D.M. Wyslouzil; U.S. Patent 3,962,403; June 8, 1976; assigned to The Superior Oil Company* nahcolite-bearing oil shale ore is heated to produce a distinct color change in the nahcolite, differentiating the nahcolite from the host oil shale for optical sorting, and such sorting is then accomplished by optical sorting means.

Nahcolite-bearing oil shale ore comes from the mine a dirty brown color. Although the nahcolite itself usually appears somewhat shinier than the remainder of the oil shale ore, it has the same basic color as the rest of the ore. The mined ore first is crushed to produce particles or fragments of less than about one inch in size, preferably between about ½ and ¾ inch in size, by conventional crushing apparatus such as a jaw crusher.

The crushed or otherwise sized ore is heated to convert the surface of the nahcolite in the ore to sodium carbonate according to the following formula: $2NaHCO_3 + Heat \rightarrow Na_2CO_3 + CO_2 + H_2O$. The time required to effect this surface conversion varies, of course, with the temperature to which the particles are exposed. A group of oil shale ore samples having a particle size distribution of:

Size	% of Sample
–¾ inch +½ inch	40
–½ inch +¼ inch	35
–¼ inch	25

were heated at the temperatures and for the times shown below to convert at least the surface of the nahcolite to sodium carbonate for optical sorting:

Temperature, °C	Heating Time
100	2–3 hours
150	30 minutes
200	15 minutes
700	20–30 seconds
1000	5–10 seconds

Heating at the higher temperatures, 700° and 1000°C is not as desirable as heating at the lower temperatures because close control of the exposure time is critical to minimize distillation and pyrolysis of the oil. In addition, increasing exposure time at the higher temperatures tends to reduce the resistance of the converted nahcolite to flaking and crumbling. The corners and edges of the oil shale fragments are particularly sensitive to pyrolysis at these high temperatures.

On the other hand, surface conversion is quite uniform at 200°C and is achieved in a reasonable time.

When nahcolite is freshly converted to sodium carbonate, it has a glossy, blue-white luster which changes to a chalky white after the converted particle has been standing in the air for some time. This change is thought to be caused by hydration and it further enhances the contrast between the converted nahcolite and the remaining oil shale. Furthermore, the oil shale tends to darken somewhat during the heating step, making the contrast even more distinct.

Following the heating (converting) step, the fragments of ore are passed through an optical sorter such as, for example, that described in U.S. Patent 3,066,797 in which the lighter colored converted nahcolite is separated from the remaining oil shale by a jet of air or other ejector means.

In one test, an ore sample having the size distribution described above was heated at approximately 150°C for one hour to convert the surface of the nahcolite to sodium carbonate. The resulting converted nahcolite product was then separated from the remaining oil shale by a Sortex model 962M optical sorting machine. Of the -¾ inch +½ inch fraction of the test sample, approximately 70% was separated as a dark fraction and approximately 30% as a light fraction. Each fraction was immersed in city water for 48 hours and occasionally agitated to dissolve both the sodium carbonate and sodium bicarbonate constituents of the respective samples. Of the dark fraction, less than 7% was soluble, while more than 26% of the light fraction was soluble under the same conditions. Of the -½ inch +¼ inch fraction, less than 4% of the dark fraction and more than 28% of the light fraction was soluble under the same conditions.

Recarbonation of Spent Shale

According to a process described by *D.M. Fenton; U.S. Patent 4,016,239; April 5, 1977; assigned to Union Oil Company of California* spent oil shale from retorting operations, containing water-soluble alkaline oxides such as calcium oxide is subjected to a recarbonation process in order to reduce its alkalinity and thereby prevent ecological damage to plant and aquatic animal life which could result from alkaline leachings derived from rain or snowfall on open dumps of such spent shale. For economic reasons, a rapid recarbonation is necessary, and such is achieved by wetting the spent shale with water containing dissolved carbonate and/or bicarbonate salts, and contacting the so wetted spent shale with an atmosphere comprising a substantial partial pressure of carbon dioxide for a period of time ranging between about 10 minutes and two hours.

In the following examples, the spent shale in all cases was derived from the retorting-gasification of a Colorado oil shale at retorting temperatures in the 850° to 1000°F range and steam-gasification temperatures in the 1200° to 1400°F range. The spent shale was a friable grey solid predominantly in the particle size range of ¼ to ¾ inch diameter with no particles larger than 1 inch diameter. Its principal chemical components were as follows: $CaCO_3$, 21 wt %; CaO, ~12 wt %; Feldspar, 14 wt %; Quartz, 24 wt %; and Na, 2 wt %. The pH of the moist surface was 12.

In all examples, the degree of recarbonation achieved is indicated by pH measurements of successive aqueous leachates. Any pH above about 8.6 is a clear indication that CaO is still being leached out.

Example 1: A 100 gram sample of the fresh, hydrated spent shale was subjected to 10 consecutive leachings at 70°F with 300 ml of distilled water. Another 100 gram sample was subjected to the same treatment after being allowed to stand for 24 hours at room temperature in one atmosphere of CO_2. The pH and total dissolved solids (TDS) of the various leachates were as follows:

Leachate No.	... Untreated Shale.... pH	TDS, ppm	.. CO_2-Treated Shale... pH	TDS, ppm
1	11.7	968	11.1	1,238
2	11.4	−	11.7	−
3	11.1	−	11.6	−
4	11.3	−	11.4	−
5	11.1	324	11.2	318
6	11.3	−	11.0	−
7	10.9	−	10.8	−
8	11.3	−	10.8	−
9	11.0	−	10.8	−
10	10.9	340	10.8	300

It will be apparent that the 24-hour treatment with CO_2 had no significant effect. After leaching with 30 volumes of water per 100 grams of spent shale, the leachates were still highly alkaline.

Example 2: Three additional 100 gram samples of the spent shale were contacted with 300 psi of CO_2 for 2 hours at various temperatures indicated below. Ten consecutive leachings at 70°F with 300 ml of distilled water gave leachates of the following properties:

Leachate No.	..... 100°C...... pH	TDS, ppm	..... 200°C...... pH	TDS, ppm	......300°...... pH	TDS, ppm
1	11.2	982	11.3	864	11.2	1,108
2	11.2	−	11.0	−	11.1	−
3	11.2	−	11.2	−	11.1	−
4	11.2	−	10.9	−	11.0	−
5	11.3	290	10.6	250	11.0	280
6	11.3	−	10.4	−	10.9	−
7	11.1	−	11.0	−	11.0	−
8	11.2	−	11.1	−	11.0	−
9	11.4	−	11.2	−	10.9	−
10	11.3	230	11.0	246	11.0	262

It is evident that even at elevated temperatures and CO_2 pressures recarbonation is very slow in the absence of water.

Example 3: Three additional 100 gram samples of the spent shale were wetted with 5 weight-percent of distilled water, then carbonated and leached as described in Example 2, with the results shown below.

Leachate No.	..... 100°C		..... 200°C		..... 300°	
	pH	TDS, ppm	pH	TDS, ppm	pH	TDS, ppm
1	9.8	646	9.3	726	10.2	670
2	10.1	–	10.2	–	10.6	–
3	9.4	–	9.7	–	10.6	–
4	9.8	–	10.0	–	10.6	–
5	10.1	162	9.8	246	10.6	206
6	9.9	–	9.4	–	10.6	–
7	8.6	–	9.2	–	10.6	–
8	8.4	–	10.0	–	10.6	–
9	9.8	–	9.3	–	10.6	–
10	10.2	98	10.3	104	10.6	136

Example 4: Three additional 100 gram samples of the spent shale were wetted with 30 weight-percent of distilled water, then carbonated and leached as described in Example 2, with the following results:

Leachate No.	..... 100°C		..... 200°C		..... 300°	
	pH	TDS, ppm	pH	TDS, ppm	pH	TDS, ppm
1	8.4	2,512	8.3	1,824	8.2	670
2	8.7	–	8.5	–	8.6	–
3	8.6	–	8.3	–	8.7	–
4	8.7	–	8.5	–	8.7	–
5	8.9	138	9.0	334	9.0	206
6	9.0	–	9.2	–	9.2	–
7	9.1	–	9.0	–	9.4	–
8	9.0	–	9.2	–	9.3	–
9	9.0	–	9.1	–	9.3	–
10	9.2	150	9.2	166	9.3	136

Comparing Examples 3 and 4, it will be seen that 30 weight-percent of distilled water during carbonation is more effective than 5 weight-percent, but no consistently acceptable pH levels were reached in either case, even at the economically impractical carbonation pressure of 300 psi.

Example 5: Five additional 100 gram samples of the spent shale were wetted with varying proportions of a tap water having a pH of about 8.0 and containing 222 mg/l of bicarbonate ions. Carbon dioxide was then bubbled through the wetted beds at atmospheric pressure for 30 minutes, and at various temperatures. The carbonated samples were then leached 10 times in succession with 300 ml portions of the tap water at room temperature, with the following results:

	.... Run No				
	1	2	3	4	5
Carbonation water, g	5	5	10	30	30
Carbonation temp, °C	22	93	22	22	93
pH of leachates					
1	8.5	10.3	8.1	8.1	8.2
2	8.7	10.3	8.4	8.1	8.4
3	9.3	10.2	8.6	8.6	7.9
4	8.6	10.0	8.6	9.4	8.6
5	9.1	10.0	8.8	9.2	8.4
6	9.2	9.8	8.6	8.6	7.8
7	8.7	9.6	8.3	8.4	7.3
8	9.1	9.5	8.7	8.5	7.8
9	8.7	9.6	8.3	8.6	8.3
10	8.5	–	8.4	–	–

Runs 3, 4 and 5 above demonstrate that the use of relatively large proportions of tap water gives satisfactory results, even with only 30 minutes carbonation time at atmospheric pressure. Runs 1 and 2 show that if insufficient tap water is used the results are unsatisfactory, especially at high carbonation temperatures.

Example 6: The procedure of Example 5 was repeated with two additional 100 gram samples of the spent shale, with the exception that in each case 0.1 gram of $(NH_4)_2CO_3$ was added to the carbonation water. The results were as follows:

	. . . . . Run No.	
	5	7
Carbonation water, g	5	30
Carbonation temp, °C	93	93
pH of leachates		
1	9.4	9.1
2	9.3	8.9
3	9.2	8.4
4	8.9	7.6
5	8.9	7.7
6	8.8	7.8
7	8.5	7.8
8	8.3	7.8
9	8.1	7.6
10	8.6	7.6

Run 7 clearly demonstrates the very satisfactory results obtained by the use of large proportions of carbonation water containing an added carbonate salt.

Bacterial Treatment of Retort Water

T.F. Yen and J.E. Findley; U.S. Patent 4,124,501; November 7, 1978; assigned to the University of Southern California describe a process for purifying oil shale retort water. Specifically, the process takes advantage of the fact that the oil shale retort water has a substantial amount of organic content and sufficient inorganic components, including sulfate, to enable the growth of anaerobic bacteria. Such bacteria, exemplified by the *Desulfovibrio* family, is added to the retort water so as to produce in the water a growth of cell biomass of the bacteria while simultaneously reducing sulfate ions to sulfide. Production of cell biomass should proceed substantially in the absence of air, preferably following purging with carbon dioxide, nitrogen or the like, to establish anaerobiasis. The cell biomass is aggregated into a flocculent mass and is removed from the retort water.

The sulfide is oxidized to sulfate either through combustion processes or by conversion with air and aerobic bacteria, such as of the *Thiobacillus* family. At least a portion of the sulfate thus produced can be recycled to the retort water so as to neutralize the retort water prior to bacterial growth. Excess sulfate can be neutralized, for example, by reaction with spent shale, that is, by reaction with the inorganic matrix of retorted oil shale. The effluent discharge from this treatment yields a water quality which not only reduces environmental damage, but also supplements industrial water requirements of the mining and retorting operation. The reacted spent shale can be combined with the removed cell biomass and used as fertilizer. Alternatively, a portion, or all of the cell biomass, can be recycled to the retort water as nutrient for growth of the bacteria.

Ammonia Recovery by Electrolysis of Retort Water

A process described by *T.F. Yen and C.-S. Wen; U.S. Patent 4,043,881; August 23, 1977; assigned to the University of Southern California* relates to oil shale treatment and more specifically to the recovery of economic values from shale oil retort water.

Specifically, the shale oil retort water is delivered to an electrolytic cell and a direct current potential is applied across the anode and cathode chambers of the cell at a current density sufficient to effect a substantial decrease in the organic compounds in the retort water in the anode chamber and to evolve a substantial amount of ammonia from the retort water in the cathode chamber. The ammonia can be recovered as a valuable product of the process and can be combined with carbon dioxide evolved from the anode chamber, as a result of the oxidative electrolysis therein, to provide an economic basis for the synthesis of urea or other valuable products.

Referring to Figure 2.14a, the process is illustrated in flow format. Oil shale retort water is provided via an inlet tube **12** to a settling reservoir **10** wherein oily liquids and the like are permitted to float to the top, with aqueous portions settling to the bottom. The retort water also contains some small suspended particles of shale oil and particles of long chain fatty acid salts. To remove such particles, the water is drawn by a pump **14** through a filtering assembly shown schematically at **16**.

Figure 2.14: Electrolytic Treatment of Shale Oil Retort Water

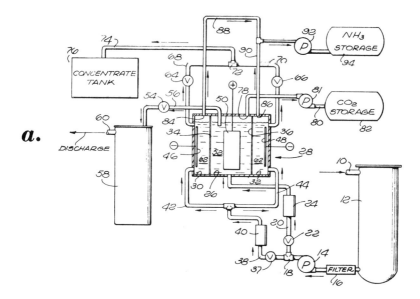

a.

(continued)

Figure 2.14: (continued)

b.

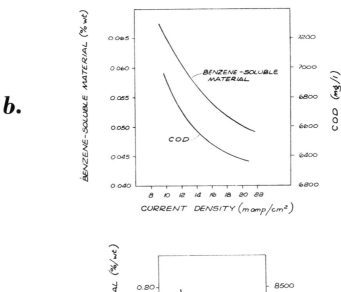

c.

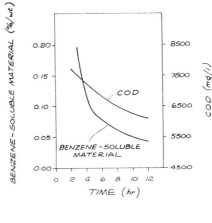

d.

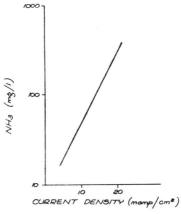

(continued)

Figure 2.14: (continued)

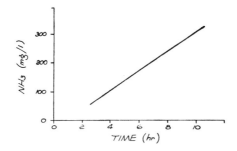

(a) Combination block form flow diagram and schematic of
   apparatus used in conducting the process
(b) Plot of benzene-soluble organic components in the anolyte
   versus current density
(c) Plot of benzene-soluble organic components in the anolyte
   versus electrolysis time
(d) Plot of ammonia generation from the catholyte versus
   current density
(e) Plot of ammonia generation from the catholyte versus
   electrolysis time

Source: U.S. Patent 4,043,881

The retort water is then pumped to a branching tee **18** on one side of which it
flows through piping **20** as controlled by a valve **22**, through a flow meter **24**
and then into the anode compartment **26** of an electrolytic cell **28**. The electrolytic cell **28** is divided into an anode chamber **26** flanked by two cathode chambers **30** and **32**. The chambers are defined by inert membranes **34** and **36**
which divide the cell **28** into the anode and cathode chambers. The membranes
are permeable to cations but are substantially impermeable to the organic components of the retort water, so as to prevent the oxidized organics from undergoing unwanted reaction at the cathode.

For example, a cation-porous membrane known as Dupont Nafion Membrane
425 (a perfluorosulfonic acid product) can be used. Alternatively, rigid porous
frits can be used, having an average porosity in the range of about 20 to 100 μ.

As the other leg from the tee **18**, the retort water flows via a valve **37** through
piping **38**, through a flow meter **40** and through branching arms **42** and **44** into
the cathode chambers **30** and **32**, respectively.

As electrodes, any commonly used electrodes can be used which are resistant
to the retort water, for example, graphite, stainless steel, copper, copper-silicon,
aluminum oxide, lead and the like. Platinum can be used for small production
runs. For large commercial installations, carbon anodes and lead sheet cathodes
can be used. In the apparatus illustrated, lead sheets define the cathodes **46**
and **48** and platinum gauze defines the anode **50**. A direct current potential is
applied by means of a source of electrical energy connected to the anodes and

cathodes, as indicated in the drawing by electrical signals. Anolyte **52** from the anode chamber **26** exhausts via a valve **54** through piping **56** into a settling column **58** from which it is discharged as required from outlet **60**. Catholyte **62** exhausts via valve **64** and **66** through piping arms **68** and **70** joined by a tee **72** to a main conduit **74** which leads into a concentrate tank **76**. Periodically, the material in the concentrate tank **76** is discharged. In the drawing, the piping arms **68** and **70** are shown above the catholyte level, but in actuality they would be directed to a lower level and the concentrate tank **76** would be at a position sufficiently below the level of liquid in the cathode chambers to permit flow of catholyte by gravity.

At the top of the anode chamber **26**, a vent **78** is provided and evolved carbon dioxide is drawn through piping **80** connected to the vent **78**, by means of a pump **81**. The evolved carbon dioxide is pumped into a carbon dioxide storage tank **82**. At the top of each cathode chamber **30** and **32**, vents **84** and **86** are provided so that evolved ammonia can be drawn through piping arms **88** and **90** by means of a pump **92**. The evolved ammonia is pumped into an ammonia storage tank **94**.

The valves **22, 37, 54, 64** and **66** can be controlled manually or can be controlled by means of servo mechanisms associated with signals obtained from the flow meters **24** and **40**, all in accordance with known engineering principles.

In operation, retort water placed in the settling reservoir **12** is pumped into the anode chamber **26** and cathode chambers **30** and **32** and is subjected to electrolysis. The current density of the applied potential generally should be above about 50 A/m^2 and can range up to 1500 A/m^2. Dwell time in the electrolytic cell should average at least about an hour at the higher levels of current density to several days if necessary at the lower levels, depending of course upon composition of the retort water, operating temperature, etc. With bench scale dimensions in which the anode is constituted by platinum gauze 5 cm^2 and the cathode is constituted by lead sheets 4 x 7 cm, under a current density of 100 A/m^2, a typical flow rate is 4 ml/sec.

Example: Electrolysis was conducted using a U-type covered cell of 500 ml total capacity. A cation permselective membrane was placed between anodic and cathodic chambers. A platinum gauze, 5 cm^2, was soldered with a 10 cm length of 20 B&S gauge platinum wire, and served as the anode. A smooth lead sheet 4 x 7 cm was used as the cathode. For purposes of measurement, a saturated calomel electrode was sealed in the anodic chamber for use as a reference electrode. Vents were provided in the roof of each chamber controlled by a stopcock, to collect gases evolved in each chamber.

Separate runs were conducted with retort water obtained from processing of Utah Green River oil shale and with retort water obtained from processing of Colorado Green River oil shale. 300 ml of retort water was filtered through a VWR Grade No. 615 filter paper and 150 ml of the filtered solution was poured into each of the anodic and cathodic chambers. Since the conductivity of the original retort water was adequate, no electrolyte was added for the electrolysis. A number of runs were made in which the current density was controlled to preselected values by varying the potential. Thus, runs were made in which the current density was at 10, 12, 14, 16 or 20 mA/cm^2 (100, 120, 140, 160 and 120 A/m^2). Electrolysis was conducted for 10 hours for each run. Additionally, further runs were conducted in which a current density of 20 mA/cm^2 was maintained for times of 3, 5, 8 and 10 hours. Upon completion of the electrolysis for each run, samples of the solution were drawn off. Each 100 ml of anodic and cathodic treating sample was lyophilized and then extracted with benzene to permit gas chromatographic and other instrumental analyses. The remaining portion of each sample was analyzed for other properties including, among others, COD (chemical oxygen demand) and color intensity.

In addition to the foregoing runs, a bench-scale continuous cell, as depicted in Figure 2.14a, was also used for the processing of some samples. Lead sheets were used as cathodes and a platinum gauze as the anode. The rate of flow was kept at approximately 4 ml per second. The other parameters were the same as those used for the batch U-type cell. The table below summarizes the results of anodic treatment of retort water at a current density of 20 mA/cm^2, at a cell voltage of approximately 15 volts, and a treatment time of about 10 hours.

	Organic Carbon	Nitrogen	Total Solid Residue	COD	Benzene-Soluble Material	Color
	. . . . (wt %)			(mg/l)	(wt %)	Intensity
Original retort water	9.16	19.48	1.68	16,600	0.48	3441
Anodic solution	0.42	1.88	1.05	6,283	0.05	255
Cathodic solution	4.04	22.98	2.01	9,991	0.24	1214

Referring to Figure 2.14b, results are shown from a series of runs made with a fixed 10 hour treatment time under various current densities. Benzene-soluble organics as well as COD are plotted versus the current density in mA/cm^2. The best mathematical representation of the data in Figure 2.14b can be written as ln COD = 8.36 – 0.13 ln I, where I is the current density in mA/cm^2 and COD is the chemical oxygen demand in mg/l.

Referring to Figure 2.14c, results are shown from a series of runs made in which the current density is fixed at 20 mA/cm^2 and in which the time of electrolysis was varied. The best mathematical representation of the data in Figure 2.14c can be written as ln COD = 8.99 – 0.025t, where t is time in hours.

In Figure 2.14d, the results are shown for collection of ammonia at different current densities at a fixed time of about 10 hours.

In Figure 2.14e, results are shown for the collection of ammonia at different treatment times under a fixed current density of 20 mA/cm^2. These plots indicate that the amount of ammonia collected is in linear proportion to the electrolysis time, but is in logarithmic proportion to the applied current density.

Upon completion of the foregoing electrolysis, over 40 to 50% of the total solid residue and 80 to 90% of the benzene-soluble organics had been removed in the anodic solution with a reduction of COD value of about 65%. Ammonia gas recovered from the cathodic chambers can be collected at an approximate value of 1,100 mg/gal of retort water. The color intensity of the retort water in the visible range has been reduced approximately 92 to 95%.

IN SITU PROCESSING OF OIL SHALE

One technique for recovering shale oil includes forming an in situ oil shale retort in a subterranean formation containing oil shale. At least a portion of the formation within the boundaries of the in situ oil shale retort is explosively expanded to form a fragmented permeable mass of particles containing oil shale. The fragmented mass is ignited near the top of the retort to establish a combustion zone. An oxygen-containing gas is introduced into the top of the retort to sustain the combustion zone and cause it to move downwardly through the fragmented permeable mass of particles in the retort.

As burning proceeds, the heat of combustion is transferred to the fragmented mass of particles below the combustion zone to release shale oil and gaseous products therefrom in a retorting and vaporization zone. Vaporized constituents of shale oil, water vapor and the like may condense on cooler oil shale in the retort below the retorting zone. The retorting zone moves from top to bottom of the retort ahead of the combustion zone, and the resulting shale oil and gaseous products pass to the bottom of the retort for collection and removal.

In preparing for the retorting process, the formation containing oil shale should be fragmented rather than simply fractured to create good and uniform permeability so that undue pressures are not required to pass the gas through the retort, and so that valuable deposits of oil shale are not by-passed owing to nonuniform permeability. The in situ retort is formed by excavating a void in the retort site, drilling blasting holes into the remaining portion of the formation in the retort site, loading explosive into the blasting holes, and detonating the explosive to expand the formation toward the void.

To promote maximum uniformity of particle size and permeability of the fragmented mass, and to minimize the quantity of explosives, the blasting holes should be reasonably accurately located with respect to each other, and with respect to the void toward which expansion occurs during the explosion. Oil shale formations in the western United States are often between 50 to 500 feet thick or even more, and are covered by a nonproductive overburden, which may be thousands of feet deep, thus often making it difficult to drill from the surface and accurately locate blasting holes in the oil shale formation. This chapter presents detailed process parameters for developing highly efficient subterranean cavities which are suitable for the retorting of oil shale and the recovery of the desired products.

FORMATION OF RETORT CAVITIES

Horizontal Sill Pillar

G.B. French and R.D. Ridley; U.S. Patent 4,118,070; October 3, 1978; assigned to Occidental Oil Shale, Inc. describe an in situ oil shale retort which is formed in a subterranean formation containing oil shale. The retort contains a fragmented permeable mass of particles containing oil shale. An open base of operation is excavated in the formation at an elevation above the fragmented mass to be formed, and an access drift is excavated to provide access to the bottom of the retort site.

The formation is explosively expanded to form the fragmented mass between the access drift and an elevation spaced below the bottom of the base of operation, leaving a horizontal sill pillar of unfragmented formation between the top of the fragmented mass and the bottom of the base of operation. The sill pillar provides a safe base of operation above the fragmented mass after it is formed. The fragmented mass is formed by, among other steps, drilling blasting holes from the base of operation down through the sill pillar and then detonating explosive in such holes to form the fragmented mass of particles in the retort below the sill pillar.

During retorting, gas is introduced into the fragmented mass through such blasting holes for establishing a combustion zone in the fragmented mass and for advancing the combustion zone through the fragmented mass. The blasting holes have separate valves located in the base of operation for use in controlling gas flow through selected regions of the fragmented mass.

Referring to Figures 3.1a and 3.1b, a fragmented permeable mass **10** of formation particles containing oil shale is in an in situ oil shale retort **12** in a subterranean formation containing oil shale. The fragmented permeable mass has vertical side boundaries **14** substantially perpendicular to each other to give the retort a rectangular horizontal cross section. The lower boundary **16** of the fragmented permeable mass slopes downwardly and inwardly (see Figure 3.1b) at an angle of about 45° and opens into the top of an elongated, substantially horizontal access drift **18** at the bottom of the retort **12**.

The access drift **18** has a gradual slope downwardly from the center of the bottom of the retort toward a sump **52** for recovering liquid products of retorting at the production level. The fragmented permeable mass also fills the portion of the access drift beneath the retort. A horizontal sill pillar **22** of unfragmented formation forms the upper boundary **23** of the fragmented permeable mass in the retort. The top of the sill pillar **22** forms the floor **24** of an open base of operation **25** spaced above the fragmented mass by a distance equal to the thickness of the sill pillar. In this example, the base of operation **25** is an excavation 12 to 14 feet high at a working level above the retort. It extends over substantially the entire horizontal cross section of the fragmented mass and opens at the left (as viewed in Figure 3.1a) to other excavations at the working level used for exploiting the oil shale deposit. Such underground workings open to a vertical shaft or horizontal adit. A plurality of vertical blasting holes **30** extend through the sill pillar. The blasting holes remain in the sill pillar after the blasting which formed the fragmented mass in the retort. The blasting holes are approximately uniformly distributed over the area of the sill pillar **22**. In a working example, the horizontal cross section of the fragmented permeable mass is square, each side being about 120 feet long; and ten inch diameter blasting holes are located at intervals of about 25 and 30 feet in a rectangular grid over essentially the entire horizontal cross section of the fragmented mass.

During operation of the retort, gas used for retorting of the oil shale is passed downwardly through the fragmented mass. An oxygen-containing gas is introduced into an upper portion of the fragmented permeable mass from the base of operation for sustaining a combustion zone in the fragmented mass and advancing the combustion zone through the fragmented mass.

Heat from the combustion zone, carried by flowing gas advances a retorting zone through the fragmented mass on the advancing side of the combustion zone. Liquid and gaseous products are retorted from oil shale in the retorting zone. The production level drift **18** provides a means for collecting and recovering liquid products and withdrawing off-gas containing gaseous products from retorting oil shale in the retort **10**.

Figure 3.1d is a horizontal cross section at the working level viewing the open base of operation **25** from above. The base of operation **25** is generally E-shaped and has a central drift **70** and a separate side drift **72** on each side of the central drift. The two side drifts are similar to each other in size and shape. Elongated roof-supporting pillars **74** of unfragmented formation separate the side drifts **72** from the central drift **70**. Short crosscuts **76** interconnect the side drifts **72** and the central drift **70** to form a generally E-shaped excavation. Other arrays of drifts and roof-supporting pillars also can be used. A branch drift **78** provides access to the base of operation **25** from underground workings at the level of the base of operation.

After the base of operation is formed, a void in the shape of a vertically extending slot is formed between the production level access drift **18** and an elevation spaced below the bottom of the base of operation. Blasting holes or shot holes **90** are drilled downwardly from the central drift **70** of the base of operation **25**. In a working example, these blasting holes are about $3^5/_8$ inches in diameter. Such blasting holes are loaded with explosive which is detonated to ultimately form the slot-shaped void. Particles of formation from forming the slot are excavated from the production level access drift **18**.

In forming the slot, the blasting holes **90** are loaded only to an elevation spaced about 40 feet below the bottom of the base of operation. In a working example, the thickness of the horizontal sill pillar **22** left unfragmented between the top of the slot and the bottom of the base of operation is about 40 feet. The tops of the holes **90** are stemmed to inhibit breakage into the sill pillar **22**. The side walls of the void formed by the slot provide vertically extending free faces within the side boundaries of the fragmented permeable mass of particles to be formed in the in situ oil shale retort site.

Figure 3.1: In Situ Oil Shale Retort

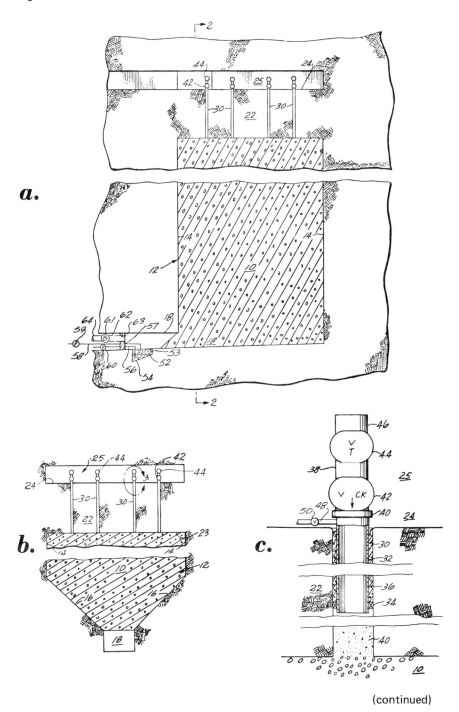

(continued)

Figure 3:1: (continued)

d.

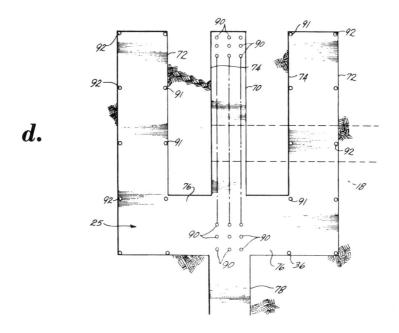

(a) Semischematic vertical cross-sectional view showing an in situ oil shale retort.

(b) Vertical cross-sectional view taken on line 2-2 of Figure 3.1a.

(c) Enlarged semischematic cross-sectional view taken within circle 3 of Figure 3.1b and showing a casing sealed in a blasting hole extending through the sill pillar in the in situ retort.

(d) Horizontal cross section at working level showing a base of operation above horizontal sill pillar in the in situ retort.

Source: U.S. Patent 4,118,070

After the slot is excavated, a remaining portion of the formation within the retort site is explosively expanded toward the void formed by such a slot. A plurality of blasting holes are drilled downwardly in the formation within the retort site from the side drifts **72** of the base of operation **25** on the working level. As illustrated, five such blasting holes, each about 10 inches in diameter, are in each of two rows parallel to the large side walls of the slot **78**. The pattern of ten blasting holes on each side of the slot is similar to the pattern on the other side. The first or inner row of blasting holes **91** is along the roof-supporting pillar **74** on the opposite side from the central drift **70** of the base of operation **25**. An outer row of blasting holes **92** is drilled downwardly along a side boundary of the fragmented permeable mass of particles to be formed in the retort site. Explosive is then loaded into each blasting hole **91** and **92** and is detonated in all of the blasting holes in a single round to form the fragmented permeable mass **10** shown in Figures 3.1a and 3.1b.

The blasting holes **91** and **92** are stemmed with inert material over the explosive to minimize overbreak of formation above the level of the explosive. Thus, as illustrated, the blasting holes are stemmed from about 40 feet below the floor of the base of operation **25**. Detonation of the explosive in the blasting holes for expanding formation toward the slot thereby leaves unfragmented formation as a 40 foot thick horizontal sill pillar **22** between the fragmented permeable mass so formed and the base of operation. The sill pillar has a horizontal extent sufficient to provide effective access to essentially the entire horizontal cross section of the fragmented mass formed in the retort **10**.

The base of operation **25** is used as a location from which to control gas flow through the fragmented mass. Separate vertical steel casings **32** are disposed in selected blasting holes. A conventional external packer **34** at the lower end of each casing seals against the casing exterior and the adjacent portion of the horizontal sill pillar **22**. The annular space between the casing and the sill pillar above the packer is filled with concrete or grout **36** commonly referred to as cement, which anchors the casing securely in the sill pillar (Figure 3.1c).

In some situations, the casing can be adequately secured by using only the packer, or the cement can be replaced by drilling mud or the like to facilitate removal of the casing after the fragmented oil shale in the retort is completely treated. The lower end of the casing is above a level in the fragmented mass where a combustion zone is established. Gas in the combustion zone can include carbon monoxide, carbon dioxide, hydrogen sulfide and water vapor. Such gases can be corrosive to steel pipe, particularly at the operating temperatures involved. By limiting the location of the lower ends of the casings to a level above the combustion zone, corrosion of the casings is inhibited.

A casing collar **40** secures an upper section **38** of the casing to the portion of the casing **32** cemented in the sill pillar. A check valve **42** and a throttle valve **44** (shown schematically in Figure 3.1c) are mounted in the upper section of the casing. An inlet section **46** connected above the throttle valve admits air from the base of operation to the fragmented mass through the throttle valve and the check valve.

An additive line **48** is sealed through the side of the casing below the check valve and throttle valve so that an additive or diluent such as steam, retorting off-gas, auxiliary fuel, additional oxygen, particulate combustible matter such as coal, or the like, can be admitted through the casing into the top of the fragmented mass.

The admission of additive or diluent is controlled by a valve **50** in the additive line **48**. The additive or diluent can be used to adjust the oxygen concentration of gas flowing into the fragmented mass through the casings. Returning to Figure 3.1a, a sump **52** in the region of the access drift **18** beyond the fragmented mass collects shale oil **53** and water **54** produced during the operation of the retort. A water withdrawal line **56** extends from near the bottom of the sump out through a sealed opening in a vertical barrier or bulkhead **57** sealed across the access drift. The water withdrawal line is connected to a water pump **60**. An oil withdrawal line **58** extends from an intermediate level in the sump out through a sealed opening in the barrier and is connected to an oil pump **59**. The oil and water pumps can be operated manually or by automatic controls to remove shale oil and water separately from the sump.

The inlet of a blower **61** is connected by a conduit **62** to an opening **63** through the barrier **57** for withdrawing off-gas from the retort. The outlet of the blower delivers off-gas from the retort through a conduit **64** to a recovery or disposal system. Thus, the access drift **18** provides means for collecting and recovering liquid and gaseous products from the in situ oil shale retort. A variety of collection and recovery techniques can be used, some of which are set forth in the prior art.

The void formed in the retort site before explosive expansion is proportioned relative to the formation expanded toward the void, so that after explosive expansion is completed, the retort is filled with fragmented particles containing oil shale which are packed against the lower surface of the horizontal sill pillar **22**. This provides support for the bottom of the sill pillar during high temperature retorting operations, and minimizes any tendency of the formation to slough from the bottom of the sill pillar.

The blasting holes remaining through the sill pillar **22** after formation of the fragmented mass can be cleaned out, reamed, and/or redrilled, if necessary, after the fragmented mass **10** has been formed. For example, the blasting holes to be used for the casings **30** can be reamed out to about 12 inches in diameter to accomodate larger casings and/or remove a layer from the hole wall which can have some damage from blasting. Other blasting holes not to be used for gas flow to the retort are sealed, such as by filling with concrete.

During retorting operations, the fragmented mass **10** is ignited through the blasting holes to establish a combustion zone across the top of the fragmented mass. Gas flow through each of the casings can be monitored during retorting and separately controlled from the base of operation to control advancement of the combustion zone through the fragmented mass. The combustion zone is advanced downwardly through the fragmented mass by introducing an oxygen-containing gas to the fragmented mass through the casings.

Hot gases flowing downwardly from the combustion zone decompose kerogen in a retorting zone in the fragmented mass of oil shale particles to produce liquid and gaseous products. The liquid products percolate through the fragmented mass on the advancing side of the retorting zone and accumulate in the sump **52** in the access drift **18**, as described above.

The oxygen-containing gas introduced through the casings can be fresh air, or air mixed with other gases, liquids and/or particulate matter. Gas flow through the fragmented mass is generated by the blower **61** which produces a lower gas pressure in the access drift **18** than in the base of operation **25**. This draws air from the base of operation **25** into the casings and into the fragmented mass. Gas flows down through the fragmented mass to the lower access level drift **18**.

The throttle valves **44** on the separate casings provide means for separately controlling the flow of oxygen-containing gas from the base of operation into selected regions of the fragmented mass to control advancement of the combustion zone through the fragmented mass. For example, prior to ignition of the fragmented mass, gas flow rate measurements can be conducted to determine the permeability distribution of the particles in the fragmented mass. Such measurements are achieved by generating gas flow across the horizontal cross-sectional extent of the fragmented mass from the top of the fragmented mass to a gas withdrawal point at the bottom of the fragmented mass.

The blower **61** in the access drift **18** draws air from the base of operation **25** down through the fragmented mass and out the access drift **18**. The rate of air flow through each casing is then measured, preferably by a conventional vane anemometer or hot wire anemometer. To simplify gas flow rate measurements, the throttle valves **44** in the casings are preferably set at the same valve opening so that the cross-sectional area provided through each valve is essentially identical.

The anemometer readings are then taken to determine the rate of flow of air through the corresponding casings. Inasmuch as the casings are distributed essentially uniformly across the face of the sill pillar, the flow rate measurements provide a reasonably accurate sampling of the permeability distribution of the formation particles essentially uniformly across the horizontal cross section of the fragmented mass.

A relatively low flow rate measurement indicates relatively low permeability in a portion of the fragmented mass, or possibly unfragmented formation present in a region of the fragmented mass. On the other hand, a relatively higher flow rate measurement indicates a relatively greater tendency for channeling in a vertically extending portion of the fragmented mass, and the magnitude of the flow rate will be substantially directly proportional to the amount of gas channeling.

After the flow rate measurements are conducted for all casings, the throttle valves **44** are adjusted in accordance with the flow rate measurements so as to adjust the volume of gas for retorting introduced through each casing. The gas flow adjustments are made by increasing throttle valve area in inverse proportion to the magnitude of the measured flow rate. Thus, in those bore holes corresponding to relatively higher gas flow rates, the throttle valves are adjusted to provide a relatively lower gas flow volume to the fragmented mass; and in those bore holes corresponding to relatively lower gas flow rates, the valves are adjusted to provide a relatively greater gas flow volume to the fragmented mass.

The valves are adjusted in relation to one another to produce an essentially uniform gas flow distribution across the horizontal cross section of the fragmented mass from its top to its bottom. As described above, this will tend to minimize the effects of channeling by equalizing the rate of gas flow through the fragmented mass and tend to produce an essentially flat and horizontal advancing combustion zone through the fragmented mass.

After the throttle valves have been adjusted in accordance with the gas flow rate measurements, the retort is ready for inlet gas to be introduced through the casings for use in sustaining and advancing a combustion zone through the retort. Hot gases flowing downwardly from the combustion zone decompose kerogen in the fragmented mass of oil shale particles to produce liquid and gaseous products. The liquid products percolate through the fragmented mass on the advancing side of the retorting zone and accumulate in the sump **52** in the access drift **18**, as described above.

If one or more portions of the fragmented mass are detected as being more permeable than another portion or other portions, resulting in nonuniform burning in the fragmented mass, or if it is found that the locus of the combustion zone is undesirable, the relative flow of gas through the various casings can be adjusted independently of one another by using the separate throttle valves. This can provide a desired gas flow gradient through the fragmented mass which can result in producing a combustion zone which is substantially flat and horizontal as it advances through the retort.

If a combustion zone is not properly advanced through the fragmented mass, the combustion zone can become skewed and/or warped. It is desirable to establish and maintain a combustion zone which is flat and uniformly transverse to the direction of its advancement to maximize yield of hydrocarbon products from oil shale in an in situ oil shale retort. If the combustion zone is skewed relative to its direction of advancement, there is more tendency for oxygen present in the combustion zone to migrate into the retorting zone, thereby oxidizing the hydrocarbon products produced in the retorting zone and reducing hydrocarbon yield.

In addition, with a skewed and/or warped combustion zone, excessive cracking of hydrocarbon products produced in the retort zone can result. By providing means for spearately controlling gas flow to selected regions throughout the horizontal cross section of the fragmented mass, the process facilitates advancing a combustion zone which is essentially flat and transverse to its direction of advancement.

Further, by using the base of operation as a plenum chamber for admission of air to the fragmented mass, all of the air introduced into the fragmented mass is drawn from the base of operation and passageways connecting it to the surface, thereby adding to the fresh air supply in those working areas. Moreover, by using the blower **61** as the means for drawing gas through the fragmented mass from the base of operation, gas pressure within the fragmented mass is reduced relative to gas pressure within the base of operation **25** mass. This inhibits leakage of off-gas from the fragmented mass into the base of operation and its surrounding underground workings.

Inasmuch as off-gas from the fragmented mass can contain a substantial amount of hydrogen sulfide and carbon monoxide, such off-gas would otherwise pose a potential hazard to operating personnel in the base of operation and other underground workings.

The check valve in each casing prevents inadvertent back flow of retorting gases into the base of operation if the blower **61** withdrawing gas from the fragment mass is temporarily shut down. There can be continued production of gas in the fragmented mass even when the blower **61** is not operating due to high temperatures which can cause further retorting. This can cause a gas pressure increase in the fragmented mass beneath the sill pillar **22** which could result in a gas pressure higher than that in the base of operation. Reverse flow of gas is inhibited by the check valves **42** in the casings which permit gas to flow into the fragmented mass from the base of operation while preventing reverse flow.

In a related process, *N.M. Hutchins; U.S. Patent 4,118,071; October 3, 1978; assigned to Occidental Oil Shale, Inc.* describes an in situ oil shale retort that is formed in a subterranean formation containing oil shale using a horizontal sill pillar. The retort, with top, bottom and side boundaries, contains a fragmented permeable mass of particles containing oil shale. A base of operation is excavated at a working level in the formation.

Means are excavated through the formation for access to a location underlying the base of operation. In one embodiment, a void in the form of a vertical slot is excavated in the site between the means for access and an elevation below the bottom of the base of operation, leaving a remaining portion which is to be expanded toward the void. This is designed to leave a horizontal sill pillar of intact formation between the top of the void and the bottom of the base of operation with a vertical thickness sufficient to maintain a safe base of operation after explosive expansion of formation to form the fragmented permeable mass of particles.

The void provides at least one free face extending vertically through the formation within the boundaries of the in situ oil shale retort site. This remaining portion is explosively expanded toward the void with a single round of explosions.

D.E. Garrett; U.S. Patent 4,045,085; August 30, 1977; assigned to Occidental Oil Shale, Inc. describes an underground in situ oil shale retort, having predetermined boundaries which contains a bed of fragmented oil shale particles having an appreciable void volume. Air passed through this bed of fragmented oil shale supports combustion of some of the carbonaceous material in the oil shale and provides heat for retorting oil.

A number of such retorts may be formed in an area and pillars are left to support the overburden. Pillars forming walls between adjacent retorts also prevent gas leakage. Oil recovery from intact oil shale pillars is enhanced by fracturing the pillars as well as fragmenting the shale in the retort. The pillars are fractured by hydraulic fracturing, electrical fracturing, liquid explosive fissuring, or the like. The fractures are propagated from access holes in the vicinity of the pillars, typically between similar holes adjacent to the next retort volume when the pillars are between retorts.

G.B. French and R.D. Ridley; U.S. Patent 4,025,115; May 24, 1977; assigned to Occidental Petroleum Corporation describe an underground in situ oil shale retort which contains a bed of fragmented oil shale particles having an appreciable void volume. Air or other retorting gas passed through this bed of fragmented oil shale supports combustion of some of the carbonaceous material in the oil shale and provides heat for retorting oil.

A number of such retorts may be formed in an area and pillars are left to support the overburden. Pillars forming walls between adjacent retorts also prevent gas leakage. Oil recovery from intact oil shale pillars between retorts is enhanced by fracturing the pillars as well as fragmenting the shale in the retort.

The pillars are fractured by detonating explosives in bore holes in the region between the retort and pillars, preferably a fraction of a second after explosive
fragmentation of the oil shale in the retort.

Slot-Shaped Columnar Voids

According to a process developed by *R.D. Ridley; U.S. Patent 4,043,596;
August 23, 1977; assigned to Occidental Oil Shale, Inc.*, a retort in a subterranean formation containing oil shale, having top, bottom and side boundaries of
unfragmented formation is formed by excavating a first portion of the oil shale
from within such boundaries to form at least one columnar void, the surface of
the formation which defines the columnar void presents at least one free face
that extends vertically through the subterranean oil shale deposit, and leaves a
second portion of the formation, which is to be fragmented by expansion toward the columnar void; within the boundaries of the retort and extending away
from a free face.

The second portion is explosively expanded toward the columnar void in one or
more segments, including at least one layer of formation parallel to a free face.
The expansion of the oil shale toward the columnar void fragments the oil shale
thereby distributing the void volume of the columnar void throughout the retort.
The columnar void can be formed by any of a number of methods, including
excavation procedures useful for forming shafts, raises and winzes. Burn-cutting
rounds, angle-cutting rounds, or combinations of angle-cutting and burn-cutting
rounds are useful for forming the columnar void.

Placement of the explosive for expanding the oil shale toward the free face of
the columnar void is preferably accomplished by drilling blasting holes through
the oil shale adjacent to the columnar void and parallel to the free face and
loading the blasting holes with the explosive. The columnar void is a slot providing two large parallel planar vertical free faces extending substantially over
the entire width of the retort to be formed; the blasting holes are arranged in
planes parallel to the free faces so the shale within the planes expands in one
direction toward each free face upon detonation of the explosive.

The columnar void extends vertically for the greater part of the height of the
retort to be formed. However, the height of the columnar void can exclude the
portion of the height of the retort to be formed attributable to workrooms, any
pillar separating a workroom from a columnar void, and any other portion of the
height of the retort being formed from which the shale is blasted to a horizontal
free face, such as a dome-shaped portion at the top boundary. In any case, the
height of the columnar void would usually be greater than three-quarters of the
height of the retort.

The explosive used for expanding the oil shale toward the planar free face of the
columnar void is detonated in an outwardly progressing sequence such that the
oil shale adjacent to the columnar void is expanded toward the free face of the
columnar void and the remainder of the explosive in the retort is detonated before the expanded oil shale adjacent to the columnar void falls appreciably due
to the force of gravity. Within the range of 10 to 20%, the especially preferred
horizontal cross-sectional area for the columnar void is about 15% of the horizontal cross-sectional area of the retort. The data collected from work in the

Piceance Basin of Colorado indicate this value provides a good balance among the various characteristics of the retort, i.e., void volume, permeability, and particle size, without having to excavate excessive amounts of shale to form the columnar void. For example, a retort having a height of about 100 feet can require a pressure drop of less than about 1 psi from top to bottom for vertical movement of a mixture of air and off-gas down through the retort at about 1 to 2 standard cubic feet per minute (scfm) per square foot of horizontal cross section of the retort, while retorts having greater heights would require proportionally larger pressure drops.

Thus, an adequate gas flow rate through retorts up to 1,000 feet in height can be provided with a pressure drop of less than 10 psi from top to bottom. In some areas of the Piceance Basin, a gas pressure of greater than 10 psi is objectionable because it results in excessive gas leakage into the intact shale around the retort.

The above percentage values assume that all the shale within the boundaries of the retort is to be fragmented, i.e., there are no intact, i.e., unfragmented regions left in the retort. If there are unfragmented regions left in the retort, for example, for support pillars or the like, the percentages would be less. The above percentage values also apply when the relationship between the size of the columnar void and the formation that is to be expanded is expressed in terms of volume, i.e., the volume of the columnar void is from about 10 to 20%, preferably about 15%, of the combined volume of the columnar void and of the space occupied prior to expansion by that portion of the formation that is to be expanded to fill both the columnar void and such space.

This method for fragmenting oil shale is useful for forming a retort of any desired dimension. When forming a retort of a relatively small cross-sectional area, a single columnar void can be excavated through the oil shale deposit in which the retort is being formed and the oil shale surrounding the columnar void expanded toward the columnar void to form the retort.

In the formation of a retort having a relatively large cross-sectional area, several columnar voids can be used; the planar free faces of the columnar voids are generally parallel. The columnar voids can be spaced through the retort being formed so that all the oil shale within the retort is fragmented and expanded toward the columnar voids. In retorts having a relatively large cross-sectional area, a portion of the oil shale can be left unfragmented in the form of vertical pillars to serve as support for the overburden, if necessary. The amount of oil shale left unfragmented in the form of pillars is taken into consideration when determining the volume of the columnar voids.

Columnar Voids

In a process described by *G.B. French; U.S. Patent 4,043,595; August 23, 1977; assigned to Occidental Oil Shale, Inc.* an in situ oil shale retort is formed in a subterranean oil shale deposit by excavating a columnar void having a vertically extending free face, drilling blasting holes adjacent to the columnar void and parallel to the free face, loading the blasting holes with explosive, and detonating the explosive in a single round to expand the shale adjacent to the columnar void toward the free face in layers severed in a sequence progressing away from the free face and to fill with fragmented oil shale the columnar void and the space in the in situ retort originally occupied by the expanded shale prior to the expansion. A room having a horizontal floor plan that coincides approximately with the horizontal cross section of the retort to be formed is excavated so as to intersect the columnar void. The blasting holes are drilled and loaded with explosive from the room. The room can lie above the columnar void, below the columnar void, or intermediate the ends of the columnar void.

In one example, the columnar void is cylindrical and the blasting holes are arranged in concentric rings around the columnar void. In another case, the columnar void is a slot having one or more large parallel, planar vertical free faces, toward which the oil shale in the retort under construction can be explosively expanded. The blasting holes are arranged in planes parallel to these faces. The resulting retort generally has a cross section coinciding with the placement of the blasting holes and a height determined for the greater part by the vertical height of the columnar void. To form a retort having a large cross-sectional area, a plurality of columnar voids can be excavated and the shale in the retort expanded toward the respective columnar voids to form a continuous fragmented permeable mass of oil shale.

Multiple Zone Design

According to a process described by *G.B. French and D.E. Garrett; U.S. Patent 4,043,598; and G.B. French; U.S. Patent 4,043,597; August 23, 1977; both assigned to Occidental Oil Shale, Inc.*, a subterranean deposit containing oil shale is prepared for in situ retorting by initially excavating a plurality of vertically spaced apart voids of similar horizontal cross sections located one above another within the deposit.

A plurality of vertically spaced apart zones of unfragmented deposit are temporarily left between the voids, each unfragmented zone having a thickness of less than about 190% of the smallest lateral dimension of the voids above and below it. Explosive placed in each of the unfragmented zones is detonated, preferably in a single round to expand each unfragmented zone into the voids on either side of it and form a subterranean room containing a fragmented mass of particles having a void volume equal to the void volume of the initial voids. Retorting of the expanded mass is then carried out to recover shale oil from the oil shale.

Figures 3.2a and 3.2b illustrate a subterranean deposit 10, such as an oil shale deposit, which is in an intermediate state of preparation for in situ recovery of carbonaceous values such as shale oil and hydrocarbon gaseous products in retorting off-gas. Generally speaking, in situ recovery is carried out by initially removing oil shale from certain volumes of the subterranean deposit and then explosively expanding a remaining portion of the oil shale in the deposit to produce a vertically extending fragmented permeable mass of oil shale particles.

The process is described in the context of a method for ultimately producing a subterranean vertical retort comprising a vertically extending room 12 (illustrated in phantom lines in Figures 3.2a and 3.2b) filled with a fragmented permeable mass of expanded oil shale particles having a uniformly distributed void volume desired for economical vertical retorting operations. The room 12 is square in horizontal cross section, and for most efficient retorting, the vertical dimension or height of the room **12** is greater than the maximum lateral dimension or width of the room.

Referring to Figure 3.2b, access to the portion of the oil shale deposit to be expanded is established by forming a horizontal tunnel, drift or adit **14** extending to the bottom of the volume to be expanded. From the adit **14**, the oil shale deposit is undercut and a volume of deposit is removed to form a lower void **20** at the bottom of the subterranean room **12** to be formed.

The material excavated from the lower void is hauled away through the tunnel **14**. The lower void **20** is preferably continuous across the width of the volume to be expanded, so that the deposit overlying the lower void is completely unsupported and defines a horizontal free face **21** of the formation immediately above the lower void. If desired, one or more pillars of unfragmented deposit can be left in the void to help support overlying deposit. Preferably, the floor plan or horizontal cross section of the lower void **20** is generally square, although the void, and also the subterranean room **12** to be formed generally can be of other horizontal cross section such as rectangular without departing from the scope of the method.

The floor **22** of the lower void is inclined downwardly in the direction of the adit **14** to facilitate the flow of shale oil in the direction of the adit during subsequent retorting operations. After the lower void **20** is excavated, or concurrently therewith, a horizontal or upwardly sloping tunnel or "lateral" **24** is excavated. The far end of the lateral opens into an upwardly inclined tunnel or raise **26**. The top **28** of the raise **26** provides access for excavating a horizontal tunnel **30** above the level of the bottom void **20**. The lateral **24** and raise **26** form a dogleg access to the tunnel **30**.

Figure 3.2: Multiple Zone In Situ Retort

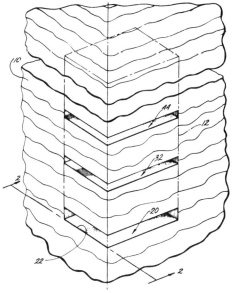

(continued)

Figure 3.2: (continued)

b.

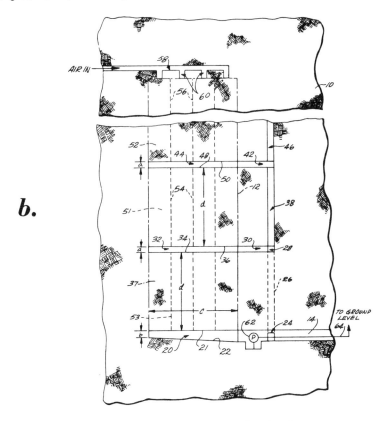

(a)   Schematic perspective view show-
      ing an oil shale deposit in an inter-
      mediate stage of preparation for in
      situ recovery
(b)   Cross sectional elevation view taken
      on line 2-2 of Figure 3.2a

Source: U.S. Patent 4,043,598

Other access can also be provided such as a sloping tunnel from the drift **14** or
a separate adit leading to the ground surface. From the horizontal access tunnel
30, oil shale is removed from the volume to be expanded to form an intermediate void **32** spaced vertically above the lower void **20**. The floor plan or horizontal cross section of the intermediate void **32** matches the horizontal cross
section and area of the lower void **20** (and the room **12** to be formed).

Thus, the intermediate void is preferably square in shape, and is substantially
directly above the lower void so that the outer edges of the two voids preferably
lie in common vertical planes. The height of the intermediate void can be less
than that of the lower void if less bulky mining machinery is used for excavation. The intermediate void also is continuous across the width of the room **12**

such that the overlying portion of the deposit is completely unsupported, thereby defining a pair of vertically spaced apart bottom and top horizontal free faces 34 and 36, respectively, adjoining intermediate void 32. The two voids 20 and 32 also define a lower zone 37 of unfragmented oil shale left within the boundaries of the subterranean room 12 between the free faces 21 and 34.

After the intermediate void 32 is formed, oil shale is removed from the deposit adjacent room 12 being formed to form a vertical raise 38 extending upwardly from the tunnel 30 to provide access for excavating a horizontal tunnel 42 above the level of the intermediate void 32. Oil shale is removed from within the boundaries of the room 12 being formed through the tunnel 42 to form an upper void 44 spaced vertically above the intermediate void 32.

The floor plan or horizontal cross section of the upper void 44 is substantially similar to the generally square horizontal cross section being formed and the lower and intermediate voids of the room 12. The upper void also is aligned with the voids below it so that the outer edges of the upper void lie in common vertical planes with the outer edges of the voids below. The upper void 44 is the same height as the intermediate void 32, and is also continuous across the width of the room 12. Thus, the part of the deposit above it is unsupported.

If desired, one or more pillars of unfragmented deposit can be left in the upper and intermediate voids to help support the overlying deposit. The upper void defines a pair of vertically spaced apart bottom and top horizontal free faces 48 and 50, respectively, on the unfragmented deposit adjoining the void. The two voids 32 and 44 also define a zone 51 of unfragmented deposit left between the free faces 36 and 48. An intact zone 52 of unfragmented deposit also is left above the uppermost free face 50.

After the multiple spaced apart voids have been excavated in the oil shale deposit, the intervening unfragmented zones 37 and 51 and the intact oil shale 52 above the upper void 44 are prepared for explosive expansion and subsequent retorting operations. Vertical blasting holes 53 are drilled in the lower unfragmented zones 37 upwardly from the lower void 20 or downwardly from the intermediate void 32.

Similarly, vertical blasting holes 54 are drilled in the upper unfragmented zone 51 from the intermediate void 32 or the upper void 44, and vertical blasting holes 56 are drilled upwardly from the upper void 44 into unfragmented deposit 52 above the upper void. If pillars have been left within the voids, blasting holes can also be drilled in them for expansion with the fragmented zones. The blasting holes are then filled from top to bottom with explosive, such as ammonium nitrate-fuel oil or other conventional explosive.

Thus, at this intermediate stage in preparation for in situ retorting explosive charges are distributed to the unfragmented zones between the voids and the unfragmented deposit on the opposite side of one of the voids from the unfragmented zone. The explosive charges within at least one of the unfragmented zones are detonated simultaneously to expand the unfragmented zone toward the previously excavated voids. This severs the oil shale from the formation to form the room 12 and fill it with a fragmented permeable mass of oil shale particles or rubble. The explosive charges are so arranged within the unfragmented zones of oil shale that the shape of the room 12 after detonation is approximately square in horizontal cross section continuously from top to bottom, as illustrated by phantom lines in Figure 3.2a. The explosive is dispersed in the unfragmented zones **37** and **51**, and in the unfragmented deposit **52** above the top void **44**.

Explosive is located sufficiently close to the free face of the zone adjoining each void that oil shale in each unfragmented zone is expanded simultaneously into both voids bordering it. Preferably all of the explosives are detonated in a single round so all unfragmented zones are expanded and all voids filled at the same time. The distributed void fraction of the permeable mass of particles in the retort, i.e., the ratio of the void volume to the total volume in the subterranean in situ retort **12**, is controlled by the volume of the excavated voids toward which the deposit is expanded. The total volume of the voids is sufficiently small compared to the total volume of the retort that the expanded oil shale is capable of filling the voids and the space occupied by the expanded shale prior to expansion.

In other words, the volume of the voids is not so large that the expanded shale occupies less than the entire space of the voids and the space occupied by the expanded shale prior to detonation of the explosives. In filling the voids and the space occupied by the unfragmented zones prior to fragmentation, the particles of the expanded shale become jammed and wedged together tightly so they do not shift or move after fragmentation has been completed. In numerical terms, the total volume of the voids should be less than about 40% of the total volume of the retort being formed to fill the voids and the space occupied by the expanded shale prior to expansion.

In one example of this process, the volume of the voids is preferably not greater than about 20% of the volume of the retort, as this is found to provide a void volume in the fragmented oil shale adequate for satisfactory retorting operation. If the void volume is more than about 20% an undue amount of excavation occurs without concomitant improvement in permeability. Removal of the material from the voids is costly and kerogen contained therein is wasted or retorted by costly above ground methods.

In another example of the process, the total height of the in situ retort or room **12** is about 110 to 120 feet. The intermediate void **32** and upper void **44** each have a height (represented by the dimension a in Figure 3.2b) of about 6 feet, and the height (represented by the dimension b) of the lower void is about 12 feet. Each unfragmented zone **37** and **51** and the unfragmented shale **52** above the top void is about 32 square feet (represented by dimension c in Figure 3.2b) in horizontal cross section, which essentially matches the horizontal cross section of the voids **20, 32** and **44**, although these can be a foot or so wider to accommodate drilling equipment near the edges.

The thickness (represented by the dimension d) of each unfragmented zone, and the upper zone **52** above the upper void is about 30 feet, i.e., about 95% of the minimum horizontal dimension of the voids. About six feet of rubble in the form of oil shale particles are backfilled in the lower void **20** prior to expansion. Explosive dispersed in blasting holes in the unfragmented zones and in unfragmented oil shale above the top void is detonated for expanding the unfragmented deposit toward the voids.

Thus, in this example, the fragmented permeable mass of particles contained in the in situ retort **12** after explosive expansion has a void volume of about 15%. This void volume is within the desired range for maximizing recovery of shale oil from the volume being retorted and providing for a minimal pressure drop from top to bottom of the vertical retort.

Multiple Adjacent Production Zones

According to a process developed by *A.T. Janssen; U.S. Patents 3,917,348; 3,917,346; and 3,917,347; all November 4, 1975; all assigned to Atlantic Richfield Company*, a permeable underground zone contains a parallel array of generally horizontal access entries communicating with the surface extending at a level beneath the top of an underground ore body or deposit. Zone entries are driven transversely from each access entry at this level, penetrating the deposit. A plurality of short crosscuts are driven in turn from each zone entry so that in combination each such zone entry and its associated crosscuts define a cavity of predetermined areal extent.

The deposit overlying each cavity is partially supported by the ribs which separate adjacent crosscuts and which project into the cavity from its side walls. Upon removal of these ribs, designated blocks of each of the overlying deposits may be expanded into their associated undercutting cavities to form a series of adjacent permeable zones.

With reference to Figure 3.3a, there is illustrated a mining layout within a subterranean ore body, for example, an oil shale formation, which has been developed in accordance with the process. At least one pair of similar vertical shafts **10** and **11** are driven at suitably spaced intervals from the surface or from an upper mining level to a selected lower level beneath the top of an ore body. A corresponding pair of main entries **12** and **13** are then driven laterally from the bottom of the shafts **10** and **11**, respectively, so that they extend in substantially the same direction and in approximately horizontal relation to each other.

The main entries **12** and **13** may be of any desired length and spacing, and the permeable zones to be developed all lie between these entries. Thus entries **12** and **13** define the perimeter or areal boundaries of the operation. If desired in connection with specific mining activities, either of main entries **12** or **13** may function as a bleeder or haulage drift.

Interconnecting adjacent main entries **12** and **13** are a series of substantially parallel spaced apart access entries **14**, only two of which are shown in Figure 3.3a for purposes of illustration. The length and number of such entries **14** are governed by the distance separating adjacent main entries **12** and **13**, the longitudinal extent of such main entries, and the selected spacing between adjacent access entries **14**. Additional shafts **10** or **11** and main entries **12** or **13** may be added if the mining layout is to be continued into contiguous areas.

Each of the access entries **14** constitutes the common trunk from which a plurality of designated permeable zones such as, for example, **15, 16, 17, 18, 19, 20, 21,** and **22** are to be developed and through which subsequent retorting operations or the like may be monitored and controlled. Each of the zones **15** through **22** is interconnected with the access entry **14** as shown through one of a plurality of zone entries **30** driven transversely from the access entry **14**.

Within the scope of this process, more than one zone entry **30** may conveniently communicate with a single permeable zone. It should further be understood that the mining layout of Figure 3.3a may constitute one of a series of vertically spaced layouts of similar form within the same general mining operation where the operation may be conducted sequentially from one layout to the next.

Any of the plurality of permeable zones to be developed in the mining layout of Figure 3.3a, such as, for example, zone **17**, may conveniently assume the form illustrated in Figure 3.3b. In this view, the rectangular or cube-shaped zone **17** is represented partially in dashed outline, as seen from the access entry **14**, to which it is interconnected by one of the zone entries **30**. The zone **17**, shown partially developed prior to expansion, comprises generally a block of ore **32** partly broken away overlaying a cavity **33** which has been mined out from the zone entry **30** in the manner to be described, leaving only one or more supporting ribs **34**.

In order to better understand the details of the mining operation whereby permeable zones may be developed, attention is directed to Figure 3.3c. Several of the zones shown in Figure 3.3a, such as, for example, zones **15, 16, 17**, and **18**, are shown, for illustrative purposes, in successive stages of development, the internal features of all such zones being identical. A zone entry **30** may be driven from the access entry **14** along a horizontal or slightly elevated path for a predetermined distance into the base of the ore body until a boundary of a designated zone, for example, zone **15**, (shown in dotted outline) is reached.

A plurality of crosscuts **35** are then driven into the deposit from the side walls of the zone entry **30** approximately at right angles as shown in the view of zone **16** in Figure 3.3c. The crosscuts **35** terminate within the ore body, also at boundaries of the designated zone **16**. The crosscuts **35** may be made short enough so that they can be conveniently mined and excavated with the use of gathering arm loaders or other equipment which is advanced within crosscuts **35** without the entry of personnel.

Figure 3.3: Method of Developing Permeable Underground Zones

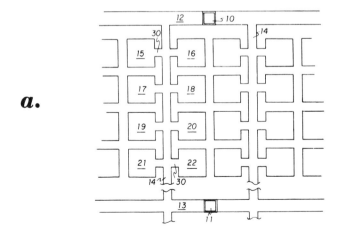

(continued)

Figure 3.3 (continued)

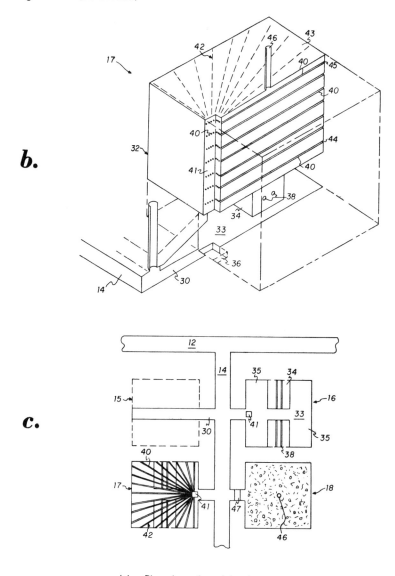

b.

c.

(a) Plan view of a mining layout
(b) Isometric view, partly broken away, of
     a permeable underground zone in prog-
     ress of development
(c) Illustration showing a plurality of per-
     meable zones in various stages of de-
     velopment

Source: U.S. Patent 3,917,348

Thus, the need for roof bolting and scaling within the crosscuts 35 is obviated. The spacing between the crosscuts 35 and the number of such crosscuts is optional; and if the total area of the cavity 33 is sufficiently small, the ribs 34 may be eliminated altogether. However, preferentially the spacing should be such that the separating ribs 34 are wider than they are high for maximum stability, as such ribs 34 partially support the overlaying block 32. The fact that the ribs 34 are integral with the side walls of the undercutting cavity 33 into which they project enhances their strength and resistance to vibration. The number of the ribs 34 is, of course, determined by the number of the crosscuts 35 which are driven from each of the zone entries 30.

The undercutting cavity 33, which is formed in the manner described above, is already coextensive with the zone to be prepared such as, for example, zone 17, less the cross-sectional area of the supporting ribs 34, which will be removed prior to expansion of the overlaying deposit. The height of the cavity 33 should be selected, in accordance with well-known principles, unnecessary to detail here, so that its void volume is sufficient to permit a desired degree of expansion of the block 32 and, if necessary, to avoid ultimate subsidence of the overburden.

If the floor of the cavity 33 is to be slanted or funneled to a liquid-gathering sump 36 as, for example, in collecting shale oil, the paths of the zone entry 30 and associated crosscuts 35 may be deviated appropriately from the horizontal. Also, within the scope of this process, the cross-sectional area of the cavity 33 may be modified so that it assumes a circular or other desired shape.

The block 32 may be expanded by methods well known to the mining art. A preferred method involves explosive removal of the ribs 34 followed by sequential explosive fragmentation of successive layers of the overlaying block 32. A technique for accomplishing such explosive fragmentation is more particularly described in U.S. Patent 3,917,346. In accordance with such preferred methods, blasting hole patterns for explosive implantation in overlaying block 32 are illustrated in Figures 3.3b and 3.3c.

A plurality of blasting holes 38 may, for example, be drilled along approximately horizontal paths through the ribs 34. Additionally, blasting holes 40 may be drilled into the overlaying block 32, horizontally or at a slight elevation, from a raise 41 extending upwardly into the deposit 32 from the roof of the undercutting cavity 33. Such blasting holes 40 may be conveniently drilled in a fan-shaped pattern 42 as illustrated in dotted outline on the top surface 43 of the block 32 at each of any desired number of spaced apart vertical levels ranging from a bottom level 44 to a top level 45.

Following the properly timed detonation of the explosive charges within the blasting holes 38 and 40, the block 32 fragments and expands into the undercutting cavity 33 to create a permeable zone such as zone 18 in Figure 3.3c. Such zones are then available for further operations such as in situ retorting, excavation, etc. In an oil shale retorting operation, for example, an air hole 46 may be drilled from the surface or an upper mining level into the top of any of the permeable zones typified by zone 18 to accommodate a source of oxygen and fuel to ignite and support combustion of the oil shale. At the same time, the zone entry 30 leading into each such zone may be sealed with a bulkhead 47 during retorting operations to eliminate passage of noxious gases into the access entry 14. Suitable conduits for recovery of carbonaceous values may easily be introduced from the access entry **14** into each zone **18** through such bulkhead **47**. If desired, any of the zone entries **30** may be extended so as to interconnect adjacent access entries **14** so that the resultant permeable zones may be operated from either of two sides.

If the mining of the zones described commences in inverse order with zones **21** and **22** and continues in sequence therefrom through zones **15** and **16**, then shaft **10** and main entry **12** may be used for hauling of excavated ore while shaft **11** and main entry **13** bleed off properly directed ventilation air. Thus, for example, in a complete system for developing and operating retort zones in an oil shale formation, zones **15** and **16** may be an initial stage of cavity development, zones **17** and **18** undergoing expansion of the overlaying deposit, zones **19** and **20** in process of retorting, and zones **21** and **22** filled with spent shale and abandoned. Ventilation air flow progresses along access entry **14** from main entry **12** to main entry **13** to insure that noxious gases are carried away from operating personnel at all times.

In order to better appreciate the practical aspect of the method described above as applied to a large scale in situ oil shale retorting operation, the following illustrative values are given. A series of four spaced apart main entries such as entries **12** and **13** may be extended equally from the bottom of a like number of vertical shafts similar to shafts **10** and **11** to form an overall square cross section mining layout of 14,880 feet on a side. This covers roughly an area of 5,000 acres.

Such a layout will accommodate approximately 204 access entries, such as entry **14**, each of which interconnects a pair of main entries and from each of which two rows of 56 permeable retortable zones, of which zone **17** is illustrative, may be developed, each approximately 75 feet on a side for a total of 22,848 retortable zones. Progressive development of such a mining layout realistically permits simultaneous operation of over 100 retortable zones over a period of 15 years.

Multiple Gallery-Type Retort Zones

According to a process developed by *T.H. Timmins; U.S. Patent 3,950,029; April 13, 1976; assigned to Mobil Oil Corporation* a retort zone is constructed so that personnel working in a gallery in the retort zone are protected against the off-gas from an adjoining gallery being retorted, but at the same time, the maximum practical amount of oil shale within the retort zone is processed to recover hydrocarbon products.

In carrying out the process, a retort zone is formed in an oil shale deposit, the retort zone being composed of two or more galleries adjacent one another within the deposit. These galleries are large areas, for example, preferably from 500 to 5,000 feet on a side, and are separated from each other by relatively thick barrier pillars, for example, greater than 50 feet.

These pillars, which in effect are actually walls, are formed by merely leaving portions of the oil shale untouched when constructing the galleries and must be thick enough to insure that there will be no leakage of gas from one gallery to another. Within each gallery are a plurality of individual retort "rooms" having dimensions preferably of from 100 to 500 feet on a side, these rooms being separated from each other within a gallery by relatively thin room walls, e.g., less than 50 feet. The rooms may be formed by conventional mining techniques wherein a portion of the oil shale within a defined room area is removed to form a void into which the remaining shale within the room area is rubblized by explosions or the like.

The room walls, which are formed by merely leaving portions of the oil shale intact, control the gas flow within each room during retorting so that high volumetric sweep efficiency can be obtained throughout the retort zone and so that the retorting gas temperature can be controlled for the best practical recovery of desired products. Also, since the room walls are relatively thin, the unretorted portions of these walls represent the smallest amount of unrecoverable products consistent with the necessary safety that must be provided during construction and retorting of the galleries.

The room walls do provide some isolation from off-gas between the rooms in a gallery, but in this method these walls do not have to be thick enough to prevent gas leakage to adjoining rooms under all circumstances. This is due to the fact that once a gallery of rooms is prepared and sealed, there will normally be no need for a worker to reenter the gallery. Further, since the barrier pillars between galleries are thick enough to prevent leakage of off-gas from one gallery to adjacent galleries, workers can safely work in or complete adjacent galleries while a previously completed gallery is being retorted.

To retort the individual rooms within a gallery, retorting gas is circulated from the surface through the rubblized shale in a room, and then either returned directly to the surface or diverted to an adjacent room to preheat the shale in that room and to cool the gas before it is returned to the surface. The off-gas can be diverted to an adjoining room by detonating explosive charges properly placed in the room walls to establish communication between rooms after a room has been retorted sufficiently to produce a high temperature (e.g., >200°F) off-gas. The explosive charges are sealed in the room walls during construction of the room. Communication passages are provided to supply the retorting gas to rooms and to remove the products resulting from the retorting.

Multiple Horizontal Units

According to a process described by *G.B. French; U.S. Patent 4,106,814; August 15, 1978; assigned to Occidental Oil Shale, Inc.,* a row of horizontally spaced apart in situ oil shale retorts is formed in a subterranean formation containing oil shale. Each row is formed by excavating at least a pair of upper and lower retort access drifts at elevations within the top and bottom boundaries of the retort sites. The access drifts extend through opposite side boundaries of a plurality of retorts in such row.

Each retort is formed by excavating upper and lower horizontal voids at the levels of the upper and lower right access drifts, respectively, such voids being excavated laterally from the access drift within the side boundaries of the retort sites. Each retort is formed by explosively expanding formation toward the upper and lower voids within the boundaries of the retort site to form a fragmented permeable mass of particles containing oil shale in each retort. Following formation of each retort, the retort access drifts on the advancing side of the retort are at least partially sealed, preferably with a mass of formation particles covered by a gas impermeable layer and backfilled with a further mass of formation particles. Referring to Figure 3.4, a system of in situ oil shale retorts 10 is formed in a subterranean formation 12 containing oil shale. Each retort, when completed by explosive expansion techniques, comprises a fragmented permeable mass of formation particles containing oil shale having top, bottom and side boundaries.

As shown in Figure 3.4a, the retorts are horizontally spaced apart in rows, leaving barriers of unfragmented formation between adjacent retorts. Each fragmented mass is rectangular in horizontal cross section. In the illustrated process each retort is also rectangular in vertical cross section. The fragmented mass in each retort 10 is, for clarity, represented in Figure 3.4a as a separate three dimensional rectangular shaped box. This drawing is semischematic with some dimensions exaggerated for clarity of illustration. For example, in a working case, the fragmented mass in a retort can be in the range of 120 to 200 feet square and the barrier of unfragmented formation between retorts can be about 30 feet or less.

Figure 3.4a illustrates the system of retorts 10 during differing stages of development. In an excavation region 14 of formation 12, the formation has been excavated prior to explosive expansion to form the retorts 10. In a retort preparation region 15 of the formation, formation has been explosively expanded to form the fragmented mass within each retort 10. In a production or retorting region 16 of the formation, retorting of the fragmented mass in each retort 10 is carried out to produce liquid and gaseous products. Excavation, explosive expansion and production in various portions of a tract can occur essentially concurrently.

In preparing the retort system, a main air level drift system 18 is excavated at an upper elevation in the formation, and a main production level drift system 20 is excavated in a lower elevation of the formation below the main air level drift system 18. One or more main retort access level drift systems are formed at elevations within the top and bottom boundaries of the in situ retorts 10 being formed. As illustrated, there are three vertically spaced apart main retort access level drift systems comprising an upper main retort access level drift system 22, an intermediate main retort level access drift system 24 below the upper main retort level drift system 22, and a lower main retort level access drift system 26 below the intermediate main access drift system 24.

The air level drift system is at an elevation above the elevation of the top boundaries of the fragmented masses being formed and the production level drift system in this example is below the elevation of the bottom boundaries of the fragmented masses being formed. As used herein, the term "level" means one of more generally horizontally extending passages or drifts.

In a working example, the main air level, production level, and retort access level drift systems extend in a rectangular pattern around the perimeter of the portion of the formation under development. The retorts 10 are developed in parallel rows extending perpendicularly between opposite parallel portions of the main drift systems. Extending along first ends of the rows of retorts 10 are a first main air level drift 18, a first production level drift, and first main upper, intermediate and lower retort level access drifts 22, 24 and 26, respectively.

Figure 3.4: Multiple Horizontally Spaced Apart In Situ Retorts

(continued)

(continued)

Figure 3.4:   (continued)

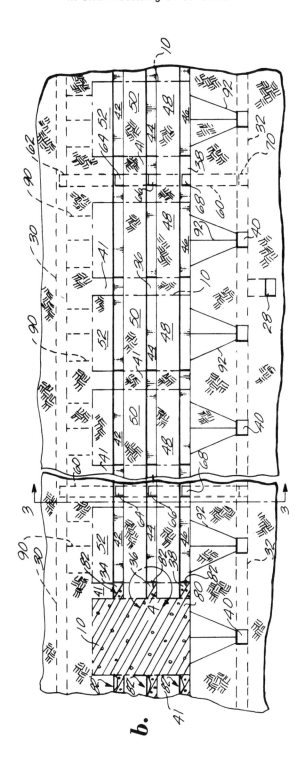

Figure 3.4:   (continued)

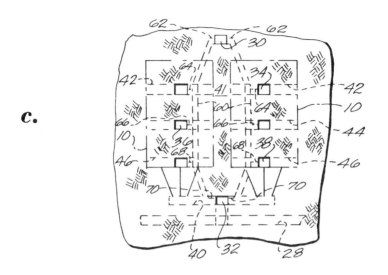

c.

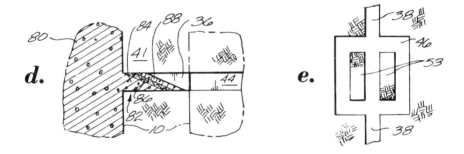

d.   **e.**

(a)   Fragmentary perspective view showing a subterranean formation con-
       taining oil shale partially prepared for in situ retorting
(b)   Fragmentary schematic view in vertical cross section showing under-
       ground workings in regions of the formation under preparation
(c)   Schematic view of vertical cross section taken on line **3–3** of Figure
       3.4b
(d)   Schematic view in vertical cross section showing a gas barrier within
       the circle **4** of Figure 3.4b
(e)   Top plan view in horizontal cross section showing an alternate method
       for forming void volumes

Source: U.S. Patent 4,106,814

Referring to Figure 3.4a, extending along second ends of the rows of retorts **10**
are second main air level and production level drifts **18″** and **20″**, respectively,

and second main upper, intermediate and lower retort level access drifts **22''**, **24''**, and **26''**, respectively. A gas collection level drift **28** extends at an elevation lower than the elevation of the production level drift system.

A variety of means for access from above ground to the air, production, and retort access drifts can be provided, such as shafts or adits. In a working case, one or more vertical shafts provide communication between the main drift systems and above ground. Such a vertical shaft or shafts can be used for ventilation of underground workings, for removal of liquid products of retorting, for transportation of workers and equipment to and from underground workings, for removing excavated formation, and the like.

A separate gas shaft provides access to the gas level drift **28**, and the gas shaft is isolated from underground workings on the other levels by unfragmented formation. The air level, production level, and upper, intermediate and lower retort access levels each includes a plurality of parallel, vertically spaced apart cross drifts **30, 32, 34, 36** and **38**, respectively, extending perpendicular to the main drifts at opposite ends of the cross drifts. There is a separate set of such upper, intermediate and lower retort access level cross drifts **34, 36** and **38** for each row of retorts **10** being formed. Each of the upper, intermediate and lower retort level access cross drifts extends through the opposite side boundaries of the retorts being formed in such a row.

The portions of the retort access cross drifts **34, 36,** and **38** extending between retorts **10** are exaggerated in length in Figure 3.4a for clarity. Moreover, only a small portion of the total number of retorts **10** in a tract is shown in Figure 3.4a for clarity. The ends of the air level, production level and retort access level cross drifts open into corresponding first and second main ventilation drifts located at opposite ends of the cross drifts. Although not shown, there can be a slight pitch or slope in each production level cross drift **32** from its longitudinal center toward the first and second main production level drifts **20** and **20''** so that liquid products produced during retorting flow toward the main production level drift system.

Each air level cross drift **30** is formed between two adjacent rows of retorts albeit at a higher elevation than the fragmented masses. That is, the air level cross drifts are in a vertical plane that lies between the side boundaries of the fragmented masses in a pair of adjacent rows of retorts. Similarly, each production level cross drift **32** also extends between two adjacent rows of retorts and at an elevation below the bottom boundaries. Each production level cross drift **32** is located directly below a corresponding air level cross drift **30**.

Each air level cross drift **30** and each production level cross drift **32** provides ventilation and/or retorting air and a liquid collection system, respectively, for two adjacent rows of retorts, i.e., for the row on either side of such drifts. To this end, a plurality of longitudinally spaced apart stub drifts **40** are excavated perpendicularly away from opposite sides of each production level cross drift **32**.

Each stub drift **40** is driven to a location below the center of a retort on one side of the production level cross drift. The stub drifts **40** are used to collect liquid and gaseous products from the retorts **10** during production and to convey the products to their corresponding production level cross drift **32** which, in turn, is used to convey liquid products to the main liquid collection drift system **20**. Gaseous products are conveyed to the gas collection drift **28**. Liquid and gaseous products of retorting reach the stub drifts **40** by way of bored holes **92** (Figure 3.4b) between such a stub drift and the bottom boundary of the fragmented mass in a retort.

The retorts in each row are formed at horizontally spaced apart locations along each set of upper, intermediate and lower retort access cross drifts **34, 36** and **38** respectively. Barriers **41** (Figure 3.4b) of unfragmented formation remain between each pair of adjacent retorts in a given row. In preparing each retort **10**, formation from within the boundaries of the retort being formed is excavated to form at least one void, leaving a remaining portion of unfragmented formation within the boundaries of the retort being formed. The remaining portion of formation is explosively expanded toward such a void to form a fragmented permeable mass of particles in the retort.

As illustrated, three vertically spaced apart horizontal voids are formed within the boundaries of each retort site. A separate void is formed at the elevation of each retort level access cross drift. A rectangular upper horizontal void **42** is excavated at the elevation of the upper retort level access cross drift **34**, a rectangular intermediate horizontal void **44** is excavated at the elevation of the intermediate retort level access cross drift **36**, and a rectangular lower horizontal void **46** is excavated at the elevation of the lower retort level access cross drift **38**.

The horizontal cross section of each horizontal void is substantially similar to that of the retort being formed. As shown, each retort level access drift extends through the opposite side boundaries of the retort site and such access drift is centered in each horizontal void. Each horizontal void has a horizontal free face having a horizontal cross section substantially larger than the horizontal cross section of the portion of the access drift extending to the void.

Each horizontal void desirably has a horizontal cross section substantially similar to the horizontal cross section of the retort being formed. The lower horizontal void **46** is formed at the bottom of the retort being formed, and the intermediate horizontal void **44** is spaced above the lower void **46**, leaving a zone of unfragmented formation **48** between the lower and intermediate voids. Similarly, the upper horizontal void **42** is formed above the intermediate void **44**, leaving a zone of unfragmented formation **50** between the upper and intermediate voids. The upper zone of unfragmented formation **52** can remain between the top of the upper void **46** and the top boundary of the fragmented mass to be formed.

The voids for each retort are substantially equidistantly spaced apart in the vertical direction and can occupy between about 15 to 25% of the total volume of the fragmented mass being formed. In a working case, each of the horizontal voids within a given retort site is substantially rectangular in horizontal cross section, with the outer edges of the voids lying in common vertical planes. In such a case, the retort level cross drifts **34, 36**, and **38** are about 30 feet wide and about 20 feet high, and the corresponding horizontal voids are excavated to about the same height. The voids are excavated about 200 feet wide and 200 feet long. The horizontal voids can be large open rooms or can include pillars **53** (shown in Figure 3.4e) for roof support, if desired. With a void volume having pillars **53**, the void is made higher in vertical dimension than a totally open void so that in each instance the void volume for the retort will be essentially the same.

It is desirable to prepare each row of retorts by essentially concurrently excavating the cross drifts for the air level, the production level and the three retort access levels. Such cross drifts are advanced or driven from the first main air level, production level and retort access level drifts **18′, 20′, 22′, 24′** and **26′** at one end of the row toward the second main drifts **18″, 20″, 22″, 24″** and **26″** at the opposite end of the row.

By connecting the opposite ends of the cross drifts to the main air level, production level and retort access level drifts, ventilation for workers in the cross drifts can be effectively provided at relatively low cost. Each production level cross drift is advanced concurrently with or ahead of its corresponding air level and retort access level cross drifts to provide an effective means for removing excavated formation as the cross drifts are being advanced. Several such cross drifts on each level can be advancing or utilized on each level for efficient utilization of men and equipment.

As excavation advances on the air level, production level and retort access level cross drifts, a number of vertically extending bypass raises **60** are formed along the length of such cross drifts. A separate bypass raise is provided for each group of four retorts in a given row. The first bypass raise **60** in each row is formed ahead of the first group of four retorts in that row. The barriers of unfragmented formation between groups of four retorts in a given row are approximately twice the width of the barriers between retorts in a cluster of four retorts to accommodate the bypass raises.

Moreover, for each pair of adjacent rows, the retorts in such rows are formed in two side-by-side groups of four retorts per row, forming clusters of eight retorts along the length of such adjacent rows. The air level and production level cross drifts lie along the middle of such clusters. In the system shown in the drawings, a separate pair of adjacent bypass raises **60** are provided for each cluster of eight retorts. The bypass raises are formed in the thicker barriers between groups of retorts.

Each bypass raise is offset laterally from its corresponding air level, production level and retort access level cross drifts. Although the configuration of each bypass raise can take many forms, in the system shown, separate horizontally extending lateral air level stub drifts **62** connect the top of each bypass raise **60** to the air level cross drift **30**. Each bypass raise then extends diagonally outwardly and downwardly towards its corresponding set of retort level access cross drifts. Separate horizontally extending lateral retort access level stub drifts **64, 66,** and **68** connect each bypass raise to the upper, intermediate and lower retort access level cross drifts, respectively.

Each bypass raise extends vertically between the elevations of the retort level cross drifts, and each lateral retort level stub drift opens into the side of the bypass raise and into its corresponding retort access level cross drift. The portion of each bypass raise below the level of the lower retort access level drift extends downwardly and outwardly to a corresponding horizontally extending lateral production level stub drift **70** which connects the bottom of each bypass raise to the side of the production level cross drift **32**. As retort preparation advances, the bypass raises **90** are used as muck passes from the air level and retort level access cross drifts. Excavated formation from driving drifts and preparing voids in retorts is dumped from these drifts downwardly through the bypass raises to the production level cross drift **32** where it can be transported by conveyors or the like through the production level cross drift to the main production level drifts for removal to ground level.

As retort preparation and drift driving continues to advance, each bypass raise previously used as a muck pass becomes available as an essentially uninterrupted ventilation air passage between the heading of the air level and retort access level cross drifts and the production level cross drift.

The bypass raises **60** are offset from the air level and the retort access level cross drifts so that there are no dangerous openings in the floors of such cross drifts. Each bypass raise is offset from the production level drift so that excavated formation or muck dumped through the bypass raise does not block the production level cross drift. After completing each set of upper, intermediate and lower voids in a given retort site, formation is explosively expanded toward such voids to form a fragmented permeable mass of formation particles containing oil shale within the boundaries of the retort.

The upper, intermediate and lower voids provide horizontally extending free faces toward which formation particles expand upon blasting. Vertical blasting holes are drilled in the zones of unfragmented formation between the upper, intermediate and lower voids. It is desirable to blast in sequence so as to form one retort at a time in a given row, advancing from one end of the row to the other. Figure 3.4b illustrates such a procedure in which formation in a retort **80** has been explosively expanded to form a fragmented permeable mass of formation particles containing oil shale.

Blasting advances from the retort **80** to the right in Figure 3.4b, one retort at a time. Between adjacent retorts the regions of unfragmented formation serve as gas barriers to prevent flow of gases between adjacent retorts. Following the explosive expansion step for forming each retort, gas barriers **82** are provided in the upper intermediate and lower retort level access cross drifts between the previously formed fragmented mass and the side boundary of the next retort being formed. The gas barriers **82** are provided to inhibit gas flow between adjacent retorts during retorting operations so that operations within individual retorts can be controlled independently of retorting operations in adjacent retorts.

It is believed that the gas barriers in the portions of the cross drifts between adjacent retorts do not need to be completely impervious to gas flow. Minor cracks or holes can be tolerated in most circumstances since pressure differentials are not large and the cross section through which gas could flow through a seal is quite small by comparison with the cross section available for gas flow through the fragmented mass in each retort.

Each gas barrier **82** is produced, in part, by the explosive expansion step which naturally forms a mass **84** of fragmented formation particles in the retort level access drift adjacent the fragmented mass just formed. In a blasting technique advancing to the right, as in Figure 3.4b, the portion of each retort level access cross drifts on the right side of each fragmented mass has a pile **84** (Figure 3.4d) of fragmented formation particles having a top surface formed substantially at an angle of repose of such particles. Each mass **84** of fragmented formation particles completely covers the openings leading from the fragmented mass to the retort level access drifts leading away from the fragmented mass. If desired, additional fragmented formation particles can be added to the top of a mass resulting from blasting. If desired, excess fragmented formation in the cross drift can be excavated to bring the face of the mass of particles approximately to the angle of repose.

The exposed face of mass **84** of fragmented formation particles is covered with a layer **86** of material which increases the amount by which the gas barrier **82** is substantially impervious to gas flow. The impervious layer **86** can be provided by pouring concrete, or shotcreting or "guniting" the face of the mass **84** of fragmented formation particles with sprayed concrete. Synthetic resins can be included or added onto the layer for further sealing or damage resistance. Reinforcing steel can be included in the concrete if desired.

A layer of impervious clay can be applied to the face of the mass **84**. A foot or so of thickness of such materials provides good durability and gas flow resistance in the impermeable layer. The impervious layer **86** serves to inhibit gas flow between the fragmented mass and the retort to be fragmented adjacent to it. The impervious layer **86** is then backfilled or covered with a top buffer layer **88** of mine run fragmented formation particles; other particles such as spent shale, crushed or ground raw shale or spent shale or clay can be used to backfill over the impervious layer **86**. Clay is desirable since it packs to form an impervious layer.

The buffer layer **88** over the impervious layer is provided to inhibit damage which might occur due to shock and impact loading transmitted to the impervious layer **86** when formation is explosively expanded for forming the fragmented mass in the next retort. In forming the next retort, the blast can cause a mass of fragmented particles to cover parts of the backfilled layer **88** of the gas barrier **82** in the cross drift between the retort being formed and the previously formed retort. A buffer layer about two feet thick can adequately protect the impervious layer from blasting damage. Thicker layers can be used if large mine run shale particles form the buffer layer.

As blasting progresses, the openings in the lateral stub drifts leading to the bypass raises **60** also are sealed. This isolates the air level, production level and retort access level cross drifts from one another. The lateral stub drifts leading to the bypass raises are sealed by dumping excavated formation particles into the drifts and pouring concrete or guniting the face of the resultant muck pile with sprayed concrete. Backfilling over the concrete can be added, if desired.

After fragmentation is completed in each row, the final preparation steps for producing liquid and gaseous products from a retort are carried out. These include drilling a plurality of feed gas inlet passages **90** diagonally downwardly from the air level cross drift **30** to the top boundary of each fragmented mass so that oxygen-containing gas can be supplied to each retort during retorting operations. Similarly, a plurality of bore holes or raises **92** are drilled upwardly from the stub drifts **40** adjacent the production level cross drift **32** to the bottom boundary of each fragmented mass for removal of liquid and gaseous products from the retorts to the production level cross drift **32**. The air inlet passages **90** and product withdrawal passages can be formed before explosive expansion if desired. During production or retorting operations, a combustion zone is established in each fragmented mass and the combustion zone is advanced downwardly through each fragmented mass by introducing a feed containing an oxygen-supplying gas to the fragmented mass. Combustion gas produced in the combustion zone passes through the fragmented mass to establish a retorting zone on the advancing side of the combustion zone wherein kerogen in the oil shale is retorted to produce liquid and gaseous products.

The liquid products and an off-gas containing gaseous products pass through the bottom bore holes **92** to the stub drifts **40** of the production level cross drifts **32** and advance to the main production level cross drifts **20** and/or **20''**. Because of the pitch or slope of such cross drift, liquid products flow toward the ends of the cross drift and are collected in a sump at each end of the production level cross drift. A pump is used for withdrawing liquid products from the sump to above ground. Off-gas is withdrawn from the gas collection drift **28** and passed to above ground.

Spaced-Apart Upright Retort Chambers

A.T. Janssen and K. Narayan; U.S. Patent 3,917,344; November 4, 1975; assigned to Atlantic Richfield Company describe a system for in situ retorting and recovery of carbonaceous values from underground formations of oil shale. A plurality of parallel access entries communicating with the surface extend horizontally at a level beneath the formation. Upright retort chambers are arranged at spaced intervals on opposite sides of each access entry.

The bottom of each chamber is interconnected with one such access entry by means of a sealed transverse tunnel. The retort chambers are ignited from the top and the carbonaceous values released from the shale by a downwardly progressing heat front are collected at the bottom. Oil recovery conduits extend from the surface through vertically directed bore holes opening into the access entry, each such conduit branching at that point to interconnect with opposite pairs of retort chambers through the sealed tunnels.

Further conduit means are provided for scavenging gaseous retort products through an annular space surrounding each of the oil recovery conduits so as to apply constant heat to the shale oil while it is being conducted to the surface. Means are also provided for insuring that a positive pressure is maintained in the access entries with respect to the bottom of the retort chambers.

Referring to Figure 3.5a, there is illustrated a pair of retort chambers **10** and **12** containing ore in a permeable, porous state, which has been formed within an underground carbonaceous formation **14**, such as, for example, oil shale. The chambers **10** and **12** may be formed by various means well-known to the art such as by explosive fragmentation and expansion. A preferred method for accomplishing such expansion is described in U.S. Patent 3,917,346.

With reference to Figure 3.5b, the chambers **10** and **12** are illustrative of any pair of such chambers interconnected with a horizontally extending access entry **16** on opposite sides thereof by means of individual transverse tunnels **18**. The access entry **16** may communicate at one or both its ends with the surface either directly through a vertical shaft or through intermediate horizontal drifts.

Figure 3.5: In Situ Retorting System

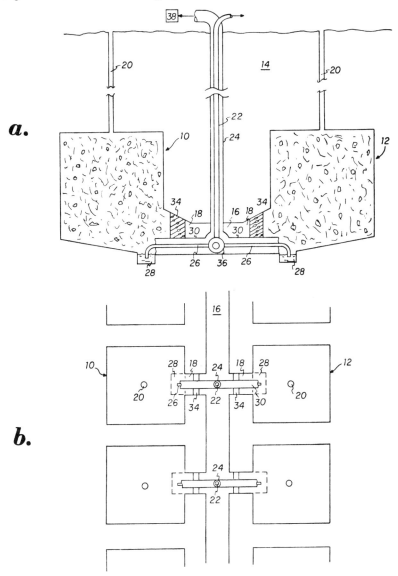

(a)   Sectional view of apparatus to facilitate the
       in situ retorting and recovery of carbonaceous
       values from an underground formation of oil
       shale
(b)   Plan view of a system for the in situ retorting
       and recovery of carbonaceous values from an
       underground formation of oil shale

Source: U.S. Patent 3,917,344

Preparatory to retorting of the chambers 10 and 12, at least one downwardly directed air hole 20 is drilled into the top of each such chamber from the surface of the earth or from an upper mining level. A source of air and fuel may then be introduced through each of the air holes 20 sufficient to establish combustion within the permeable mass in the chamber 10 or 12.

A pair of concentric conduits consisting of an inner oil recovery conduit 22 and an outer gas recovery conduit 24, encased within a suitable bore hole, lead vertically downward from the surface into communication with the access entry 16 between the chambers 10 and 12. At this point, a pair of branching oil pipes 26 interconnect the bottom of each oil recovery conduit 22 with an oil sump 28 situated in the sloping floor of each of the chambers 10 and 12 adjacent the respective tunnels 18. Preferably the floor of each chamber 10 and 12 is sloped with an approximately 10% grade downwardly toward the sump 28. In similar fashion a pair of larger open-ended, branching gas-collecting pipes 30 surround the branch oil pipes 26 and interconnect the base of the gas conduit 24 with the bottom of the chambers 10 and 12 respectively through the tunnels 18.

In order to prevent the passage of noxious gases between the interior of chambers 10 and 12 and the access entry 16, suitable means are provided for sealing the tunnels 18, such as bulkheads 34. Each of the bulkheads 34 may be, for example, several feet in thickness and constructed of timber and sand or concrete. Typical construction may include a board frame on the side facing the chambers 10 or 12 with a steel reinforcement on the opposite side facing the access entry 16, the latter to be removed after the chamber 10 or 12 is completely produced and abandoned. Suitable openings are provided in the bulkheads 34 to accommodate passage therethrough of the respective gas-collecting pipes 30 in a substantially air-tight fashion.

In operation, chambers 10 and 12 may be retorted in any known manner as, for example, by means of a downwardly directed heat front. As the kerogen in the ore in these chambers is pyrolyzed and releases its carbonaceous values, liquid oil flows to the sumps 28. An oil pump 36 may be positioned within the access entry 16 at the juncture of the base of each oil recovery conduit 22 and its associated branch oil pipes 26 so that these liquids are driven to the surface through the conduit 22.

At the same time, a vacuum pump 38 at the surface may be operably interconnected with each of the gas-collecting conduits 24 so as to effectively remove gas evolved in the retort operation from the base of each of the chambers 10 or 12. These gases flow into and occupy the annular space between the branch gas-collecting pipes 30 and the branch oil pipes 26. Thereafter such gases fill the corresponding space between the oil recovery conduit 22 and the gas recovery conduit 24. In this manner, heat is applied to the liquids evolved from the retort process from the time they reach the sumps 28 until recovery at the surface.

At the surface, the gases from the gas-collecting conduit 24 may be applied at the top of other retort chambers adjacent to chambers 10 and 12 for the purpose of preheating or, if sufficiently hot, for directly retorting such adjacent chambers. In a complete large scale shale oil recovery operation, it may be desirable to develop and retort, in progressive fashion, a plurality of adjacent chambers such as chambers 10 and 12 in accordance with this process. A practical and feasible mining layout well adapted for this purpose is described in more detail in U.S. Patent 3,917,348. Under these circumstances it may be desirable and economical to associate more than two individual retort chambers, for example, four or six, with a single common oil recovery conduit 22 and associated gas-collecting conduit 24. In such a case, a corresponding increase occurs in the number of branch oil pipes 26 and gas-collecting pipes 30. Also, it will then be desirable to direct such branch pipes 26 and 30 for some distance along the access entry 16 to arrive at their junction with the respective bases of a strategically located pair of concentric oil and gas conduits 22 and 24.

The shale oil evolved from a retorting operation as described will tend to thicken rapidly as it cools. Thus, one of the features of this process is that constant heating is applied to the oil from the point of its collection at the base of the retort chambers to the point of its recovery at the surface. The closer a downwardly directed progressing combustion front moves toward the bottom of the retort chamber, the hotter the gases become which are evolved and hence the more effective will be the heating accomplished by the process.

Although the gas-collecting conduits 30 may be tightly fitted within suitable openings in the bulkheads 34, it may be advisable to provide additional safeguards so that a positive pressure exists within the access entry 16 to protect working personnel against noxious gases, such as carbon monoxide. It will be convenient, therefore, to adjust the inflow of compressed air through each of air holes 20 in conjunction with the operation of the vacuum pumps 38 so that a slight vacuum is created at the bottom of each of the retort chambers 10 and 12.

It may further be desirable for ecological reasons or because of uneven terrain to confine the structural equipment normally positioned above the retort chambers 10 or 12 or like zones to an upper subterranean level. Thus, for example, the vacuum pumps 38 and the upper outlets of air holes 20, oil recovery conduits 22, and gas-collecting conduits 24 can all fall within such a subterranean level.

Permeability Control in Rubble Pile

A process described by *R.D. Ridley; U.S. Patent 3,951,456; April 20, 1976; assigned to Occidental Petroleum Corporation* provides a method for avoiding channeling of retorting fluids in in situ carbonaceous value retorting by selectively controlling the bulk permeability of a retort rubble pile to promote fluid flow throughout the entire retort. More particularly, the process provides a method for controlling the distribution of bulk permeability of a rubble pile in an in situ retort by progressively increasing the bulk permeability from the shortest to the longest path between a retorting fluid entrance and an exit.

Communication is established between the rubble pile and a source of retorting fluid. Communication is also established between the rubble pile and a carbonaceous value collector. The communication to the rubble pile for the collector is spaced by at least a portion of the rubble pile from the retorting fluid entrance into the pile. At an exit for the retorting fluid from the rubble pile, communication is established for the retorting fluid to a destination for the fluid. The radial distribution of the bulk permeability of the rubble pile is developed in such a manner that the resistance to retorting fluid flow through the rubble pile along retorting fluid paths through the pile is at least approximately equal along each path. The rubble pile thus developed is retorted to extract organic carbonaceous values with the retorting fluid, or at least with the aid of the retorting fluid. The retorted carbonaceous values are then collected in the collector. The retort is preferably vertical to avoid the problems attendant with horizontal retorting, of channeling due to void development at the top of the retort and vertical bands of debris having different bulk permeabilities.

The problem of vertical channeling is particularly acute in in situ retorts having low length-to-diameter ratios and it is here, therefore, that the process finds its greatest application. To take advantage of gravity and prevent retorted liquid values from entering a combustion zone in the retort, retorting is accomplished progressively from the top to the bottom of the retort.

The retorting fluid is typically air to provide oxygen for a combustion zone within the retort. Within the combustion zone shale oil value residuals, say, carbon, are burned to develop heat energy which retorts shale ahead of it in a retorting zone. The retorting fluid can also be superheated steam, recycled flue gas from the retort, or flue gas from an adjoining retort. The retorted values will collect at the bottom of the retort where they are transferred to the value collector by a pump. Typically, the retorted values will be freed from the shale in both gas and liquid states. Vaporized values will condense on the cold rubble into droplets at the base of the retort. The liquid droplets will agglomerate there.

Communication between the source of the retorting fluid and the rubble pile and from the rubble pile to the destination of the retorting fluid is conveniently accomplished by conduits. These conduits enter the top of the retort for the entering retorting fluid and leave the base of the retort for the exiting retorting fluid. A conduit may also be provided between the base of the retort and the collector, which is typically located on the surface above the subterranean deposit being retorted.

The rubble pile is developed by undercutting. The deposit to be retorted is undercut to promote a condition where the remaining roof is susceptible to free collapse, explosively induced collapse, or both. However, because of the adjustment in the resulting pile's bulk permeability, the easiest technique is through explosives. With the material removed from the undercut, the volume of the deposit to be retorted is free to expand into a larger volume constituted of its original volume and the volume of the undercut.

The bulk permeability of the rubble pile may be controlled through explosive charge placement or by leaving a dome of rubble at the terminus of the shortest path between the retorting fluid entrance and exit. The size of the individual fragments of shale can also be controlled by the explosive charges and can be used to develop the desired bulk permeability variation. It is possible, of course, to use combinations of these. Typically, the floor of the undercut is contoured to provide collection drainage for the retorted values.

According to a process described by *D.D. Heald; J.C. McKinnell and M.A. Lekas; U.S. Patent 3,980,339; September 14, 1976; assigned to Geokinetics, Inc.*, subterranean mineral deposits, such as oil shale, are prepared for in situ retorting by selectively mining out an area at the base of the deposit leaving an overlying deposit supported in a suitable manner such as by a plurality of pillars. The overlying deposit is expanded in any suitable manner into the underlying area in a fashion to create a predetermined distribution of permeability from an area of low permeability to an area of high permeability. An inlet is provided at the low permeability area and an outlet at the high permeability area. A suitable medium is introduced into the deposit at the low permeability end for extracting and forcing mineral values from the deposit toward the outlet end for recovery.

Formation of Rich and Lean Zones

A.E. Lewis; U.S. Patent 4,017,119; April 12, 1977; assigned to The U.S. Energy Research and Development Administration describes a method for rubblizing an oil shale deposit that has been formed in alternate horizontal layers of rich and lean shale. The process includes the steps of:

> driving a horizontal tunnel along the lower edge of a rich shale layer of the deposit;
> sublevel caving by fan drilling and blasting of both rich and lean overlying shale layers at the distal end of the tunnel to rubblize the layers;
> removing a substantial amount of the accessible rubblized rich shale to permit the overlying rubblized lean shale to drop to tunnel floor level to form a column of lean shale;
> performing additional sublevel caving of rich and lean shale towards the proximate end of the tunnel;
> removal of a substantial amount of the additionally rubblized rich shale to allow the overlying rubblized lean shale to drop to tunnel floor level to form another column of rubblized lean shale;
> similarly performing additional steps of sublevel caving and removal of rich rubble to form additional columns of lean shale rubble in the rich shale rubble in the tunnel; and
> driving additional horizontal tunnels in the deposit and similarly rubblizing the overlying layers of rich and lean shale and forming columns of rubblized lean shale in the rich, thereby forming an in situ oil shale retort having zones of lean shale that remain permeable to hot retorting fluids in the presence of high rubble pile pressures and high retorting temperatures.

Since oil shale deposits generally are composed of rich and lean layers, the process leads to substantial mixing, in a gross sense, of the rich and lean shale by formation of a series of columns throughout the rubblized deposit, thereby minimizing the effect of plastic flow of rich shale at retorting temperatures, typically 400° to 500°C, and high pressures; shale deposits are often in the range of 2,000 feet thick.

The rich shale starts to deform around 300°C, while the lean shale does not significantly compress or flow at retorting temperatures and rubble pile pressures so that hot fluid passages throughout the rubblized deposit are maintained open during retorting. The shale fragments are also formed of an optimum size to maintain open passages at the various depths by monitoring the fragment size during blasting at each level. Sublevel caving and partial rubble removal provides automatic access to rubble fragments for examination as to size so that the drilling and blasting of overlying shale layers may be continuously modified to attain the optimum size fragments.

Successive Rubblizing and Combustion

W.P. Acheson, H.H.A. Huygen and R.P. Trump; U.S. Patent 4,015,664; April 5, 1977; assigned to Gulf Research & Development Co. describe a method for recovering shale oil and gas from subsurface oil shale deposits in which free space is formed in the shale deposit and relieved blasting toward the free space from first shot holes drilled into the shale from the ground surface fills the free space with rubble. In situ combustion of the rubblized shale decomposes organic material in the shale to form shale oil and gas, which are conveyed by combustion products through the shot holes to the surface, and leaves a weak, easily compressible spent shale.

After the in situ combustion, shale surrounding the spent shale is rubblized by explosives detonated in second shot holes blasting toward the previously retorted zone. The second shot holes, which also are drilled from the surface into the shale, are spaced laterally from the first shot holes. The rubblized shale is then retorted by in situ combustion. The successive rubblizing and in situ combustion steps can be repeated to move the combustion operation laterally through the shale deposit.

W.A. Hoyer; U.S. Patent 4,091,869; May 30, 1978; assigned to Exxon Production Research Company describes a method for enhancing recovery of carbonaceous materials from subterranean hydrocarbon-containing deposits. Initially, a first rubble pile in a carbonaceous deposit is retorted to liquefy and vaporize the carbonaceous materials. After a substantial portion of the carbonaceous materials are removed from this first rubble pile, a second rubble pile contiguous to the first pile is formed such that a portion of the second rubble pile occupies a portion of the space occupied by the first rubble pile. This second rubble pile is then retorted and the carbonaceous materials removed.

This process may be progressively repeated to systematically remove carbonaceous material from other portions of the subterranean deposit. In one example of this process, initially from about 5 to about 30% by volume of the shale in a first zone of an oil shale deposit zone is mined to create a void or cavity. The remaining shale is then blasted into the void space to create a rubble pile. Communication is established with the upper level of the rubblized deposit and a suitable high temperature, gaseous medium is introduced which will cause the rubble pile to release the carbonaceous materials as a liquid and/or vapor by downward flow of the gaseous medium.

The released carbonaceous materials are recovered from the base of the rubble pile. A second zone of the deposit contiguous to the first rubble pile is then fragmented and expanded by detonating an explosive charge such that the resulting rubble pile occupies a portion of the first zone. The carbonaceous material in the second rubble pile is retorted and removed in a manner similar to the shale oil recovery from the first rubble pile.

Thermomechanical Fracturing

A process described by *J.R. Bohn and D.J. Pearson; U.S. Patent 4,083,604; April 11, 1978; assigned to TRW Inc.* relates to a method for producing a fracturing pattern in subsurface oil shale deposits. Non-steady-state thermal stresses arise as a result of transient temperature gradients in a body and the corresponding differential thermal expansion which cannot be accommodated by geometrically compatible displacement within the body. These stresses continually adjust themselves in such a way that the internal forces in the body are self-equilibrating and the displacements are compatible. If, in the process, either the stresses or the strains reach some critical value, failure may occur.

In general, either fracture or excessive deformation may be taken as the critical failure mode. The expression "thermal shock" has been defined by materials investigators as catastrophic brittle fracture which occurs as a result of high tensile stresses which are generated at the cooler side of transiently heated bodies. These same tensile forces might instead produce excessive deformation in a body if the material were strong enough to resist fracture, or if it were ductile rather than brittle. Even if the deformation were not excessive during a single heating and cooling cycle, multiple cycling can lead to an accumulated deformation which eventually will become excessive.

One mode of failure for in situ processing involves both plastic flow and fracture near the heated surface of the body. Regions of checking or cracking have been noted near the heated surface where compressive plastic flow has occurred during heating. It has recently been discovered that the reversal of stress at the hot surface, from compressive to tensile, and the reversal of plastic flow from compressive to tensile, occurs not when the body cools, but earlier in the cycle, i.e., as soon as the temperature gradient begins to disappear. This will happen even if the overall temperature of the body is still increasing, as might be the case during sustained heating.

Thus, the heated surface material might be put into tension, which would be multiaxial tension in most cases, while it is still very hot to the point of approaching melting, and ductile fracture or hot tearing would very easily take place. Cracking of this nature could also lead to loss of material at the hot surface which might be mistaken for compressive spallation in any posttest evaluation.

In order to apply the theoretical considerations previously set forth, a core sample from the deposit which is to be extracted is subjected to a heating schedule to determine the thermomechanical characteristics of the deposit material. Generally, more extreme thermal gradients will lead to more extensive fracture and a smaller average particle size, while larger average particle sizes will result from more gradual thermal gradients.

These thermomechanical fractures will occur in three principle modes. In one mode, the hot retort wall (or surface of a boulder or rock) is put into compression compared to the cooler surrounding strata, and failure occurs in compression by buckling or spallation. In another mode, the hot inside wall is put into compression compared to the cooler surrounding strata which then fail in tension. In the third mode, the hot inside wall is put into compression and undergoes plastic flow during the period when the thermal gradient is relatively high.

As the heat spreads outward and the thermal gradient becomes less steep, a more distant material heats up, expands, and causes a tensile hot tearing failure at the hot inner wall. It should be noted that with the proper temperature versus time cycles that it is possible to preferentially comminute large boulders, blocks, and the cavity walls while exercising a lesser size reduction effect on smaller pieces of rubble. This is because the surface area to volume ratio of the former is smaller than that of the latter. Because of this, the former rocks can be subjected to larger thermal gradients for longer periods of time than is the case with smaller rubble which heats up in its interior relatively rapidly. As a result, the proper temperature versus time cycles can yield a more uniform rubble bed with fewer huge blocks which are wasted resource because of inefficient extraction, and fewer fines which greatly decrease bed permeability, hence greatly increase the process system's capital and operating costs.

Thermomechanical control of fracture can be applied to oil shale deposits to effect proper rubblization of the deposits so that mineral and hydrocarbon value extraction may be optimized. One particular area which has rich oil shale deposits as well as rich mineral deposits, is the Piceance Creek Basin in northwestern Colorado. This area contains recoverable oil shale, nahcolite, and dawsonite and lends itself to an integrated in-place process that first extracts nahcolite and is followed by shale oil recovery, alumina recovery, and finally, residual fuel values recovery.

In order for as much as possible of the mineral and hydrocarbon values to be recovered, the process must be conducted in a sequence of specific steps. In the first step, a core hole is drilled into the shale deposit, and the core is extracted. The core sample is then subjected to controlled heating combined with strain measurements and computation to determine the thermomechanical characteristics of the minerals and hydrocarbon values in the deposit.

When the thermomechanical characteristics of a particular portion of the deposit have been determined, an injection well and producer wells are sunk into the deposit. These may be coaxial, i.e., in the same hole, such as a reamed out bore hole. Steam is injected into the shale deposit to fracture the deposit according to the fracturing parameters of temperature versus time determined by the core sample tests and calculations and to remove the nahcolite mineral by leaching. The nahcolite leach, together with the thermomechanical fracturing, will produce a rubblization of the shale deposit which will render the deposit permeable and porous.

Upon completion of the nahcolite removal, the resulting gas-tight chamber may be tested to determine if sufficient rubblization has occurred. If further rubblization is required, the chamber may be exposed to further thermal cycling so as to produce the desired particle size which will result from the further fracture of the rubble. By continual monitoring of the rubble in the chamber, close control may be exercised over the chamber conditions.

After creating porosity in the formation by leaching the water-soluble nahcolite from the shale zone, and by inducing thermomechanical fracture, the chamber is pumped dry and in situ retorting of the oil shale can be accomplished by the circulation of a hot, pressurized, nonoxidizing fluid, such as heated low molecular weight hydrocarbon gas, steam, heated retort off-gas, comprising H_2, CO, N_2, CO_2, and mixtures thereof from the injection well through the permeable shale bed and out the producing well. During the retorting process, heat is transferred from the hot fluid to the shale, causing the kerogen and dawsonite to decompose according to the following idealized reactions.

(1)   kerogen $\longrightarrow$ bitumen $\longrightarrow$ oil + gas + residue

(2) $2NaAl(OH)_2CO_3 \longrightarrow Na_2CO_3 + Al_2O_3 + 2H_2O + CO_2$

(3) $NaAl(OH)_2CO_3 \longrightarrow NaAlO_2 + CO_2 + H_2O$

Neither reaction (2) nor (3) represents the sole mechanism for dawsonite decomposition, although it is known that reaction (3) is the predominant one at the higher temperatures and reaction (2) is almost nonexistent at temperatures above 650°F.

The in situ retorting process should be carried out in the temperature range of 660° to 930°F, and preferably between 800° and 850°F. These temperature ranges will permit rapid completion of the oil evolution from the raw shale, and the decomposition of dawsonite to chi-alumina which occurs about 660°F. In addition, cooccurring with the dawsonite is the nordstrandite which forms difficult to leach gamma-alumina at temperatures above 930°F. The retorting of oil shale at temperatures in the range of 800° to 850°F leads to a quality shale oil product with a typical pour point about 25°F, an API gravity of about 28° and a nitrogen content of less than 0.8 wt % according to Hill and Dougan in *The Characteristics of a Low-Temperature In-Situ Shale Oil*, Quarterly of the Colorado School of Mines, Volume 62, No. 3, July 1967.

In contrast, the shale oil from high temperature retorting can have a pour point of as high as 90°F and API gravity of about 20° and a nitrogen content of approximately 4 wt %. Thus, the shale oil product from the low temperature process may be readily transported to refineries by a pipeline, and on site upgrading becomes optional.

If the recovery of hydrocarbon values is not as great as estimated, thermal cycling may be performed using the retorting gas as the medium. Constant monitoring of the permeability of the shale bed should be conducted to note changes in pressure versus flow relation. Excessive comminution with its accompanying high pressure drop should be avoided.

Water Leaching and Explosive

P.J. Closmann; U.S. Patent 3,957,306; May 18, 1976; assigned to Shell Oil Co. describes a process for forming a rubble-containing cavity within a water-soluble mineral-containing subterranean oil shale. A relatively areally extensive void is formed in or above an upper portion of the oil shale by selectively leaching solids from a water-soluble mineral-rich layer in that location.

A relatively areally extensive permeable zone and/or void is formed within or contiguous with a lower portion of the oil shale by selectively leaching solids from a relatively water-soluble mineral-rich zone in that location. An explosive is displaced into the lower void or permeable zone and detonated, to fragment the adjacent oil shale by the action of the direct and reflected shock waves and the displacement of solids into the cavity.

The process is particularly applicable to regions of the Piceance Basin of Colorado in which significant intervals of oil shale are overlain by two halite beds. One such bed, the lower halite zone, is in or adjacent to the upper portion of

Figure 3.6: Explosive-Aided Oil Shale Cavity Formation

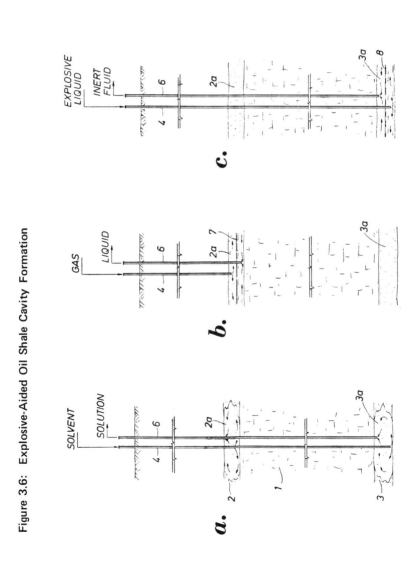

Source: U.S. Patent 3,957,306

a relatively thick layer of normally impermeable water-soluble mineral-containing oil shale. The upper halite zone is located considerably higher, near a portion of oil shale that has been naturally water-leached to become an aquifer capable of delivering large amounts of water. In these regions the oil shale layer is commonly about 500 or more feet thick and usually contains or is contiguous with the "Greeno" layer of nahcolite. In addition, there is a significant amount of nahcolite throughout the oil shale interval, particularly along the bedding planes. The Greeno layer often maintains a thickness of several feet for areal distances in the order of miles. The lower halite zone is similarly relatively thin and significantly areally extensive.

Figure 3.6a shows an early stage of the application of the process to such a portion of an oil shale deposit. A relatively thick layer of oil shale 1 contains an overlying or upper-portion-located halite layer 2, and a lower-portion-located nahcolite-rich zone 3. At least one well is drilled into those layers and is equipped with conduits 4 and 6. Such conduits can be installed in one or more boreholes and arranged, by means of packers or the like, to selectively conduct fluids into and out of the layers 2 and 3. As shown by the arrows, a solvent, such as a hot aqueous fluid, is inflowed through conduit 4 and outflowed through conduit 6 to selectively leach out an areally extensive void 2a in the halite layer 2 and areally extensively void or permeable zone 3a in the nahcolite-rich zone 3.

Figure 3.6b shows a particularly preferred case in which a low density, highly compliant fluid, such as a gas or a relatively light hydrocarbon, is displaced into an upper portion of the zone 2a while the aqueous liquid used to solution-mine that void is displaced out through conduit 6. Such a displacement is preferably continued until the gas/oil interface 7 is substantially contiguous with the bottom of the void.

In the stage shown in Figure 3.6c, an explosive liquid having a relatively high density is flowed into a bottom portion of the cavity 3a. This displaces fluid, such as the aqueous solution remaining after the formation of the void or permeable zone, out through conduit 6. Such a displacement is preferably continued until the interface 8 between the explosive liquid and the inert fluid is substantially contiguous with the top of the zone. The so-displaced explosive liquid is detonated, for example, by conventional means.

Figure 3.6d shows a relatively extensive fragmented zone 9 resulting from such a detonation. The well borehole of the one or more wells is redrilled or cleaned out to the extent necessary and conduits 4 and 6 are reinstalled and arranged for circulating a solvent in and a solution out. The solvent is preferably a hot aqueous liquid which is injected near the bottom of the fragmented zone. The solution is preferably withdrawn from near the top of the fragmented zone.

Inlet Gas Means

R.D. Ridley; U.S. Patent 4,047,760; September 13, 1977; assigned to Occidental Oil Shale, Inc. describes an in situ oil shale retort for a subterranean oil shale formation which has an inlet gas access provided to an end of the retort through which gas is supplied to initiate and advance a retorting zone through the in situ retort for converting kerogen in the oil shale to liquid and gaseous products. A zone of fragmented oil shale fills the in situ retort and extends from the inlet gas access means to the product recovery end of the in situ oil shale retort. The zone of fragmented oil shale has a length from the inlet gas access means to the product recovery end of the in situ retort in the range of from about two to five times the width of the zone of fragmented oil shale and an average void fraction of about 10 to 25% of the volume of the zone of fragmented oil shale.

In a typical example, the in situ retort is square and has a width of about 32 feet and a height of about 82 feet with a flat top boundary and a flat bottom boundary. The inlet gas access to the in situ retort is at about the center of the top boundary. A zone of fragmented oil shale having a void volume of about 15% of the volume of the zone of fragmented oil shale fills the in situ retort and extends from the inlet gas access to the bottom of the in situ retort.

The cavity filled with fragmented oil shale is formed by excavating about 15% of the oil shale within the volume that is to become the cavity. The remaining oil shale is blasted in a single round to form the cavity and simultaneously fill it with fragmented oil shale. A product recovery zone is provided in a tunnel connected to the bottom of the in situ retort. A sump for collecting liquids produced in the in situ retort is provided in the product recovery zone and a bulkhead through which conduits extend to remove liquids from the sump and gases from the product recovery zone is provided in the tunnel.

A combustible gaseous mixture of fuel and air or other oxygen-supplying gas is supplied through the inlet gas access means to the top of the in situ retort and ignited to establish a combustion zone at the top of the in situ retort. After the fragmented oil shale in the combustion zone has reached ignition temperatures, combustion is maintained and advanced toward the bottom of the in situ retort by supplying an oxygen-supplying gas to the combustion zone. The flue gas from the combustion zone is moved through the in situ retort on the advancing side of the combustion zone to establish a retorting zone on the advancing side of the combustion zone. The kerogen in the retorting zone is converted to liquid and gaseous products as the combustion zone and retorting zone advance through the in situ retort. The products, including shale oil, are recovered from the product recovery zone.

Fluid Communication

A process described by *J.C. Knepper and E.L. Grossman; U.S. Patent 4,120,355; Oct. 17, 1978; assigned to Standard Oil Company (Indiana)* relates to subterranean oil shale in situ retorting and methods for providing communication with underground retorts. Figure 3.7 shows an integrated oil shale retorting operation where both surface and subterranean oil shale retorting is conducted.

Subterranean in situ oil shale retorts **2, 3** and **4** are located within oil shale formation **1**. In situ retorts **2, 3** and **4** generally have slanted bottoms to allow for the drainage of produced shale oil through sloping tunnels **7, 9** and **32** respectively. These tunnels lead to separation zones **8, 10** and **33** respectively, where oil, gas, and water are separated.

These in situ retorts are formed by well-known techniques. Generally, a limited amount, about 5 to 40%, of the area to be retorted is removed to provide porosity. The surrounding formation is then rubblized explosively to provide a mass of relatively uniformly-sized particles of oil shale. In situ retorts **2** and **3** are filled with rubblized oil shale **6** and **22** respectively.

Figure 3.7: Fluid Communication for In Situ Shale Retort

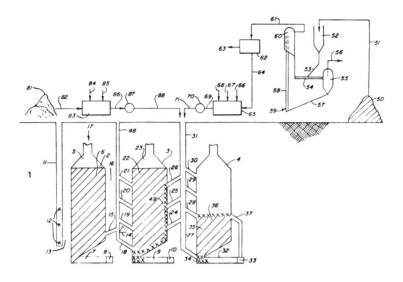

Source: U.S. Patent 4,120,355

This rubblized mass oil shale is retorted by passing a hot retorting fluid through the rubblized mass to release shale oil from the shale. This is commonly done by generating the gases within one or more retorts. Fuel can be injected into the top of the retort to initiate combustion. After combustion of the rubblized mass has been initiated, commonly air, or air plus water, or air plus off-gases from an operating retort, are passed downwardly through the retort to provide a flame front with advancing hot retort gases. These gases provide for the retorting of the oil shale and the production of shale oil.

The oil shale which has been removed from underground formations to provide for porosity for in situ retorts is commonly brought to the surface. This mass of oil shale **50** can then be ground or broken up to the appropriate size and re-torted in surface retorts. This oil shale can be passed through line **51** to vessel or hopper **52** which then passes the oil shale through line **53** to mixer **54**. In mixer **54**, fresh shale is contacted with hot spent or partially spent shale and heat is transferred to the fresh shale.

The mixture of shales is then passed into vessel **55** where shale oil is recovered from the shale and passed out of line **56** to recovery. Spent or partially spent oil shale is then passed to the bottom of vessel **55** through line **57** for further treatment, especially the removal of carbon. Pipe **58** is an elongated lift pipe which transfers spent or partially spent shale upward while air and/or fuel is passed upwardly through the same pipe from point **59**. In this lift pipe carbon on the shale is oxidized and the temperature of the spent shale is raised signifi-cantly. It is preferred to operate this lift pipe at a temperature of about 1200° to about 1500°F in order to produce a suitable spent shale for slurry backfilling.

The lift pipe is preferably operated at about 1300°F. Spent shale passes into vessel **60** and a portion of the hot spent shale then passes down to mixer **54** wherein it is contacted with fresh shale and transfers heat thereto. Off-gases containing some spent oil shale pass from vessel **60** through line **61** to electrostatic precipitator **62** which separates finely divided spent oil shale from off-gases. The off-gases are passed out through line **63**. The spent shale is then passed from electrostatic precipitator **62** through line **64** to slurry tank **65**. There it is contacted with water **66** and optionally small amounts of clay **67** or other additives **68** which modify various properties of the slurry.

The slurry is then passed through line **69** and can optionally be passed through pump **70**, such as a mud pump, through line **71** for injection into in situ retorts. In many cases, the slurry from slurry tank **65** can be injected down-hole without need for a slurry pump. In order to form drainage paths in in situ retorts for the passage of water, finely divided sand is introduced. This sand **81** is passed through line **82** to slurry tank **83** where water **84** and optionally additives **85** are added. The slurry is passed through line **86** through optional slurry pump **87** through line **88** for injection in in situ retorts.

Communication with underground retorts can be provided a number of ways. For example, a drill hole **11** approximately 4" in diameter, is drilled through the solid formation almost immediately adjacent to retort **2**. Intact oil shale **13** yet remains between the drill hole **11** and retort **2**. Explosive charges **12** are placed in drill hole **11** and exploded to provide communication from the surface through drill hole **11** into retort **2**.

In a similar manner, communication can be provided to the in situ retorts by directional drilling. Drill hole **48** is drilled down through solid intact oil shale formation **1**. At the appropriate depth, the drill hole is angled toward retort **2** through the use of a wedge **14** which has been placed downhole. This well-known often-used method of directional drilling provides lateral access through unmined intact oil shale area **16** into retort **2**. By the various techniques multiple lateral communication is formed with the retorts as communications **18**, **19**, **20**, **21**, **24**, **25** and **26** to subterranean in situ retort **3** and communications **27**, **28**, **29** and **30** to subterranean in situ oil shale retort **4**.

Either or both the slurries from lines **88** or **71** can pass through these communications into the in situ retorts. The sand slurry is intended to provide drainage paths to remove water from aqueous slurries of spent shale from surface retorting. In retort **3**, an approximately vertical layer or path of sand or sand slurry **49** has been provided. This approximately vertical drainage path allows the drainage of water from shale slurry placed within retort **3** down the side of the retort and across the slanted bottom and down through the normal path where product flows.

It is preferred to have sand slurry or sand or porous material provided at the bottom of the retort for good drainage. In retort **4** a porous layer **34** has been placed at the bottom of the retort. On top of this porous layer, a layer of shale slurry **35** from surface retorting has been placed. After some solidification of layer **35**, a layer of sand slurry **36** is placed approximately horizontally across the top of the shale slurry. After allowing enough time to ensure the stability of layer **36**, further layers of spent shale slurry and sand slurry can be placed successively on top of layers **35** and **36**. A small tunnel **37** is shown to provide a path for water draining through sand layer **36** from in situ retort **4**. This small tunnel **37** can provide a path for water to drain out, for example, to a separation zone **33** to provide for the recovery of the water. The water can be sent to water purification, combined with water from in situ retorts, or used for process water.

G.H. Watson and T.L. Speer; U.S. Patent 4,131,416; December 26, 1978; assigned to Standard Oil Company describe a process for the slurry backfilling of subterranean in situ oil shale retorts. The improvement comprises introducing a slurry of sand and water into the subterranean retort so as to form drainage paths for the removal of water from the slurry of spent shale and water.

The overall process for the subterranean in situ retorting of oil shale and disposal of spent shale from surface retorting comprises forming a subterranean in situ retort so that the subterranean retort contains a mass of rubblized oil shale; passing a retorting fluid through the rubblized mass so as to substantially retort the mass and recover hydrocarbons; cooling the subterranean retort; introducing a slurry comprising water and spent oil shale from surface retorting into the subterranean retort; and introducing a slurry comprising water and a material capable of forming a porous structure at one or more points in the subterranean retort so as to form one or more drainage paths for the removal of water from the slurry of water and spent shale from surface retorting. In this way the spent shale from surface retorting is effectively disposed of and a mechanically and environmentally suitable underground formation is established.

Cementation to Minimize Plastic Flow

According to a process described by *A.E. Lewis and R.G. Mallon; U.S. Patent 4,096,912; June 27, 1978; assigned to The U.S. Department of Energy,* in an in situ oil shale retorting process, plastic flow of hot rubblized oil shale is minimized by injecting carbon dioxide and water into spent shale above the retorting zone. These gases react chemically with the mineral constituents of the spent shale to form a cement-like material which binds the individual shale particles together and bonds the consolidated mass to the wall of the retort.

This relieves the weight burden borne by the hot shale below the retorting zone and thereby minimizes plastic flow in the hot shale. At least a portion of the required carbon dioxide and water can be supplied by recycled product gases.

Example: Raw oil shale was first crushed to 0.375 inch pieces and then loaded into a cylinder 3 inches in diameter by 9 inches tall. The cylinder was fitted with a piston resting on top of the crushed shale and subjected to a constant load of 50 psi. Provision was made for simultaneously heating the shale and flowing selected gases through it, always under a compressive load of 50 psi.

First, the crushed shale was retorted by heating in nitrogen to 500°C at a rate of 2°C/min. Heating was continued at 2°C/min for 30 min while gradually changing from flowing nitrogen to air; shale temperature was about 550°C at the onset of pure air flow. Air flow was maintained for the next 2½ hours while continuing to heat at 2°C/min until a temperature of 800°C was reached, thereby burning off the remaining char. The shale was held at 800°C under nitrogen flow for 24 hours thereby decomposing the carbonate minerals, and then cooled gradually to 100°C under nitrogen. The gas flow was then changed from nitrogen to a mixture of 85 mol percent CO_2 plus 15 mol percent H_2O. The shale was held at $100°C$ under flowing CO_2/H_2O for the next 6 hours. The recovered shale specimen was then subjected to unconfined compressive loading in a stress/strain test. The test results showed that this shale specimen carried a maximum load of 166 lb in unconfined compression, indicating that the burned shale in an in situ retort can be bonded into a load-bearing member of appreciable strength.

Experiments also showed that burning off the carbonaceous char remaining on the retorted shale is necessary for interparticle bonding. It was also found that the strongest bond resulted when the gas environment during cementation was a mixture of carbon dioxide and water vapor. The resulting bond is much weaker if either the carbon dioxide or the water vapor is absent.

Thus, the process affords a method for minimizing plastic flow of hot, rubblized oil shale during in situ retorting. By chemically reacting the burned oil shale in the upper part of the retort with carbon dioxide and water, the burned shale is cemented in situ. Such cementation greatly reduces the rubble pressure in the lower portion of the retort, thereby reducing the problem of loss of permeability due to creep.

Near-Surface Cavity Preparation

A. Zvejnieks; U.S. Patent 4,063,780; December 20, 1977; assigned to AZS Corp. describes a method of processing oil shale to recover liquid or gaseous products which comprises constructing longitudinally sloping trenches excavated in a mineral deposit which is relatively impermeable in relation to the crushed oil shale. The crushed shale is placed into the sloping trenches and covered with a compacted layer of clay or other relatively impermeable and essentially inorganic minerals.

The oil shale is then ignited at the upper end of the trench. Air is introduced at points along the upper end of the trenches and as the retorting zone moves longitudinally downward in the sloping trenches, the liquid and gaseous materials are withdrawn at points located at the lower end of the trenches.

According to a process described by M.A. Lekas; U.S. Patent 4,037,657; July 26, 1977 subterranean carbonaceous deposits, such as oil shale that are located at or close to the surface, are prepared for retorting by drilling blast holes from the surface into the deposit, and blasting, creating a rubble pile that reaches the surface. The surface is sealed by suitable means, and the oil shale is retorted in place.

Where a stratum of barren rock lies between the carbonaceous deposit and the surface, the blast holes are drilled and blasted in such a manner as to maximize the fragmentation of the carbonaceous deposit, and minimize the fragmentation of the overlying barren stratum. Where overburden conditions are not suitable for treatment by this method, the overburden is removed by strip-mining methods, and the carbonaceous deposits are exposed for treatment by the method described above.

RETORTING PROCESSES

Ignition Techniques

R.S. Burton, III; U.S. Patent 3,952,801; April 27, 1976; assigned to Occidental Petroleum Corporation describes a technique for igniting the oil shale rubble pile in an in situ oil shale retort. A gas-air burner is lowered through a hole to a plenum over the oil shale to be ignited. An excess of air is passed through the hole and around the burner so that it is kept cool as the flame from it impinges on the rubble pile. The air also transfers heat downwardly into the rubble pile and provides oxygen for combustion of carbonaceous material in the shale. Preferably the burner is in a cylindrical housing having a flame exit at its lower end so that a hot flame is ejected downwardly.

Figure 3.8 illustrates in vertical cross section and partly schematically, a burner arrangement for igniting a rubble pile in an in situ oil shale retort. Only the very uppermost portion of the retort volume 10 is indicated. This retort volume is simply cross-hatched as earth, however it will be understood that the volume is filled with irregularly shaped particles of expanded oil shale, ordinarily fragmented by detonation of explosives.

Above the ceiling 11 of the retort volume there is an overburden of intact rock 12. The thickness of this overburden is arbitrary and may be a few tens of feet in some retorting arrangements and may be hundreds of feet in others. A cylindrical hole 13 is bored through the overburden 12 to the top of the rubble pile. This hole may be formed either before or after blasting to form the rubble pile of expanded shale, but is usually made subsequent to blasting. Such a hole may be made by conventional drilling techniques and reamed out to the desired size.

A larger diameter plenum 14 is formed at the lower end of the hole 13 with its lower end in communication with the top of the rubble pile. This plenum may extend below the ceiling into the rubble for some distance, however, a principal portion of the plenum will ordinarily be formed in intact rock to assure that the plenum remains open. If a hole of any substantial height is formed in the rubble pile, the irregular pieces of rock may collapse into the hole and block it. It is therefore generally undesirable to form any great length of the plenum in the rubble pile itself. Some of the plenum is desirable in the rubble pile to assure fluid communication with appreciable void volume between the oil shale particles and minimize air flow resistance. The larger the cross section of the plenum, the less need be in the rubble pile for these purposes.

Such a plenum may be formed prior to blasting to form the rubble pile, however, the uncertainty that it will remain intact is such that it is preferable to form the plenum after blasting. If it is formed prior to blasting, it should be inspected to assure that an appropriate plenum remains after blasting. Inspection can be by remote television, for example.

The plenum is typically formed by lowering a conventional expanding underreamer or chambering tool down the hole 13 and reaming out an enlarged diameter. An appreciably enlarged plenum can be formed in this manner. For example, with a 10 inch diameter bore hole, a plenum in the range of 17 to 27 inches can be made with conventional tools. The length or height of the plenum need be only sufficient to accommodate a burner lowered therein and assure that particles of rubble do not sufficiently block the lower end of the plenum to inhibit the passage of combustion air therethrough. After a suitable plenum is assured, a burner **16** is lowered down the hole by cable **17** connected to a winch **18** above the overburden. Preferably the burner is lowered to a point that it is substantially completely in the plenum so that there is no obstruction of the hole **13** which would inhibit the passage of air therethrough.

This is not necessary in all cases and if small enough in diameter, the upper portions of the burner can be in the hole **13** without unduly constricting air flow. Further, the quantity of air needed during ignition of the rubble pile may be less than needed during retorting thereof. Air is forced down the hole into the rubble pile from any conventional blower or other air supply **19**, indicated schematically in Figure 3.8.

Figure 3.8: Ignition Technique for Oil Shale Retort

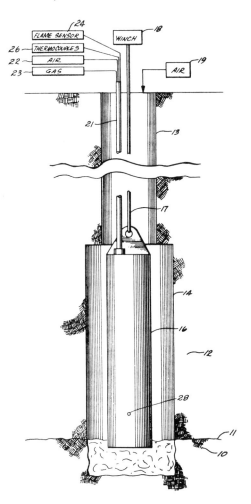

Source: U.S. Patent 3,952,801

A utility umbilical **21** is connected to the burner **16** and extends up the hole **13** for operation of the burner. Compressed air **22** and a combustible gas **23** are fed down hoses in the umbilical for combustion in the burner. Propane, butane, natural gas, flue gas from oil shale retorting, or other combustible materials such as oil can conveniently be used. It will also be apparent, of course, that oxygen-enriched air or mixtures of air and retorting flue gas can be used for either air supply **19** or **22**.

A conventional flame sensor **24** is also connected to the burner to assure that ignition of the combustible gases has occurred and that heating of the oil shale is proceeding. Thermocouples may also be provided in the burner and a thermocouple measuring circuit **26** is also connected through the umbilical **21**. The thermocouples in the burner monitor the temperature near the lower end where the most severe heating is encountered. This permits the operator to reduce the air and fuel supply to the burner to lower the rate of heat generation or, if desired, to increase the quantity of air flowing down the hole and around the burner to provide additional cooling.

A strong flame is directed out of the lower end of the burner to impinge on the top of the rubble pile in the oil shale retort. This burning is conducted until a substantial volume of oil shale has been heated above its ignition temperature so that the combustion in the rubble pile is self-sustaining. This vast amount of heat would rapidly destroy the burner and elements within it if steps were not taken to keep it cool. Air from the supply **19** is therefore forced down the hole at a sufficient rate that the cool air flow around the burner **16** maintains it at a safe operating temperature.

It is also desirable to force some of the air from the air supply **22** into the upper portion of the burner for cooling the interior. A hole or holes **28** near the bottom of the burner discharge additional cooling air into the region surrounding the burner. This air mixes with the air forced down the hole. This internal cooling of the burner with air that is mixed with the air surrounding it significantly reduces the internal temperature of the burner.

It will be noted that the secondary air passed down the hole around the burner provides the oxygen for combustion of the carbonaceous material in the oil shale heated by the burner. It also carries heat of the flame into the bed of oil shale particles for heating a substantial volume of the bed. As heating of the shale continues, a greater portion of the total heat adjacent the top of the retort comes from combustion of carbonaceous materials as compared with the quantity of heat from the burner and eventually the combustion in the retort becomes self-sustaining. At this point the burner can be turned off and withdrawn from the hole and retorting conducted in the normal manner with air or other gas passed down the hole **13**.

According to a process described by *W.J. Bartel and R.S. Burton, III; U.S. Patent 4,027,917; June 7, 1977; assigned to Occidental Petroleum Corporation*, an in situ oil shale retort is ignited by directing a combustible inlet gas mixture into an ignition zone extending across the top of the in situ retort and igniting the combustible mixture to create a combustion zone in the in situ retort. The ignition zone has a sufficient volume of interconnected open spaces for the movement of inlet gas through the ignition zone with minimal pressure loss, and the in situ retort below the ignition zone has sufficient void volume that inlet gas can be introduced into the ignition zone and moved downwardly through the in situ retort to the bottom. After ignition of the combustible mixture, additional quantities of a combustible mixture are directed into the ignition zone to maintain the combustion zone. Flue gases generated in the combustion zone are moved from the combustion zone toward the bottom of the in situ oil shale retort to establish a retorting zone on the advancing side of the combustion zone. When a self-sustaining combustion zone is established, introduction of combustible mixture can be terminated and an oxygen-supplying gas introduced.

C.Y. Cha; U.S. Patent 4,005,752; February 1, 1977; assigned to Occidental Petroleum Corporation describes a procedure for igniting an in situ oil shale retort with flue gas from an earlier retort. Towards the end of oil shale retorting, the flue gas from an in situ retort has a substantial fuel value so that it can be burned for generating heat. This fuel gas is conveyed to the entrance to a second retort and burned to initiate retorting. Even after retorting of the bed of particles in the first retort is completed, a fuel-rich flue gas can be obtained and used for ignition of a subsequent retort. In either case the prior retort has a large bed of hot spent oil shale particles through which air is passed to burn carbonaceous material therein. Hot flue gas from the earlier retort can also be used for preheating.

Multistage Operation

W.J. Bartel and R.S. Burton, III; U.S. Patent 4,072,350; February 7, 1978; assigned to Occidental Oil Shale, Inc. describe a method of processing oil shale in which an in situ oil shale retort comprising an elongated cavity containing a fragmented permeable mass of formation particles containing oil shale is formed in a subterranean formation containing oil shale to recover liquid and gaseous products. Access to the cavity is by a drift or conduit at each end of the cavity and through a drift at an intermediate position.

A processing zone is established in the fragmented mass at one end of the cavity and processing gas is introduced at that end of the retort and heating of the fragmented mass of formation particles is conducted from that end towards the other end. Initially, off-gas is withdrawn at the intermediate drift. When the processing zone passes the intermediate drift, processing gas is introduced through the intermediate drift and off-gas including gaseous products is withdrawn by way of the drift at the other end. As the processing zone passes the intermediate drift, processing gas is introduced at one end and off-gas is withdrawn from the other end of the retort.

Referring to Figure 3.9, the numeral **10** indicates generally a subterranean formation containing oil shale. Such a formation may be hundreds of feet below the ground surface. An upper level drift, adit, tunnel **12**, or the like, is mined or otherwise formed at a level in or above an upper portion of the oil shale formation. An intermediate level drift or tunnel **13** is mined or otherwise formed at an intermediate elevation in the formation **10**, the intermediate level drift **13** terminating in an excavated void, room or chamber **17**, which has a horizontal cross section which corresponds to the desired cross section of the retort being formed. A lower level tunnel or drift **18** is provided at a lower portion of the formation, or even beneath the oil-shale-rich portions of the formation. A vertical shaft or raise **28** or other columnar void is formed which extends from the

end of the drift **18** vertically upward through the chamber **17** to a level immediately below the drift **12**. The volume of the room **17** and columnar void
28 collectively are a fraction of the volume of formation to become the retort
corresponding to the desired void fraction of the fragmented permeable mass of
formation particles in the retort.

Thus, for example, if the retort is to contain a fragmented permeable mass of
formation particles having an average void fraction of 15%, the volume of the
room and raise total 15% of the final volume to become the retort. Explosive
is placed in the volume of formation to become the retort surrounding the
raise. This is used to explosively expand the formation in a concentric zone
about the raise **28** to form a retort comprising a cavity **26** containing a fragmented permeable mass of formation particles containing oil shale. Because the
void space of the room and raise is then distributed between the particles of the
fragmented mass of formation, the mass of particles substantially fills the entire
cavity.

After the explosive expansion of formation, a plurality of gas supply conduits
or openings **39** are drilled from the upper level drift **12** to distribution points
at the top of the retort. Air or other processing gas is conveyed from a suitable
blower or pump **40** to the gas supply conduits **39**. A conduit **41** in the intermediate level drift **13** extends through a bulkhead **34** into communication with
an intermediate portion of the retort (the chamber **17** having been filled with
fragmented formation particles formed in the blasting process). Initially, the
conduit **41** at the intermediate level is used to exhaust flue gas or off-gas from
the retort.

Figure 3.9: Multistage Operation of In Situ Retort

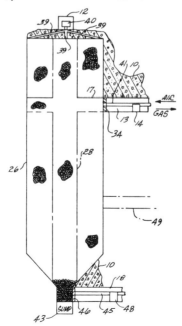

Source: U.S. Patent 4,072,350

A blower **14** is preferably connected to the conduit **41** in the intermediate drift and can be used to help withdraw off-gas from the retort during this first stage of operation while processing gas is being introduced at the upper end of the retort. The blower can also be connected to supply air or other processing gas to the retort in a second stage of operation.

The top of the mass of formation particles is ignited by initially mixing a combustible gas or other fuel with air admitted through the gas supply openings **39** to form a flame for igniting carbonaceous material in oil shale in the mass of particles. Once oil shale is ignited and a combustion zone is established, the combustible gas is discontinued and only a combustion supporting processing gas is introduced through the gas supply openings.

A combustion supporting processing gas, which contains oxygen, can be air directly from the atmosphere, air mixed with recycled off-gas or other combustible gas, or with inert gas or water vapor so as to have a reduced oxygen content, or air enriched with oxygen. Also, the processing gas can be substantially oxygen-free, and the processing gas can be added as hot gas to the retort for retorting the oil shale, or can be added as cool gas for transferring existing heat from hotter to cooler formation particles along the length of the retort. When the processing gas is oxygen-free, there is no combustion zone in the retort.

The economics obtained by multiple stage operation of the retort as described are not governed solely by the nature of the processing gas, but a gas containing oxygen is the preferred processing gas for most in situ retorting, and the most preferred processing gas is a mixture of air and water vapor. The heat of combustion of oxygen with carbonaceous material in the oil shale provides heat which is transferred by gas flow to heat the formation particles downstream of the combustion zone. This heating decomposes kerogen in the oil shale and drives off liquid and gaseous hydrocarbons as products from the oil shale.

The zone being heated below the combustion zone is known as a retorting zone and is the principal region in which kerogen is decomposed to produce useful shale oil. Heating of the particles to establish a retorting zone can also be provided by passing hot inert gas through the retort. Similarly, once a sufficient mass of formation particles has been heated above the retorting temperature (about 700° to 1000°F), the heat can be transferred along the length of the retort for appreciable distances by flow of processing gas without adding heat of combustion.

Thus, a processing zone comprising a combustion zone and a retorting zone is gradually moved along the length of the in situ retort by flowing processing gas introduced on one side of the processing zone and off-gas withdrawn on the opposite side. During the first stage of the processing operation, an off-gas including gaseous hydrocarbon product is removed through the conduit **41** in the intermediate level drift **13** while the liquid hydrocarbon products and water percolate to the bottom of the retort and are collected in a sump **43**. It is a principal purpose of operation of the retort to recover these liquid hydrocarbon products as shale oil.

When the processing zone advances to the level of the intermediate drift **13**, flow through the conduit **41** is terminated and off-gas is withdrawn through a conduit **45** at the bottom of the cavity. A pump or blower **48** is preferably connected to the conduit **45** at the bottom of the retort to assist in withdrawing off-gas. Thus, in this transition stage of the processing operation, processing gas flows in one end of the retort and off-gas flows out the other end of the retort. After the processing zone has passed the level of the intermediate drift **13**, flow of processing gas through the gas supply conduits **39** at the top is terminated and processing gas is introduced through the conduit **41** at the intermediate level. Off-gas is withdrawn at the bottom end of the retort through the conduit **45**. This provides a second stage of operation of the retort with processing gas being introduced at the intermediate portion of the retort and off-gas being withdrawn from the bottom of the retort. This mode of operation can be continued until processing is completed.

When formation in the retort volume is blasted to form a fragmented mass of formation particles in the cavity, there can be some nonuniformity of void volume distribution because of the room or void **17**. Formation adjacent the room at the intermediate level can move radially inwardly towards the center raise **28** or can move longitudinally inwardly towards the void to fill it with oil shale formation particles.

This can result in a somewhat higher average void volume or void fraction in this region of the mass of formation particles than in portions of the retort remote from the intermediate level drift. This is advantageous since the higher void fraction permits better processing of off-gas distribution across the full width of the retort than if the void fraction were rather low. This minimizes disturbance of the shape of the processing zone which is preferably nearly planar.

If desired, another intermediate access can be provided to the retort by way of a drift **49** illustrated in phantom in the figure. In such an example, processing gas can be introduced through the upper intermediate drift **13** during the second stage of processing and off-gas withdrawn from the lower intermediate drift **49**. Thereafter, processing gas can be introduced through the lower intermediate drift and off-gas withdrawn through the bottom of the retort. Any number of desired intermediate levels of access to the retort can be provided as desired. Processing gas is introduced and off-gas withdrawn through an adjacent pair of access means during the principal stages of retorting.

During the transition operation while the processing zone passes one of the access means, processing gas can be introduced and off-gas withdrawn through the two access means adjacent thereto to avoid disturbing the shape of the processing zone, which is preferably maintained substantially planar and transverse to the principal length of the retort.

By operating the retort in a series of stages where gas is passed through less than the full length of the retort, the flow resistance or pressure drop is minimized and the energy required for pumping gas through the retort is also minimized. During each stage of operation, the gas is passed through a portion of the length of the retort in a downstream direction from the previous portion.

The following is an illustrative example of a method of operating an in situ oil shale retort of the kind described above having access means in fluid communication with a portion of the fragmented permeable mass of formation particles intermediate the top and bottom of the retort. A combustible gas and air mixture introduced into the top of the retort is ignited by means known in the art as, for example, described in U.S. Patents 3,952,801 and 3,990,835. After ignition of oil shale, the flow of the gas and air mixture is discontinued and retorting proceeds with the introduction of a flow of air through the gas supply conduits **39** at the top of the retort. In the first stage of operation, off-gas is withdrawn through the side conduit **41** in the intermediate level tunnel **13** during a first period of time. Shale oil produced during retorting trickles down through the fragmented mass of particles to the sump in the oil collection system at the bottom of the retort from where it is withdrawn to storage.

When the processing zone comprising a combustion zone and a retorting zone comes near the side conduit, the side conduit is closed and for a second period of time, air is admitted through the upper gas supply conduits **39** and off-gas is withdrawn through conduit means **45** at the bottom of the retort. The approach of the processing zone to the intermediate level tunnel **13** is sensed by an increase in the temperature of the off-gas exiting from the side conduit **41**, or by thermocouples placed in the retort near the side conduit.

After the processing zone has passed the side conduit, it is reopened and air is introduced therethrough for a third period of time. The introduction of air through the gas supply inlets **39** at the top is discontinued when desired, as when it is not desired to heat incoming air or other retorting fluid by passing it through the hot retorted shale above the side conduit **41**. When the combustion zone has moved downwardly below the side conduit **41** at a distance of about 20 feet, in this case, the introduction of air at the top through the gas supply inlets **39** is discontinued. It is found in this case that the pressure drop between top and bottom of the retort is about 4 psig, whereas between the side conduit **41** and the bottom the pressure drop is about 2 psig.

Therefore, the processing of oil shale by this method can be conducted with greater ease when air or other gases can be withdrawn or introduced through a conduit in the side of the retort, intermediate its ends. Also, shale oil is satisfactorily recovered from the oil shale in the retort. Off-gas can be withdrawn through both the side conduit and the bottom conduit **45** during the processing of oil shale in the portion of the fragmented mass of particles in the retort which is above the side conduit **41**. The introduction of gas through the gas supply conduits **39** at the top can be reduced or discontinued when air is admitted through the side conduit or at any time thereafter.

As described above, a plurality of access means can be provided along the side of a retort between its ends. Air or other processing gas can be introduced into the retort through one or more inlets upstream from the combustion zone, an off-gas can be withdrawn through one or more outlets downstream of the combustion zone. Processing gas, with or without air, can be passed or recycled through the retort for the purpose of achieving processing of the oil shale.

Steam Leaching and Combustion

D.A. Hill, D.J. Pearson, E.P. Motley, T.N. Beard, and J.L. Farrell; U.S. Patent 4,065,183; December 27, 1977; assigned to TRW Inc. describe an in-place process for extracting water-soluble minerals to develop the porosity and permeability in oil shale, generating and recovering oil from the artificially leached chamber, and the subsequent leaching of water-insoluble minerals. This process is most applicable to oil shale deposits lying beneath gas-tight geological formations. To effect the process, at least one hole is drilled through the gas-tight structure into the shale deposit. Hot water, preferably steam, is pumped into the shale formation dissolving water-soluble minerals which are removed to the surface. Removal of the water-soluble materials renders the oil shale porous and permeable to hot gases which change the kerogen to bitumen which then decomposes into oil, gas, and tarry residue.

Simultaneous with the decomposition of the kerogen, is the decomposition of certain other water-insoluble minerals, e.g., dawsonite. In the penultimate step, the retort chamber is flushed with a solvent-surfactant to recover the hydrocarbon values and the decomposed mineral values. A tertiary hydrocarbon recovery comprises the final step in which pyrolysis of the residue produces a low Btu gas from the residual hydrocarbon values. When processing of the retort chamber is complete, the pipes are severed at the next level to form another gas-tight retort chamber. The process is repeated until substantially all of the oil shale deposit is worked.

Pressure Swing Recovery System

A process described by *D.J. Pearson and J.R. Bohn; U.S. Patent 4,059,308; November 22, 1977; assigned to TRW Inc.* involves pressure cycling of gases in an in-place process for extracting water-soluble minerals from an oil shale bed, generating and recovering oil from the artificially leached chamber produced by the mineral extraction, and the subsequent leaching of minerals which were water-insoluble before retorting.

This process can be used in conjunction with the process set forth in U.S. Patent 4,065,183. This process uses cyclic pressure swings of the process gases used in each of the recovery steps. Generally, these pressure swings may vary on the order of one cycle per minute to one cycle per day and have magnitudes of ±35% of the ambient pressure in the chamber. In the absence of pressure fluctuations, process gases become stagnant in the blind fractures or cracks, i.e., those fractures or cracks which are open only at one end.

When the pressure is cycled, the process gas is forced into and drawn out of the blind fractures, providing fresh processing gas and improved heat transfer with each cycle. Thus, the removal of the hydrocarbon, carbon monoxide, and hydrogen values or minerals is greatly enhanced. This effect is most clearly visualized by considering an empty blind crack. When filled with steam, the steam condenses to stagnant water, saturated with soluble minerals. Under constant pressure conditions, leaching would cease.

If the pressure is reduced, some of the water in the crack will boil, thereby expelling the saturated water, and making the crack accessible to fresh steam on the next pressure upswing. These effects, improved material and heat transfer, can also be obtained by pressure swings even when there is no phase change; since PV = nRT, the pressure swings will move process gas, products, and heat in blind cracks far more effectively than under stagnant constant pressure conditions.

Multistratum Reservoir

P. Bandyopadhyay and V.W. Rhoades; U.S. Patent 3,978,920; September 7, 1976; describe a method for recovering liquid hydrocarbons from a hydrocarbon-bearing subterranean formation wherein the formation comprises an upper permeable hydrocarbon-bearing stratum overlying a lower permeable hydrocarbon-bearing stratum and wherein the hydrocarbon-bearing strata are separated by a semi-permeable stratum which is substantially permeable to oxygen but not substantially permeable to water. The process involves combusting a portion of the hydrocarbons in the formation.

According to the process, the lower hydrocarbon-bearing stratum is ignited near the locus of the injection well, and oxygen-containing gas is injected into the lower hydrocarbon-bearing stratum to combust the hydrocarbons in the locus of the injection well and form a combustion front, an oxygen-containing gas is injected into the lower hydrocarbon-bearing stratum and an aqueous fluid is injected into the upper hydrocarbon-bearing stratum to maintain and move the combustion front between the injection well and the production well and to prevent or mitigate channeling through the upper hydrocarbon-bearing stratum.

Production Well Throttling to Control Combustion Drive

P. Bandyopadhyay and V.W. Rhoades; U.S. Patent 3,999,606; December 28, 1976; assigned to Cities Service Company have found an improved method for recovering liquid hydrocarbons from a hydrocarbon-bearing subterranean formation involving combusting a portion of the hydrocarbons in the formation. According to the process, oil production rate is improved by increasing the pressure of the condensing steam front preceding the combustion front, as by throttling the production wells.

Also, combustion front movement in the formation can be controlled by retarding the advance toward or away from at least one of a plurality of production wells by throttling gas production from that production well to increase the gas pressure therein. According to one preferred case, throttling is effected in accordance with the following relationship. The rate of oil production is given by:

$$q_o = \frac{7.08 \, k_o h \, \Delta P}{\mu_o(T) \, \ln \frac{r_e}{r_w}}$$

h is pay thickness, ft; r_e is drainage radius, ft; r_w is wellbore radius, ft; ΔP is pressure differential, psi; μ_o is oil viscosity, cp; T is temperature, °F; k_o is permeability to oil, darcy; q_o is oil rate, bpd; for a given k_o, h, r_e and r_w

$$q_o = \frac{C \Delta P}{\mu_o \, (T)}$$

where C is a constant. This, if ΔP_1 and T_1 are the pressure differential and temperature prior to back pressure, and if ΔP_2 and T_2 are the pressure differential and temperatures after applying back pressure, the ratio of oil rates can be calculated as follows:

$$\frac{q_{o_1}}{q_{o_2}} = \frac{\Delta P_1}{\mu_o(T_1)} \times \frac{\mu_o(T_2)}{\Delta P_2} = \frac{\Delta P_1}{\Delta P_2} \times \frac{\mu_o(T_2)}{\mu_o(T_1)}$$

Thus, oil production can be maintained or only minimally decreased as a result of optimum throttling according to the process.

Example: To illustrate the process, a center injection well and four outlying production wells in an inverted five-spot configuration are drilled and completed into a formation of about 6,000 ft of depth. The formation is approximately 20 ft thick and is composed of a porous and permeable sand reservoir containing a near saturation in the porous spaces with a very heavy bituminous petroleum and reservoir aqueous fluid.

Air injection is started into the injection well, and the formation in the vicinity of the injection well is ignited. Following a burning period of several weeks, water in controlled amounts is injected into the injection well to enhance recovery. Production of liquid hydrocarbons and combustion gas is effected from the production wells. A gaseous back pressure is maintained on the production wells in accordance with the relationship provided above.

It is observed that one of the production wells exhibits an increase in production of hydrocarbons and combustion gases in comparison to the other three production wells. The temperature in the vicinity of the well rises and the temperature of the fluids produced also rises. The percent of oxygen in the produced gas increases relative to the concentration of oxygen, carbon dioxide, and carbon monoxide in comparison to the other three production wells. These relative changes indicate that the firefront is channeling or differentially moving toward the production well exhibiting these changes.

The production well exhibiting the changes is throttled back exerting a gaseous back pressure in accordance with the relationship provided above, but five pounds gauge of gaseous pressure higher than the other production wells. In response, it is noted that production of liquid hydrocarbons is only minimally inhibited, but after a matter of several weeks, the other wells start exhibiting temperature, pressure, production, and analyses characteristics similar to the more throttled wells. Thus, differential movement of the firefront is corrected and enhanced recovery is obtained according to the process.

Combined Combustion Techniques

V.D. Allred; U.S. Patent 4,084,640; April 18, 1978; assigned to Marathon Oil Company describes a process in which cocurrent and countercurrent techniques to retort the shale in a nonoxidizing atmosphere achieve some in situ cracking which upgrades the quality of the recovered oils, and improves thermal efficiency by recovering most of the sensible heat from the retorted shale.

In situ combustion for the recovery of shale oil from oil shale formations can be effectively accomplished using a process in which retorting is carried out in a rubblized or fractured formation by initiating the combustion in an intermediate zone between the oxidant injection and the production facies of the formation. Under these conditions a combustion zone will move through the formation toward the point of oxidant injection so long as the temperature is high enough to cause spontaneous ignition and fuel is available to support combustion.

Concurrently, the hot oxygen depleted gas stream will move downstream forming a heat front (hot zone) into the production side of the ignition zone preheating the shale to retorting temperatures and forming a second shale oil producing zone. Upon reaching the oxidant injection zone, the combustion zone will reverse itself and burn back through the formation toward the production point consuming all of the fuel remaining on the formation as is typical of cocurrent combustion and also supplying the additional heat required to complete the downstream retorting.

Initiation of a combustion zone at an intermediate point in the shale formation being processed gives the most desirable combination of the cocurrent and countercurrent combustion process. That is: the oily matter being educed from the shale is produced in a hot nonoxidizing gas stream over a prolonged period of time so that the larger blocks of shale can be completely retorted; cracking of the oil takes place to produce a lighter gravity, lower pour point oil which will not plug the formation as it passes beyond the downstream retorting zone; and the fuel of the carbonaceous residue and sensible heat of the retorted shales are all effectively utilized.

Laser Retorting

According to a process described by *H.S. Bloomfield; U.S. Patent 4,061,190; December 6, 1977; assigned to The U.S. National Aeronautics and Space Administration* oil shale formations are retorted in situ and gaseous hydrocarbon products recovered by drilling two or more wells into an oil shale formation underneath the surface of the ground. A region of the oil shale formation is fractured by directing a high energy laser beam into one of the wells and focusing the laser beam onto the region of the oil shale formation from a laser optical system.

Compressed gas is forced into the well through which the laser beam was directed at the site of the fracture which supports combustion in the flame front ignited by the laser beam in the fractured region of the oil shale, thereby retorting the oil shale.

Figure 3.10 shows a vertical cross section of ground **1** containing an underlying oil shale formation **3**. A wellbore **5** is drilled into the ground **1** which penetrates into the underlying shale deposit **3**, and is provided with two ducts **6** and **7**. Central duct **6** functions as a protective housing for a laser beam **13**, a beam turning mirror **17**, and a beam focusing mirror **19**. Outer duct **7** provides a housing for annular region **10**. If housing **7** is smaller in diameter than well **5**, an annular region **11** is established by annular wall **22**.

The well **5** is shown as directed vertically downward through a shale deposit. However, such a well could also be directed horizontally through a shale deposit such as through the face of a cliff. It is not critical or necessary that either duct **6** or **7** be located concentrically within well **5**. The diameter of well **5** is not critical, although the diameter of central duct **6** should be greater than ten times the beam diameter. The depth of well **5** is only dependent upon the depth of the shale deposit or how far into the shale deposit the laser beam is to be directed.

At least one wellbore **20** is drilled into the shale deposit for the eventual recovery of gaseous hydrocarbon products which permeate through fracture zone **2** from wellbore **5** to wellbore **20**. The central duct **6** provides the channel by which the laser beam can be directed down into the wellbore and focused onto the desired portion of the oil shale formation. Thus, laser beam **13** from laser **15** is reflected by beam turning mirror **17** down into the central duct **6** of the wellbore.

Figure 3.10: In Situ Laser Retorting of Oil Shale

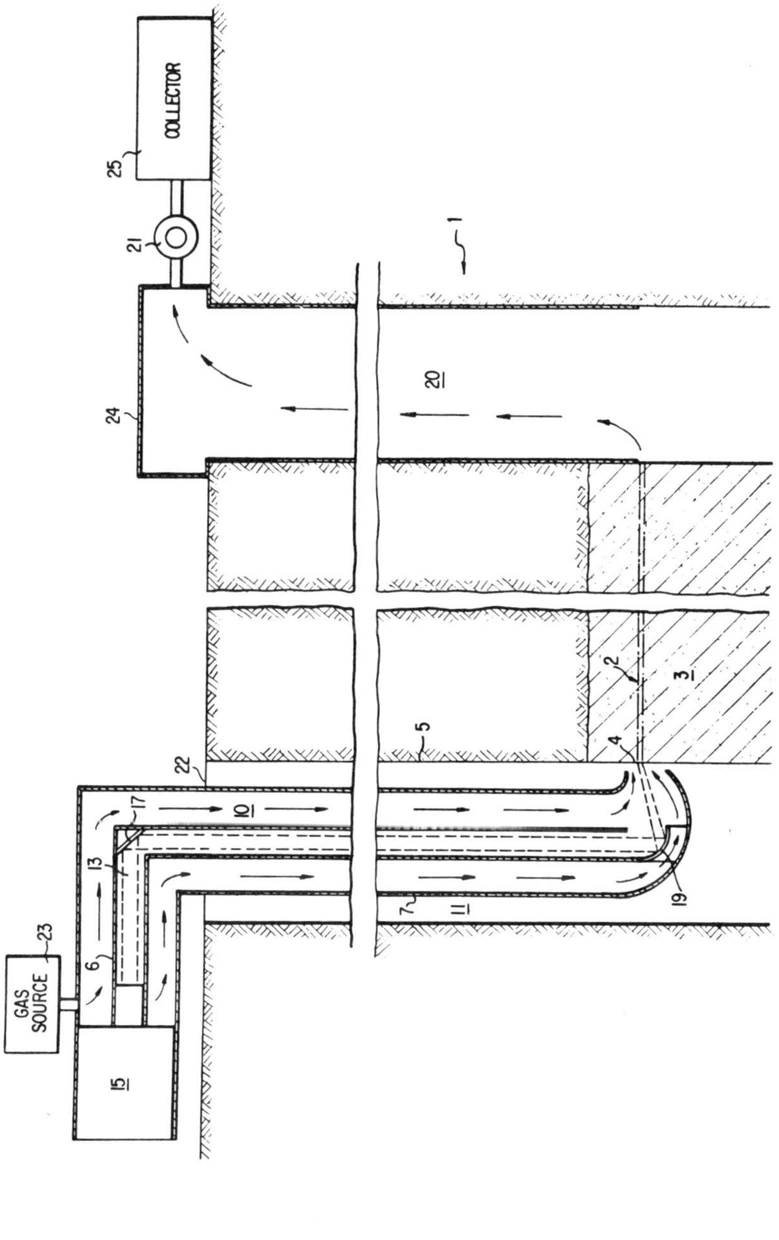

Source: U.S. Patent 4,061,190

Beam turning mirror 17 can be eliminated by placing the laser in a vertical position above the central core, thereby directing the beam directly down the central core of the well. The beam is then reflected at the desired fracture point 4 in the shale formation 3 by a focusing mirror 19 which directs the focused laser beam to a spot in the oil shale formation.

It is important that the laser beam strike the side of the wellbore 5 at an angle so that the slag generated in the fracture can flow from the fractured zone. The oil shale is rapidly heated by the focused beam to high temperatures by the action of the focused beam which causes fracturing of the region 2 of the shale formation which initiates combustion in the oil shale formation.

The focusing mirror is placed at the desired level in the well and fixedly attached to duct 7. The reflecting and focusing mirrors are fabricated from uncooled, low absorption reflecting materials which are compatible with the high flux beams used. The only important consideration is that the mirrors be capable of withstanding high flux densities. The laser beam which is reflected from the focusing mirror into the shale deposit is focused to an extent which is a function of the depth of the well and the original beam flux density. The beam is directed into the shale deposit for a time sufficient to cause fracturing and ignition of a layer of shale.

The first annular region 10 functions as a means for conducting a pressurized gas into the oil shale formation. The gas in addition to supporting combustion and functioning as a carrier gas for heated shale oil effluent, also functions to cool and clean the last focusing mirror 19. The gas must be capable of supporting combustion and therefore is an oxygen-containing gas such as air or oxygen. The gas should be relatively dry, i.e., low water content.

The gas could possibly contain a combustible component such as methane to aid in the combustion process, although such a combustible component raises problems because of the possibility of an explosion. The gas is injected into the well 5 under a pressure sufficient to maintain combustion in the shale zone from a suitable gas source 23. The flow of pressurized gas is continued only as long as the continuation of combustion is desired.

The focused laser beam generates a hole in the shale formation whose horizontal depth within the shale is increased until the stress gradient on the shale exceeds the strength of the shale. When this point is reached, the shale fractures preferentially parallel to the bedding plane. The introduction of the pressurized gas at the point of the shale fracture 4 supports a flame front which can advance through the fractured zone in the shale formation. The laser beam is turned off when the fracture extends between the wellbores.

The gaseous hydrocarbon product which is evolved by the retorting of the shale zone and is withdrawn through an adjacent well 20 closed by a cover 24 and is collected in a suitable collector 25 and processed for further use. A vacuum pump 21 can be used to facilitate removal and collection of the evolved gases from an adjacent well 20 and to direct the flame front selectively to the adjacent well 20. Since the gaseous hydrocarbon product is a complex mixture of materials, the manner in which the gas is subsequently processed is dependent on what types or blends of hydrocarbon products and hydrocarbon-containing gases are desired. The liquid hydrocarbon products produced in the process are not recovered and are allowed to remain in the well.

Low Head Fans for Frontal Advance Units

N. Daviduk, D.W. Lewis and M.T. Siuta; U.S. Patent 4,018,280; April 19, 1977; assigned to Mobil Oil Corporation describe an in situ retorting process for recovering hydrocarbon from a retort zone formed in a oil shale deposit wherein the power required for circulating retorting gas is substantially reduced during the latter stages of the process.

Figures 3.11a and 3.11b show an oil shale deposit **10** in which a gallery or retort zone **11** has been formed. The retort zone may be formed by any known technique, e.g., a portion of the oil shale can be mined out to establish a cavity into which surrounding shale is then rubblized by means of explosives or the like. For a more complete description of such techniques, see U.S. Patent Numbers 3,011,776; 2,481,051 and 1,919,636.

Figure 3.11: In Situ Retorting Process

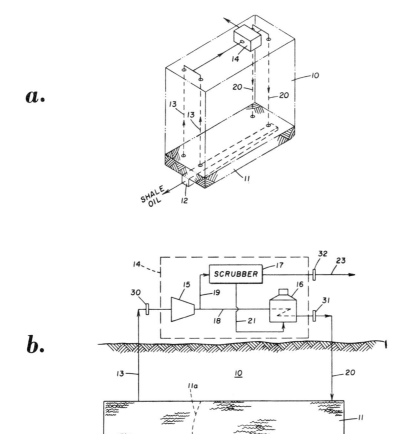

(continued)

Figure 3.11: (continued)

c.

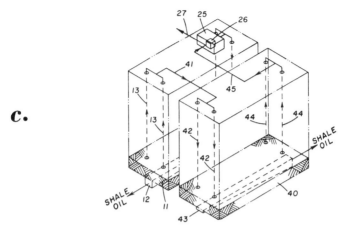

(a) Perspective view of a retort zone within an oil shale deposit
     undergoing an in situ retorting process
(b) Schematic view of the process shown in Figure 3.11a
(c) Perspective view of a modification of the process shown in
     Figure 3.11a

Source: U.S. Patent 4,018,280

In the process, a retorting gas is heated and circulated through retort zone **11**
to recover hydrocarbons from the rubblized shale within the zone. This retorting
gas is comprised of the gaseous products recovered from the retorting operation
itself. Gas may be temporarily supplied from an external source for start-up
operations. The retorting gas gives up heat to the shale as it is circulated through
and the gaseous hydrocarbons formed from the kerogen in the zone flow along
with the retorting gas back to the surface. The liquid hydrocarbons formed
from the kerogen flow downward by gravity through the rubblized shale into
sump **12** or the like from which they can be recovered through a well or the
like.

Looking now at Figure 3.11b, as the retorting operation is commenced, the off-
gas exits from zone **11**, flows to the surface through outlets **13**, and passes into
surface retorting unit **14**. Although only one retorting unit is shown in detail,
it should be recognized that the actual size and number of such units will be
dictated by the particular retort operation involved. Retorting units **14** are
basically comprised of compressor means **15**, heating means **16**, a gas treating
means (e.g., scrubber **17**), and the associated piping.

The compressor means, which is preferably comprised of one or more commercially available centrifugal compressors, boosts the pressure of the off-gas stream
to a value necessary to overcome the pressure drop which occurs in the piping,
the heating means, and the rubblized shale in the retort zone, thereby providing
the pressure required to insure continued circulation of gas through the retort
system.

The off-gas stream is split after it passes through compressor means **15** into a first portion which flows through line **18** to heating means **16** and a second portion which flows through line **19** to gas treating means **17**. The gas flowing through line **18** comprises the retorting gas which is recycled back to retort zone **11** through inlets **20** after it is heated by the heating means. The heating means is preferably one or more gas-fired furnaces which heat the retorting gas to a temperature, e.g., 1175°F, capable of retorting the shale in the retort zone. The gas flowing through line **19** is treated by means **17** to remove unwanted diluents, e.g., an amine scrubber may be used to remove the ammonia, hydrogen sulfide, and a large percentage of the carbon dioxide.

A part of this treated gas is supplied through line **21** to the heating means to serve as fuel therefor. The excess gas from treating means **17** flows through line **23** and may be used to generate electrical power, sold as industrial gas, or put to any other suitable use.

Surface retort units **14** are used to start the retorting operation and are used to heat and circulate the retorting gas until sufficient heat is available in the retort zone to complete the retorting operation without any further external heating. This condition occurs from the externally heated gas giving up heat to the shale as the gas moves through the retort zone. The shale holds a substantial portion of this heat and as more and more heated gas is circulated, the retorting front **11a** moves away from inlets **20** toward outlets **13**. The spent portion of the shale behind the retorting front increases in temperature and accepts less and less heat from the externally heated gas as the gas passes therethrough. Accordingly, the temperature of the off-gas from the outlets begins to rise as the retorting front moves further into the retort zone.

Based on a heat and material balance which includes such factors as the size of the retort zone, oil content of shale, inlet temperature and rate of retorting gas, etc., the time of switch over to frontal advance units is calculated to determine when there will be sufficient heat available in the spent portion of the shale behind retort zone to complete the retorting zone without further external heating of the retorting zone. Compressors **15** must be designed so that this temperature is below the maximum allowable suction inlet temperature of the compressors. At this point, there is no need to continue to externally heat the retorting gas since unheated gas flowing through the retort zone from the inlets to the outlets will pick up heat from the spent shale behind the retorting front and will be hot enough when it reaches the front to advance same through the remainder of the retort zone.

Since the retorting gas no longer needs to be heated externally, furnaces **16** are no longer required; and since the major pressure drop in the circulation path is due to the furnaces, there is no longer a need for the expensive and power-consuming compressors. Therefore, when the temperature of the off-gas reaches a condition indicating that no further external heat is needed (this normally occurring when approximately two-thirds of the retort zone has been retorted), surface retort unit **14** is replaced with frontal advance unit **25** (see Figure 3.11c). This frees the expensive, surface retort unit for use in retorting another zone (not shown). The frontal advance unit is comprised of one or more commercially available low head fans **26** which are capable of circulating the required volume of retorting gas to advance front **11a** but which require substantially less power to operate than did compressors **15**.

For example, in a particular retorting operation in accordance with the process, a single 48-inch suction, pedestal type 150,000 ACFM (actual cubic foot per minute) centrifugal compressor unit requires approximately a 7,000 horsepower electrical motor to provide the differential head necessary to insure proper gas circulation through furnaces 16 and zone 11. A low head fan capable of handling the same volume of gas, i.e., 150,000 ACFM, and generating sufficient circulating pressure with no furnaces present requires only approximately a 2,500 horsepower motor.

To summarize, surface retorting unit 14 is used to start the retorting and frontal advance unit 25 is used to complete the method. Compressor means 15 is needed to develop the pressure necessary to force the retorting gas through the high pressure drop heating means 16 where the gas is heated to high temperature before it is injected into retort zone 11. When the temperature of the off-gas from the retort zone indicates that adequate heat is available in the zone to complete retorting operations, surface retorting unit 14 is replaced with frontal advance unit 25 which circulates the necessary gas with substantially less power requirements. Although the retorting gas is not externally heated when the frontal advance unit is in use, the gas picks up sufficient heat from the previously retorted portion of the retort zone as it moves from inlets 20 to outlets 13 to thereby continue the advance of the heat front through the retort zone.

To aid in replacing surface retorting unit 14 with frontal unit 25, both the units are portable in that the units are preferably skid mounted (not shown) and the piping has common flanging as at 30, 31, 32 (Figure 3.11b) so that the units may be exchanged as easily as possible. For most commercial-sized operations, the size and weight of these units will be substantial and since they will likely be transported in rough terrain, tracked vehicles or those having large diameter wheels will likely be required.

When the retorting operation of the process reaches the point where the surface retorting unit is replaced with the frontal advance unit, off-gas from outlets 13 is routed into a second retort zone 40 by means of piping 41 and inlets 42. The off-gas from zone 11 passes through the rubblized shale in zone 40 and gives up heat to preheat zone 40 and aids in eventual retorting of zone 40. Also, this cools the off-gas so that it can be more easily handled at the surface. Still further, the heavier hydrocarbons in the hot off-gas condense in relatively cool zone 40 and can be recovered later from sump 43.

After the off-gas from zone 11 passes through zone 40, it flows to the surface through outlets 44 and via piping 45 is fed into frontal advance unit 25. That portion of the gas that is to be recirculated is fed to the suction of low head fan 26 within unit 25 while any excess gas is split off through line 27 for suitable deposition. Circulation of the off-gas is continued through frontal unit 25 until the retorting process in zone 11 has been completed.

Buffer Zone of Retorted Oil Shale

A process developed by *C.Y. Cha; U.S. Patent 4,126,180; Nov. 21, 1978; assigned to Occidental Oil Shale, Inc.* concerns a method for recovering liquid and gaseous products from an in situ oil shale retort in a subterranean formation containing oil shale, where the in situ retort contains a fragmented permeable mass of formation particles containing oil shale.

According to this method, a buffer zone of hot retorted oil shale containing residual carbonaceous material is established in the fragmented permeable mass by passing a hot processing gas through at least a portion of the fragmented permeable mass. The hot processing gas is substantially free of free oxygen and has a temperature at least as high as the retorting temperature of oil shale in the fragmented mass.

Thereafter, a combustion zone advancing through the fragmented permeable mass is established in the buffer zone. A combustion zone feed containing oxygen is introduced into the fragmented mass on the trailing side of the combustion material in retorted oil shale in the buffer zone. This advances the combustion zone through the fragmented mass and retorts oil shale to liquid and gaseous products in a retorting zone on the advancing side of the combustion and buffer zones. The thickness of the buffer zone is sufficient for reaction of most, and preferably at least 80%, of the oxygen in the combustion zone feed with residual carbonaceous material in retorted oil shale in the buffer zone. With such a buffer zone, oxidation of hydrocarbon products produced in the retorting zone is minimized.

The hot processing gas can be generated by burning a fuel. The fuel, which can be burned in the fragmented permeable mass containing the buffer zone, can be a fuel-containing gas. A fuel-containing gas can be generated by introducing an oxygen-containing gas into a second fragmented permeable mass of formation particles containing hot retorted oil shale.

Gas Introduction and Blockage

A process described by *W.J. Bartel, R.S. Burton, III and C.Y. Cha; U.S. Patent 4,119,345; October 10, 1978; assigned to Occidental Oil Shale, Inc.* is directed toward an improved method for recovering values from an in situ oil shale retort in a subterranean formation containing oil shale, the in situ retort containing a fragmented permeable mass of formation particles having side boundaries, a first end boundary, and a second end boundary. The method comprises passing a measuring gas through the fragmented mass between the first and second end boundaries of the fragmented mass. The unit pressure drop of the measuring gas is measured in a first portion of the fragmented mass between the first end boundary and an intermediate location between the first end boundary and the second end boundary of the fragmented mass.

The unit pressure drop is also measured in a second portion of the fragmented mass between the intermediate location and the second end boundary. This is done to determine if the unit pressure drop of the measuring gas is substantially greater in the first portion than in the second portion of the fragmented mass. If the unit pressure drop of the measuring gas is substantially greater in the first portion than in the second portion of the fragmented mass, a processing gas is introduced to the retort at an intermediate location between the first portion of the fragmented mass and the second end boundary of the fragmented mass for processing oil shale in the retort in the second portion of the fragmented mass.

This leaves unprocessed oil shale in the first portion of the fragmented mass. The first end boundary of the fragmented mass can be the top of the retort and the second end boundary of the fragmented mass can be the bottom of the retort.

Alternatively, the first end boundary of the fragmented mass can be the bottom of the retort and the second end boundary of the fragmented mass can be the top of the retort.

Water Injection

According to a process described by *C.Y. Cha; U.S. Patent 4,089,375; May 16, 1978; assigned to Occidental Oil Shale, Inc.* a combustion zone is advanced through an in situ oil retort in a subterranean formation containing oil shale. The retort contains a fragmented permeable mass of formation particles containing oil shale. The combustion zone is advanced through the retort by introducing into the retort on the trailing side of the combustion zone a retort inlet mixture comprising liquid water, at least sufficient fuel to vaporize the water, and sufficient oxygen to oxidize the fuel for vaporizing the water and to form a gaseous combustion zone feed containing water vapor and oxygen. The gaseous combustion zone feed is introduced into the combustion zone to advance the combustion zone through the fragmented mass of particles and produce combustion gas in the combustion zone.

Liquid and gaseous products are produced in the retort by passing the combustion gas generated in the combustion zone and any unreacted portion of the combustion zone feed through a retorting zone in the fragmented mass of particles on the advancing side of the combustion zone. Heat transferred from the combustion zone to the retorting zone retorts oil shale to produce gaseous and liquid products. The liquid products and a retort off-gas containing the gaseous products, combustion gas, gas from carbonate decomposition, and any gaseous unreacted portion of the retort inlet mixture are withdrawn from the retort from the advancing side of the retorting zone.

The liquid products include hydrocarbon product and water. Portions of the hydrocarbon product and/or the water can be used to supply at least a portion of the fuel and/or water of the retort inlet mixture. Preferably, the retort inlet mixture is introduced into the retort at a sufficient rate to form gaseous combustion zone feed having a superficial volumetric flow rate of from about 0.1 to about 2 standard cubic ft/min (SCFM) per square foot of cross-sectional area of the fragmented permeable mass being retorted, and more preferably, from about 0.5 to about 1 SCFM per square foot of cross-sectional area of the fragmented permeable mass being retorted.

At such a total combustion zone feed rate, the retort inlet mixture introduced to the retort preferably contains sufficient oxygen that the combustion zone feed contains from about 1 to about 20% oxygen, and more preferably from about 10 to about 15% oxygen by volume. Because of its ready availability, air is the preferred source of oxygen.

Preferably the retort inlet mixture contains sufficient water that the gaseous combustion zone feed contains from about 10 to about 50% water vapor by volume, and more preferably from about 20 to about 40% water vapor by volume. Preferably, the combustion zone is maintained at a temperature greater than about 900°F, and more preferably greater than about 1100°F, to ensure fast retorting in the retorting zone, but less than about 1800°F to prevent fusion of the oil shale.

A related process described by *C.Y. Cha and R.D. Ridley; U.S. Patent 4,036,299; July 19, 1977; assigned to Occidental Oil Shale Inc.* is a method of retorting fragmented oil shale in an in situ retort comprising: establishing a combustion zone in the fragmented oil shale in an in situ oil shale retort; introducing into the combustion zone, in the direction in which the combustion zone is to be advanced, a gaseous feed mixture comprising an oxygen-supplying gas and water vapor; generating combustion product gases in the combustion zone, which together with unreacted feed mixture gases form a flue gas which passes through the retort in the direction of the advancement of the combustion zone, thereby retorting the oil shale on the advancing side of the combustion zone to produce liquid and gaseous products. Liquid product and retort off-gas comprising gaseous products and flue gases are withdrawn from the in situ oil shale retort at a point on the advancing side of the combustion zone.

This process provides a method for retorting fragmented oil shale in an in situ oil shale retort by which the temperature of the combustion zone can be controlled, heat is more efficiently transferred from the combustion zone to fragmented oil shale in the retorting zone, the yield of liquid product is increased, and the heating value of the off-gas is improved. The volume of water withdrawn from the in situ oil shale retort is greater than the volume of water attributable to combustion and retorting and can be attributed to condensation of water vapor on the oil shale on the advancing side of the retorting zone.

The quantity of water vapor in the retort off-gas is less than the water vapor introduced into the in situ oil shale retort and the water which is attributable to retorting and combustion. The reduced quantity of water vapor can be attributed to condensation of water vapor on unretorted oil shale on the advancing side of the retorting zone and the separation of water vapor from gases in the in situ oil shale retort.

Oil Collection System

According to a process developed by *R.D. Ridley; U.S. Patent 4,007,963; Feb. 15, 1977; assigned to Occidental Petroleum Corporation* an in situ oil shale retort is provided with a sealed space at the bottom in which liquids produced in the in situ retort and retort off-gases are separated. The separated liquids and retort off-gases are removed from the sealed space through a bulkhead provided in an access tunnel leading to the sealed space which can be a portion of the tunnel. A sump is provided in the floor of the access tunnel inside the sealed space for collecting liquids. Trenches extending from the bottom of the in situ retort into the sump are provided for directing liquids from the in situ retort to the sump.

The trenches are backfilled with large shale particles to prevent blocking of the trenches when the oil shale in the retort is explosively fragmented. Conduits extending through the bulkhead and into the sealed space are provided for removing liquids from the sump and retort off-gases from the sealed space above the liquid level.

Referring to Figure 3.12, the numeral **10** indicates generally a subsurface formation of oil shale which typically might be 50 to 1,000 ft in thickness. An overburden **12** of rock lies between the top of the oil shale formation and the ground surface.

Figure 3.12: Oil Collection and Recovery System

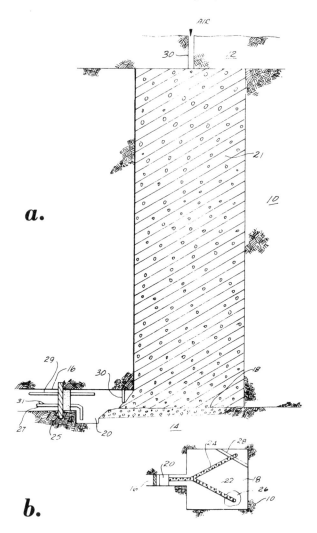

(a) Schematic sectional view of an in situ retort for oil shale
(b) Plan view of the floor of the in situ retort

Source: U.S. Patent 4,007,963

The underlying rock **14** extends below the oil shale formation. It is preferred that the in situ oil shale retort extend the full height of the oil shale formation so that maximum amount of shale oil can be recovered. In some cases, the retort may extend for less than the full height of the formation because of factors of no importance in practice of this process.

In other examples the top or bottom of the in situ retort may be in rock out-side of the oil shale formation. For purposes of exposition herein, the height of the in situ retort illustrated in Figure 3.12a corresponds to the full height of the oil shale formation 10. To form the in situ retort illustrated in Figure 3.12a an access tunnel 16 in communication with the ground surface directly or by way of a shaft is excavated at the bottom of the oil shale formation. A portion of the oil shale is excavated over all or some of a suitable region, for example, 35 to 120 feet square, adjacent the bottom of the oil shale formation.

The floor 18 of the excavated region is sloped slightly downwardly toward the access tunnel to provide drainage into a sump 20 excavated in the floor of the tunnel. The oil shale from the excavated region is removed through the tunnel. However, unless extensive chipping and smoothing work is done, the floor may have substantial depressions and ridges formed as a result of the blasting and excavation operations.

In the process, to avoid smoothing and shaping of the floor and yet provide com-plete drainage and avoid accumulation of appreciable amounts of liquid within the in situ retort, one or more trenches, two of which are indicated at 22 and 24 in Figure 3.12b, are formed in the floor of the excavated region. The trenches extend from the larger depressed areas in the floor, such as indicated at 26, or from areas separated from the access tunnel by a ridge, such as indicated at 28. The trenches can be cut in the rock floor of the excavated region by conventional techniques, such as mechanical cutting or blasting. The trenches are desirably made relatively narrow, so that the bottom of the trenches can easily be made uniform and formed with a gradual slope of the order of $\frac{1}{2}$% grade or more ex-tending into the sump.

The trenches are then filled with rubble consisting of fairly large shale particles. If desired additional large shale particles can be piled over the trenches or other areas of the floor. Shale particles having diameters of 5 to 10 inches and rela-tively free of fine particles are desirable for filling the trenches while providing sufficient interconnected open spaces between the shale particles in the trenches for free flow of liquids through the trenches. Backfilling the trenches with sized rubble prevents fragmented oil shale formed during the formation of the in situ retort from blocking the trenches and preventing liquid flow therethrough.

The in situ retort is then formed by placing explosives in the oil shale formation above the excavated region in a pattern such that when the explosives are deto-nated, the overlying oil shale is fragmented into relatively small pieces to form an enclosed volume of fragmented oil shale 21 within the oil shale formation. Thus, the in situ oil shale retort has boundaries of essentially undisturbed or unfragmented oil shale containing oil shale fragments produced by blasting. The fragmented oil shale substantially fills the volume from which it is formed, plus the excavated region at the bottom. The in situ oil shale retort can be formed by any of a variety of techniques having no effect on practice of this process. One technique is described, for example, in U.S. Patent 3,661,423.

Before the explosives are detonated, the sump 20 is excavated in the floor of the access tunnel. The sump is spaced away from the excavated region in the volume to become the in situ retort far enough to be out of reach of the normal fall of the fragmented oil shale into the tunnel when the explosives are detonated.

Thus the sump remains substantially clear of fragmented oil shale from the in situ retort. If desired, the sump can be excavated after the oil shale in the retort is blasted, but this complicates formation of the trenches.

After fragmenting the oil shale to form the in situ oil shale retort, a bulkhead 25 is positioned in the tunnel 16 to separate the remainder of the access tunnel from the in situ retort. The bulkhead is anchored in the floor, wall, and ceiling of the access tunnel to form a substantially gas-tight barrier. The steel bulkhead can be anchored to the floor, walls, and ceiling of the access tunnel with cement. The bulkhead may be provided with a hatch to permit entrance to the sealed space adjacent the in situ retort. The inside of the steel bulkhead is then lined with firebrick or other suitable heat-resistant material to insulate the bulkhead from high temperatures produced within the in situ retort during the retorting process.

A fire wall may also be placed away from the bulkhead or may be between the sump and the in situ retort if adequate fluid flow passages are provided and the trenches are not thereby blocked.

In order to remove the liquids such as shale oil and water which accumulate in the sump 20 during the retorting process, a conduit 27 is provided which extends through the bulkhead 25 and part way down into the sump. The conduit preferably extends through the access tunnel to the ground surface. Suitable pumping equipment is used for withdrawing liquids from the sump and moving the liquids through the conduit to the surface. Since both water and shale oil accumulate in the sump during the retorting process, the conduit preferably extends only part way between the top and bottom of the sump so that the shale oil can be withdrawn from the sump without withdrawing water accumulated at the bottom of the sump.

A separate conduit may be provided for withdrawing water through the bulkhead and from the bottom of the sump. If desired, both water and shale oil can be withdrawn through a single conduit and separated outside of the bulkhead. The liquids can be withdrawn continually, or conventional floats or other sensors can be provided in the sump so that liquids can be withdrawn intermittently. Preferably an opening 31 such as a Y, is provided in the liquid conduit so that it can be cleaned out if plugged during retorting.

In addition to the conduit 27, a large diameter gas conduit 29 extends through the bulkhead 25 between the sealed space and the balance of the access tunnel. The gas conduit has a gas collecting opening above the liquid level in the sump for withdrawing retort off-gas from the in situ retort. It is convenient to locate the gas conduit near the ceiling to avoid interference with other conduits and provide adequate working room. It is only important that the gas conduit be above the sump to avoid accidental withdrawal of liquids through the gas conduit. Preferably the gas conduit is connected to an exhaust fan or pump so that withdrawal of retort off-gas from the bottom of the retort is aided and there is little danger of the retort off-gas escaping into the access tunnel outside of the bulkhead.

In addition to spacing the sump 20 well away from the in situ retort beyond the normal fall of fragmented oil shale from the in situ retort, a suitable baffle 30 may be provided in the tunnel 16 between the sump and the in situ retort.

The baffle **30** (which may be old crawler tractor treads) is suspended from the ceiling of the tunnel and is spaced above the floor of the tunnel, permitting liquids and gases to flow underneath the baffle. The baffle acts to protect the conduits and sump from pieces of fragmented oil shale thrown into the tunnel when the explosives are detonated during formation of the in situ retort. With the trenches from the excavated region formed with a downward slope in the direction of the sump **20**, liquids which are formed during the retorting process flow from the in situ retort along the tunnel and into the sump, from which they are withdrawn throught the conduit **27**.

The fragmented oil shale in the in situ oil shale retort is retorted by advancing a retorting zone from the top to the bottom of the in situ retort by gas introduced through a conduit **40** at the top. Liquids, such as shale oil and water, are collected in the sump in the sealed area between the bulkhead **25** and the in situ retort **21** and are withdrawn through the bulkhead through the liquid conduit **27**. Off-gas is withdrawn through the larger gas conduit **29**.

In one example of this process, a square in situ oil shale retort is formed in a subterranean oil shale formation. An access tunnel is driven into the oil shale formation and a square room extending from the access tunnel is excavated in the volume of the oil shale formation to become the in situ retort. The room is about 35 feet square, and has a height of about 20 ft. The floor of the room is approximately horizontal and on about the same horizontal level as the floor of the access tunnel. Trenches having widths of about 2 ft and bottoms sloping toward the tunnel are excavated from low points in the floor of the in situ retort to the area where a sump is to be formed in the floor of the tunnel. The trenches are filled with irregular oil shale particles having diameters of about 5 to 10 inches.

The sump is excavated in the tunnel with the in situ retort side of the sump being about 20 feet or more from the entrance to the room to prevent fragmented oil shale from filling the sump when the oil shale is blasted to form the in situ oil shale retort. Explosives are then placed in the oil shale formation above the room for expanding the oil shale and filling room and resulting in situ retort with fragmented oil shale. The explosives are detonated to fragment the oil shale and from the in situ retort.

A bulkhead with a hatch is anchored in the access tunnel about 10 ft from the tunnel side of the sump to provide a sealed space connected to the in situ oil shale retort. Liquid removal conduits are welded or otherwise sealed through the bulkhead and dip into the sump. A retort off-gas removal conduit is also welded through the bulkhead and provided with an opening for collecting retort off-gas from the space above the top of the sump. A conduit is also provided for introducing retorting gas to the top of the in situ oil shale retort.

A combustible mixture of fuel and an oxygen-supplying gas is introduced to the top of the in situ retort and is ignited to form a combustion zone at the top of the in situ retort. A supply of the combustible mixture is maintained at the top of the in situ retort to supply fuel and oxygen to the combustion zone for about 1 week. At the end of about 1 week, the supply of fuel to the combustion zone is terminated and a supply of oxygen-supplying gas, such as air or air diluted with off-gas, is supplied to the combustion zone. Oxygen reacts with carbonaceous material in shale in the in situ retort which has been heated to

900°F or more by previous combustion, and supplied additional heat to the in situ retort. As the inlet gas moves through the combustion zone, oxygen is depleted and the gas is heated. As the gas moves downwardly from the combustion zone heat is transferred from the combustion zone to the fragmented oil shale below it, to form a retorting zone where the shale is heated to a sufficient temperature for retorting. Kerogen in oil shale in the retorting zone in the in situ retort is converted to liquid such as shale oil and water, and product gases. As the gas moves through the in situ retort, it becomes a mixture of flue gases from the combustion zone and product gases from the retorting zone which are carried through the in situ retort to the sealed space connected to the bottom of the in situ retort.

These retort off-gases are withdrawn from the sealed space through the gas conduit extending through the bulkhead. The liquids produced in the retorting zone percolate downwardly through the in situ retort, flow through the trenches in the floor, and are collected in the sump provided in the sealed space connected to the in situ retort. The liquids are removed from the sump through the liquid removal conduit extending through the bulkhead.

Handling System for Feed and Products

According to a process described by *G.B. French, W.J. Bartel, R.D. Ridley, C.Y. Cha and R.S. Burton, III; U.S. Patent 4,014,575; March 29, 1977; assigned to Occidental Petroleum Corporation* an underground room in substantially undisturbed shale is filled with fragmented oil shale particles for in situ retorting. A comprehensive system is provided for feeding air to the top of the retort and recovering oil and flue gas from the bottom of the retort. The oil is separated from admixed water and both are recovered. Flue gas is withdrawn from the bottom of the retort, scrubbed clean and a portion may be recycled through the retort while another portion is vented or burned in a turbine. Means are also provided for passing scrubbed gas through a second spent shale retort prior to venting, burning or recycle.

Figure 3.13 illustrates in block diagram form a comprehensive system for handling the feed and products of an in situ oil shale retort. As illustrated, there is an underground active retort **10** which is in the form of a subterranean room filled with oil shale particles. The room and bed of particles are preferably created simultaneously by explosives. The room is surrounded by substantially undisturbed shale which is relatively impervious so that substantial amounts of fluids do not leak in or out of the active retort. At the bottom of the retort there is a lateral tunnel **11** containing a sump **12** in the floor in which liquids from the retort can collect. The tunnel is closed beyond the sump by any suitable bulkhead, and a flue gas line **13** is in fluid communication with the bottom of the retort.

The active retort is ignited by liquified petroleum gas **14** and compressed air **16** fed down to a burner **17** at the top of the retort. Access to the top of the retort is provided by a bore hole through the undisturbed shale, and the burner is temporarily lowered down the hole and operated until a sufficient volume of shale has been heated above its self-ignition temperature. The burner can then be withdrawn and the retort operated in its normal retorting mode.

Figure 3.13: Handling System for Feed and Products

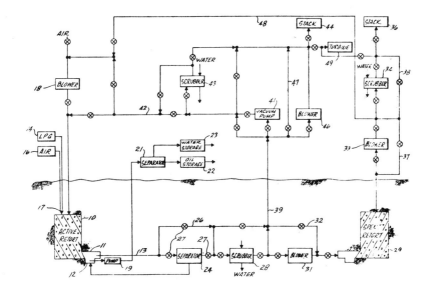

Source: U.S. Patent 4,014,575

In the illustrated arrangement, the retort is indicated to be a substantial distance below the ground surface, and the bore hole may extend from the surface down to the top of the retort. Many elements of the system such as the LPG and air supplies are located at the ground surface. It will be apparent that if desired, access to the top of the retort can be from a tunnel above the retort, and some of the system elements may be located underground or at the ground surface at the end of the tunnel. Generally speaking, substantial volumes of gas are being handled, and it is desirable to keep the gas flow distances short to minimize line pressure drops and friction losses.

Compressed air is supplied to the top of the retort by a blower **18**; a conventional Roots type blower may advantageously be used for this purpose. The air from the blower passes to the top of the retort by way of the bore hole through the undisturbed shale from the surface to the top of the retort. The volume of air blown through the retort is in the order of 0.5 to 2.5 SCFM/ft^2 of cross-sectional area of the retort. High pressures are not required, since the pressure drop through the retort is ordinarily in the order of only a few psi.

The air flowing down through the retort from the blower supports combustion in the oil shale in a conventional manner, so that oil is retorted from the shale. Oil flows from the bottom of the retort into the sump **12**. Water may also accumulate in the sump from a variety of sources including water deliberately added to the retort, water leaking into the retort from subterranean aquifers, or condensed products of combustion and decomposition of water-bearing minerals. The oil-water mixture is removed from the sump by a pump **19** which typically is controlled by a float in the sump since, at times, continuous operation of the pump may not be required.

The pump 19 is, along with other equipment hereinafter mentioned, preferably located in a tunnel near the bottom of the retort. The oil-water mixture is pumped to the ground surface where it goes to a separator 21. The separator can provide a simple gravity separation of oil and water; however, it is found that strong emulsions of oil in water and water in oil ordinarily are encountered. Conventional means for breaking this emulsion may also be included in the separator to improve the efficiency of separation. Oil so separated is conveyed to an oil storage reservoir 22 from which it is conveyed to pipeline, trucking, refinery, or like facilities for usage.

The water from the separator is conveyed to a water storage pond 23. This water is "sour water" containing soluble materials from the oil and retort and should not be imposed on the environment without purification. It is, however, water that is useful in continued operation of the retorting system and may be recirculated for cooling, scrubbing and other water usage purposes. Flue gas from the bottom of the retort is first passed through a conventional separator 24 for removal of entrained water and oil which are returned to the sump 12. A bypass 26 is provided around the separator and is controlled by valves 27. This permits temporary bypassing of the separator for maintenance, cleaning or the like.

Throughout Figure 3.13, numerous valves for control of the fluids in the system are illustrated. The same symbol is used for these valves as for the valves 27 and in general, these will not be specifically mentioned in the description, since their uses are readily apparent to one skilled in the art. These valves may be automatically controlled in some cases so as to be responsive to pressure, temperature, flow rate or the like, or may be manually operated. Flue gas from the separator then passes through a conventional Venturi scrubber 28 which also serves to reduce the content of aerosols and some water-soluble materials in the flue gas. Preferably both the separator and Venturi scrubber are located in the tunnel near the bottom of the retort so that preliminary cleaning of the flue gas occurs promptly and removed material may be returned to the sump.

In one mode of operation it may be desirable to pass the flue gas through a second spent retort 29. This second retort is one in which oil shale has been previously retorted to decompose the kerogen. It, too, is a subterranean room filled with a bed of fragmented oil shale particles. This retort has been previously operated in the same general manner as the active retort so that the shale particles are spent and are in the form of a solid ash which may have substantial quantities of unburned carbon distributed therein. In general, the spent retort can be considered identical to the active retort except for the fact that it is filled with spent shale. The temperature in the spent retort can range anywhere from ambient temperatures up to several hundred degrees Fahrenheit.

There are a variety of reasons for running the flue gas through the spent retort, including enhancement of the fuel value by enrichment from remaining carbonaceous material in the spent retort, removal of sulphur dioxide and other contaminants including aerosols by contact with the substantial surface area of spent shale, and the like. Preferably, the flue gas is passed through the spent retort from the bottom to the top to minimize the distance that the flue gas must travel between retorts. A blower 31 in the tunnel adjacent the bottoms of the two retorts 10 and 29 withdraws gas from the active retort and causes it to flow through the spent retort.

This blower provides the principal force for the pressure drop in the spent retort. A bypass **32** is provided around the blower, since under some conditions, natural convection in the spent retort and withdrawal of gas from the top can effect a substantial flow of flue gas through the spent retort without the blower. Such operation is ordinarily practiced only temporarily during maintenance of the blower.

Flue gas from the top of the spent retort **29** is withdrawn by a gas blower **33** ordinarily located at the ground surface. Flue gas from this blower is passed through a final water scrubber **34** for removal of any remaining aerosol, water-soluble materials, or dust that may be present in the flue gas. The flue gas may then be passed to a vent stack **36** and vented to the atmosphere, preferably with flaring of the gas to consume combustible materials and reduce odorous products, if any. It might be noted that additional combustible gas may be added to the flared flue gas to assure a sufficient flame temperature. A bypass **37** is provided around the gas blower **33** so that if the gas pressure from the underground blower **31** is sufficient, gas may flow from the spent shale retort without further assistance.

Likewise, the final flue gas scrubber has a bypass **38** to permit bypassing during operation wherein substantially all noxious materials are removed by the Venturi scrubber and spent retort. Temporary bypassing is also available in case of needed maintenance of the final flue gas scrubber **34**.

Gas from the bottom of the active retort after aerosol separation and preliminary scrubbing may be withdrawn by a line **39** extending from the tunnel to the ground surface. A vacuum pump **41** is connected to this line so that a less than atmospheric pressure may be maintained at the bottom of the active retort if desired. The vacuum pump outlet is connected by a recycle line **42** to the air inlet to the top of the active retort **10**. This recycle of flue gas from the vacuum pump can be either upstream or downstream from the inlet air blower **18** depending on the relative pressures prevailing in the system.

A water scrubber **43** is also connected to the outlet of the vacuum pump so that if desired recycled gas can be further scrubbed prior to being put back into the top of the active retort. The scrubber is particularly useful if, as indicated in the figure, a portion of the flue gas is conducted to a vent stack **44** for flaring or venting to the atmosphere. A blower **46** is also connected to the flue gas line **39** so that in the alternative flue gas can be diverted directly to the vent stack if the vacuum pump is not operating. A bypass **47** is also provided to the stack to provide venting of the bottom of the retort in a situation where both the vacuum pump and blower are not operating. It will also be noted that after passing through the spent retort, flue gas can be recycled from the blower **33** to the air inlet by a line **48**. This permits an alternative mode of operation wherein flue gas modified by passage through the spent retort is recycled instead of flue gas directly from the active retort.

Flue gas from either the scrubber **34** connected to the spent retort, or the scrubber **33** connected to the outlet of the active retort can be conducted to a conventional gas turbine **49** for production of power. When the heating value of the flue gas is sufficiently high, it can be burned in a turbine or other power generating device so that electric power can be generated for operating various equipment at the retorting site.

Substantial amounts of energy can be contained in this flue gas which is advantageously employed for generating power rather than simply flaring or venting to the atmosphere. It is preferred that the flue gas to the turbine be water scrubbed prior to use so that sulfur-bearing materials are substantially completely removed for inhibition of corrosion of the turbine.

Uniform Gas Flow

According to a process described by *R.S. Burton, III, C.Y. Cha and R.D. Ridley; U.S. Patent 3,941,421; March 2, 1976; assigned to Occidental Petroleum Corporation* an in situ oil shale retort containing a cavity filled with broken particles of oil shale is formed within the subsurface oil shale formation and air is forced down through the cavity to sustain combustion of the top layer of oil shale particles. The products of combustion are withdrawn through a plurality of transverse exhaust pipes at the bottom of the cavity, the exhaust pipes each being provided with a series of holes along the length of the pipes within the cavity, the holes being graded in size to compensate for the pressure drop along the length of the pipe so as to provide substantially equal volume of gas flow through each of the openings.

Referring to Figure 3.14, number **10** indicates generally a subsurface formation of oil-bearing shale of the type commonly found in the Rocky Mountain region of the United States. An in situ retort is provided in the oil shale formation by means of a substantially horizontal access tunnel **12** which communicates with the surface of the ground. The inner end of the tunnel is excavated and enlarged to form an upwardly extending chamber **14**. The chamber is blasted or otherwise cut out of the oil shale formation, and the shale material excavated in forming the chamber is removed through the tunnel. A sump **16** is provided in the floor of the tunnel outside of the chamber and serves as a collection point for the liquids driven off from the oil shale during the retorting process.

After the chamber is formed, pipes for exhausting the gaseous products are run into the lower portion of the chamber. In the figures, three parallel pipe sections **18, 20** and **22** are shown, but the number of pipes may be increased, depending upon the size of the retort chamber. The three parallel pipes are brought out through the tunnel where they are preferably connected to a common outlet pipe **24** through a manifold and separate control valves **26, 28,** and **30,** respectively. The three valves can be individually adjusted to modify the gas flow in the respective pipes. The outlet pipe may be connected to a suitable pump or blower.

The respective pipes **18, 20,** and **22,** within the chamber **14,** are provided with a series of holes, as indicated at **32,** distributed along the undersides of the pipes. The pipes are supported off the bottom of the chamber on mounds of rock fill placed under the pipes to the depth of approximately one foot. The lower part of the chamber is then filled with oil shale particles to a depth of 4 to 5 feet, completely covering over the pipes with a protective layer of oil shale, as indicated at **36.** By placing the holes **32** on the underside of the pipes, gases are able to enter the pipes through the coarse rock fill **34** on which the pipes are supported while, at the same time, the holes are protected against being clogged by solid particles or liquids during the retorting process.

Figure 3.14: Controlling Gas Flow in an In Situ Retort

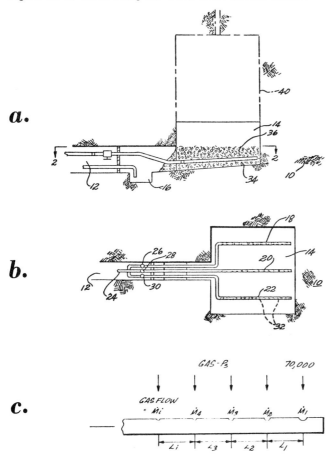

(a)   Sectional view in elevation of an in situ retort
(b)   Cross-sectional view taken substantially on the line **2–2** of
        Figure 3.14a
(c)   Cross-sectional view of one of the exhaust pipes used in ex-
        plaining the operation of the process

Source: U.S. Patent 3,941,421

Once the exhaust pipes are in place in the manner described hereinabove, blasting charges are set in the oil shale formation above the chamber **14**. An enlarged cavity is formed in the oil shale formation by setting off the charges, the
enlarged cavity forming an upward extension of the chamber. This enlarged
cavity, indicated at **40**, is filled with particles of oil shale formed during the
blasting operation.

The pipes **18, 20** and **22** are preferably made of an 8-inch diameter pipe having a very thick wall, for example, Schedule 80 pipe, to withstand the force of the blasting operation. The pipe is further protected from damage by the overlying layer **36** of oil shale which is put in place before the blasting operation.

Once the blasting operation is completed, vents are opened to atmosphere in the top of the retort cavity to permit air to be drawn into the cavity at the top. The oil shale is ignited and burning proceeds. The hot product gases are drawn down through the cavity and out the exhaust pipes. By adjusting the valves, the flow rate through the respective pipes can be balanced to produce uniform burning.

Referring to Figure 3.14c, a distributor pipe is shown with a series of orifices numbered **1** through **i** spaced at intervals **L** along the pipe. According to the process, the size of the orifices are selected so that the mass flow rate M_i through each orifice is made equal to that of all the other orifices by changing the orifice diameter of the orifices to compensate for pressure drop along the interior of the pipe.

Postretorting Technique

According to a process described by *C.Y. Cha; U.S. Patent 4,105,072; August 8, 1978; assigned to Occidental Oil Shale* for recovering liquid and gaseous products from an in situ oil shale retort containing a fragmented permeable mass of particles containing oil shale, a heated zone is established in an upper portion of the fragmented mass. For a period of normal retorting operation, an oxygen-containing gas is introduced to the fragmented mass on the trailing side of the heated zone at a sufficient rate for advancing the heated zone downwardly through the fragmented mass and liquid products and a relatively lean off-gas containing gaseous products are withdrawn from the bottom of the retort.

Thereafter, for a period of postretorting operation, the introduction of gas to the fragmented mass is reduced to a rate such that a relatively rich off-gas is withdrawn from the retort. The rich withdrawn off-gas preferably has a heating value of at least about 75 Btu/scf. The reduced rate of introduction includes substantial closing of an end of the retort or introduction of gas at a rate less than about 10% of the rate of introduction of gas to the retort during normal retorting operation. Relatively rich off-gas from postretorting operation is preferably withdrawn from the top of the retort and can be used for igniting another retort or for sustaining a secondary combustion zone in a second retort.

Sound Monitoring

W.B. Elkington; U.S. Patent 4,082,145; April 4, 1978; assigned to Occidental Oil Shale, Inc. describes a process for determining the locus of a processing zone such as a combustion zone advancing through a fragmented permeable mass of particles in an in situ oil shale retort in a subterranean formation containing oil shale.

The method comprises the step of monitoring for sound produced in the retort. Preferably sound is monitored at at least two locations, and more preferably at three locations, in a plane substantially normal to the direction of advancement of the processing zone through the fragmented mass to determine if the processing zone is flat and uniformly transverse to its direction of advancement.

Monitoring can be effected by placing one or more sound transducers in a conduit extending into the fragmented mass and/or in a well extending through the formation adjacent the retort. Also, a sound transducer can be placed directly into the fragmented mass. A plurality of sound transducers can be placed at a plurality of selected locations spaced apart from each other or a single sound transducer can be moved to a plurality of locations within a conduit or well to track a processing zone as it advances through a retort.

The sound transducers are sensitive to sound intensity and sounds characterizing a combustion zone and/or a retorting zone for distinguishing them from each other and for distinguishing their sounds from those produced in other portions of an in situ oil shale retort. Monitoring such characteristic sounds provides a way of determining the locus of a processing zone in an in situ oil shale retort. For determining the locus of a combustion zone, the sound transducers can be sensitive to sound at a frequency characteristic of sound produced by burning of hydrocarbons.

Underground Weir Separator

According to a process described by *P. Albulescu and J.F. McMahon; U.S. Patent 4,119,349; October 10, 1978; assigned to Gulf Oil Corporation and Standard Oil Company (Indiana)* gaseous and liquid products discharged from the outlet of an in situ retort for the retorting of oil shale are delivered into an underground separating chamber located substantially at the level of the bottom of the retort.

The lower portion of the separating chamber is divided by a weir into a first sump adjacent the inlet end of the separating chamber and a second sump adjacent the outlet end of the separating chamber. Oil and water separate in the first sump and the oil overflows the weir into the second sump. Water is withdrawn at a level below the oil in the first sump and pumped to the surface. Oil is withdrawn from the second sump and pumped to the surface separately from the water.

The apparatus and method of this process minimize formation of difficult to separate emulsions of aqueous liquid and shale oil. The location of the separating chamber at the level of the bottom of the retort results in the delivery of liquids into the first sump at a high temperature that favors separation of the shale oil and aqueous liquids. The large volume of the separating chamber, particularly in the preferred design, reduces the velocity of gases to improve disengagement of droplets of liquids from the gases.

The weirs will generally have a height of approximately 25 ft to form sumps of large volume to give adequate time for the liquids at the high temperature to separate into an oil phase and an aqueous liquids phase. The low rate of heat loss to the formation surrounding the chambers as compared to heat loss to the atmosphere in a surface separator results in the shale oil retaining its high temperature and low viscosity that favors rapid and effective separation. The separate delivery of the oil and the aqueous phase to the surface avoids the vigorous mixing that encourages emulsification that occurs on delivering the liquid products of retorting through a single delivery line.

Emulsion Breaking Technique

R.S. Burton, III; U.S. Patent 4,109,718; August 29, 1978; assigned to Occidental Oil Shale, Inc. describes a technique for breaking the very strong emulsion of shale oil and water produced by an in situ oil shale retorting process so that separate shale oil and water phases can be recovered. The emulsion is broken by heating it to a temperature of at least about 120°F and holding at a temperature in the range of from 120° to 180°F for about one day. Preferably the shale oil and water are held in the range of from 130° to 150°F for about one day and the phases separated by gravity. Heat for the process can be obtained by injecting water into a spent in situ oil shale retort for generating steam and transferring heat from the steam to the emulsion.

Off-Gas Recycling

C.Y. Cha and R.D. Ridley; U.S. Patent 3,994,343; November 30, 1976; assigned to Occidental Petroleum Corporation describe a process which is suitable for in situ retorting of oil shale particles, with retorting proceeding downwardly through a bed of broken pieces of shale. When a single bed is being retorted, air is passed downwardly after ignition until a hot zone trailing the combustion zone has built up to some predetermined thickness, for example, 20 ft having a temperature over 1000°F. Thereafter off-gas from the bed is recycled downwardly without air.

Reaction of the recycle gas with the heated spent shale increases the heating value of the resultant off-gas. The transfer of heat without combustion increases the yield of oil. When the maximum temperature in the bed drops to a predetermined temperature above the self-ignition temperature of the shale, air is again introduced to reestablish a combustion zone and build up a hot zone. Retorting continues with alternating combustion and recycling periods through the entire bed.

When multiple beds of oil shale particles are retorted air is passed downwardly through one of the beds to maintain a combustion zone until a sufficient hot zone trailing the combustion zone has been produced. Air is then passed through a second bed of oil shale particles and at least a portion of the off-gas from the second bed is recycled through the first bed for cooling the hot zone, increasing the heating value of the off-gas, and retorting additional oil. Additional beds of oil shale particles can be included in series with combustion zones being intermittently established in each of the beds, alternatingly with cooling by recycled off-gas.

Prevention of Off-Gas Leakage

C.Y. Cha, R.D. Ridley and R.S. Burton, III; U.S. Patent 4,076,312; February 28, 1978; assigned to Occidental Oil Shale, Inc. describe a process and apparatus for preventing leakage of gases from an in situ oil shale retort to avoid dangers from such leakage. Specifically, the retorting process is carried out by withdrawing off-gas from the fragmented mass in the in situ oil shale retort on the advancing side of the retorting zone at a rate sufficient to reduce pressure within the in situ oil shale retort on the advancing side of the combustion zone to less than the ambient pressure in tunnels adjacent the retort. Thus any leakage between the retort on the advancing side of the combustion zone and surrounding spaces is into the retort, thereby preventing leakage of gas from the retort on the advancing side of the combustion zone. Preferably off-gas is withdrawn from the retort at a rate sufficient to reduce the pressure in all locations of the retort to less than the ambient pressure in tunnels adjacent the retort to prevent all leakage from the retort.

Referring to Figure 3.15, an in situ oil shale retort 10 is in the form of a cavity 20 formed in an unfragmented subterranean formation 14 containing oil shale. According to the shale oil recovery process described in U.S. Patent 3,661,424, the retort is formed by providing an access drift or tunnel 18 from the surface through the subterranean formation. The tunnel section 18 illustrated in the drawing may be a part of a tunneling system extending to a plurality of retorts such as the retort 10.

Figure 3.15: Vertical Cross Section of an In Situ Oil Shale Retort

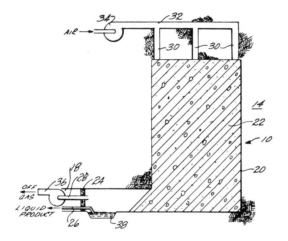

Source: U.S. Patent 4,076,312

The access tunnel 18 is used while mining out a portion of the formation within the site of an in situ oil shale retort. After the mining operation, formation remaining within the retort site is fragmented and explosively expanded by explosive charges to form the cavity 20 containing a fragmented permeable mass 22 of formation particles containing oil shale. The tunnel 18 is then blocked off at the entrance to the cavity by suitable blocking means such as a concrete barrier or bulkhead 24 through which an outlet conduit 26 and a gas withdrawal pipe 28 extend. The conduit 26 is used to recover liquids from the retort, and the pipe 28 is used to withdraw off-gas from the retort.

During the retorting operation of the retort 10, a combustion zone is established in the retort by igniting a portion of the fragmented mass. The combustion zone is advanced through the fragmented permeable mass by introducing a gaseous feed containing an oxygen-supplying gas such as fresh air or air mixed with other gases into the in situ oil shale retort through inlet means communicating with the upper region of the retort such as a primary inlet conduit 32 in fluid communication with one or more secondary inlet conduits 30. The gaseous feed can be caused to flow into the retort by means such as a blower 34. As the gaseous feed flows through the fragmented mass in the retort, oxygen oxidizes carbonaceous material in the oil shale to produce combusted oil shale and combustion product gases.

An effluent gas from the combustion zone comprising combustion product gases produced in the combustion zone, any unreacted portion of the gaseous combustion zone feed, and gases from carbonate decomposition is passed through the fragmented mass of particles on the advancing side of the combustion zone. Heat carried by the effluent gas establishes a retorting zone on the advancing side of the combustion zone. As oil shale is retorted in the retorting zone, kerogen is converted to liquid and gaseous products.

Liquid products formed in the retorting zone collect in a sump 38 at the bottom of the tunnel 18 to be withdrawn through the conduit 26 for further processing. An off-gas, which contains gaseous products, combustion product gases, gas from carbonate decomposition, and any unreacted portion of the gaseous combustion zone feed, passes from the retort on the advancing side of the retorting zone into the portion of the tunnel 18 inside the barrier 24 and is then withdrawn through the barrier into the pipe 28 for further processing. The barrier seals the retort from the balance of the tunnel to prevent gas communication.

The blower 34, by forcing air under pressure into the retort, was heretofore relied on to force gas to flow downwardly through the retort and out through the pipe 28. It has been found, however, that the surrounding formation is not always completely impervious to the flow of gases out of the retort. As a result some of the combustion zone effluent gas and off-gas can escape from the retort so that a part of these gases leak into drifts, shafts and other tunnels such as the access tunnel 18.

Since the access tunnel can be part of a common network of tunnels, drafts, shafts, and the like, used to mine and service other retorts within the same oil shale deposit, accumulation of product gases in this tunneling system presents a hazardous condition.

According to the process, gas withdrawing or pumping means such as a blower or vacuum pump 36 are provided on the withdrawal pipe 28. The withdrawing means has sufficient capacity for reducing pressure within at least a portion of the retort adjacent the tunnel 18 to a pressure less than the ambient pressure in the tunnel to prevent leakage from the retort into the tunnel.

Since gas on the advancing side of the combustion zone is substantially free of free oxygen, and contains poisonous carbon monoxide and noxious or toxic sulfurous compounds, leakage of gas on the advancing side of the combustion into tunnels adjacent the retort can present a serious problem. Therefore, preferably the withdrawing means has sufficient capacity to reduce the pressure within all of the retort on the advancing side of the combustion zone to less than the ambient pressure in tunnels adjacent the retort, such as the access tunnel 18, to prevent leakage of dangerous gases from the retort into such tunnels. It is within the contemplation of this process to maintain a continous flow of gas through the retort with the entire retort at or less than the ambient pressure in all tunnels adjacent the retort to prevent leakage from the retort. If desired, the entire retort can be maintained at subatmospheric pressure.

The process can be used with alternate approaches in use for forced ventilation of mine tunnel systems. In one approach, the mine tunnels are pressurized by forcing fresh air through some of the passages and permitting air to exhaust freely through others. With another technique, air is exhausted from one passage with entry of fresh air into other passages by natural circulation. In the first technique, a pressurized mine results where the pressure within the workings is higher than ambient pressure at the altitude outside the mine. In the second system, the pressure in the tunnels is less than external ambient pressure.

In practice of this process, leakage of gases from the retorts into the mining tunnels is prevented with both of these ventilation approaches by maintaining pressure in the portion of the retort adjacent the tunnels at less than the adjacent ambient pressure in the tunnels. There is sufficient pumping capacity that the pressure in the retort is lower than that in the tunnels, and when the tunnels are at subambient pressure, the pressure in the retort is lower than the ambient pressure outside the entire tunnel system.

According to one version of the process, the gas withdrawing means on the withdrawal pipe 28 is capable of reducing the pressure at the bottom of the retort to 2 to 3 psi below the ambient pressure within the access tunnel 18, which is maintained at or above atmospheric pressure. At the same time, the blower 34 is operated such that the pressure at the top of the retort is at or slightly below or slightly above the atmospheric pressure. Thus, the blower is operated to overcome the normal pressure drop within the oxygen-containing gas introduction system provided by the inlet conduits 32 and 30. In this way the blower 34 and pumping means 36 operate to provide a continuous flow of gases through the retort.

This arrangement provides adequate oxygen-containing gas to maintain combustion in the combustion zone while at the same time producing a flow of combustion gases through the retort and maintaining a pressure less than the ambient pressure in adjacent tunnels on at least the advancing side of the combustion zone. Thus any leakage of gas between the portion of the retort on the advancing side of the combustion zone and the tunnel 18 or other adjacent tunnels results in flow into the retort rather than out of the retort. In this manner, leakage of off-gas out of the retort into surrounding spaces is prevented.

TREATMENT OF OFF-GASES FROM RETORT

Cooling System

According to a process described by *G.B. French; U.S. Patent 4,022,511; May 10, 1977; assigned to Occidental Petroleum Corporation* a retort off-gas cooling zone is provided in an in situ oil shale retort at the product outlet end of the in situ oil shale retort. The retort off-gas cooling zone has a sufficient thermal capacity to reduce the temperature of the retort off-gas moving through the cooling zone to a temperature below which the temperature of the retort off-gas will not deleteriously affect the product collection and removal apparatus in the product collection zone. Oil shale in the retort off-gas cooling zone having an average kerogen content lower than the average kerogen content of the oil shale in the in situ retort provides an in situ retort having a high yield of products based on the recoverable products in the in situ retort.

Kerogen in the in situ oil shale retort is converted to shale oil by moving a heated gas through a retorting zone in the in situ retort and toward the product outlet end of the in situ retort. The movement of heated gas through the retorting zone is continued until the retort off-gas moving from the product outlet end of the in situ retort to a product collection zone is at a temperature above which the gas will deleteriously affect product collection and removal apparatus in the product collection zone.

A feature of the process is the formation of the retort off-gas cooling zone adjacent to the bottom of an in situ retort in a stratum of shale having a low kerogen content. Fragments of such shale may be present in the in situ retort. As the retorting zone moves down through the in situ retort, the intact oil shale bordering the in situ retort is also partially retorted. However, when the movement of hot gas through the retorting zone is terminated, the shale adjacent to the bottom of the in situ retort remains substantially unretorted because there is a minimal flow of gas for heating it. Since this shale has a low oil content, there is little loss of yield based on recoverable product from the in situ retort. The fragmented shale in the retort off-gas cooling zone adjacent to the bottom of the situ retort can be formed from the low kerogen content oil shale of the stratum without backfilling.

Reduction of Oil and Water

G.B. French; U.S. Patent 4,029,360; June 14, 1977; assigned to Occidental Oil Shale, Inc. describes a method for reducing water and oil content of oil shale retort flue gas by collecting the flue gas in a conduit at the bottom of the retort and passing it upwardly through an elongated conduit in heat transfer relation with relatively cool overburden a sufficient distance to lower the flue gas temperature to less than the dew point of the flue gas so that water is condensed in the conduit and oil and water aerosols are collected on the walls of the conduit. The oil and water flow to the bottom of the conduit and are recovered underground.

Figure 3.16 is a semischematic vertical cross section drawn without regard to scale since, in general, relative dimensions are not of significance in practice of this process. As illustrated, there is an underground retort **10** in the form of a room in substantially undisturbed shale. The interior of the room is filled with a rubble pile of fragmented oil shale particles. This bed of oil shale particles and the room are created essentially simultaneously by means of explosives. Air is passed downwardly through a conduit **11** to enter the top of the retort **10**. The air passes downwardly through the retort for supporting a combustion zone moving slowly downwardly through the bed of oil shale particles. The heat from combustion retorts the shale oil which flows from the bottom of the room into a sump **12** in a laterally extending tunnel **13**. Oil and water are recovered from the sump **12**.

The retort is sealed from the tunnel beyond the sump by a gas-tight bulkhead **14** which is typically a steel plate cemented into the rock or a concrete barricade. A conduit **16** extends through the bulkhead for collecting flue gas adjacent the bottom of the retort. The conduit may end in the tunnel near the bulkhead or may be extended in the form of one or more perforated pipes into the lower portion of the bed of oil shale particles in the retort. The flue gas is preferably passed through a separator and/or Venturi scrubber **17** for removing substantial amounts of entrained oil and water.

Figure 3.16: Recovery of Oil and Water from In Situ Oil Shale Retort Gas

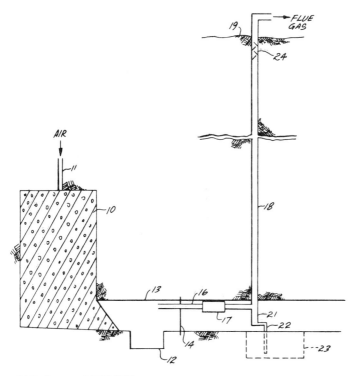

Source: U.S. Patent 4,029,360

The flue gas then passes to an elongated substantially vertical conduit **18** extending upwardly from the tunnel to the ground surface **19**. At the ground surface the flue gas may pass to a vacuum pump, gas scrubbers, vents, recycle lines and the like which are not of concern in practice of this process. The vertical conduit may typically extend 500 ft or more from the level of the tunnel **12** to the ground surface **19**. Throughout this distance it is passing through relatively cool overburden that overlies the beds of shale to be retorted.

Typically, for example, this is a relatively impervious marlstone and, if desired, the conduit can be simply a borehole through the solid rock so long as means are provided for sealing the end portions to minimize leakage. Alternatively, the borehole may be provided with a casing in the manner of oil wells so that the flue gas is actually flowing inside a pipe in the borehole. In a typical case, an eight-inch pipe may be passed through a 10¾-inch borehole. Such an arrangement effectively eliminates any possibility of leakage of the flue gas but reduces the rate of heat flow from the flue gas into the rock formations. Even so, heat transfer is sufficient between the upwardly flowing flue gas and the relatively cooler overburden around the conduit **18** that the temperature of the flue gas is dropped well below its dew point.

This temperature reduction in the flue gas causes condensation of water on the walls on the conduit. In addition, the flue gas is in turbulent flow and aerosols are contacting the conduit walls. Appreciable quantities of oil and reusable water, therefore, collect on the inside walls of the conduit. These liquids flow downwardly in the conduit and eventually collect in a standpipe **21** at the bottom of the conduit. The standpipe is located below the collection conduit so that it is out of the gas flow path.

A pipe **22** from the bottom of the standpipe leads to an underground sump **23** (the sump is indicated in dotted lines since it is preferably displaced laterally from the main tunnel **13** so as not to interfere with other operations). The oil and water coming out of the flue gas in the vertical conduit **18** are recovered from the underground sump. The lower end of the pipe **22** to the sump may be left open since the pressure in the conduit may be less than the ambient pressure in the tunnel and so long as liquid remains in the underground sump there is no leakage and liquids flow from the standpipe automatically. Alternatively, if a higher pressure is present in the conduit, the lower end of the pipe may be left open under a sufficient head of liquid in the sump to prevent gas leakage. Alternatively, a float-controlled valve may be provided in the recovery pipe.

In a typical oil shale retorting operation, the vertically extending conduit **18** may be an 8-inch pipe as mentioned above. The gas flow velocity through the pipe may be in the order of 6,000 to 10,000 ft/min. The total length of the conduit **18** is preferably in the range of 500 to 1,000 ft. If it is less than about 500 ft, the volume of rock available for heat flow may be too low for needed heat dissipation.

Towards the end of the operation the temperature of the flue gas at the bottom of the retort during normal retorting operations is in the order of about 140°F. After passing through the elongated vertical conduit through the relatively cool overburden the temperature of the flue gas may be lowered to the order of 60° to 70°F. This substantial cooling of the flue gas causes a large condensation of water on the walls of the conduit. Further, turbulent flow of gas through the conduit brings oil and water aerosols into contact with the walls where they are removed and run down the walls with the collected water. The oil is recovered as a saleable product and the water recovered from the underground sump is used in various retorting operations.

Since the flow rate of gas through the vertical conduit is moderately high, small droplets of oil or water may be entrained and carried upwardly. This effect can be minimized by providing demisters in the conduit so that droplets impinge and coalesce on surfaces from which they drain to the walls of the conduit and eventually back to the sump at the bottom. Baffles may be introduced in the conduit to assure turbulent flow and direct flow such that the droplets are caused to impinge on the walls. Restrictions or other means may also be employed for modifying flow velocity in some regions of the conduit so that coalescence of the droplets and condensation of materials is enhanced. A broad variety of such measures for reducing the vapor and entrained aerosol content of the gas flow-ing in the conduit will be apparent to one skilled in the art. The baffles, de-misters, etc., are preferably located near the top of the conduit as indicated schematically at **24** in the drawing so that gas cooling has occurred and any aerosol content of the gas is fully developed.

R.S. Burton, III and G.B. French; U.S. Patent Reissue 29,553; February 28, 1978; assigned to Occidental Oil Shale, Inc. describe a technique for cooling the flue gas or off-gas from the bottom of an in situ oil shale retort. The gas is collected in a conduit that has a vertical portion through which the gas flows upwardly. It is then withdrawn from the retort through a gas-tight bulkhead. Water is sparged downwardly through the vertical portion of the conduit for cooling and cleaning the gas. Means are provided for draining the sparged water into a sump at the bottom of the retort wherein oil and water are collected. Water and oil are separated and the water may be recycled for additional cooling.

Removal of Acidic Impurities

A process described by *D.E. Honaker; U.S. Patent 4,117,886; October 3, 1978; assigned to Standard Oil Company (Indiana)* relates to the retorting of oil shale and the purification of off-gases from oil shale retorting, including combustion products of off-gases from oil shale retorting.

The process for removing acidic impurities from off-gases generated in the re-torting of oil shale or in the combustion of off-gases comprises contacting a rubblized mass of oil shale which has been substantially depleted in hydrocar-bonaceous materials with water, so as to extract basic components from the mass; and contacting off-gases, which were generated during the retorting of oil shale and which contain acidic impurities, with the water containing basic com-ponents so as to substantially remove the acidic impurities from the off-gases.

The oil shale which is substantially depleted in hydrocarbonaceous materials may be spent shale from surface or in situ retorting. For example, spent shale which is removed from Tosco, Lurgi or Paraho retorts may be contacted with water in a reactor or an extraction zone for a time sufficient to extract basic components from the spent shale. The water containing basic component is then used to remove impurities from off-gases generated during the surface or in situ retorting of oil shale.

Figure 3.17 is a schematic diagram of an oil shale retorting process with purifica-tion of off-gases. In situ retorts **2** and **5** are located within oil shale deposit **1**. These retorts can be formed by any well known mining technique, preferably by sublevel caving. Rubblized oil shale within in situ retorts is retorted by passing a hot retorting gas through the rubblized mass so as to free shale oil from the deposit. The hot retorting gases are commonly formed by passing air, air plus steam, or air plus recycle off-gases through the rubblized mass in an in situ re-tort. A burner may be needed to initiate combustion.

Air **10** can be passed through access way **9** into in situ retort **2** so that the rub-blized mass oil shale within the retort is effectively retorted. Oil, water, and off-gases are then passed through collection area **3** to separation zone **4**. After in situ retort **2** is substantially depleted in hydrocarbonaceous material, retorting is stopped. Water **11** is then passed through access way **9** into the hot rubblized mass within in situ retort **2**. Because this hot mass of spent shale holds a great deal of heat and because the surrounding rock formation serves as an insulator, a great deal of heat is present to vaporize water added to the rubblized mass. Water is converted into steam and is passed through collection area **3** to separation zone **4**.

The steam is then passed through line **13** to compressor **14** where it is compressed for passage through line **15** for use in retorting other in situ retorts such as in situ retort **5**. After in situ retort has cooled from the introduction of water, the water can exist as a liquid. Water then injected into the rubblized mass of oil shale or spent oil shale in in situ retort **2** will then suspend or extract basic materials from the retorted mineral. The water containing basic components is then removed by collection area **3** and passed to separation zone **4**. The water containing basic components is then passed through line **17** for use in the purification of off-gases.

When forming in situ retorts, approximately 5 to 40% of oil shale is mined, removed from the formation and brought to the surface. This rubblized mass of oil shale **30** is then passed through line **31** to surface retort **32** where it is contacted with hot retorting gases to release shale oil. During this retorting, off-gases are formed which are passed out of retort **32** through line **33**, shale oil **34** is recovered, and spent retorted oil shale is removed through line **35**. The spent retorted oil shale can be introduced into vessel **36** where it can be contacted with water **37** so that basic components can be extracted or suspended by the water and this water solution containing basic components can be passed out of reactor **36** through line **39** for use in off-gas scrubbing. Spent shale **38** which has been extracted or contacted with water is then passed out of reactor **36**.

Figure 3.17: Oil Shale Retorting and Off-Gas Purification

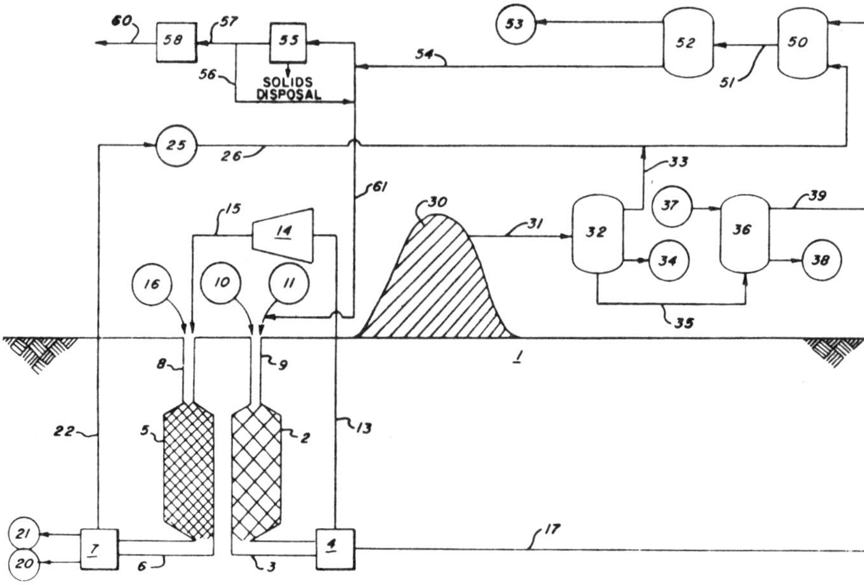

Source: U.S. Patent 4,117,886

In situ retort **5** is a retort undergoing retorting. Air **16** and steam from line **15** are passed through access tunnel **8** into in situ retort **5** where a rubblized mass of oil shale is effectively retorted. Shale oil, water, and off-gases are then collected in zone **6** and passed to separation zone **7**. Separation zone **7** is commonly a simple gravity separator which separates water from oil from gases. Water **20** is removed from the separation zone. Shale oil **21** is also removed from separation zone **7**. Off-gases are passed from the separation zone through line **22** for cleanup. In some cases, these off-gases are first treated in zone **25** to remove dust, entrained oil, etc. The off-gases are then treated for purification.

In this process diagram, off-gases from surface retort **32** and line **33** are combined with off-gases from in situ retort **5** in line **26** for purification. The combined off-gas stream is passed into reactor **50** along with water containing extracted or suspended basic components. Water containing basic components from in situ retort **2** and line **17** are combined with water with extracted and suspended basic components from surface retorting from line **39** and passed into reactor **50**. After sufficient contacting between off-gases and water containing basic components to achieve a satisfactory level of purification, the contents of reactor **50** are passed through line **51** and through separation zone **52** where purified off-gases are separated from the aqueous phase.

The off-gases are then passed out of reactor **52** to other processing **53**. This other processing can be energy recovery through combustion and use of power turbines, use as diluent in retorting other in situ retorts, and other uses. The aqueous phase removed from reactor **52** is then passed via line **61** to the spent retort **2** for regeneration and recirculation. A purge stream is removed from the circulation loop to control suspended solids concentration and sent to a solid separator **55** wherein insoluble solids are recovered and used or disposed of. A clear aqueous phase is returned through line **56** to the circulation loop for regeneration. A soluble purge stream **57** is withdrawn at a rate to control the soluble salt concentration and sent to **58** for recovery and/or treatment before being passed through line **60** to disposal.

Oxidation of Hydrogen Sulfide

According to *L.E. Compton; U.S. Patent 4,086,963; May 2, 1978; C.Y. Cha; U.S. Patent 4,086,962; May 2, 1978 and L.E. Compton and W.H. Rowan; U.S. Patent 4,082,146; April 4, 1978; all assigned to Occidental Oil Shale, Inc.* the hydrogen sulfide concentration of a gas is reduced by reacting hydrogen sulfide in the gas with oxygen in the presence of raw oil shale. The ratio of sulfur dioxide to sulfur produced by this reaction depends upon the molar ratio of oxygen to hydrogen sulfide present. Sulfur is the predominant product when hydrogen sulfide is reacted in the presence of oil shale with less than about 1 mol of oxygen for each 2 mols of hydrogen sulfide.

Referring to Figure 3.18a, an in situ oil shale retort **8** is in the form of a cavity **10** formed in an unfragmented subterranean formation **11** containing oil shale. The cavity contains an expanded or fragmented permeable mass **12** of formation particles. The cavity **10** can be created simultaneously with fragmentation of the mass of formation particles **12** by blasting by any of a variety of techniques. A method of forming an in situ oil retort is described in U.S. Patent 3,661,423.

A conduit **13** communicates with the top of the fragmented mass of formation particles. During the retorting operation of the retort **8**, a combustion zone is established in the retort and advanced by introducing a gaseous feed containing an oxygen-supplying gas, such as air or air mixed with other gases, into the in situ oil shale retort through the conduit **13**. As the gaseous feed is introduced to the retort, oxygen oxidizes carbonaceous material in the oil shale to produce combusted oil shale and combustion gas. Heat from the exothermic oxidation reactions carried by flowing gases advances the combustion zone through the fragmented mass of particles.

Combustion gas produced in the combustion zone, any unreacted portion of the oxygen-supplying gaseous feed and gases from carbonate decomposition are passed through the fragmented mass of particles on the advancing side of the combustion zone to establish a retorting zone on the advancing side of the combustion zone. As oil shale is retorted in the retorting zone, kerogen is converted to liquid and gaseous products.

There is a drift **14** in communication with the bottom of the retort. The drift contains a sump **16** in which liquid products are collected to be withdrawn for further processing. An off-gas containing gaseous products, combustion gas, gases from carbonate decomposition, and any unreacted portion of the oxygen-supplying gaseous feed is also withdrawn from the in situ oil shale retort **8** by the way of the drift **14**. The off-gas can contain large amounts of nitrogen with lesser amounts of hydrogen, carbon monoxide, carbon dioxide, methane, higher hydrocarbons, water vapor, and sulfur compounds such as hydrogen sulfide. The off-gas also can contain particulates and hydrocarbon-containing aerosols. It is desirable to remove at least a portion of the hydrogen sulfide from the off-gas so the off-gas can be used as fuel gas for power generation in a work engine such as a gas turbine, or if the off-gas is flared, to limit the sulfurous emission.

The retort illustrated in Figure 3.18a has not yet had retorting and combustion operations completed. The retort contains a fragmented permeable mass of formation particles containing raw oil shale. As used herein, the term "raw oil shale" refers to oil shale which has not been subjected to any processing affecting the chemical composition of the oil shale.

As gas stream **18** containing hydrogen sulfide, such as off-gas from an active oil shale retort, and a gas stream **19** containing oxygen, such as air, are introduced concurrently through the conduit **13** to the retort **8**. There is sufficient differential pressure between the top and bottom of the retort to cause the gas streams to flow through the conduit **13**, which is in communication with the upper boundary of the fragmented mass of raw oil shale particles in the retort **8**, and downwardly as one combined gas stream through the retort to be withdrawn from the retort through the tunnel **14** which is in communication with the bottom of the retort.

For economy, the conduit to be used for introducing oxygen-supplying gaseous feed to the retort **8** during a retorting operation is utilized for introducing the gas streams **18**, **19** into the retort. Similarly, the tunnel to be used for withdrawing off-gas from the retort during a retorting operation is utilized to withdraw purified gas from the retort.

When the hydrogen-sulfide-containing gas is off-gas from an active oil shale retort, oil aerosols and/or particulates which can be contained in the off-gas can
be removed from the off-gas prior to introduction into the retort. This is done
to prevent deposition of oil and/or particulates on the fragmented mass of oil
shale particles in the retort, which can reduce the activity of the particles in removing hydrogen sulfide from the off-gas.

As the hydrogen-sulfide-containing gas stream **18** and the oxygen-containing gas
stream **19** pass through the retort, hydrogen sulfide is oxidized to sulfur dioxide
and/or sulfur. Oxidation of hydrogen sulfide in contact with oil shale has been
demonstrated to occur at appreciable rates even at temperatures as low as 75°F.
This overall result is surprising because hydrogen sulfide is not oxidized at appreciable rates at temperatures less than its spontaneous ignition temperature of
550°F without use of a catalyst. It was not expected that raw oil shale would
promote the oxidation of hydrogen sulfide.

It has been found that the lower the temperature at which the hydrogen sulfide
and oxygen are reacted, the higher the ratio of sulfur to sulfur dioxide at least
initially produced by the oxidation reaction. At temperatures less than about
300°F, even at molar ratios of oxygen to hydrogen sulfide greater than 3:2, over
90% of the hydrogen sulfide is at least initially oxidized to form elemental sulfur. Even at temperatures as high as 450°F, over half the hydrogen sulfide oxidized is at least initially oxidized to elemental sulfur.

Figure 3.18: Oil Shale Retorting

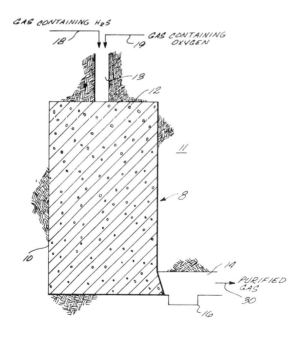

(continued)

Figure 3.18: (continued)

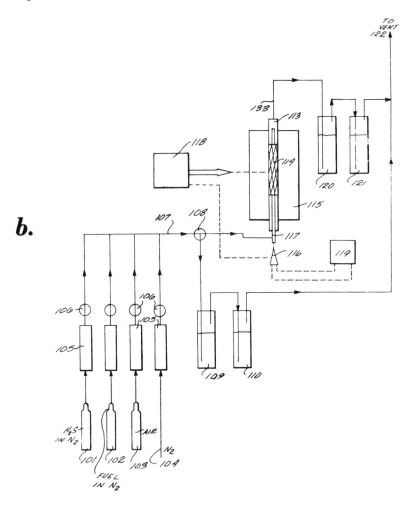

b.

(a)   Vertical cross section of an in situ oil shale retort containing
       combusted oil shale being used for oxidizing hydrogen sulfide
       contained in a gas stream
(b)   Apparatus used for demonstrating the efficacy of the process

Source: U.S. Patent 4,086,963

The hydrogen-sulfide-containing gas **18** can contain fuel value components such
as when the gas is off-gas from an in situ oil shale retort. Off-gas from an in
situ oil shale retort can contain fuel value components such as hydrogen, methane and other hydrocarbons, and carbon monoxide. To avoid oxidation of such
fuel value components, preferably the formation particles contacted by the fuel
value components are at a temperature less than their spontaneous ignition

temperature. The spontaneous ignition temperature of the fuel value components is dependent upon the conditions at which the formation particles are contacted by the fuel value components, i.e., the spontaneous ignition temperature of fuel value components is dependent upon such process parameters as the total pressure and the partial pressure of oxygen and the fuel value components in the retort.

As the temperature at which hydrogen sulfide contacts oil shale in the presence of oxygen increases, the rate at which hydrogen sulfide contained in the gas stream **18** is oxidized to sulfur and sulfur dioxide increases with all other process conditions maintained constant. If there is insufficient residence time in the retort **8** to achieve a desired degree of conversion, the hydrogen sulfide and oxygen-containing gases can be passed through additional retorts containing raw oil shale in series and/or parallel, or recirculated several times in a single retort to achieve maximum removal.

At temperatures greater than about 300°F, the molar ratio of oxygen reacted with hydrogen sulfide in the presence of oil shale affects the ratio of sulfur to sulfur dioxide produced. The higher the molar ratio of oxygen reacting with the hydrogen sulfide, the lower the resulting molar ratio of sulfur to sulfur dioxide from oxidation of hydrogen sulfide. This can be understood with reference to the stoichiometry of the following two reactions:

(1) $$2H_2S + O_2 \longrightarrow 2H_2O + 2S$$
(2) $$2H_2S + 3O_2 \longrightarrow 2H_2O + 2SO_2$$

Thus at a molar ratio of oxygen to hydrogen sulfide of 1:2, all the hydrogen sulfide in the gas **18** can be converted to sulfur, and at a molar ratio of 3:2 all of the hydrogen sulfide can be converted to sulfur dioxide. Therefore, by adjusting the ratio of oxygen to hydrogen sulfide introduced to the retort, the molar ratio of sulfur to sulfur dioxide produced from hydrogen sulfide should be controllable.

It should be understood that even at molar ratios of oxygen to hydrogen sulfide of 1:2 and lower, some sulfur dioxide results from the oxidation of hydrogen sulfide, thereby leaving some hydrogen sulfide unoxidized. Similarly, even at molar ratios of oxygen to hydrogen sulfide of 3:2 and greater, some sulfur is at least initially produced from the oxidation of the hydrogen sulfide.

An advantage of oxidizing hydrogen sulfide at a temperature less than 300°F and an oxygen to hydrogen sulfide molar ratio of about 1:2 or less is that production of elemental sulfur is favored. Therefore, the purified gas can contain a lower concentration of sulfur compounds than the hydrogen-sulfide-containing gas introduced into the retort because the elemental sulfur formed can deposit in the retort. Also, a portion of the deposited sulfur can be recovered and sold as a valuable commodity.

The sulfur dioxide and sulfur produced from the reaction of oxygen and hydrogen sulfide can combine with constituents of the oil shale to yield solid sulfur-containing materials such as pyrites. It has been found that the percent of hydrogen sulfide oxidized by contacting oil shale in the presence of oxygen gradually decreases as the oil shale is exposed to hydrogen sulfide. However, it appears that percent conversion asymptotically approaches a constant effective level.

The gas stream **30** withdrawn from the retort has a relatively lower hydrogen sulfide concentration than the hydrogen-sulfide-containing gas **18** introduced into the retort **8** due to oxidation of hydrogen sulfide in the retort. It also can have a lower total sulfur compound content because of solid sulfur deposited on the mass of oil shale particles in the retort.

The hydrogen-sulfide-containing gas and oxygen-supplying gas can be introduced separately into the retort, or can be substantially homogeneously mixed prior to introduction into the retort. Mixing can be accomplished by any of a number of methods. Mixing can be effected with devices such as jet mixers, injectors, fans and the like.

The hydrogen-sulfide-containing gas **18** can inherently contain sufficient oxygen such that an oxygen-containing gas is not required. For example, off-gas from an in situ oil shale retort can contain 0.2% by volume oxygen and 0.16% by volume hydrogen sulfide. Thus off-gas can inherently contain sufficient oxygen to oxidize 83% of the hydrogen sulfide contained therein to sulfur dioxide and water.

The following controls and examples demonstrate the efficacy of raw oil shale in promoting the oxidation of hydrogen sulfide at low temperatures. The apparatus for conducting controls 1–4 is shown in Figure 3.18b. Bottled gas was provided in three tanks, **101, 102,** and **103.** Tank **101** contained 1.2 vol % hydrogen sulfide in nitrogen. Tank **102** contained 27 vol % CO_2, 4.5 vol % CH_4, 2.9 vol % H_2, and 4.2 vol % CO in nitrogen. This is about the same ratio as these gases are present in off-gas from an oil shale retort. Tank **103** contained air. Dry nitrogen was provided from line **104.**

Gases from tanks **101, 103** and line **104** were metered with flow meters **105** and control valves **106** and blended together to form 0.0464 cfm at 75°F of a gas mixture in line **107** containing 18 vol % oxygen, 0.10 vol % H_2S, and 71.9 vol % nitrogen. The gas mixture in line **107** passed to a three way valve **108** where a portion was intermittently diverted to a first water trap **109**, and then to a first sodium hydroxide trap **110** having a pH of 14. The first water trap **109** was used to determine the amount of hydrogen sulfide which dissolved in water at the gas compositions, flow rates, and trap configurations used. The first sodium hydroxide trap **110** was used to determine the inlet hydrogen sulfide concentration.

The gas mixture not diverted passed to a $7/8$-inch inner diameter quartz reactor **113** containing a bed **114** of oil shale particles. The temperature of the oil shale bed was maintained at a desired level with a single zone, 1-inch internal diameter electric furnace **115**. Shale bed temperatures were scanned with a thermocouple probe **116** inserted in a thermowell **117**. The temperature in the bed was controlled by means of a temperature controller **118**, and temperature was monitored with a temperature indicator **119**.

Effluent gas from the shale bed passed via line **133** to a second set of water **120** and sodium hydroxide **121** traps, and then was vented through line **122** to a hood. Elemental sulfur formed by the oxidation of hydrogen sulfide departed in line **133**.

The second water trap **120** served to remove sulfur dioxide from the reactor effluent and the second sodium hydroxide trap **121** removed unreacted hydrogen sulfide from the reactor effluent.

The sulfur content in the four traps was determined using a KIO_3 titration to a starch-iodine end point. For the sodium hydroxide traps **110** and **121**, the sample was acidified with hydrochloric acid prior to titration. The SO_2 concentration of the effluent gas as measured with the second water trap **120** was adjusted for the amount of H_2S known to dissolve in the trap as determined with the first water trap **109**.

For controls 1–4, 70 g of 1-mm diameter glass beads were used in the reactor. The reactor temperature used for each control is listed in the table below. The traps were periodically sampled to determine the hydrogen sulfide and sulfur dioxide content of the effluent from the reactor.

The percentage by weight of hydrogen sulfide removed from the feed, the percentage by weight of hydrogen sulfide converted to sulfur dioxide and the ratio of elemental sulfur to SO_2 produced from the H_2S are presented in the table for one hour after initiation of feed to the pyrolysis reactor. The values in the table assume that all hydrogen sulfide in the gas mixture feed to the reactor which is not in the effluent as sulfur dioxide or hydrogen sulfide was converted to elemental sulfur.

Example 1: Using the apparatus of Figure 3.18b, a reactor feed gas mixture having a composition by volume of 28% CO_2, 5% CO, 4.5% CH_4, 4.2% H_2, 0.10% H_2S, 0.5% O_2 and the balance N_2 was introduced to the reactor **114** at a rate of 0.0464 cfm at 75°F. The reactor contained a 70 g charge of –3 +8 mesh raw Colorado shale. The percent hydrogen sulfide removal was determined using the method described for controls 1–4 at 20, 60 and 100 minutes after initiation of feed to the reactor.

The results, which are presented in the table, clearly show that raw shale was effective in promoting oxidation of hydrogen sulfide in the presence of oxygen. However, even at temperatures up to 500°F hydrogen sulfide was not oxidized by contacting glass beads in the presence of oxygen.

It was noted that no measurable amount of the carbon monoxide, methane, and hydrogen introduced into the quartz reactor was lost. This indicates that raw oil shale can be used to effectively remove hydrogen sulfide from a gas stream containing components having fuel value without deleteriously affecting the fuel value of the gas stream.

Example 2: Off-gas generated in an in situ oil shale retort at a rate of 1,046 scfm containing a varying concentration of hydrogen sulfide in the range of from 1,500 to 3,000 ppm by volume hydrogen sulfide is combined with 12.8 scfm of air (molar ratio of O_2 to H_2S of 3:2 at 3,000 ppm H_2S content of the off-gas). The combined gas stream is introduced into the top of an in situ oil shale retort in the south/southwest portion of the Piceance Creek structural basin in Colorado. The retort contains a fragmented permeable mass of particles containing raw oil shale. The cross-sectional area of the retort is 1,055 ft^2 and the retort is 113 ft high. Gas is withdrawn from the bottom of the retort. The withdrawn gas has a lower H_2S concentration than the combined gas introduced to the retort.

Reactor Charge	Reactor Temperature (°F)	H₂S Removal .... Minutes.....		
		20	60	100
		......(%)......		
Control 1	Glass Beads	300	–	3	–
Control 2	Glass Beads	400	–	0	–
Control 3	Glass Beads	500	–	3	–
Control 4	Glass Beads	650	–	48	–
Example 1	Raw Wyoming Shale	300	52	30	15

Removal of Sulfur Dioxide

According to a process developed by *R.D. Ridley; U.S. Patents 4,093,026; June 6, 1978 and 4,125,157; November 14, 1978; both assigned to Occidental Oil Shale, Inc.*, sulfur dioxide is removed from a process gas, such as oxidized off-gas from oil shale retorting, by passing the process gas through a fragmented permeable mass of particles containing treated oil shale and including alkaline earth metal oxides. The fragmented permeable mass of particles can be in an in situ oil shale retort in a subterranean formation containing oil shale. The fragmented mass includes water, which can be provided by introducing water to the fragmented mass. The water combines with alkaline earth metal oxides in the fragmented mass and sulfur dioxide in the process gas.

Preferably the fragmented permeable mass contains a stoichiometric excess of alkaline earth metal oxides and/or hydroxides relative to the sulfur dioxide in the process gas when the process gas is passed through the fragmented permeable mass of particles to permit quick removal of the sulfur dioxide from the process gas and to insure that a high proportion of the sulfur dioxide is removed from the process gas.

The water in the fragmented mass can be introduced into the mass either alone, or it can be mixed with the process gas. Preferably water is removed from effluent gas from the fragmented mass and the removed water is recycled into the fragmented mass.

OTHER IN SITU RECOVERY PROCESSES

Molecular Sulfur and Benzene Recovery

According to a process described by *R.B. Duke; U.S. Patent 3,929,193; Dec. 30, 1975; assigned to Marathon Oil Company*, organic matter is recovered from organic mineral-containing deposits, e.g., oil shale, by contacting oil shale with elemental sulfur and an extraction fluid at temperatures in the range of from 200° to 1000°F. Ideally, the extraction fluids should not react substantially with the elemental sulfur.

The experimental extractions are carried out in a high-pressure autoclave into which the extraction fluid is pumped upflow through a bed of oil shale. Pressure on the system is maintained by a back pressure relief valve. The shale oil extract is collected in high-pressure cylinders which can be isolated from the extraction system, depressurized, and the shale oil-extraction fluid mixture collected.

The reactor is filled with a known amount of preassayed oil shale in either lump or core form. Under the desired operating pressure, 300 ml of extraction fluid is charged to liquid-fill the reactor. The flow rate through the reactor is then adjusted and the reactor heated rapidly to the desired extraction temperature. When sulfur is used, it is dissolved in the extraction fluid and pumped along with the latter to the reactor.

When the reactor reaches the desired temperature, the product reservoir is drained. The oil recovered during warmup is not used in the subsequent yield calculations. The initial time of the reaction, i.e., zero time, is taken the moment the extraction unit reaches the desired temperature. Subsequent time measurements are also taken from this reference point. Samples are then taken periodically and the oil yield determined.

The shale oil yields are determined by first filtering or centrifuging the shale oil-extraction fluid mixture to remove the small amount of insoluble matter carried along in the extractate. The extract is then distilled to separate the extraction fluid from the shale oil. The shale oil is subsequently vacuum dried to a constant weight to ascertain the yield. When sulfur is used to promote the extraction, some unreacted molecular sulfur is carried over into the product. To compensate for this, each shale oil sample is analyzed for sulfur. The shale oil yields are then reported on a sulfur-free basis.

Example 1: The extraction apparatus is filled with lump-size oil shale (-½ +10 mesh) and extracted with benzene at 625°F and 1,500 psig. The oil shale had a Fischer assay of 33.4 gal/ton (12.45 wt % oil). The results are shown in Figure 3.19a.

Figure 3.19: Extraction Process

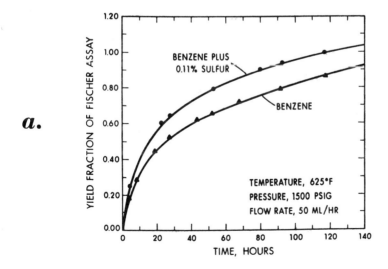

a.

(continued)

Figure 3.19: (continued)

b.

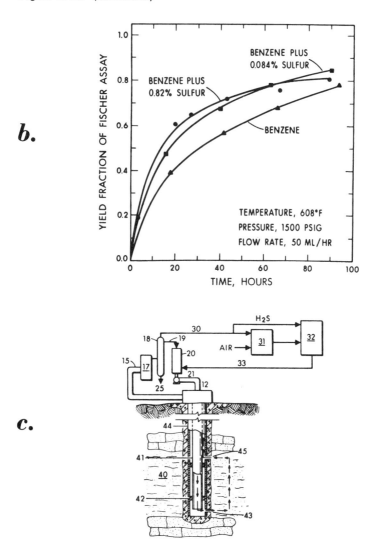

Source: U.S. Patent 3,929,193

Example 2: The extraction apparatus was filled with the same oil shale described in Example 1. The extraction was then carried out at the same temperature and pressure stated in Example 1; the benzene, however, contained 0.11% sulfur. The results are also shown in Figure 3.19a.

Example 3: The extraction apparatus was filled with the same oil shale described in Example 1 and extracted with benzene at 608°F. The results are shown in Figure 3.19b.

Example 4: The extraction apparatus was filled with the same oil shale described in Example 1 and extracted with benzene containing 0.084% sulfur at 608°F. The results are shown in Figure 3.19b.

Example 5: The extraction apparatus was filled with the same oil shale described in Example 1 and extracted with benzene containing 0.82% sulfur at 608°F. The results are shown in Figure 3.19b.

Example 6: Referring to Figure 3.19c, an extraction fluid containing sulfur is injected through inner well pipe **41** at a temperature of about 600°F to the bottom of the well where a packer **42** causes it to exit through a perforation **43** into an oil shale formation **40** which has previously been fractured by conventional techniques, e.g., explosive fracturing, leaching of sodium-containing minerals, mining, mining and explosive rubblizing, etc., in order to render the formation permeable to the flow of fluids. The hot extraction fluid, together with extracted shale oil removed from the formation enter the annular well pipe **44** through a second, higher, perforation **45**.

The mixture flows upward to the surface and into pipe **15**, and then into settling tank **17** to remove the inorganic residue. Centrifuges or filters may be used in the place of or in addition to the settling tank. The extractate is then transferred to the fractionator **18** from which a bottoms fraction **25** of shale oil is withdrawn for refinery processing. An overhead of H_2S **30** is withdrawn from the top of the fractionating tower **18**, oxidized to SO_2 in burner **31** to which air is fed, and then fed together with another portion of H_2S to reactor **32** in which H_2S and SO_2 react to form elemental sulfur for recycle through line **33**.

Fractionation tower **18** also separates the extraction fluid used in the process and recycles it to line **33** through line **19** where it is recombined with sulfur in tank **20**. Pump **21** then injects this benzene-sulfur mixture after heating, back into inner pipe **41**, repeating the process.

Hydrogen Sulfide and Carbon Dioxide Treatment

According to a process described by *A.H. Pelofsky; U.S. Patent 3,915,234; October 28, 1975; assigned to Cities Service Research & Development Company* hydrocarbon values are recovered from a subterranean deposit of oil shale by introducing a mixture of H_2S and CO_2 in water under pressure into the deposit. This is preferably accomplished by introducing water, CO_2 and H_2S into the deposit through wells extending into the deposit. Introduction of water, CO_2 and H_2S is continued until the pressure in the deposit at the point of introduction is increased to between about 200 and 1,000 psi above the formation pressure of the deposit. The deposit is then shut in until the pressure drops to less than about 50 psi above formation pressure, at which time hydrocarbon values, usually in the form of kerogen, may be recovered from the deposit.

In a preferred example, the sequence of injection of H_2S, CO_2 and water under pressure, followed by shutting in until pressure drops, is continued until the acids have penetrated the deposit throughout spheres of a radius between 50 and 500 feet about the points of introduction.

It is also preferred that the CO_2 and H_2S dissolved in water be introduced into the deposit as a saturated aqueous solution, between about 30 and 70 vol % of which comprises a saturated solution of CO_2 with the remainder being a saturated aqueous solution of H_2S.

Hot Fluid Injection into Solvent-Leached Shale

Numerous subterranean oil shales are mixed with water-soluble minerals. Such shales comprise substantially impermeable, kerogen-containing, earth formations from which shale oil can be produced by a hot fluid-induced pyrolysis or thermal conversion of the organic solids to fluids. A series of patents typified by T.N. Beard, A.M. Papadopoulos and R.C. Ueber; U.S. Patents 3,739,851; 3,741,306; 3,753,594; 3,759,328 and 3,759,574 describe procedures for utilizing the water-soluble minerals in such shales to form rubble-containing caverns.

In the caverns the oil shale is exposed to a circulating hot aqueous fluid that converts the kerogen to shale oil while dissolving enough mineral to expand the cavern and expose additional oil shale. In such a process, the heat transfer is aided by injecting the hot fluid into an upper portion and withdrawing fluid from a lower portion of the cavern.

A process described by *P.J. Closmann and M.J. Tham; U.S. Patents 3,967,853; July 6, 1976 and 3,880,238; April 29, 1975; both assigned to Shell Oil Company* relates to producing shale oil from a subterranean oil shale formation which contains or is contiguous with an areally extensive layer of water-soluble mineral. A plurality of cavities are formed in horizontally spaced locations surrounding a central well within the subterranean oil shale formation.

Portions of the areally extensive layer of water-soluble mineral are solution mined to form a generally horizontal void that interconnects the cavities and the central well. The shale oil is recovered by circulating hot fluid into the cavities, through the void connecting them with the central well and out through the central well.

U.S. Patent 3,880,238 describes a process for producing shale oil by circulating hot fluid into and out of a cavity in a subterranean oil shale formation in which the tendency for the fluid flow path to become plugged is reduced by injecting both a hot solvent fluid and a hot nonsolvent gas at rates adjusted to reduce the rate of disaggregating the oil shale into fine solid particles and to keep the cavity substantially free of liquid.

In the process, a plurality of cavities are interconnected with each other and a central well. The cavities are treated concurrently to produce shale oil from an areally extensive portion of the oil shale formation while maximizing the control of the fluid circulation and providing a relatively complete sweep of the formation. Where desirable, the rate of oil shale disaggregation can be controlled in the manner described in U.S. Patent 3,880,238 to avoid the plugging of the flow path.

The composition of the circulated fluid can be adjusted to provide proportions of hot solvent fluid and hot nonsolvent gas that maintain a selected rate of expansion of the cavity walls without causing an unduly rapid disaggregation of oil shale to fine solids. In such a fluid, the hot solvent may consist essentially of steam while the hot nonsolvent gas consists essentially of the products of an underground combustion.

"Water-soluble inorganic mineral" refers to halites or carbonates, such as the alkali metal chlorites, bicarbonates or carbonates, which compounds or minerals exhibit a significant solubility (e.g., at least 10 g/100 g of solvent) in generally neutral aqueous liquids (e.g., those having a pH of from 5 to 8) and/or heat-sensitive compounds or minerals, such as nahcolite, dawsonite, trona, or the like, which are naturally water-soluble or are thermally converted at relatively mild temperatures (e.g., 500° to 700°F) to materials which are water-soluble. The term "water-soluble-mineral-containing subterranean oil shale" refers to an oil shale that contains or is mixed with at least one water-soluble inorganic mineral, in the form of lenses, layers, nodules, finely-divided dispersed particles, or the like.

A "cavern" or "cavity" (within an oil shale formation) refers to a relatively solids-free opening or void in which the solids content is less than about 60% (preferably less than about 50%) and substantially all of the solids are fluid-surrounded pieces which are substantially free of lithostatic pressure, due to the weight of the overlying rocks.

In the process, the cavities can readily be formed by available means. A small cavity is formed by drilling a borehole. It can be enlarged by under-reaming, solution-mining, hydraulic or explosive fracturing, or the like operations. Where desirable, acids and/or viscous fluids can be utilized to dissolve and/or entrain solids to increase the volume of solid-free space within a cavity.

The solution-mining of water-soluble minerals by circulating hot aqueous fluid through an initially relatively small cavity (such as an under-reamed portion of a borehole) is a particularly preferred procedure for concurrently expanding the volume of a cavity and leaching the water-soluble minerals to form a permeable oil shale rubble within the cavity. The T.N. Beard and P. vanMeurs U.S. Patent 3,779,602 describes a particularly suitable process of solution-mining bicarbonate minerals by circulating hot water at a pressure that is optimized for enhancing the growth of a permeable rubble-containing cavity. The L.H. Towel and J.R. Brew U.S. Patent 3,792,902 describes such a solution-mining process in which plugging due to mineral precipitation is minimized by injecting an aqueous diluent into downhole portions of the outflowing fluid.

In general, the solution-mining fluid can be substantially an aqueous liquid (which is preferably slightly acidic or neutral) that tends to dissolve the water-soluble mineral without damaging the well conduits. Such a fluid is preferably circulated at a temperature, of from 200° to 400°F, exceeding the temperature of the adjacent portions of the subterranean oil shale formation.

Where the cavity in the oil shale formation is initially a substantially vertical section of a well borehole, the leaching fluid is advantageously injected into the cavity at a point near the bottom, with the mineral-laden solution being withdrawn from a point near the top. The points of injection and withdrawal can be reversed and the flow rate can be cyclically changed, both in direction and rate. The leaching is preferably continued to provide a cavity that contains a permeable oil shale rubble and has a suitable volume. As the leaching fluid contacts the oil shale in and along the walls of the cavity, soluble materials are dissolved from the contacted portions. This imparts permeability. Where the distribution of the water-soluble mineral is nonuniform, the leaching out of streaks or layers may cause the collapse of chunks of oil shale that become more permeable as the leaching continues. Along the walls, the rate of leaching tends to decrease with increases in the size of the cavity.

In general, the mineral-leaching should be continued until the cavity radius is on the order of 40 to 50 ft or more, preferably at least 100 ft. The cavity vertical height should approximate the thickness of the oil shale deposits and should be at least 200 ft, and preferably at least about 500 ft. The average permeability of the pieces of leached oil shale formation within the cavity and along the innermost portions of the cavity walls should be at least about 1 and preferably 10 or more darcies (1,000 to 10,000 or more millidarcies).

The minerals dissolved during the leaching operation can, of course, be recovered and can provide valuable by-products to the recovery of shale oil. In general, during the leaching process, some, but relatively small amounts of shale oil is entrained with and can be recovered from the fluid being circulated to effect the leaching operation.

A hot solvent fluid suitable for use in the process is one which is heated to a temperature of about 500° to 700°F and, at that temperature, has a significant miscibility with at least one of the organic or inorganic solid or liquid components or pyrolysis products of a water-soluble-mineral-containing oil shale. Such fluids preferably contain, or consist essentially of, steam at a temperature and pressure causing condensation within the cavern. Such fluids may also include or comprise hydrocarbons such as benzene, toluene, shale oil hydrocarbons, oil-soluble gases such as carbon dioxide, mixtures of such fluids, or the like.

A hot nonsolvent gas suitable for use in accordance with this process, can comprise substantially any gas which is heated to a temperature of at least about 500°F and at that temperature has a relatively insignificant miscibility with any of the organic or inorganic solid or liquid components or pyrolysis products of a water-soluble-mineral-containing oil shale. Such a gas preferably has a solubility of less than about 1 part per hundred in such solid or liquid components or pyrolysis products. Suitable nonsolvent gases include nitrogen, natural gas, combustion gases, methane (substantially free of higher hydrocarbons), mixtures of such gases, and the like.

Particularly where steam is used as the hot solvent fluid, the hot nonsolvent gas can be injected at temperatures higher than about 700°F, for example, to enhance the rate of revaporizing the steam condensate and the drying out of the cavern.

In a preferred example of the process, the borehole of the central well, through which the shale-oil-containing hot fluid is produced, is cases or lined in a manner that restricts the rubbling or disaggregating of the earth formations that form the wall of the borehole. This can be effected by means of methods or devices known to those skilled in the art. For example, one or more strings of casings or liners can be run in and cemented, the borehole walls can be heat-treated to carbonize the organic components, the inorganic components can be thermally glazed or coated with materials that are resistant to the temperature and solvent effects of the outflowing fluid, etc.

Figure 3.20a shows a portion of an oil shale formation **1** which contains or is contiguous with a water-soluble layer **2**, such as the Greeno nahcolite layer that is commonly encountered in the lower portion of oil shale formations in Colorado. Wells **3**, **4** and **6** are drilled into the soluble layer **2**. An open channel **7** (comprising an areally extensive void in the space occupied by layer **2**) is formed by solution-mining portions of the soluble mineral so that the channel interconnects the wells. The channel can be formed by means of known procedures and materials.

Figure 3.20: Production of Shale Oil with Circulating Hot Fluid

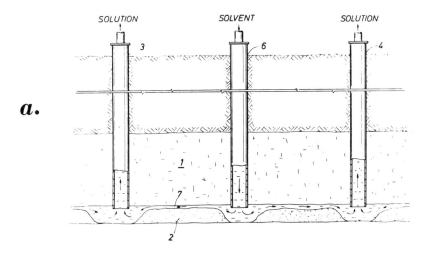

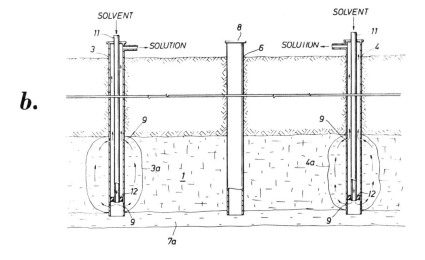

(continued)

Figure 3.20: (continued)

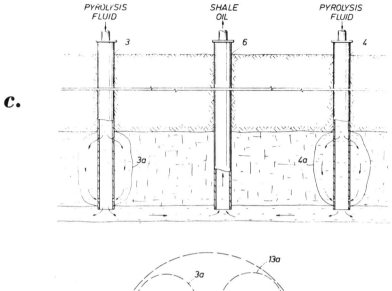

c.

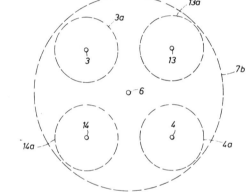

d.

(a)–(c)   Schematic illustrations of portions of subterranean oil
          shale formation
(d)   Plan view of a well pattern suitable for use in the proc-
      ess

Source: U.S. Patent 3,967,853

For example, near well portions can be leached out by initially extending tubing strings into each of the wells so that hot aqueous fluids can be circulated
to leach out portions of the soluble mineral around each well. The fluids in
the leached portions can then be pressurized to form generally horizontal fractures along the soluble mineral boundary and extend the fractures between the
wells. A solution of the soluble-mineral solvent can then be circulated in through
well **6** and out through wells **3** and **4**, as shown by the arrows in Figure 3.20b,
to form the well-interconnecting channel **7**.

As shown in Figure 3.20b, the well-interconnecting channel 7 can be leached out to form a substantially solids-free areally extensive void space 7a that interconnects the wells. Such a void space can conduct a relatively large volume of fluid without requiring a high velocity of flow.

The boreholes of wells 3 and 4 can be readily converted to cavities within the oil shale formation 1. During this operation the well 6 can be closed in, as indicated by the cap 8, so that the fluid in well 6 and the passageway 7a remain substantially static. In forming the cavities, the casings in the wells 3 and 4 can be penetrated by perforations 9. Such wells can be equipped with tubing strings 11 and packers 12, so that solvents and solutions can be circulated along the walls of the boreholes as shown by the arrows. Such circulations of hot aqueous solvents mine or leach the water-soluble minerals present in the oil shale formation. In effect, this expands the walls of the boreholes into cavities of increasing diameters, as indicated by the dashed lines and lines 3a and 4a.

Figure 3.20c shows a later stage of the process. Hot pyrolysis fluid is circulated in through the cavities around wells 3 and 4 while shale-oil-containing fluid is circulated out through the central well 6. As known to those skilled in the art, the tubings and packers 11 and 12 can be removed (as shown) or retained within the wells, with certain advantages and disadvantages accompanying either procedure. In general, the injected fluid is (a) preferably at least predominately a hot nonsolvent gas that pyrolyzes the kerogen in the rubble in and along the walls of the cavities 3a and 4a into which the walls of the boreholes of wells 3 and 4 have been expanded, and (b) is injected at a rate such that the wall-expansion continues without an undue amount of disaggregation of the oil shale into fines.

Figure 3.20d shows an essentially five-spot pattern of cavities and wells for use in the process. The wells 3, 4 and 6 are supplemented by wells 13 and 14. All of the wells are interconnected by the areally extensive passageway 7, which has been extended beyond the cavities, as indicated by the broken line 7b. The cavity walls 3a, 4a, 13a and 14a can be expanded until they extend substantially as close as desired to each other. Although the process can be conducted with one or more pairs of the cavities interconnected, it is generally preferably to leave sufficient "pillars" of untreated oil shale to prevent undue subsidence of the oil shale and the overlying earth formations. Multiples of such patterns of cavity-surrounded central wells, having ratios of cavities to central wells of at least one may be used in the process.

A number of related processes pertaining to producing shale oil from relatively permeable leached zones within a subterranean oil shale deposit by the use of hot fluids have been developed by *P.J. Closmann; U.S. Patents 3,888,307; June 10, 1975 and 4,026,359; May 31, 1977; M.J. Tham; U.S. Patent 3,987,851; October 26, 1976; M.J. Tham and P.J. Closmann; U.S. Patent 3,894,769; July 15, 1975 and P.J. Closmann, G. Drinkard, E.H. Street, C.C. Templeton and M.J. Tham; U.S. Patent 3,945,679; March 23, 1976; all assigned to Shell Oil Company.*

Steam Treatment and Extended Soak Period

According to a process described by *A.H. Pelofsky; U.S. Patent 3,882,941; May 13, 1975; assigned to Cities Service Research & Development Co.* hydrocarbons are recovered from oil shale deposits by introducing hot fluids into the deposits through wells and then shutting in the wells to allow kerogen in the deposits to be converted to bitumen which is then recovered through the wells after an extended period of soaking. The process thus comprises the steps of:

(a)   introducing heat energy in the form of hot fluids not containing oxygen into the deposit through one or more wells extending into the deposit, the heat energy being introduced in quantities sufficient to heat the deposit in the vicinity of the wells to more than about 50°F above its transition temperature and until the pressure at the bottom of the wells is from at least 200 to 1,000 psi above the formation pressure of the deposit;

(b)   then shutting in the wells until the temperature in the vicinity of the wells drops to less than about 50°F above the transition temperature of the deposit and until the pressure at the bottom thereof drops to less than about 50 psi above formation pressure, with the shutting in period lasting from about two weeks to about six weeks;

(c)   repeating steps (a) and (b) for a period of from one to ten years; and

(d)   producing bitumen through the wells.

Steam-Driven Excavating Unit

A process described by *G.M. Garte; U.S. Patent 3,941,423; March 2, 1976;* involves the use of apparatus in which high pressure steam is employed to drive engines mounted on the apparatus by which the screw action is effected causing the apparatus to descend through the shale bed. Steam, preferably in combination with compressed air, is also supplied to the interior of the apparatus at temperatures of approximately 900°F for reaction with the constituents of the shale to effect pyrolysis of the shale, with the separated oil being thereafter directed from the apparatus for treatment above surface.

In accordance with the process, the shale during the descent of the apparatus through the shale seam is directed to the interior of the apparatus through a crusher plate which functions to comminute the shale in order to facilitate the extraction process. As steam is admitted to the interior of the apparatus, the oil is extracted from the shale, due to the pressure and temperature conditions resulting from the steam admission, with the vaporized shale oil being withdrawn from the periphery of the apparatus and conveyed to separation equipment mounted on the surface. The remaining spent shale is forced through an upper grinding plate as the apparatus descends whereby the spent shale remains in situ during the operation of the apparatus.

When the apparatus has descended through the shale belt, the drive engines and consequently the screw action is reversed and the apparatus is propelled by its own grinding action upwardly through the spent shale until the apparatus reaches the surface. There is thus no hole or opening formed in the surface as such, and the apparatus can be moved to an adjoining area and the operation repeated. Several units can be assembled together to increase the productivity in a specified area of operation.

Thus, the oil extraction apparatus is relatively portable and is constructed and arranged to descend through the earth propelled by its own grinding action. The apparatus in normal operation descends to the bottom of the shale seam and can thereafter be reversed for upward movement to the surface with the spent shale remaining in the area as the apparatus ascends.

Anaerobic Microorganisms

S. Ghosh and D.L. Klass; U.S. Patent 4,085,972; April 25, 1978; assigned to Institute of Gas Technology describe a process for recovering underground fossil fuel deposits wherein the deposit is contacted with an aqueous medium of anaerobic microorganisms for a time sufficient to produce particles of the deposit containing both the organic fossil fuel and inorganic matrix of a size capable of forming a slurry with the aqueous medium for pumping to the ground surface. At the ground surface, the particulates are separated from the aqueous medium of anaerobic organisms, the particulates further processed by efficient surface techniques to separate the organic carbon and hydrocarbon component from the inorganic matrix.

The aqueous medium of anaerobic organisms is recycled to the underground fossil fuel deposit for further production of the slurry forming particles of the deposit. Spent inorganic matrix may be added to the aqueous medium of anaerobic organisms to provide solid support and nutrient for the organisms and to maintain the desired pH. Such use of the spent inorganic matrix provides a useful service for the waste from the organic carbon and hydrocarbon recovery process.

Example 1: Colorado oil shale containing 11.7 to 15.8% organic carbon and 19.87% volatile matter by weight and having more than 70 wt % particle size of 2.0 to 2.8 mm in diameter was mildly mixed by a magnetic agitation bar in an aqueous slurry with facultative anaerobes provided by an inoculant of municipal digested sewage sludge for 45 days at 35°C and a pH of 7.1. The oil shale particle sizes were reduced to 0.1 mm and less, and a gas containing 90% methane was produced at a yield of 2.5 scf of methane per pound of oil shale volatile matter. This example shows the size reduction of the oil shale which takes place as a result of the anaerobic microorganism activity and the high methane content gas produced as compared to 55 to 60% methane content gas usually obtained.

Example 2: An aqueous slurry of microorganisms provided by digested municipal sewage sludge and spent inorganic matrix from kerogen recovery from oil shale is pumped down a hole to an underground fossil fuel deposit. The slurry contains about 15 wt % anaerobes and about 30 wt % spent inorganic matrix which provides solid support and nutrient for the organisms and maintains the pH at less than about 7.0. The fossil fuel deposit temperature is about 40°C and after a fossil fuel deposit contact time of 70 days a slurry is pumped from the deposit to the ground surface and contains particulates of the underground deposit of organic fossil fuel and inorganic matrix having an average particle size of about 10 mm. The particulates are separated for processing to separate the organic carbon component, and the anaerobes together with a suitable amount of spent inorganic matrix are recirculated to the underground deposit as an aqueous slurry.

Hot Aqueous Alkaline Liquids and Fluid Circulation

A process described by *G. Drinkard; U.S. Patent 4,026,360; May 31, 1977; assigned to Shell Oil Company* relates to producing shale oil from a subterranean oil shale formation which has a composition at least similar to those encountered in the Piceance Creek Basin in Colorado and contains an interconnected network of relatively permeable channels formed by the natural fracturing or leaching of the formation. At least one pair of wells is opened into the formation and is operated so that fluid flows between them along a selected path within the oil shale formation. The composition, pressure and temperature of the so-flowed fluid is adjusted

(a)   to cause the oil shale to be contacted by a relatively hot aqueous alkaline liquid that hydrothermally converts oil shale mineral components to particles of water-swellable clay-like material that are dispersed along the flow path, and

(b)   to subsequently contact the so-dispersed particles with a relatively electrolyte-free aqueous liquid that swells the clay-like materials and reduces the permeability of the earth formations within the flow path.

Shale oil is then produced by circulating fluid into and out of a portion of the oil shale formation which is bounded by a flow-confining barrier formed by at least one such path of reduced permeability.

Samples of generally sand size particles of a Green River oil shale formation were heated at the temperatures indicated in Table 1 under aqueous liquid solutions at the indicated compositions. The fluid pressures were about the minimum needed to keep substantially all of the aqueous fluid liquid. Where the fluid status was static, the fluids were kept quiescent and where the status was flow, the aqueous liquid phase was changed by displacement of equal portions of solutions of the same initial concentration during the test.

Table 2 shows the results of the above tests on the crystalline components of the oil shale samples, as indicated by an x-ray diffraction analysis. The mineral components are indicated in percentages by weight.

The concentration of clay refers to the clay-like mineral material that was produced during the treatment. Typical samples of the untreated raw shale contained only the indicated proportions of feldspar and calcite along with 15% quartz, 35% dolomite, 17.5% nahcolite, and 17.5% dawsonite. Thus, it is apparent that significant proportions of clay-like minerals were formed by hydrothermal conversion of the mineral components during the interaction between the oil shale samples and the hot aqueous alkaline liquids.

Table 1

Run	Temperature ($^\circ$F)	Duration (days)	Fluid Description	Fluid Status
4-A	554	35	aqueous phase:5% Na_2CO_3	static
4-B	554	35	aqueous phase:5% Na_2CO_3	flow
4-C	554	49	aqueous phase:5% Na_2CO_3	static
4-D	554	49	aqueous phase:5% Na_2CO_3	flow

(continued)

Table 1: (continued)

Run	Temperature (°F)	Duration (days)	Fluid Description	Fluid Status
6-1	617	20	aqueous phase:5% Na_2CO_3	static
6-2	617	20	aqueous phase:5% Na_2CO_3	flow
6-3	617	22	aqueous phase:5% Na_2CO_3	static
6-4	617	22	aqueous phase:5% Na_2CO_3	flow
7-1	482	5	aqueous phase:5% Na_2CO_3	static
7-2	482	10	aqueous phase:5% Na_2CO_3	static
7-3	482	10	aqueous phase:5% NaOH	static
7-4	482	30	aqueous phase:5% Na_2CO_3	static
8-A	482	14	aqueous phase:5% Na_2CO_3	static
8-B	482	24	aqueous phase:5% Na_2CO_3	static

Table 2

Run	Feldspar	Calcite	Analcite	Clay
Raw shale	10	20	—	—
4-A	30	20	20	30
4-B	20	20	30	30
4-C	25	25	10	40
4-D	10	20	50	20
6-1	20	20	25	35
6-2	25	20	15	40
6-3	25	30	15	30
6-4	10	35	30	25
7-1	10	45	25	20
7-2	10	45	25	20
7-3	15	35	20	30
7-4	15	35	20	30
8-A	10	45	25	20
8-B	10	45	25	20

To illustrate the permeability effects of such clay-like materials, a laboratory experiment was conducted in which a sample of Green River oil shale, pretreated in an aqueous sodium-alkaline solution at approximately 600°F for a time sufficient to form clay-like materials, was tested for permeability to brine and water.

The so-treated samples were made into reconstituted cores for use in a permeability apparatus by lightly tamping it into a split mold containing a cylindrical opening 1 inch in diameter by about 2½ inches long. The core thus produced was then frozen, removed from the mold, and placed in a rubber-sleeve Hassler-type holder. A thin wafer of porous Alundum (K >10 darcies) was used to confine the ends of the core. Isostatic pressure of 35 psi was applied to the sample and the core was saturated with a synthetic brine containing 25,000 ppm NaCl. Permeability to a flowing brine of the same high electrolyte composition was measured over a three-hour period. Permeability decreased from about 66 millidarcies (md) to a stable level of about 28 md during the flowing through the core of about 26 to 36 cc of the brine.

After this phase of the test, the flooding liquid was changed to fresh water and additional permeability measurements made for approximately two hours. During this time permeability decreased from about 28 to less than 4 md during the flowing through the core of about 35 cc of the fresh water. This behavior illustrates the permeability control achievable by conversion of shale using alkaline solutions followed by treatment with low salinity water.

Typical results of dispersive x-ray analysis of similarly treated oil shale samples have shown the major effect of such a conversion to be the formation of clay-like material resembling montmorillinite. The permeability decreases observed in the above tests are believed to arise from swelling of this material in the presence of fresh water in the same way that natural montmorillinite swells and closes off permeability.

Plasma Arc

S.L. Camacho and L.J. Circeo, Jr.; U.S. Patent 4,067,390; January 10, 1978; assigned to Technology Application Services Corporation describe an apparatus and method which utilizes a plasma arc torch as a heat source for recovering useful fuel products from in situ deposits of coal, tar sands and oil shale.

When applied to tar sands and oil shale, the torch is lowered in a shaft into the deposit and serves as a heat source to allow the entrapped oil in the tar sand or the kerogen in the oil shale to flow to a reservoir for collection. When economically justified, the carbonaceous matter in the tar sands or oil shale deposits may be partially or completely pyrolyzed and recovered as gaseous fuel products.

Monitoring means for continuously analyzing selected properties of the fuel products enable the operator to control the operating parameters within the shaft.

SHALE OIL REFINING
AND PURIFICATION PROCESSES

As a result of the increasing demand for light hydrocarbon fractions, there is much current interest in economical methods for recovering liquid hydrocarbons from oil shale on a commercial scale. Various methods for recovery of hydrocarbons from these deposits have been proposed, but the principal difficulty with these methods is their high cost which renders the recovered hydrocarbons too expensive to compete with petroleum crudes recovered by more conventional methods.

Moreover, the value of hydrocarbons recovered from oil shale is diminished due to the presence of certain contaminants in the recovered hydrocarbons and the form of the recovered hydrocarbons. The chief contaminants are sulfurous, nitrogenous, and metallic compounds which cause detrimental effects with respect to various catalysts utilized in a multitude of processes to which the recovered hydrocarbons may be subjected. These contaminants are also undesirable because of their disagreeable odor, corrosive characteristics, and combustion products. Also the oil obtained from tar sands is heavier and more viscous than conventional petroleum crudes and has properties resembling those of residual materials. About 50% of the hydrocarbon fraction recovered from tar sands boils above 1000°F and cannot be pumped in a conventional crude pipeline because of the relatively high pour point and viscosity.

Additionally, as a result of the increasing demand for light hydrocarbon fractions, there is much current interest in more efficient methods for converting the heavier hydrocarbon fractions recovered from oil shale into lighter materials. The conventional methods of converting heavier hydrocarbon fractions into lighter materials, such as catalytic cracking, coking, thermal cracking and the like, always result in the production of more highly refractory materials.

It is known that such heavier hydrocarbon fractions and such refractory materials can be converted to lighter materials by hydrocracking. Hydrocracking processes are most commonly employed on liquefied coals or heavy residual or distillate oils for the production of substantial yields of low boiling saturated products and to some extent of intermediates which are utilizable as domestic fuels, and still heavier cuts which find uses as lubricants. These destructive hydrogenation processes or hydrocracking processes may be operated on a strictly thermal basis or in the presence of a catalyst.

However, the application of the hydrocracking technique has in the past been fairly limited because of several interrelated problems. Conversion by the hydrocracking technique of heavy hydrocarbon fractions recovered from oil shale to more useful products is complicated by the presence of certain contaminants in such hydrocarbon fractions. The presence of sulfur- and nitrogen-containing and organo-metallic compounds in crude oils and various refined petroleum products and hydrocarbon fractions has long been considered undesirable.

This chapter describes a number of developments for the combined retort and hydrocracking of shale oil as well as for the removal of certain contaminants.

COMBINED RETORTING AND REFINING PROCESSES

Retorting and Hydrocracking Using Activated Spent Shale

P.H. Gifford, II; U.S. Patent 4,001,105; January 4, 1977 describes a process for the simultaneous retorting and in situ hydrocracking of carbonaceous materials in general as, for example, oil shale, coal, tar sands, and lignite. The catalytic effects of activated spent shale are utilized to produce the desired results, i.e., a high yield of either low boiling liquid hydrocarbons or of a gas suitable for the subsequent production of methane or synthetic natural gas, or a significant yield of both.

The process is performed by first producing a catalytically reactive mass in a reaction zone. This is a startup step and needs to be performed only during the startup. The reaction zone is filled with raw shale, and using steam and oxygen, the raw shale is retorted to a white, nonagglomerating spent shale which is activated when held above a minimum temperature of from $1000°$ to $1100°F$. This assures a finite rate of carbonate decomposition in the presence of water.

Raw oil shale or a mixture of raw oil shale and other carbonaceous materials to be liquefied and/or gasified is added continuously to the reactive mass. In the case of mixtures, spent oil shale may be substituted for raw oil shale where just the catalytic value, as opposed to the hydrocarbon value, of the shale is desired. The source of this spent shale may be any one of the existing oil shale processes. The point of introduction of this carbonaceous feed must be upstream of the activated spent shale which was provided in the startup step.

Steam and oxygen are added simultaneously and continuously to the reactive mass. The steam is required for two reasons: (1) it is believed to be associated with the catalytic cracking activity of the activated spent shale, and (2) it reacts with the coke, char, or carbonaceous residue to produce the hydrogen required. The oxygen is added to supply the heat duty of the process. If the steam and oxygen or their reaction products do not provide sufficient agitation of the reactive mass to assure adequate solids mixing of the reactive mass, then other means of agitation must be employed. Such means could be, for example, mechanical agitation or the use of a recycle of a portion of the gaseous products to the bottom of the bed.

From the reactor is withdrawn continuously a low molecular weight hydrocarbon product and the spent material. The low molecular weight hydrocarbon product may be either a low boiling liquid of from about 30° to 60°API or a gas suitable for the subsequent production of methane or synthetic natural gas, or both. The spent material, whose composition should be similar to that of the reactive mass in the reaction zone, should be essentially free of any carbonaceous residue.

In essence, this process actually includes three process variations, a liquefaction variation, a gasification variation, or a combination of the two. It is to be understood, however, when operated in either mode, liquefaction or gasification, some of the compliment product is obtained. When it is operated mainly as a liquefaction process, it is the purpose of this process to produce a low boiling, stable crude of from about 30° to 60°API from the volatile constituents of both the oil shale and the other carbonaceous materials being fed. This is believed to be accomplished through the catalytic cracking of the normally heavy thermal decomposition products, followed by the in situ hydrogenation of these cracked products. Although there is another possible mechanism, it is believed that the hydrogen is supplied through the catalyzed steam-carbon reaction, this carbon coming mainly from the lesser reactive char or coke which is normally left behind as a residue in other existing processes.

When operated mainly for the gasification of the carbonaceous feeds, it is the purpose of this process to produce a gaseous product which is suitable for the subsequent production of methane or synthetic natural gas at thermal efficiencies much higher than are obtained by the prior art processes. This again is believed to be accomplished through the more severe hydrocracking of the normally volatile constituents of the carbonaceous feeds with the hydrogen again coming from the catalyzed steam-carbon reaction. The distribution between liquid and gaseous products is determined mainly by the severity of operation, and the severity of the reaction zone, as used in this process is related primarily to the temperature of the reaction zone, but concentration of catalyst per unit volume of reactive mass is also a part of severity. The higher the severity the greater will be the percentage of gaseous products produced.

Hydroretorting

S.A. Weil, P.B. Tarman and D. Punwani; U.S. Patent 4,003,821; January 18, 1977; assigned to the Institute of Gas Technology describe a process for producing hydrocarbon liquid in preference to gases from oil shale. The shale is introduced at the top of a reaction chamber which includes an upper oil shale preheat zone having a temperature not more than about 950°F, a hydroretort reaction zone at a temperature of about 850° to 1250°F and a lower hydrogen preheat zone to recover heat from spent shale. Solids from the shale are passed downwardly through the chamber so that the shale, and particularly the oil therein, is gradually heated to the reaction temperature over a relatively extended period of at least 10 minutes so as to inhibit the formation of a carbon residue.

A hydrogen-rich gas, containing hydrogen in excess of stoichiometric amounts needed for the hydroretorting of the oil in the shale, is passed upwardly in the reaction chamber and countercurrent to the shale solids passing downwardly. A hydroretorting reaction is promoted in the reaction chamber between the oil or organic material in the shale and the hydrogen so as to produce predominately distillable hydrocarbon liquids and a low proportion of low molecular weight paraffinic hydrocarbon gases. The process can be controlled to maximize production of aliphatic and alicyclic hydrocarbon liquids which may be utilized for wide variety of purposes including gasification for the production of synthetic pipeline-quality gas from oil shale.

Prehydrogenation and Hydroretort Zone

H.R. Linden, P.B. Tarman and H.L. Feldkirchner; U.S. Patent 3,922,215; November 25, 1975; assigned to American Gas Association, Inc. describe a process for the production of hydrocarbon liquids and gases from oil shale comprising the steps of gradually preheating oil shale in a preheat and prehydrogenation zone to a temperature of about 700° to 950°F in the presence of hydrogen-rich gas without substantial production of liquid and gas in the preheat and prehydrogenation zone, then destructively distilling the preheated and prehydrogenated oil shale in a hydroretort zone at a temperature of about 850° to 1250°F in the presence of hydrogen-rich gas to form aliphatic and alicyclic hydrocarbon liquids and low molecular weight paraffinic hydrocarbon gases from the preheated and prehydrogenated organic hydrocarbon portion of the oil shale.

The hydrogen-rich gas may be passed countercurrent in thermal exchange relation to the spent shale to recover heat from the spent shale heating the hydrogen-rich gas for passage countercurrent and in thermal exchange relation to fresh oil shale in the preheat and prehydrogenation zone. The improvement of this process lies in the exceptionally high conversion of the organic component of oil shale to products of high value including high yields of readily distillable liquids comprising a high proportion of aliphatic and alicyclic hydrocarbon liquids and to low molecular weight paraffinic hydrocarbon gases. The process can be controlled, if desired, to maximize production of aliphatic and alicyclic hydrocarbon liquids.

Example: Oil shale having a Fischer Assay of 24 gallons per ton was crushed into particles of about one-half inch in size. The crushed shale, at ambient temperature of about 77°F, was introduced into a vessel having an upper preheat and prehydrogenation zone, a hydroretort zone in the middle and a heat recovery zone in the lower portion. These zones are separated by two decks, one between the bottom of the preheat and prehydrogenation zone and the top of the hydroretort zone and the other between the bottom of the hydroretort zone and the top of the heat recovery zone. Solid flow by gravity through these zones was controlled by a solids flow controller at the spent shale exit in the bottom of the heat recovery zone. The entire system operated at a total pressure of 1,000 psia and lock hoppers were used to introduce the crushed shale to the upper end of the preheat and prehydrogenation zone and moved through this zone countercurrent to hydrogen-rich gas.

Hydrogen-rich gas containing 93.9 mol percent hydrogen was introduced at a rate of 4.3 mols per hour at a temperature of 950°F to the bottom of the preheat and prehydrogenation zone through a gas distributor. The shale was introduced at the rate of 100 pounds per hour for a residence time of about 15 minutes flowing countercurrent to the hydrogen-rich gas. The shale left the preheat and prehydrogenation zone at a temperature of 850°F and entered directly to the top of the hydroretort zone. About 0.6 pound per hour of hydrocarbon oils having a carbon/hydrogen ratio of 6.95/1 and about 0.34 pound per hour of water were formed in the preheat and prehydrogenation zone. The oil and water were removed from the hydrogen-rich gas leaving the top of the preheat and pre-hydrogenation zone and the oil was fed directly to a gas phase hydrogasifier.

The shale was further heated in the hydroretort zone to 1100°F by a combination of cocurrent flow with hydrogen-rich gas introduced to the top of the hydroretort zone at 1350°F and by direct firing of fuel and oxygen within the zone. 0.12 pound per hour of the aromatic liquids produced in the gas phase hydrogasifier were used as fuel for this purpose. 0.5 mol per hour of gas containing hydrogen were supplied to more than satisfy the chemical requirements for complete hydroretorting. This gas was removed from the top of the preheat and prehydrogenation zone and after liquids removed, was heated to 1350°F and introduced to the top of the hydroretort zone. The residence time of the shale in the hydroretort zone was about 5 minutes. The output of the hydroretort zone showed that 90.8% of the organic carbon in the shale had been converted, 82.7% to hydrocarbon liquids having a C/H ratio of 7.4/1 and 8.1% to low molecular weight paraffinic hydrocarbon gases.

The spent shale was removed from the bottom of the hydroretort zone to the top of the heat recovery zone wherein it was cooled to 150°F by countercurrent flow with hydrogen-rich gas recycled from the preheat and prehydrogenation zone, 3.8 mols per hour of gas containing 93.8 mol percent hydrogen were recycled from the preheat and prehydrogenation zone at 100°F, heated to 792°F in the heat recovery zone and further heated to 950°F by a furnace in the recycle line bypassing the hydroretort zone and fed to the bottom of the preheat and prehydrogenation zone. 0.51 mol per hour of 94.4% hydrogen-rich make-up gas was added to the hydrogen-rich gas fed to the bottom of the heat recovery zone. 10.3 pounds per hour of hydrocarbon liquids from the hydroretort zone and 1.2 pounds per hour of water were separated from the product gases by cooling.

The hydrocarbon liquids were then fractionated and the low boiling hydrocarbon fraction produced at the rate of 4.2 pounds per hour and having a C/H ratio of 7.0/1 were fed, together with the product gases from the separator, to a recycle type gas phase hydrogasifier operated at 1400°F. Hydrocarbons having a C/H ratio of 7.0/1 or less limit the carbon deposition in the hydrogasifier. The high boiling hydrocarbon fraction produced at the rate of 6.0 pounds per hour and having a C/H ratio of 7.7/1 were fed to a partial oxidation plant for producing hydrogen-rich gas make-up for use in the process. The product of the hydrogasifier at 1400°F was passed in thermal exchange relation with the hydrogen-rich gas removed from the top of the preheat and prehydrogenation zone prior to its introduction to the top of the hydroretort zone, heating such hydrogen-rich gas from 100° to 1350°F and cooling the product of the hydrogasifier to 720°F.

After passing through this heat exchanger, the gaseous product was further cooled and 0.034 pound per hour of water and 0.73 pound per hour of aromatic liquids were removed. Then 0.012 mol per hour of carbon dioxide and 0.010 mol per hour of hydrogen sulfide were removed and the gas methanated resulting in dried pipeline-quality gas having a gross heating value of 951 Btu/scf and containing less than 0.1% carbon monoxide. 1.58 scf of pipeline-quality gas containing 92.8 mol percent methane was produced per pound of dry shale.

According to a related process described by *H.R. Linden, P.B. Tarman and H.L. Feldkirchner; U.S. Patent 3,929,615; December 30, 1975; assigned to the American Gas Association, Inc.* the production of hydrocarbon gases from oil shale comprises the steps of gradually preheating oil shale in a preheat and prehydrogenation zone to a temperature of about 700° to 950°F in the presence of hydrogen-rich gas without substantial production of liquid or gas in the preheat and prehydrogenation zone, then hydrogasifying the preheated and prehydrogenated oil shale in a hydrogasification zone at a temperature of about 1200° to 1500°F in the presence of hydrogen-rich gas to form predominately low molecular weight paraffinic hydrocarbon gases from the preheated and prehydrogenated organic hydrocarbon portion of the oil shale.

The hydrogen-rich gas may be passed countercurrent in thermal exchange relation to the spent shale to recover heat from the spent shale heating the hydrogen-rich gas for passage countercurrent and in thermal exchange relation to fresh oil shale in the preheat and prehydrogenation zone. The improvement of this process lies in the exceptionally high conversion of the organic component of oil shale to products of high value having high content of low molecular weight paraffinic hydrocarbon gases.

Fluidized Bed Hydroretort

A process described by *A.A. Gregoli; U.S. Patent 4,075,081; February 21, 1978; assigned to Cities Service Company* eliminates the retorting stage of conventional shale upgrading, by subjecting crushed shale to a hydroretorting treatment in an upflow, fluidized bed reactor, such as that used for the hydrocracking of heavy petroleum residues. Broadly, the process for extracting oil from oil shale comprises the steps of: (a) crushing the shale; (b) mixing the crushed shale with a hydrocarbon liquid to give a pumpable slurry and heating at least one of the reactor feed component streams; (c) introducing the slurry, along with a hydrogen-containing gas, into an upflow, fluidized bed reactor at a superficial fluid (liquid plus gas) velocity sufficient to move the mixture upwardly through the reactor; (d) hydroretorting the oil shale; (e) removing the reaction mixture from the reactor as total overhead effluent; and (f) separating the reactor effluent into two or more components.

This process, in eliminating conventional thermal retorting, concurrently eliminates the internal combustion feature common to several of the retort systems. Since carbonate decomposition, common to retorting, is minimized in the process by the use of reaction temperatures lower than those used in retorting, the gas product from this process has a greater heating value, due to a minimum of CO_2 resulting from combustion and carbonate decomposition. Also, due to the exothermic nature of the hydroretorting reactions, less input in energy is required per barrel of product obtained. The products, having less unsaturation than products obtained by prior art retorting processes, have improved stability.

There is no upper or lower limitation on the grade of oil shale that can be treated. A liquid recycle stream is used as a primary means of heating incoming feed material, as opposed to the mechanical movement and mixing of hot spent shale or hot metal balls of prior art retorting processes. The yield (per ton of feed material) from this process is higher than for prior art processes.

Retorting and Cracking

A process described by *J.C. Morrell; U.S. Patent 3,954,597; May 4, 1976* relates to unitary and continuous process to produce the desired products, divided for clarity of description, into two sections: (a) retorting section, and (b) cracking section, the first comprising a retorting section which in one principal aspect may be an essentially tubular vertical retort, or in another aspect a horizontal rotating retort sloping downwardly, in which in any event the oil shale is heated indirectly by the hot gases of combustion, and are kept separate from the oil vapors and gases from the oil shale.

The hot combustion products of the fuel in general move upwardly and out of direct contact with the shale. The fuel in general is producer gas made from the spent oil shale and/or coke from the cracking section, and alternatively hydrocarbon gases both from the retort and cracking section of the process. All of which fuels in general furnish the heat to support the entire operation including refining, steam generation and power production generally, including electricity. The oil vapors (and gases) from the oil shale pass into a fractionator and/or partial condenser which is directly connected to the oil shale retort and wherein the light oil distillate and water (from the oil shale) are condensed, separated and collected as an overhead product.

The major portion of the shale oil, i.e., the hot-liquid condensate from the bottom of a fractionator and/or partial condenser which is the charging stock for the cracking section, may be pumped by a high-pressure hot-oil pump together with the hot reflux condensate from the dephlegmator of the cracking section through the highly heated cracking tubes, and into one of the reaction and coking chambers wherein the coke from the reaction is deposited and accumulated until ready for switching to another chamber for periodic cleaning and removal of the coke.

The vapors leaving the reaction chamber pass into the dephlegmator of the cracking section where the overhead cracked or pressure distillate containing the unrefined product of the process is condensed and collected and separated, and the hot heavier reflux condensate from the dephlegmator of the cracking section is continuously recycled, together with the major portion of the hot shale oil from the fractionator of the oil shale retort section, to produce on a continuous basis the desired products of the process.

The retort section including the fractionator, etc., both at relatively high temperatures of the process, is under substantially atmospheric pressure or may be made slightly less (by use of a suction fan) to avoid leakage; whereas the cracking section of the process is entirely under a relatively high superatmospheric pressure throughout the system; and all the heating elements and those directly attached thereto, e.g., the heater or cracking tubes, reaction or cracking chambers, and dephlegmator are at relatively high temperatures. The by-products of the process other than those used as fuel, e.g., those produced from spent oil shale and their uses are obviously secondary to those of the principal process.

According to a related process described by *J.C. Morrell; U.S. Patent 4,105,536; August 8, 1978* oil shale is partially dehydrated prior to retorting. Both the dehydrating and retorting steps are carried out by heat treatment in rotating horizontal cylindrical vessels heated by indirect heat exchange with hot gas.

The vapors withdrawn from the retorting step are fractionated to yield products including a heavy conversion oil. The process permits the transport of the shale oil product by pipeline to the refinery where it may be refined into products, utilizing cracking and refining equipment, and in addition, to facilitating transportation as well as defining operations at the refinery, and simplifying the operations at the mine.

The latter is a very important factor in the development of a full scale fuel distillate industry from oil shale comparable in capacity to the present day operation in the petroleum industry.

Oil Extraction and Cracking in Presence of Hot Sand

According to a process described by *A.M. Leas; U.S. Patent 4,008,145; Feb. 15, 1977* solid fuel in a crushed or shredded state is conveyed into the top of an oil extractor, where oils are extracted, phenolics, organo-nitrogen compounds and sulfurous materials are decomposed to steam, ammonia and hydrogen sulfide with hydrogen transfer operating to increase the rate of removal of oils from the solid fuel, the hot fuel gases are removed to a unit where the hydrogen sulfide is removed and desulfurized low Btu gas recovered.

The solid-oil slurry remaining in the extractor is removed to a hydrocracker where high molecular weight compounds are cracked to lower molecular weight compounds. The thus-treated solid-oil slurry is removed to a reactor, admixed with hot, circulating sand with the resultant cracking producing fuel gas, and vaporized diesel and gasoline fuels. The vaporized fuels are filtered and separated, the gasoline fraction further extracted in a fractionator and removed as product.

The diesel fraction is hydrogenated and returned to the oil extractor for further recycling, the higher heat content fuel gas in the solids reactor removed with the vaporized diesel and gasoline fuels is diverted, a portion thereof removed to the diesel hydrogenator and the hydrocracker, with the remainder conveyed to a desulfurization caustic treater and reconveyed to a desulfurization caustic treater and removed from the system.

The solids in the reactor adhere to downwardly flowing hot sand into a gasification zone where the carbon is gasified with steam, oxygen, and carbon dioxide, the ash separated from the sand by the upward force of the gases and collected in annular collection zones at the bottom of the reactor, the sand removed to lower pressure storage or lock-bins for recycling with the carbon dioxide removed and recycled after desulfurization with cobalt oxide, and the ash removed for treatment to remove soluble alkali metals and removed from the system.

SHALE OIL REFINING

Thermal Cracking

F.E. Wynne, Jr.; U.S. Patent 4,057,490; November 8, 1977 and J.D. McKinney, R.T. Sebulsky and F.E. Wynne, Jr.; U.S. Patent 4,080,285; March 21, 1978 both assigned to Gulf Research & Development Company describe a process for the noncatalytic thermal cracking of shale oil in the presence of a gaseous diluent and an entrained stream of inert heat carrier solids. The cracking process is directed towards the recovery of gaseous olefins as the primarily desired cracked product, in preference to gasoline range liquids. At least 15 or 20% of the feed oil is converted to ethylene. While ethylene is the single most prevalent gaseous product most of the feed oil is converted to both other gaseous products and to liquid products. Other valuable hydrocarbon gaseous products include propylene and 1,3-butadiene. Other C_4's and ethane are also produced. Hydrogen is recovered as a valuable nonhydrocarbon gaseous product. Liquid products are produced in the cracking process by combination of intermediate olefinic material in the reactor and can comprise 40 or 50 weight percent or more of the total product.

Recovered liquid products include benzene, mixtures of benzene, toluene and xylenes (BTX), gasoline boiling range liquids and light and heavy gas oils. The economic value of the various gaseous and liquid hydrocarbon products is variable and depends upon prevailing market conditions. Coke is a solid product of the process and is produced by polymerization of unsaturated materials. Most of the coke formed is removed from the process as a deposit upon the entrained inert heat carrier solids.

In the thermal cracking operation, a stream of hot solids supplied at a temperature above the average thermal cracker temperature is mixed with feed oil and a gaseous diluent, such as steam or other vapor, both supplied at a temperature below the average cracking temperature. There is no need to charge gaseous hydrogen to the thermal cracker. The components in the resulting mixture of feed oil, gaseous diluent and entrained solids flow concurrently through the thermal riser at an average riser temperature of 1300° to 2500°F (704° to 1371°C) for a residence time between about 0.05 and 2 seconds. Endothermic cracking occurs in the thermal cracker so that the highest temperature occurs near the inlet of the riser, with the temperature falling slightly and gradually along the length of the riser.

The thermal cracking reactor is elongated and has a high length to diameter ratio in the range of 4:1 to 40:1, generally, or 6:1 to 20:1, preferably. The reactor can be disposed either vertically or horizontally. Direction of flow is not important and in a vertically disposed riser flow can be directed either upwardly or downwardly. Most commonly, the reactor will be an elongated riser with preheated feed oil, steam diluent and hot solids flowing concurrently upwardly or downwardly through the riser at a sufficiently high velocity that the heat carrier solids are carried in entrained flow through the riser by flowing vapors. More than 98 or 99% of the hot solids flowing to the riser are recirculated solids. Essentially the only solids bled off from the solids circulation system are solids or ash contained in the feed oil or very fine solids resulting from attrition of the heating solids.

The size of the entrained solid particles is not important as long as the solids are sufficiently small that there is little or no slippage between the inert solids and the flowing gases. Henceforth, for convenience the thermal cracking reactor will be considered to be a vertical upflow riser with steam as the diluent vapor.

The thermal reactor is to be distinguished from a coil thermal cracking reactor which does not utilize hot solids as an internal heat carrier agency but wherein feed oil and steam diluent flow occurs through a coil disposed in a radiant, reflective furnace chamber enclosing an open flame.

Example: Tests were performed to compare thermal cracking of a hydrodesulfurized petroleum heavy gas oil, a hydrodesulfurized petroleum residual oil and a nonhydrotreated and nonfiltered retorted shale oil. Following is the analysis of the feed heavy gas oil, both before and after hydrodesulfurization.

Desulfurized Kuwait Heavy Gas Oil

	..Hydrodesulfurization..	
	Before	After
Flash point (°F)	–	230.0
Viscosity SUS at 210°F	–	44.2
Pour point (°F)	–	+90.0
Carbon residue ramsbottom (wt %)	–	0.09
Aniline point (°C)	–	87.0
API gravity	–	28.0
Specific gravity 60/60°F	–	0.887
Carbon (wt %)	85.07	86.69
Hydrogen (wt %)	12.05	12.69
Sulfur (wt %)	2.83	0.10
Nitrogen (wt %)	–	0.047
Nickel (ppm)	–	0.10
Vanadium (ppm)	–	<0.10
Hydrocarbon types (vol %)		
Isoparaffin	–	14.2
Normal paraffin	–	3.1
Cycloparaffin	–	34.8
Noncondensed	–	21.6
Condensed	–	13.2
2 ring	–	6.9
3 ring	–	3.0
4 ring	–	1.7
5 ring	–	0.8
6 ring	–	0.7
Aromatics	–	45.2
Benzenes	–	17.7
Distillation, D1160: at 760 mm (°F)		
Volume Percent		
10	–	669.2
30	–	755.6
50	–	820.4
70	–	874.4
90	–	944.6
EP	–	1005.8

It is seen from the above table, that the accomplishment of nearly complete desulfurization of a heavy gas oil resulted in an increase in hydrogen content in the oil equal to 0.64 weight percent of the oil. A similar degree of hydrodesulfurization of residual oil results in an increase of hydrogen content in the oil equal to about 1.5 weight percent of the oil. Following is an analysis of hydrodesulfurized residual oil.

Hydrodesulfurized Residual Oil

Flash point (°F)	197.6
Pour point (°F)	+5
Carbon residue (wt %)	2.23

(continued)

Aniline point (°C)	92
API gravity	25.8
Carbon (wt %)	87.27
Hydrogen (wt %)	12.47
Sulfur (wt %)	0.14
Nitrogen (wt %)	0.087
Nickel (ppm)	0.2
Vanadium (ppm)	<0.1
Hydrocarbon types (wt %)	
Saturates	47.8
Aromatics	46.9
Polar compounds	5.3
Hydrocarbon types (vol %)	
Saturates	46.4
Alkanes	15.3
Naphthenes	31.1
Noncondensed	18.5
Condensed	12.6
Aromatics	48.3
Benzenes	18.9
Distillation, D1160: at 760 mm (°F)	
Volume Percent	
5	538
10	587
20	660
30	722
40	777
50	833
60	892
70	970
80	1055
90	1086
95*	769

*at 10 mm

Following is an analysis of the nonhydrotreated and nonfiltered shale oil.

Tosco Shale Oil

Flash point (°F)	100
Viscosity, SUS: sec at 100°F	162
Pour point (°F)	+75
Carbon residue (wt %)	3.54
API gravity	20.7
Specific gravity 60/60°F	0.9297
Carbon (wt %)	84.52
Hydrogen (wt %)	11.14
Sulfur (wt %)	0.70
Nitrogen (wt %)	1.99
Total oxygen (wt %)	1.32
Water and sediment (vol %)	0.4
Neutralization number (TAN)	1.0
Ash (wt %)	0.67
Nickel, calculated (ppm)	4.1
Vanadium, calculated (ppm)	0.5

(continued)

Distillation (°F)

Over point	263
Vol % condensed at	
<1	284
3	320
10	392
14	428
17	464
21	500
23	518
27	554
33	590
66.5 residue after	590
0.5 loss	–

Following are one set of conditions employed during the thermal cracking tests.

Feed Oil	Hydro-desulfurized Residual Oil	Shale Oil	Hydro-desulfurized Heavy Gas Oil
Operating conditions, °F			
Feed preheat	302	305	312
Solids preheat	1,735	1,735	1,758
Riser, average	1,513	1,511	1,537
Lower riser inlet	1,517	1,493	1,638
Upper riser outlet	1,465	1,477	1,499
Primary quench	1,188	1,197	1,202
Steam-to-feed, wt ratio	0.997	0.981	0.987
Solids-to-feed, wt ratio	10.1	10.4	10.0
Reactor pressure, psia	24.16	24.30	24.28
Reactor velocity, ft/sec	30.19	29.78	27.94
Reactor residence time, sec	0.334	0.341	0.331

Figures 4.1a, 4.1b and 4.1c show the yields of the various products obtained by thermal cracking in the presence of entrained hot, inert solids of hydrodesulfurized petroleum heavy gas oil, hydrodesulfurized petroleum residual oil and non-hydrotreated shale oil at the indicated ratios of steam to feed oil. As shown, increasing steam to oil ratios favorably affect ethylene and other yields. Cracking severities are expressed in terms of methane yield. Cracked products represented in the table include ultimate ethylene yield (ethylene plus 0.8 times the sum of ethane and acetylene), single pass ethylene yield, coke, hydrogen, C_2H_2, C_2H_6, C_3H_4's, C_3H_8, propylene, 1,3-butadiene, C_4's other than 1,3-butadiene, aromatics (BTX), gasoline, furnace oil and residual oil.

Figure 4.1b shows the surprising result that at a similar steam to oil ratio and cracking severity the nonhydrotreated shale oil produces approximately as high a hydrogen yield as is obtained from both the hydrotreated residual oil and the hydrotreated heavy gas oil, even though the feed shale oil has a lower hydrogen content than either of the other two oils. Figure 4.1b also shows that at a similar steam to oil ratio and cracking severity the shale oil provides approximately as high a propylene and 1,3-butadiene yield as the other two feedstocks. Propylene and 1,3-butadiene are both valuable by-products in the ethylene cracking operation.

Figure 4.1: Thermal Cracking of Shale Oil

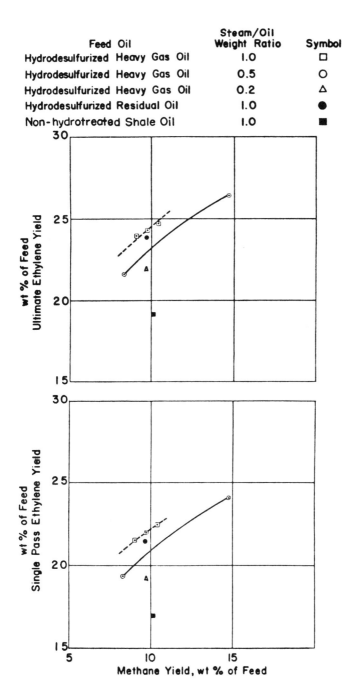

a.

(continued)

Figure 4.1: (continued)

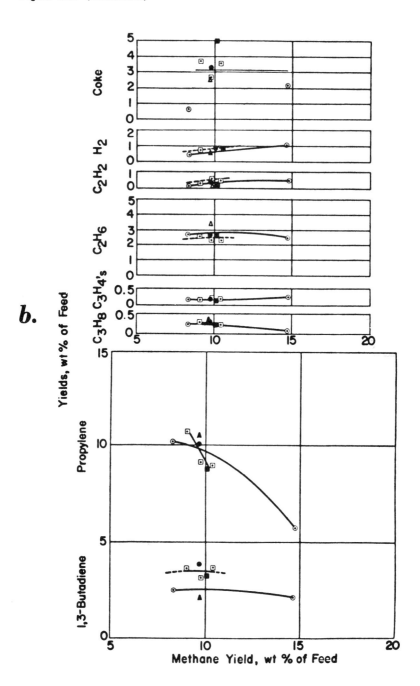

(continued)

Figure 4.1: (continued)

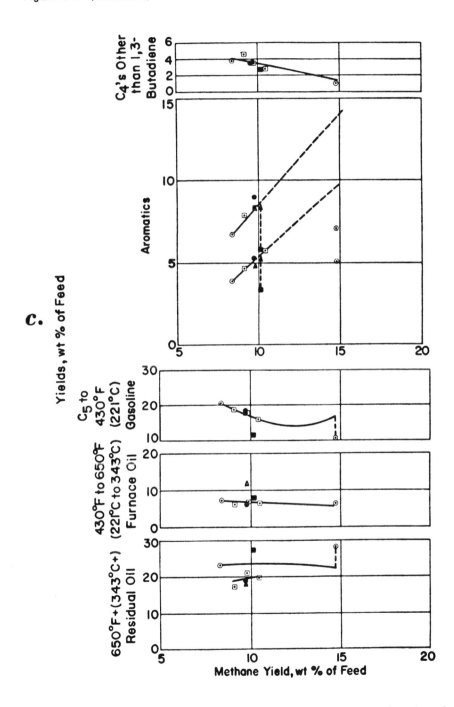

(continued)

Figure 4.1: (continued)

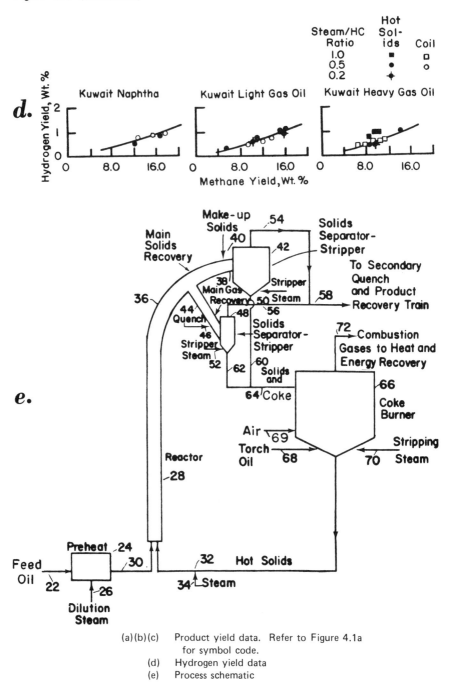

(a)(b)(c)   Product yield data. Refer to Figure 4.1a
             for symbol code.
(d)   Hydrogen yield data
(e)   Process schematic

Source: U.S. Patent 4,080,285

Figure 4.1d shows hydrogen yields obtained when thermally cracking three oils; a nonhydrotreated naphtha; a hydrodesulfurized light gas oil and a hydrodesulfurized heavy gas oil, each oil being cracked both in a coil without hot solids and in a riser with hot solids. Figure 4.1d shows that the hydrogen yield declines in the coil cracker as the boiling point of the feed oil increases but that the hydrogen yield remains constant in the hot solids riser cracker as the boiling point of the feed oil increases. Figure 4.1d therefore indicates that the high hydrogen yield obtainable during thermal cracking of the relatively high boiling shale oil feedstock of this process is specific to the use of a hot solids thermal cracker.

The process is illustrated in Figure 4.1e. As shown in Figure 4.1e, shale feed oil entering through line 22 passes through preheater 24, is admixed with dilution steam entering through line 26 and then flows to the bottom of thermal cracking reactor 28 through line 30. A stream of hot regenerated solids is charged through line 32 and admixed with fluidizing steam entering through line 34 prior to entering the bottom of riser 28. The oil, steam and hot solids pass in entrained flow upwardly through riser 28 and are discharged through a curved segment 36 at the top of the riser to induce centrifugal separation of solids from the effluent stream.

A stream containing most of the solids passes through riser discharge segment 38 and can be mixed, if desired, with make-up solids entering through line 40 before entering solids separator-stripper 42. Another stream containing most of the cracked product is discharged axially through conduit 44 and can be cooled by means of a quench stream entering through line 46 in advance of solids separator-stripper 48.

Stripper steam is charged to solids separators 42 and 48 through lines 50 and 52, respectively. Product streams are removed from solids separators 42 and 48 through lines 54 and 56, respectively, and then combined in line 58 for passage to a secondary quench and product recovery train, not shown.

Coke-laden solids are removed from solids separators 42 and 48 through lines 60 and 62, respectively, and combined in line 64 for passage to coke burner 66. If required, torch oil can be added to burner 66 through line 68 while stripping steam is added through line 70 to strip combustion gases from the heated solids. Air is charged to the burner through line 69. Combustion gases are removed from the burner through line 72 for passage to heat and energy recovery systems, not shown, while regenerated hot solids which are relatively free of coke are removed from the burner through line 32 for recycle to riser 28.

In Situ Hydrogen Generation Using Water and Catalyst

J.D. McCollum and L.M. Quick; U.S. Patents 3,948,754; April 6, 1976; 3,948,755; April 6, 1976 and 4,005,005; January 25, 1977; all assigned to Standard Oil Company (Indiana) have developed a process for recovering hydrocarbons from oil shale or tar sands solids and simultaneously for cracking, hydrogenating, desulfurizing, demetalating, and denitrifying the recovered hydrocarbons, which comprises contacting the oil shale or tar sands solids with a water-containing fluid at a temperature in the range of from about 600° to 900°F in the absence of externally supplied hydrogen and in the presence of an externally supplied catalyst system containing a sulfur- and nitrogen-resistant catalyst selected from the group consisting of at least one soluble or insoluble transition metal compound, a transition metal deposited on a support and combinations thereof. The density of water in the water-containing fluid is at least 0.10 g/ml, and sufficient water is present to serve as an effective solvent for the recovered hydrocarbons. Essentially all the sulfur removed from the recovered hydrocarbons is in the form of elemental sulfur. In this process, hydrogen is generated in situ.

The density of water in the water-containing fluid is preferably at least 0.15 g/ml and most preferably at least 0.2 g/ml. The temperature is preferably at least 705°F, the critical temperature of water. The oil shale and tar sands solids and water-containing fluid are contacted preferably for a period of time in the range of from about 1 minute to about 6 hours, more preferably in the range of from about 5 minutes to about 3 hours and most preferably in the range of from about 10 minutes to about 1 hour.

The weight ratio of the oil shale or tar sands solids-to-water in the water-containing fluid is preferably in the range of from about 3:2 to about 1:10 and more preferably in the range of from about 1:1 to about 1:3. The water-containing fluid is preferably substantially water. The oil shale solids have preferably a maximum particle size of one-half inch diameter, more preferably a maximum particle size of one-quarter inch diameter and most preferably a maximum particle size of 8 mesh.

The catalyst preferably is selected from the group consisting of ruthenium, rhodium, iridium, osmium, palladium, nickel, cobalt, platinum and combinations thereof and most preferably is selected from the group consisting of ruthenium, rhodium, iridium, osmium, and combinations thereof. The catalyst is present in a catalytically effective amount which is equivalent to a concentration level in the water in the water-containing fluid in the range of from about 0.02 to about 1.0 weight percent and preferably in the range from about 0.05 to about 0.15 weight percent.

Preferably the catalyst system contains additionally a promoter selected from the group consisting of at least one basic metal hydroxide, basic metal carbonate, transition metal oxide, oxide-forming transition metal salt and combinations thereof. The promoter promotes the activity of the catalyst in cracking, hydrogenating, desulfurizing, demetalating, and denitrifying the hydrocarbon fraction and directs selectivity between generating hydrogen in situ and cracking the hydrocarbon fraction. The transition metal in the oxide and salt is preferably selected from the group consisting of a transition metal of Group IV-B, V-B, VI-B and VII-B of the Periodic Chart and is more preferably selected from the group consisting of vanadium, chromium, manganese, titanium, molybdenum, zirconium, niobium, tantalum, rhenium, and tungsten and is most preferably selected from the group consisting of chromium, manganese, titanium, tantalum and tungsten.

The metal in the basic metal carbonate and hydroxide is preferably selected from the group consisting of alkali and alkaline earth metal and more preferably is selected from the group consisting of sodium and potassium. The ratio of the number of atoms of metal in the promoter to the number of atoms of metal in the catalyst is preferably in the range of from about 0.5 to about 50 and most preferably in the range of from about 3 to about 5.

Denitrogenation Using Cracking Catalyst

According to a process developed by *R.H. Smith; U.S. Patent 4,090,951; May 23, 1978; assigned to Atlantic Richfield Company* syncrude feed containing nitrogen is mixed with at least one material which is effective both to adsorb nitrogen compounds from the syncrude feed and to serve as a catalytic cracking catalyst for the syncrude feed, the mixing of the adsorbent with the feed helping form two phases, a first phase composed essentially of a first low nitrogen syncrude product and the second phase composed essentially of the adsorbent and high nitrogen syncrude feed. The second phase is subjected to catalytic cracking conditions which produce a second low nitrogen syncrude product.

Figure 4.2 shows syncrude feed in pipe 1 which feed is at least one hydrocarbonaceous liquid (full range or one or more cuts thereof) obtained from tar sands, normally solid coal, and/or oil shale, i.e., syncrude. This feed contains an amount of nitrogen that is to be reduced. Depending upon the desired use of the syncrude product, the syncrude feed stream can contain widely varying amounts of nitrogen, e.g., from about 10 ppm to about 10 weight percent. That is to say that the initial quantity of nitrogen in the syncrude feed can be any amount, including that which initially appears to be quite low.

Figure 4.2: Denitrogenation of Syncrude

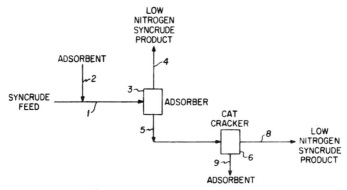

Source: U.S. Patent 4,090,951

The feed in pipe 1 is mixed with an adsorbent by way of pipe 2 and the mixture then passes into adsorber 3. A mixing chamber can be employed if desired. The adsorbent is employed in the feed in pipe 1 in an amount effective to serve both to adsorb nitrogen compounds and later to serve as a catalyst for the feed present in the catalytic (cat) cracking unit. The adsorbent can be any material which serves the above double requirement and preferably selected from the group consisting of acid treated alumino-silicates, amorphous synthetic silica-alumina and crystalline silica-alumina, as is well-known in the art and described in greater detail in *Catalytic Processes and Proven Catalysts* by C.L. Thomas, Academic Press (1970). Of course, mixtures of two or more of such materials can be employed in this process. The adsorbent is generally employed in an amount of at least about 5 weight percent based on the total weight of the syncrude feed to which it is added, the maximum amount of adsorbent employed being dictated only by economics and not by operability of the process. The syncrude feed and adsorbent are mixed in pipe **1** as well as in adsorber **3** at ambient conditions of temperature and pressure and for a time sufficient to allow formation of the two phases, the first phase being essentially a low nitrogen syncrude product and the second phase being a mixture essentially of adsorbent and high nitrogen syncrude. The low nitrogen syncrude product generally contains at least 20% lower nitrogen concentration than the high nitrogen feed in the second phase. The first phase is removed from the adsorber by way of pipe **4** while the second phase is separately removed from adsorber **3** by way of pipe **5** and passed through cat cracker **6**.

In cat cracker **6** a mixture of adsorbent and high nitrogen syncrude is subjected to cracking conditions of from about 650° to about 1000°F. The residence time is sufficient to crack the hydrocarbonaceous materials present and form a low nitrogen syncrude product which also has a nitrogen content at least 20 weight percent lower than that of the high nitrogen syncrude material in pipe **5**. This additional low nitrogen syncrude product formed in cat cracker **6** is removed by way of pipe **8** for use as desired, including, but not limited to, combination with the product in pipe **4**. Adsorbent is separately removed from cat cracker **6** by way of pipe **9**.

Example: A process is carried out similar to that shown in Figure 4.2 wherein a shale oil feed containing 2.17 weight percent nitrogen is mixed with an adsorbent, which is a commercial synthetic zeolite cracking catalyst composed of aluminosilicates. Equal weights of the adsorbent and shale oil feed were mixed at conditions of 350°F and atmospheric pressure and allowed to set in an adsorber for 15 minutes at essentially quiescent conditions. After separation of the solid adsorbent from the mixture, a low nitrogen syncrude phase remains which contains 1.35 weight percent of nitrogen and essentially no adsorbent. The adsorbent contains high nitrogen syncrude containing 4.50 weight percent nitrogen.

The adsorbent-high-nitrogen syncrude phase mixture is separately subjected to cracking conditions of 925°F, 10 psig, and a weight hourly space velocity of 1.0 pound feed oil per pound of catalyst per hour. During this catalytic cracking step the high nitrogen syncrude is cracked and denitrogenated to form a low nitrogen syncrude product containing at least 10 weight percent less nitrogen than in adsorbent containing high nitrogen syncrude and is removed as an additional product of the process separate from the adsorbent catalyst present in the cat cracker.

In related work *R.H. Smith; U.S. Patent 4,071,435; January 31, 1978; assigned to Atlantic Richfield Company* describes a method for reducing the nitrogen content of a syncrude feed obtained from at least one of oil shale, tar sands, and coal wherein the syncrude is mixed with an extractant-catalyst which is effective for extracting nitrogen materials from the syncrude feed and also effective as a hydrocracking catalyst for the syncrude feed. The mixing helps form a first phase composed of a first low nitrogen syncrude product and a second phase composed of the extractant-catalyst and high nitrogen syncrude feed, separating the first and second phases from one another, and hydrocracking the second phase to produce a second low nitrogen syncrude product.

The extractant-catalyst is employed in the feed in an amount effective to serve both to extract nitrogen compounds and later to serve as a catalyst for the feed present in the hydrocracker. The extractant-catalyst can be any material which serves the above double requirement, and preferably is selected from the group consisting of halides (chlorine, fluorine, bromine and iodine) of zinc, cadmium, mercury, lead, and copper. The extractant-catalyst is generally employed in an amount of at least about 5 weight percent based on the total weight of the syncrude feed to which it is added, the maximum amount of extractant-catalyst employed being dictated only by economics and not by operability of the process.

Moving Bed Hydroprocessing Reactor

According to a process described by *R.F. Anderson; U.S. Patent 3,910,834; October 7, 1975; assigned to Universal Oil Products Company* crude oil petroleum derived from oil shale or tar sands and containing large amounts of highly abrasive particulate matter, such as rock dust or sulfated ash, is hydroprocessed in a dual function moving bed reactor which simultaneously removes particulate matter by the filter action of the catalyst bed. The effluent from the moving bed reactor is then separated and further hydroprocessed in fixed bed reactors with fresh hydrogen added to the heavier hydrocarbon fraction to promote desulfurization.

The preferred process utilizes a moving bed reactor followed by a fractionation step to divide the wide boiling range crude oil produced from the tar sand into two separate fractions. The lighter fraction is hydrotreated for the removal of residual metals, sulfur and nitrogen, while the heavier fraction is treated or cracked in a second fixed bed reactor operated at higher severity conditions. The hydrogen that is not consumed in the moving bed reactor is passed through to the fixed bed reactor processing the lighter fraction of the charge stock. A higher purity hydrogen stream is charged to the second moving bed reactor processing the heavy fraction of the moving bed reactor effluent to maintain a higher hydrogen partial pressure for more effective desulfurization of this heavier material.

The reactors may be operated at different conditions of pressure and temperature as dictated by product slate, feed composition, and economics. The residual metals still in the effluent of the moving bed reactor will cause deactivation of the catalyst in the next reactor to which it is charged. Since the great majority of the metals and particulate matter in the reactor effluent will be in the heavier fraction leaving the separation zone, the reactor treating this fraction will have greater problems of deactivation and plugging than the reactor processing the lighter fraction. To obtain all the advantages inherent in long periods of continuous operation, a moving bed reactor may be used to process this heavier fraction.

The light fraction removed from the separation zone may also be either processed in a fixed bed or moving bed reactor may be fractionated prior to any further treatment. Either of these fractions may be recycled to the initial moving bed reactor as a second stream charged to the top of the reactor to prevent fluidization or lifting of the catalyst bed by the charge stream entering the bottom of the reactor.

Electrolytic Hydrogenation

T.F. Yen and C.-S. Wen; U.S. Patent 4,043,884; August 23, 1977; assigned to the University of Southern California describe a means for recovering economic values of oil shale by electrolytic hydrogenation by first leaching the carbonate matrix from the shale and subjecting the resultant residue to reductive electrolysis. Leaching out the carbonate components develops the porosity and permeability of the residue, increasing the extent of its internal surface and providing an interconnected pore structure which aids in releasing the bridge portions of the kerogen (i.e., amides, cycloalkadines, esters, and heterocyclic compounds).

The released bridge components of kerogen serve as proton-donors for further electrolytic refining. The reduced residue can be separated from the electrolyzed slurry, for example, by centrifugation, to yield an upgraded product. Electrolysis is preferably conducted at a current density above about 50 amperes per square meter of anode surface (50 A/m²) for a period of at least an hour, or for several days, if necessary, at low current density. A current density of up to 300 A/m² can be used. The following example illustrates the application of the process.

Oil shale such as obtained from the Green River formation, can be ground to pass a 100 to 150 mesh screen, U.S. Standard. For example, 10 grams of such a shale can be extracted wtih 100 ml of benzene to remove soluble organic material (bitumen). The extracted shale can be treated with 7.4% hydrochloric acid for 24 hours and the leached material Soxhlet extracted with a mixture of benzene:methanol (4:1) for 48 hours to remove the soluble bitumen. The resultant residue can then be treated with a 1:1 by volume mixture of concentrated hydrofluoric acid (48%) and hydrochloric acid (37%), followed by filtration and washing of the residue repeatedly with boiling water until the filtrate is neutral. The residue can then be dried, e.g., at 75°C in an oven for several hours, to obtain a kerogen concentrate.

Electrolytic hydrogenation of kerogen concentrate obtained as above was carried out in a 250 ml flask with three necks which were fitted with reducing tube adaptors. The center adaptor was fitted with a thermometer which could be immersed in the solution. An aluminum sheet was sealed through one end adaptor neck, into the flask, and had a surface of 12 centimeters square immersed in the electrolyte, serving as the cathode. A carbon rod, 3.5 centimeters long and 0.5 centimeters in diameter, was used as the anode, passed by a lead through the other end neck.

A sample of 1 gram of the foregoing kerogen concentrate in 100 ml of ethylene diamine containing 1.4 grams of lithium chloride was placed in the flask. A current was applied and kept constant at 50 mA/cm² by adjustment of the potential, which was in the range of 70 to 80 volts. During electrolysis, the flask was kept at a constant temperature of about 35°C by application of an ice bath. Electrolysis was conducted for 30 hours.

To isolate the products, the reduced mixture was poured into 100 ml of ice water and the reduced kerogen was separated from the mixture by centrifugation. Washing and centrifugation were repeated until the washings had a pH of 8, as shown by test paper. The residue was then transferred to a round flask, dried by a stream of nitrogen and placed in an oven at 75°C. A portion of the solid residue was analyzed by infrared spectroscopy and an elemental analysis was obtained. The remaining portion of the solid residue was Soxhlet extracted with heptane for 10 hours and then dried and extracted again with a mixture of benzene:methanol (volume 4:1) for 48 hours. The heptane and benzene:methanol extracts were analyzed by gas chromatography using a 10' x ⅛" glass column packed with 5% Carbowax 20M on Chromosorb W. The centrifuged liquid layer from the electrolyzed mixture was evaporated to 50 ml and neutralized with carbon dioxide gas to a pH of 8, then extracted with heptane and chloroform. The extracts were analyzed with gas chromatography and infrared spectroscopy.

The gas chromatogram of the heptane soluble extract from the reduced kerogen showed the extract to be composed of predominantly normal alkanes having from 22 to 28 carbon atoms. Identification of peaks was accomplished by co-injection of known standards and by comparison of the chromatographic retention times of each compound with those of standard kits. The distribution of the normal alkanes is presented in the table below.

n-Alkane	Relative Quantity
C_{19}	0.01
C_{20}	0.03
C_{21}	0.15
C_{22}	0.39
C_{23}	0.72
C_{24}	1.00
C_{25}	0.90
C_{26}	0.70
C_{27}	0.60
C_{28}	0.38
C_{29}	0.23
C_{30}	0.18
C_{31}	0.15
C_{32}	0.08

The total yield of the heptane-soluble product was about 3.7% of the original kerogen concentrate. The extract of the benzene:methanol-soluble fraction of reduced kerogen consisted of an orange-brown, semisolid material which was about 6.4 weight percent of the original kerogen concentrate. The following table compares elemental components of the original kerogen concentrate to that of reduced samples.

	Original Kerogen Concentrate	..Reduction Samples..	
		1*	2**
Carbon (wt %)	68.60	40.71	40.55
Hydrogen (wt %)	8.42	6.41	6.47
Nitrogen (wt %)	3.48	3.25	3.34
Sulfur (wt %)	2.41	0.14	0.22
H/C atomic ratio	1.47	1.82	1.84

*Reduced sample obtained from washings and centrifugations.
**Reduced sample obtained after heptane and benzene:methanol extraction.

The calculation of the atomic ratio of hydrogen to carbon is on an ash-free basis. Some of the loss of sulfur is likely caused by elimination of sulfur from heterocyclic organic structures.

The heptane and chloroform extracts from the liquid layer were analyzed by gas chromatography which showed the presence of normal C_{20-22} alkanes present among a group of peaks.

It will be seen that electrolytic reduction of kerogen concentrate is a powerful technique to break down the crosslink matrix of kerogen. The decrease of sulfur content is an important advantage and normal alkane extracts from reduced kerogen offers a feasible large-scale electrolytic solvent refining process.

Short Residence Time Low Pressure Hydropyrolysis

M. Greene; U.S. Patent 4,048,053; September 13, 1977; assigned to Cities Service Company describes a process for upgrading solid fuel-derived tars produced by short residence time low pressure hydropyrolysis of coal.

The process comprises the following steps: adding liquid carbonaceous material into a first reaction zone of a reactor having at least two reaction zones, and a pressure of between atmospheric pressure and 450 psia; adding hot hydrogen to the stream of carbonaceous material to affect a reaction with same to produce reaction products; quenching the mixture while insuring that the total residence time varies from about 2 milliseconds to about 2 seconds; removing at least a portion of the reaction products from the quenched mixture; introducing the residual carbonaceous material into a subsequent reaction zone and repeating the foregoing steps for the subsequent reaction zone, and introducing carbonaceous tars produced directly into a fluid coking zone to obtain gas, upgraded tars, and hot coke.

The process, involving short heat-up (preferably between 500°C/sec and 1°C/sec) and quench times, results in improved yields of desirable carbonaceous tar products to be directly introduced into a fluid coker, no problems of catalyst addition or removal, simplified apparatus, and improved process reliability.

The heart of the process resides in a concept of producing and upgrading tars produced from a short total residence time of the carbonaceous material at low pressure in each reaction zone of the reactor; this residence time includes heat-up, reaction, and quench times. This short residence time contrasts sharply with other high pressure hydrogenation processes involving catalyst and solvents wherein relatively long residence times are involved and the reaction mixture is quenched outside the reactor.

Removal of Inorganic Solids

R.N. Lucas; U.S. Patent 3,929,625; December 30, 1975; assigned to Petrolite Corporation describes a process for removing predominantly inorganic solids from shale oil produced by the high-temperature retorting of oil shale. A surface active chemical aid (a polyoxyalkylene derived nonionic polymeric surfactant) is intermixed with the shale oil. Then, water in the amount between 10 and 30 volume percent of the shale oil is dispersed throughout the shale oil. The resulting dispersion is resolved in an electric field into a purified shale oil phase and an aqueous phase carrying the removed solids. Examples of the chemical aid are oxypropylated, oxyethylated, polyethylene amine and oxypropylated, oxyethylated butyl phenol formaldehyde resin.

The utility of the process was carefully evaluated in the laboratory and in the field. In the laboratory, a test procedure was derived for testing the effectiveness of the process. Mixing facilities were provided wherein the surface active chemical aid, or water, or both, could be mixed into the shale oil. The resulting mixture of dispersion was introduced continuously into a pilot plant electric treater which provided an electric field with a gradient of about 5 kilovolts per inch and facilities to remove separately purified shale oil and aqueous phases. The shale oil was adjusted in temperature to 200°F. The dispersion was passed through the electric treater at a relatively constant flow of conventional rate magnitude. The surface active chemical aid was employed in amounts of 300 parts per million. Water was intermixed at 20% by volume into the shale oil.

The shale oil was passed in one run through the laboratory equipment without the addition of a chemical aid or water. The electric treater exhibited acceptable electric characteristics but removed only 25% of the solids from the shale oil. Then, 20% by volume of water was added into the shale oil (but no surface active chemical aid). The resulting dispersion was passed through the electric treater. The electric treater did not remove any solids from the shale oil. It exhibited overloaded electrical characteristics in this run. The same run was repeated with the addition of sodium silicate (a powerful wetting agent) in an attempt to remove solids. No significant change in the result was obtained.

Next, a surface active chemical aid (diglycolic ester of oxypropylated, oxyethylated butyl phenol formaldehyde resin) was mixed at 300 ppm with the shale oil. Then, 20% by volume of fresh water was dispersed into the shale oil. The resulting dispersion was passed into the electric treater for its resolution electrically. The solids content of the purified shale oil was analyzed. Analysis indicated a 93% removal of the solids from the shale oil. The electrical behavior of the treater was acceptable.

Sulfur Removal by Reaction with Polysulfides

A process described by *R. Swanson; U.S. Patent 4,018,572; April 19, 1977* involves desulfurizing fossil fuels such as coal or oil by reacting such fuels with a nonvolatile agent which removes much of the sulfur and produces a compound which can be recycled after its decomposition into nonpolluting sulfur and the reconstituted original agent, and by reduction of the sulfur content of fossil fuels prior to their combustion by means of alkali metal sulfides in either melt conditions or in aqueous solution followed by thermal decomposition of the resulting higher sulfur content polysulfide into nonpolluting sulfur and a lower sulfur content polysulfide.

The process basically comprises contacting fossil fuels with a sulfur compound which is a nonvolatile sulfur unsaturated sulfide or polysulfide of the alkali metals or with hydrogen polysulfides. The unsaturated sulfides or polysulfides of the alkali metals will dissolve elemental sulfur, will remove sulfur from many organic compounds, dissolve certain water-insoluble metal sulfides and form higher sulfur content alkali metal polysulfides. The form considered to be sulfur saturated for sodium is the tetrasulfide, for potassium it is the pentasulfide, for cesium and rubidium the hexasulfide.

Though additional sulfur will dissolve in these saturated forms, the above forms represent what is generally considered the limit of sulfur which combines with each of these alkali metals with formation of definite compounds. When these sulfur saturated compounds are made with the sulfur derived from the fossil fuels, they can be thermally decomposed into lower sulfur content polysulfides of the alkali metals with elemental sulfur separating from this melt. The temperatures required to decompose the various polysulfides are as follows from the saturated forms.

	Temperature (°C)
Potassium tetrasulfide	>300
Potassium trisulfide*	–
Potassium disulfide**	>850
Monosulfides***	–
Sodium trisulfide†	–
Sodium disulfide	550

   *Cannot be produced directly thermally
  **Which temperature decomposes the tetrasulfide
 ***Cannot be produced thermally
   †Does not exist

The existence of sodium pentasulfide is questionable and its production in the process is not preferred. Therefore, the tetrasulfide is considered the sulfur saturated sodium form. At least two forms of sodium tetrasulfide exist and one of these forms appears capable of forming a pentasulfide of definite chemical composition.

In melt condition, the potassium polysulfides are preferred to the sodium polysulfides. In aqueous solutions, the ability of potassium to gather sulfur is somewhat greater than that of sodium and the recycling of the polysulfides is much easier with potassium. With sodium, the sulfur is distilled from the melt at 550°C whereas the sulfur is molten at just over 300°C with the potassium pentasulfide decomposition.

In aqueous solution, there is little difference between sodium and potassium in their ability to remove sulfur from the fossil fuels.

IN SITU PROCESSING OF TAR SANDS

Petroleum is found in subterranean formations or reservoirs in which it has accumulated, and recovery of conventional petroleum is achieved by penetrating these reservoirs with wells and permitting the fluid to flow to the surface as a result of natural pressure existing in the reservoir, or by pumping the fluid to the surface in instances where insufficient natural pressure exists to force it to flow to the surface. There are many reservoirs which contain petroleum too viscous to be pumped from the formation under normal circumstances. When such formations are encountered, production is possible only by means of some process of supplemental recovery, commonly referred to as secondary or tertiary recovery, in which energy is supplied to the formation to force the petroleum to move, and heat and/or a solvent is supplied to the formation to reduce the viscosity of the petroleum so it will flow.

The most extreme example of formations which contain petroleum too viscous to recover by conventional means are the so-called tar sands or bitumen sands, such as those located in the western United States, western Canada, and Venezuela. These formations are known to contain huge reserves of bituminous petroleum, but the bituminous petroleum contained therein is too viscous to be recoverable by conventional techniques.

The state of the art for the recovery of bitumen from tar sand deposits can be generally classified as strip mining or in situ separation. Strip mining requires removal of the overburden by mechanical means and the mixture of bitumen and sand that constitutes the tar sand deposit is then similarly removed by mechanical means and transported to a surface processing plant for separation of bitumen and sand. In situ separation processes make use of techniques for separating the bitumen from the sand within the tar sand deposit itself, so the bitumen in some modified form may be transported to the surface with at least a major portion of the sand left in the tar sand deposit.

Techniques generally proposed for in situ separation may be classified as thermal or emulsification processes. The thermal techniques include in situ combustion, (fire flooding), and steam flooding. Emulsification processes may also involve

259

the use of steam plus some additional chemical to promote emulsification of the high viscosity bitumen so that it may be transported to the surface where the emulsion is resolved into bitumen and water. A number of processes involving the in situ use of hydrocarbon solvents for extracting or diluting the tar sand formation have also been developed. Although many in situ separation techniques have been proposed in the prior art, none have really been both economically and technically successful.

Since only a small portion of the tar sands are recoverable by surface mining techniques, it is all too clear that if these energy values are to be recovered for this generation and those to come they must be recovered by in situ techniques.

HOT AQUEOUS FLUID DRIVE

Horizontal and Ascending Hole Pattern

V.G. Verty, P.G. Voronin, E.I. Gurov, V.S. Zubkov, N.I. Melnichuk, G.G. Miller, V.N. Mishakov, V.S. Sukrushev, L.M. Ruzin, and V.P. Tabakov; U.S. Patent 4,099,783; July 11, 1978 describe a method for thermoshaft oil production which comprises the provision of a combination of mining holes above an oil-bearing bed which are inclined at from 1° to 3° to the horizon. Then injection holes are drilled from these mining openings for feeding a heating medium into the bed. After that, a slope and a footway leading to the bottom part of the oil-bearing bed are constructed, and a production gallery is provided within the bottom part of the bed. Horizontal and ascending holes are drilled from the production gallery for oil production.

A heating medium is fed into the injection holes for uniform distribution over the entire volume of the oil-bearing bed and for displacement of oil into the horizontal and ascending production holes towards the production gallery and the oil is fed up to the surface.

Referring to Figure 5.1, a combination of mining openings **1** are provided at an overburden level **2** above the roof of a production oil-bearing bed **3**. The plane of the mining openings is inclined at about 1° to 3° to the horizon.

Then vertical injection holes **4** and inclined injection holes **5** are drilled from the mining openings **1** for feeding a heating medium into the bed, such as steam. The steam may be suitably supplied to the bed **3** by a boiler house **14** via a steam-supply pipe or hole **15**. Subsequently, a slope **6** and a footway **7** leading to the bottom part of the oil-bearing bed are constructed, and a production gallery **8** is provided within the bottom part of the bed. Horizontal production holes **9** and ascending production holes **10** are drilled from the production gallery **8**. Other supporting equipment for an oil field comprise suitable hoisting and ventilation shafts **16** and **17**, respectively.

The production oil-bearing bed **3** is heated to 50° to 95°C by feeding a heating medium, such as steam, into the bed at regular intervals through the system of injection holes **4** and **5** of the overburden level **2**.

Upon reaching the abovementioned temperature, oil is recovered at regular intervals without suspending the intermittent steam supply into the bed. Then hot

water, and subsequently cold water, is fed to replace the steam at regular intervals while continuing the oil recovery through the production holes **9** and **10** at
regular intervals.

Figure 5.1: Thermoshaft Oil Production

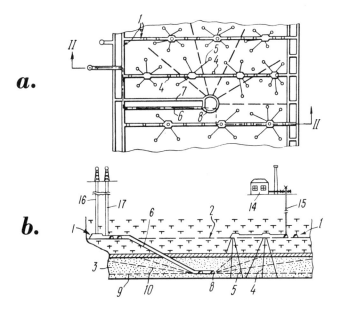

a.

b.

(a) An area of mining openings with vertical and
     inclined injection holes in a top, plan view
     (the mining openings are conventionally
     shown in one horizontal plane); and
(b) Cross-sectional view taken along the line II-II
     in Figure 5.1a

Source: U.S. Patent 4,099,783

Due to the provision of the dense network of the injection holes **4** and **5**, the
oil-bearing bed **3** is uniformly and rapidly heated over its entire volume. This
is facilitated by the presence of cracks in the bed **3**. Upon the temperature
raise in the bed, the oil viscosity is lowered and its mobility is improved.

Pressure difference between the injection holes **4** and **5** and the production holes
9 and **10**, capillary impregnation and gravity contribute to the oil displacement
from the rock blocks of the bed into the cracks and therefrom into the production holes **9** and **10** towards the production gallery **8** located within the bottom
part of the bed.

A large opening area of the bed with the production holes **9** and **10** and injection holes **4** and **5**, as well as the abovementioned factors, enable a substantial
reduction of the filtration resistance to the oil flow in the bed **3**.

The inflow of fluid into the developed network of the horizontal production holes **9** and ascending production holes **10** is effected as a result of both the pressure difference between the injection holes **4** and **5** and the production holes **9** and **10** and gravity. The provision of the horizontal production holes **9** and ascending production holes **10** facilitates the operating conditions, eliminates the necessity of permanent attendance of the operating staff in the production gallery **8** and allows for automation of the oil production process.

There is also no need for frequent repair operations in the production holes **9** and **10** since the sand effluent from the bed **3** is washed off them with the oil and water. A large number of injection holes **4** and **5** and a large opening area of the production bed **3** with the injection holes **4** and **5** eliminate the need for injecting a heating medium under high pressure so that the danger of steam breakthrough into the mining openings **1** is reduced, if not completely eliminated.

Oil production through the system of horizontal and ascending production holes **9** and **10** permits a better utilization of the natural cracking of the bed **3** with predominant vertically oriented cracks. Insofar as the oil recovery and heating medium supply are effected from different levels, labor conditions and safety of the operating staff are improved.

Closed-Loop Flow Path

A process described by *D.J. Anderson, C.F. Kirkvold, P. Pisio and J.R. Lishman; U.S. Patent 3,994,341; November 30, 1976; D.J. Anderson, P. Pisio and C.F. Kirkvold; U.S. Patent 4,008,765; February 22, 1977; P. Pisio and C.F. Kirkvold; U.S. Patent 4,019,575; April 26, 1977 and D.J. Anderson; U.S. Patent 4,037,658; July 26, 1977; all assigned to Chevron Research Company* is directed to a method of assisting the recovery of viscous petroleum from a petroleum containing formation and is particularly useful in those formations where communication between an injection position and a recovery position is difficult to establish and maintain. The method of assisting the recovery of viscous petroleum from a petroleum-containing formation is particularly useful in a formation having a large vertical dimension.

A substantially vertical passage, such as a well or shaft, is formed through the petroleum-containing formation. A closed-loop flow path is provided from the earth's surface through a substantial portion of the formation penetrated by the vertical passage. A recovery path is formed for flowing petroleum out of the formation. This path may be located in the vertical passage near the bottom thereof or it may be located in a separate nearby well. A hot fluid is circulated through the closed-loop flow path to heat the viscous petroleum in the formation adjacent at least a portion of the vertical passage to form a potential passageway for fluid flow through the formation, and a drive fluid is injected into the upper portion of the formation through the potential passageway to promote flow of petroleum to the recovery portion near the bottom of the vertical passage.

In a preferred form, the hot fluid which is flowed through the flow path is steam, and the drive fluid used to promote movement of the petroleum is also steam. In some situations, other fluids such as gas or water may be useful drive fluids. Depending on certain conditions, the hot fluid and the drive fluid are injected simultaneously. Under other conditions, the hot fluid and the drive fluid are injected intermittently or alternatively. The injectivity of the drive fluid into the formation is controlled to some extent by adjusting the flow of hot fluid through the flow path member. In this manner, the sweep efficiency of the drive fluid in the formation may be improved.

Figure 5.2a shows a substantially vertical passage formed through a petroleum-containing tar sand **14**. The vertical passage may be a shaft or well. Thus, the shaft, generally indicated by the number **10**, has been cased by means of casing **24**. A wellhead **30** is located at the upper end of the casing **24**. A hollow tubular member **18** extends through the wellhead **30** to a position near the lower part of the tar sand **14**. An end plate **21** closes off the bottom of the tubular member. A flow pipe **20** extends down the interior of tubular member **18** and cooperates with the tubular member **18** to form a closed-loop flow path through at least a portion of the tar sand.

Figure 5.2: Recovery Process Using Closed-Loop Flow Path for Hot Fluid

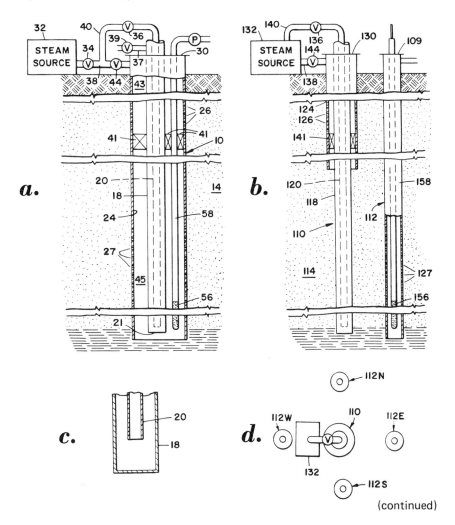

(continued)

Figure 5.2: (continued)

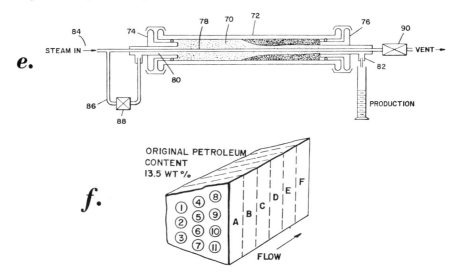

e.

f.

(a)   Elevation view partially in section illustrating the apparatus assembled
         for use in recovering viscous petroleum from an underground forma-
         tion.
(b)   Elevation view partially in section illustrating an alternative arrange-
         ment of the apparatus.
(c)   Enlarged partial view of a portion of the apparatus of Figure 5.2a.
(d)   Plan view illustrating a potential well layout.
(e)   Elevation view partially in section illustrating apparatus used in con-
         ducting demonstrations.
(f)   Perspective view of a block of tar sand flooded in accordance with
         the process showing position of core samples taken after the flood.

Source: U.S. Patent 3,994,341

A source of hot fluid such as a steam source **32** is connected to flow pipe **20**
by means of conduits **38** and **40** through valves **34** and **36**. The steam source
32 is also connected to the interior of casing **24** by means of conduit **38** through
valve **44**. Steam is circulated through the formation out of direct contact therewith by flowing down flow pipe **20** and up the annulus between the outside of
the flow pipe **20** and the tubular member **18**. Fluid leaves this annulus via conduit **37** and valve **39**. A production pump is located in the interior of the casing to move produced fluids to the surface via flow line **58**.

The outside of tubular member **18** and the production flow line **58** are both
packed off by packing means **41** to effectively form an upper injection chamber
43 and a lower production chamber **45** inside casing **24**. Upper perforations **26**
and lower perforations **27** are formed in the casing to permit communication between the interior of the casing and the formation. In operation, it is usually
desirable to first introduce steam into the annulus **43** of the casing of shaft **10**

to attempt to obtain injection of steam into formation **14** through perforations **26**. In most instances, in viscous tar sands little or no injection is obtained. Steam is then flowed through a closed-loop flow path via flow pipe **20** and tubular member **18** by appropriate manipulation of valves **34, 36, 44** and **39**. The steam or hot fluid flowing in the flow path formed of pipe **20** and tubular member **18** heats the viscous petroleum in tar sand formation **14** to reduce the viscosity of at least a portion of the petroleum adjacent the casing occupied by tubular member **18**. This provides a potential passage for flow of the drive fluid or steam into the formation via annulus **43** and perforations **26**.

By suitably controlling the flow in the flow path **20, 18** and the formation **14**, a good sweep efficiency can be obtained and oil recovery maximized through perforations **27** in recovery position **45**. Thus when the steam flowing in the flow path establishes injectivity for the drive fluid into the formation and results in some production of petroleum from the producer steam, flow through the flow path is terminated to prevent breakthrough of the drive fluid. If injectivity of the drive fluid becomes undesirably low, then additional steam is flowed through the flow path to reestablish the desired injectivity.

Figure 5.2b is an elevation view partially in section, and illustrates an alternative form of apparatus. As shown, two closely spaced-apart wells **110** and **112** are formed and penetrate a tar sand formation **114**. Well **110** includes a string of surface casing **124** which extends at least into the upper portion of the tar sand **114**. The surface casing **124** is provided with a wellhead **130**. A tubular member **118** extends through the wellhead and down through the tar sand. An inner flow pipe **120** cooperates with the tubular member to form a closed-loop flow path for hot fluid through the formation. Thus, steam from steam source **132** is circulated through the flow path via conduit **140** and valve **136**. Returning condensate through tubular member **118** may be removed via a crossover connection for reheating and recirculating, if desired.

The annulus of the tubular member **118** in the casing is packed off by packing means **141**. Steam may be injected into formation **114** from steam source **132** via conduit **138**, valve **144** and perforations **126**. A nearby production well **112** is provided with perforations **127** in the lower portion of the formation for recovery of petroleum moved there by the injected steam. A suitable pump **156** and flow line **158** are used to move it to the surface.

Figure 5.2d is a plan view and illustrates a potential field layout. A central injector well **110** is surrounded by four producers **112N, 112E, 112S** and **112W**. Figure 5.2e is an elevation view partially in section and illustrates apparatus used in conducting demonstrations in accordance with the process. As shown, a sand pack **70** of Athabasca tar sand was encased in a suitable elongated core tube **72**. The core tube was provided with suitable end plates **74** and **76** for receiving a hollow tubular member **78**. The apparatus is also arranged for steam injection into the face of the sand pack through conduit **80** and for collecting proceeds of the sand pack flood through conduit **82**.

A steam source **84** is connected to the tubular member **78** and to the sand pack face through tubing **86** and control valve **88**. A down-stream control valve **90** controls flow of steam through the central tubular member **78**. Thus, assisted recovery operations can be demonstrated utilizing the apparatus shown in Figure 5.2e.

Figure 5.2f is a perspective of a block of Athabasca tar sand showing a number of core positions for cores taken longitudinally through the core block. The cores are identified by number and flow plane as indicated. The tar sand block was flooded. The cores were taken after the flood and analyzed for residual petroleum.

The table below indicates the residual viscous petroleum weight by core position and plane of the cores of Figure 5.2f. The original block contained 13.5% by weight of viscous petroleum. As is evident from the table, a substantial weight percent of a viscous petroleum was recovered when the cores were flooded in accordance with the process.

Core Analysis—Weight Percent Residual Petroleum

Core Position	. . . . Plane.					
	A	B	C	D	E	F
Left Side						
1	3.8	5.5	5.9	6.5	8.2	7.2
2	3.7	4.4	5.4	4.3	7.3	5.7
3	3.9	4.2	5.2	5.7	4.6	7.9
Center Line						
4	3.7	4.4	5.2	4.9	8.8	9.0
5	3.7	4.8	3.7	4.3	7.3	7.1
6	3.7	3.9	4.1	4.2	6.7	5.4
7	3.8	4.7	4.0	5.0	4.5	4.9
Right Side						
8	4.2	5.2	6.0	6.4	10.9	9.5
9	3.8	4.4	5.8	4.5	7.0	7.3
10	3.9	4.2	5.8	4.3	6.0	6.2
11	4.1	5.1	7.1	5.4	5.2	5.8

Further with respect to Figures 5.2e and 5.2f in order to demonstrate the process, it was necessary as a first step to set up an apparatus containing Athabasca oil sand having a zero effective permeability to steam. To do this, a 1 inch i.d. by 12 inch long quartz tube was used. The tube was packed with Athabasca oil sand containing about 13% by weight viscous petroleum and about 4% water. Fittings were attached to both ends of the tube and a conventional steam drive applied to the oil sand at a pressure of 75 psi and a temperature of 320°F.

It was found during the early runs that 50% of the petroleum was recovered because of unrealistic permeability to steam, and so the runs did not successfully simulate Athabasca conditions. It was found later that by using a ½ inch diameter solid steel rod, 12 inches long, as a tool for ramming the oil sand very tightly in the tube, the room temperature air permeabilities were reduced to less than 50 millidarcies, a much more realistic value for viscous petroleum-containing formations. In this region of permeability, conventional steam drive did not work and the steam front advanced only about 1 inch into the tube and no farther, since the initially mobilized petroleum blocked off any communication, thereby reducing the effective mobility to zero. These conditions were reproducible on a satisfactory basis.

The process was then demonstrated using the apparatus shown schematically in Figure 5.2e. Figure 5.2e shows a partially completed demonstration in accordance with the process. The in-place tubular member **78** has been heated by opening the heating annulus control valve **90** allowing steam to pass through. This immediately provides steam injectivity at the drive end of the tar sand pack **70** and viscous petroleum produced immediately at the producing end. Recoveries in these experiments ranged from 48 to 52% by weight of the total petroleum in place. Residual petroleum was determined in every case by exhaustive solvent extraction at the end of each run. In some demonstrations, too much heat was allowed to pass through the tubular member **78**, thereby creating an annulus outside the tubular member of very high mobility, allowing premature steam breakthrough and giving rather poor recoveries, on the order of only 30% of the total petroleum in place.

In a related process, *D.J. Anderson, C.F. Kirkvold and P. Pisio; U.S. Patent 3,994,340; November 30, 1976; assigned to Chevron Research Company* have found that the recovery of viscous petroleum from tar sands is assisted using a substantially vertical passage from the earth's surface which penetrates the tar sand and has extending therefrom a lateral hole containing a flow path isolated from the tar sand for circulating a hot fluid to and from the vertical passage to develop a potential flow path into which a drive fluid is injected to promote movement of the petroleum to a production position.

According to a process described by *D.J. Anderson; U.S. Patent 4,120,357; October 17, 1978; assigned to Chevron Research Company* a production well is formed through the petroleum-containing formation and a casing string having a production opening near its lower portion is inserted into the production well to provide a production flow line in the production well from a position adjacent the production opening to the earth's surface. A tubular member is inserted into the production well to form a closed-loop flow path from the earth's surface to the lower portion of the formation and back to the earth's surface.

A hot fluid is circulated through the closed-loop flow path to heat the viscous petroleum in the formation adjacent at least a portion of the production well to form a first potential passageway for fluid flow through the formation. A plurality of injection wells are linearly spaced apart from the production well and communicate with the upper portion of the formation. The first of the injection wells is positioned for injection of hot drive fluid into the first potential passageway for fluid flow in the formation and the remaining injection wells are linearly spaced apart from the first injection well and each other at least a distance equal to the distance between the production well and the first injection well.

A hot drive fluid is injected through the first injection well in the upper portion of the formation into the first potential passageway to promote flow of petroleum to the production opening near the bottom of the casing string of the production well and to form a second potential passageway for fluid flow in the formation communicating with the next adjacent linearly spaced apart injection well.

The injection of hot drive fluid through the first injection well is stopped when significant breakthrough of hot drive fluid occurs into the production well. Injection of hot drive fluid through the next adjacent linearly spaced apart injection well and then into the second potential passageway for fluid flow in the formation is started to promote flow of petroleum to the production well.

Progressively thereafter, hot drive fluid injection is stopped at a given injection well as significant hot drive fluid breakthrough occurs at the production well, and started at the further next adjacent linearly spaced apart injection well.

P. Pisio and C.F. Kirkvold; U.S. Patent 4,020,901; May 3, 1977; assigned to Chevron Research Company describe an arrangement for recovering viscous oil from a tar sand formation having a large vertical dimension including a substantially vertical lined shaft extending through the tar sand formation. A first opening is formed in the lower portion of the shaft lining and at least one lateral hole extends into the formation through the first opening. A plurality of tubular members are positioned in the lateral hole to provide both a closed-loop flow path for fluid flow from the shaft into and out of the hole out of contact with the formation and a separate flow path for production fluids from the hole into the shaft.

A steam source is connected to the tubular members forming the closed-loop flow path. A second opening is formed in the shaft lining and a steam injection conduit extends through the second opening into the formation. The steam injection conduit is connected to the steam source for injecting steam into the formation.

Water and Induced Pressure

A process described by *R.C. Terry and X.T. Stoddard; U.S. Patents 4,019,578; April 26, 1977; 4,058,164; November 15, 1977 and 4,022,280; May 10, 1977* relates to the recovery of petroleum from tar and heavy oil sands in which one or more injection passages and two or more removal passages are established between the surface of the ground and an underground petroleum deposit. Hot water is injected into the petroleum deposit at a temperature above the pour point temperature of the petroleum substance, and heat is transferred until the petroleum substance becomes flowable. Under the influence of induced pressure, the petroleum substance is made to flow countercurrent to the flow of heat, with the petroleum substance captured at the surface of the ground.

Referring to Figure 5.3a, two wells **11** and **12** are drilled from the surface of earth through the overburden **13** to the top of the pay zone **14**. A casing **16** is set and cemented at **17** into place. The amount of cement used should be enough to assure a hermetic seal between the pay zone and the surface of the earth. Well diameter could be, for example, nine inches and the casing diameter could be, for example, seven inches. The wells are then deepened by drilling through pay zone **14** and into water-bearing stratum **15** so that the wells penetrate, for example, the top five feet of the water-bearing stratum.

Tubing **18** with a diameter of, for example, two and seven-eighths inches is set within well **11** with the bottom of the tubing located, for example, three feet from the bottom of the hole. Tubing **18** contains valve **20** and is suspended by wellhead **19**. Wellhead **19** also contains flow line **21** which contains valve **22**. Well **12** is fitted with wellhead **23** which contains flow line **24** which in turn contains valve **25**. The complete system is hermetically sealed.

In this arrangement fluids can be made to flow under the influence of differential pressure through tubing **18**, annulus **26**, flow line **21** of well **11**, flow line **24** and water-bearing stratum **15**.

The process begins by opening valve **20** and injecting hot water at a temperature of, for example, 330°F under pressure, for example, of 175 psi into tubing **18** at a rate of 300 gpm. Valves **22** and **25** are opened to the extent necessary to permit expulsion of air or other fluids as the circulating system pressure builds up. As soon as water begins to flow out of flow line **21**, valve **22** is closed and valve **25** is opened fully.

The water being injected in stratum **15** through tubing **18** begins to displace water in the aquifer, and due to differential pressure the water column in well **12** will rise until flow is established through flow line **24**. Initially the temperature of the water exiting through flow line **24** will be substantially the temperature of the water in stratum **15**, for example, 60°F. As circulation continues the temperature of the water exiting through flow line **24** will gradually increase, and due to heat losses in the circuit will stabilize at a temperature of 150°F.

The water entering stratum **15** is substantially hotter than the water within the stratum, thus is less dense, and by comparison more buoyant. Therefore, the injected water will tend to override the cooler water in stratum **15**, and will tend to circulate near the oil-water contact **27**.

The circulating hot water at or near the oil-water contact **27** will lose heat to the cooler overlying pay zone **14**. The heavy oil nearest the circulating water will increase in temperature from, e.g., 60°F to its pour point temperature of, e.g., 100°F in a relatively short time, and traces of oil will begin to show in the water exiting through flow line **24**. With continuing circulation the temperature of the lower section of pay zone **14** will rise to the point that its heavy oil content will become quite flowable. This condition will be signaled at the surface of the ground by increasing shows of oil in the water exiting through flow line **24**.

With continued circulation of hot water a portion of the lower section of pay zone **14** will be heated to a temperature at or above the pour point temperature of the entrapped heavy oil crude, for example, a temperature of 100°F or above. This heated portion of pay zone **14** is indicated on Figure 5.3a as the material between oil-water contact **27** and the dotted line **28**. The heavy oil crude in the described lower portion of pay zone **14** is now at or above its pour point temperature and is in flowable condition.

The heated heavy oil crude, although of similar specific gravity as the injection water, is of different physical characteristics compared to the water, and the heavy oil crude will coalesce into a multiplicity of droplets of varying size. These droplets of heavy oil crude have a bulk density somewhat less than a corresponding volume of water and are more buoyant. In this mode the droplets of heavy oil crude will migrate to the highest permeable point in the fluid column. While the exact mechanism of the movement of heavy oil crude droplets is not well known in the prior art, it is believed that buoyancy is attained by a combination of differential density and surface tensions.

With mobility attained in the heavy oil crude by continuing addition of heat, the droplets will migrate in part toward well **12** in the sweep of circulating water, but more particularly upward in the annulus **26** of well **11** under the influence of buoyancy. The droplets ascending in annulus **26** will displace the hot water in annulus **26** to a substantial degree and will tend to agglomerate in the uppermost portion of annulus **26**. The uppermost portion of annulus **26** also tends to be the hottest location for the accumulation of heavy oil crude due to the transfer of heat from the hot injection fluid through the wall of tubing **18**.

Figure 5.3: Recovery of Petroleum from Tar Sands

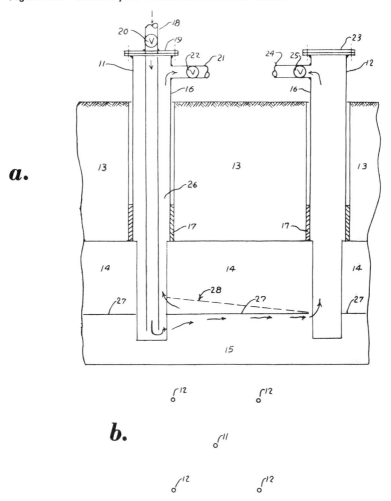

(a)   Diagrammatic vertical cross section taken through a portion of the earth showing a pair of wells, the overburden, the heavy oil or tar sands stratum and the water-bearing sands stratum.

(b)   Plan view of a possible well pattern.

Source: U.S. Patent 4,019,578

The hot heavy oil crude may now be recovered through flow line **21** by opening valve **22** where the existing fluids are composed, for example, of 95% hot heavy oil crude and 5% water. Temperature of the fluids exiting through flow line 21 can be, for example, 200°F or higher. A portion of the heavy oil crude may be recovered through flow line 24 where the exiting fluids are composed of 95% water and 5% heavy oil crude at a temperature of 150°F.

The exiting fluids from flow lines 21 and 24 are directed to above ground facilities where the hot heavy oil crude is separated from the water using methods common in the petroleum industry. As a practical matter the separated crude oil is directed to storage tanks and then to market, while the separated water is saved for reheating and recycling through the hot water injection circuit.

By continuing the injection of hot water into the pay zone 14 the temperature boundary 28 will gradually ascend generally in parallel to line 28 as shown in Figure 5.3a. With the heavy oil crude removed from the lower portion of pay zone 14 by the mechanisms described above, a substantial amount of porosity and permeability of the host rock will be opened to the passage of fluids and the oil-water contact 27 also ascends generally parallel to ascending temperature boundary 28. In order to provide maximum heat transfer from the circulating hot water, tubing 18 is raised periodically so that the bottom of tubing 18 is near the ascending oil-water contact boundary 27.

As the process continues water will invade into the portion of pay zone 14 wherein the heavy oil crude has been mobilized and in part removed. While water preferentially wets the host rock compared to the heavy oil crude, the process of doing so can sometimes be too slow for commercial purposes. The thin film of oil adhering to the surfaces of the host rock can at times be a substantial percentage of the original oil in place. In the process suitable additives commonly used in conventional petroleum water floods can be mixed with the injection water to break the film of oil adhering to the surfaces of the host rock, allowing a substantial amount of the residual oil to be produced.

Thus it may be seen that an immobile heavy oil crude can be mobilized by the process, that a substantial amount of the crude in place can be conditioned so that it will migrate toward the source of heat and thus be increasingly more flowable, and that substantial deposits of heavy oil crude and tar sands bitumen can be unlocked and recovered at the surface of the ground.

Air Pressurization Wells

According to a process described by *C.D. Woodward; U.S. Patent 3,905,422; September 16, 1975; assigned to Texaco Inc.* at least one injection well is drilled in the formation and a plurality of production wells are arranged symmetrically around the injection well, and a thermal recovery fluid such as steam, heated air, a mixture of steam and air or hot water is injected into the injection well to heat the formation within the pattern defined by the production wells so as to mobilize the viscous petroleum contained in the formation within the pattern.

A plurality of air pressurization wells are drilled around the production wells in a generally symmetrical fashion, and air is injected into the air pressurization wells at a pressure from about 10 to 90% of the pressure at which the thermal recovery fluid is being introduced into the injection well. As a consequence of the air pressurization step, a pressure gradient is formed around the pattern which serves to confine the thermal recovery fluid, thereby improving the capture efficiency and the thermal efficiency of the thermal recovery operation. Air injection also preexposes the subterranean formation to air at a low temperature, thereby pretreating the formation so as to render it more responsive to oil recovery by thermal means such as steam, in situ combustion, or low temperature oxidation recovery. After the main thermal recovery fluid has broken through at the production wells in the pattern, the production wells are converted to thermal recovery fluid injection wells, the air pressurization wells are converted to new production wells, and the thermal recovery operation is extended outward to the area previously pretreated by air pressurization.

I.S. Bousaid and M.F. Fontaine; U.S. Patent 3,946,808; March 30, 1976; assigned to Texaco Inc. describe a method for operating an in situ combustion process in a petroleum-containing reservoir wherein a plurality of air injection wells are spaced so that the approximate distance between the wells will be twice the distance at which the flux of air to the burning front from a single injection well becomes negligible.

Perforated Liner for Injection Well

According to a process described by *J.H. Striegler and E.P. Howell; U.S. Patents 3,960,213; June 1, 1976; 3,960,214; June 1, 1976; 3,986,557; October 19, 1976 and 4,007,788; February 15, 1977; all assigned to Atlantic Richfield Company*, bitumen is recovered from a subterranean tar sand formation by the following multistep method. First, an injection well is drilled to the formation and extended into the formation. Subsequent thereto, a perforated liner is inserted into the injection well extending the entire length and having the perforations provided in the portion of the injection well in contact with the formation.

Next, a plurality of production wells are drilled and completed into the formation positioned above and along the length of the injection well. Thereafter, a heated fluid is circulated through the injection well contacting the formation via the perforations thereby reducing the viscosity of the bitumen contained therein rendering it mobile. Subsequently, the mobilized bitumen is recovered through the plurality of production wells.

Figure 5.4 illustrates the earth's surface **10** from which a wellbore having a first section **12** has been drilled to penetrate a subterranean tar sand formation **14** and having a horizontal section **16** extending a desired distance therethrough. Figure 5.4 further shows wellbores **20** through **26** drilled and completed to penetrate the subterranean tar sand **14** and positioned above and along the horizontal section **16** of wellbore **12**. Continuous liner **30**, having perforations located between points **32** and **34**, is shown extending the entire length of the wellbore.

The process is started with a single-ended wellbore having a first section **12** and horizontal section **16** penetrating the subterranean tar sand formation **14**. Initially, first section **12** is drilled to penetrate the tar sand formation **14** and horizontal section **16** is provided for a suitable distance into the formation. The injection well is then provided with continuous liner **30** having perforations between points **32** and **34**. Subsequently, vertical wellbores **20** through **26** are drilled and completed to penetrate the subterranean tar sand formation **14** and are positioned above and along, at suitable intervals, the horizontal section **16**.

After completion of drilling, circulation of a heated fluid such as steam or hot water is begun through the injection well, contacting the formation via the perforations. The circulation, initially, of heated fluid is done at such pressures to cause breakthrough into wellbores **20** through **26** for fluid communication.

As the heated fluid is circulated through the single-end wellbore and contact is made with the formation via the perforations, the temperature of the formation is raised and the bitumen contained therein is rendered mobile. The mobilized bitumen is recovered by the driving force of the circulating fluid. After initial breakthrough to the wellbores **20** through **26**, the wellbores are plugged back to a shallower depth in the tar sand away from horizontal section **16** and circulation of heated fluid is continued. In the operation of the process, care should be taken in correlating the fluid composition, the fluid flow rate and the rate at which the fluid temperature is raised above the reservoir temperature, so that an adequate rate of flow is maintained at pressures that remain below the fracturing pressure of the formation.

Figure 5.4: Vertical Section of Subterranean Tar Sand Formation

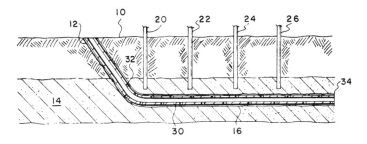

Source: U.S. Patent 3,960,213

The diameter and length of the injection well is not critical and will be determined by conventional drilling criteria, the characteristics of the specific formation, and the economics of a given situation. The diameter of the production wells is not critical and will be determined by conventional drilling criteria, etc. The production wells, however, must at least extend from the surface into the tar sand formation. The optimum number of and distance between production wells is a balance of economic criteria. Perforation size will be a function of other factors such as flow rate, temperature and pressures employed in a given operation. However, the injection well, in order to most efficiently exploit the effects of gravity in recovering the bitumen should be extended into the formation at a position near the bottom.

Perforated Pipes

L.C. Rabbitts; U.S. Patent 4,101,172; July 18, 1978 describes a method of in situ extraction of bitumen from an oil sands body. The method comprises sinking an access shaft through the oil sands body, driving an access drift in the rock strata underlying the oil-sands body, delineating a rectangular block of oil sands in the body by drilling and blasting the oil sands body to provide substantially vertical planes of fractured oil sands on all four sides of an enclosed mining room.

The mining room should be capable of retaining liquids and gases under pressure and comprises solid pillar walls, providing generally upwardly extending bores in the block of oil sands from the access drift in the body. Perforated pipes are provided in those portions of the bores in the block, the perforations of the pipes being dimensioned to prevent sand particles from the block passing through.

The permeability of the block of oil sands within the room is increased by fracturing the block, flooding the mining room with a hot fluid at a temperature and for a residence time sufficient to raise the temperature of the block by an amount to cause the bitumen to become flowable with the fluid and removing the fluid-bitumen mixture so formed from the block. The passage of fluid through the bed is via the perforated pipes.

Control of Steam Quality

E.E. Gomaa; U.S. Patent 4,093,027; June 6, 1978; assigned to Chevron Research Company describes an improved steam drive method for recovering oil from a hydrocarbon-containing formation. The quality of the injected steam is controlled to a value so that steam of a quality of between 35 and 45% enters the formation from the injection well. The process is particularly useful in relatively thick hydrocarbon-containing formations having at least 30 feet of hydrocarbon-containing interval. An injection well is provided with apparatus for injecting steam and a producing well is completed for producing oil from the formation at a location spaced apart from the injection well. The steam is formed and the quality of the steam is adjusted to provide 35 to 45% quality steam for injection into the formation. The steam is continuously injected into the formation while maintaining this quality and oil is produced from the production well.

Condensible Foam

A process described by *R.B. Needham; U.S. Patent 4,068,717; January 17, 1978; assigned to Phillips Petroleum Company* involves injecting steam into an injection well penetrating the reservoir sufficiently to fracture the tar sand and provide passage for the steam through the tar sand to a production well piercing the tar sand reservoir. Steam is provided at sufficient heat to mobilize heavy oil from the permeated tar sand and a pressure sufficient to maintain competency of the formation to permit continued flow from the injection well to the production well.

Injection of surfactant into the tar sand reservoir is used to produce a condensible foam which aids in maintaining back pressure on the injected steam within the tar sand reservoir to maintain the competency of the formation and to cause further permeation of the formation by the steam. Foam can be produced of strength sufficient to permit pressure to be applied in the tar sand reservoir capable of further fracturing the reservoir.

Example 1: Consider two wells completed in a tar sand spaced 330 feet apart drilled to a depth of 1,500 feet. A fracture is created between the two wells by using conventional means such as hydraulic fracturing, or by injecting steam at pressures greater than the fracturing pressure. About 75,000 barrels of water are injected as steam at about 400°F to clean the tar out of the fracture and heat a zone about 2 feet on either side of the fracture. Since the cleaned out portion outside the fracture (about 0.5 ft wide) is essentially unconsolidated sand, the steam permeability in this 0.5 ft wide section will be about 4,000 md. Because of the presence of the heated tar in the zones 2 ft on either side of the fracture the steam permeability in this zone will be about 200 md. Thus the steam injected will flow over 70% in the 0.5 ft cleaned out section and only 30% into the adjacent heated zones which extend out 2 ft from the fracture.

By injecting 320 barrels of water containing 9,000 lb of foaming agent Bio Soft B-40 (a sodium linear alkylate sulfonate, Stepan Chemical Co.) with the steam, a foam is created largely in the cleaned out 0.5 ft section. After creation of the foam in excess of 90% of the subsequent steam will be injected into the adjacent heated zones as a result of the presence of the foam in the cleaned out section. Less than 10% of the steam will enter the 0.5 ft section filled with foam.

Example 2: To illustrate the benefit of injecting steam both into the injection well and the normally producing well, less heat will be required to cause a hot path to be created between the two wells of Example 1. By heating through only one well as in Example 1, the amount of steam to heat the fracture and the two adjacent 2 ft zones would be about 75,000 barrels of water as steam at 400°F. Only about 30,000 total barrels of water as steam at 400°F are needed to heat a path between the wells, provided about half the steam is injected into each well. The benefits of creating foam by injecting into both wells are similarly illustrated since only about half as much foaming surfactant (approximately 4,500 lb) is needed to create foam from one well to the other provided the injection of the foaming agent used is about equally split between the two wells.

Cone-Shaped Gravel Pack

J.C. Allen and B.G. Harnsberger; U.S. Patent 4,124,074; November 7, 1978 and B.G. Harnsberger; U.S. Patent 4,066,127; January 3, 1978; both assigned to Texaco Inc. describe a process which comprises basically

(1) washing out a cavity in the formation to the bottom thereof,

(2) pouring a graded gravel into the cavity for building a conical-shaped gravel pack,

(3) running a screen down through the apex of the cone to the cavity bottom to bury the screen,

(4) ejecting hot fluids into the cavity for melting bitumen from the tar sands, and

(5) flowing the melted bitumen through the gravel pack and screen for filtering out sand and gravel from the melted bitumen for recovering the bitumen at the surface.

Figure 5.5a shows a well **10** having a casing **11** extending down through the usual shale formation **12**, for example, to a tar sand formation **13**, which formation may extend down to bedrock **14**. A preferred mechanism for washing out or forming a cavity in the well through the unconsolidated oil-bearing or tar sand formation comprises the following elements. A high pressure fluid supply pipe **15** extends from a suitable source **16** on the surface of high pressure, high velocity, hot aqueous fluids, as hot water, down through the well **10** to a hydraulic nozzle **17**. Nozzle **17**, shown here as a double nozzle, for example, has two 180° oppositely positioned openings for ejecting the high velocity fluids horizontally and is rotatable about bearing housing **18**. Thus as the double nozzle ejects hot and high pressure, high velocity fluid in the tar sand formation immediately under the lower end of the casing, the nozzle is slowly rotated and lowered until reaching the lowermost, bedrock position illustrated in Figure 5.5a. Immediately upon ejection of the hot fluids from the nozzle, a slurry **19** of spent fluids, sand, and bitumen is washed out and up the well to exhaust through a conduit at the surface where the bitumen is recovered therefrom. After a cavity **20** is formed, the nozzle **17** and supply pipe **15** are removed.

In the next basic method step, a gravel pack slurry supply pipe **21**, Figure 5.5b, is lowered into the well from a suitable source of graded gravel **22** at the surface. A predetermined amount of graded gravel pack slurry **23**, substantially less than the amount of sand and bitumen removed when forming the cavity, is measured out. A stream of the gravel pack slurry **23** is poured down into the cavity **20**, Figure 5.5b. The resulting cone-shaped mound on sand pack **24** is formed on the surface of the bedrock **14**. Surplus fluids in the cavity **20** are pushed out exhaust conduit **19**, Figure 5.5b.

The natural slope of a typical conical pile of wet sand is 22° as verified by the National Tank Company Handbook. Small graded gravel, such as that passing through a 20 to 40 [holes per linear inch (2.5 cm)] mesh, i.e., for fine aggregates, is sand.

Figure 5.5c illustrates the system for producing bitumen from tar sands in its last stage of being formed. After the conical-shaped gravel pack **24** is poured, a sieve or screen **25** is buried in the center of the vertex of the cone to the bottom or bedrock. The illustrated screen **25** preferably has a screw bit or muleshoe thread **26b** fixed to the bottom thereof for facilitating boring of the screen down through the vertex of the cone. Alternately, the screen may be driven down vertically into the vertex of the cone for being buried therein.

A production tube or string **26** is lowered to the bottom from a tank on the surface with the cylindrical screen **25** mounted over a perforated lower end **26a** of the production string. In the configuration of Figure 5.5c, the high pressure hot aqueous fluids are supplied from a suitable source **16** on the surface for passing through injection tube **27** to the well casing **11** from which the hot fluids are ejected into the well cavity **20** for melting and flowing the melted bitumen and tar sands from the tar sand formation through the gravel pack **24** toward the screen **25**. Only the melted bitumen and wash fluids pass through the gravel pack, screen, and perforated production tube end for passing up through the production string **26** to the collection tank at the surface.

A typical formation with the completed gravel pack **24** is illustrated in Figure 5.5c for a 2-inch diameter production tube. Here the oil-bearing formation is 20 ft (6 m) thick and the gravel pack **24** has a height of 6 ft (1.8 m) and a radius of 15 ft (4.5 m). The volume is 1,385 ft^3 (39.57 m^3).

In tar sand formations as unconsolidated oil-bearing sands, the conventional gravel pack over the screen utilizes a small size gravel to prevent oil sand flow which results in low oil flow and provides too low oil flow for good commercial production.

Figure 5.5: Gravel Pack Formation

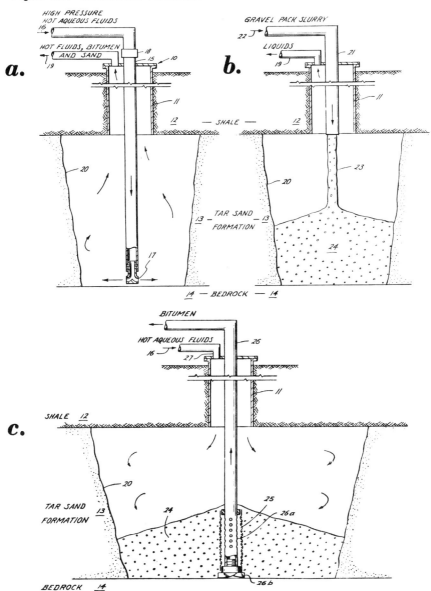

(a)   Schematic vertical sectional view of a well through a subterranean reservoir of tar sands illustrating the first step of washing out a cylindrical cavity down through the tar sand formation to the bottom.

(b)   Well of Figure 5.5a when pouring the cone of gravel for forming the sand pack in the cavity.

(c)   Well of Figure 5.5b after the screen is buried in the cone and the sand pack is finished and bitumen is being produced with the circulation of hot fluids.

Source: U.S. Patent 4,124,074

This process overcomes this problem by providing a larger surface area of the gravel pack for formation fluids to flow through. This larger surface is the surface of the cone-shaped gravel pack, i.e., about 761.5 ft² (68.5 m²) in the example. The surface of the conventional cylinder gravel pack having a 2-ft diameter and a 6-ft height is 37.7 ft², about $\frac{1}{20}$ the area of the new gravel pack. Thus for the same gravel pack permeability, the well productivity is greatly increased.

Gravel Packing

J.T. Payton; U.S. Patents 4,114,691; September 19, 1978 and 4,114,687; September 19, 1978; both assigned to Texaco Inc. describes a method for producing oil from a subterranean reservoir of tar sands as unconsolidated oil-bearing sands. The method comprises basically

(1) setting a screen in an open hole, the screen being large enough to pass a majority of the formation sand and small enough to retain a packing material,

(2) running a wash pipe through the screen for connecting to a lateral nozzle in a hole in the bottom of the screen for washing out a cavity around the screen,

(3) dropping a weight down the wash pipe for breaking off the nozzle for enlarging the screen bottom opening, and

(4) ejecting a consolidating gravel packing material through the large bottom opening for forming a consolidated gravel pack around the screen for primary production, or

(5) agglomerating the gravel pack with chemicals such as resins, plastics, or jelly for secondary recovery production.

Figure 5.6a shows a well **10** having a casing **11** extending down through the usual shale formation **12**, for example, to a tar sand formation **13**, which open hole well portion **14** in the formation is drilled down to bedrock **15**. A preferred mechanism for washing out or forming a cavity in the well through the unconsolidated oil-bearing or tar sand formation comprises the following elements.

Figures 5.6a and 5.6b show a liner screen **16**, wash pipe **17**, and a hydraulic double nozzle **18**, which has two 180° oppositely positioned openings for ejecting high velocity fluids horizontally or laterally and is rotatable about bearing housing **19**, Figure 5.6b. The nozzle is connected to a cap **16a** on the bottom of the screen **16** with two or more shear pins **20**, Figure 5.6a, for example. The top of the screen **16** is packed off against the bottom of the casing and extends down through the tar sand or unconsolidated petroliferous formation **13** to the bedrock, for example. This screen is large enough to pass a majority of the formation sand and small enough to retain a gravel packing material.

Following packing of the screen in the open hole, a wash pipe **21**, Figure 5.6b, is lowered internally of the screen **16** to connect to the bottom of the screen and accordingly to the double nozzle **18**. The high pressure fluid supply wash pipe **17** extends from a suitable source **21** on the surface of high pressure, high velocity, hot aqueous fluids, such as water, down through the well **10** to the cap **16a** and the hydraulic double nozzle **18**. Nozzle **18** has two 180° oppositely positioned openings for ejecting the high velocity fluids horizontally and is rotatable about bearing housing **17**. Thus as the double nozzle ejects hot and high pressure, high velocity fluid in the tar sand formation immediately under the lower end of the casing, the nozzle is slowly rotated and lowered until reaching the lowermost, bedrock position illustrated in Figure 5.6b. Immediately upon ejection of the hot fluids from the nozzle, a slurry **22** of spent fluids, sand, and bitumen is washed out and passes through the screen and then up the annulus **23** in the well formed between the wash pipe and the well walls to exhaust through a conduit at the surface where the bitumen is recovered therefrom. After a cavity **24**, Figure 5.6b, is formed the double nozzle **18** is removed by pumping a ball **25** down the wash pipe to shear pins **20**, Figure 5.6c, to knock the nozzle out of the cap **16a** in the bottom of the wash pipe and screen.

A predetermined amount of consolidating graded gravel pack slurry **26**, Figure 5.6e, substantially equivalent to the amount of sand and bitumen removed when forming the cavity, is then measured out. Without stopping the flow of fluids into the well, a stream of the consolidating gravel pack slurry **26** is pumped down into the cavity **24** out of the bottom of the cap **16a** and the wash and packing materials supply pipe **17**. The gravel pack slurry circulates up and around in the cavity **24** to deposit on the screen **16** forming the consolidated gravel pack **26a**. The liquid portion of the slurry **26** passes through the screen and up the annulus **23** to exit from pipe **27** at the surface.

Figure 5.6: Sand Consolidation

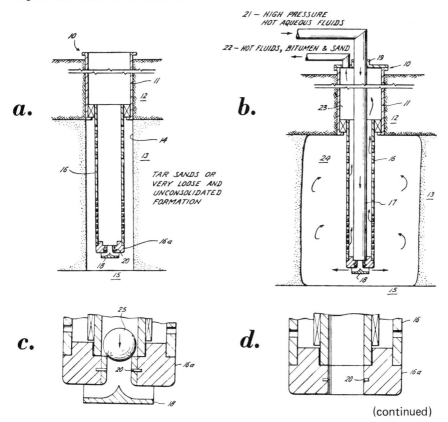

(continued)

Figure 5.6:   (continued)

e.

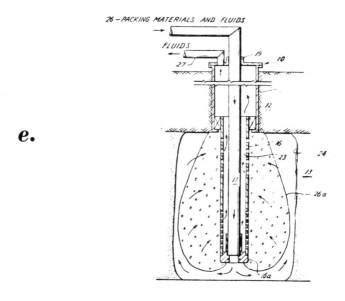

f.

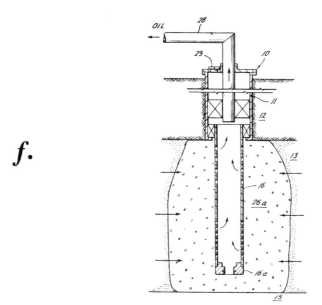

(continued)

Figure 5.6: (continued)

g.

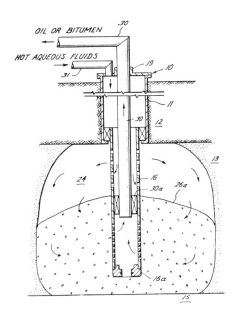

(a)   Schematic vertical sectional view of a well through a subterranean
        reservoir of tar sands illustrating one of the first steps of setting a
        screen in the open hole down through the tar sand formation to
        the bottom thereof and packing it off against the casing.
(b)   Well of Figure 5.6a after a wash pipe has been run through the screen
        for connecting to a nozzle at the screen bottom.
(c)   Well of Figure 5.6b after the cavity has been washed out with a hori-
        zontal nozzle and a weight is dropped to break away the nozzle.
(d)   Well of Figure 5.6c with the nozzle broken out for injecting a consoli-
        dated gravel pack material.
(e)   Injection of the consolidated gravel pack material.
(f)   Well producing primary crude oil.
(g)   Modified gravel pack in the well consolidated around the screen by
        various consolidating materials such as hot aqueous fluids, a jell, or
        other consolidating chemicals for secondary recovery production.

Source: U.S. Patent 4,114,691

The wash pipe **17**, Figure 5.6e, is then removed and replaced with an oil outlet
pipe **28**, Figure 5.6f, packed in the casing **11**. Exit pipe **27**, Figure 5.6e, is removed and the opening on top of the well sealed with a cap **29**, Figure 5.6f.
Primary oil then flows through gravel pack **26a** and into screen **16** for passage
through the oil outlet pipe **28** to the surface for gathering and/or storage.

When the primary oil ceases to flow, secondary recovery is required for continued oil production. Production tubing **30**, Figure 5.6g, is then substituted
for the oil outlet pipe **28**, Figure 5.6f, and packed off midway down the screen
16 with packer **30a** so that oil entering the lower half of the screen may flow,

as by being pumped, up through the production tubing **30** to the surface for gathering and/or storage. An injection tube **31** is inserted in the opening formerly closed by cap **29** for injecting secondary recovery fluids, such as hot aqueous fluids including steam, either saturated or superheated, or hot water, etc.

Accordingly, in configuration of Figure 5.6g, the high pressure hot aqueous fluids are supplied from a suitable source on the surface for passing through injection tube **31** to the well casing **11** and annulus between the screen and production tubing, through the upper perforated portion of the screen above the packer **30a** through which the hot fluids are ejected into the well cavity **24** for first spreading the gravel pack out and below the level of the packer **30a**. Then the hot aqueous fluids melt and flow the melted bitumen and tar sands from the tar sand formation through the gravel pack **26a** toward the screen **16**. Only the melted bitumen and wash fluids pass through the gravel pack and screen, to the production tube for passing through the production string **30** to the collection tank at the surface.

A typical formation with the completed consolidated gravel pack **26a** is illustrated in Figure 5.6g for a 2-inch (5.08 cm) diameter production tube. Here the oil-bearing formation is 20 ft (6 m) thick and the gravel pack **26a** has a height of 6 ft (1.8 m) and a radius of 15 ft (4.5 m). The volume is about 4,200 ft^3 (120 m^3).

Vibrating Probe to Fluidize Sand

A process developed by *J.S. Adamson; U.S. Patent 4,109,715; August 29, 1978* involves circulating steam, solvent or fluids through a material such as sand while constantly agitating the material to scrub and wash entrained substances such as oil, bitumen or the like free; then the substances are carried back to the surface. A vibrating probe assembly is utilized which is highly maneuverable and which fluidizes the sand immediately surrounding it thus facilitating the movement of the probe and assisting in the scrubbing and separating action of the solvents or steam upon the sand.

The probe includes means for extending it into the sand to the bottom of a wellbore so that the vibration in conjunction with the probe configuration moves the probe through the sand in a horizontal plane or, if desired, up and down at an angle from the horizontal. The voids remaining in the clean sand are filled with water so that the probe floats on the surface of the water. The substances which have been separated from the sand normally float on the water to the wellbore and then may be elevated to the surface by the pressure of the steam, solvent or fluid circulation.

Hydraulic Mining

D.A. Redford; U.S. Patent 3,951,457; April 20, 1976; assigned to Texaco Exploration Canada Ltd., Canada has found that bitumen may be recovered from subterranean tar sand deposits by a hydraulic mining technique wherein the tar sand is contacted by hot water or steam which may also contain an alkaline substance such as sodium hydroxide or ammonium hydroxide, plus a noncondensable gas. One means for accomplishing this process employs an injection string capable of both rotation and axial movement, equipped near its lower end with jet nozzles which direct the aqueous hydraulic mining fluid as one or more jet streams against the tar sand deposit face. A separate communication path to the surface of the earth facilitates movement of the injected hydraulic mining fluid with bitumen dispersed therein to the surface for further processing. The injection string is constructed so as to permit its simultaneous rotation and vertical movement as the aqueous hydraulic mining fluid is injected down the injection string and out through the jet nozzles so that a stream of fluid sweeps the tar sand deposits. A noncondensable, nonoxidizing gas such as nitrogen, methane or carbon dioxide is injected simultaneously to support the weight of the overburden, to enhance pumping action, and to insure that the cavity formed in the tar sand formation is gas filled, so the jets of fluid can penetrate deep into the formation.

Hydraulic Mining from Tunnel

A process described by *R.W. Johns; U.S. Patent 4,076,311; February 28, 1978* relates to the hydraulic underground mining of bituminous sands, oil shales and other friable mineral deposits. Accordingly, the process involves the provision of a tunnel complex at or near the base of the deposit, in which tunnels are driven parallel one with the other, and spaced a substantial distance apart.

An exemplary distance would be in the region of 2,000 ft. Hydraulic excavators are driven outwardly from the sides of the tunnels until the excavator heads are in a position substantially midway between adjacent tunnels. The excavators are arranged in a multiple array at spaced intervals along the tunnels, these intervals being adjusted such that there is interaction during operation, between adjacent excavator heads. The excavators may be positioned in two or more tiers by insertion into the deposit at differing angles from the operating tunnel, such that interaction between excavators is in two dimensions, horizontal and vertical.

By systematic and programmed reciprocating movement of the individual excavators over a progressively enlarging active zone, interacting between excavators is increased to three dimensions, horizontal, vertical, and lateral, thus effectively extending the active zone and increasing the volume of material being excavated. The ejector head, in addition to being provided with a multiplicity of nozzles through which fluid may be ejected at high pressure, also includes an intake or suction nozzle through which the fluidized sand, or slurry may be removed from the active zone.

The excavating nozzles are additionally spaced around the excavator head so that, at any time, certain nozzles are excavating below the intake nozzle to provide and evacuate a space into which oversized material can accumulate without plugging the intake. The nozzles are additionally spaced at predetermined angles relative to the excavator head so that they excavate both ahead of the intake nozzle and laterally thereof. In this manner, the excavation is both advanced, and expanded laterally.

Hydraulic Mining Using Steam Jets

C.A.R. Lambly and C.T. Draney; U.S. Patent 3,957,308; May 18, 1976; assigned to Bechtel International Corporation have found that subterranean tar sands can be more effectively extracted if exposed surfaces of adjacent cavities formed in a tar sands formation are continuously wetted so that water can penetrate the tar sands and cause the latter to spall and break off in blocks. This action is believed to be caused by water penetrating the formation through capillary action along paths of preferential wettability, causing adjacent portions of the formation to be essentially lubricated so that the binding forces between them diminish to the point where some of the tar sands portions separate from the formation and fall as blocks and loose tar sands into and toward the bottoms of the corresponding cavities while the remaining formation is left temporarily intact and presents new surfaces to be wetted to effect further spalling and so on. This action can be accelerated by the presence of heat, such as results from the introduction of hot water or steam.

This process is directed to a method of mining tar sands based upon the above determinations, and the method is preferably carried out by the performance of the following steps:

(1) Forming a tunnel or series of tunnels in the rock formation underlying the tar sands formation or near the bottom of the tar sands formation;

(2) Forming openings extending upwardly from the tunnel or tunnels at a plurality of locations and entering the tar sands and thus initiating the formation of a cavity in the tar sands at each such location;

(3) Wetting the exposed tar sands surfaces in each cavity. This can be done by directing a stream of water against the exposed tar sands surfaces or by spraying water into each cavity in a manner such that the water will create and maintain a moist atmosphere. The moisture in the moist atmosphere may include suspended droplets of water. In the alternative, the moist atmosphere may be saturated with respect to water at an elevated temperature relative to the ambient temperature of the tar sands so that condensation will occur on the surfaces of the tar sands;

(4) Maintaining wetting so that the water on the exposed tar sands surfaces in each cavity permeates the surface of the formation, including blocks of tar sands resulting from spalling, along paths of preferential wettability and/or by capillary action, so that adjacent portions of the formation will be lubricated and certain of the portions will spall and slough from the formation as blocks and chunks and gravitate toward the bottom of the corresponding cavity;

(5) As the blocks or chunks of tar sands from spalling and sloughing rest in each cavity, disintegration of the blocks and chunks is accomplished by the wetting action of the water in the cavity;

(6) Converting the disintegrated tar sands to slurry form by streams of water introduced under pressure or by other mechanical action. While the water introduced to cause spalling and sloughing may be introduced separately from that introduced for slurrying, water for both purposes may be introduced as a single stream;

(7) Directing the slurried tar sands out of the cavities by gravity flow through pipes to pumps in the tunnels and then to a processing plant;

(8) Maintaining constant wetting of all exposed tar sands surfaces to continue the spalling, sloughing, disintegrating, slurrying, and slurry-

removing steps to cause each cavity to continue to enlarge so that, as each cavity grows in size, the ability of the roof thereof and of the walls between adjacent cavities to support the weight of the remaining tar sands formation and that of the overburden is diminished, and deformations of the remaining formation will occur by:

(a)   Gradual subsidence through plastic flow of the walls into adjacent cavities; and

(b)   Collapsing of the roof when its span between supporting walls becomes too great to enable it to withstand its own weight and the weight of the overburden.

The tar sands masses which enter each cavity as a result of (a) and (b) are subjected to the wetting and mechanical action of the water such that disintegration and slurrying occur in the same manner as that for the tar sands blocks loosened by spalling and sloughing, and thus become part of the slurry formed and flowing from the cavity;

(9)   The foregoing mining procedure in any given cavity continues until all, or essentially all, of the tar sands have been removed, and is discontinued at such time as the overburden reaches the bottom of the cavity. By thus progressively mining out adjacent rows of cavities, the tar sands within a subterranean formation can be progressively and systematically removed and while being so removed, the overburden will be caused to subside in a controlled and orderly manner.

According to a process described by *C.A.R. Lambly and C.T. Draney; U.S. Patent 3,934,935; January 27, 1976; assigned to Bechtel International Corporation* tar sand and other similar oil-bearing formations are mined from below by building one, but usually at least two tunnels, in the underlying stratum underneath the tar sand formation and drilling substantially a line of raises, bore holes, or channels (all called channels here) from the tunnels into the tar sand formation. Oscillating and/or rotating high pressure jet stream nozzles are introduced through the channels into the tar sand formation, so as to direct high pressure, high velocity streams of fluid, e.g., hot water, above the underlying stratum into the tar sand formation, forming a slurry of fluid, sand and bitumen. The jet streams are usually directed in horizontal planes, but such planes could be inclined if deemed necessary or desirable.

The slurry flows downwardly, is gathered and directed through pipes, through the tunnel to a separation plant, which separates the bitumen from the sand and fluid, e.g., water.

The jets are spaced apart in a predetermined pattern at a distance somewhat less than twice their effective distance, so that the areas covered by the jet streams overlap to insure that tar sand pillars, which would support overlying formations of tar sand and overburden, are not left in the tar sand formation. As a cavity is created and enlarged in the tar sand formation, the tar sands above the cavity fall into the cavity in the path of the jet stream and are slurried. Each jet stream forms a large cavity interconnecting with adjacent cavities to form a large chamber. Successive rows of jet streams are initiated so that there is a continually receding chamber as the tar sands are eroded away. When the tar sand formation can no longer support the overlying formation above the chamber, the formations will cave into the chamber.

SOLVENT LEACHING AND FLUID FLOW

Aromatic Solvent, Carbon Dioxide and Solubilizing Agent

J.C. Allen; U.S. Patents 4,071,458; January 31, 1978 and 4,068,716; January 17, 1978; both assigned to Texaco Inc. has developed a method for recovering petroleum from subterranean, viscous petroleum-containing formations including tar sand deposits. The formations are penetrated by at least one injection well and by at least one production well comprising:

(a)   establishing a fluid communication path in the formation between the injection well and the production well;

(b)   injecting via an injection well a slug of an aromatic hydrocarbon solvent saturated at pressures ranging from 100 to 1,000 psi with a material selected from the group consisting of carbon dioxide, a gaseous hydrocarbon and mixtures thereof into the communication path;

(c)   injecting via the injection well an oil-displacing fluid selected from the group consisting of hot water, steam and superheated steam; and

(d)   recovering petroleum from the formation via the production well.

Example 1: A tar sand deposit is located at a depth of 450 ft and it is determined that the thickness of the formation is 65 ft. It is also determined that the petroleum is in the form of a highly bituminous hydrocarbon, and its viscosity at the formation temperature is much too high to permit recovery thereof by conventional means. An injection well is drilled to the bottom of the formation, and perforations are formed between the interval of 490 to 515 ft, i.e., the bottom of the petroleum saturated zone.

A production well is drilled approximately a 330 ft distance from the injection well, and perforations are similarly made slightly above the bottom of the petroleum saturated zone. The production well is also equipped with a steam trap so that only liquids can be produced from the formation, and vapors are excluded therefrom.

A fluid communication path low in the formation is formulated by fracturing the formation using conventional hydraulic fracturing techniques, and injecting a gravel sand mixture into the fracture to hold it open and prevent healing of the fracture.

Following the fracturing operation, the formation optionally may be heated by injecting hot water at a temperature of 205°F into the formation and continuing the injection until the temperature of the water produced at the production well rises to about 195°F, indicating that the communication path is open and is heated uniformly between the two wells.

In the next step, 2,500 barrels of benzene saturated with carbon dioxide at a temperature 60°F and 500 psig is injected into the formation at this same pressure and at a rate of 10 barrels per minute. After the benzene saturated with carbon dioxide is injected via the production well into the formation, the injection of 80% quality steam at a temperature of 417°F and a pressure of 285 psig is commenced at the rate of 15,000 lb/hr. The production of viscous oil via the production well gradually increases as injection of the oil-displacing fluid is continued and at the end of 30 days production of the viscous hydrocarbons is significantly increased over production of similar wells in the same formation utilizing only steam injection.

Example 2: In this example, viscous oil is recovered from a tar sand at a depth of 730 ft and having a thickness of about 28 ft. An injection well is drilled to the bottom of the hydrocarbon bearing structure and the casing perforated in the interval of 735 to 745 ft. In a like manner a production well drilled at a distance of about 400 ft from the injection well is perforated at a depth of 730 to 740 ft, i.e., the center of the tar sand formation at that location.

In the next step, a fluid communication path is formed by fracturing the formation in both wells using conventional hydraulic fracturing technique. A gravel-sand mixture is injected into the formation to hold it open and to prevent healing of the fracture. A total of 3,400 barrels of toluene saturated with carbon dioxide at a temperature of 60°F and a pressure of 500 psig is injected into the formation at the same pressure and at a rate of 10 barrels per minute. Following the injection of the carbon dioxide-saturated toluene, the injection of superheated steam (temperature 600°F, pressure 300 psig) containing about 0.01% by weight of solubilizing agent of the formula:

$$(CH_2CH_2O)_sH$$
$$|$$
$$-N-(CH_2CH_2O)_tH$$

where s plus t is about 14, is commenced at the rate of 13,000 lb/hr. Production of viscous oil from the production well is continued and at the end of 12 days the rate of production is substantially greater than with steam injection alone.

Gas-Saturated Hydrocarbon Solvent and Steam Injection

A process described by *J.C. Allen; U.S. Patent 4,026,358; May 31, 1977; assigned to Texaco Inc.* involves the steps of injecting a hydrocarbon solvent saturated with a gas, followed by the establishment of a heat wave or thermal sink in the formation, followed by a soak period. Thereafter, the formation is produced to recover the hydrocarbons. By the process, thermal and compositional gradients are created within the formation which result in improved sweep efficiency and thus lead to increased recovery of hydrocarbons.

In one illustration of the process, an injection well is completed in the formation and suitable offset wells, arranged in a five-spot pattern, are completed as production wells. Thereafter, a solvent saturated with gas or having gas dissolved therein such as naphtha saturated with natural gas or methane is injected via the injection well. The amount of solvent injected should be in the range of about 0.1 to 20% of the reservoir pore volume. Once this amount has been injected, solvent injection is terminated and a thermal sink is created in the formation.

This thermal sink can be established, for example, by the injection of steam, saturated or superheated, the temperature of the steam being such that the formation in the vicinity of the injection wellbore is heated to about 400° to 800°F. In the example, to attain a temperature in the desired range adjacent the injection well, approximately 5,000 barrels of saturated steam at a temperature of 500°F are injected.

Once the desired thermal sink is established, the steam or the air injection, dependent upon the method used, is terminated, and the reservoir undergoes a soak period. The amount of heat generated and the subsequent length of the soak period can be computed from heat and mass transfer calculation by methods known to those skilled in the art.

The production period is continued until the rate indicates the cycle should be repeated. Optionally after the production period, the formation may be water flooded, thereby scavenging any residual heat and further producing the formation.

Alternating Steam and Solvent Treatments

A process described by *C.B. Barry; U.S. Patents 3,946,810; March 30, 1976; 3,881,550; May 6, 1975 and 3,945,435; March 23, 1976; all assigned to The Ralph M. Parsons Co.* provides solvent stimulation of hydrocarbon deposits having extremely high viscosities, such as found in the Peace River region of Canada.

This process involves the use of a hot solvent generated from product on site to recover hydrocarbon product values from heavy crudes or bitumens. The hot solvent is injected into the deposit and functions to reduce deposit viscosity by demulsifying viscous emulsions of crude-in-water and water-in-crude, solvent cutting of crude and raising the temperature of the crude. The solvent also solubilizes production restricting precipitated waxes and asphaltenes. The solvent can be used to remove scale deposited from produced water, sand deposited around wellbores, and drilling and completion damage. The solvent is introduced at a temperature of from 200° to 650°F and is preferably depentanized naphtha of up to an 800°F end point.

This naphtha has substantial quantities of aromatics, the aromatics being useful in the dissolving of asphaltenes and waxes. The solvent may be manufactured from recovered bitumen by topping or by a combination of topping with visbreaking or reforming. Surfactants may be added to the solvent to prevent deposition of asphaltenes on deposit formations by keeping surfaces in the formation water wettable. Suitable surfactants are butylamines or mixed alkyl phenols.

The preferred form of this process involves the use of both solvent and steam extraction of hydrocarbon values from tars or bitumens typified by the Peace River deposits. This is done by either injecting steam and solvent vapors and liquids continuously into the formation or by cyclic injection of steam and hot solvent. With steam, thermal reduction in crude viscosity results and reservoir fluids expand. There will be some, though limited, distillation of hydrocarbons by the steam from heat and partial pressure reduction. With the decrease in viscosity, gravity drainage is promoted. The steam pressure, about 1,500 psia at injection, will strongly drive crude towards production wells.

The steam-solvent process retains the production resulting from thermal stimulation of deposits by the steam while eliminating or minimizing production restrictions occasioned by viscous emulsions, precipitated waxes and asphaltenes, scale and sand deposition, and drilling and completion damage.

When steam and solvent are used together, the difficult problem of solvent-crude mixing is not present because the steam is a low viscosity fluid which will rapidly fill all available voids in the reservoir and carry solvent with it. The solvent can then function more completely throughout the formation.

Fluid Carrier Recovery System

According to a process described by *G.M. Barrett; U.S. Patent 4,033,412; July 5, 1977* the problem of separating the oil-solvent mixture or solution from the sand has been simplified. A suitable carrier, such as water, is pumped into the tar sand in sufficient volume that the water fills the cavities in the tar sand and further flows back up to or substantially adjacent the surface of the earth through a flow passage in the earth down to the tar sand deposit. Then when a suitable solvent is introduced into the tar sand, the solvent dilutes the oil to the extent that droplets of oil-solvent mixture or solution are released from the sand and these droplets float in the carrier up to the earth's surface through the flow passage. The oil is thus separated from the sand in situ so that the sand need not be handled at all.

Further, because the oil-solvent mixture or solution freely floats upwardly within the carrier to above the surface of the carrier, no pumping of the oil-solvent mixture or solution per se is required. Basically, all that is required is that sufficient volumes of the carrier (water) are flowed underground to maintain a carrier level within the flow passage above which it is desired to have the oil-solvent mixture or solution float for recovery purposes and to continuously supply sufficient quantities of solvent to effect a reduction in the viscosity of the oil so that it will free itself from the sand and float in the carrier.

Cycling of Fluid Injection and Soaking

According to a process described by *R.H. Widmyer; U.S. Patent 4,034,812; July 12, 1977; assigned to Texaco Inc.* a hot fluid such as steam is injected into the formation and pressure maintained thereon for a period of time to heat the viscous petroleum in the immediate vicinity of the wellbore, which causes the unconsolidated mineral grains to settle to the bottom of the formation with the viscous oil located on the top of the settled grains.

The injection pressure maintenance phase is then terminated and petroleum is recovered from the upper portion of the formation. Numerous cycles of hot fluid injection, soak, followed by production of petroleum from the upper portion of the cavity are required to exploit a reasonable aerial extent of the formation by this method.

The separation is enhanced by introducing a solvent material for the viscous petroleum which has a specific gravity substantially less than the specific gravity of petroleum, such as a low molecular weight hydrocarbon solvent, or introducing a fluid which is immiscible with petroleum and which has specific gravity substantially greater than the specific gravity of the viscous petroleum, such as a dense brine which settles to the bottom portion of the cavity and displaces petroleum upward. Both treatments may be employed simultaneously for optimum recovery.

Example: A tar sand deposit is located under an overburden whose thickness is 250 ft. The tar sand deposit is 75 ft thick. The petroleum present in the formation is so viscous that it is totally immobile at formation temperatures. The sand which comprises approximately 60% of the volume of the formation, is unconsolidated and only partially in grain-to-grain contact. A well is drilled to the bottom of the formation and casing set through the entire interval.

Perforations are formed about midway between the top of the formation and the center of the formation, and another set of perforations are formed approximately 10 ft from the bottom of the formation. A tubing string is run into the casing, the end of the tubing string being positioned approximately even with the lower set of perforations. A packer is set above the end of the tubing string between the sets of perforations, to isolate the annular space between the tubing string and the casing.

Air is injected into the upper perforations, and the tubing string which is in fluid communication with the lower perforations is open to the atmosphere initially in order to establish some fluid permeability since the initial permeability of the tar sand deposit is found to be exceedingly low. Air injection is continued for at least 24 hours, after which steam is injected into the upper perforation with the tubing string open to the atmosphere until it is determined that steam is flowing from the tubing string to the atmosphere. The tubing string is then connected with the steam source and steam is injected into both the upper and lower perforations simultaneously. The steam quality is 80%, the maximum steam temperature is approximately 366°F (186°C).

The injection pressure gradually rises and the injection rate is curtailed when the bottom hole pressure approaches about 150 psig, since this is the predetermined maximum safe injection pressure. The injection flow rate is gradually reduced and only enough steam is injected to maintain the bottom hole pressure at about 150 psig for the duration of the soak period during which time heat transfer from the injected steam to the petroleum and mineral matrix is accomplished with sand settling to the lower portion of the zone adjacent the formation affected by the injected steam at the same time. The soak period is approximately 7 to 10 days during this first cycle.

In order to facilitate separation of petroleum from the sand and to aid in the settling to a lower portion of an affected zone, an oil field brine is obtained which has a specific gravity of 1.15. Approximately 1% surfactant is added to the brine in order to reduce the interfacial tension between the brine and the viscous petroleum, which aids in the separation thereof. Since any surfactant used in this process must be stable in the presence of high salinity and high temperature, the surfactant utilized was the ammonium salt of a sulfonated, ethoxylated nonphenol containing six ethoxy groups per molecule. This is effective in the high salinity, high temperature embodiment to which it will be subjected. The brine-surfactant mixture is then heated to a temperature 200°F prior to injecting it into the formation. The hot surfactant-brine mixture is introduced into the lower portion of the formation via the tubing, so it saturates the sand area from the bottom up, displacing the heated viscous petroleum in an upward direction as the brine saturates the sand mass.

The heated viscous petroleum is displaced upward and into the annular space through perforations in the casing in the upper portion of the formation, to the surface of the earth. The end point for this cycle is determined when brine is detected, since it indicates that all of the petroleum which has been mobilized in the first phase of the operation has been displaced into the well. At this point, fluid production is terminated and another cycle of steam injection is initiated.

As the zone in which the oil-saturation has been decreased and the permeability has been increased expands with each cycle, a greater amount of heating fluid as well as other fluids injected into the process will be required in each new cycle than in the preceding cycle. This must be considered during the course of operation of the process, and also offers a means for monitoring the effectiveness of the process in extending the treated zone outwardly from an injection well.

As the affected zone increases greater quantities of injected fluid are required to fill up and saturate the affected area in each new cycle before any appreciable heating of the petroleum formation surrounding the affected area will be possible. In a large field in which a number of wells are being treated simultaneously and sequentially using this process, there will be a point reached where the process would be converted to a throughput mode in which steam or other heated fluid is injected into one well to move through a communication zone to a remotely located well, so hot fluid injection in the one well and oil production from another well can continue simultaneously.

If the process is applied to a formation by means of a number of wells, and the formation dip is appreciable, the development and expansion of the cavity will be updip, so subsequent wells should be located updip from the original wells in order to take advantage of tendency for the cavity to develop preferentially updip from the injection point.

Solvent and Carrier Gas

J.C. Allen; U.S. Patent 4,008,764; February 22, 1977; assigned to Texaco Inc. has found that viscous petroleum including bitumen may be recovered from viscous petroleum-containing formations including tar sand deposits by injecting into the formation a gaseous mixture of a carrier gas and a hydrocarbon solvent which is liquid at reservoir conditions. Suitable materials for the solvent include paraffinic hydrocarbons having from 5 to 10 carbon atoms such as pentane, hexane, etc., as well as naphtha, natural gasoline, carbon disulfide, and mixtures thereof.

Suitable carrier gases include nitrogen, carbon dioxide, methane, ethane, propane, butane, hydrogen, anhydrous ammonia, hydrogen sulfide, ethylene or propylene. For example, nitrogen may be passed through a vaporizer to vaporize pentane, and then the gaseous mixture injected into a subsurface tar sand deposit. Viscous petroleum or bitumen absorbs the liquid solvent from the gaseous phase until sufficient solvent is absorbed to make the petroleum sufficiently mobile that it will flow into the production well. Production may be taken from a remotely located well or from the same well as was used for injecting the gas-solvent mixture. The use of paraffinic hydrocarbons such as pentane or hexane in application of this process to tar sand materials does not result in plugging of formation flow channels caused by precipitation of asphaltic materials. The carrier gas and/or the solvent may be heated prior to injection into the formation to increase the solvency rate and vapor pressure of the solvent. The solvent may be displaced by injecting water, hot water or steam into the formation.

The process is best understood by referring to Figure 5.7 in which viscous petroleum-containing formation 1 is penetrated by injection well 2 and production well 3. Perforations 4 and 5 establish fluid communication between the wells and the formation 1. On the surface, vaporizer 6 is fed by carrier gas via line 7 and by liquid solvent through line 8. Initially, all of the liquid solvent and carrier gas will be supplied from external makeup sources, although recycling of both produced solvent and carrier gas reduces the inventory of these fluids.

Solvent is added to vaporizer 6 only as needed to maintain the level up to a preselected level. Carrier gas is bubbled into the liquid solvent via nozzles 9, so that a uniform distribution of gas bubbles in the liquid is achieved to insure maximum gas-liquid solvent contact. The gaseous phase is saturated with solvent vapors, and only gaseous materials are allowed to exit through line 10. Baffles 11 aid in achieving efficient mixing and prevent liquid solvent from exiting the vaporizer.

Figure 5.7: Oil Recovery Method Using Carrier Gas and Solvent

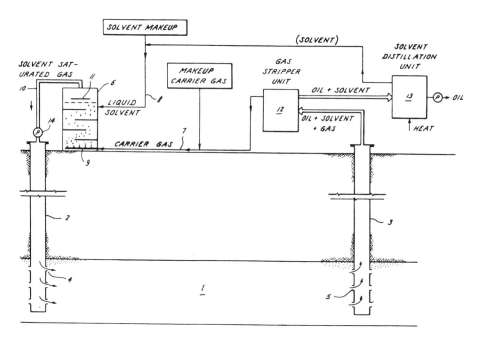

Source: U.S. Patent 4,008,764

The gaseous effluent from vaporizer **6**, comprising carrier gas and vaporized solvent, passes via line **10** and is pumped by compressor **14** into injection well **2**. The gaseous mixture of carrier gas and solvent enters the formation and flows through the flow channels in the formation. Solvent is absorbed directly into the viscous petroleum from the gaseous phase. The carrier gas serves the essential additional purpose of maintaining transmissibility by maintaining the formation flow channels open.

The viscosity of the viscous petroleum gaseous solvent decreases until flow of petroleum is initiated. Contact between solvent and viscous petroleum is achieved in a very uniform manner throughout the formation between the injection well and the production well, as contrasted to liquid solvent injection where maximum solvent-petroleum mixing occurs near the injection well, with much of the petroleum between the contact point and the production well being essentially uncontacted by solvent.

The petroleum-solvent mixture flows toward production well **3** being driven by the injected gas. The fluid enters well **3** via perforations **5**, and is pumped to the surface. Some carrier gas is produced simultaneously with petroleum and solvent. It is usually desirable to separate the gas and petroleum by means such as gas stripper **12**. The stripped gas is recycled through vaporizer **6**. The produced fluid then passes through a solvent separator unit. Thermal distillation unit **13** accomplishes the separation. Solvent recycling is desirable for economic reasons. If a central surface processing plant is to be used, as will be the case for tar sand operations, for example, the separation of solvent from the petroleum may be accomplished in the central processing plant.

After the process described above has proceeded for a period of time, gas-solvent injection can be terminated and a drive fluid such as water, hot water or steam may be injected to displace the residual petroleum and solvent toward the production well.

Example: The following is a pilot field example. A tar sand deposit is located at a depth of 200 ft and the thickness of the deposit is 70 ft. Since the ratio of overburden thickness to tar sand deposit thickness is greater than one, the deposit is not economically suitable for strip mining. It is determined that the most attractive method of exploiting this particular reservoir is by means of carrier gas vaporized solvent flooding.

A commercial grade natural gasoline is available at an attractive price in the area, the composition of this material being 90% C_6 through C_9. This material is essentially all liquid at reservoir pressure and temperature, so it is quite suitable for use as the liquid solvent.

Flue gas available from a steam generator operating nearby in the field is passed through a filter and a scrubber to remove particulate matter and corrosive materials, and the scrubbed flue gas, which is approximately 86% nitrogen and 14% carbon dioxide, is used as the carrier gas.

A multiple baffle gas vaporizer unit capable of handling 50,000 scf of gas per hour is installed near the injection well and connecting lines are added so that carrier gas and liquid solvent may be introduced into the vaporizer and gaseous effluent pumped to the injection well. The nitrogen-carbon dioxide carrier gas and the solvent are both heated to a temperature of 120°F prior to introduction into the vaporizer. The gaseous effluent is compressed to a pressure of 150 psi and injected into the formation. Production of carrier gas is obtained within 20 days from the production well, which is located 100 ft from the injection well. Oil production begins 10 days after the carrier gas first appeared. Produced gas comprising the injected carrier gas and a small amount of methane is stripped from the produced fluid and recycled through the vaporizer unit. Solvent is removed from the produced fluid by distillation for recycling through the vaporizer.

After production has continued for 12 months, the gas:oil ratio begins to rise. Gas analysis indicates that the solvent content is beginning to increase, indicating absorption of solvent by formation petroleum has reached an equilibrium. Gaseous fluid injection is terminated and hot water is injected into the injection well to displace additional petroleum and solvent. The petroleum production rate increases rapidly and remains high for several months, and then decreases as the injected hot water begins to break through. The injection of hot water is stopped after the water-oil ratio rises above about 50.

According to a related process described by *J.C. Allen and D.A. Redford; U.S. Patent 4,109,720; August 29, 1978; Texaco Inc. and Texaco Exploration Canada, Ltd., Canada* petroleum may be recovered from viscous petroleum-containing formations including tar sand deposits by injecting into the formation a solvent which is liquid at formation conditions and simultaneously therewith injecting a substance which will remain totally gaseous at the pressure and temperature conditions existing within the reservoir.

The presence of noncondensible gas in the formation into which solvent is being injected prevents formation of an impermeable bitumen bank which blocks the further flow of fluids through the formation. The gas should be essentially unreactive with the solvent and formation fluids in order to obtain the desired benefits. Examples of suitable gases include methane, ethane, nitrogen, carbon dioxide, and mixtures thereof.

A process described by *J.C. Allen and C.D. Woodward; U.S. Patent 4,042,027; August 16, 1977; assigned to Texaco Inc.* involved first injecting into the tar sand formation a paraffinic hydrocarbon at a temperature below 300°F which precipitates asphaltic material from the asphaltic petroleum in the formation.

Next, solvent injection is terminated and air is injected into the formation, and the formation is ignited to accomplish in situ combustion within the tar sand reservoir utilizing the precipitated asphaltic materials for fuel for the in situ combustion reaction. Reaction temperatures higher than normal in situ combustion temperatures are produced, facilitating thermal cracking and in situ hydrogenation to upgrade the produced crude within the tar sand reservoir.

Formation of Highly Permeable Zones

A process described by *A. Brown, C.H. Wu and J.H. Park; U.S. Patent 3,983,939; October 5, 1976; assigned to Texaco Inc.* concerns a method for recovering viscous petroleum from subterranean viscous petroleum-containing formations, and especially those formations which are relatively thick and which may have one or more high permeability strata which makes normal recovery methods ineffective because of channeling of the recovery fluid through the high permeability strata, thereby bypassing substantial amounts of petroleum.

The first step involves forming a high permeability zone in the upper portion of the formation, preferably at or near the top, which extends laterally across the top of the formation. Next, a similar high permeability zone is formed in the lower portion of the formation, preferably at or near the bottom of the formation, similarly extending laterally throughout the full portion of the formation to be exploited. At least two wells are then drilled into the formation, and separate communication means are established between the surface of the earth and each of the two high permeability zones in each of the wells.

A heated fluid is injected into the lower high permeability zone by at least one of the wells, and preferably is injected into one well to flow through the zone and out the other so as to heat the lower high permeability zone to a temperature substantially higher than the original ambient temperature of the formation. A solvent is introduced into this heated zone, which solvent has a boiling point intermediate between the temperature to which the high permeability zone has been heated and the ambient temperature existing in the portion of the formation above the heated high permeability zone in the lower portion of the oil formation. The solvent vaporizes upon contacting the heated zone and the vapor phase solvent freely moves up into the formation.

The gaseous phase solvent may dissolve directly into the viscous petroleum contained in the intermediate zone, or it may condense as it cools and dissolve in the viscous petroleum, or both may occur simultaneously within various portions of the intermediate zone of the petroleum formation. The result is that solvent is introduced into the intermediate zone in sufficient depth to reduce the viscosity of the petroleum in that zone by a significant degree. A gaseous substance is then introduced into the upper high permeability zone by one or more wells, sufficient to increase the pressure therein to a value substantially greater than the pressure existing in either the intermediate zone or the bottom high permeability zone. The gaseous material may be a solvent such as carbon dioxide or low molecular weight hydrocarbons, or a relatively inert gas may be utilized.

The gaseous substance present in the upper high permeability zone forces the mixture of viscous petroleum and solvent downward into the bottom high permeability zone, where it may be displaced by a suitable fluid to the remotely located production well, from which it is produced to the surface of the earth.

Communication Path

J.C. Allen and D.A. Redford; U.S. Patent 3,913,672; October 21, 1975; assigned to Texaco Inc. and Texaco Exploration Canada, Canada and D.A. Redford; U.S. Patent 3,908,762; September 30, 1975; assigned to Texaco Exploration Canada Ltd., Canada have found that a stable, permeable communication path may be established between wells drilled into and completed in a subterranean, viscous petroleum-containing formation such as a tar sand deposit. The process requires that there be appreciable gas permeability or a high permeability streak within the formation. The permeable streak may be a naturally occurring high permeability streak or one which is formed by means of conventional hydraulic fracturing and propping according to techniques well known in the prior art. The process utilizes a solvent which is effective at dissolving essentially all of the hydrocarbon portion of the tar sand deposit, and a gas which is highly soluble in the solvent.

Examples of solvent suitable for use in the process include aromatic solvents such as benzene, toluene, and xylene, carbon tetrachloride, certain halogenated hydrocarbons, carbon disulfide and mixtures thereof. Gases suitable for use in the process include carbon dioxide, methane, nitrogen, air, and their mixtures. Gas is dissolved in the solvent or the solvent is saturated with the gas at a pressure up to a value in pounds per square inch numerically equal to the overburden thickness in feet.

The gas-saturated solvent is injected into the permeable formation or into the propped fracture or naturally occurring high permeability streak within the formation. Injection continues until that portion of the formation into which the gas-saturated solvent is injected is pressurized to a preselected pressure not exceeding a value in pounds per square inch equal numerically to the overburden thickness in feet.

Once the pressure within the portion of the formation contacted by the gas-saturated solvent reaches the desired value, injection is terminated and bitumen is recovered from the portion of the formation by solution gas drive, and the mixture of bitumen and solvent together with the liberated gas is produced to the surface of the earth. This will enlarge the permeability zone; however, repetitive treatments are usually required to achieve the desired extent of enlargement to form a stable communication path. Recovery of bituminous petroleum by more conventional, high efficiency techniques such as steam injection, steam emulsification drive, combined thermal-solvent, or in situ combustion operations may be undertaken using the communication path.

D.A. Redford and J.C. Allen; U.S. Patent 3,913,671; October 21, 1975; assigned to Texaco Inc. and Texaco Exploration Canada, Canada have discovered that the production and recovery of viscous petroleum or bitumen from subterranean viscous petroleum-containing formations including tar sand deposits, may be improved by employment of a method which permits contacting immobile hydrocarbon deposits in the formation in the vicinity of the production well so as to facilitate removal thereof from the formation.

In the process, at least one production well is completed so as to provide a separate flow path from the surface, so that a treating fluid may be introduced into a portion of the petroleum formation, the fluid being capable of removing at least a portion of the immobile hydrocarbon materials.

In one preferred case, the annular space between the production tubing and the well casing is utilized for the separate flow path for introducing the treating fluid into the formation. Heated, aqueous fluid such as hot water or steam or superheated steam which melts the immobile, solid-like hydrocarbon materials. so that they will flow into the production wellbore and be produced to the surface of the earth are introduced via the flow path. The aqueous heating fluid may be injected into the portion of the formation adjacent to the production well on a timed program basis, or only when the production rate has decreased, indicating the presence of immobile hydrocarbon materials obstructing the flow of petroleum from the formation. Continuous injection of the aqueous heating fluid into the formation may also be employed in order to prevent deposition of obstructing hydrocarbon materials.

SOLVENT EXTRACTION

Trichlorofluoromethane

C.D. Smith and D.V. Keller, Jr.; U.S. Patents 4,027,731; June 7, 1977 and 3,941,679; March 2, 1976; both assigned to Otisca Industries, Ltd. describe hydrocarbon recovery processes of the solvent extraction type. Liquid trichlorofluoromethane is utilized as the extraction solvent. It has been found that the bitumen found in tar sands and the kerogen in oil shales dissolve readily in this medium, permitting the hydrocarbon values to be easily separated from the mineral solids of the geological composite. The solvent can be removed by a simple and conventional distillation step, by stripping, etc., to isolate the hydrocarbons.

Trichlorofluoromethane is not flammable. It has low boiling and freezing points (ca 75° and −168°F, respectively), a low heat of vaporization and low viscosity and surface tension, all of which are desirable. The compound does not react with hydrocarbons; and it is nontoxic and noncorrosive, available in large quantities at reasonable cost, and almost completely recoverable in the course of the extraction process.

In the process apparatus, the extraction solvent is preferably circulated in counterflow relationship to the composite being extracted both within each reactor and in the system as a whole, the latter goal being accomplished by employing the liquid effluent from each extraction stage as the solvent for the preceding stage. This makes the most efficient use of the solvent, which is important from an economic viewpoint and, also, maximizes the concentration of the hydrocarbons in the liquid delivered to the system component where the solvent is separated from the hydrocarbons. This latter factor is important in that it minimizes the amount of solvent which must be separated and, therefore, the energy required to recover and cost of recovering the solvent.

The apparatus for in situ recovery of hydrocarbons includes submersible pumps in the formation being produced and equipment for pumping extraction solvent into the formation. The solvent percolates downwardly through the formation, separating the hydrocarbons from the mineral solids to produce a liquor which is lifted to the surface by the submersible pumps.

Above ground is a concentrator where fines unavoidably pumped to the surface with the liquor are removed and the concentration of the hydrocarbons in the liquor is increased. Also located above ground is equipment for cleaning the solids, for separating the extraction solvent from the hydrocarbons, and for recovering this solvent and any solvent which vaporizes in the various system components.

Chlorofluorocarbon Solvents

C.D. Smith and D.V. Keller, Jr.; U.S. Patent 4,067,616; January 10, 1978; assigned to Standard Oil Company describe methods of and apparatus for recovering bitumen from tar sands and the like in which the tar sand is mechanically dislodged from the formation in which it is deposited and in which a solvent for the bitumen is mixed with the mined material to reduce the viscosity of the bitumen and thereby facilitate the transfer of the mined material to an operation where the bitumen is separated from solid components of the tar sand.

Figure 5.8a depicts a system **20** for recovering bitumen from a tar sand formation **22** underlying overburden **24**. The tar sand is removed from formation **22** by mining apparatus **26** embodying and constructed in accord with the principles of the process. As shown in Figure 5.8a, the formation can be attacked from a vertical outcropping or stripped face **28** or from a vertical, lined shaft **30**. In both cases the mining operation is preferably initiated at the bottom of formation **22**. This promotes the efficiency of the operation because, as tar sand is removed from formation **22**, material above it will tend to flow down into the resulting void, bringing it within the reach of the mining apparatus without redirecting or relocating the latter.

Referring to Figures 5.8a and 5.8b, the tar sand dislodged by mining apparatus **26** is conveyed from the mining apparatus down a chute **34** into a crusher **36** adjacent the working face where the top size of the tar sand is reduced to facilitate its further handling. Preferably the tar sand is wet ground. A solvent is in this case sprayed onto the material in crusher **36** through nozzles **37** to facilitate the comminution process. From crusher **36** the tar sand flows into a slurry tank **38** equipped with an agitator **40**. Here, the tar sand is slurried with a fluorochlorocarbon solvent to further facilitate the subsequent movement of the tar sand.

A slurry pump **42** pumps the resulting slurry through conduit **43** to an extractor **44**, typically located on the surface and preferably of the character described in U.S. Patent 3,941,679. Here, the tar sand slurry is contacted with additional solvent introduced through conduit **46** to separate the bitumen constituents of the tar sand from its solid components. From the extractor, the bitumen-laden solvent flows through conduit **48** to a stripper **50**, again preferably of the construction described in U.S. Patent 3,941,679, where the solvent is removed to isolate the bitumen.

Not all of the solvent need be removed. Instead, enough can be left so that the bitumen can be readily pumped to a refinery or other processing operation. In fact the stripping step can be eliminated and all of the solvent retained for this purpose. The mineral solids from which the bitumen is separated in extractor **44** are transferred to a dryer **52** where the solvent still associated with the solids is removed. The solids are then typically conveyed back to the mining site and spread to compensate for subsidence resulting from the removal of the tar sand.

Solvent recovered from dryer **52** and stripper **50** and that evolved in extractor **44** is conveyed through conduits **56, 58** and **60** to a purge/condenser unit identified by reference character **62** in Figure 5.8a. Here, noncondensibles are stripped from the solvent, and it is liquefied. From unit **62** the solvent is recirculated through main conduit **64** and branch conduits **66, 68** and **70** to mining apparatus **26**, crusher **36**, and slurry tank **38** to complete the cycle.

Figure 5.8: Mining and Processing Technique for Tar Sands

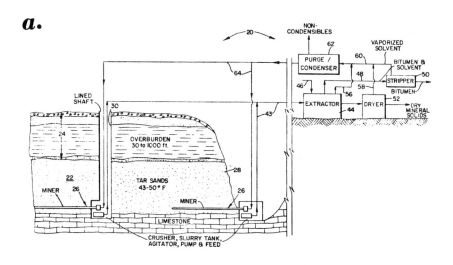

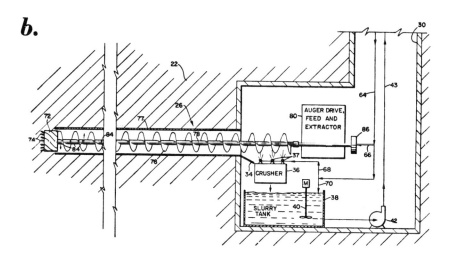

(a)   Pictorial view illustrating the mining of tar sands.
(b)   Primarily schematic, vertical section through mining apparatus
        employing the principles of the process.

Source: U.S. Patent 4,067,616

Referring specifically to Figure 5.8b, mining apparatus **26** is basically similar to the auger type miners commercially used in the mining of coal. Apparatus **26** includes a mining head **72** with teeth **74** for dislodging tar sand from formation **22**, helical conveyor **76** for conveying the dislodged material to shaft **30** or the face of outcrop **28** through a casing **77**, an elongated shaft **78** to which the miner head and conveyor are fixed, and a drive mechanism **80** for rotating the miner head and conveyor via shaft **78**. Mining apparatus **26** differs from a conventional auger type miner in that the conveyor **76** is surrounded by a casing, in that shaft **78** is hollow, and in that nozzles or apertures **84** are provided in the forward end of the shaft; i.e., the end adjacent miner head **72**. Also, the mining apparatus has a manifold **86** providing fluid communication between solvent supply line **66** and shaft **78**.

The fluorochlorocarbon solvent is circulated through shaft **78** to its forward end where it is discharged through nozzles or apertures **84** and mixed with the mechanically dislodged tar sand by conveyor **76** as the tar sand is dislodged from formation **22**. This reduces the viscosity of the dislodged material from over a million centipoises to a few hundred centipoises at most, producing two salutary effects. One is to significantly facilitate the flow of the tar sand from the miner head through casing **77** to crusher **36**; the other is to significantly reduce the power required to drive the conveyor and cutter head.

Mining apparatus as just described is capable of removing material as far as 200 to 300 ft away from an outcropping such as **28** or a shaft such as **30**. In such circumstances, multiple casing sections and conveyor flights are required. Auger type miners with extractors for recovering conveyor flights from one mining operation and transferring them to the next are available (see, for example, *Coal Mining and Processing,* March, 1974, p 46 et seq) and the same mechanism can with only minor changes be used to transfer casing sections.

An important feature of the casing is that it can be extended to cover virtually all the auger or none of it, depending on the bed mining and material handling requirements and thereby the operator can selectively mine the ore bed. As the auger removes tar sands there will be a flow into the void created by the auger, that in vertical section would have characteristics similar to solids flow in a bin, in that on an angle relatively similar to the angle of repose of the material, a dead area will be established which can be mined, by simply extending or retracting the auger head and the casing an appropriate distance. Similarly, any tendency towards rat-holing or channeling can be circumvented by manipulating the extension of the casing and the auger. By utilizing joints in the casing that are liquid and vapor tight any potential for media loss or migration into the ore bed would be eliminated.

Finally, the extension of the casing would remove the active mining area a sufficient distance to reduce or eliminate shear forces that could affect the vertical shaft structure or in the case of mining against a high wall reduce or eliminate the potential for ore or overburden material from collapsing on the equipment building. Trichlorofluoromethane is several times as dense as air and consequently diffuses only slowly into the surrounding environment. Accordingly, the loss of solvent by evaporative diffusion in enclosed spaces such as at the bottom of a shaft is so small that it can be ignored, a feature of practical importance. In operating in a more open area such as from a vertical outcrop, the equipment can readily be hermetically encased and any solvent which evaporates circulated to the purge/condenser unit and recovered.

Sequential Treatment with Paraffin Liquid Hydrocarbon

J.C. Allen; U.S. Patent 3,978,926; September 7, 1976; assigned to Texaco Inc., has found that a paraffin liquid hydrocarbon such as n-pentane is excellent as a solvent for bitumen and in fact superior in some cases to aromatic hydrocarbons for extracting bitumen. The effectiveness of the use of paraffin hydrocarbons can be shown in the following tests wherein n-pentane was used to extract bitumen by capillary imbibition and gravity drainage. In demonstrating the process in the laboratory, a recovery of 92% was obtained by sequential contacting and extraction of bitumen from a Utah tar sand permeability plug.

In the test the plug was placed in a jar, n-pentane was added to bring the level to ¼ inch above the bottom of the plug, and the jar was then closed and left for 24 hours. Rapid imbibition of the pentane occurred and simultaneously therewith bitumen extraction occurred by gravity drainage. The following table shows the recovery by sequential extraction:

Extraction	Recovery, %
1	59
2	71
3	80
4	83
5	87
6	88
7	92
8	92

The results show that the bitumen-containing core rapidly and spontaneously imbibed the paraffin liquid hydrocarbon which very effectively extracted substantially all of the bitumen by capillary imbibition and gravity drainage in a series of sequential extractions.

Any paraffin liquid hydrocarbon can be used as the solvent providing it has a low viscosity and low molecular weight. Preferred hydrocarbons are normal paraffins having from 3 to 7 carbon atoms per molecule that are liquid at formation conditions. In particular, n-pentane has been found to be very effective. A typical example for recovery of bitumen from tar sands by imbibition and sequential extractions using a paraffin liquid hydrocarbon is provided in the patent.

Multiple-Component Solvent System

According to a process described by *J.C. Allen, C.D. Woodward, A. Brown, and C.H. Wu; U.S. Patent 4,007,785; February 15, 1977; assigned to Texaco Inc.* petroleum may be recovered from viscous petroleum-containing formations including tar sand deposits by contacting the formation with a heated multiple-component solvent for the petroleum. At least one solvent component is a normally gaseous material such as methane, ethane, propane or butane and at least one component is normally liquid, such as pentane and higher molecular weight hydrocarbons. The solvent mixture is heated to a temperature in excess of ambient temperature, and preferably from 100° to 500°F prior to injection into the formation.

The multiple-solvent is introduced under sufficient pressure that it is substantially all liquid at the injection conditions. Recovery of petroleum and solvent may be from the same well as is used for injection or from a remotely located well. When the pressure in a portion of the formation contacted by the solvents is reduced below the bubble point pressure of the solvent-bitumen solution, the solvents vaporize to provide a solution gas oil recovery mechanism. The normally liquid components dissolve in the petroleum and reduce the petroleum viscosity.

A process described by *A. Brown, C.H. Wu; and D.T. Konopnicki; U.S. Patent 4,004,636; January 25, 1977; assigned to Texaco Inc.* involves injecting into the formation a multiple-component solvent for the petroleum and a thermal fluid. At least one solvent component is gaseous at the temperature and pressure of the petroleum reservoir such as carbon dioxide, methane, ethane, propane, butane or pentane, and at least one component is liquid at the reservoir conditions, such as hexane and higher molecular weight aliphatic hydrocarbons or aromatic hydrocarbons such as benzene.

The multiple-solvent injection is continued with no production until the pressure is from 50 to 250% above the vapor pressure of the solvent, at which pressure the solvent mixture is substantially all in the liquid phase. Recovery of petroleum and solvent is from a remotely located well by reducing the pressure in the portion of the formation contacted by the solvents to a value from 5 to 100% above the vapor pressure of the gaseous solvent.

A fluid heated to a temperature above the boiling point of the solvent, such as steam, is then injected into the same well as was used for solvent injection. The heated fluid raises the temperature of the solvent on contact therewith, causing vaporization of the gaseous component, which gaseous solvent expands to force viscous petroleum with liquid solvent dissolved therein toward the production well. In formations having oil saturation greater than 50%, this oil saturation should first be reduced to a value below 50% to prevent plugging.

Solvent Vapors

W.G. Routson; U.S. Patent 4,022,277; May 10, 1977; assigned to The Dow Chemical Company describes an in situ solvent fractionation process for recovering bitumens from unconsolidated tar sands. The process consists of:

(1) introducing hot solvent vapors in a formation consisting essentially of a bitumen-containing tar disposed among discrete sand particles; the vapors being so composed and at such a temperature as to condense, upon contact with unfractionated tar in the formation, to form a liquid and to selectively dissolve bitumens out of the tar as a more soluble fraction;

(2) allowing the resultant solution of bitumens to drain below the level at which the hot vapors contact unfractionated tar and collecting it, thereby leaving in place a less soluble bituminous fraction of the tar as an undissolved residue capable of supporting itself and the sand particles among which it is disposed;

(3) removing the collected solution from the formation; and

(4) recovering the dissolved bitumen content of the solution.

Preferably, the process is regulated so that the undissolved residue constitutes at least 5 wt % of the unfractionated tar.

In a particularly preferred mode of operation the vapors are introduced to, and the solution removed from, the formation, both through the same bore; optionally, the bore passes through the formation and is bottomed in an underlying stratum. In this case, the underlying stratum is impermeable or the portion of the bore (wall and bottom) therein and the zone of contact between the layers is rendered impermeable by appropriate procedures of known types; for example, by horizontal fracturing, injection of a curable resin solution and curing.

In a more economic and highly preferred mode of operation, the hot vapors comprise a hydrocarbon obtained by distilling, cracking or otherwise treating bitumens recovered from the formation. The temperature of the hot solvent vapors upon introduction to the formation is preferably within the range of from about 90° to 150°C, most preferably within the range of 95° to 120°C.

Example: Solvent Effectiveness Tests — An open-top container is set up with boiling solvent at the bottom, a cooling coil around the top for a condenser, and an opening so that a sample in a wire screen basket can be lowered into the heated vapors. Any solvent condensing on the sample runs down through the screen and is caught in an aluminum dish suspended below the basket but above the liquid. Samples are prepared from irregular small pieces of the tar sand by placing them in a mold and compressing them to 6,000 psi to form a cylinder about 1 inch long and 1 inch in diameter.

The tared sample in the wire basket is lowered into the solvent vapors until no more condensation occurs, usually less than one-half hour. Then the sample is removed, cooled and weighed. Any sand removed with the solvent is separated and weighed and the residual sand (the leached sample) is weighed. The sum of these weights is subtracted from the original sample weight to find the weight of the tar extracted from the sample. The leached sand sample from the basket is then broken down and thoroughly washed with Chlorothene (1,1,1-trichloroethane) to remove any residual tar. The final sand weight is used to calculate the original total tar content and then the percent recovered by the solvent vapor being tested.

Cores cut from undisturbed tar sands are also extracted by this method and the results are comparable, within experimental error, to those obtained with the pressure-molded samples. Solvents of different types and having different boiling points were tested with five different tar sands and one asphalt rock.

The vapor compositions and temperatures employed and the results obtained are given in the following table. (Samples suspended in steam vapor at 100°C for an hour gave no recovery. The sample did not even slump. Heating the sample for 2 hours at 200°C also gave no recovery.)

In the following table the data indicated that the boiling point of the solvent is more critical for extraction than the type or types of hydrocarbon in the solvent. Solvents boiling above 90°C recovered more than 90% of the bitumen from Athabasca tar sand and solvents boiling at or above 115°C recovered 90% or more bitumen from the two California tar sands tested. On the other hand, solvents boiling below 80°C recovered less than 50% of the bitumen in all cases and below 50°C there was almost no recovery.

Effect of Solvent Composition and Vapor Temperature on Bitumen Recovery Percents of Tar and Sand Leached and Lost from Sample

Solvent Component	Proportion (%)	Boiling Temp (°C)	Athabasca, Canada Tar	Athabasca, Canada Sand	Edna, CA Tar	Edna, CA Sand	Santa Cruz, CA Tar	Santa Cruz, CA Sand	Asphalt Ridge, UT Tar	Asphalt Ridge, UT Sand	P.R. Springs, UT Tar	P.R. Springs, UT Sand	Sunnyside, UT Tar
Pentane	100	36	0	—	—	0.9	—	—	—	—	—	—	—
Hexane	100	69	46	2.0	—	—	—	—	—	—	—	—	—
Benzene	100	81	37	5.7	—	—	—	—	—	—	—	—	—
Hexane/heptane	50/50	80–83	57	9.8	—	—	—	—	—	—	—	—	—
Hexane/xylene	50/50	85	76	7.2	—	—	—	—	—	—	—	—	—
Benzene/octane	75/25	86	50	9.9	—	—	—	—	—	—	—	—	—
Benzene/toluene	75/25	86–87	60	8.5	—	—	—	—	—	—	—	—	—
Benzene/xylene	75/25	86–88	52	4.3	—	—	—	—	—	—	—	—	—
Hexane/toluene	50/50	86–90	70	16.6	27	2.4	43	3.8	36	20.6	11	0.2	20
Hexane/heptane	25/75	90	88	13.4	—	—	—	—	—	—	—	—	—
Benzene/octane	50/50	94	94	12.2	—	—	—	—	—	—	—	—	—
Heptane	100	99	81	13.0	—	—	41**	3.7	78	39.8	51	0.0	25
Benzene/toluene	50/50	99	94	9.9	—	—	—	—	—	—	—	—	—
Isooctane	100	100	95	0.8	—	—	—	—	—	—	—	—	—
Heptane/toluene	50/50	103	97	37.1	46	10.8	64	13.6	88	29.8	46	0.3	39
Isooctane/toluene	50/50	104	96	32.3	—	—	—	—	—	—	—	—	—
Toluene	100	111	96	28.3	78	26.3	76	7.2	51 / 64***	13.1	61	0.9	36
Octane/toluene	50/50	115	96	41.2	92	19.0	91	8.4	87	25.2	95	12.1	32
Isooctane/xylene	50/50	116	97	34.4	—	—	—	—	—	—	—	—	—
Heptane/xylene	50/50	117	96	25.4	—	—	—	—	—	—	—	—	—
Heptane/xylene	25/75	122	98	38.2	—	—	—	—	—	—	—	—	—
Octane	100	127	96	21.2	96	24.4	88**	9.8	89	33.9	96	9.1	48
Octane/o-xylene	50/50	131	98	55.7	—	—	—	—	—	—	—	—	—
m-Xylene	100	139	98	40.9	96.5	31.5	99	26.6	90	31.6	—	—	—
p-Xylene	100	139	93	—	—	—	—	—	—	—	—	—	52
Decane	100	175	98	55.6	—	—	—	—	—	—	—	—	53
Pentadecane	100	254	100†	—	—	—	—	—	—	—	—	—	—

*Asphalt rock; cut cores.
**Aliphatic solvent anomaly.
***Aromatic solvent anomaly.
†Sand collapse resulted.

Samples from the Santa Cruz area in California did show some solvent-type discrimination. Pure naphthenic solvents were 10 to 20% less effective than aromatic or mixed solvents of the same boiling points. This presumably is attributable to the higher asphaltene content of the Santa Cruz tar sands. In contrast, bitumen from Asphalt Ridge, Utah did not extract as well with aromatics as with aliphatics at corresponding temperatures.

Countercurrent Hydrocarbon Vapors

R.R. Dewell; U.S. Patent 4,067,391; January 10, 1978 describes a method of extracting highly viscous nonfracturable oil from earthen deposits. The process involves a plurality of radially extending horizontal conduits which direct heated hydrocarbon vapors into the formation. The vapors are selected to have a boiling point above the pour point of the viscous oil. Thus, as the vapors rise in the formation, they will be in heat exchange relationship with the viscous oil to cause the latter to flow downwardly. In addition to the thermal exchange of energy, the vapors will move toward molecular equilibrium with the viscous oil formation. This latter action will cause the vapors to strip off the more volatile, lower boiling components, from the descending liquid oil.

The liquid oil, on the other hand, will condense the less volatile, higher boiling point fraction of the vapors. The total effect is one of rectification which establishes a distinct temperature gradient in the formation and results in complete dissemination of the vapors from the bottom to the top. Because the temperature is maximized at the point of withdrawal of the liquefied oil, removal of the oil is facilitated. To this end, a plurality of second conduits, radially extending and horizontally disposed, are placed in the formation to carry off the liquefied oil. By allowing the liquefied oil to accumulate to a degree at the bottom of the formation and locating the openings for extracting the liquid below the vapor outlet openings, a pool is formed which seals off the vapor from extraction openings, thereby preventing the vapors from returning until condensed as liquid.

The process is particularly designed for use with highly viscous, unfracturable oil formations characterized by the oil being present in the formation at a temperature below its pour point; the oil representing the matrix phase of the formation and any sand present representing a discontinuous phase; an absence of horizontal layers of clay, shale, and other substances within the formation which would be impermeable to the flow of hydrocarbon vapors; and the residual sand resulting after dissolution of the oil phase being permeable to hydrocarbon vapors. Such deposits are normally found at depths of no greater than about 500 feet.

In the preferred form of the process, naphtha will be employed as the hydrocarbon extractant, although it is to be understood that other hydrocarbons having boiling points substantially within the range of approximately 100° to 400°F can be utilized. This will include hydrocarbons having a molecular weight approximately within the range of 70 to 150 which will include the C_5 through C_{11} hydrocarbons.

Examples of suitable hydrocarbons which can be utilized in the process are: pentanes, hexanes, naphtha, toluene, gasoline, and light distillates. Petroleum naphtha is a preferred extractant because of its availability.

OXIDATION AND COMBUSTION

Activation of Labile Groups Associated with Bitumen

A process described by *D.A. Redford and D.L. Mitchell; U.S. Patent 3,938,590; Feb. 17, 1976; assigned to Texaco Exploration Canada Ltd., Canada* makes use of the fact that there are naturally occurring labile groups associated with the bituminous petroleum which can be activated by being contacted with an oxidizing gas. After the labile groups have been activated, an alkalinity agent such as ammonium hydroxide or gaseous ammonia is utilized to neutralize the oxidized groups, thereby converting them to the water-soluble form so that they may aid in the formation of an oil-in-water emulsion during subsequent process steps.

Gaseous ammonia is an especially preferred step since it serves as the neutralization agent and also to expand the zone of gas permeability, thereby extending the contact area of the fluids injected subsequently. Steam is thereafter injected, in order to heat the bituminous petroleum to render it more mobile and form an oil-in-water emulsion. The surface active compounds generated by the oxidative gas and the ammonia gas reaction cause the formation of the oil-in-water emulsion, increasing the bituminous petroleum concentration in the emulsion and resulting in the production of little or no water-in-oil emulsion. Ammonia may be injected simultaneously with the steam. Alternatively, steam injection alone may be continued awhile, with brief interruptions during which time ammonia or a mixture of steam and ammonia is introduced into the formation.

Production is in the form of a fluid comprising an oil-in-water emulsion in which the bituminous petroleum is the discontinuous phase. The pressure differential is reduced. The petroleum content of the emulsion will be in the range of from about 9 to about 15% by volume. Essentially no free bitumen or water-in-oil emulsion is produced.

Example: A tar sand deposit is located under an overburden thickness of 650 feet, and the tar sand deposit is 80 feet thick. Two wells are drilled to the bottom of the deposit, the wells being 75 feet apart. Both wells are completed in the bottom 5 foot section of the tar sand deposit, and a gravel pack is formulated around the slotted liner on the end of the production tubing in each well to restrain sand flow into the wells.

Air is injected at an initial low rate into one well and the other well is held open to the atmosphere. The initial air injection rate into the first well is 250 standard cubic feet per hour. This rate is maintained until an indication of air production is obtained from the remotely located well. The air injection rate is increased at the rate of about 10% every two hour period until an injection rate of 1,000 standard cubic feet per hour is obtained. This level of air injection is continued for 24 hours to ensure an adequate air-swept zone has been established in the formation.

A mixture of approximately 50% natural gasoline which is predominantly C_5 through C_7 saturated hydrocarbons, and 50% mixed aromatic solvent, which is predominantly benzene and toluene, is pumped into each well at a pressure of 300 pounds per square inch until the injection rate drops materially, indicating the maximum penetration has been achieved. The pressure is released and solvent with bituminous petroleum dissolved therein is pumped out of each well.

Solvent injection into each well is again performed to a maximum pressure of 300 pounds per square inch, followed by a cycle of production of solvent with bituminous petroleum dissolved therein. Solvent is then injected into one well and it is determined that solvent is flowing readily into the other well, indicating that well-to-well communication has been established. Solvent injection is continued for approximately one week, which depletes the air-swept zone, ensuring that a good stable communication path has been established between the two wells.

The next phase of the operation comprises introduction of an oxidizing gas into the communication path to oxidize the labile groups in the petroleum. A mixture of essentially pure oxygen and 80% quality steam is injected into both wells and the pressure is maintained at 450 psi for two days. This ensures that good contact and penetration into the tar sand material adjacent to the communication zone is achieved. The pressure is then relieved and the gas is allowed to flow out of the well. Some bitumen is produced during this interval, and this material is removed from the wells.

Essentially pure ammonia gas is then introduced into each well and the pressure raised to 400 pounds per square inch. The pressure is maintained, injecting ammonia as necessary to increase the pressure to its desired maintenance level for 1½ days.

After the prolonged ammonia contact phase is completed, the pressure is again released and the ammonia gas purged from the interval. A steam generator is installed, and boiler feed quality water passed to the generator to produce 85% quality steam at a temperature of 375°F. A mixture of steam and ammonia at a ratio of approximately 0.3 standard cubic foot of ammonia per pound of steam is introduced into one well, with production of gases and liquids being taken from the adjacent well. This ratio is maintained for 24 hours, after which the ratio of ammonia to steam is reduced to approximately 0.2 standard cubic foot per pound of steam, and this ratio is maintained continually throughout the remainder of the recovery operation.

Because of the relatively low pressure differential between the wells as a result of the pretreatment, it is possible to maintain the steam injection rate at 2,000 barrels of steam per day per well. An emulsion of bituminous petroleum in water is produced from the adjacent well, the bituminous petroleum content averaging around 13% by volume. This is readily resolved into essentially pure bitumen and water by contacting the produced liquid with a mineral acid. The bituminous petroleum separated from the emulsion is essentially free of emulsified water, so that no further treatment is necessary.

A series of three laboratory runs were performed to substantiate the process. The cell used in all three runs was a section of steel pipe, 18 inches in diameter and 15 inches long. One inch diameter wells were included, one for fluid injection and one for production, each well being positioned 3 inches from the cell wall and 180° apart. The top of the cell was equipped with a piston and sealing rings by means of which hydraulic pressure can be imposed on tar sand material packed in the cell to simulate overburden pressure.

The cell was packed with tar sand material. A clean sand path, approximately ⅛ inch thick and 2 inches wide was formed between the wells to serve as the communication path. The tar sand material was compressed under hydraulic pressure for several days. In run 1, steam was injected into the cell and bitumen produced from the production well.

The cumulative production was recorded as a function of time and also as a function of pore volumes of steam injected. As can be seen from curve **1** in Figure 5.9, the oil recovery as a percentage of the oil originally in place reached a value of about 24% at 5+ pore volumes of steam.

A second run in a cell packed as described above, was run using a mixture of steam and air. Curve **2** shows that the percent oil recovery is substantially better than with steam alone (curve **1**) at all values of pore volumes of steam injected.

Run 3, which corresponds to this process, was run in a similarly prepared cell. The bitumen was exposed to air, steam, and liquid ammonium hydroxide. As shown, the air-steam-ammonium hydroxide run of curve **3** is substantially superior to either the steam or steam plus air run. (Steam volume for curve **3** was corrected for the volume of ammonium hydroxide). At a value of two pore volumes of steam injected, a reasonable commercial level, the recovery for steam was about 18%; for steam and air it was about 26%; and for steam, air and ammonium hydroxide it was about 36%.

Figure 5.9: Laboratory Data for Oil Recovery Process

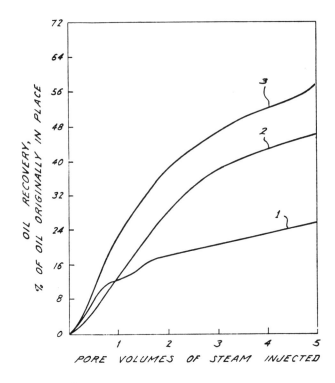

Source: U.S. Patent 3,938,590

In addition to the increased oil recovery, it was observed that the pressure differential between the injection wells was substantially less for run 3 than for either run 1 or 2. Furthermore, the produced fluid was substantially all in the form of an oil-in-water emulsion whereas appreciable amounts of water-in-oil emulsion was produced in runs 1 and 2.

Low-Temperature Oxidation Processes

A process described by *P.J. Cram and D.A. Redford; U.S. Patent 4,114,690; Sept. 19, 1978; assigned to Texaco Exploration Canada Ltd., Canada* relates to the recovery of low API gravity, viscous oils and bitumen from tar sands by the use of a low-temperature oxidation. The process involves the injection of a mixture of an oxygen-containing gas and steam at a temperature corresponding to the temperature of saturated steam at the pressure of the formation wherein the free oxygen in the oxygen-containing gas to the steam is maintained in the range of 0.03 to 0.13 mscf/bbl.

To illustrate the process, a series of laboratory runs was performed using a tar sand from the McMurray formation in Alberta, Canada. A laboratory cell approximately 15 inches long and 18 inches in diameter was packed with from 170 to 190 pounds of tar sand. Generally, a communication path consisting of clean 20–40 fracturing sand was provided between the wells during the packing. The cell was equipped for operating at controlled temperatures up to about 420°F and pressures up to about 300 psi and contained simulated suitable injection and production wells. The cell was also equipped with many thermocouples so that both temperatures throughout the cell could be measured and heat transfer rates could be calculated.

The injection system was provided with a manifold allowing for the injection of separate streams of fluid as, for example, steam and air which could be mixed at the injection well. The producing system was provided with the necessary control and measurement instrumentation to monitor and analyze the produced fluids. Porosity of the tar sand pack was determined from the equation:

$$\phi = 1 - (\rho_{bs}/2.65)(1 - \omega_{fb} - \omega_{fw})$$

where ρ_{bs} is the density of the tar sand and ω_{fb} and ω_{fw} are the weight fractions of bitumen and water, respectively. By knowing the porosity, quantities of fluids injected and produced could therefore be expressed in terms of pore volumes (PV).

In a typical run generally a preliminary injection period was conducted wherein either air or steam was injected for a short period of time to insure that fluid communication between the wells was present. Thereafter a mixture of an oxygen-containing gas and steam was injected in which the ratio of the free oxygen in the oxygen-containing gas to the steam was known and controlled. The ratio was expressed in terms of thousand standard cubic feet of oxygen per barrel of steam, measured as liquid water (mscf/bbl).

Low-temperature oxidation was established in the formation at a temperature of about 417°F, corresponding to the temperature of the injected saturated steam. In the runs described, injection of the mixture of the oxygen-containing gas and steam was continued until a desired cumulative pore volume of steam had been injected. In some runs as much as 4 pore volumes of steam were injected. The table below shows the results, tabulated in terms of cumulative recovery and cumulative oxygen/steam and air/steam ratio and pore volumes of steam injected.

Oil Recovery and Cumulative Free O_2/Steam Ratio at Given Injected Pore Volumes (PV) of Steam

Run No.	Fluids Injected	. . . . .2 PV Steam			. . . . .4 PV Steam			. At Termination of Run. .		
		Cum Free-O_2/ Steam . . (mscf/bbl) . .	Cum Air/ Steam	Cum Recovery (% OOIP)	Cum Free-O_2/ Steam . (mscf/bbl) . .	Cum Air/ Steam	Cum Recovery (% OOIP)	Cum Free-O_2/ Steam . . (mscf/bbl)	Cum Air/ Steam	Cum Recovery . . (% OOIP)
1	steam	0	0	15.2	0	0	21.2	0	0	31.4
2	air/steam	0.016	0.08	18.0	0.022	0.11	26.2	0.030	0.15	35.2
3	air/steam	0.034	0.17	26.8	0.036	0.18	46.4	0.034	0.17	62.3
4*	air/steam	0.048	0.24	27.7	0.052	0.26	42.4	0.048	0.24	46.7
5**	air/steam	0.128	0.64	28.0	0.130	0.65	37.4	0.132	0.66	39.2
6**	air/steam	0.280	1.40	27.1	0.148	0.74	39.5	0.130	0.65	40.6

*Air injected briefly prior to injection of air/steam mixture.
**Steam injected briefly prior to injection of air/steam mixture.

A straight steam run (Run 1) has been included for comparison with runs utilizing a mixture of an oxygen-containing gas (air) and steam. The results demonstrate that the use of a mixture of air and steam yields increased recovery of bitumen as compared with using steam only. The results show that with 2 pore volumes of injected steam, maximum bitumen recovery is realized when the cumulative air to steam ratio is in the range of about 0.15 to 0.65 mscf of air per barrel of steam or 0.03 to about 0.13 mscf oxygen per barrel of steam. Furthermore, with the cumulative recovery measured at the termination of the run it may be seen that the highest recovery occurred when the cumulative air-to-steam ratio was in the range of 0.16 to 0.25 mscf/bbl or about 0.035 to 0.050 mscf oxygen per barrel of steam.

In the table the results of Run 6 show that the cumulative bitumen recovery at both pore volumes and termination pore volumes of injected steam were comparable to the recoveries from the other runs. It is seen that Run 6 had a much higher air/steam ratio, namely 1.4 mscf per barrel at 2 pore volumes. Considerable difficulty was experienced during this run caused by plugging and excessive carbonization of the bitumen, manifested by a gradual decrease of the injectivity of the fluid mixture.

Numerous necessary remedial measures were taken in an effort to continue the run, so that results could be obtained at higher pore volumes of injected steam. These measures included reversing the flow and adjusting injection rates. Nevertheless, the higher ratio could not be maintained and decreased during the run. The results indicate clearly that at too high an air/steam ratio, operational difficulties may be experienced. Consequently, too high an air/steam ratio is undesirable.

The results are also plotted in Figures 5.10a and 5.10b. In Figure 5.10a, bitumen recovery is plotted vs the air/steam ratio (mscf per barrel) at 2 pore volumes injected steam. The results indicate a significant increase in recovery occurs after a ratio of about 0.15 mscf air per barrel of steam has been realized. In Figure 5.10b, bitumen recovery is plotted vs air/steam ratio (mscf per barrel) for given pore volumes of injected steam.

Figure 5.10:   Low-Temperature Oxidation Process

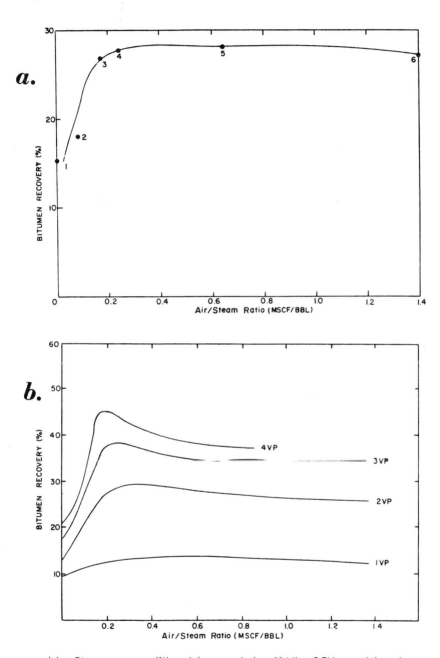

(a)   Bitumen recovery (%) vs air/steam ratio (mscf/bbl) at 2 PV steam injected.
(b)   Bitumen recovery (%) vs air/steam ratio (mscf/bbl) for several PV of injected steam.

Source: U.S. Patent 4,114,690

The results again indicate that maximum recovery is obtained after about 0.15 mscf air per barrel of steam has been realized, and further show that maximum recovery is obtained when the air/steam ratio is in the range of 0.15 to 0.65 mscf/bbl.

It is postulated that in the low-temperature oxidation process the oxygen combines with the bitumen to form various oxidation products such as aldehydes, ketones and acid. Furthermore, the temperature of this low-temperature oxidation process is controlled by the performance of the liquid water phase and the saturated steam so that the temperature is controlled and maintained below about 500°F. The improved performance over that when steam only is injected may be attributed to better distribution of the heat generated by the low-temperature oxidation process and to the creation of flow channels with minimum formation of carbonized portions of the bitumen.

An important element of the process is that liquid water must be present to absorb the heat of oxidation so as to control the temperature and improve the heat distribution. Without this water present, uncontrolled combustion of the bitumen could occur that would result in heavy deposition of carbonized bitumen and subsequent plugging of the formation.

The importance of controlling the air/steam ratio and the use of low ratios may be demonstrated by the following calculations relating to heat generation. The heat released by the low-temperature oxidation reactions per mol of oxygen when produced water is in the liquid phase, are as follows: carboxylation or formation of CO_2, 105 kcal/mol O_2; carboxylation or formation of CO, 90 kcal/mol O_2; hydroxylation, 90 kcal/mol O_2; and hydroperoxidation, 30 kcal/mol O_2.

For the purpose of an approximate calculation, an average heat release may be assumed to be 95 kcal/mol O_2. At an air/steam ratio of 0.2 mscf/bbl, and assuming all the injected oxygen is utilized, the relative heats generated by the oxidation of bitumen and by the condensation of steam would be:

$$
\underset{\substack{200 \\ \text{(scf air)}}}{200} \times \underset{\substack{0.21 \\ (O_2 \text{ content} \\ \text{of air})}}{0.21} \times \underset{\substack{1.195 \\ \text{(mol/scf)}}}{1.195} \times \underset{\substack{95 \\ \text{(kcal/mol } O_2)}}{95} \times \underset{\substack{4.19 \\ \text{(kJ/kcal)}}}{4.19} \times \underset{\substack{0.94 \\ \text{(Btu/kJ)}}}{0.94} = 18.9 \text{ mBtu}
$$

The latent heat of steam at 300 psig is:

$$
\underset{\substack{1 \\ \text{(bbl steam)}}}{1} \times \underset{\substack{350 \\ \text{(lb/bbl)}}}{350} \times \underset{\substack{805.9 \\ \text{(Btu/lb)}}}{805.9} = 282.1 \text{ mBtu}
$$

Thus, at an air/steam ratio of 0.2 mscf/bbl, the heat contribution of the oxidation processes will be some 6.7% of the latent heat of steam. At an air/steam ratio of 0.60 mscf/bbl, this contribution would rise to 20%. Also, if the steam injected is less than 100% quality, the relative contribution due to oxidation will be somewhat higher. It is concluded that the heat contribution provided by the oxidation reactions is a significant factor in the low-temperature oxidation process.

A number of related processes for the recovery of low API gravity oils or bitumen from a subterranean formation have been described in the recent patent literature. These include: *P.J. Cram and D.A. Redford; U.S. Patents 3,993,132;*

November 23, 1976; 4,046,195; September 6, 1977; both assigned to Texaco Exploration Canada Ltd., Canada; D.A. Redford and S.M. Creighton; U.S. Patent 4,006,778; February 8, 1977; D.A. Redford; U.S. Patent 3,978,925; September 7, 1976; both assigned to Texaco Exploration Canada Ltd., Canada; I.S. Bousaid; U.S. Patent 3,976,137; August 24, 1976; and J.C. Allen; U.S. Patents 4,024,915; May 24, 1977; and 3,964,546; June 22, 1976; all assigned to Texaco Inc.

Sequential Combustion and Air Injection

J.C. Allen and Y.-M. Shum; U.S. Patents 4,059,152; November 22, 1977; and 3,991,828; November 16, 1976; both assigned to Texaco Inc. describe a method for recovering hydrocarbons such as low gravity viscous crude oil or bitumen from a subterranean reservoir penetrated by at least one injection well and at least one production well comprising the steps of:

(a)   injecting superheated steam into the formation via the injection well;

(b)   terminating injection of the superheated steam and initiating injection of air to establish an in situ combustion front in the reservoir;

(c)   continuing injection of the air to support the in situ combustion front and resuming injection of superheated steam at the injection well;

(d)   terminating injection of the superheated steam and initiating injection of water along with the air to continue an in situ combustion front;

(e)   terminating air injection to discontinue the in situ combustion front while continuing to inject water into the injection well and;

(f)   producing hydrocarbons from the production well.

The following table lists the reservoir injection data that were used in a computational model:

Reservoir Data	
Formation thickness, ft	26
Thermal capacity, Btu/ft^3 °F	35
Thermal conductivity, Btu/hr ft °F	1
Gravity of crude oil, °API	18.6
Initial reservoir temperature, °F	80
Kh, darcy-ft	1.1
Distance between injection well and producing well (in an inverted 5 spot), ft	320
Injection Data	
Injection pressure, psig	500
Producing well pressure, psig	200
Superheated steam injection rate, bpd, at 700°F	400
Superheated steam injection + air injection:	
Steam, bpd at 700°F	400
Air, MMscfd	1.84

(continued)

Hot water injection + air injection
Hot water, pbd at 200°F   400
Air, MMscfd   1.84

Computations may best be displayed by the graphical representations of Figures 5.11a through 5.11d. Figure 5.11a shows the leading edge of the saturated steam zone as distance from the injection well versus time. Curve 1 of Figure 5.11a represents superheated steam alone. The curve 2 segment is for super-heated steam plus air from 72 to 144 days of the operation. Curve 3 is for superheated steam and air or air and 200°F water injection after 144 days have elapsed.

It is noted that the introduction of in situ combustion speeds up the advance of the thermal front. Combination of in situ combustion with superheated steam drastically increases the velocity of the thermal front which increases the oil recovery and production rates. A distinct advantage is obtained by augmenting superheated steam with in situ combustion. All oil-bearing formations have a vertical permeability distribution. Therefore, injected fluids traverse through only a minor portion of the vertical interval taking the path of least resistance. The oil-bearing beds adjacent to the invaded thermal zones are heated, however, and a substantial amount of oil is produced therefrom.

Heat transport from the hot zone to the cooler uninvaded zone varies directly with the temperature of the hot zone, the areal extent of the hot zone and the time of the uninvaded zone's exposure to the hot zone.

Figure 5.11: Thermal Recovery Method

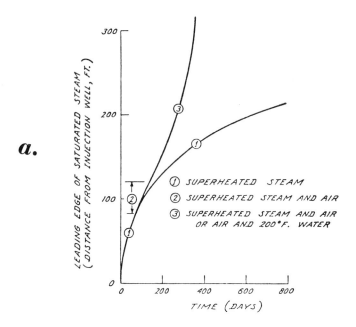

(continued)

Figure 5.11: (continued)

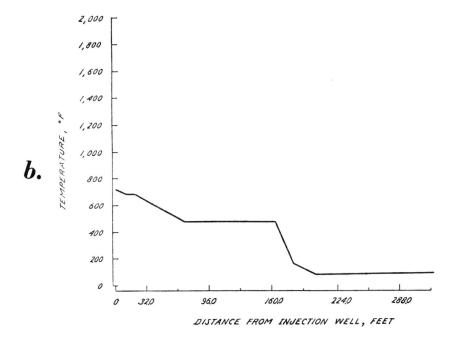

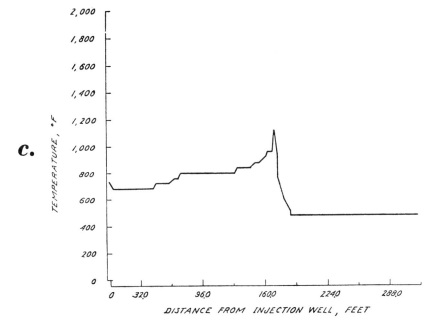

(continued)

FIGURE 5.11: (continued)

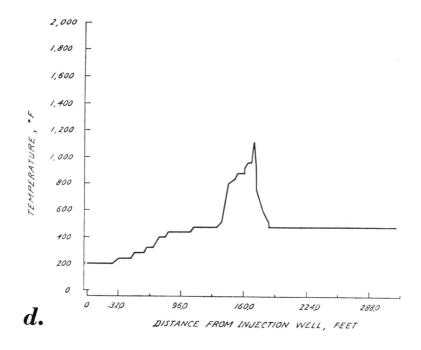

d.

(a)   Thermal Advance—time relations
(b)   360 days superheated steam
(c)   72 days superheated steam, 288 days superheated steam plus air
(d)   72 days saturated steam, 72 days saturated steam plus air, 216 days
       air and 200°F water

Source: U.S. Patent 4,059,152

The dramatic increase in thermal front advance rate as shown by Curve **3** over Curve **1** of Figure 5.11a is evident. Figure 5.11b shows the computer calculation of a temperature profile from the injection well to a production well 320 feet apart. After 360 days of injecting superheated steam at 700°F, formation is heated to that value (700°F) for only a short distance from the injection well. A rather long saturated steam temperature plateau is established, however, the formation is heated only halfway to the production well.

Figure 5.11c is also a plotted temperature profile for 360 days of thermal drive. For this case, however, 72 days of superheated steam injection was followed by superheated steam plus air injection for another 288 days for a total of 360 days as in Figure 5.11b. A study of Figure 5.11c discloses that a much higher thermal front advance rate has been obtained over that of Figure 5.11b which was for superheated steam alone. Also, much more heat is introduced into the formation. This is determined by integration of the curve. Also a much higher temperature difference (ΔT) over a greater areal extent exists. The higher thermal front advance rate and the greater amount of heat in the formation increase oil production rate and recovery directly. The great difficulty in propagating any thermal front in a piston-like manner makes the higher ΔT extremely effective in heating, moving and recovering oil in the adjacent uninvaded oil saturated bed.

The superiority over the simple wet combustion process which consists of in situ combustion followed by in situ combustion and water injection is proven by comparing the results in Figure 5.11c with the results in Figure 5.11d. Although the advance rate of the saturated steam front is the same for the wet combustion process, the amount of heat in the formation and areal extent of a very high temperature gradient between swept and unswept zones are much higher for the process of Figure 5.11c than for the wet combustion process of Figure 5.11d. This increases oil recovery and production rate in the case of this process.

Superheated Steam and Combustion Drive

A process described by *J.C. Allen; U.S. Patent 4,083,404; April 11, 1978; assigned to Texaco Inc.* relates to a method for recovering petroleum from subterranean, viscous petroleum-containing formations including tar sand deposits, the formations being penetrated by at least one injection well and by at least one production well, comprising:

(a) establishing a fluid communication path in the formation between the injection well and the production well;

(b) injecting via an injection well a fluid comprising superheated steam and air under pressure into the formation whereby in situ combustion is initiated in the formation providing heat and pressure for driving the petroleum in the formation toward the production well; and

(c) recovering petroleum from the formation via the production well.

Such an injection well is shown in Figure 5.12. In this arrangement three strings of concentrically located tubing, that is **10**, **11**, and **12**, are employed inside of casing **9**. Closed-end tubing string **10** penetrates the well to a depth above perforations **13**. A smaller open-end tubing string **12** penetrates the closed-end tubing **10** to a depth just above that of the closure in tubing string **10**. Tubing string **11** which has a larger diameter than string **10** penetrates the oil-bearing formation and is equipped with perforations **13** which are positioned so that they open into the oil-bearing zone. Well casing **9** is seated at a point just below the top of the oil-bearing formation and is open at the lower end.

Steam of about 80% quality is formed in generator **20** and passed via line **22** into the annular space **21** between tubing strings **10** and **12**. As the steam passes down this annular space the walls are heated and the steam which condenses collects at the bottom of closed-end tubing **10** after which the condensate is returned to steam generator **20** via tubing **12** and line **24**. Steam from steam boiler **26** having a temperature below that of the steam flowing in line **22** is injected via line **28** into annular space **30** where it is superheated as it passes downwardly through annular space **30**. This superheated steam is then forced into the oil-bearing formation via perforations **30** of tubing strings. Air is injected into the annular space between casing **9** and tubing **11** and enters the oil-bearing formation at **34**. Thus, in the above-described well arrangement the injection well serves as a superheater.

Figure 5.12:   Oil Recovery Process

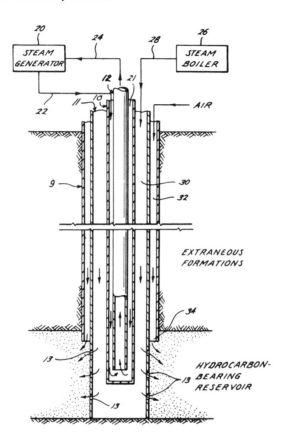

Source: U.S. Patent 4,083,404

Example: A tar sand deposit is located at a depth of 875 feet and it is determined that the thickness of the formation is 120 feet. It is also determined that the petroleum is in the form of a highly bituminous hydrocarbon, and its viscosity at the formation temperature is much too high to permit recovery therefrom by conventional means. An injection well is drilled to the bottom of the formation, and perforations are formed between the interval of 850 to 875 feet, i.e., the bottom of the petroleum-saturated zone.

A production well is drilled approximately 600 feet distance from the injection well, and perforations are similarly made slightly above the bottom of the petroleum-saturated zone. The production well is also equipped with a steam trap so that only liquids can be produced from the formation, and vapors are excluded therefrom.

A fluid communication path which is low in the formation is formed by fracturing the formation using conventional hydraulic fracturing techniques, and injecting a gravel-sand mixture into the fracture to hold it open and prevent healing of the fracture.

In the next step a fluid comprising a mixture of about 50 wt % steam and about 50 wt % air at a temperature of about 1000°F and at a pressure of about 300 psig is introduced into the formation at the rate of 5,000 lb/hr via the previously prepared fluid communication path. Injection of the steam-air mixture is continued and the production of viscous oil via the production well commences after about 30 days and gradually increases and injection of the oil-displacing fluid is continued. At the end of 60 days production of the viscous hydrocarbons is significantly increased over production of similar wells in the same formation utilizing only steam injection.

N-Methyl-2-Pyrrolidone and Furfural Pretreatment

According to a process described by *J.C. Allen and C.D. Woodward; U.S. Patent 3,874,452; April 1, 1975; assigned to Texaco Inc.* viscous, asphaltic petroleum may be effectively recovered from subterranean viscous, asphaltic petroleum containing formations such as tar sand deposits by first injecting into the tar sand formation a quantity of N-methyl-2-pyrrolidone or furfural or a mixture which precipitates asphaltic material from the bituminous petroleum portion of the petroleum formation.

Next, solvent injection is terminated and air is injected into the formation, and the formation is ignited by heating or other means to initiate in situ combustion within the petroleum formation utilizing the precipitated asphaltic materials for fuel for the in situ combustion reaction. Reaction temperature higher than normal in situ combustion temperatures is produced, facilitating thermal cracking and in situ hydrogenation to upgrade the produced crude within the tar sand reservoir.

Example: A tar sand deposit is discovered at a depth of 350 feet, and it is determined that the thickness of the tar sand deposit is 60 feet. Production wells are drilled on a square grid pattern approximately 400 feet apart, and injection wells are drilled in the center of each square grid pattern. It is determined that the hydrocarbon content of the tar sand deposit is relatively high, but the viscosity of the hydrocarbon material is too high to recover any part thereof by conventional production means. That is to say, the hydrocarbon material is essentially immobile at reservoir conditions, and some treatment to reduce the viscosity of the hydrocarbons must be undertaken in order to recover any part thereof.

It is determined that the permeability of the tar sand deposit averages about 30%, and so the total pore volume in each square grid pattern will be:

$$0.30 \times 400 \times 400 \times 60 = 2,880,000 \text{ cubic feet}$$

Since the sweep efficiency of a pattern such as described above is 70% and the vertical conformance is 50%, the total swept area will be:

$$0.7 \times 2,880,000 \times 0.50 = 1,008,00 \text{ cubic feet}$$

It is determined that furfural is available at low cost in the area, which is satisfactory as the asphalt precipitation solvent. A 0.2 pore volume slug or 20,160 cubic feet (155,800 gallons) of this material is injected into the injection well. Care is taken to avoid exceeding approximately 350 pounds per square inch injection pressure, since it is desired to accomplish injection of the deasphalting solvent into the tar sand deposit without causing a fracture to occur, which would interfere with sweep efficiency of the formation. Injection of the solvent is completed in approximately 200 days.

After completion of solvent injection, air compressors are placed in operation and air is injected into the injection well at the maximum rate possible without exceeding 350 pounds per square inch. After air injection for approximately 24 hours, the well bore is subjected to heating by a 100 kW downhole electric heater to initiate the combustion reaction. Since the injection well bore is perforated essentially the entire thickness of the tar sand interval, a relatively long heating element is positioned adjacent to these perforations so that air entering the perforations is heated to a temperature approximately 500°F, which is sufficient to heat the formation so as to initiate the combustion reaction.

It is only necessary to heat the formation utilizing this electric heater for approximately 36 hours in order to initiate a stable combustion reaction within the formation, which can thereafter be propagated without additional extraneous heat being supplied to the formation. The electric heater is then removed from the injection well bore, and air injection is continued without interruption.

After air injection has been continued for approximately 600 days, calculations indicate that slightly more than half of the volume to be swept by the injected fluid should have been contacted by the injected air. Air injection is then terminated, and water injection is initiated to sweep the burned out area of the tar sand deposit, scavenging heat therefrom and pushing the previously injected air the rest of the way through the formation. The production well bore temperature begins to increase after approximately 800 days, and the water/oil ratio also increases indicating the approach of the injected water. The produced water is utilized for a period as injection water, but after the water/oil ratio exceeds about 30, the water injection of the operation is terminated.

Ignition System

C.E. Howard, D.G. Calvin and R.W. Pitts, Jr.; U.S. Patent 4,079,784; March 21, 1978; assigned to Texaco Inc. describe a method for heating a well or for initiating an in situ combustion operation to recover petroleum from a well in a subterranean reservoir, and a method for assembling an ignition system for the in situ combustion. The ignition system comprises an elongated combustion chamber suspended from a hollow electrical cable which supplies both electrical means and fuel gas to the chamber.

Air inlet ducts in the walls of the combustion chamber receive air from the annular space between the hollow cable and the wellbore tubing. An electrical ignitor is temporarily energized to ignite the fuel-air mixture in the air inlet cylinder. An adjacent thermocouple is responsive to a flameout for reenergizing an ignitor manually such that burner operation is interrupted only momentarily.

The gas fired burner **10** is illustrated schematically in Figure 5.13a, and in more detail in Figures 5.13b and 5.13c in cross section as being suspended from hollow cable **11**, in the well tubing **13**, the well tubing being centered in and spaced from the well casing **33**, with spacers **50**. The gas burner **10** comprises a combustion chamber **14**, an air inlet cylinder **19**, and an electrical chamber **15**, having an ignitor relay **16**, and a hollow cable electrical and natural gas connecting chamber **17**.

Well tubing **13**, Figure 5.13a, is centered in the well casing **33** with the spacers **50**, only two spacers or centralizers being shown for clarity. A pump seating nipple **12**, is formed on the internal surface of the well tubing **13** for supporting a liquid pump for producing crude oil, as in a reverse or counter-current flow well, for example.

Figure 5.13: In Situ Combustion Process

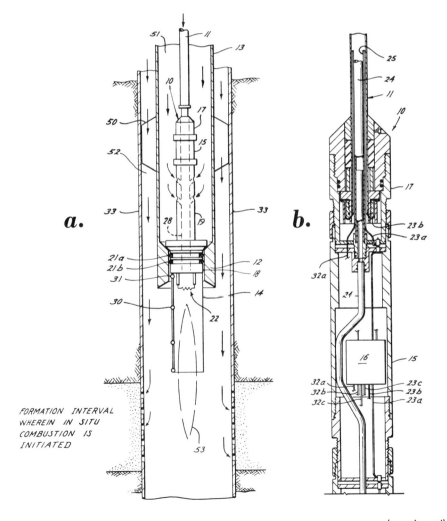

(continued)

Figure 5.13: (continued)

c.

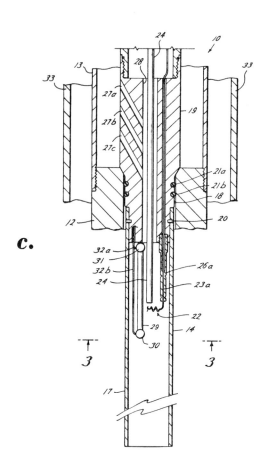

d.

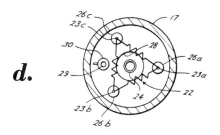

(continued)

Figure 5.13 (continued)

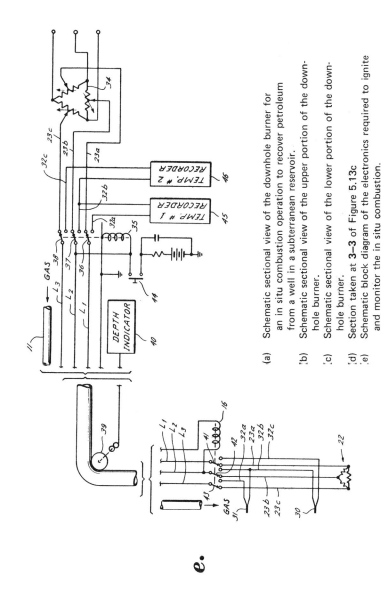

(a) Schematic sectional view of the downhole burner for an in situ combustion operation to recover petroleum from a well in a subterranean reservoir.

(b) Schematic sectional view of the upper portion of the downhole burner.

(c) Schematic sectional view of the lower portion of the downhole burner.

(d) Section taken at **3–3** of Figure 5.13c.

(e) Schematic block diagram of the electronics required to ignite and monitor the in situ combustion.

Source: U.S. Patent 4,079,784

After flow of all liquid petroleum has ceased and heat is desired to reduce the viscosity of the remaining petroleum for increased flow for increased production, the pump is removed and the gas fired burner **10** lowered into well tubing **13** to rest on the pump seating nipple **12** or the lower end of the air inlet cylinder. Seals are provided between a reduced diameter portion **18**, Figures 5.13a and 5.13c, of the thick walled cylinder **19** such as, but not limited to, O-rings **21a**, and **21b**.

The hollow cable, Figure 5.13a, centered in well tubing **13** forms a primary or combustion air supply annulus duct **51**. The well tubing centered in well casing **33** forms a secondary air supply annulus duct **52** in which air is pumped down from the surface in annulus **52** for being heated by the flame **53**. The hollow cable per se forms the natural gas fuel supply duct, a fuel supply duct **24** illustrated in Figures 5.13b and 5.13c being deleted in Figure 5.13a for clarity.

Figures 5.13b and 5.13c, enlarged vertical sectional schematic views of the burner, provide more details thereof. The combustion chamber, Figure 5.13c, comprises a hollow, open-ended cylinder sheath (such as a ceramic sheath) with one end tightly fitted over the reduced diameter portion **18** of a thick walled air inlet cylinder and secured thereto with pins **20**, or the like. The reduced diameter portion fits down inside the pump seating nipple until the burner comes to rest on the beveled portion where the diameter of the thick walled air inlet cylinder increases to full size. An ignitor **22** shown schematically in Figure 5.13a, actually comprises three nicrome wire heater elements connected in delta as illustrated in Figures 5.13d and 5.13e.

Connected to the three intersections of each of the three elements of the ignitor are wires **23a**, **23b**, and **23c**, each wire being in an electrical insulator **26a**, **26b**, and **26c**, respectively, Figure 5.13d. All three insulators and their respective wires are mounted in the end of the cylinder reduced diameter portion, Figure 5.13c, which extends internally of the combustion chamber ceramic sheath **14**. The wires **23a**, **23b**, and **23c**, pass up through the thick walled cylinder, through the relay **16**, Figure 5.13b, in the electrical chamber **15**, through the hollow cable electrical and natural gas connecting chamber **17**, and into the walls of the insulated wire sheathed hollow cable **11** to the surface where they are connected to the burner ignitor control system disclosed hereinafter.

The hollow cable is a reelable armored type hose having an armor-wire outer covering, a coiled-spring inner wall stiffener, and at least three separately insulated electrical conductors embedded between two layers of impervious plastic material forming the walls of the hose, such as in U.S. Patent 3,800,870. This hose or cable is capable of withstanding high pressure, particularly in its use for supplying natural gas, or the like, from the surface down to the combustion chamber. Thus the cable carries the necessary electrical wiring for the ignitor and the thermocouples.

Natural gas is supplied directly to the combustion chamber **14**, Figures 5.13a and 5.13c at the location of the ignitor heater **22** from the gas supply tube or fuel conduit **24**, Figure 5.13c, which extends down through the burner and the hollow cable from a suitable supply at the surface.

Primary air for the gas fired burner, Figures 5.13a and 5.13c is pumped down in the annulus **51**, formed between the well tubing and the hollow cable.

As this pressurized air arrives at the top of the thick walled air inlet cylinder **19**. it passes through transverse and downwardly sloping air inlet ports **27a, 27b,** and **27c,** to a large axial cylindrical duct **28** in the air inlet cylinder **19**. This duct **28** has the fuel supply tube **24** mounted in the center thereof as it traverses the full length of the air inlet cylinder from which the fuel supply tube protrudes a substantial distance to eject the natural gas into the ignitor heater **22**. The air from the inlet ports empties into the duct **28** or annulus formed therein by the centered fuel supply tube. The pressurized air from these ports is forced down the annulus and expands into combustion chamber **14** while mixing with the natural gas at ignitor heater **22**, thereby providing a combustible mixture.

A thermocouple support tube **29**, extends downwardly from the lower end of the air inlet cylinder close to and past the ignitor heater. One thermocouple **30** is mounted on tube **29** below the ignitor heater at the end of the tube and thermocouple **31** is mounted on tube **29** at the base of the tube adjacent the air inlet cylinder **19**. Wires **32a, 32b,** and **32c** from the two thermocouples pass up to the relay **16** of the burner **10**. From the relay, wires L_1, L_2, and L_3 extend to control relay **35** at the surface.

Three conductors in the wall of the hollow cable provide current for ignition and temperature monitoring of the burner. More specifically, a three-phase electrical power source **34**, having three output leads **23a, 23b,** and **23c**, supplies 208 volt ac 3-phase current, for example, to wires L_1, L_2, and L_3 respectively in the walls of the hollow gas supply cable **11** through relay **35** having three, 3-pole, double-throw, latching switches **36, 37,** and **38**.

Relays **16** and **35** are current pulse activated step relays. Capacitor **c** is discharged through the relay coils when push button switch **44** is pressed. Latching switches **36, 37,** and **38** of step relay **35**, switches electrical lines L_1, L_2, and L_3 between the heater wires and the recorder wires. Cable **11** is lowered over pulley **39**, for example, into the well to the desired depth as indicated by the depth indicator **40** and the pump seating nipple **12**.

Relay **35** is connected in parallel with relay **16**. Relay **16** down in the burner, likewise is illustrated in Figure 5.13e, having latching switches **41, 42, and 43** for connecting wires L_1, L_2, and L_3, respectively, to either the nicrome wire heater **22** through wires **23a, 23b,** and **23c** or to the two thermocouples **30** and **31** through wires **32a, 32b,** and **32c**. Recorders **45** and **46** show instant readouts of the temperatures encountered in the burner **10**. Manual push button switch **44** thus may connect the electrical power source **34** to the ignitor heater **22** with the relays **16** and **35** set as illustrated in Figure 5.13e, or it may connect the recorders **45**, and **46** to the thermocouples **30**, and **31** by actuation of the relays to their other positions. Thermocouple **30** detects the temperature of the flame below the ignitor while thermocouple **31** detects the temperature of the upper portion of the rest of the ignitor sensitive to excessive heat.

Briefly, in operation, for introducing heat to the formation in order to reduce the viscosity of the petroleum so that it will flow more readily for recovery, the burner **10** is lowered down into the well to rest on the pump seating nipple **12**, Figure 5.13c, and to be sealed therein by O-rings **21a,** and **21b**. Natural gas is pumped down at a predetermined pressure through the hollow cable **11** to the combustion chamber **14** while the precise amount of primary air is pumped down

the annulus around the hollow cable to inside the combustion chamber to provide an explosive mixture therein. Power source **34**, Figure 5.13e, also at the
surface, is then actuated with the manual push button switch **44** and relays **35**
and **16** set as illustrated in Figure 5.13e, to activate the heater ignitor wire coil
element **22** for a few seconds to ignite the combustion mixture in the combustion chamber **14**, Figure 5.13c, deep in the well.

After a sufficient time period has lapsed to ensure ignition of the burner **10**, push
button switch **44** is actuated momentarily for a few seconds. Instantly relays
35 and **16** flip their respective three switches to the other positions from that
illustrated in Figure 5.13e to thereby disconnect the power source **34** from the
ignitor **22** and to interconnect the temperature recorders **45** and **46** with their
respective thermocouples **30** and **31**.

After the heater is lighted deep in the well, additional air is required to heat the
formation or reservoir. This additional air is pumped down from the surface in
larger annulus **52**, Figure 5.13a, between the well tubing **13** and the well casing
33. As this air passes down and around the full length of the heater **14** and a
portion of the flame, it becomes very hot. This heated air is then transferred to
the formation interval, as illustrated in Figure 5.13a, and with continued burning,
in due course in situ combustion results and is sustained for as long as desired.

Recorder **45** would then be indicating the temperature of combustion in the combustion chamber and recorder **46** would be indicating the temperature at which
the upper portion of the burner is being exposed to, as is the vulnerable electronic
equipment therein. When the combustion chamber temperature drops below
combustion temperature, a flameout is noted immediately and after it is determined that the gas and air supplies are adequate, the switch **44** is manually actuated or pushed to flip both relays **35** and **16** and their respective three switches
each to disconnect the recorders **45** and **46** from the thermocouples **30** and **31**
and to interconnect the power source **34** with the ignitor to relight the burner.

After adequate time has lapsed for ignition, the process is repeated by actuating
push-button switch **44** again. If too high a temperature is recorded on recorder
46 from the thermocouple **31** indicating the electrical portion of the burner
may be approaching a too high or critical temperature, the air velocity in annulus
51 is increased for cooling of the burner.

ELECTRODE WELLS

Electrical Conduction and Pressure

According to a process by *T.K. Perkins; U.S. Patent 3,958,636; May 25, 1976;
assigned to Atlantic Richfield Company* bitumen is produced from a subterranean
tar sand formation while heating the formation via electrical conduction between
a plurality of wells completed therein by the following multistep process. First,
a high back pressure is maintained on the wells. Next, a fluid which is immiscible with the bitumen is injected into the tar sand formation through at least
one of the wells. Thereafter, the bitumen is produced from at least one of the
wells. The steps of maintaining a high back pressure and injecting of the fluid
may be employed once only or simultaneously as desired to attain the desired
production rate during electrical heating of the formation.

Referring to Figure 5.14, a plurality of wells **11** and **13** have been drilled into the subterranean tar sand formation **15**. Each of the wells **11** and **13** have been completed so they may be operated as either injection or production wells. Specifically, the wells have a string of casing **17** that is inserted in the drilled bore hole and cemented in place with the usual foot **19**. A perforate conduit **21** extends into the subterranean tar sand formation **15** adjacent the periphery of the wellbore that was drilled thereinto. Preferably, the casing **17** includes a lower electrically insulated conduit for constraining the electrical current flow to the subterranean tar sand formation as much as is practical.

Figure 5.14: Electrode Well

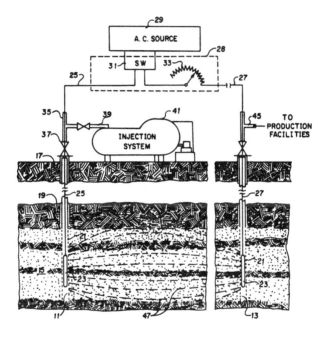

Source: U.S. Patent 3,958,636

The perforate conduit **21** may be a casing having the same or a different diameter from casing **19**, or it may be a large diameter tubing inserted through the casing **19**. As illustrated, the perforate conduit **21** comprises a separate string of conduit extended from the surface for better preserving the heat content of an injected immiscible fluid.

Each of the wells **11** and **13** has an electrode **23**. The respective electrodes **23** are connected via electrical conductors **25** and **27** with surface equipment **28** and a source of electrical current, illustrated as alternating current (ac) source **29**. The electrical conductors **25** and **27** are insulated between the electrodes **23** and the surface equipment. The surface equipment **28** includes suitable controls that are employed to effect the predetermined current flow. For example, a switch **(SW) 31** and voltage control means, such as rheostat **33**, are illustrated for controlling the duration and magnitude of the current flow between the electrodes 23 in the wells 11 and 13 by way of the subterranean tar sand formation 15. It is preferred that the alternating current source 29 be adjusted to provide the correct voltage for effecting the current flow through the subterranean tar sand formation 15 without requiring much power loss in surface control equipment, exemplified by rheostat 33. The respective electrical conductors 25 and 27 are emplaced in their respective wells 11 and 13 with conventional means. As illustrated, they are run through lubricators 35 in order to allow alternating or simultaneous heating, and injection and production, without having to alter the surface accessories, such as changing the configuration of the well heat 37, with its valves, etc. Well 11 is connected with an immiscible fluid injection system by way of conduit 39. The injection system 41 comprises a storage tank for injecting fluid which has a specific resistivity less than that of the connate water in place.

The perforate conduit 21 in well 13 is connected to surface production facilities by way of a second surface conduit 45. The production facilities (not shown) are those normally employed for handling viscous crude oils; they include heater treaters, separators, and heated storage tanks as well as the requisite pumping and flow facilities for handling the bitumen. The production facilities also are connected with bitumen processing facilities, such as are employed in the processing of the bitumen recovered from the tar sand formation by surface mining techniques, or otherwise.

In operation, the wells 11 and 13 are completed in the tar sand formation 15 in accordance with conventional technology. Specifically, bore holes are drilled, at the desired distance and patterning, from the surface into the subterranean tar sand formation 15. Thereafter, the casing 17 is set into the formation to the desired depth. As illustrated, the casing 17 may comprise a surface string that is cemented into place immediately above the tar sand formation. Thereafter, a second string of casing, including an insulated perforate conduit 21, is emplaced in the respective bore holes and completed in accordance with the desired construction. For example, a perforate conduit 21 may have its foot cemented in place, or it may be installed with a gravel pack or the like to allow for expansion and contraction and still secure the desired injectivity and productivity.

In any event, the electrodes are thereafter placed in respective wells. For example, the tar sand formation may be from 100 to 300 feet thick and the respective electrodes 23 may be from 50 to 100 feet or more in length. The electrodes 23 are continuously conductive along their lengths and are connected with the respective electrical conductors 25 and 27 by conventional techniques. For example, the electrodes 23 may be of copper based alloy and may be connected with copper based conductors 25 and 27 by suitable copper based electrical connectors.

Thereafter, the alternating current source 29 is connected with the conductors 25 and 27 by way of the surface control equipment, illustrated simply as switch 31 and rheostat 33. If the desired current densities are obtainable without the use of the rheostat, it is set on the zero resistance position to obtain the desired current flow between the wells.

Immediately, upon beginning heating, a high back pressure is held on the wells utilized for the injection of the immiscible fluid. The pressure held on the injection wells should be in the range of from about 100 to about 2,000 psi. However, the pressure should be kept below that which is sufficient to lift the overburden, ordinarily referred to as the fracturing pressure.

The fracturing pressure not only limits the injection pressure but also limits the pressure and temperature for maintaining the water envelopes on the sand grains for conductivity. It is recognized that the pressure that will effect fracturing with a given overburden depth may be determined in accordance with conventional petroleum engineering technology. A safe and over-simplified figure may be taken as one-half pound per square inch (psi) for each foot of overburden depth. Thus, an overburden depth of 1,200 feet will safely sustain an injection pressure, or a pressure necessary to retain saturation around a well, of 600 psi. Ordinarily, a somewhat higher pressure may be employed once the geology of a given overburden site is properly investigated. For example, if there is 1,000 feet of overburden on the tar sand formation 15, the injection pressure will probably not exceed 500 psi.

Since there will be a high current density immediately adjacent each of the electrodes 23, the temperature will tend to increase more rapidly in this area. Accordingly, it is desirable to inject the immiscible fluid around each of the wells in order to keep the conductivity high in this region. It is preferable to inject an immiscible fluid having a density greater than that of the in-place bitumen and water in order to obviate the necessity of repeated injections of fluid. The current flow through the tar sand formation to heat the tar sand formation 15 and the bitumen therewithin depends on the connate water envelopes surrounding the sand grains.

Accordingly, the temperature in the regions of highest current densities, for example, in the regions immediately about and adjoining the wells, should not be so high as to cause evaporation of the water envelopes at the pressure that is sustainable by the overburden. Expressed otherwise, the predetermined electrical current should be maintained low enough to prevent drying of the tar sand formation 15 around the wells 11 and 13.

The electrical current will flow primarily through the tar sand formation, although some of the electrical energy will flow through the bitumen-impermeable shales, as illustrated in the dashed lines 47. The voltage and current flow are adjusted to effect the desired gradual increase in temperature of the tar sand formation 15 and the bitumen therein without overheating locally at the points of greatest current density. For example, the current may run from a few hundred to 1,000 or more amperes at the voltage drop between the electrodes 23 in the wells 11 and 13. This voltage drop may run from a few hundred volts to as much as 5,000 or more volts.

As the bitumen is heated, it begins to have a greater mobility in the tar sand formation 15. Once the yield point of the bitumen is reached in the tar sand formation or at least the temperature at which plastic flow begins at the pressure that can be imposed at the injection well is reached, mobility begins to make feasible in situ separation.

The complicated and interrelated events that determine mobility and, hence, productivity, require that the electrical heating prior to commencing further production methods such as steam drive must be long enough to get an overall mobility of the bitumen that is high enough to sustain a minimum flow-through from the one or more injection wells to the one or more production wells. If the predicted temperature at the midpoint intermediate of the two wells is inadequate to sustain the minimum flow-through, the electrical heating will have to be continued. Thus, empirically, if mobility of the bitumen will sustain a minimum throughput of at least 30 barrels per day, the drive methods are economically preferred over the electrical heating, and the injection of driving fluids is begun without the electrical heating.

While heating is continued, the bitumen is produced from the production well **13** by conventional techniques. For example, if it has been rendered mobile enough to flow readily, the pressure will be sufficient to cause production of the heated bitumen out of the production well **13** without requiring pumping facilities. On the other hand, with shallow overburdens, it may be economically feasible to install pumping equipment for pumping the bitumen from the production well **13**. As illustrated, the pressure is employed to effect flow of the hot bitumen from the production well **13** and to the production facilities through surface conduit **45**.

Example: The following example is given to demonstrate a typical process carried out as described with respect to Figure 5.14. The exemplified tar sand formation had an averaged thickness of 100 feet with an overburden of 1,000 feet in the pattern area. The tar sand formation had an averaged permeability of 700 millidarcies with the overburden and underburden being impermeable shales. The tar sand formation had an averaged porosity of 0.33 with an initial bitumen saturation of 12% by weight, when averaged. The averaged electrical resistivity, in ohm-meters at 50°F, were, respectively: tar sand, horizontally 30, vertically 90; overburden, 10; underburden, 50.

The geological formations adjacent the tar sand, as well as the tar sand formation **15**, had an initial temperature of 50°F, an averaged thermal conductivity of 0.6 Btu/ft/hr/°F, and an averaged thermal volumetric heat capacity of 44 Btu/ft^3/°F.

The exemplified pattern was a five-spot over 10 acres. The electrical heating time was 3 years, and the average electrical power input level for the pattern was 3,100 kilowatts. Thus, the total electrical input per pattern was 82 x 10^6 kilowatt hours. A back pressure of 700 psi was held on the injection well for the heating period. 6,000 gallons of 10 wt % NaCl brine were injected at the start of the heating period. The temperature adjacent the respective injection and production wells, equivalent to wells **11** and **13**, was 466°F. The minimum temperature at the midpoint between the injection and production wells was 160°F to attain the desired mobility of the bitumen. The bitumen had measured viscosities at different temperatures as follows: 50°F, 2 x 10^6 cp; 160°F, 1,500 cp; and 466°F, 5.4 cp. The total pattern productivity during the heating period was 150 barrels per day.

Injection, Production and Electrode Wells

According to a process described by *J.C. Todd; U.S. Patent 4,084,637; Apr. 18, 1978; assigned to Petro Canada Exploration Inc., Canada-Cities Services, Ltd., and Imperial Oil Limited, Canada* a method of producing viscous materials from subterranean formation comprises a plurality of steps. At least two wells are drilled and completed into the subterranean formation that contains the viscous material. At least one of the wells is completed as an injection well and one of the wells is completed as a production well. A plurality of electrode wells are drilled into the subterranean formation with the plurality of electrode wells being generally arranged in a pattern to define at least one path between the production well and the injection well with the length of the path being substantially greater than the distance between the production well and the injection well. The electrode wells are spaced apart along the path at distances that are substantially less than the distance between the production well and the injection well. A voltage is applied across the adjacent pairs of electrode wells to cause an electrical current to pass through the subterranean formation between each adjacent pair of the electrode wells.

As the electrical current passes through the subterranean formation, the viscous material is heated to thereby lower the viscosity of such material. Following the heating of the subterranean formation in the vicinity of the path formed by the electrode wells, a driving fluid is injected through the injection wells to migrate along the path and force the material having a reduced viscosity toward the production well. The material is produced through the production well and by continuing to inject a heated fluid through the injection wells, substantially all of the viscous material in the subterranean formation can be heated to lower its viscosity and be produced from the production well.

Quasitoroidal Conductor Envelope

S.T. Fisher and C.B. Fisher; U.S. Patents 4,008,761; February 22, 1977; 4,008,762; February 22, 1977; 3,972,372; August 3, 1976; and 3,989,107; November 2, 1976 describe a method of heating hydrocarbons in situ in an underground hydrocarbon deposit such as bituminous sands or oil shale. A selected part of the deposit is heated by electrical induction coils arranged in a quasitoroidal configuration to temperatures high enough to facilitate extraction. The coils are preferably comprised of interrupted rectangular turns. A series of generally concentric quasitoroidal configurations can be used to heat large volumes. A hexagonal honeycomb array of such configurations can be used to heat deposits underlying very large surface areas.

Figure 5.15a illustrates schematically an example of an inner quasitoroidal envelope constructed in accordance with the process. Within a hydrocarbon deposit, inner vertical conductor segments 1 are connected by upper horizontal conductor segments 3 and lower horizontal conductor segments 4 to outer vertical conductor elements 2. In Figure 5.15a, for example, six turns are illustrated each turn being composed of two vertical conductor elements 1 and 2 and two horizontal conductor elements 3 and 4 so as to form a substantially rectangular turn.

The turns are arranged at angles of 60° to one another to define a generally hexagonal configuration, with the outer vertical conductor elements 2 lying at the apexes of a notional regular hexagon. The inner conductors 1 also lie on the apexes of an inner notional hexagon. By notional hexagon is meant that there is no actual structure defining the entire perimeter of the hexagon; only the apexes of the respective hexagons are defined by physical structures.

The upper horizontal conductive elements 3 are shown interconnected by a conductive annular ring 7 to a terminal 5 for connection to one terminal of a source of alternating current. The inner vertical conductors 1 extend vertically upwards, from their respective points of connection to lower horizontal connectors 4, to an annular connecting conductor 9 which is connected to a terminal 6 for connection to the other terminal of the source of alternating current.

Figure 5.15: Induction Heating Technique

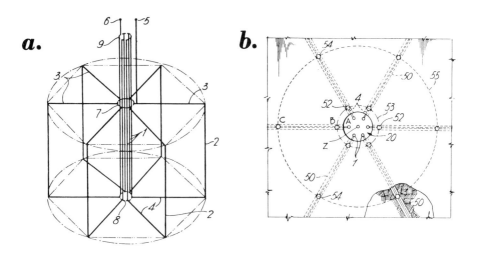

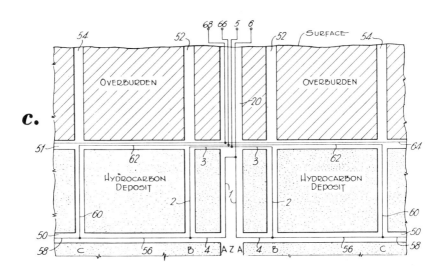

(continued)

Figure 5.15: (continued)

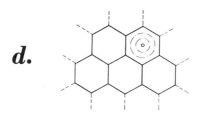

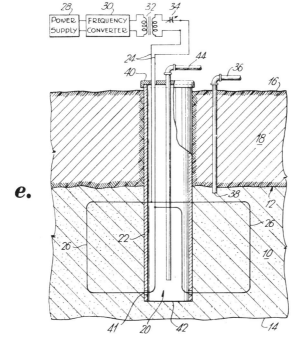

(a)   Schematic diagram showing the coil structure for a quasitoroidal
       envelope.
(b)   Schematic plan view of a portion of the surface of the earth, il-
       lustrating a preferred manner of locating vertical drill holes and
       horizontal tunnels.
(c)   Schematic sectional view of the portion of the earth to which Fig-
       ure 5.15b relates, illustrating a preferred horizontal and vertical
       tunnel arrangement.
(d)   Schematically illustrates a grid arrangement on the earth's surface
       for the practice of a preferred hydrocarbon exploitation tech-
       nique.
(e)   Illustrates the heating of bituminous sands or oil shales

Source: U.S. Patent 4,008,761

The conductors **1** are insulated from the annular ring **7** and from the upper horizontal conductor elements **3** so that at the inner upper corner of each rectangular turn there is a discontinuity. This of course is essential in order that current flow around the parallel-connected rectangular turns. The term "interrupted turn" is sometimes used herein to indicate that such a discontinuity is present.

When alternating current is applied to terminals **5** and **6**, an electromagnetic field is generated by the rectangular coils. The electromagnetic field tends to permeate a quasitoroidal space which differs from a true toroidal space not only because of the drop-off in field between conductive turns (especially at their outer extremities) but also because of the interrupted rectangular turn configuration in distinction from the usual circular coil configuration which would appear in conventional small-scale toroidal inductors.

The quasitoroidal space has an inner annular radius defined by the radius of the conductive connecting ring **7** (or by the radius of the notional circle on which the junction points of conductors **1** with conductors **4** lie). The outer radius of the quasitoroidal space is defined by the outer vertical conductor elements **2**. The upper limit of the quasitoroidal space is defined by a notional horizontal annular surface in which the upper conductor elements **3** lie. A similar notional annular surface in which the lower conductor elements **4** lie defines the lower boundary of the quasitoroidal space. Thus the turns formed by the inner and outer vertical conductor elements **1** and **2** and the upper and lower horizontal conductor elements **3** and **4** together form a quasitoroidal envelope which substantially surrounds the quasitoroidal space defined above.

Obviously the more turns that are used in the envelope, the more closely the actual electromagnetic field will extend throughout the entire quasitoroidal space surrounded by the envelope. However, bearing in mind that tunnelling or drilling is required for the introduction of each of the conductor elements into an underground hydrocarbon deposit, a trade-off must be made between the efficiency of generation of the electromagnetic field within the quasitoroidal space and the economies obtained by minimizing the number of holes or tunnels drilled or excavated.

In the discussion which follows it will be assumed that the number of turns may be as few as six, which facilitates the formation of a hexagonal honeycomb grid for the extraction of hydrocarbons from an entire hydrocarbon deposit too large to be heated by a single arrangement according to the process. However, some other number of conductors may be utilized in appropriate situations, and empirical evaluation of the effectiveness of the number of turns initially employed will undoubtedly be made in particular applications to determine whether a greater or fewer number of turns might be suitable. Obviously additional tunnels and drill holes can be provided to increase the number of turns as required.

While in the example of Figure 5.15a, the upper conductors **3** and the lower conductors **4** have been illustrated as being horizontal, it is to be understood that the orientation of these conductors may vary to accord with the angle of inclination of the upper and lower limits respectively of the underground hydrocarbon deposit required to be heated.

There is a practical upper limit on the ratio of the outer radius of the quasitoroidal envelope defined by vertical conductors **2** to the inner radius of the quasitoroidal envelope defined by the location of the inner vertical conductor elements **1**. For this reason, it may be desirable to provide a further quasito-roidal envelope surrounding that illustrated in Figure 5.15a. Such further quasi-toroidal envelope could utilize as its innermost vertical conductor elements the conductor elements **2** of Figure 5.15a. Figure 5.15b illustrates in plan view the appropriate configuration both of vertical drill holes and horizontal tunnels in which the required coil segments can be located. Obviously only one of the two horizontal tunnels can be shown in plan view; one of any pair of horizontal tun-nels of course will generally directly lie below the other horizontal tunnel in the pair.

In a central vertical circular cylindrical shaft **20**, the innner vertical conductors **1** are located. Extending radially outwardly from the shaft **20** are horizontal tunnels **50** which are assumed to be the lower horizontal tunnels required for the location of the lower horizontal conductors **4**. The upper horizontal tunnels would then lie directly above tunnels **50**. Intersecting with the horizontal tun-nels **50** are vertical drill holes **52** in which vertical conductors **2** are located. The conductor arrangement thus defines an inner quasitoroidal envelope whose outer periphery is generally defined by a notional cylindrical surface shown in plan view by a broken line circle **53** and whose inner periphery is the notional cylindrical surface defined by conductors **1**.

The next quasitoroidal envelope surrounding the inner quasitoroidal envelope formed by conductors **1, 2, 3** and **4** will then be generated by extending the tunnels **50** radially outwardly from the drill holes **52** and sinking further vertical drill holes **54** which lie again on a notional cylindrical surface indicated in the plan view of Figure 5.15b by broken line circle **55**. These drill holes **54** thus necessarily lie at the apexes of a further hexagon larger than that defined by the drill holes **52**. The inner vertical conductors for the outer quasitoroidal envelope are conveniently the already-placed vertical conductors **2** located in the drill holes **52**.

This achieves an economy both in drilling and in conductor utilization. If a fur-ther quasitoroidal space is to be defined, the tunnels **50** can be extended further radially outwardly, a further set of vertical drill holes provided, and appropriate extensions of the horizontal conductors and appropriate insertions of additional vertical conductors provided. The inner conductors for such hypothetical outer quasitoroidal envelope would be the conductors provided in the drill holes **54**.

If the center of shaft **20** is indicated by **Z**, then the inner radius of the inner quasitoroidal envelope will be **AZ** where **A** lies on the circle defined by the inner vertical conductors **1**. The outer radius of the inner quasitoroidal envelope will be **BZ**, where **B** lies on the circle defined by vertical conductors **2** located in drill holes **52**. The outer next adjacent quasitoroidal envelope has an inner radius **BZ** and an outer radius **CZ**, where **C** lies on the circle defined by drill holes **54**.

A further appreciation of the scheme of Figure 5.15b can be had by referring to the schematic elevation view of Figure 5.15c, which is a section of the earth along one of the horizontal tunnels **50**.

Extending radially outwardly from the central shaft **20** are the lower horizontal tunnels **50** located at or near the bottom of a hydrocarbon deposit which is sep-arated from the surface of the earth by an overburden layer. A set of upper horizontal tunnels **51** extend radially outwardly from the central vertical shaft **20** at or near the upper limit of the hydrocarbon deposit. A first set of drill holes **52** define the outer limit of the innermost quasitoroidal space to be surrounded by the quasitoroidal conductive envelope. A further set of vertical drill holes **54** spaced radially outwardly from the drill holes **52** define the outer limit of the second quasitoroidal space. Further vertical drill holes (not shown) could be provided yet further radially outwardly from the shaft **20** to define the outer limit of yet a further quasitoroidal space.

Conductor elements **1, 2, 3** and **4** are shown connected to surface terminals **5** and **6** for connection to a source of alternating current in the manner previously described with reference to Figure 5.15a. It can be seen that the inner vertical conductors **1** lie generally along the periphery of the central shaft **20**, that the vertical conductors **2** lie in drill holes **52** within the hydrocarbon deposit, that upper horizontal conductors **3** lie in the upper horizontal tunnels **51**, and that the lower horizontal conductors **4** lie in lower horizontal tunnels **50**.

To provide the rectangular turns required for the adjacent outer quasitoroidal envelope, tunnels **50** and **51** are shown extending radially outwardly beyond vertical tunnels **52** to intersect an outer set of vertical drill holes **54**. Horizontal conductor elements **4** can be continued as horizontal conductor elements **56** lying between drill holes **52** and **54**. Vertical conductor elements **60** located in drill holes **54** are connected between horizontal conductor elements **56** and further horizontal conductor elements **62** located in upper horizontal tunnels **51**. The interrupted rectangular turns therefore comprise conductor elements **2, 56, 60** and **62** for this quasitoroidal envelope. The upper horizontal conductor elements **62** are connected to a terminal **66**. Alternating current would then be applied across terminals **5** and **66** to energize the intermediate quasitoroidal envelope.

The horizontal conductors **4** and **56**, can be further extended as conductor elements **58** to an outer set of vertical drill holes in which an outer set of vertical conductors may be located. These vertical conductors can then be connected to horizontal conductors **64** located in tunnel extensions **51** which in turn are connected to terminal **68** at the surface. Alternating current can then energize such outer quasitoroidal envelope by being applied across terminals **66** and **68**, it being perceived that the outer toroidal envelope utilizes as its innermost vertical conductors the vertical conductors **60** located in drill holes **54**. This kind of progressive drill hole and circuit extension can be continued indefinitely to an outer economic limit.

It is of course necessary in the arrangement above-described to make sure that the conductors **3, 62, 64**, etc., located in horizontal tunnel **51** are insulated from one another. The selection of the tunnel **51** as containing a plurality of horizontal conductors whereas tunnel **50** contains just one continuing horizontal conductor is arbitrary; the reverse arrangement might in some circumstances be preferred. Furthermore, it may be preferable in some circumstances to continue the vertical conductors upwardly through drill holes **52** and **54**, etc., and then to make surface connections from these drill holes rather than via the horizontal tunnels **51**.

The coil arrangement of Figures 5.15a, 5.15b, and 5.15c has been illustrated as involving a parallel connection between the turns. This is expected to be the most appropriate manner of interconnection of the turns, but a series coil connection could be substituted in a particular situation if considered appropriate by the designer. The manner in which a series connection can be arranged is within the ordinary skill of an electrical engineer.

The size of the tunnels **50** and **51** and the drill holes **52, 54** and of the central shaft **20** have been exaggerated for purposes of convenience of illustration. It is to be expected that these holes will be as small as possible to be consistent with the use that is to be made of them. The central shaft **20** for example will be utilized not only for the location of the conductors **1** and the connecting lines from terminals **5, 6, 66, 68,** etc., but also will probably be required as a construction shaft into which men and machinery will enter for the purpose of excavating horizontal tunnels **50** and **51**.

The central shaft **20** may also be utilized to extract at least a portion of the hydrocarbon deposit through appropriate conduits. The drill holes **52** and **54** may conceivably be utilized not only for the location of the vertical conductor elements but may also conceivably be utilized for the injection of fluid into the hydrocarbon deposit or the extraction of at least a portion of the hydrocarbons from the deposit. In the event that gas under pressure is required to be injected into the deposit in order to facilitate extraction of hydrocarbons, it may be required to stop-up some of the vertical drill holes **52, 54,** etc., to prevent the unwanted escape of gas from the hydrocarbon deposits. Alternatively, the holes might be used to house the gas injection pipes, provided of course that they do not interfere with the induction coils.

Figure 5.15d illustrates a hexagonal honeycomb grid, each hexagonal section thereof comprising a plurality of quasitoroidal envelopes of the type illustrated in Figure 5.15b. The number of quasitoroidal envelopes within any one hexagon will be determined by the economies of the situation, since generally speaking, it is expected that an outer radial limit for the outer periphery of a given quasitoroidal envelope will be reached beyond which it is uneconomical to arrange further drill holes, tunnels, or conductor elements. However, the hexagonal arrangement of Figure 5.15d permits as much of the underground hydrocarbon deposit as economically possible to be effectively exploited.

In Figure 5.15e, a schematic illustration of a structure suitable for heating bituminous sands or oil shales is illustrated. For simplicity, only the innermost quasitoroidal conductor configuration is illustrated, but the description to follow can be applied, mutatis mutandis, to outer quasitoroidal envelopes.

An oil shale or bituminous sand deposit **10** is shown having an upper boundary **12** and a lower boundary **14**. The formation **10** is separated from the earth's surface **16** by an overburden layer **18**. A central shaft generally indicated as **20** is provided from the surface to the bottom or a point near the bottom of the oil shale formation **10**. For structural strength and sealing of the shaft, the shaft walls are generally provided with an annular concrete reinforcing layer **22** and the shaft is capped by a conventional well-cap **40**.

Electrical conductors **24** extend from the surface power supply and into the shaft **20** for connection to rectangular electric induction coil **26**. This rectangular coil **26** extends outwardly from the shaft **20** to surround an annular quasitoroidal volume of the oil shale formation **10**. Electricity is supplied to the conductors **24** from a power supply **28** (e.g., a generator driven by a turbine which may be powered by a portion of the extracted hydrocarbons), whose output may optionally be passed through a frequency converter **30**, a transformer **32**, or both, depending upon the desired operating parameters for the system and upon the frequency and voltage at which the output from power supply **28** is available. A series-connected tuning capacitor **34** is also provided to resonate the circuit so as to facilitate maximum energy transfer to the volume of oil shale encompassed by the induction coil **26**.

An injection pipe **36** may optionally be provided for injecting water into the hot formation for the purpose of generating steam when hydrocarbon extraction has been substantially completed, or for injecting gas under pressure into the formation to facilitate extraction of the hydrocarbons, or may be used to inject catalysts into the formation to facilitate cracking of residual coke after volatile fractions have been extracted via suitable communicating holes **41** in the shaft lining and via extraction pipe **44**. Note that the lower end **38** of the pipe is located just above and outside the induction coil **26**, since if the pipe **36** were made of metal and the pipe penetrated the volume encompassed by induction coil **26**, the result would be the undue absorption of energy by the pipe **36** within the heated volume with attendant risk of damage to the pipe, burning of adjacent kerogen, etc.

One or more pipes **36** may be provided as required, and instead of being located in separate drill holes, could conceivably be provided within the shaft **20** and directed radially outwards through suitable openings in the concrete layer **22** into the interior of the formation.

Alternating current is passed through the coil **26** at a frequency, voltage and amperage sufficient to heat the selected portion of the deposit within the annular quasitoroidal envelope formed by the induction coil **26** to a desired temperature at which the method of extraction selected by the user is implemented.

Electrolyte Circulation

In accordance with a process developed by *A.L. Barnes; U.S. Patent 3,931,856; January 13, 1976; assigned to Atlantic Richfield Company* a subterranean formation intermediate a plurality of electrode wells completed therein is heated by electrical conduction and includes the steps of drilling and completing a satellite well in the formation adjacent an electrode well, and injecting water containing dissolved electrolyte into the formation via the electrode well having an adjacent satellite well, establishing fluid communication between the electrode well and the satellite well, and thereafter circulating the water between the electrode well and adjacent satellite well.

Thus, in the process, the in situ fluid and the formation are preheated to mobilize the viscous oil in the formation, by heating with a predetermined electrical current for a predetermined time interval. Production of the mobilized oil intermediate the electrode and satellite wells is effected through either the electrode well or satellite well to provide for fluid communication between them. The electrolyte solution circulation between the electrode and satellite wells effectively increases the size of the electrode by providing a larger area of high electrical conductivity than is possible without the satellite well.

With the size of the electrode increased, the area of heating is correspondingly increased between the electrode wells which allows more power to be transmitted to the formation in the form of heat energy. Thereafter, for production, it may be necessary to inject a drive fluid such as steam or hot water into the formation via either the electrode or satellite well.

In one example, the circulation of the electrolyte solution is effected by withdrawing the solution from the satellite well and passing it through a heat exchanger on the surface and reinjecting the cooled solution down the electrode well past conductors (such as cables) therein and through the formation to the satellite well to complete the cycle. The circulation of solution past the conductors in the electrode well allows the current capacity to be increased severalfold by maximizing heat transfer. Corrosion inhibitors may be needed in the solution if cable is uninsulated. Contact between copper and steel should be avoided to prevent electrolytic corrosion.

The following example illustrates applicability of this process to effect the lowering of the electrical resistance of a formation.

Example:

Formation thickness, ft	50
Formation porosity, %	30
Water saturation, %	30
Oil saturation, %	70
NaCl content of water, % by weight	1
Electrical resistivity of formation water at formation temperature, ohm-meters,	0.3
Electrical resistivity of formation, ohm-meters	140
Oil viscosity, cp	100
NaCl content of injected electrolyte solution, % by weight	5
Electrical resistivity of injected electrolyte solution at formation temperature, ohm-meters	0.06
Distance between satellite well and electrode well, ft	30

A 421 bbl volume of the electrolyte solution is injected into the formation through the electrode bore hole. This injected volume of solution banks up and displaces the formation water which in turn displaces part of the oil, reducing its saturation from 70 to 50%. Initially, the injected electrolyte solution travels through the porous formation a distance of about 10 ft from the center of the wellbore and occupies 50% of the pore space within this 10 ft radius. In addition, in the interval space from 10 to 12.6 ft, the oil saturation is reduced from 70 to 50% by the banked-up formation water.

In this interval space, because formation water occupies 50% of the pore space, formation resistivity is reduced from 140 to 63 ohm-meters. In the 10 ft interval adjacent the wellbore, the resistivity is reduced another five-fold because the injected electrolyte solution has a resistivity one-fifth that of the formation water. Therefore, in the 10 ft interval adjacent the wellbore, the formation resistivity is reduced from 140 to 12.6 ohm-meters.

The effect of the pressure differential created by the adjacent satellite wells causes the electrolyte solution to migrate toward the satellite well. Subsequently, after preheating and production of initial expansion, the electrolyte solution fills the region between the electrode and the satellite wells reducing the formation resistivity to 12.6 ohm-meters, thereby obtaining an enlarged effective electrode area of high conductivity to improve electrical connection with other electrode wells completed in the formation. Upon establishment of communication between the electrode well and the satellite well, the electrolyte solution is continuously withdrawn from the formation through the satellite well, passed through a heat exchanger and reinjected through the electrode wellbore to complete the cycle of the circulation system.

The water containing the dissolved electrolyte may be injected concurrently or intermittently with the electrical conduction to establish and maintain the region of high electrical conductivity. When it is injected concurrently with heating, precaution should be taken to ensure that no electrically complete conductive path is established intermediate the high voltage electrodes and the injection conduits which may pose hazards to operating personnel.

Electrical Conduction with Variable Current

W.C. Pritchett; U.S. Patent 3,948,319; April 6, 1976; assigned to Atlantic Richfield Company describes a method and apparatus for heating a subterranean formation by a multistep process. First, a plurality of wells are drilled into and completed within a subterranean formation from the surface of the earth in a predetermined pattern. Respective electrical conductors, including electrodes, are emplaced in the wells and connected electrically with the subterranean formation and a source of current at the surface. Thereafter, the subterranean formation is heated by electrical conduction under conditions such that the electrical current flowing at different subterranean points varies at different times because of different current flow patterns induced, to attain more nearly uniform heating of the subterranean formation within the predetermined pattern of the wells.

The electrical conductivity may be as a result of direct current flowing from one electrode to another under a given electromotive force, or voltage potential. On the other hand, the electrical conduction may be effected as a result of alternating current flow through the subterranean formation between respective electrodes. With either direct or single phase current sources, the current flows through the same areal portion of the subterranean formation over a period of time with the switching being effected, manually or automatically, at the surface by switching means.

In one example of this process, a multiphase alternating current is flowed through the formation intermediate a plurality of at least three electrodes. The electrodes and multiphase current source are connected in one or more predetermined multiphase configurations such that the electrical current changes as the phase voltages change on the respective electrodes. With the multiphase current sources, the current flows through an areal portion of the subterranean formation for a period of time.

Fluid may be produced to the surface through the respective production wells as the fluids migrate thereto, alone or under the influence of induced pressure gradients.

TAR SANDS SEPARATION PROCESSES

It has been estimated that there are in excess of 915 billion barrels of bitumen in 19 major deposits of what are commonly known as "tar sands" (The Major Tar Sand Deposits of the World," Phizackerley and Scott, Panel Discussion No. 13, Topic No. 1, The World Petroleum Congress, Mexico City, April 1967). By 1973, petroleum production had diminished sufficiently with respect to demand to generate a world energy crisis. Irrespective of the vagaries of international politics, there is an ever increasing demand for petroleum with an ever decreasing availability which threatens a worldwide depression.

There are major tar sand deposits in the following eight nations: Canada, Venezuela, the United States, Malagasy, Albania, Trinidad, Rumania and the U.S.S.R. By far, the greatest deposits are located in the province of Alberta, Canada in an area of approximately 30,000 square miles commonly referred to as the Athabasca Tar Sands.

Tar sand deposits may lie either exposed or covered with an overburden of varying thicknesses up to approximately 3,000 feet. Of the 700 billion barrels of crude oil estimated to lie in the Athabasca fields, approximately 15% is free of overburden. Additionally, substantial deposits exist in eastern Venezuela, Kentucky and Utah which are also free of overburden and total in the millions of barrels.

The composition of the bitumen which permeates the sand varies specifically with respect to location but the various bitumens have many common characteristics. Merely by way of illustration, the Athabasca tar sands comprise fractions ranging from a totally saturated colorless oil having a molecular weight of 360 to a brown-black solid asphaltene with a molecular weight of approximately 2,500. Additionally, there are oil fractions ranging from totally saturated hydrocarbons through a series containing gradually increasing proportions of aromatics ("Athabasca Oil Sands," K.A. Clark, Research Council of Alberta, 1963). The various compositions of most of the significant deposits of tar sands have been published in the *Encyclopedia of Chemical Technology*, Second Edition, Volume 19, page 698.

Unlike crude oil deposits which lie in pools, the bitumens in tar sands are not subject to common well-drilling techniques, although a Frasch Process approach appears viable. The sand appears as a tacky to relatively solid black mass and in some instances relatively hard. There are virtually no deposits of free liquid petroleum.

A typical arrangement of tar sand particles discloses a water envelope proximal to the sand particle containing extremely fine solid particles. The water envelope is covered by a continuous bitumen film which interengages with the bitumen film of adjacent sand particles, to form a cohesive mass generally as illustrated in the *Encyclopedia of Chemical Technology*, Second Edition, Volume 19, page 693. Thus, the bitumen constituent of the tar sands first must be separated from the sand particles and thereafter refined to produce the various usual petroleum distillate fractions.

The published literature clearly demonstrates that over a period of approximately 47 years, extensive research has been undertaken to develop an economically efficient method for the recovery of bitumen from tar sands without notable success. By 1963, Dr. K.A. Clark, who by then had spent 43 years researching this problem, settled upon a hot water process combining the use of steam, sodium hydroxide and centrifugal force. The Great Canada Oil Sands Limited, a subsidiary of the Sun Oil Company, expended approximately $235,000,000 on the development of the Clark process which has not achieved significant commercial success.

Additionally, the Canadian Department of Mines and Technical Surveys developed a pilot plant separation process employing cold water and kerosene as a solvent. The kerosene is used in ratios of one-to-one by weight to the bitumen in the feed while the total water added to the process is 2 to 3 times the weight of the feed. Soda ash and wetting agents were also added.

The first step in the cold water process is disintegration of the sand feed mass in a pebble mill together with water, kerosene and other reagents. The pebble mill effluent is mixed with additional water, and fed to a rake classifier to separate the bulk of the sand from the liquid phase. The liquid phase is thickened to concentrate the oil.

The hot water process of Clark includes a wide variety of extremely complicated control conditions and is effected by variations in the composition of the tar sand, particularly its clay content. It is estimated that the overall efficiency of recovery of the Clark hot water process is no greater than 6 to 8%.

Another hot water process has been tested on a laboratory scale by the United States Bureau of Mines as applied to tar sands found in the United States. This process is distinctly different from the hot water process of Clark because a solvent is employed. In the U.S. process, a 33° API fuel oil containing 20 to 25% by volume aromatics is added as a solvent in one-to-three weight ratio based upon the feed bitumen content. The product of this process closely resembles the product derived from the Canadian Mines Branch cold water process. Additionally, it has been found that tar sands which include relatively large concentrations of iron and calcium salts, such as tar sands found in deposits at Edna, California, cannot be extracted by the Clark or U.S. hot water process. This chapter includes over 60 recently developed processes for the separation of bitumen from tar sands.

HOT WATER PROCESSES

Hydroseparation Liquid Distributor in Frusto-Cone Design

H.J. Davitt; U.S. Patent 3,954,415; May 4, 1976; assigned to Sun Oil Company of Pennsylvania describes an improved separation cell suitable for use in a hot water method for extracting bitumen from tar sands. The improvement lies substantially in the hollow inverted frusto-cone-shaped bottom of the cell having a means for injecting hydroseparation liquid into the cavity formed by the frusto-conical bottom.

Figure 6.1a illustrates the hot water extraction process in flow diagram form as generally shown in Canadian Patent No. 841,581 with the improvement of the incorporation of the hydroseparation hot water extraction cell of this process. Figure 6.1b is an illustration of the detail of one mode of the hot water extraction cell.

Referring to Figure 6.1a, bituminous tar sands are fed into the hot water extraction system through line **1** where they first pass into conditioning zone **18**. Water and steam are introduced from **2** into the conditioning zone along with recycled middlings from line **14** and are mixed with the sands. Total water so introduced is a minor amount based on the weight of the tar sands and generally is in the range of 10 to 45 wt % of the mixture. Enough steam is introduced to raise the temperature in the conditioning zone to within the range of 130° to 210°F and preferably above 170°F and most preferably about 185°F.

Figure 6.1: Extraction Vessel

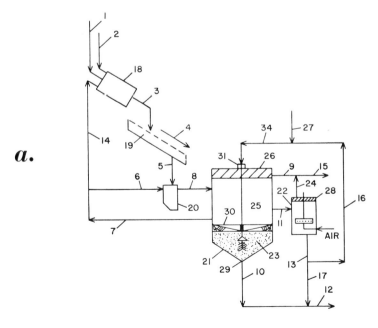

a.

Flow diagram

(continued)

Figure 6.1: (continued)

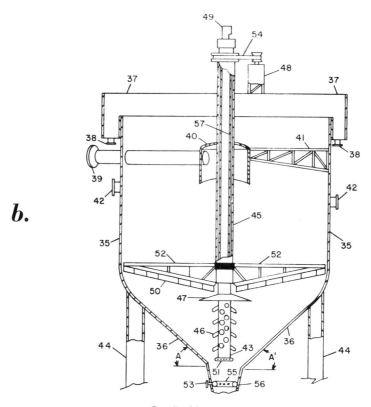

b.

Detail of hot water extraction cell

Source: U.S. Patent 3,954,415

The water added into the mixing zone as indicated can include a middlings re-cycle drag stream which can be withdrawn from primary extraction zone **21** and transferred via line **7** into line **14** and thereafter into conditioning vessel **18** as indicated in the drawing.

An alkaline reagent can also be added to the conditioning zone in the amount of 0.1 to 3.0 lb/ton of tar sand. The amount of such alkaline reagent preferably is regulated to maintain the pH of middlings layer **25** in the separation zone **21** within the range of about 8.0 to 8.5. The quantity of alkaline reagent that needs to be added to maintain the pH in the desired range can vary from time to time as the composition of the tar sands obtained from the mine site varies. Alkaline reagents suitable for use include caustic soda, sodium carbonate, or so-dium silicate although any of the other alkaline reagents known in the art for this application can be used if desired.

The mixture from conditioning zone **18** can be transferred via line **3** to screen **19** where oversized matter such as rock and tar sand or clay lumps are removed as indicated at **4**. The pulp then passes as indicated via line **5** into sump **20** where it is diluted with additional water from line **6** which can also be recycled middlings withdrawn from extraction zone **21** as well as fresh water which can be added to line **6** from an outside source not shown.

The addition of water to the pulp in sump **20** dilutes the pulp to a pumpable viscosity so that it can easily be transferred into separation zone **21** via line **8** as shown. Additional water can also be added to screen **19** to wash pulp through the screen and act as a diluent for the pulp if desired. In normal practice, the total amount of water added to the tar sand pulp as liquid water and steam prior to the separation step should be in the range 0.2 to 3.0 lb of water per lb of tar sand being processed. The water requirements for the separation zone, of course, are contingent upon the quantity of silt and clay which the tar sands contain as compared to the bitumen content of the tar sands.

Separation zone **21** includes the improved hydroseparation features which are the contributions of the process. Separation zone **21** is illustrated as containing the upper froth layer **26**, the middlings layer **25**, and the sand tailings layer **23**. The hydroseparation liquid distributor is located within the sand tailings layer **23**. Separation zone **21** also contains sand rake **30** as well as exit means **29** having a withdrawal outlet pipe **10** which feeds into line **12** which thereafter is utilized to discard the sand tailings layer from separation zone **21**. Also, means for rotating sand rake **30** is indicated at **31**. Hydroseparation liquid is transferred into extraction cell **21** via line **34** which carries hydroseparation liquid from lines **27** and/or **16**.

In separation zone **21**, the slurry mixture normally separates into an upper bitumen froth layer as indicated by **26**, a middlings layer indicated by **25**, and sand tailings layer indicated by **23**. The bitumen froth is recovered from separation zone **21** via line **9**. The tailings layer of extraction zone **21** containing sand and the hydroseparation liquid medium is withdrawn via line **10** through exit **29** and transferred into line **12** for discard. A first middlings drag stream can be withdrawn from separation zone **21** via line **7** for transfer into line **14** or line **6** as the abovementioned recycle diluent for the tar sands pulp.

A second middlings stream can be withdrawn from separation zone **21** and transferred via line **11** into scavenger zone **22**. Additional bitumen froth **28** is recovered from the middlings stream in zone **22** via air flotation. The additional froth **28** from zone **22** is transferred via line **24** into line **15** wherein it is combined with the froth recovered from the separation zone **21** via line **9**. The combined froths can thereafter be processed to usable synthetic petroleum in the manner known in the art.

A depleted middlings stream from scavenger zone **22** is withdrawn via line **13**, and, if desired, all or part of this stream can be transferred via line **16** into line **34** for use in the primary extraction zone **21** as the hydroseparation liquid. Also, the scavenger tailings can be transferred from line **13** into line **17** and thereafter into line **12** for addition to the primary cell tailings to be discarded, if desired.

Referring to Figure 6.1b, a hot water extraction cell is a tank having a circular vertical wall **35** with middlings outlets **42** located generally midway between the top end and bottom end of the wall. Disposed on the upper end of the tank is an overflow launder **37** having outlets **38** for transfer of the overflow liquids from the launder for further processing.

The tank contains a hollow inverted frusto-conical shaped bottom **36**. The larger opening of the frusto-cone is attached to the lower end of the vertical wall **35**. The smaller opening of the frusto-cone is attached to exit means **56**. Exit **56** provides a means for removing the sand tailings layer from the bottom of the cell. Disposed within the cavity formed by the frusto-conical bottom of the cell is a hydroseparation liquid distributor **43**. Hydroseparation liquid distributor **43** can be a hollow tube having an inlet means at one end for receiving hydroseparation liquid and also having distribution outlets **46** as indicated for dispersing the liquid into the bottom of the cell.

Situated immediately above the uppermost distribution outlet **46** on the hydro-separation liquid distributor **43** is shed baffle **47**. This baffle is generally in the shape of an inverted saucer or frusto-cone and is provided to inhibit a channel being formed between the middlings zone (**25** in Figure 6.1a) and the discharge cone **56** of the cell through the sand tailings layer (**33** in Figure 6.1a) in the bottom of the cell. In normal operation, the level of the sand tailings layer in the cell is maintained at a point between the sand rakes **50** and the uppermost part of shed baffle **47**.

The hydroseparation liquid distributor can also contain outlets in the form of a perforated flange **51** on the end of distributor **43**. The flange outlets are arranged to provide hydroseparation liquid to the exit opening in the bottom of the cell to aid the free flow of sand from the cell. Also, located within exit cone **56** is a perforated cone flush pipe **55** or similar fluid delivery means which provides additional flushing fluid to exit cone **56** to aid in transferring sand tailings from the separation cell. Fluid is supplied to the cone flush means by inlet **53** attached to the cone flush pipe and located outside of exit cone **56**.

Also, disposed in the cell is sand rake **50** attached to support arms **52** which in turn are affixed to the central rotating shaft **45** centrally disposed within the cell. This central rotating shaft **45** to which the sand rake **50** is attached is powered by means of drive belt **54** which is connected to power source **48**. Connected to the hydroseparator distributor is delivery means **57** which can be a hollow tube through which the hydroseparator liquid is provided to the distributor. In one aspect of the apparatus, the hydroseparator liquid delivery means **57** is concentric with and located within hollow rotating shaft **45**. The hydroseparation delivery means is supplied by line **49** connected thereto which is supplied by line **34** of Figure 6.1a.

One important aspect of the apparatus is the slope of the sides of the frusto-conical bottom. As shown, this slope is indicated by angle A which is the external angle between the side of the frusto-conical bottom and a plane perpendicular to the axis of the cone. This angle is herein defined as slope of the bottom of the tank. To facilitate continuous flow of sand tailings on the bottom of the cell to the exit therein, this angle should be at least 15°. The most effective angle for this cell bottom is in the range of 30° to 60° and most preferably the angle is at about 45°.

Tar sands pulp is delivered to the separation cell via feed inlet means **39** which communicates with feed well **40** centrally disposed within the separation cell.

Feed well **40** is supported by support means **41** attached to cell wall **35**. The entire separation cell is supported by support means **44**.

The sand rake in the cell serves to prevent sand buildup along the cell walls which, if permitted, could interfere with the normal operation of the cell. The cell is operable without having sand rakes but the use of the raking system is preferable. Also, the shed baffle **47** located above the hydroseparation liquid distributor is not absolutely essential to the operation of the cell. However, a cell containing the shed baffles **47**, as shown in Figure 6.1b, is preferable.

The improved hot water extraction cell incorporates the inverted hollow frusto-conical bottom having a hydroseparation liquid distributor located within the cavity of the frusto-conical bottom of the cell and near the sand tailings exit of the cell. In the operation of the cell, it is also below the surface of the sand tailings layer in the bottom of the cell.

By this unique combination of a hydroseparation liquid distributor within a hollow inverted frusto-cone shaped bottom, bitumen-rich middlings material is not lost through the bottom sand tailings discharge means of the cell thereby improving recovery of bitumen from the tar sands feed.

Closed-Cycle, Single-Stage Extraction Vessel

W.J. Rosenbloom; U.S. Patent 3,875,046; April 1, 1975 describes a process for extracting oil from tar sand containing fines using extraction and phase separation techniques. A closed-cycle, single-stage process uses only one extraction vessel in which tar sand is contacted by an extractant, such as water containing a wetting agent and/or a solvent, and recycle water in a fluidized bed condition which avoids disturbing fines attached to the tar sand particles. Fines exiting the extraction vessel in a water phase are agglomerated and reintroduced to the bottom of the extraction vessel where they are filtered out by the extracted sand passing downward in the vessel.

The solvent may be vaporized to enhance contact and assure complete recovery. Steam is advantageously introduced to the extraction vessel to scour the sand particles free of solvent. The usual process control additives may be included in the recycle water. The sand and fines tailings are essentially free of pollutants.

Referring to Figure 6.2 tar sand is fed into the processing system, shown at **10**, into a mixer **14** which may be of the simple low energy type such as a rotary cement mixer. Hot water from the water recycle system is also fed into the mixer through a line **12**. Sufficient hot water, plus steam if needed, is added to form a fluid slurry. The temperature within the mixer is preferably maintained at the lowest possible temperature for suitable fluidity. Within the mixer **14** gentle mixing to prevent disruption of the clays and other fines attached to the sand particles takes place. That the mixing be sufficiently gentle to avoid displacement of the fines is important in the process and is in distinction from previously known processes which deliberately mull, aerate or grind the tar sand. The tar sand-water slurry flows from the mixer **14** to a screen **18** via the line **16**. On the screen **18** oversize material may be removed and discarded via a conveyor **20**. It is also important that this screening not disrupt the clays and other fines attached to the sand particles. The screened slurry is then fed through a line **22** to the top of the extractor vessel **24**. Within the extraction vessel an internal downcomer **26** assures that the tar sand-water slurry is fed to a level below the oil-solvent collection layer (hydrocarbon phase) and preferably to a point below the water-contaminants layer.

Figure 6.2: Extraction Process

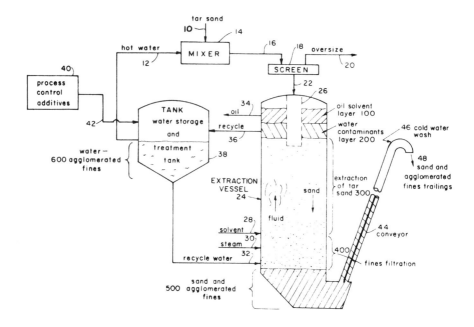

Source: U.S. Patent 3,875,046

The extraction liquid, or extractant, may be hot water, or it may be water to which has been added wetting agent, dispersing agent, etc., in order to facilitate extraction of the oil. Also, solvent of the type customarily used in such extraction processes may desirably be introduced to the extraction vessel **24** via a line **28** at a point near the lower portion of the extraction vessel. Steam is also introduced, indirectly or directly, into the extraction vessel **24** at a point near the bottom of the vessel via a line **30** which is located below the point of introduction of the solvent.

After start-up, once the process has reached steady-state operation, there exists a recycle stream containing water and contaminants such as clay and other fines from the extraction process. This recycle stream may also contain slight amounts of additives, such as wetting agents, dispersing agents, flocculants, and caustic for pH control, used for process control. This recycle stream is introduced to the extraction vessel **24** at a point below the points of introduction of the solvent and steam through a line **32**.

The extraction process within the extraction vessel operates as follows. The up-flowing extractant liquid, including the recycled water, adjusted for the most suitable pH and containing wetting or dispersing agents, and dissolved salts, if necessary, for increased density, and solvent acts to release the tar or heavy oil from the sand and cause it to rise to an upper oil-solvent liquid layer in the extraction vessel. This hydrocarbon phase is shown schematically and referenced by **100**. Since the extraction is countercurrent, the tar sand becomes more depleted in oil as it continues in its downward path in the extraction vessel while becoming exposed to leaner solvent and solvent vapor until practically all oil is removed and the sand is wetted with the solvent only.

As the sand continues its downward path in the extraction vessel **24** below the point of solvent introduction via the line **28**, it is heated by steam introduced via the line **30**. The heating by steam may be accomplished directly or indirectly; however, the introduction of live steam is preferred because it allows for the use of induction nozzles which provide an intimate mix with the sand particles. The steam scours the remaining solvent and other chemicals off of the sand particles and the amount of steam necessary to accomplish this is used. Should this scouring be insufficient to remove all solvent, additional steam is added until the sand temperature is above the boiling point temperature of the solvent, which has a boiling point temperature lower than the boiling point temperature of the circulated liquid, in order to vaporize the solvent.

The solvent vapor rises with the flowing liquid and condenses on the cooler down-coming sand. The oil-solvent phase constitutes the uppermost layer in the extraction vessel and is removed as a relatively clean hydrocarbon phase containing a reduced amount of contaminants via the line **34**. This hydrocarbon phase may then be further refined, if desired, and separated into a solvent fraction and a product tar fraction for a refinery feed. The solvent fraction from such further refining may then be reintroduced to the system as makeup solvent entering via the line **28**. The water phase containing fines such as silt and clay and other contaminants in addition to additives is an intermediate layer, shown at **200**, between the oil-solvent phase and the sand extraction zone. This phase, which may also contain some dispersed hydrocarbon, is removed via a line **36** to a storage and treatment tank **38**.

In the storage and treatment tank **38** this recycle material is sampled and its pH, wetting agent and salt content, and flocculating agent composition adjusted, if needed. This adjustment is accomplished through the introduction of additives from suitable supply tanks illustrated generally by the representative tank **40** feeding into the water storage and treatment tank **38** via a line **42**. The water storage and treatment tank **38** is selected so as to provide sufficient retention time for agglomeration of the fines in a quiescent zone incorporated in the tank.

The agglomerated fines concentrated in the recycle waste are represented at **600**. The length of time of agglomeration will, of course, be dependent upon the particular clays and other fines found in the tar sand and may vary. Agglomeration is aided through the addition of flocculating agents. The incidence of collision of the particles to improve adherence in agglomeration may be enhanced by the incorporation of a vibrator, such as a sonic vibrator, as is known in the art. The treated liquid containing concentrated agglomerated fines exits the storage and treatment tank **38** via a line **32** for reintroduction into the extraction system. Under some circumstances the tank may not be required and agglomeration in the layer will be sufficient. As previously mentioned, hot water may be removed from an upper phase in the water storage and treatment tank **38** via line **12** for addition to the tar sand in the mixer **14**. Also, any minor amount of oil dispersed in the water phase may be permitted to separate here and withdraw from the top, if desired.

The tar sand is contacted with the up-flowing stream including all of the solvent, recycle water and steam introduced to the extraction vessel as is shown generally at **300**. Here the relative velocities of the down-flowing sand and up-flowing steam should be such that the tar sand is fluidized sufficiently to permit good effective tar sand-extractant contact but insufficiently active to dislodge fines which are attached to the sand particles. This is an important aspect of the process since it reduces the amount of fines which must be removed in the water phase and helps assure that the hydrocarbon phase has a minimum of fines. Thus, many fines can remain with the sand as fines attached to the sand particles.

The sand, which is free of solvent and soluble chemicals following the steam scouring, continues its down-flow against the incoming recycle water containing concentrated agglomerated clay and silt fines. As shown at **400**, the sand particles are merely sufficiently suspended and fluidized to act as a filter medium for removing agglomerated fines from the recycle steam. The fluid velocity in the extraction vessel will vary with the other process conditions which are dependent upon the composition of the tar sand and the nature of the extractant fed to the system. In any event, the velocity should be great enough only to permit uniform distribution of the extractant and desirably kept as low as possible for good extraction contact.

The sand containing the filtered silt, clay and other agglomerated fines settles to the bottom of the extraction vessel **24** where it is represented at **500**. Here it may be removed either by a drag type conveyor **44**, such as a screw conveyor, or pumped away as a slurry. The drag type conveyor is preferred in that it allows the removal of sand tailings containing a minimum amount of water and avoids the need for pumping abrasive slurries. Furthermore, any water remaining with the sand is likely to be hot and contain the additives of the system. These can be recovered by adding a cold water back-wash to the conveyor via a line **46** at the point of discharge **48**. As a consequence, not only are heat and conditioning chemicals retained in the system, but the sand and agglomerated fines tailings disposed of are free of possible pollutants.

Extraction Cell with Deflection Baffles

A process described by *R.A. Baillie, H.J. Davitt and D.E. Rose; U.S. Patent 3,986,592; Oct. 19, 1976; assigned to Great Canadian Oil Sands Limited, Canada* relates to an improved separation cell specifically designed for use in the hot water process for treating tar sands.

The separation cell comprises a circular tank with a bottom and a rotatable center shaft on the vertical axis of the tank from the top towards its bottom, an inlet means for charging tar sands pulp, an overflow recovery means at the top of the tank and a sand rake attached to the center shaft. The cell is also provided with a discharge outlet at the center of the lowest portion of the bottom of the cell for removing water and solids. The improvement of the process comprises a combination of two or more deflecting shed baffles one of which is located immediately above the sand rake and is referred to as the lower or lowest baffle. All baffles are concentric with the vertical shaft running through the cell. The lower shed baffle is located immediately above the sand rake support arms and can extend from the shaft to a point between the end of the sand rakes and their connecting point on the rotating shaft. The other baffles can be located between the lower shed baffle and the feed well along the vertical shaft. The lower shed deflecting baffle can be described as preferably being a saucer-shaped member preferably having a skirt at the outer periphery thereof and placed in an inverted position upon the sand rakes so that the skirt extends downward from the outer periphery of the saucer to a point between the baffle and the bottom of the tank.

The upper deflecting baffles can be defined as inverted saucer-shaped members concentric with the vertical shaft and located thereon between the feed well and the lower shed baffle immediately above the sand rake support arms. This improvement to the separation cell provides that when fresh tar sands pulp is fed into the cell, part of the feed which normally channels toward the bottom outlet is first deflected by the upper baffle into the intermediate portion of the cell. The remaining tar sands which continue to fall towards the sand outlet are deflected by the lower shed baffle into the middlings portion of the cell. This improvement increases residence time of most of the tar sands processed therein and thereby improves the separation of bitumen from the sand.

In Figure 6.3a, bituminous tar sands are fed into the system through line **1** where they first pass to a conditioning drum or muller **18**. Water and steam are introduced from **2** and mixed with the sands. The total water so introduced is a minor amount based on the weight of the tar sands processed and generally is in the range of 10 to 45 wt % of the muller mixture. Enough steam is introduced to raise the temperature in the conditioning drum to a temperature in the range of 130° to 210°F and preferably to above 170°F. Suitable alkaline reagent can also be added to the conditioning drum usually in amount of from 0.1 to 3.0 lb/ton of tar sand.

The amount of such alkaline reagent preferably is regulated to maintain the pH of the middlings layer in separator zone **21** within the range of 7.5 to 9.0. Best results seem to be obtained at a pH value of 8.0 to 8.5. The amount of the alkaline reagent that needs to be added to maintain a pH value in the range of 7.5 to 9.0 may vary from time to time as the composition of the tar sands as obtained from the mine site varies. The best alkaline reagents to use for this purpose are caustic soda, sodium carbonate or sodium silicate, although any of the other suitable alkaline reagents can be used if desired.

Mulling of the tar sands produces a pulp which then passes from the conditioning drum as indicated by line **3** to a screen indicated at **19**. The purpose of screen **19** is to remove from the tar sand pulp any debris, rocks or oversized lumps as indicated generally at **4**. The pulp then passes from screen **19** as indicated by **5** to a sump **20** where it is diluted with additional water from **6** and a middlings recycle stream **7**. Recycling of the middlings is not essential in all cases, particularly when the clay content of the tar sands is high. In this event a relatively high rate of fresh feed water introduction through **6** can be employed to compensate for the high clay content while a correspondingly high rate of transfer of middlings layer through line **11** as hereinafter described can be maintained. Under these circumstances recycling of the other stream of middlings through line **7** to the sump or conditioning drum is not required.

Figure 6.3: Hot Water Extraction Cell

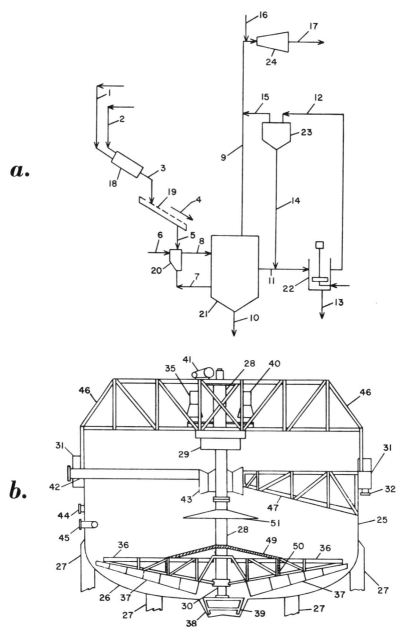

(a) Schematic representation of the hot water process
(b) Elevation view, partly in section, of the separation cell

Source: U.S. Patent 3,986,592

Modifications that may be made in the process as abovedescribed include sending a minor portion of the middlings recycle stream from line 7 through a suitable line to the conditioning drum 18 to supply all or a part of the water needed therein other than that supplied through condensation of the steam which is consumed. Also, if desired, a stream of the middlings recycle can be introduced onto the screen 19 to flush the pulp therethrough and into the sump.

The pulped and diluted tar sands are pumped from the sump 20 through line 8 into the separation zone 21. The separation zone comprises the improved settling cell of the process and will be described more in detail in reference to Figure 6.3b. The cell contains a relatively quiescent body of hot water which allows for the formation of a bitumen froth which rises to the cell top and is withdrawn via line 9, and a sand tailings layer which settles to the bottom to be withdrawn through line 10. An aqueous middlings layer between the froth and tailings layer contains silt and clay and some bitumen which failed to form froth. In order to prevent the buildup of clay in the system, it is necessary to continually remove some of the middlings layer and supply enough water in the conditioning operations to compensate for that so removed.

The amount of bitumen remaining in the middlings layer appears to be more or less related to the percentage of clay and/or silt present in the tar sands being processed, varying directly with the amount of clay and/or silt present. For example, typical oil recovery values for the froth from tar sands in which 15% of the mineral matter is less than 44 microns and from sands in which 25 to 30% is less than this size are respectively, 85% and 60%. For commercial operation it is highly desirable to obtain increased recoveries over such values as these which are obtainable heretofore by the hot water process. This is particularly true when the tar sands as mined contain a relatively high proportion of clay and silt components.

The oil-rich middlings stream withdrawn from separator 21 through line 11 is sent to a scavenger zone 22 wherein an air flotation operation is conducted to cause the formation of additional bitumen froth. Bitumen froth is passed from the scavenger zone 22 through line 12 to a froth settler zone 23. An oil-lean middlings stream is removed and discarded from the bottom of the scavenger zone 22 via line 13.

In the settler zone 23, the scavenger froth forms into a lower layer of settler tailings which is withdrawn and recycled via line 14 to be mixed with oil-rich middlings for feed to the scavenger zone 22 via line 11. In the settler zone, an upper layer of upgraded bitumen froth forms above the tailings and is withdrawn through line 15 and mixed with primary froth from line 9 for further processing. The use of gravity settling to upgrade scavenger cell froth is described in Dobson, Canadian Patent No. 857,306.

The combined froths are at a temperature of about 160°F. They are heated with a steam and diluted with sufficient naphtha or other diluent from 16 to reduce the viscosity of the bitumen for centrifuging in zone 24 to produce a bitumen product 17 suitable for further processing.

Details of the separation cell 21 are shown in Figure 6.3b. The cell consists of a tank 25 which can be employed in various forms. The tank shown is circular with an upwardly concave bottom 26 set on supports 27 and provided with rotatable shafts 28 and 30 arranged concentrically to one another on the vertical axis of tank 25. The tank is provided with an overflow launder 31 which is positioned at the top of the tank, peripherally around its circumference. This launder 31 is provided for receiving froth which is then discharged into an overflow outlet 32 for conveying through line 9 to the centrifuge zone 24 of Figure 6.3a.

The sand rake positioned on center shaft 28 consists of a plurality of support arms 36 with connected blades 37 which direct sand to the discharge cone 38 which is connected to the sand tailings discharge line 10 of Figure 6.3a. The cone scraper 39 is an optional feature of the cell and is attached to shaft 30 which is driven by motor 35. Shaft 28 is driven by motor 40. The lifting device and motor 41 provide another alternative feature in the cell and can be used to raise and lower the sand rake 36 to adjust to the level of the sand tailings layer. The pulp feed conduit 42 is attached to line 8 of Figure 6.3a and provides for delivering tar sands pulp through the tank 25 to the feed well 43 which is supported by feed well support 47.

The upper middlings conduit 44 is provided at the side of the tank 25 for conveying oil-rich middlings to line 11 of Figure 6.3a for secondary recovery in scavenger zone 22. The lower middlings conduit 45 is positioned at the side of the tank at a point lower than the upper middlings conduit 44. The lower middlings conduit removes middlings to line 7 for recycle to the sump 20. The recycle is used to maintain the viscosity or density of the middlings contained in the tank 25. Although only one lower middlings conduit 45 and one upper middlings conduit 44 are shown, a plurality of conduits provided around the circumference of the tank can be utilized. 46 is a walkway and handrail.

Attached to shaft 28 with which it is concentric and also attached to the sand rake support arms 36 is the lower shed deflection baffle 49 with the downwardly extending skirt 50 attached to the outer periphery of the baffle. This baffle is preferably saucer-shaped and in an inverted position. The baffle extends outwardly from the shaft thereby providing a means by which a part of the tar sands exiting from the feed well 43 is inhibited from channeling directly from the feed well into tailings exit 38.

Also attached to shaft 28 is one or more upper shed deflecting baffles 51 defined as inverted saucer-shaped members affixed to and concentric with the center shaft and located at any point between the feed well 43 located in the upper portion of the separation cell and the lower shed baffle 49 located immediately above the sand rake support arms 36. Although only one upper shed deflecting baffle is shown in Figure 6.3b, this is merely illustrative and represents at least one baffle and can be defined to include two to ten shed baffles.

The following example defined in connection with Figure 6.3a, illustrates, in a general way, a hot water process utilizing the separation cell. On an hourly basis a sufficient amount of the tar sands to give 1,000 tons in the feed after screening is fed via base line 1, along with 300 tons of water and steam fed via line 2, into a conditioning drum 18. The mixture is heated to about 180°F while being mulled. The resulting pulp is passed through a screen 19 which rejects material of a size ¾ inch and larger as indicated at 4. At a sump 20 the screened pulp is mixed continuously with hot water from line 6 at 190°F in the amount of 500 tons and with a middlings recycle stream from line 7 in the amount of 2,000 tons. The diluted pulp is then pumped via line 8 to a separation zone 21 which comprises a single tank with an upwardly concave bottom. The tank also contains rotatable center shafts connected to a sand rake and has a shed deflection baffle attached to the shaft at the bottom of the tank. The sand rake rotates at about 0.5 rpm. In the cell the diluted pulp separates into a bitumen froth which floats to the top of the tank which overflows into a launder and into a sand layer which falls to the bottom of the tank and is raked to a discharge outlet.

Sand tailings are removed from the tank at the rate of about 1,020 tph and froth is removed from the launder at a rate of about 40 tph. A bitumen content in the froth corresponding to a recovery of more than 60% of the bitumen in the original tar sands is obtained. A stream of oil-rich middlings in the amount of 740 tph is withdrawn from the tank through an outlet **44** and transferred via line **11** to a scavenger zone **22** where it is subject to air flotation. Additional oil froth is obtained from the secondary recovery in an amount of 170 tph and is withdrawn via line **12**. About 965 tph of oil-lean middlings are withdrawn and discarded from zone **22** via line **13**. The secondary froth is settled in separation cell **23** and added to the primary froth in line **9** via line **15** to give a recovery of oil from the tar sands of an overall value of greater than 90%.

Digester and Flotation Cell

A process described by *J.D. Miller and J.E. Sepulveda; U.S. Patent 4,120,776; October 17, 1978; assigned to University of Utah* relates to separating bitumen from Utah tar sands or tar sands with a negligible connate water content. Bitumen displacement from the sand grains of the tar sands is accomplished by digesting the tar sands under controlled conditions. The controlled conditions in the digester include the percent solids, the pH range as determined by the concentration of the particular wetting agent, and the temperature. A high shear force field in the digester is obtained by maintaining the percentage of solids in the range of 65 to 80%, and, in no case less than 50%. The wetting agent in the digester is maintained in the range of 0.2 N to 1.0 N with the most effective range being 0.5 N to 0.8 N.

The temperature of the aqueous/solids mixture in the digester is maintained above 70°C and, preferably, near the boiling point of the aqueous solution. After digestion, separation is achieved in a separation or flotation cell wherein additional water serves as a diluent to lower the solids concentration below about 50% solids and the temperature to near ambient. Preferably, the pH in the flotation cell is maintained above pH 10. Air is diffused into the separation cell to assist in lifting the bitumen to the surface where it may be collected.

Disc Recycling Centrifuge System and Transfer Agent

G.P. Canevari; U.S. Patent 3,893,907; July 8, 1975; assigned to Exxon Research and Engineering Company describes a centrifuging method of separating oil or bitumen from tar sands which utilizes a relatively small quantity of transfer agent and which results in relatively high yields of oil or bitumen. In accordance with the general features of the process, a tar sand froth is centrifuged to provide an overflow effluent comprising an oil or bitumen phase and an underflow effluent comprising water and bitumen-wetted solids. The underflow effluent is reintroduced into the centrifuge in a recycling circuit and a water-wetting transfer agent is combined with the underflow effluent in the recycling circuit to cause the solids to become water-wet and transfer from an oil/water interface to a water phase which is then rejected.

In accordance with more particular features of the process, the underflow effluent is recycled in a disc centrifuge and a water-wetting transfer agent is mixed and contacted with the recycled underflow. The transfer agent is mixed in the recycle circuit in an amount ranging from about 0.01 to 1.0 wt % and preferably between about 0.1 and 0.5 wt %. The underflow effluent represents a concentrate to which a relatively small amount of transfer agent is added in order to obtain the desired wetting relative to the quantity which would be required when added to the input to the stage.

The quantities of transfer agent added to the underflow in the recycle circuit is on the order of one-tenth of that quantity which would be required to be added to a froth which is initially charged to the inlet of the centrifuge to provide a substantially equivalent separation. A significant reduction in the material and cost of the separation thus accompanies the enhanced separation.

A demulsifying agent is also added to the inlet to the centrifuging stage for enhancing the separation of the bitumen oil from the tar sand froth. A recycling disc-type centrifuge is provided having means for increasing contact of the recycled underflow and thereby enhancing separation.

Example 1: Whole tar sands were slurried with hot water (180°F) and mixed. The residue, or washed sands, were then mixed with 3 parts of water to produce a 25% solids concentration slurry. An amount of tetrasodium pyrophosphate "transfer agent" was added equivalent to approximately 0.5 wt % based on the total liquid-solid slurry. This treated slurry was then mixed in a Waring blender for approximately 20 seconds to simulate the contacting/mixing that would occur in the underflow recycle. The mixture was then transferred to a laboratory centrifuge and maintained at 1,000 *g* for 2 minutes. At the end of this interval, free bitumen was observed floating on the surface of the centrifuge tube.

The following illustrates the degree of bitumen recovery by this process: bitumen content of tar sand feedstock, 10.4%; bitumen content of residue tar sand after lab hot water wash, 0.48%; and bitumen content of tar sand after treatment by transfer agent, 0.06%. Therefore, effectiveness of bitumen recovery from tailings =

$$\frac{0.48 - 0.06}{0.48} = 87.5\%$$

Example 2: In a repeat laboratory simulation experiment, the pH of the hot water wash was adjusted to 9.5 by the addition of approximately 1 wt % NaOH. Subsequent experimental steps described in Example 1 were repeated and yielded the following results: bitumen content of tar sand feedstock, 10.4%; bitumen content of residue tar sand after lab hot water (pH = 9.5) wash, 0.12%; and bitumen content of residue tar sand after treatment by transfer agent, 0.03%. Therefore, effectiveness of bitumen recovery from tailings =

$$\frac{0.12 - 0.03}{0.12} = 75\%$$

In this second example, a more complete recovery of bitumen had been obtained in the extraction step. Hence, the recovery of the smaller amount of bitumen remaining in the tailing is more difficult (75% vs 87.5%) but still practical.

Two-Stage Separation System

A process described by *L.M.O. Cymbalisty; U.S. Patent 3,935,076; January 27, 1976; assigned to Canada-Cities Service, Ltd., Atlantic Richfield Canada Ltd. and Gulf Oil Canada Ltd., Canada* involves the hot water process for recovering bitumen from tar sand. The aqueous slurry of tar sand is introduced into a first vessel, termed the sand separation cell, containing a body of hot water. The coarse sand settles out and is discharged as tailings. The top product, comprising bitumen, water and fine sand, is transferred to a second vessel, termed the froth formation cell, containing a second body of hot water.

In this latter cell, the bitumen forms froth and is recovered, and the fine solids and some water are recycled to the lower end of the sand separation cell. Because the coarse sand has previously been removed in the sand separation cell, good distribution of the feed across the cross-sectional area of the froth formation cell is achieved. This leads to good recoveries and froth quality. By recycling the fines from the froth formation cell to the vicinity of the tailings outlet of the sand separation cell, the fines can be eliminated from the system without the need for a middlings dragstream, as is required in the prior art.

Superatmospheric Pressure Aeration

H.J. Davitt; U.S. Patent 3,963,599; June 15, 1976; assigned to Sun Oil Company of Pennsylvania describes a method for improved recovery of bitumen from aqueous streams associated with the hot water process for extracting bitumen from tar sands. It has been discovered that by aerating an aqueous stream containing bitumen at a pressure above atmospheric, suddenly reducing the pressure on the mixture and settling the mixture at a pressure lower than the pressure at which the stream was aerated, improved recovery of bitumen is obtained.

More particularly it has been discovered that by aerating an aqueous stream of tar sands pulp at superatmospheric pressure or aerating an effluent discharge stream from a hot water process for extracting bitumen from tar sands at superatmospheric pressure and thereafter settling the aerated stream at a lower pressure, improved recovery of bitumen is realized.

In one mode of the process, it has been discovered that by aerating a mixture of bitumen, minerals and water, at a temperature in the range of 40° to 200°F at a relatively high pressure, e.g., above atmospheric, and thereafter settling the mixture at a lower pressure, the recovery of bitumen froth from the stream is enhanced. It has been found that by aerating a tar sands pulp under pressure and thereafter settling the pulp in a hot water extraction vessel at a lower pressure, e.g., atmospheric pressure, recovery of bitumen froth is improved when compared to settling a pulp without the relatively high pressure aeration step.

Further, it has been discovered that the efficiency of the hot water extraction process can also be increased if the middlings stream normally found in the hot water extraction primary settling vessel is subject to relatively high pressure aeration and subsequently settled at a lower pressure. Also it has been found that treating bitumen-containing effluent discharge streams in this manner provides a means of recovering bitumen from those streams.

Example 1: In the hot water extraction process practiced as described in Canadian Patent No. 841,581, tar sands containing approximately 9% bitumen are fed into a hot water extraction process at the rate of 2,000 tph. A total of approximately 1,000 tph of hot water and 60 tph of steam are added to the tar sands in the conditioning stage. In the primary settling step of this process, approximately 117 tph of froth are recovered. In the secondary froth extraction process known as the air scavenger zone, approximately 38 tph of froth are recovered providing a total of 155 tph of bitumen recovered. An evaluation of this process points out that the primary separation vessel provides about 65% recovery of the bitumen in the feed material and the secondary bitumen recovery phase provides an additional 21% recovery with the total recovery overall being approximately 86% of the bitumen fed to the process.

Example 2: As a means of comparison, substantially identical tar sands as described in Example 1 above are fed into a hot water extraction process as in Example 1 at the rate of 2,000 tph. A total of approximately 1,000 tph of hot water and 60 tph of steam are added to the tar sands in the conditioning stage. The tar sands-water mixture is thereafter aerated at a pressure of 45 psig for about 2 minutes while being transferred through a pipe to a primary settling zone maintained at atmospheric pressure. The aerated mixture prior to entering the settling zone passes through a constriction in the line to effect a sudden release of pressure as the mixture enters the settling zone.

Approximately 137 tph of bitumen froth are recovered in the primary settling zone. The middlings material from the settling zone is transferred to an air scavenger zone where an additional 25 tph of bitumen froth is recovered to provide a total recovery of 162 tph of bitumen from the process. Thus, by this process 90% of the bitumen in the tar sands fed into the process is recovered, which represents a substantial improvement over the prior art as illustrated in Example 1.

Aerated Scavenged Middlings as Conditioner

J.C. Anderson; U.S. Patents 4,018,665; April 19, 1977; and 3,951,779; April 20, 1976; both assigned to Great Canadian Oil Sands Ltd., Canada describes a process which comprises utilizing the bitumen-depleted middlings stream recovered from an air scavenger zone to dilute the tar sands-water mixture prior to separating bitumen from the tar sands in the primary extraction zone of a hot water process for recovering bitumen from tar sands. Bitumen-depleted middlings material recovered from an air scavenger zone of the hot water process contains entrained air bubbles as a result of the scavenger zone aeration. When this aerated stream is added to a tar sand-water mixture prior to separation in a hot water extraction cell, the air bubbles added via the middlings stream aid in flotation of bitumen in the extraction cell thereby improving recovery of bitumen therefrom.

Normal recovery of bitumen from tar sands in the primary extraction zone of the above-defined hot water process lies in the range of 80 to 90 wt % based on the quantity of bitumen in the tar sands. By the improvement of the process, an increase in recovery of bitumen from the primary extraction step in the order of 0.5 to 1.0% and above can be realized.

Thus, the process provides an improved process for the recovery of bitumen from tar sands comprising the steps:

(1) forming a mixture of tar sands and water including that of the specified recycle stream of aerated bitumen-depleted middlings material;

(2) settling the mixture in a separation zone to form an upper bitumen froth layer, a middlings layer containing water, silt, clay and bitumen, and a sand tailings layer;

(3) separately removing the bitumen froth layer and the sand tailings layer;

(4) passing a stream of middlings layer into an air scavenger zone and aerating the stream to provide additional bitumen froth;

(5) recovering the froth from the scavenger zone; and

(6) removing the bitumen-depleted middlings stream from the air scavenger zone and utilizing at least a part thereof as the recycle stream in forming the mixture of step (1).

J.C. Anderson and H.J. Davitt; U.S. Patent 3,969,220; July 13, 1976; both assigned to Great Canadian Oil Sands Limited, Canada and Sun Oil Company of Pennsylvania describe a hot water process for extracting bitumen from tar sands comprising forming a mixture of tar sands and water, settling the mixture in a primary extraction zone to form an upper bitumen froth layer, a middlings layer, and a sand tailings layer, and passing a part of the middlings layer to an air scavenger zone to recover additional bitumen. The improvement comprises aerating the mixture of tar sands and water before separating bitumen froth from the mixture in a gravity settling zone. This aeration can be accomplished by adding an aerated recycle middlings stream to the tar sands-water mixture prior to the settling step.

Heating and Deaeration

T.C.A. Hann; U.S. Patent 4,033,853; July 5, 1977; assigned to Great Canadian Oil Sands Limited, Canada has developed an apparatus suitable for collecting, heating and deaerating raw bituminous froth prior to upgrading that froth to synthetic crude oil. Raw bituminous froth normally contains 30 to 70 volume percent air and is reasonably viscous at the temperature at which it is normally recovered, i.e., 120° to 180°F. Therefore, it is very difficult to transfer froth by ordinary methods such as pumping. However, if the froth is heated, and deaerated and diluted with a less viscous hydrocarbon liquid prior to transferring the froth from the recovery area, the treated froth is substantially easier to upgrade to synthetic crude oil.

Referring to Figure 6.4, bituminous froth containing 30 to 70% by volume of air is transferred from hot water extraction separation cells **10** to collection zone **12** via lines **11** and **14**, respectively. The froth is quite viscous at 150°F having a viscosity of about 2,000 cp. The froth flows by gravity to collection zone **12**. Froth collection zone **12** can be any vessel suitable for storing liquids which has an inlet and an outlet for the addition and withdrawal of liquids. Preferably the inlet **27** is located in the upper part of zone **12** and the outlet **26** is located in the lower section thereof. By this arrangement withdrawal of liquids from the zone can be aided by gravity.

Figure 6.4: Apparatus for Heating and Deaerating Bituminous Froth

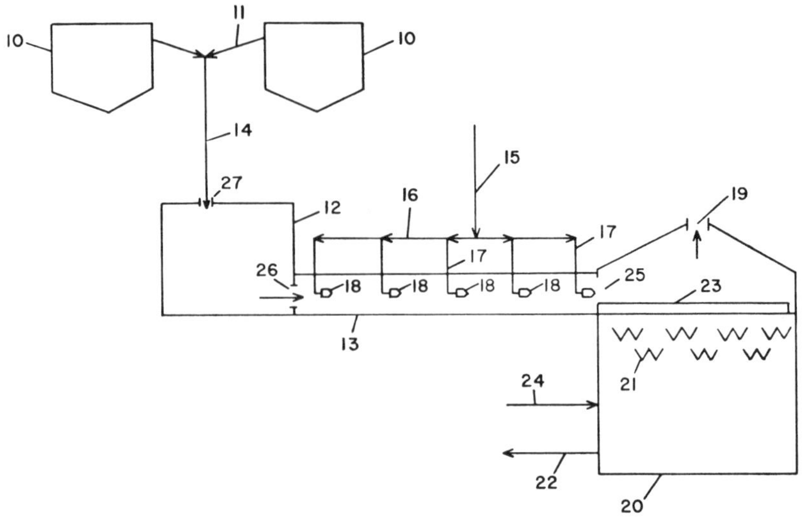

Source: U.S. Patent 4,033,853

Communicating with the outlet **26** of zone **12** is conduit **13** wherein the froth is heated and transferred to deaeration zone **20**. Conduit **13** can be a pipe or tube suitable for transporting liquids. Disposed within conduit **13** are steam injection means **18** which can be any nozzle suitable for providing steam under pressure into conduit **13**. Steam injection means **18** are positioned in conduit **13** to provide steam under pressure directed towards the outlet end of the conduit thereby propelling the froth through the conduit while concurrently heating the froth. Steam is supplied to injection means **18** via line **15**, **16** and **17**, respectively.

As noted above, the inlet end of conduit **13** communicates with the outlet **26** of zone **12**. The outlet of conduit **13** communicates with the inlet means of deaeration zone **20** at inlet **25**. Conduit **13** can be parallel to the plane of the horizontal axis or can be disposed at an angle of up to 10° from the horizontal axis with the outlet of the conduit being above the inlet. When a liquid such as bituminous froth is heated in conduit **13** the entrapped air rises to the upper section in the conduit and tends to migrate to the highest level in the conduit. Thus, preferably the conduit has its outlet raised higher than the inlet to promote flow of gas pockets in the direction of the outlet rather than in the inlet direction.

Deaeration zone **20** can be any tank or other facility suitable for storing liquids having an inlet means **25** in the upper end and a liquid withdrawal means **22** at the lower end. Also zone **20** can be an open top tank or have a top with a vent **19** as illustrated in the figure. Disposed in the upper end of deaeration zone **20** is distributor means **23**, which serves to disperse the froth preferably over the entire cross section of deaeration zone 20 thereby permitting the froth to cascade down over baffles 21 into the lower section of deaeration zone 20. Distribution means 23 can be any of the various structures such as a box with a perforated bottom or a series of channels having weirs whereby the froth overflows the weir onto the baffles 21.

Air bubbles formed in the froth as a result of the steam injection are released from the froth as it cascades over the baffles in zone 20. The heated deaerated froth collects in the lower section of zone 20 wherein it can be mixed with a liquid hydrocarbon diluent from line 24 and transferred by pumping or other means for further processing via exit line 22.

The improvement realized in the apparatus and method substantially lies in the transfer of the froth via injected steam propulsion from the collection zone to the deaeration zone through the heating transfer conduit. Also, the deaeration zone provides efficient release of entrapped gasses from the froth by the cascading effect achieved through the distribution means within the deaeration zone. The distribution means within the deaeration can be any arrangement which disperses the heated froth over the cross section of the deaeration zone.

S.K. Opoku; U.S. Patent 3,998,702; December 21, 1976; assigned to Great Canadian Oil Sands Limited, Canada describes a method and apparatus for upgrading bituminous froth recovered via hot water extraction of tar sands. Specifically, it has been discovered that collecting bituminous froth in a special collection apparatus affixed to a hot water extraction separation cell provides bituminous froth with substantially improved flow properties and pumping characteristics. The apparatus of the process comprises an improved hot water extraction separation cell launder which contains a plurality of steam injection means for concurrently heating and deaerating the bituminous froth as it is collected in the launder prior to being further processed. Also, the process provides a gravity flow conduit in which bituminous froth can be heated and deaerated while being transferred from a separation cell to a collection zone.

Stagewise Dilution with Liquid Hydrocarbon

F.C. Stuchberry and A.E. Backstrom; U.S. Patent 4,035,282; July 12, 1977; assigned to Shell Canada Limited, Canada and Shell Explorer Limited have found that diluent losses can be reduced and a higher quality bitumen product obtained in the bitumen recovery phase of the hot water, tar sands separation process wherein bituminous froth is diluted with a liquid hydrocarbon and subject to a two-stage centrifuging, if the liquid hydrocarbon solvent is added in stagewise fashion before each centrifuging stage such that no more than 90% of the total solvent charge is added to the bituminous froth prior to the first centrifuging stage.

By staging the liquid hydrocarbon solvent dilution of the bituminous froth in the manner described, inherent diluent losses in the first stage of centrifuging are reduced since less of the total diluent requirement for bitumen recovery is passed through this centrifuging stage. Further, since less liquid hydrocarbon solvent is added to the bituminous froth prior to the first stage centrifuging, less water-hydrocarbon diluent emulsion is formed in that stage and the consequent loss of emulsified diluent in the second stage centrifuging is reduced. Finally, by staged addition of diluent to the bituminous froth, much better control over the final diluent to bitumen ratio is possible since the quality of diluent added to the diluted bituminous froth prior to second-stage centrifugation can be varied to compensate for differences in the quality and quantity of bituminous froth passed to the bitumen recovery phase of the process in continuous plant operation.

Better control of the final diluent to bitumen ratio not only produces a high quality bitumen product, but also allows a smaller quantity of diluent to be used since it is unnecessary to maintain a larger than required diluent to bitumen ratio as a safety factor against variations in bituminous froth composition and feed rate which is required when diluent is added at a single point in the process. Smaller diluent volumes in the centrifuging stages lead to supplemental economic advantages in the overall process because fewer and/or smaller centrifuges are needed to purify a given volume of bitumen and less energy is required for downstream removal of diluent from the bitumen stream.

The liquid hydrocarbon solvent used to dilute the bituminous froth in the process is rather conventional in nature, it only being required that the solvent be substantially nonmiscible with water and be sufficiently volatile to be readily recoverable from the bitumen by distillation. Preferably, the hydrocarbon solvent should not be so volatile that it presents a potential safety hazard in the process. Suitable liquid hydrocarbon solvents include those boiling in the 200° to 600°F range such as naphthas, kerosenes, gas oils, light cycle oils and other intermediate refinery fractions. Preferably the liquid hydrocarbon solvent is naphtha.

Preferably, this solvent charge is divided such that between about 75 and about 85% of the total solvent employed is added to the bituminous froth prior to first-stage centrifuging. By dividing the solvent flow in this preferred manner, adequate viscosity reduction and separation of larger mineral particles is assured in the first centrifuging stage while at the same time minimizing solvent losses through the centrifuging process.

Ketones as Deemulsifier

J.L. Moyer; U.S. Patent 3,884,829; May 20, 1975; assigned to Great Canadian Oil Sands, Ltd., Canada has discovered that the method of purifying bitumen froth by centrifuging the froth to remove water and mineral matter can be substantially enhanced by the addition of a C_{3-7} ketone to the froth prior to the centrifuging procedure. Specifically, it has been discovered that by the addition of a C_{3-7} ketone to a petroleum naphtha diluent which is thereafter added to the bitumen froth, the efficiency of the centrifuging step is substantially improved to provide a bitumen product having a substantial quantity of the water and mineral impurities removed.

The ketone additives are the C_{3-7} ketones including acetone, 2-butanone, 2-pentanone, 3-pentanone, 2-hexanone, 3-hexanone, 2-heptanone and 3-heptanone. The ketone used should be at least slightly soluble in water. The preferred ketones are acetone and 2-butanone. As a practical matter, the ketone additive should have a boiling point lower than 500°F. The C_{3-5} ketones including acetone, 2-butanone, 2-pentanone and 3-pentanone are the preferred ketone additives in the method and compositions of this process.

Example 1: A liter of bituminous froth containing 38 volume % water and 4 volume % mineral matter is diluted with 500 ml of petroleum naphtha having a boiling range of 150° to 480°F. The mixture is agitated until substantially homogeneous and subsequently a 100 ml aliquot is withdrawn and subjected to centrifugal forces for 20 minutes in a centrifuge rotating at 1,700 rpm. The aliquot is observed to separate into three separate phases which are 1 ml of solids, 15 ml of water and 84 ml of froth.

Example 2: A bituminous froth identical to the froth of Example 1 is prepared in the same manner with the exception that the naphtha diluent contains 50 volume % acetone. The froth is centrifuged as in Example 1. The product after centrifuging comprises three phases which are 3.5 volume % mineral matter, 34 volume % water with some acetone dissolved therein and the remainder froth.

Reduction of Water Content in Froth

R.A. Baillie; U.S. Patents 3,900,389; August 19, 1975 and 3,901,791; August 26, 1975; both assigned to Great Canadian Oil Sands Limited, Canada describes a method for upgrading bituminous froth recovered from tar sands via hot water extraction techniques. The essence of the process is the combined steps of centrifuging diluted bitumen froth and subsequently settling the centrifuge froth product at an elevated temperature in the range of 300° to 1000°F using a liquid hydrocarbon diluent boiling in the range of 350° to 750°F. These combined steps provide efficient processing of the froth at substantially good volume throughput rates. Also, because of its higher boiling range, less diluent is lost in aqueous waste streams by the process as compared to methods using diluents having a lower boiling range.

Example: Referring to Figure 6.5, a raw bitumen froth provided via line **11** is diluted with a hydrocarbon diluent having a boiling range of 350° to 750°F added via line **12** into line **13**. The diluted froth is transferred to scroll centrifuge **15** via line **14**. The feed to scroll centrifuge **15** can also contain recycled tailings from hereinafter defined autoclave settling zone **19** which are provided by line **22** into line **14**. Scroll centrifuge **15** provides a tailings stream containing water and mineral matter which is removed via line **16** and discarded. Also, a scroll centrifuge froth is recovered via line **17** and transferred to heat exchange **18** wherein the froth is heated to a temperature in the range of 300° to 1000°F and thereafter transferred into autoclave settling zone **19**.

In autoclave settling zone **19**, the froth is permitted to settle to provide an upper bitumen froth layer, a lower tailings layer containing mineral matter, water, and bitumen, and an intermediate water layer substantially comprised of water containing minor quantities of bitumen and mineral matter. The bitumen froth product substantially reduced in mineral matter and water is recovered via line **20** from autoclave settling zone **19**. Water is recovered from autoclave settling zone **19** via line **21** and can be discarded or recycled to other processes requiring the use of fresh water.

The lower layer in autoclave settling zone **19** is comprised of mineral matter and water and some bitumen and is withdrawn via line **22** and transferred to line **14** where it can be combined with the diluted froth feed being fed to scroll centrifuge **15**. Alternately, the tailings from autoclave settling zone **19** withdrawn via line **22** can be discarded via line **27**.

Figure 6.5: Processing of Bitumen Froth

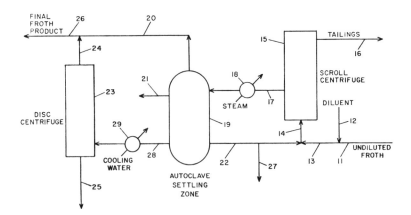

Source: U.S. Patent 3,900,389

In autoclave settling zone **19**, a substantial separation of bitumen from water and mineral matter is accomplished. Further, the tailings from this autoclave separation zone can be recycled to the scroll centrifuge and thus provide additional bitumen recovery. The product withdrawn via line **20** is of sufficient quality to be suitable for coking, hydrovisbreaking, or any of the many petroleum refining techniques normally applied to this type of feed material. Typically, this final bitumen froth product contains at least 96% hydrocarbon and no more than 0.5% mineral matter and 3.5% water. The advantages of this froth refining technique are particularly realized in the greater volume throughput of froth as well as the improved quality of the bitumen froth product as compared to other well-known techniques.

Thus, generally the process comprises (1) diluting a bitumen froth containing mineral matter and water with a liquid hydrocarbon boiling in the range of 350° to 750°F; (2) centrifuging the diluted froth to provide a centrifugal tailings stream and a centrifuge froth product; (3) settling the centrifuge froth product in an autoclave settling zone at a temperature in the range of 300° to 1000°F and a pressure in the range of 0 to 1,000 psig; and (4) recovering a bitumen froth product substantially reduced in mineral matter and water from the settling zone. This process can additionally and optionally include the step (5) recovering a tailings product from the settling zone comprised of mineral matter, water, and bitumen and recycling the tailings to the centrifuge of step (2).

Dry Distillation of Residue as Heat Source

R. Rammler, P. Schmalfeld and H.-J. Weiss; U.S. Patent 4,098,674; July 4, 1978 and R. Rammler and H.-J. Weiss; U.S. Patent 4,054,492; October 18, 1977; both assigned to Metallgesellschaft AG, Germany describe a process for the recovery of hydrocarbonaceous materials from tar sand. The process comprises subjecting a part of the tar sand to hot water extraction by mixing it with hot water, the solids and bitumen being separated and the latter treated further, and carrying out a dry distillation of another part of the tar sand which is thereby heated to temperatures above 400°C, the gaseous and vaporous distillation products being cooled and condensed. This process is characterized in that at least a portion of the thermal energy required for hot water extraction originates in the dry distillation waste heat. This process is further characterized in that the solid coke-like residue recovered from the further treatment of the bitumen from hot water extraction is used as fuel in the dry distillation and in that the wet solids recovered from hot water extraction are mixed with the dry distillation residue to form a solid product which can be transported on belt conveyors.

The dry distillation of tar sand, oil shale or other bituminous or oil-bearing materials is described, for instance, in the German Patents 1,809,874 and 1,909,263 and in the corresponding Canadian Patents 920,080 and 928,654. In this process a finely granulated heat carrier, heated to about 600° to 800°C, is mixed with the material to be distilled so that a mixing temperature of above 400°C, usually between 450° and 650°C, is established. At this temperature the bituminous or oil-bearing material is distilled followed by cooling and condensation of the vapors. The finely granulated distillation residue or an external granulated material with a grain size of preferably between 2 and 15 mm can be used as heat carrier. The processes yield dry solid residue, and a large portion of the thermal energy can be recovered from the hot gases, vapors and residue.

Referring to Figure 6.6, rotary drum 1 is supplied with tar sand through feed line 2, and with hot water and steam through feed lines 3 and 4, respectively, the tar sand being mixed with water and heated. The mixture, through line 5, enters separator 6 where initial separation of liquid and solids takes place. The bulk of the solids is discharged as a sludge with about 40% water through line 7, while the bituminous material containing little solids and water is withdrawn from separator 6 and supplied through line 8 to a further separation step 9 consisting of centrifuges.

Figure 6.6: Combined Hot Water Extraction and Dry Distillation Process

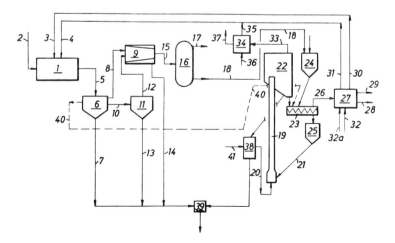

Source: U.S. Patent 4,098,674

A bitumen/water sludge is withdrawn from the middle of separator **6** and routed through line **10** to a further separator **11** for separation into bitumen and sludge. The bitumen still containing little dust and water is supplied through line **12** also to separation step **9** where it is purified, jointly with the bitumen coming directly from separator **6**, to a dust content of about 1% and a water content of about 5%. The sludge from separator **11** is withdrawn through line **13**. The sludge occurring in separation step **9** is withdrawn through line **14** and combined with the sludge from lines **7** and **13**.

The bituminous materials extracted from the tar sand require aftertreatment to increase the yield of valuable low-boiling hydrocarbons. Therefore, through line **15** they enter coker **16** where they are heated and partially cracked. The heating temperatures range between about 550° and 650°C. The distillate produced in coker **16** passes out line **17**. At the same time, a considerable quantity of petroleum coke is produced.

As the starting material usually contains dust and sulfur compounds, the coke produced in coker **16** also contains ash and sulfur. Its further use is therefore problematic, but it can be employed as fuel for the dry distillation of the tar sand which will be described later on. For this purpose the coke, after passing through a grinding and/or screening facility, is supplied preferably through line **18** to storage bin **24** for the dry distillation tar sand feed. It is also possible to supply this coke directly to mixer **23** or to pneumatic conveying pipe **19** by paths not shown in the figure.

In the conveying pipe finely granulated solids consisting of circulating heat carrier and freshly produced distillation residue are carried upwards and thereby heated. The heat is supplied by burning carbon already contained in the distillation residue and petroleum coke from coker **16** with the addition of preheated air from line **20**. The sulfur content of the coke is not of disadvantage because the distillation residue used as circulating heat carrier usually contains sufficient calcium and/or magnesium oxide to absorb the SO_2 formed. When required, some lime and/or dolomite can be added to the feedstock (tar sand).

The distillation residue heated to about 600° to 800°C on ascending in pneumatic conveyor pipe **19** enters collecting bin **22** where it is separated from the combustion gases and accumulated in the bin lower section. The hot distillation residue is fed to mixer **23** which is preferably of the known double-shaft type or a rotary drum. This mixer is also supplied with an appropriate quantity of tar sand from storage bin **24** so that a mixing temperature of about 450° to 650°C is established at the end of the mixer. At these temperatures the volatiles are distilled from the tar sand. This devolatilization of the tar sand is continued in downstream postdevolatilizing vessel **25**.

The gaseous and vaporous products from the distillation zone proper, namely, mixer **23** and vessel **25**, are withdrawn through line **26** and, after preliminary dedusting, fed to condensation unit **27** where the desired product oil and gas are recovered and discharged through lines **28** and **29**. The waste heat from condensation unit **27** is utilized for the generation of hot water (line **30**) and steam (line **31**) from makeup water from line **32** and boiler feed water from line **32a**.

The combustion gases at about 600° to 800°C from collecting bin 22 are fed through line 33 to boiler 34 where steam (line 35) is generated from boiler feed water from line 36, and the combustion gases are cooled. The cooled waste gases leave boiler 34 through line 37 and are finally purified in a dust collector, not shown in the figure, before they are discharged to atmosphere.

The hot distillation residue is withdrawn from collecting bin 22 and, after cooling in air preheater 38, fed to mixer 39 to which the sludge from hot water extraction from lines 7, 13 and 14 is also charged. Air enters air preheater 38 through line 41 and flows at elevated temperature through line 20 to pneumatic conveying pipe 19. The distillation residue leaves air preheater 38 at about 150° to 300°C. As this distillation residue is water-free, it is suitable for mixing with wet residue which takes place in mixer 39. From mixer 39 the residue mixture can, for instance, be carried on belt conveyors to the dump. This eliminates the usual large settling basins for the sludge from hot water extraction which create an ever increasing environmental pollution problem.

The first separation step of hot water extraction consisting of rotary drum 1 and separator 6 yields a beneficiated tar sand from which part of the solids has been removed through line 7. This concentrated intermediate product is equally suitable for further processing in the dry distillation unit. The figure therefore shows phantom draw-off line 40 which leads to mixer 23 of the dry distillation unit and which indicates the possibility of feeding beneficiated tar sand to dry distillation, either in addition to the crude tar sand or as the sole feed material.

Dual Control System for Tailings Outlet

G.R. Lorenz; U.S. Patent 4,107,029; August 15, 1978; assigned to Canadian Minister of Energy, Mines and Resources, Alberta Syncrude Equity, Ontario Energy Corporation, Imperial Oil Limited, Canada-Cities Service, Ltd. and Gulf Oil Canada Limited, all of Canada has found that controlling the rate of withdrawal of tailings from a hot water process primary separation vessel with a rake torque sensor is attended by problems when the feed to the vessel is high in fine solids content.

It was also found that a nuclear density gauge was much better at controlling the withdrawal with the high fines feed, but did not work as well as rake torque control with low fines feed. Therefore the withdrawal is now controlled with a rake torque sensor when the vessel is receiving low fines feed and a density gauge when it is receiving high fines feed.

Referring to Figure 6.7, there is shown a primary separation vessel 1 having a launder 2 for removal of froth, a middlings conduit 3 for removal of middlings, and a tailings conduit 4 for removal of tailings. A rake 5, having a drive shaft 6, is centrally mounted in the vessel in conventional fashion. The rake is rotated by an electrically driven drive system 7. The rate of withdrawal of tailings is controlled by a constricting valve 8 downstream of a constant speed tailings pump 9. The constricting valve 8 is operated by a valve control 10 responsive to either a torque sensor 11, connected to the rake shaft 6, or a nuclear density gauge 12 attached to the tailings conduit 4. A torque sensor model 1104 (Lebow Associates Inc.) and a density gauge (Ohmart of Canada) have been successfully used for this purpose.

Figure 6.7: Dual Control System for Tailings Outlet of Separation Vessel

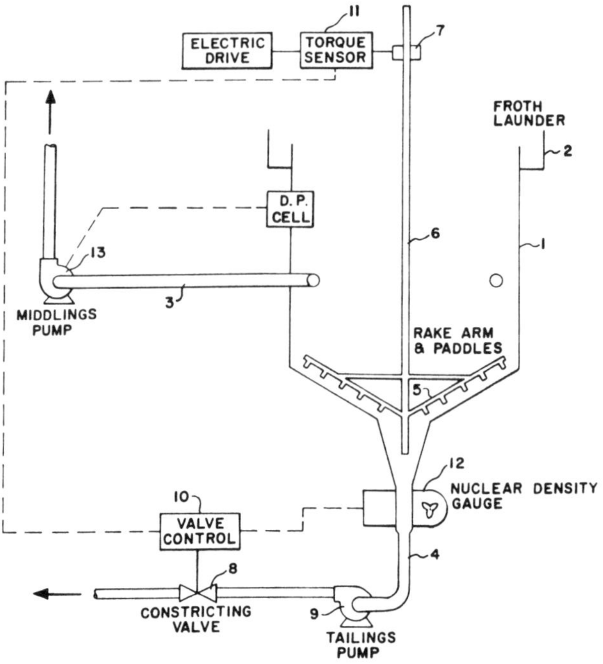

Source: U.S. Patent 4,107,029

A variable speed pump **13**, controlled by a differential pressure liquid-froth interface sensor, is used to withdraw middlings from the vessel to maintain the interface level generally constant. The process was developed as a result of observing the unstable operation and other known problems arising from feeding high fines feed to the vessel, and recognizing that the rake torque control was inaccurate in this environment. Experimentation showed that a nuclear density gauge could properly control the tailings withdrawal and that improved bitumen recoveries are obtained by using the gauge on the high fines feed. This is demonstrated by the following table, showing the results obtained when bituminous sands from the same source were processed at the same process conditions.

Samples Processed with Rake Torque Control

... Bituminous Sands ...		Primary	Combined
Bitumen	−325	Recovery	Recovery
.... (%)			
6.4	25.8	24.5	83.3
6.9	19.7	12.1	66.0
7.0	26.2	12.2	71.5
6.5	24.9	14.0	77.7
7.8	19.2	19.0	63.5

Samples Processed with Density Gauge Control

... Bituminous Sands ...		Primary	Combined
Bitumen	−325	Recovery	Recovery
......................(%)........................			
7.7	19.5	64.4	87.1
8.7	16.6	33.8	83.6
9.0	12.8	44.2	85.1
7.8	14.7	48.9	88.4
8.6	15.4	41.0	85.1

In this experience, rake torque control on the tailings outlet of the primary separation vessel is the preferred operating mode for bituminous sands containing less than 15 to 20% of the total solids as fines.

In related work, S. McQuitty; U.S. Patent 4,105,537; August 8, 1978; assigned to Canadian Minister of Energy, Mines and Resources, Alberta Syncrude Equity, Ontario Energy Corporation, Imperial Oil Limited, Canada-Cities Service, Ltd. and Gulf Oil Canada Limited, all of Canada describes a system for handling the underflow from a primary separation vessel. The process involves, for operating control and safety, a variable-speed close-coupled pump directly connected to the underflow of the primary separation vessel (PSV). The desired discharge density of the PSV is 70 to 80% solids in order to minimize bitumen losses. For a good pumping system, the pump discharge density should be less than 65% solids to avoid settling out of the solids in the downstream conduit. Therefore it is necessary to dilute the PSV underflow before it reaches the pump.

Secondary flotation tailings, a dilute stream containing a high proportion of fine solids, is used for this purpose. The solids content of the PSV underflow is monitored by one of two alternative systems, a torque recorder on the PSV rake shaft or a density gauge on the PSV underflow conduit. The former is used when the PSV is being fed low fines tar sand, the latter when it is treating high fines tar sand. The close-coupled pump speed is adjusted relative to the solids content measurement to keep it at the desired 70 to 80% level.

The density of the stream at the pump discharge is also monitored and the measurement is used to control the amount of secondary flotation tailings added. By the use of the controlled-speed, close-coupled pump, a closed system for controlling underflow density is provided. By using secondary tailings as diluent, water requirements for the process are reduced and a pumpable mixture is provided from which the solids do not readily settle out.

COLD WATER PROCESSES

Granular Sulfur and Water

A process described by E.J. Fuller; U.S. Patent 4,094,768; June 13, 1978; assigned to Exxon Research & Engineering Co. relates to a relatively low temperature process for recovering bitumen from tar sands which includes mixing the tar sands with granular sulfur and water in the presence of air thereby forming a sulfur-bitumen agglomerate which floats on the water and is then separated from the water and sand. The bitumen is recovered from the agglomerate by heating the sulfur-bitumen agglomerate to melt the sulfur and then separating the molten sulfur from the hot bitumen.

Example 1: 5 parts by weight of Athabasca tar sand containing 10 wt % bitumen were added into each of three glass containers. To each container was added an equal amount by weight of water at room temperature. Elemental sulfur having a particle size ranging from about 1 to 10 microns was added to two of the containers in an amount shown in the table on the following page and all three containers were closed and well shaken by hand. The containers were about ¾ full. The observations of this experiment are listed in the table, and show that the best visible agglomeration of the bitumen by the sulfur took place in container B wherein the bitumen completely agglomerated with the sulfur thereby releasing clean, bitumen-free sand and clean water.

Example 2: This experiment was conducted to study the effect of the amount of bitumen removed from Athabasca tar sands (as a sulfur-bitumen agglomerate) as a function of the amount of sulfur used in the process. The sulfur had a particle size of about 5 microns and water/tar sand ratio was approximately 2/1 by weight. The experiments were conducted at a temperature of 40°C (104°F) in a manner similar to that used in Example 1. That is, progressively increasing increments of sulfur were added to a series of glass containers along with tar sand and water. The containers were about ¾ full, were stoppered and shaken by hand. The sulfur-bitumen agglomerate floated on top of the water and the sand settled on the bottom. The containers were then frozen, broken and the sulfur-bitumen agglomerate separated from the water and sand. The sulfur-bitumen agglomerate was extracted with pentane in order to determine the bitumen content thereof. The results are plotted in Figure 6.8 and show the optimization of bitumen removal as a function of the amount of sulfur used via the relatively low temperature flotation process of this process.

Figure 6.8: Sulfur Flotation of Tar-Sand Bitumen at 104°F

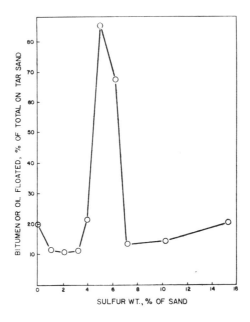

Source: U.S. Patent 4,094,768

	. . . . .Container.		
	A	B	C
Tar sand weight, g	5.0	5.0	5.0
Water weight, g	5.0	5.0	5.0
Sulfur weight, g	0	0.5	0.235
	. . . . .After Shaking.		
Surface of water	black, oil emulsion	clean	some emulsion particles ~$\frac{1}{8}$" diameter
Surface of sand	black, fine grains throughout	large black, single agglomerate; sand flows away	some particles on surface sand
Glass surface above water level	oil, sticky film	no film; isolated clumps of agglomerate	some agglomerates stuck to glass

Alkali Metal Silicate Catalyst

According to a process described by *J.W. Willard, Sr.; U.S. Patent 3,951,778; April 20, 1976; assigned to CAW Industries, Inc.* bituminous sands are intimately contacted with an aqueous medium containing a catalytically effective amount of a special catalyst to separate the bitumen at temperatures below the decomposition point of valuable hydrocarbons contained therein. Usually the temperatures of separation are not higher than 100°C and preferably are about 40° to 90°C. The catalyst may be prepared by steps including admixing a water-soluble alkali metal silicate with an aqueous medium containing carefully controlled amounts of dissolved water-soluble substances which are sources of calcium ion and magnesium ion, reacting the same to produce an aqueous colloidal suspension of the reaction product, admixing a micelle-forming surfactant with the aqueous medium, and agitating the aqueous medium containing the colloidal particles and surfactant to form catalyst-containing micelles.

Example 1: This example illustrates one preferred method for preparing the catalyst used in the process. Anhydrous calcium chloride in an amount of 0.66 g and magnesium sulfate heptahydrate in an amount of 1.32 g were dissolved in two liters of deionized water with stirring and warming until solution was complete. Then 95 g of sodium silicate pentahydrate having a molecular ratio of sodium oxide to silicon dioxide of 1:1 were added to the solution with stirring and continued warming to produce a white colloidal suspension of the reaction product.

After setting for 10 minutes, the colloidal suspension was heated to 80°C and sulfated castor oil in an amount of 50 g was added with stirring. The average molecular weight of the sulfated castor oil was 940 and it contained 50% water. The turbidity lessened somewhat as the colloidal suspension was heated at 80° to 90°C for one hour with vigorous stirring to produce catalyst micelles. The aqueous suspension of catalyst micelles thus prepared had a viscosity similar to that of water.

Example 2: This example illustrates the separation of bitumen from freshly mined unweathered bituminous sand taken from a deposit near Vernal, Utah known as Asphalt Ridge. The average bitumen content was 12.8 wt % as determined by extraction with carbon disulfide. The as-mined bituminous sand was reduced in particle size to –4 mesh and 64 lb thereof was soaked overnight at room temperature in 8 gallons of a diluted aqueous catalyst suspension. The diluted aqueous catalyst suspension was prepared by adding 1,000 gallons of water to one gallon of the catalyst suspension as prepared in accordance with Example 1. The bituminous sand was thoroughly penetrated by the diluted catalyst suspension and the bonds between the sand particles and bitumen were broken, thus allowing removal of the bitumen by gentle agitation.

The admixture of the aqueous catalyst suspension and the soaked bituminous sand was placed in a vessel and heated to 30°C with gentle agitation provided by a laboratory-type stirrer. At this temperature, a light oil separated and floated to the surface of the catalyst suspension which covered the bituminous sand. The first oily fraction was removed by skimming. The temperature was increased to 50°C and the gentle agitation was continued. A second oily fraction separated and floated to the surface of the catalyst suspension and was also removed by skimming. A third oily fraction was separated by raising the temperature to 75°C with continued gentle agitation.

The third oily fraction rose to the surface and was removed by skimming. The temperature of the catalyst suspension was then raised to 90° to 95°C with continued gentle agitation. The remainder of the bitumen separated and floated to the surface and was recovered by skimming. The residual sand was substantially free of bitumen as determined microscopically and thus the separation was complete.

The three oily fractions and the final heavy bitumen fraction were examined. It was found that the lightest oily constituents were recovered in the first fraction, an intermediate oily fraction was recovered as the second fraction, and a viscous heavy oil fraction was recovered as the third fraction. The final fraction did not have substantial oily properties and resembled tar or asphalt. Thus, the process is capable of removing substantially the entire bitumen content from the bituminous sand and, at the same time, fractionating the same into a plurality of fractions of increasing molecular weight and viscosity.

Example 3: This example illustrates the unique ability of the aqueous catalyst suspension in penetrating large pieces of bituminous sand and breaking the bonds between the bitumen and the sand particles. Pieces of the bituminous sand of Example 2 having a diameter of approximately four inches are soaked overnight in diluted aqueous catalyst suspension prepared in accordance with Example 1. The pieces of bituminous sand are thoroughly penetrated by the catalyst suspension and may be disintegrated by gentle agitation to release the bituminous content. The soaked pieces of bituminous sand are treated in accordance with Example 3 to recover the bitumen content. Comparable results are obtained and thus it is not always necessary to reduce the bituminous sand to small pieces in instances where sufficient time can be allowed for the catalyst suspension to penetrate the larger particles.

Alkali Metal Bicarbonate

A.R. Globus; U.S. Patent 4,120,777; October 17, 1978; assigned to Guardian Chemical Corporation describes a process for the recovery of bituminous tar-like materials from tar sands. The process includes mixing the tar sands with water, mildly heating the same in the presence of an alkali metal bicarbonate, gently mixing the mixture and while the mixture is warm, removing the recovered bituminous materials.

Example 1: Into a suitable mixing vessel there are charged 100 ft^3 of sand and 200 ft^3 of water previously heated to about 95°F, and 2% $KHCO_3$ based upon the weight of the sand-water mixture. The slurry thus formed is gently mixed and an exothermic reaction is initiated bringing the temperature to 130°F. In about ½ hour, the temperature begins to drop and there are formed three layers in the mixing vessel, the recovered tar forming the top layer, which is then withdrawn.

Example 2: The procedure of Example 1 is repeated except that the water layer is also withdrawn and charged with CO_2 under slight pressure and the thusly treated water recycled for another sand treatment.

Example 3: The procedure of Example 1 is repeated except that there is added to the sand 0.5 wt % of 1-(lauryldimethylammonio) acetate.

Sodium Silicate Wetting Agent

J.B. Fairbanks, Jr. and G.C. Brimhall; U.S. Patent 4,017,377; April 12, 1977 describe a process which includes the steps of passing the tar sand through or subjecting the same to a diluent, to reduce the internal fluid friction or viscosity of the oil layers surrounding each sand particle, and then bringing together the "sand," i.e., the sand particle plus its thinned oil layer, and an aqueous bath having a slightly raised specific gravity and also a wetting agent.

The purpose for the wetting agent is to allow the sand particles to fall to the bottom of the processing tank as sludge. The raised specific gravity of the water, which is still substantially less than that of seawater, causes the released globules or droplets of oil to be accelerated rapidly to the surface of the water, thereby escaping recapture or admixture with the descending sand particles. The now dilute oil is recovered, separated, and the diluent is reused in the tank. As to the wetting agent, sodium silicate is preferably used; optionally, Treatolite or another type of wetting agent may be employed. The following tests made are illustrative.

Uniform amounts of crushed tar sands, approximately filling an 8-oz cup, were placed in each of 6 containers labeled No. 1 to No. 6. 114 ml of clear diesel fuel as a diluent was premixed with the tar sands. Then 116 ml of an aqueous solution (No. 1) was added to containers No. 5 and No. 6 and the latter agitated for 30 seconds. The aqueous solution contained one drop, per ounce of water, of 40% sodium silicate solution and one-eighth ounce of soda ash per gallon of water (here equalling a specific gravity of 1.001).

In a separate container 50 ml of Great Salt Lake brine water was diluted with 150 ml of cold tap water to approximate the concentration of ocean water, and this (No. 2 solution) was added to containers No. 2 and No. 3 which were agitated for 30 seconds. All containers were allowed to stand for approximately 3 minutes. 160 ml of warm solution (No. 1) abovedescribed, at 90°F was added to container No. 4 and such container agitated for 30 seconds. Agitation was used to shorten the time of stratification and separation.

Containers No. 5 and No. 6 received additions of the abovedescribed (No. 1) aqueous solution, including the soda ash and sodium silicate. Container No. 1 received 150 ml of warm, equivalent ocean water (No. 2) and was agitated for 30 seconds. All containers were then allowed to stand for 3 minutes. The following results were obtained. Containers No. 5 and No. 6 showed clear separation and stratification of oil at the top, clear water in the center, and fairly clean white sand at the bottom. Container No. 4 showed excellent clean separation and stratification of tar and oil on top, clear water in the center, and fairly clean white sand at the bottom. Containers No. 1, No. 2 and No. 3 showed slight incomplete separation, sands were not clean in appearance, and the water and oil emulsion which resulted did not separate.

The crux of the process, therefore, is to provide a solvent whereby to reduce the viscosity and specific gravity of the oil trapped in a tar sand particle, and then raising the specific gravity of the water bath such that its specific gravity is between that of the now dilute oil and that of the sand particle. Hence, upon supplying the necessary wetting agent to effect an initial separation of the sand particle from the oil, then the dilute recovered oil bubbles rapidly upwardly through the water, whereas the sand drops down. The lighter the diluent, such as naphtha, the more effective the separation.

Ammonium Hydroxide in Tannic Acid Solution

E.B. Myers; U.S. Patent 3,953,317; April 27, 1976 describes compositions and methods for separating bituminous constituents from bitumen-bearing sands, commonly known as "tar sands" in which the composition comprises the product resulting from the addition of ammonium hydroxide with an aqueous solution of tannic acid. The method comprises the efficient intermixing, preferably by agitation, of the tar sands with the composition until the desired separation of the sand from the bituminous fraction is achieved, the rate of separation being increased by increasing the temperature of the composition, and separating the bituminous fraction from the composition.

Example 1: 2.0 g of tannic acid were added to 75 g of water. No ammonium hydroxide was added. Rather, the tannic acid solution without ammonia was heated to approximately 60°C and 50 g of tar sands derived from deposits in Athabasca Canada (18% bitumen) were introduced and agitated by hand for 2 to 3 minutes with very little separation of the bitumen fraction. Thereafter 0.293 g ammonia as 29% ammonium hydroxide was added to the tannic acid-tar sand mix without any significant increase in the separation of the bitumen fraction.

Example 2: 25 ml of an aqueous solution of tannic acid bearing 0.042 g of tannic acid per ml were added to 2.2 ml of 29% ammonium hydroxide. The resultant composition was added to 50 g of tar sand of the character of Example 1 having approximately 18 wt % bitumen. The entire mixture was then heated to approximately 90° to 95°C and moderately agitated with a mechanical agitator. Bitumen fraction separation commenced at approximately 65°C and at 90° to 95°C the sand sample appeared to be substantially completely separated from the bitumen fraction.

Example 3: 4.2 g of tannic acid were mixed with 100 ml of water. 4.4 ml of 29% ammonium hydroxide were added. The resultant composition was diluted to the extent that there was but 0.0139 g of tannic acid per ml of the composition. 50 g of tar sand of the character of Example 1 were then added to the diluted composition and the mixture heated to 90° to 95°C. Separation commenced at 60° to 70°C with moderate mechanical agitation with substantially complete separation at 90° to 95°C.

Separation of the mother liquor and bitumen fraction from the solid sand is a matter of choice depending upon other process parameters. The basic principals of the separation of solids from liquids are well known and need not be detailed further. Separation of the bitumen fraction from the mother liquor of ammonium tannate may be achieved by any one of a number of well-known techniques applicable to the separation of oily liquid hydrocarbons from a water-based diluent. These include decantation, centrifugation, distillation, absorption in mixed solvents, etc.

The ammonium tannate does not appear to suffer significant degradation during the separation process particularly if protected from actinic light. It is contemplated that any industrial process employing ammonium tannate would include techniques for recycling the ammonium tannate and for protecting it from degradation due to light and/or oxidation.

SOLVENT EXTRACTION PROCESSES

Hydrocarbon Under Supercritical Conditions

D.F. Williams and T.G. Martin; U.S. Patent 4,108,760; August 22, 1978; assigned to Coal Industry (Patents) Limited, England describe a process for the extraction of oil shales and tar sands which process comprises heating the shale in the presence of an extractant in the gas phase at a temperature within the range 350° to 550°C to extract extractable constituents, separating the extractant and extract from the residue, recovering the extract from the extraction and recycling the extractant for further use. The extraction is preferably carried out at a temperature within the range of 370° to 450°C and the shale is preferably crushed to a size smaller than 1.5 mm.

The solvent/shale ratio may be within the range 1:1 to 30:1 and is preferably within the range of 2:1 to 10:1. The extraction pressure should be above the critical pressure and may be within the range of 500 to 10,000 psi and preferably within the range of 1,000 to 3,000 psi.

Suitable solvents include aromatic hydrocarbons having a single benzene ring and preferably not more than 4 carbon atoms in substituent groups, e.g., benzene, toluene, xylene, ethyl benzene, isopropyl benzene and tri- and tetramethyl benzenes. Thus, virtually the whole of the bitumen in tar sands can be extracted with benzene at or above 290°C or with toluene above 320°C. A very high proportion of the kerogen in oil shales, particularly those shales such as Colorado shales which release all their kerogen on heating, can be extracted with aromatics containing 2 to 4 carbon atoms in substituent groups at about 440°C.

By way of example, a number of shales were analyzed and then subjected to extraction in accordance with the process. The materials subjected to extraction were as follows: Colorado oil shale, Scottish oil shale and Athabasca tar sands. Before commencing extraction, a sample of each material was analyzed and the results are shown in Table 1 on the following page.

Gray-King assays of the oil shales and tar sands was then carried out on a dry basis and as a gas analysis. The results are shown on the following page in Tables 2 and 3.

In each case extraction was conducted by the use of toluene, pentane or acetone at temperatures within the range of 350° to 550°C and at pressures of 1,500 psi. The residue and the extract were collected and subjected to analysis. Table 4 shows Examples 1 to 5 with analysis details. The analysis of the gas produced in the process is set out in Table 5.

Table 1: Ultimate Analyses of Oil Shales and Tar Sands

	H$_2$O, ar	Ash, db	C	H	O	N	S	Cl	CO$_2$
	.... (%).		. . . . (% dry basis)						
Colorado oil shale	0.5	60.6	17.5	2.4	1.0	0.55	0.90	nil	17.1
Scottish oil shale	1.9	69.8	21.5	2.9	3.7	0.55	1.10	nil	0.43
Athabasca tar sands	2.9	89.1	8.3	0.9	1.2	0.10	0.45	nil	0.04

Table 2: Gray-King Assays of Oil Shales and Tar Sands

	Coke	Tar	Liquor	Gas	Gas Vol (ml/100 g of sample, dry basis)
	. . . . (% by wt dry basis)				
Colorado oil shale	79.9	14.8	0.8	3.2	3,190
Scottish oil shale	79.3	14.8	2.8	2.3	2,280
Athabasca tar sands	90.5	8.4	0.5	0.8	620

Table 3: Gray-King Assay Gas Analyses

	H$_2$	O$_2$	N$_2$	CH$_4$	CO	CO$_2$
	. . . . (% dry basis)					
Colorado oil shale	41.0	—	—	26.3	7.1	25.6
Scottish oil shale	38.9	—	—	38.2	4.0	18.9
Athabasca tar sands	11.0	—	—	10.1	0.0	78.9

Table 4: Gas Extraction Data and Product Yields

Ex. No.	Charge	Solvent	Temp (°C)	Extraction Time (min)	Solvent/ Dry Coal Ratio	Solvent Flow (g/min)	. .Percent Yield . . Extract	Residue . . .(dry basis) . . .
1	Colorado oil shale	toluene	395	60	20.3	31.6	16.6	82.3
2	Colorado oil shale	toluene	440	60	18.1	28.1	18.9	78.7
3	Scottish oil shale	toluene	440	60	19.4	27.2	19.0	80.1
4	Athabasca tar sands	toluene	395	30	11.0	30.8	9.3	88.0
5	Athabasca tar sands	pentane	230	60	—	—	7.9	89.7

Table 5: Gas Extraction Product Analyses

Ex. No.		H$_2$O, ar	Ash, db	C	H	O	N	S	Cl	CO$_2$
		. . . . . (%)		. . . . (% dry basis)						
1	Colorado oil shale									
	Extract	—	—	83.0	10.3	2.6	2.20	1.75	0.03	—
	Residue	0.3	72.9	3.2	0.7	—	—	—	—	27.3
2	Colorado oil shale									
	Extract	—	—	83.4	10.2	2.3	2.25	1.60	0.05	—
	Residue	0.3	75.6	1.9	0.30	—	0.15	0.65	0.03	21.5
3	Scottish oil shale									
	Extract	—	—	85.5	10.5	1.5	1.35	0.90	0.03	—
	Residue	0.7	85.9	7.8	0.8	—	0.40	1.00	0.02	0.75
4	Athabasca tar sands									
	Extract	—	—	84.0	10.3	1.3	0.40	3.85	0.09	—
	Residue	0.3	98.4	0.5	0.1	—	0.02	0.10	nil	0.28
5	Athabasca tar sands									
	Extract	—	—	83.2	10.6	1.2	0.30	4.25	nil	—
	Residue	0.2	97.8	1.25	0.20	—	0.05	0.15	nil	0.07

Light Naphtha-Methanol Solvent System

According to a process developed by *M. Farcasiu and D.D. Whitehurst; U.S. Patent 4,046,668; September 6, 1977; assigned to Mobil Oil Corporation*, extraction of organic constituents from tar sands is accomplished by a double-solvent system of light naphtha and methanol. The addition of heat to the extraction zone is not normally required because the extraction temperature may be as low as about 50°F. Rapid decrepitation of the tar sand aggregate occurs, followed by separation of two layers of solution. The heavy asphaltenes are partitioned between the interface of the two solutions and on the fluid surface.

Further product separation of the liquid layers following extraction of hydrocarbons and organic materials from the tar sand is a unique feature of this process. Depending on the water content of the tar sand, the separation may occur simultaneously with the extraction or may be accomplished by the addition of a small quantity of water, at least about 1% to the binary extract. After removal of the upper, light naphtha fraction by decantation, the major portion of the methanol fraction is separately withdrawn. The remaining portion is filtered through the sand. This deposits all of the asphaltenes on the sand. The light naphtha fraction is separated to avoid filtration thereof through the sand. The methanol fraction is much easier to filter than the whole binary mix.

It is believed that the effectiveness of the double-solvent system is based on the ability of methanol to penetrate the water layer surrounding the sand grains of the tar sand aggregate. By contrast, it is known that a solvent, such as hexane, works ineffectively in a water system and penetration of the aggregate water layers by such a solvent is difficult. The methanol penetration of the water layer is beneficial in reducing the interfacial tension between the double solvent/tar-sand oil phase and the solid phase so that the fine sand grains separate more readily from the hydrocarbon organic matter phase.

Moreover, the separation of the binary solvent/tar-sand oil mixture into a light naphtha phase and a methanol phase results in a favorable distribution of the extracted hydrocarbon organic matter between the phases, in addition to improving the performance of the later filtration step. The most desirable nonpolar components of the extracted constituents are recovered from the light naphtha phase, the more polar, soluble constituents are recovered from the methanol phase and the less desirable asphaltenes are withdrawn with the sand.

The solid asphaltenes deposited on the surface of the sand may also be recovered. For example, the sand fraction with deposited asphaltenes may be combusted or burned with oxygen-containing gas and thus used as source of energy for the process. Alternatively, the asphaltenes deposited on the sand surface may be further recovered as by extraction by an aromatic solvent. Aromatic compounds especially effective for such further extraction are aromatics benzene and pyridine. Alternatively, the majority of the asphaltenes may be recovered by decantation or other method of withdrawal of oil liquids followed by filtration to remove entrained asphaltene particles.

An important aspect of the process is the ease with which the particular duel solvents may be recovered due to the large differences in the boiling point between the solvents, the respective extracts and the good filtration properties of the methanol layer.

High Shear Liquid Phase Separation

B.T. Porritt, L.A. Johanson, and K.L. Noall; U.S. Patent 4,096,057; June 20, 1978; assigned to New Energy Sources Company describe an apparatus and method for recovering bituminous products from tar sands wherein an impellor is used to create a high shear environment in a liquid phase. The high shear environment causes the masses of tar sand to be rapidly reduced by attrition to sand particles and also rapidly strips the bituminous product from the finely divided detritus and sand resulting from this abradent action.

The apparatus includes a vessel which is divided into an attrition zone enclosed by a screen member, a sand separation zone and a product recovery zone. The vessel accommodates liquid which is, advantageously, a solvent into which the agglomerated masses of tar sands are introduced. The liquid is impelled vigorously upwardly into the attrition zone to create a high shear environment by which the tar sand masses are reduced by attrition into sand particles coated with the bituminous matrix material of the tar sand. The separated grains of sand are also stripped of the bituminous product by the high shear environment. The cleansed sand passes through the screen member surrounding the attrition zone into the sand separation zone. The liquid and the bituminous product removed from the sand pass to the product recovery zone.

Countercurrent Flow Using Hydrocarbon Solvent

H.E. Alford and J.C. Saunders, Jr.; U.S. Patent 4,067,796; January 10, 1978; assigned to Standard Oil Company describe a process for the recovery of bitumen from tar sand comprising dissolving the bitumen in a solvent. The improvement comprises conducting the bitumen recovery in a vessel containing a liquid comprising an organic phase which contains a water-immiscible hydrocarbon solvent capable of dissolving the bitumen and an aqueous phase, and processing the tar sand by introducing the tar sand into the organic phase of the liquid and subsequently conducting the tar sand into the aqueous phase. The process gives very substantial savings in the hydrocarbon solvent and provides a spent tar sand effluent that can be readily discharged to the environment. Broadly, the process provides for a countercurrent flow of tar sand and solvent with a very efficient method of removing the solvent from the spent tar sand.

The Vessel: A column measuring 3.1 m in height and having an internal diameter of 5 cm was equipped with the following inlets, outlets and mixers: 13 cm from the top of the column, a liquid product overflow outlet, 60 cm from the top of the column an inlet for tar sand, 3 mixers located 1, 1.7 and 2.6 m from the top of the column, an inlet for solvent entry at 2.8 m and an exit port for water and spent tar sand in the bottom of the column. The hydrocarbon-water interface in the column was located 1.9 m from the top. The water to make up the aqueous phase was introduced with the tar sand.

Example 1: Product Quality — Tar sand containing about 8% bitumen was conditioned with water by mixing 1,000 parts by weight of tar sand with 4.04 parts by weight of 10% Na_2CO_3 solution, 114.5 parts of fresh water and 181.5 parts of recycle water. The conditioning took place at 66°C for 5 minutes with constant stirring. The conditioned tar sand was then introduced into the column described above containing water and kerosene. In addition to the tar sand slurry, 80 parts by weight of kerosene were also added. The column was operated at a temperature of 82°C. The products from the column were 1,044.5 parts of dewatered sand, 181.5 parts by weight recycle water and 154 parts of bitumen solution. The analyses of the various products are shown in the table below:

| | .... Product Analysis, wt %.......... | | | |
Product	Kerosene	Bitumen	Water	Solids
Bitumen Solution	49.8	49.8	0.2	0.2
Recycle Water	0.55	0.55	97.3	1.6
Dewatered Sand	0.31	0.31	11.78	87.6

It is seen from the data above that the process produces a very high recovery of bitumen from tar sand.

Examples 2 through 4: Effectiveness of Various Solvents — Three solvents were compared in their effectiveness for the recovery of bitumen from tar sand. The tar sand was conditioned for 15 minutes at 68°C at a pH of 9 using a water/tar sand ratio of 0.4. Recycle water was used. In the extraction, a solvent/tar sand ratio of 0.15 was used and the column was operated at 82°C. The effect of various solvents on the hydrocarbon remaining on the sand is shown in the table below. The results stated include the small amounts of solvent that remained on the sand.

Example	Solvent	% Original Hydrocarbon Remaining on Sand
2	#2 Furnace oil	55.0
3	Water white distillate	43.0
4	Kerosene	11.8

Example 5: Effect of Solvent Ratio — Using the conditions of Examples 2 through 4 and a solvent of water-white distillate, the effect of the solvent ratio was considered. Example 3 shows 43.0% of the hydrocarbon remaining on the sand at a solvent ratio of 0.15. Reducing the solvent/tar sand ratio to 0.10, the hydrocarbon remaining on the sand was reduced to 38.6%.

Examples 6 and 7: Effect of Tar Sand Feed Rate — Tar sand was conditioned for 10 minutes at 66°C at a pH of 8 using recycle water and a 0.3 water to tar sand ratio. Kerosene was used as the solvent in a ratio of kerosene to tar sand of 0.11. The column was operated at a temperature of 82°C. The amount of hydrocarbon remaining on the sand at two different feed rates is shown in the table below:

Example	Tar Sand Feed Rate (g/hr)	% Original Hydrocarbon Remaining on Sand
6	3,600	16.7
7	20,000	38.9

Various other experiments were run on the conditioning of the tar sand prior to use in the process. The tar sand recovery tended to increase as the water/tar sand ratio in the conditioning increased, with the best results being obtained at a water/tar sand ratio of 0.4. Experiments conducted on the pH indicated that a pH of about 7 to 8 was preferred. The experiments on the time allowed for conditioning indicated better recovery with increased time of conditioning, with the best results being obtained at a conditioning time of 15 minutes. The experiments with conditioning temperature indicated that 66°C was preferred.

Rotary Separator and Extracting Device

P. Kraemer and O. Meresz; U.S. Patent 4,098,648; July 4, 1978 describe a rotary separator, which is specially adapted for extraction of bituminous materials from tar sands or shale, and comprises an inclined vessel having a helical conveyor attached to it, provided with apertures at the radially outer portion of the helical flights. Material introduced at the bottom is conveyed upwardly, and solvent washes downwardly to dissolve out the bituminous material. The apertures in the helix permit downward passage of liquid but prevent substantial downward passage of solids. A solvent recovery vessel is provided for recovering residual solvent from the separated solids.

With reference to Figure 6.9a, the apparatus comprises a rotatable generally cylindrical washer vessel **10**. As shown, it is mounted at an incline to the horizontal, in practice about 5° to 18° and is rotatable about its longitudinal axis, using suitable driving means.

At its lower end **11**, the washer vessel is rotatably supported on ring bearing **12** and at its upper end on ring bearing **13**. The lower end **11** of the vessel **10** is provided with an annular end plate **14**. It has two lower compartments, the first and lowermost **15** which is bounded at its lower extremity by annular end plate **14**, and the second and uppermost **16** which is bounded by a second annular plate **17** at its lower end, common with lowermost compartment **15**, and at its upper end by third annular plate **18**. The lowermost compartment **15** is provided with an exit pipe **19**, through which liquid solution deposited in compartment **15** can be led off. Second compartment **16** is provided with a scoop device **20** secured to the inner surface of the cylindrical vessel wall.

Upwardly of the second compartment **16**, and bounded by annular plate **18** at its lower end, the washer vessel **10** has a main chamber **21**. The main chamber **21** has disposed therein, rigidly affixed to the internal cylindrical wall, an open centered helical ribbon **22** of substantially constant helical pitch. The pitches of the open helix **22** effectively divide the main chamber **21** into a plurality of successive upwardly disposed zones. The radially outer portions of the helix **22** are apertured.

A tar sands introduction means is provided at the lower end **11** of the washer vessel **10**. This introduction means comprises a hopper **23**, into which bituminous tar sand is fed by means of a conveyor **24** from storage. While in hopper **23**, the tar sand is wet with small amounts of solvent by solvent inlet nozzle **23a**. A pair of crushing rollers **25**, **26** with radial crushing teeth are disposed at the bottom exit from the hopper **23**, through which the wetted tar sand can leave the hopper **23** and drop into closed inlet conduit **27**.

Scrapers **28** are provided to scrape the bottom surfaces of rollers **25**, **26** to prevent adherence of the tar sand to the rollers as they rotate. A diaphragm pump **29** moves the material forwardly through the inlet conduit **27**. The inlet conduit **27** extends forwardly through the central apertures in annular plates **14**, **17** and **18**, and terminates at its forward end at the lower end of main chamber **21** of vessel **10**.

Figure 6.9: Rotary Separating and Extracting Devices

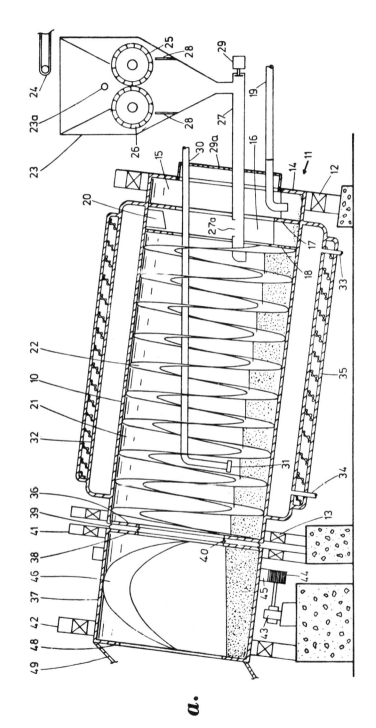

a.

(continued)

Figure 6.9: (continued)

b.

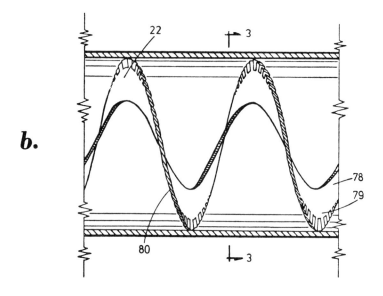

c.

d.

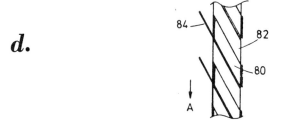

(continued)

Figure 6.9: (continued)

e.

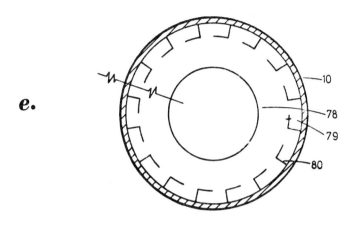

f.

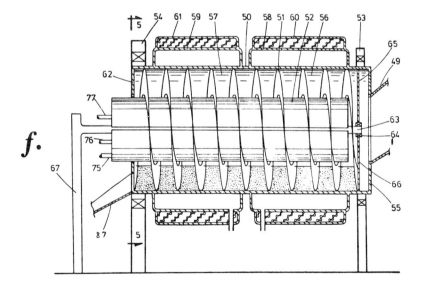

(continued)

Figure 6.9: (continued)

g.

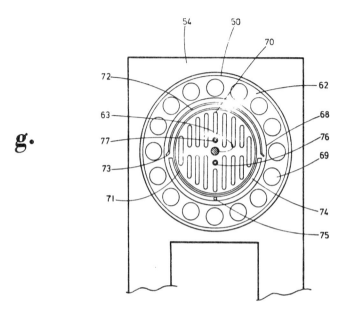

(a)   Longitudinal cross-sectional view of a washer vessel and associated parts
(b)   Detailed cross section of a portion of the washer vessel of Figure 6.9a, showing the helix in place
(c)   Edge view of a fragment of the radially outer edge of the helix
(d)   Edge view similar to Figure 6.9c
(e)   Cross section on the line 3–3 of Figure 6.9b
(f)   Longitudinal cross-sectional view of a residual solvent recovery vessel and associated parts for use in conjunction with the washer vessel of Figure 6.9a
(g)   View along the line 5–5 of Figure 6.9f

Source: U.S. Patent 4,098,648

Thus, wetted tar sand is pretreated with solvent, reduced to suitable consistency by crushing rollers **25, 26** and then delivered via conduit **27** to the lower end of main chamber **21**, into the pitch of the helix **22**. A bearing seal **29** is provided which is stationary with respect to the cylinder **10**, but closes the aperture in the end plate **14**, to prevent solvent vapor escape. Conduit **27** and exit pipe **19** pass through sealed apertures in seal **29a**.

A solvent inlet pipe **30** is provided, extending from a source of solvent supply not shown. Pipe **30** extends through a sealed aperture in bearing seal **29a**, through the central apertures in annular plates **14, 17, 18** and through the open center of the helix **22**, to a position about three-quarters of the way towards the upper end of the main chamber **21**. The solvent inlet pipe terminates in an outlet nozzle **31** which extends downwardly but at an angle to the vertical. The main chamber **21** and the chamber **16** of the vessel **10** are surrounded by a heat exchange jacket **32** provided with a fluid inlet conduit **33** and a fluid outlet **34** for heating the main chamber by hot fluid supply. The heat exchange jacket **32** is lined on its exterior surface with an insulation layer **35**. The upper end of the main chamber is defined by an upper annular end plate **36**.

Flexibly connected to the upper end of main chamber **21** is a generally cylindrical vibrating chamber **37**. The vibrating chamber **37** is of generally the same diameter as main chamber **21**, and is mounted substantially coaxially therewith. At its lower end, vibrating chamber **37** is bounded by an annular end plate **38**, generally the same as upper end plate **36** of main chamber **21**. The vibrating chamber **37** is flexibly connected to main chamber **21** by means of flexible accordion-type circular sleeve connectors **39, 40** of oil-resistant rubber, for example, so that the connection between chambers **37** and **21** is substantially fluid-tight but permits vibration of chamber **37** relative to rotating chamber **21**.

Vibrating chamber **37** is adapted to be rotated about its axis, along with main chamber **31**, and is mounted in respective lower rearward ring bearing **41** and upper forward ring bearing **42**. To impart vibration to the chamber **37** as it is rotated, there is provided a vibrating motor **43** driving a gear **44** which engages a ring gear **45** on the exterior of the chamber **37**. The vibrating chamber **37** is provided, secured to its inner cylindrical surface, with a half turn of an open centered helix **46**. The helix **46** is arranged in the same sense as the helix **22** of the main chamber **21**, so as to continue conveyance of material in an upward direction on rotation together of chambers **21** and **37**. The pitch of helix **46** is much larger than the pitch of helix **22** in the main chamber **21**, so that material delivered to chamber **37** has a period when it is vibrated but not agitated.

The forward upper end of vibrating chamber **37** is provided with an annular end plate **48**, to the forward end of which is journalled an exit chute **49** connecting to the residual solvent recovery vessel **50** illustrated in Figure 6.9f. The end plate **48** rotates with the cylinder **10**, while chute **49** remains stationary. With reference to Figure 6.9f, the vessel **50** for recovering residual solvent comprises a rotatable cylinder having affixed to the inner cylindrical surface an open centered helix **51**. A stationary, generally cylindrical condenser unit **52** extends longitudinally of the vessel **50**. The vessel **50** is generally horizontal and is rotatably supported in a rear ring bearing **53** and a forward ring bearing **54**.

At its rearward end, the vessel **50** has an annular end plate **55** to which the end of exit chute **49** is journalled, to allow passage of material from chamber **37** to vessel **50**. The material, which is sand contaminated with residual solvent, is deposited in the rearward end of rotating vessel **50**, into the pitch of the helix **51**. It is conveyed forwardly as the vessel **50** and helix **51** rotate.

The vessel **50** is effectively divided into a first heating zone **56** and a second cooling zone **57**. A heating jacket **58** surrounds the heating zone **56**, and has suitable inlets for the circulation of heated fluid. A cooling jacket surrounds the cooling zone **57**, and has suitable inlets for circulation of cold fluid. The heating jacket **58** and cooling jacket **59** are provided on their outer surfaces with respective insulation layers **60, 61**. The material entering the rearward end of the vessel **50** is conveyed successively through heating zone **56** and cooling zone **57**. The forward end of the vessel **50** has an annular end plate **62** which rotates with the vessel. The condenser **52** has a central axle **63** by means of which it is supported at each end of the vessel **50**. At the rearward end, the axle **63** has a bearing **64** by means of which it is supported on radial arms **65**, **66** secured to the cylindrical surface of the vessel **50**. At its forward end, it is rigidly supported on a post **67**. Thus, the condenser remains stationary as the cylinder **50** is rotated.

The form of the upper end plate **62** and condenser **52** are also illustrated in Figure 6.9g, which is a view along the line **5–5** of Figure 6.9f. The cylindrical vessel **50** is rotatably mounted in bearing **54**. The end plate **62** of vessel **50** has a central aperture **68** through which the condenser **52** extends, and a series of circumferentially spaced apertures **69** arranged around its rim. The condenser **52** has a central axle **63** for support purposes, and a plurality of interconnecting fluid-circulating condenser pipes **70** surrounded by a metal cylinder **71**. The condenser is also provided with an upper cover plate **72** with deflector formation **73** at its lower edges, and a lower collector tray **74**. In operation, the solvent is condensed and collected in tray **74**, from which it is led out through outlet pipe **75**. Cover plate **72** prevents sand, moved up the walls of cylindrical vessel **50** as it rotates, from entering condenser collector tray **74**. Inlet and outlet conduits **76**, **77** for fluid circulation through the condenser pipes **70** are provided.

With reference to Figures 6.9b, 6.9c, 6.9d, and 6.9e, it is seen that the helix **22** in the washer vessel **10** has an open center, and a radially inner solid, fluid-impervious portion **78** and a radially outer portion **79** with a series of circumferentially spaced slotted apertures **80** therethrough. These slots **80** are arranged obliquely to the longitudinal axis of the helix **22**, and present a tortuous passage through the helix flights, for liquid flow. The openings are presented generally away from the direction of travel of material conveyed upwardly by the helix **22**.

Direct flow of material through the slots **80**, parallel to the axis of the helix **22**, is not permitted. The slots **80** are defined by parallelogram-shaped formation **81**, the faces **82** of which in the direction of forward conveyance of material by the helix **22** extend in the direction **A** of rotation of the helix **22**. The formation **81** thus defines entrances for the slots **80** which present an oblique angle **83** to the material being conveyed by the rotating helix.

In the alternative form shown in Figure 6.9d, the parallelogram formations **82** are provided with spring steel strips **84** further overlying the entrances to the slots **80**, so that again the material being conveyed by the helix as it rotates in direction **A** is met by an oblique angle formation defining the entrance to the slotted aperture **80**.

The operation of the apparatus, as illustrated, is described as follows. Vessels **10** and **50**, with their associated annular end plates and associated helices **22**, **51** are set rotating at a suitable speed, which is fast enough to raise the solids part way up the side of vessel **10**, but not to sling it around in vessel **10**. Chamber **37** with its associated helix **46** is set rotating at the same speed as chambers **10** and **50**, and is set vibrating, at a frequency of about 30 to 100 cycles per second. Tar sand material is conveyed by conveyor **24** into hopper **23**, where it is mixed with about 1 part by weight of solvent per 1 part by weight of organic bituminous material in the tar sand, determined by previous analysis, supplied through nozzle **23a**. This is sufficient solvent to produce a homogeneous material, capable of forming a weak sheet which will break up into particulate form under its own weight.

The tar sand thus wetted with solvent is fed through rollers **25, 26** where mixing and homogenizing is effected and is dropped into pipe **27**, in which it falls in generally particulate form. Then, it is pumped into the lower end of the main chamber **21** of rotating washer vessel **10**. At the same time, solvent is delivered to the upper part of chamber **21** via solvent pipe **30** and nozzle **31**. Tar sand is conveyed upwardly by helix **22** so that the upward direction through washer vessel **10** is the downstream direction with respect to the direction of flow of solid material to meet a downwardly flowing stream of solvent. The solvent dissolves the tar or bitumen, and the solvent-bitumen solution moves downwardly through the various zones of the main chamber **21**.

Since the solution is lighter than the undissolved sand, the solution effects a thorough washing of the solids before it finds its way through the apertures **80** of the helix **22**, which are located at the radial outer edge of the helix, i.e., at the bottom thereof. Passing through these downwardly located slots and downwardly to the bottom of the inclined cylinder **10** is against the natural tendency of the solution to float on the sand, so that it substantially increases the washing efficiency. Rotating cylinder **10** and helix **22** cause continuous tumbling and mixing of the tar sand and solvent, with countercurrent washing to effect maximum extraction of bitumen by the solvent.

The rotation of cylinder **10** tends to cause solid material to rise part way up the walls of the cylinder and fall back, with a continuous tumbling action. However, the liquid solution remains disposed in the bottom of the rotating cylinder, due to its greater fluidity. The liquid is free to flow through the oblique slots **80** in the helix, since it is fluid enough to be able to follow the tortuous path. The solid material, however, will not pass through the slots **80** because of their tortuous arrangement, and because the slots are angularly disposed with overlying formation **82** or **84** at their entrances to trail against the solid material as the helix rotates relative to the solid material.

Thus, the solids brush across the forward surfaces **82** and **84** and have no component of motion permitting them to enter the angled slots **80**. This separation action is assisted by the thixotropic characteristics of the material. Since the solids will tend to be disposed part way up the wall of the rotating cylinder **10**, the nozzle **31** delivering the solvent is directed at an angle to the vertical, to impinge initially upon the solid mass.

At the bottom of the main chamber **21**, the bitumen-solvent solution overflows through the central aperture in plate **18** into compartment **16**, the apertured plate **18** thus constituting a weir. Here, it is subjected to the action of scoop **20**, which rotates with the rotating cylinder **10**, picks up residual sand settled in chamber **16** and drops it into pipe conveyor **27**, which is apertured at **27a** for this purpose, to mix with fresh incoming tar sand for delivery back to the main chamber **21**.

The solution of bitumen extracted from the tar sand then overflows through the aperture in plate **17**, into the lowermost compartment **15** of the rotating cylinder **10**. From compartment **15**, the solution is pumped off through pipe **19** communicating with the upper portion of the solution to refinery or storage. The solution so obtained contains only very small amounts of extremely fine insoluble inorganic matter, which can be settled out on storage.

The arrangement, as described, provides for extremely efficient washing and extraction of the organic content of the tar sand by the countercurrent action of the solvent and the tumbling agitation and conveying of the cylinder **10** and associated helical conveyor **22**. The separation is facilitated by the arrangement of the apertures **80** at the bottom of the helix flights, and angularly to prevent solid passage, as described. Heating can be applied to main chamber **21**, if desired, by means of heating jacket **32** to adjust the rate of extraction of the tar sand.

As the solid material reaches the upper end of main chamber **21**, it comprises sand substantially completely free from bituminous material. However, the sand has substantial amounts (about 25% of its own weight) of solvent adhering to it, largely through surface tension effects. For an economic and acceptable tar sands extraction process, it is necessary that this solvent be recovered and reused, and that the sand be substantially free from residual solvent before it is returned to the environment.

This solvent-bearing sand is conveyed by the helix **22** out through the aperture in upper end plate **36** into chamber **37**, which is both rotating and vibrating. In this chamber, it has a period when it rests under vibration and rotation of the chamber only, free from agitation by the helix **46**. As illustrated, the pitch of helix **46** is at least twice that of helix **22** in the main chamber **21**, and vibrating chamber **37** and main chamber **21** rotate at the same speed. Thus, sand delivered from main chamber **21** has at least half a revolution during which it is not tumbled by the helix, but rests on the rotating cylinder wall under vibration. This causes substantial amounts of the residual solvent to rise above the sand and return to main chamber **21**. The solvent content of the sand is thus reduced to about 12%.

The 12% solvent content of the sand leaving vibrating chamber **37** is still unacceptably high, both in terms of economic solvent losses and sand contamination. Therefore, the sand from vibrating chamber **37** is conveyed by helix **46** out through apertured end plate **48**, down chute **49** and into the heated zone **56** of residual solvent recovery unit **50** (Figure 6.9f). Heat is supplied to heating jacket **58**, raising the temperature in heated zone **56** to about 200°F, either by hot fluids or induction heating, etc. The sand is agitated by the tumbling action of the helix **51** as vessel **50** rotates, and the solvent is evaporated from it. Solvent vapor enters between the cover plate **72** and the pan **74** of the condenser, collects in pan **74** and is pumped out of pipe **75**. The configuration of cover plate **72** prevents sand, which may be carried up the wall of rotating cylinder **50**, from falling into the solvent in pan **74**.

The sand is substantially totally free from residual solvent by the time it reaches the cooling zone **56** of vessel **50**. Cooling water is supplied to jacket **59**, so that the sand is cooled to ambient temperature by the time it is conveyed by helix **51** out of the apertures **69** in end plate **62** and down exit chute **87**. The heat extracted from the hot sand is then recovered in the water of the cooling jacket. This process and apparatus can be operated continuously to give substantially complete extraction of bitumen from tar sand, minimal solvent consumption and clean cool sand ready for return to the environment.

Perforate Bed and Chlorinated Solvent

T.A. Pittman and J.L. Woods; U.S. Patent 4,029,568; assigned to Minerals Research Corporation describe a method of recovering oil and oil sands, wherein the system is operated without the need of water or in general even of heat, at least in appreciable quantities. The method includes providing crushed ore, crushed preferably to particulate size, on a perforate bed or support and then spraying the so-crushed oil sands ore with a selected solvent at from 1 to 100 psi gauge pressure such that an oil-containing solution can be collected beneath such support.

Thereafter, the oil is recovered by vaporizing the solvent and condensing the solvent for reuse. Upon vaporization of the solvent, the oil and lighter fractions remain and can be introduced into a refinery or distillation column for recovering desired fractions from the recovered oil or bitumen and also for producing a separate fraction so that the same can be used as an energy source to supply the necessary heat required as well as power for the mechanical equipment used. In the process of selecting and utilizing solvents, it is preferred that methylchloroform, trichloroethylene, or perchloroethylene be used.

Trichloroethylene, Surfactant and Polyelectrolytes

A process described by *N.F. Blaine; U.S. Patents 4,057,485; Nov. 8, 1977; and 4,046,669; Sept. 6, 1977* involves the utilization of trichloroethylene as a solvent in a solvent extraction process for removing tar from the sand particles of tar sands. The process is conducted at relatively mild conditions of from about 70° to 800°F and 0 to 200 psig, typically 300°F and 50 psig, preferably using 1 to 20 ppm surfactant to reduce film strength between tar and sand particles, and 1 to 20 ppm polyelectrolytes to relieve any problems from fine-particle electric charges.

The amount of solvent utilized is dependent principally on the size of the contact vessel, process conditions and percentage of tar in the sand. Generally, the amount of solvent transferred to the contact vessel is from 3 to 10 times the amount of tar on a weight basis. A typical weight ratio of gross solvent transferred to the contact vessel to the amount of tar in the tar sands is 5:1 and ratios of 3:1 to 7:1 are common. It should be understood, however, that the amount of make-up solvent compared to the amount of tar is minimal, i.e., less than 5%, generally less than 2%, and the solvent loss any higher than the above is due to equipment or other mechanical failures.

The use of the solvent herein, particularly trichloroethylene, has been found to result in higher tar yields and lower solvent loss. Tar yields of over 99 volume percent recoverable from tar sands have been found by the use of the solvent herein, particularly trichloroethylene. Generally, solvent losses are less than 0.5 volume percent.

The removed oil having a typical gravity of 10° to 12°API is removed from the side of the vessel and may be heated, and transferred to a distillation column for separating light ends from heavy ends of the oil for further processing. Some distillation and refinery operations may be desired at the site of the solvent extraction process which may be close to the tar sand fields for improving transportation costs.

Liquid Separation Promoter

According to a process described by *G.J. Snell and R.H. Long; U.S. Patent 4,094,781; June 13, 1978; assigned to The Lummus Company*, a tar sands extract containing sand is mixed with a liquid promoter to enhance and promote the separation of sand from the tar sands extract by a gravity difference separation technique to thereby recover an essentially sand-free liquid product which can be employed for the production of valuable liquid products. The liquid which is employed to enhance and promote the separation of insoluble material is generally a hydrocarbon liquid having a characterization factor (K) of at least about 9.75 and preferably at least about 11.0 wherein:

$$K = \sqrt[3]{T_B/G}$$

wherein T_B is the molal average boiling point of the liquid (°R); and G is specific gravity of the liquid (60°F/60°F).

The characterization factor is an index of the aromaticity/paraffinicity of hydrocarbons and petroleum fractions as described by Watson and Nelson, *Ind. Eng. Chem.* 25, 880 (1933), with more paraffinic materials having higher values for the characterization factor (K). The promoter liquid which is employed is one which has a characterization factor (K) in excess of 9.75. The following table provides representative characterization factors (K) for various materials:

Anthracene	8.3
Naphthalene	8.4
425° to 500°F coal tar distillate	8.8
550° to 900°F coal tar distillate	9.1
600° to 900°F coal tar distillate	9.0
400° to 450°F coal tar distillate	9.4
Benzene	9.8
Tetrahydronaphthalene	9.8
o-Xylene	10.3
Decahydronaphthalene	10.6
Cyclohexane	11.0
425° to 500°F boiling range kerosene	11.9
n-Dodecylbenzene	12.0
Propylene oligomers (pentamer)	12.2
Cetene	12.8
Tridecane	12.8
n-Hexane	12.9
Hexadecane or cetane	13.0

The most preferred promoter liquid has a 5 volume percent distillation temperature of at least about 425°F and a 95 volume percent distillation temperature of no greater than about 500°F. It is to be understood that the promoter liquid may be a hydrocarbon; e.g., tetrahydronaphthalene, in which case the 5 volume percent and 95 volume percent distillation temperatures are the same; i.e., the hydrocarbon has a single boiling point. In such a case, the boiling point of the hydrocarbon must be at least about 350°F in order to meet the requirement of a 5 volume percent distillation temperature of at least about 250°F and a 95 volume percent distillation temperature of at least about 350°F. The promoter liquid is preferably a blend or mixture of hydrocarbons in which case the 5 volume percent and 95 volume percent distillation temperatures are not the same. The

5 volume percent and 95 volume percent distillation temperature may be conveniently determined by ASTM No. D 86-67 or No. D 1160 with the former being preferred for those liquids having a 95 volume percent distillation temperature below 600°F and the latter for those above 600°F.

Example: 1,000 g of tar sands extract, having the inspection data compiled in the table below, are preheated to 250°F and charged to a 2,300 ml electrically heated, stainless steel shaker bomb. The shaker bomb is outfitted with a multiplicity of valved side draw-off nozzles as well as a valved bottom draw-off nozzle. With shaking, the contents of the shaker bomb are quickly heated to 550°±10°F. 600 g of promoter liquid (K = 11.5; 5 volume percent distillation temperature of 310°F and 95 volume percent distillation temperature of 400°F) are then quickly added via a pressurized addition bomb and the mixture is heated to 550°±10°F with shaking. The contents of the bomb are allowed to settle at 550°±10°F for 1.5 hours.

An overflow product is withdrawn from a side draw-off nozzle located in the lower portion of the shaker bomb and collected in a preweighed 1 gal container, which is vented through a water-cooled reflux condenser. An underflow product is now withdrawn through the bottom draw-off nozzle and is collected in a 1 qt preweighed container which also vents through an external water-cooled reflux condenser. 1,060 g of overflow product and 525 g of underflow product are collected in the experiment. The sand content of the overflow product, as measured by an ASTM D482-74 ash determination, is found to be 0.03 wt %.

A Fischer assay is run on a representative 100 g aliquot sample of underflow prepared in accordance with the above procedure. This technique is basically a batch bench-scale coking method and thus provides preliminary simulation of coke yields which would be expected in commercial coking processes. The Fischer assay gas, liquid product, and char yields are 2.0 wt %, 81.5 wt %, and 16.5 wt %, respectively. An overall clean oil yield of 90.3±0.3 wt % is calculated from the Fischer assay results. Clean product yield is considered to be the feedstock oil weight minus Fischer assay gas plus char yield scaled to the actual amount of overflow product in the calculation.

A 262.5 g representative aliquot sample of underflow prepared above is vacuum distilled in a 500 ml round-bottom distillation flask at 5 mm Hg absolute pressure. This laboratory vacuum distillation experiment was terminated when 175.0 g of composite vacuum distillate was collected. The vacuum residue had a softening point of 332°F. An overall promoter-liquid-free clean liquid product of yield of 81.0±0.3 wt % is calculated for the case where underflow, prepared in accordance with the subject example, is vacuum stripped to a vacuum residue softening point of about 332°F. This overall clean liquid product yield corresponds to the experimental data observed in the underflow vacuum stripping experiment.

Analysis of a Typical Moisture-Free Tar Sands Extract or Bitumen

Specific gravity at 110/60°F	1.014
Ash, wt %	1.4
Conradson carbon, wt %	13.6
Sulfur content, wt %	4.2
Nitrogen content, wt %	0.4

Vacuum Distillation Data (ASTM)

Vol % Distilled	Overhead Temperature in °F*
0	450
5	532
10	598
20	721
30	820
40	899
50	990**

*Corrected to 760 mm Hg absolute pressure
**The wt % of residue (+990°F) was 56.3

The process is particularly advantageous in that liquid product suitable for up-grading to a crude oil can be recovered from a tar sands extract without the necessity of preliminarily coking the entire extract. In addition, there is obtained improved sand-free liquid yields.

Solvent and Water Freezing Technique

J.H. Park and J.C. Allen; U.S. Patent 3,993,555; November 23, 1976; assigned to Texaco Inc. describe a method for extracting bitumen from the tar sand at or near the surface of the earth comprising contacting the tar sand with a bitumen solvent having a freezing point below the freezing point of any water in the tar sand, separating the dissolved bitumen solvent and any attendant water from the sand and lowering the temperature of the bitumen solvent and the attendant water to a point which will freeze the water. The frozen water is then separated from the dissolved bitumen and the solvent by conventional means such as centrifuging or filtering.

Referring to Figure 6.10a, mined tar sand is carried by conveyor **1** and deposited in a tank **2** which contains toluene at about –10°F. The mined tar sand and cold toluene are thoroughly mixed and sand is removed at **3** and ice at **11** by gravity separation and settling. The tar and toluene are then transported to a filter **4** to remove additional sand and crystalline ice. The upgraded tar and toluene mixture is then moved to another chiller **5** wherein the temperature is once again lowered to about 0°F.

After this chilling operation, the tar and toluene mixture is moved to a centrifuge **6** where any additional sand and ice crystals are removed. The now sand- and ice-free tar and toluene mixture is routed through a heat exchanger to raise its temperature from about 5° to 130°F wherein this hot tar and toluene mixture is introduced into a distillation tower **8** and the toluene and petroleum are separated. The petroleum from the tar sand is removed at **9** and the toluene is the overhead at about 250°F.

This toluene is routed through heat exchanger **7** to raise the temperature of the incoming tar and toluene mixture to the distillation tower. After emerging from the heat exchanger at about 50°F, the recovered toluene is introduced into a chiller **10** wherein the temperature of the toluene is lowered to –10°F. This toluene is then routed back into the first phase separator **2** to be mixed with more incoming tar sand.

Figure 6.10: Oil Recovery Process Using Cold Solvent

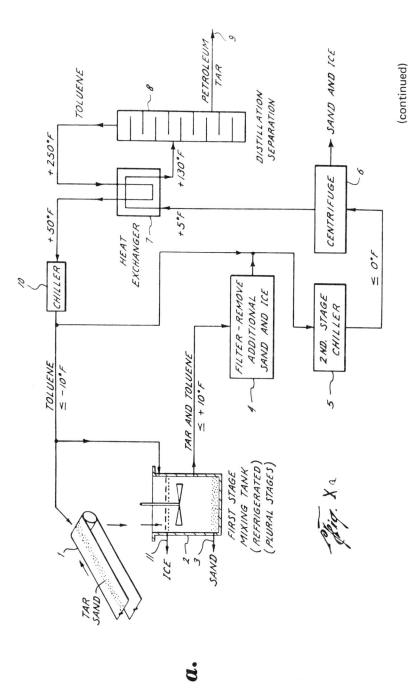

(continued)

Figure 6.10: (continued)

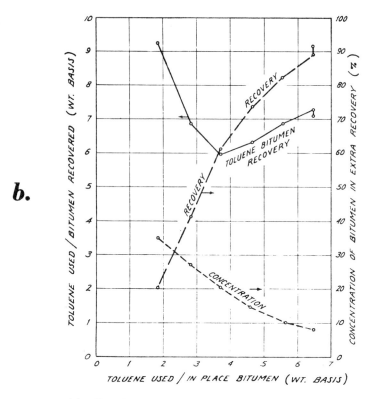

b.

(a)   Flow diagram
(b)   Extraction of Athabasca Tar from tar sand by multiple
       stage leaching at -2°F

Source: U.S. Patent 3,993,555

Example: A series of multistage extractions (by leaching) were performed at
-2°F. A sample (214 g) of Athabasca tar sand was treated with toluene by
stages at -2°F. The sample contained 13.23 wt % tar and had dried out since
it contained only 3% water and about a 20% gas saturation.

Figure 6.10b shows a recovery of 91%, an efficiency of 7.3 barrels of toluene
per barrel of bitumen recovered and a tar concentration in the toluene extract
decrease from 35 to 8% from the first to sixth stage.   Initially, 2 units of toluene were required to obtain a supernatant liquid. The final points were obtained by permitting the system to warm to room temperature, washing with
water and recovering additional supernatant extract.

The efficiency can be increased by washing with water earlier such as after treating with 2 to 4 units of toluene. Note that the maximum efficiency, without washing with water, occurred at 3.7 parts of toluene per part of original in-place tar.

According to a process described by *P.L. Paull and F.C. Armistead; U.S. Patent 4,003,432; January 18, 1977; assigned to Texaco Development Corporation,* a competent permeable communication zone connecting injection and production wells completed in a tar sand which communication zone will be rigid and will not tend to slump or heal may be developed by injecting a fluid in the injection well under such pressure so as to fracture the tar sand formation between the injection well and the production well and circulating a fluid between the injection and production wells which is at a temperature sufficiently low to freeze the water in tar sands. The fluid may contain propping agents to hold the fracture surfaces apart.

This procedure will rigidify the hydrocarbon portion of the tar sand formation in the vicinity of the fracture zone as well as freeze the water in the tar sand formation. Once the fracture is established, a solvent for the hydrocarbon in the tar sands may be circulated preferably at a temperature below the freezing point of the water in the tar sands to extract the bitumen.

Solvent Slurry and Water Separation

According to a process described by *G.R. Peterson, M.C. Hicks, and P.W. Schwartz; U.S. Patent 4,110,194; August 29, 1978; assigned to Intermountain Oil Research, Inc.,* mineral materials, containing bituminous oil in one form or in another, are intimately mixed with a hydrocarbon solvent which has a specific gravity less than that of water and which is capable of dissolving the bituminous oil contained in the mineral materials. The mixing is continued for a time sufficient for the solvent to extract essentially all the bituminous oil from the mineral materials, thereby forming a slurry which comprises solid particles of the mineral material suspended in the oil-rich solvent.

The oil-rich solvent is then separated from the solid particles of mineral material by feeding the slurry into a body of water beneath the surface thereof. Preferably, a stream of the slurry is continuously introduced into the body of water through a distributor means positioned wholly beneath the surface of the water. The distributor means is adapted to direct the incoming slurry downwardly into the water. The solid particles of mineral material contained in the slurry settle to the bottom of the body of water, and the oil-rich solvent rises and forms a supernatant layer on the surface of the body of water. Introducing the slurry stream beneath the surface of the water has been found to be particularly advantageous in obtaining a rapid, efficient separation of the solid particles of mineral material from the oil-rich solvent.

The solid particles of mineral material settle to the bottom of the body of water and are removed by a mud pump, auger, or other mechanism capable of transporting a dense slurry of the particulate material from the body of water. Water is continuously added to the body of the water to replace that which is withdrawn with the wet mineral material. The oil-rich solvent is skimmed from the surface of the body of water, and the bituminous oils are recovered therefrom.

The separation of the oil-rich solvent from the solid particles of mineral material is particularly effective when the slurry stream is introduced into the body of water through a distributor member which comprises a hollow cone having an upwardly directed apex, a downwardly directed, open base, and a plurality of openings through the sidewalls thereof. The slurry is jetted downwardly from the apex of the distributor, and as the hydrocarbon solvent phase separates from the particulate mineral material, it rises to the top of the body of water through the openings in the sidewalls of the distributor. The gradual reversal of the direction of flow of the oil-rich solvent, from its initial downward flow as it is introduced into the body of water to its ascent through the body of water, has been found to have a pronounced, beneficial effect on the rate of separation of the particulate material from the solvent, as well as on the efficiency of the separation. In accordance with this process, the oil-rich solvent which is removed from the surface of the body of water contains only very small amounts of solid particles of mineral material in the form of fines. The fines can be removed from the oil-rich solvent by conventional filtration and/or by centrifugal separation.

It has also been found advantageous to utilize high-speed mixing of the oil-bearing mineral materials and the hydrocarbon solvent. Preferably, the solvent and the mineral materials are mixed in a mixing vessel having an agitation impeller operating at a rotational speed of at least about 1,200 rpm, with the tip speed of the impeller being from about 6,000 to 9,000 fpm. The high-speed mixing results in very rapid extraction of the bituminous oil from the mineral materials. Essentially complete extraction is obtained with residence times as short as 30 seconds in the mixer. Because of the high-speed mixing and rapid extraction of bituminous oil from the mineral materials, the process is adapted to an integrated, continuous mode of operation.

C.A. Irani, E.W. Funk, E. Gomez, and R.L. Espino; U.S. Patent 4,036,732; July 19, 1977; assigned to Exxon Research and Engineering Company describe a process for the extraction of bitumen from tar sands which comprises contacting the tar sand in an extraction zone with a paraffinic hydrocarbon solvent having from 5 to 9 carbon atoms at a ratio of from 2 to 10 parts solvent per part of bitumen present in the tar sand, maintaining the asphaltene fraction of the tar sands in suspension, separating a major portion of the solvent which contains a major amount of the bitumen dissolved therein along with the suspended asphaltene fraction from the extracted sand, passing the extracted sand along with a minor portion of the solvent and a minor amount of bitumen into a water-contacting zone and therein contacting the extracted sand with sufficient water at a temperature of at least 100°F to separate substantially all of the minor amount of bitumen and the minor portion of solvent from the sand, separating the major solvent portion from the suspended asphaltenes and distilling the solvent from the major solvent portion to recover the major amount of bitumen.

In a preferred example, the extract from the water-contacting zone is centrifuged to separate fines and water from the bitumen and solvent, the minor amount of bitumen is removed from the solvent, e.g., by distillation and may be burned to provide heat for the process. The process contemplates separating the minor amount of bitumen as a low-metals bitumen fraction, thus useful as a clean burning fuel. The metal contaminants of the tar sand are removed with the asphaltenes and discarded.

It has been found that the process allows recovery of 97% or more of the bitumen which is present in the tar sands of which 83% or more is recovered as a high-grade fraction (the major portion described above). The difference, that is 14% bitumen, which differs from the initial fraction, is still of a significantly high grade as to be conveniently burned for energy to supply to the process. The major amount of bitumen will contain less than 130 ppm of vanadium, 65 ppm of iron, and 65 ppm of nickel; these are important criteria for downstream processing. Solvent losses in this process are as little as 0.7% by weight or less in one cycle.

Example 1: 500 g of fresh tar sands from Mildred Lake were sprayed with 25 ml of aqueous solution containing 200 ppm of phenol. This slurry was then contacted with normal heptane at a solvent/bitumen weight ratio of 4 and a temperature of 25°C. After 3 minutes contacting time, the liquid extract was withdrawn. The remaining sand, with residual solvent and bitumen, was contacted with 500 ml of water at 55°C. The water displaced the bitumen and solvent giving an oil phase above the water phase with no intermediate emulsion phase. Clean sand formed below the water phase. It was found that 2.3% of the total bitumen was lost with the sand and that 0.4% of the total heptane was lost. The bitumen layer from the water wash was centrifuged sufficiently to remove sand and water and was then combined with the liquid extract from the heptane contacting.

Subsequent centrifugation of this extract at 27°C and 1,700 rpm removed small quantities of clay and 9.54 g of asphaltenes (corresponding to 14.9% of the total bitumen). These asphaltenes have a Conradson carbon of 35%, a V content of 640 ppm, a Ni content of 350 ppm and a Fe content of 500 ppm. Following this centrifugation, heptane was removed from the dissolved bitumen by distillation and 56.99 g of deasphalted bitumen were recovered (corresponding to 82.3% of the total bitumen). The table below shows the properties of this major bitumen fraction.

Properties of Tar Sand Bitumens (Deasphalted)

Gravity, °API	
60°F	10.6
Viscosity, cs	
100°F	2,986.0
210°F	62.05
V, ppm	110
Ni, ppm	52
Fe, ppm	60
Conradson carbon, %	9.5

These results show that the major bitumen fraction obtained in this process is of a higher quality and can be used as a feed for hydrocarbon conversion processes.

Example 2: 1,000 g of fresh Athabasca tar sands from Mildred Lake were sprayed with 50 g of cold water. These wet tar sands were then contacted with n-heptane at a 4/1 solvent to bitumen weight ratio and at 20°C. The liquid extract containing solvent, dissolved bitumen and suspended asphaltenes was then passed to a conventional settler. The extract was settled at 90°C for 10 minutes; the liquid phase was then removed, and the solvent stripped off by distillation. The resulting deasphalted bitumen had a vanadium concentration of 113 ppm.

In another run where the settling was carried out at 20°C, the resulting deasphalted bitumen had a 185 ppm vanadium concentration for the same settling time. The asphaltenes precipitated by settling at a temperature of 90°C contain greater than 250 ppm of vanadium and also a small fraction of oils and resins entrained with the asphaltenes. The overall yield of deasphalted bitumen is 83% and of asphaltenes, 14%. The water wash step is the same as that used in Example 1 and again for water at 55°C solvent losses are less than 1%, and bitumen losses below 3%. This example demonstrates that a deasphalted bitumen can be obtained by the process by using simple equipment and avoiding the use of centrifuges or filters.

Example 3: The fresh tar sands were initially slurried with added water amounting to approximately 5% of the initial weight of the tar sands. The solvent was then added and the mixture agitated at 25°C. The liquid extract was then poured off the tar sand bed. Water at 55°C was then added to the tar sands and again the mixture was well stirred. Clean sand fell to the bottom and a hydrocarbon phase formed above the water phase; no emulsion formed.

The hydrocarbon phases were centrifuged to remove the asphaltenes plus suspended fines and water. The hydrocarbon phase from the solvent extraction has only a small quantity of fines, and is free of sand. The hydrocarbon phase from the water wash is similar to the froth produced in the hot water extraction process, except diluted by solvent. This phase contains both sand and water which are removed by centrifugation. The water-washed sand was contacted with benzene to remove the residual solvent and bitumen. Bitumen losses were determined by weight and the solvent loss by chromatographic analysis. The table below shows a summary of the experiments.

Solvent	Solvent Bitumen	DAB* Asphaltenes	Solvent Loss, %	Bitumen Loss, %
Hexane	4	5.6	0.4	2.3
Heptane	2	6.9	0.85	4.3
Heptane	3	5.5	1.02	2.7
Heptane	4	5.2	0.85	3.1
Heptane	5	5.0	0.86	2.1
Heptane (dry)	2	7.0	1.86	5.06

*Deasphalted Bitumen.

The following are the important conclusions: (1) High solvent recovery requires that the water envelope be maintained; this is the reason for the added water. Results in the table above show that for dry tar sands the solvent losses are high. This is due to the wetting of the sand by the solvent. (2) Solvent losses are based on the percent of total solvent used in the extraction. Thus, the percent tends to decrease with increasing solvent/bitumen ratio. Therefore, it does not appear that solvent losses are related to the total amount of solvent used. (3) The split between DAB/asphaltenes changes with the solvent/bitumen ratio used in the extraction. Also, the product characteristics change.

Ultrasonic Energy and Stirring

L.I. Hart, Jr., J.J. Schmidt-Collerus, and L.R. Burroughs; U.S. Patents 4,054,506; October 18, 1977; and 4,054,505; October 18, 1977; both assigned to Western Oil Sands Ltd. describe a method of removing bitumen from tar sand for subsequent recovery of the bitumen. The method comprises contacting tar sand with an excess of solvent in which the bitumen is soluble, the contacting being performed within a vessel wherein simultaneously the solvent is being stirred and ultrasonic energy is being applied, the ultrasonic energy being of an intensity sufficient to break apart any connections between sand granules and to remove bitumen from the sand granules to thereby permit the bitumen so removed to go into solution in the solvent for subsequent removal of the solvent-plus-bitumen and recovery of the bitumen. Stirring within the vessel reduces residence time required for removal of the bitumen from the tar sand by constantly changing that portion of the solvent directly in contact with the surface of the tar sand to thereby cause even loading of all of the solvent with the bitumen. The vessel utilized can be a column through which the tar sand falls as ultrasonic energy is applied and stirring occurs therein.

Example: A chunk of tar sand weighing about 110 g is placed in a beaker and covered with 50 ml (about 2 times the dead volume of the tar sand) of a solvent comprising a reagent grade mixture by volume of 23% ethylbenzene, 14% orthoxylene, 55% meta-xylene, and 8% para-xylene. The solvent is kept stirred with a small stirring blade operated by a small stirring motor at a speed of 15 rpm. The stirring blade keeps the solvent circulating, but does not contact the tar sand. Immediately thereafter, a sonic head of ½" diameter is placed in the solvent and 60 kilocycles of sonic energy is applied for a period of 60 seconds to break apart any connections between sand granules and to concurrently remove from the sand granules bitumen which goes into solution in the solvent.

The resulting solvent-plus-bitumen is then decanted for subsequent recovery of the bitumen. To indicate the effectiveness of the sonic energy, further experimentation is shown in Table 1, below, comparing the bitumen recovered from the above decantation against four subsequent consecutive respective 30 ml amounts of the same solvent put in contact with the tar sand for respective 30-second periods and then, respectively, decanted. Acetone is used in Extraction No. 6 of Table 1 to remove all solvent from the remaining sand.

Table 1: Extraction of Tar Sands*

Extraction Number	Amount of Solvent (ml)	Extraction Time	Extracted Bitumen (wt %)
1 (sonic used)	50	60 sec	11.5
2	30	30 sec	13.4
3	30	30 sec	14.3
4	30	30 sec	14.4
5	30	30 sec	14.7
6	30**	30 sec	14.7
Total	200	3.5 min	14.7

*At ambient temperature and slow stirring utilizing sonic energy in the first extraction.
**Acetone.

Analysis of the above tar sand shows that the total amount of bitumen present originally by weight percent is 14.7. Table 1 shows that 78% of the total bitumen content was removed from the tar sand and in solution in the solvent 60 seconds after the procedure began.

To contrast the results in Table 1, a second procedure, the solvent extraction method, was undertaken using a second sample of tar sand, the same solvent, and the same amount of stirring, but without using sonic energy. The results of this procedure are shown in Table 2 on the following page.

Table 2: Extraction of Tar Sands*

Extraction Number	Amount of Solvent (ml)	Extraction Time (hr)	Extracted Bitumen Wt (%)
1	110	4	8.5
2	30	3	11.0
3	30	3	12.4
4	30	3	13.1
5	30	3	13.1
6	30**	3	13.5
Total	260	19	13.5

*At ambient temperature and slow stirring without utilization of sonic energy.
**Acetone.

Analysis of the above tar sand shows that the total amount of bitumen present originally by weight percent is 13.5. Table 2 shows that even with additional solvent and 4 hours of contact of solvent with the tar sand, only 63% of the total bitumen content was removed from the tar sand and in solution in the solvent. Further, at Extraction No. 5, 16 hours into the procedure, a small amount of bitumen still had not been removed from the tar sand. This is contrasted to Extraction No. 5 of Table 1 wherein, after only 3 minutes into the procedure, all of the bitumen was removed from the tar sand.

To demonstrate the effectiveness of using stirring in addition to using ultrasonic energy in relation to bitumen uptake by the solvent, experiments were conducted in which bitumen was extracted from tar sand by using ultrasonic energy both with and without stirring in a large beaker. The ultrasonic energy frequency used was 25 kHz, and the quantity of bitumen extracted from the tar sand was measured as a function of time.

90 g of ¼" diameter pellets of tar sand were placed in 250 ml of petroleum condensate (raw gasoline). An ultrasonic application of 25 kHz frequency was applied as was a stirrer blade rotating at 1,000 rpm. Small samples of bitumen-plus-solvent were removed at 15, 30, 60, 120, and 300 seconds. A second identical experiment, with the exception of the stirring, was also undertaken, with small samples likewise at 15, 30, 60, 120, and 300 seconds. Each set of bitumen-plus-solvent samples was then analyzed for bitumen uptake. This analysis was performed with a Beckman DG spectrophotometer measuring the light transmittance at a wavelength of 500 nm. The quantities of bitumen extracted from the tar sand and in solution in the solvent, with and without stirring, are compared in Table 3, below.

Table 3: Percent Comparison of Bitumen Contained in Solvent

Time (sec)	With Stirring (Wt % of Solution)	Without Stirring (Wt % of Solution)
15	1.44	0.42
30	2.40	0.64
60	3.06	0.63
120	3.27	1.01
300	3.99	1.96

The improved results, with stirring, are due to the removal of the bitumen film away from the surface of the tar sand by macroscopic mixing which effectively introduces cleaner solvent to the tar sand surface which in turn increases the mass transfer driving force. Comparison of the results outlined in Table 3 shows that stirring enhances bitumen recovery and, because tar sand is an agglomerate, stirring consequently decreases the time required to disintegrate this agglomerate and enhance bitumen uptake by the solvent, thus significantly decreasing the residence time required for the uptake.

Agglomerating Technique

A process described by *F.W. Meadus, B.D. Sparks, I.E. Puddington, and J.R. Farnand; U.S. Patent 4,057,486; November 8, 1977; assigned to Canadian Patents and Development Limited, Canada* is directed to the separation of mineral solids from hydrocarbons, particularly bitumens of kerogens, the mixtures thereof usually occurring naturally as tar sands, oil sands, oil shales, etc. The mineral solids are finely divided, or are rendered so by pulverizing, grinding, etc. The mineral solids are caused to agglomerate into discrete, compact units (substantially free of the hydrocarbon) which are readily separated mechanically.

The method of separating siliceous solids usually including clay from hydrocarbons or bitumens of deposits or mixtures thereof, the solids being in finely divided form, comprises:

(1) Distributing an organic solvent or diluent for the hydrocarbons into the mixture in sufficient amounts to dissolve or disperse the hydrocarbons and provide a liquid slurry;

(2) Providing an aqueous agglomerating liquid in the diluted mixture in total amounts of from about 8 to 50% by weight of the feed mixture;

(3) Agitating the multiphase mixture severely enough and, for a sufficient time, to contact intimately the aqueous liquid and the siliceous solids, continuing agitation until the aqueous liquid and the hydrophilic siliceous solids form into discrete, compact agglomerates;

(4) Separating the compact agglomerates from the organic phase; and

(5) Recovering the hydrocarbons and solvent or diluent.

Example 1: A sample of tar sands from Great Canadian Oil Sands (with 25% being fines of –325 mesh) was mixed with kerosene and water in the following proportions (all parts by weight): tar sands, 30 parts (7.6% H_2O); kerosene, 49 parts; and water, 2 parts containing NaOH to pH 9.5. This mixture was shaken in a closed partially filled container for 30 minutes. After this agitation, balls of the sand and clay had formed ranging in diameter from about 1.5 to 12 mm. These balls were compact, easily separated and appeared free of bitumen.

Example 2: Tar sand, kerosene and water were mixed in a stirred blender in the following proportions (all parts by weight): tar sand, 120 parts (7.6% H_2O); kerosene, 200 parts; and water, 5 parts NaOH to pH 9.5. The bitumen largely dissolved and initial small agglomerates formed. This mixture was then transferred to a rotating drum and subjected to controlled agitation for 15 minutes. The tumbling action in the drum could be controlled to produce round, compact balls with a narrow size distribution. Uniform larger agglomerates of about 2 mm diameter were removed from the drum and washed with kerosene. The petroleum fraction was virtually free of water and solids, while the agglomerates contained 3.6% organic material and 11.7% water.

Example 3: A blender was used to mix the following (all parts by weight): tar sands, 200 parts (7.6% H_2O); aliphatic hydrocarbon solvent, 200 parts (Varsol); and water, 8 parts. This mixture was then transferred to a rotating drum where it was less violently agitated for 15 minutes to form larger round compact agglomerates of about 2 mm diameter. The agglomerates were washed with 140 parts of kerosene and the combined organic phase recycled to contact tar sand feed. After four cycles, no change in results was observed, indicating that at this solvent to tar sands ratio extensive recycling of solvent is desirable.

Agglomeration Using Rotatable Drum

According to a process described by *F.W. Meadus, B.D. Sparks, and I.E. Puddington; U.S. Patent 3,984,287; October 5, 1976; assigned to Canadian Patents and Development Limited, Canada,* a rotatable drum having an interior which tapers in a horizontal direction has a first port at the smaller end for receiving particulate tar sands or coal, and an agglomerating liquid, e.g., water, and a second port at the larger end for receiving an organic-material-separating liquid, e.g., Varsol, with which the agglomerating liquid is immiscible.

The first port is, for example, larger than the second port so that the separating liquid will drain from the drum through the first port. A conveying means delivers the particulate material and agglomerating liquid into the drum interior, and the separating liquid forms a slurry so that inorganic residue from the particulate material is formed into ball agglomerates as it tumbles along the drum and the ball agglomerates overflow through the second port while the separating liquid fed into the second port separates organic material from the particulate material in the drum and overflows through the first port.

Pipeline Slurry Processing

A process described by *M. Wicks, III; U.S. Patent 3,925,189; December 9, 1975; assigned to Shell Oil Company* involves transporting tar sands from an open pit tar sand to a processing plant and partially recovering hydrocarbons in transit.

The system **11** shown in Figure 6.11a comprises a conveyor belt **12** driven by a pair of rollers **13** and **14**, coupled to suitable motive means, for feeding hydrocarbon-containing solids such as tar sands into a jet-type mixer **15**. Hydrocarbon-containing solids such as tar sands may be those which have been extracted from a subterranean formation, such as the Athabasca tar sands of Canada, Indian Knob tar sands in San Luis Obispo County, California, Utah's Green River Desert tar sand deposits, by any suitable means, such as open pit mining, or the Green River oil shale deposits of Colorado which on recovery must be rubblized into particles of 2 to 5,000 microns suitable for forming a slurry with a suitable solvent.

Mixer **15**, as shown in detail in Figure 6.11b, includes a hopper **16** which communicates at its upper end with the upper portion of belt **12**. Thus, tar sands carried by belt **12** are deposited into hopper **16** of mixer **15** as illustrated in Figure 6.11b.

Figure 6.11: Pipeline Processing

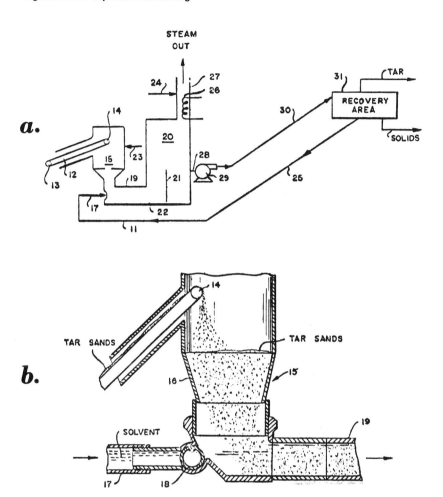

(a)   Schematic diagram of system
(b)   Detail of a portion of the apparatus of Figure 6.11a

Source: U.S. Patent 3,925,189

A suitable solvent such as an aromatic and/or aliphatic solvent, e.g., toluene, benzene, xylene, phenol, aliphatic naphthas, e.g., Shell's Tolusol having the following properties: specific gravity at 60°F, 0.737; distillation range 205° to 220°F; aniline cloud point 120°F; aromatic, 11 vol %; is introduced under pressure through inlet **17** past flow valve **18** where it mixes with the tar sands from hopper **16** to form a tar sands-solvent slurry. This slurry is removed from mixer **15** through outlet **19**. From outlet **19**, the slurry preferably passes into a surge tank **20** (Figure 6.11a) so as to provide an opportunity for vapor disengagement from the slurry and also give some additional contact time for tar leaching. Tank **20** consists of a substantially cylindrical vessel having a baffle plate **21** across its diameter and extending vertically upward from the lower wall **22** of tank **20**. Tank **20** and baffle **21** are preferably of stainless steel. In order to exclude air from both mixer **15** and tank **20**, purge stream inlets **23** and **24**, for introducing oxygen-free gas, communicate with the interiors of mixer **15** and tank **20**, respectively.

Any suitable inert gas may be used, e.g., steam, N_2, CO_2, etc.; however, steam is preferred since a small amount may be added to the slurry so as to improve filtration rates. If it is found that steam condensate from the steam introduced into mixer **15** causes the tar sand particles to stick together, nitrogen may be used as the mixer purge gas and small amounts of water can be introduced as liquid into the solvent return line **25** or into mixer **15** directly by any suitable means so as to achieve correct proportions of tar sands and solvent in the slurry. A vapor condenser **26** is preferably located in a steam outlet **27** which communicates with the interior of tank **20** for minimizing solvent losses and permitting inert gases to leave system **11**.

A surge tank outlet **28** communicates with tank **20** for removing the slurry; the slurry is flowed through suitable pumping means **29** and is preferably pumped uphill (i.e., at an angle to the horizontal of 2° to 45° and preferably between 5° and 15°) along a slurry pipeline **30** of 2 to 40 inch diameter, preferably 6 to 24 inch diameter, the slurry flowing at a velocity within the range of 3 to 20 ft/sec which can be several thousand feet to several miles, e.g., 1,000 to 15,000 ft to a recovery area **31**.

Any remaining tar and solids will be recovered from the slurry at the recovery area **31**. Solvent return line **25** communicates with the recovery area **31** for removing solvent therefrom under gravity flow. The solvent return line **25** communicates with inlet **17** for introducing solvent back into mixer **15**.

As an example of the operation of the process tar sands extracted from the subterranean formation are fed from conveyor belt **12** into mixer **15**. As shown in Figure 6.11b, the tar sands are mixed with a suitable solvent introduced under pressure through inlet **17**. In this manner, a tar sands-solvent slurry is flowed out of mixer **15** through outlet **19**. The slurry is then flowed into surge tank **20** at a velocity sufficient to keep all of the slurry in suspension. For example, a 15 ft diameter cylindrical surge tank, 14 ft high, at high capacity provides 60 seconds surge time at maximum flow and thus 60 seconds contact time for tar desorption from the sand. In this manner, tar is partially leached from the slurry and condensed vapors are removed through outlet **27**.

The partially leached slurry is then preferably pumped uphill at relatively high flow velocities through a slurry pipeline **30** to the recovery area **31**. The residence time of the slurry in the pipeline **30** promotes further leaching of the tar from the tar sands in the slurry. At the recovery area **31**, any remaining tar is recovered from the slurry by means well known in the art. The solids (i.e., the sand and other waste materials) are also recovered and removed at the recovery area **31**. The slurry flowing within pipeline **30** can flow in a variety of ways or flow regimes dictated primarily by average flow velocity, particle size and weight, fluid properties and pipe size and orientation, all of which are described in detail.

Example: Based on a maximum tar sand flow of 56,000 tons per stream day, the following dimensions are preferred for the system:

Item	Remarks
Line **30**	14-inch pipe with 0.406-inch wall thickness
Line **25**	14-inch pipe with 0.406-inch wall thickness resulting in the obtaining of a solvent at a minimum of 60 psig pressure at the solids-liquid mixing point by gravity return of the liquid
Pumping means **29**	Two 1,500 horsepower piston-type slurry pumps
Lift range of line **30**	300 to 600 feet (at an angle of approximately 5° to 7° to the horizontal)
Pipe length range	3,500 to 5,000 feet
Tar sand	Flow rate range of 34,000 to 56,000 tons per stream day; solid specific gravity, 2.6; and solid concentration in solvent, 40% by volume
Solvent	Tolusol
Slurry properties (Tolusol-tar liquid solution)	Viscosity, 3 to 4 cs at 80°F; specific gravity, 0.9

It can be seen from the foregoing that the transportation of tar sands in a liquid in which they are soluble enables tar sands to be transported from the area in which they were mined to a recovery area while leaching some of the hydrocarbons from the tar sands thereby lowering the recovery cost in the remainder of the process. Any additives which might improve the operations in the recovery area may be mixed during the transportation of the slurry. The residence time for leaching tar from the slurry may be controlled by varying the velocity and solids concentration in a given length and size pipeline. For open-pit mining operations, for example, the length of the pipeline is adjusted as required by merely adding more pipe length segments as the mining operations proceed.

Processing Tank and Conveyor System

J.B. Fairbanks, Jr. and G.C. Brimhall; U.S. Patent 3,951,749; April 20, 1976 describe a apparatus for processing tar sands to recover bitumen without the use of heat or steam. The apparatus includes a processing tank having a concave, upwardly facing bottom constructed for receiving the upper flight of an endless conveyor.

Structure is provided for admitting tar sands onto the feed end of such conveyor and for discharging the same at the discharge end. Stirrer means are provided as needed, above the endless conveyor, for maintaining in solution the very fine tar sand particles, this to effect as efficient a recovery of oil as possible. A baffle is constructed to separate recovered oil, disposed as a layer over the aqueous bath of the tank, from the discharge end of the tank and the spent sands coming upwardly thereat. In one example, the processing tank is constructed for towing by a vehicle and, in another case, the bottom of the tank is constructed to separately contain diluent for preprocessing the tar sands to be fed into the main tank proper.

Separation of Coarse Sand Particles

R.G. Murray and B.J. Gikis; U.S. Patent 4,120,775; October 17, 1978; assigned to Natomas Company describe a solvent extraction method in which a well comminuted tar sand is first mixed with a liquid hydrocarbon solvent to form a dilute bitumen solution in which, by means of suitable agitation, the coarse as well as the fine solid particles present are well dispersed. This dispersion flows downwardly from the agitation zone and through a shallow conduit, generally rectangular in cross section and having an opening extending across its bottom portion over which the dispersion passes.

During the short residence time of the dispersion over the opening, the coarse sand particles, which under the influence of gravity fall faster than the fines, selectively drop out of the dispersion and pass through the conduit opening into an underlying sand-receiving chamber. The latter is continuously provided with solvent which wells up into the bitumen solution passing overhead, which still contains the fines portion of the dispersion, and thus supports the solution. The coarse sand particles separated out in this fashion are collected, solvent-washed and freed of solvent. The residual bitumen solution, containing bitumen, solvent and fines, is in part recycled to the tar sand receiving zone, while the balance is conventionally processed (preferably by centrifuging) to separate out all or most of the fines before being sent to a solvent recovery column where the solvent is stripped from the bitumen. The recovered solvent can be employed to wash the bitumen from the collected coarse sand particles. The bitumen product fraction recovered can be worked up in any desired manner.

Combined Recovery of Fertilizers and Kerogen Materials

According to a process developed by *M.L. Anthony; U.S. Patent 4,130,474; December 19, 1978; assigned to Shoilco, Inc.*, fertilizers and kerogen materials are extracted from crushed oil shale utilizing a low temperature dekerosing (kerogen removal) solvent phase followed by a second fertilizer extraction phase using water as solvent. Process control factors are effective in producing delamination of the crushed oil shale resulting in high yield of kerogen and fertilizer values. The shale residue is not disintegrated and constitutes an ecologically acceptable soil conditioner and land restoration residuum.

Proper blending of the various extracts and residues results in a wide variety of commercial fertilizer products. Bitumens and fertilizer materials may also be extracted from tar sands of both the hard, stony and soft variety and again a nonpetroleum solvent, low temperature extraction process is used in a first step to recover the bitumen fraction. The solvent is totally recovered and recycled. Thermal energies are also recycled resulting in high overall efficiency. The sand residuum or dross is clean and uncontaminated, constituting a water-wettable land restoration medium with plant nutrient value imparting arable character. A second step may be employed to selectively leach fertilizers, notably phosphates and potash. Leaching is accomplished by the use of water, which is recovered and recycled.

Recovery of Zircon and Rutile

A process described by *R.A. Baillie, L.F. Schmoyer, and T.E. Skarada; U.S. Patent 3,990,885; November 9, 1976; assigned to Great Canadian Oil Sands Limited,*

Canada is directed to the recovery of zircon and rutile from bituminous tar sands. The process includes the steps of recovering a mineral-containing bitumen froth from a separation process for the treatment of bituminous tar sands, diluting the froth with a liquid hydrocarbon diluent, centrifuging at least a portion of the mineral-containing diluted bitumen froth to produce a bitumen product and a waste stream comprised of heavy minerals including zircon and rutile, as well as bitumen, diluent, and water. Subsequently, the heavy mineral stream is mixed with a solvent to remove the bitumen and other contaminants adhered to the surface of or mixed with the metal particles. The clean particles are subsequently washed with hot water.

COKING AND REFINING PROCESSES

Subdivision of Slurry for Coking and Fractionation

According to processes described by *D.O. Hanson; U.S. Patent 4,071,433; Jan. 31, 1978; and P.H. Gifford, II; U.S. Patent 4,071,434; January 31, 1978; both assigned to Phillips Petroleum Company*, tar sand is blended in a melt tank with oil to form a slurry. The slurry is subdivided in a centrifugal zone into two streams, one containing coarse sand particles and the other containing fine sand particles. The stream containing coarse sand is passed through a solid separation zone in which sand is removed. Any residual bitumen is removed from solids by kerosine. The kerosine wash is combined with the filtrate stream. The stream containing fine solid particles is introduced into a coker where sand particles act as nuclei in the formation of coke.

The vapor stream produced in the coker is introduced into the bottom section of the fractionator thereby supplying most of the heat requirements for product separation. The filtrate of the fine sand stream is fed into the fractionator at intermediate points. The fractionator produces gas and oil fractions, which are recovered as products. Heavy gas oil can be recycled to the melt tank and heavy bottoms can be recycled to the coker. Kerosine from the kerosine wash promotes reflux in the upper section of the fractionation zone.

Referring to Figure 6.12, suitably pulverized tar sand is introduced to the melt tank **10** by **15** and blended by agitator **18** with a suitable starting solvent such as gas oil or diesel fuel introduced by **20**. If necessary, to aid in dissolution of bitumen from the sand the blend can be heated by passing heating liquid through a jacket **25**. Water contained in the sand is evaporated from the melt tank removed by **12**, condensed and disposed of.

Once the slurry becomes pumpable, it is transported to a centrifugal classifier **30** via **35**. In the centrifugal classifier, the slurry is subdivided into an overflow stream **40** containing fine sand particles and an underflow stream **45** containing coarse sand particles. Although any of a variety of classifiers [described in *Unit Operations of Chemical Engineering*, W.L. McCabe and J.C. Smith, 2d Edition, pp. 930 to 931 (1967)] can be used in connection with this process, a Dorr-Oliver, Inc. classifier is usually employed.

Coarse solids are removed in a coarse solids removal zone which comprises a hot oil filter **50**. The details of the operation of hot oil filters (also referred to as rotary drum filters) can be found in *Chemical Engineers' Handbook* by R.H.

Perry, 5th Edition (1973). The sand trapped in the filter **50** is washed with kerosine introduced by **51**. Make-up kerosine is brought by **52**. The washed sand is passed into a sand drier **53** via **54** and therein organic materials are vaporized and sand is taken out of the system by **55**. The essentially particle-free filtrate of stream **45**, kerosine wash and vaporized organic materials brought from the drier **53** by **56** are passed via **60** to a heater **62** and therefrom via **62** to the mid-section of the fractionator **65**.

Therein kerosine helps to reflux the upper section of the column and to scrub out entrained fine sand particles that may have entered via vapor stream **90**. The amount of heat supplied by heater **62** is sufficient to maintain the temperature which permits under the pressure maintained in the fractionation zone **65** separation of materials introduced therein into an overhead, intermediate cuts and bottoms.

Figure 6.12: Oil Recovery Process

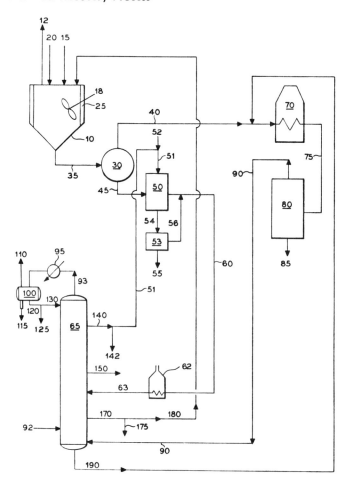

Source: U.S. Patent 4,071,433

The overflow stream **40** is passed into a coker preheat furnace **70** and from there it is introduced to coker drum **80** via **75**. In the coker drum **80**, the stream is separated into coke, formed around sand particles acting as nuclei, and vapors. The coke is withdrawn by **85** and vapors are withdrawn by **90**. A more detailed description of the coking process can be found, for example, in "Diagram of Delayed Coking Process," W.L. Nelson, *Petroleum Refinery Engineering*, McGraw-Hill (1958). Vapor stream **90** is fed into the bottom of the fractionator **65** to supply the heat for reboiling. Further heating is provided by live superheated steam introduced by **92**.

The fractionator **65** is maintained at such operating conditions as to separate the feed into overhead, intermediate cuts of kerosine, light and heavy gas oils and heavy bottoms. The overhead comprising mainly gas, steam and gasoline is taken off by **93** and passed through a condenser **95** to an accumulator **100**. Gas is removed from the accumulator by **110**; water is removed by **115** and gasoline stream withdrawn by **120** is subdivided into **125** and **130**. The former is recovered as product and the latter is returned to the top of the column as reflux. The light gas oil cut taken off by **150** is recovered as product. A part of the kerosine stream **140** is recycled via line **51** to the hot oil filter **50** and the rest is withdrawn as product via **142**. A portion of the heavy gas oil withdrawn by **170** is recovered as product via **175** and a portion thereof is recycled by **180** to the melt tank **10**. The heavy oil cut is recycled via **180** to the melt tank **10** and heavy bottoms stream **190** is recycled to the furnace **70** via **40**.

Example: In the system as shown in Figure 6.12, 50,000 tons per day (tpd) of tar sand containing 11 wt % of bitumen, 83 wt % of sand and 6 wt % of water is introduced into a melt tank **10** where a slurry is produced with oil recycled from the fractionator at a rate of 50,000 tpd. The melt tank **10** is maintained at 400°F (204°C), a temperature sufficient to evaporate 3,000 tpd of water. The slurry is passed from the melt tank at a rate of 97,000 tpd to a centrifugal classification zone **30**. The melt tank stream **35**, entering zone **30**, comprises 41,500 tpd of sand and 55,500 tpd of organics.

The zone **30** subdivides the melt tank stream **35** into an overflow stream **40** comprising 8,060 tpd of flow and an underflow stream **45** comprising the remainder of the melt tank slurry: 39,010 tpd sand and 49,930 tpd organics. The overflow stream **40** contains 2,490 tpd of sand having diameter equal or less than 44 microns; sand of that diameter comprises about 6 wt % of the total sand in the slurry. The underflow stream **45** is introduced into the hot oil filter **50** having filter area of 48,000 ft² which retains coarse solids so that the filtrate stream leaving the hot oil filter contains 39 tpd solids and 53,571 tpd organics.

The solids trapped by the oil filter **50** are washed with a kerosine wash **51** introduced to the filter at the rate of 5,000 tpd. A portion of the kerosine wash is combined with the filtrate stream and a portion (1,559 tpd) is removed from the hot oil filter **50** together with the sand (38,971 tpd). The filter cake, removed from the hot oil filter, is then introduced into a sand drier **53** from which 1,520 tpd of kerosine and any water contained therein is evaporated and 38,971 tpd of sand together with 39 tpd of organics are removed from the system by **55**.

The filtrate stream together with kerosine wash and evaporated kerosine stream **56**, comprising together 39 tpd solids and 53,371 tpd organics, is heated in heater **62** and introduced into the mid-section of the fractionator **65**. The overflow stream 40 is heated in preheat furnace 70 and introduced to a coker 80 where 1,225 tpd of coke is formed around sand particles acting as nuclei and from which 9,315 tpd vapor is withdrawn by 90 and fed to the bottom of the fractionator 65 where its heat is used for reboiling the column. The bottom temperature of the column is maintained at 650°F (343°C); the pressure is 20 psia (138 kPa). Superheated steam is added at the rate of 9 mol/mol of hydrocarbon vapor to reduce the hydrocarbon partial pressure to 2 psia (13.8 kPa). The feed is separated into various fractions taken off from the column in the following amounts via the designated lines:

Line	Product	Tons/Day
110	Noncondensible gases	372
125	400 EP gasoline	1,630
140	Kerosine	1,080
150	Product light gas oil	700
170	Product heavy gas oil	463

The heavy gas oil is recycled to the melt tank at the rate 50,000 tpd, and the heavy bottoms is recycled to the coker at the rate of 5,000 tpd. Kerosine is recycled to the hot oil filter at the rate of 5,000 tpd.

Coking Using Hot Solids Recycle

According to a process described by *P.C. Flynn; U.S. Patent 4,082,646; April 4, 1978; assigned to Petro-Canada Exploration Inc., Province of Alberta, Department of Energy and Natural Resources, Alberta Syncrude Equity, Ontario Energy Corporation, Imperial Oil Limited, Canada-Cities Service, Ltd., and Gulf Oil Canada Limited, all of Canada*, coked solids, produced by coking of tar sands, are contacted in a first zone with air and the minimum amount of supplemental fuel needed to burn all the coke. Part of the hot clean mineral solids produced is then discarded; the balance is moved into a second zone. Here, supplemental fuel is burned to increase the temperature of the solids. The hot solids from the second zone are recycled to the coking stage.

In the process, by modifying the typical configuration of the burning zone, two improvements are introduced. First, the quantity of supplementary fuel is reduced for reasons that will become evident hereinafter. Secondly, the flue gases are concentrated so that removal of the unwanted components is simplified and, therefore, made less expensive.

Example: With reference to Figure 6.13, 1 kg of tar sand feed, comprising 11.6 wt % bitumen, 4.4% water and 84% solids, is added to a coker zone 1. Here, it is mixed with 5.64 kg of hot solids recycle coming from a fuel burner zone 2. The two streams reach an ultimate temperature of about 525°C, whereupon hydrocarbon and water vapors are released and pass out of the zone. Approximately 12% of the hydrocarbons in the feed forms noncondensable gases, 72% is vaporized to condensable gases, and the balance forms a coke layer on the grains of solids. 6.50 kg of coked solids are conveyed from the coker zone 1 into a coke burner zone 2. Here, they are mixed with 0.16 kg of air and burned to remove the coke. Burning is conducted to produce a 2:1 CO_2 to CO ratio in the flue gas. The clean solids leave the coke burner zone at a temperature of about 575°C. About 0.176 kg of flue gas is produced, containing contaminants including H_2S and fine particulates.

Figure 6.13: Direct Coking Processes

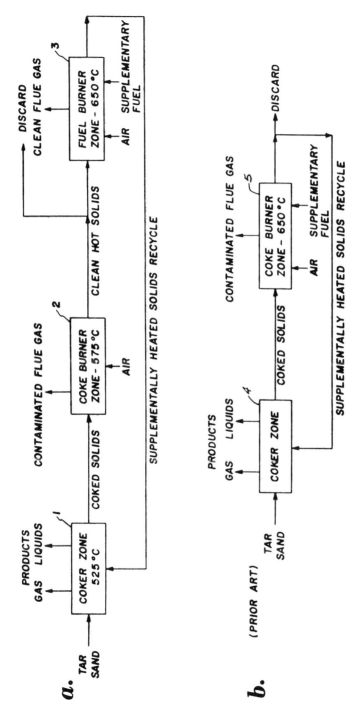

(a) Schematic showing a direct coking operation of this process
(b) Schematic showing a prior art example of a direct coking operation for tar sands

Source: U.S. Patent 4,082,646

Approximately 0.84 kg of clean hot solids (i.e., an amount equal to the solids introduced in the feed) is preferably discarded from the stream leaving the coke burner zone 2. The remaining 5.64 kg of hot clean solids are introduced into a fuel burner zone 3. Here, 0.20 kg of air and 0.013 kg of refinery fuel gas are combusted completely to raise the temperature of the solids to 650°C. Approximately 0.211 kg of flue gas is produced from the fuel burner zone 3. This flue gas is essentially free of contaminants and can be released directly to the atmosphere. The 5.64 kg of solids at 650°C produced from the zone 3 are recycled to the coker zone 1.

For purposes of comparison, the results of a direct coking operation in accordance with the prior art are now described. Again, 1 kg of the same tar sand feed is introduced into the coker zone 4 and mixed with 5.64 kg of recycled solids at 650°C. The 6.50 kg of coked solids from the coker zone 4 are conveyed into a burner zone 5. Here, the solids require 0.016 kg of refinery fuel gas and 0.40 kg of air for combustion of the coke, at a CO_2 to CO ratio of 2:1 and the gas at a CO_2 to CO ratio approaching infinity to produce clean solids at 650°C, part of which is recycled to the coker zone 4. Approximately 0.43 kg of contaminated flue gas is produced from the burner zone 5. From the foregoing, it will be noted that there is a significant concentration of contaminants in the flue gas from the combustion of the coke, and a reduction of supplementary fuel consumption when this process is practiced.

Fluidized Bed Reactor

According to a process described by *P.H. Gifford, II; U.S. Patent 4,094,767; June 13, 1978; assigned to Phillips Petroleum Company,* fresh (raw) tar sands are preheated and injected into the fluidized bed of a tar sand reactor means into an area of the fluidized bed below the top of the bed. The bitumen contained in the fresh tar sand input stream is reacted under substantially reducing conditions in the presence of steam, recycle and combination gases, such that the bitumen is converted to vaporous hydrocarbonaceous materials to some extent by vaporization and at least to some extent by cracking, leaving a coked sand.

Hot gases are removed overhead from the fluidized bed and passed in heat exchange with fresh tar sands, or with air which is thus preheated air and then is used in heat exchange with fresh tar sands, prior to adding the thus preheated tar sands into the fluidized bed. The partially cooled off-gases are separated to recover a raw oil as product, while the separated gases are recycled at least in part to the base area or heat recovery zone of the reactor means. The recycle gases are passed upwardly through the downwardly moving bed of hot spent sand, thus returning heat into the reactor decoking and cracking zones. Steam and oxygen are injected into the fluidized bed in the decoking area above the spent sand cooling zone, and below the input area in the cracking zone for fresh tar sand.

Thermal efficiency is obtained in the process from the incoming recycle off-gas which in turn recovers heat from the spent sand which would otherwise escape from the system. The hot recycle gases, combustion products from decoking, and steam provide a substantially reducing atmosphere for the conversion of bitumen to vaporous products. These reducing conditions are believed to be advantageous in permitting recovery of more of the bitumen as useful products than is otherwise possible.

Gasification of Solid Residue

According to a process described by *D.A. Redford; U.S. Patent 4,026,357; May 31, 1977; assigned to Texaco Exploration Canada Ltd., Canada*, solid hydrocarbon materials contained in a subsurface, porous, permeable formation may be converted to a gaseous form and thereby transported to the surface by contacting the material with a gas, which is at least 40% oxygen, in combination with a moderating fluid such as steam or carbon dioxide to convert the carbonaceous material to carbon monoxide and hydrogen. In a preferred case, essentially pure oxygen is injected into the formation and sufficient heat is applied to the formation at the point of oxygen injection to initiate an in situ combustion reaction, after which the extraneous heat source is removed and oxygen injection is continued to propagate a high temperature reaction zone within the formation. A moderating fluid is then injected simultaneously or intermittently with the oxygen, the moderating fluid being steam, water or carbon dioxide.

The moderating fluid serves to reduce the oxidation reaction temperature and, consequently, ensures that the predominant products of the reaction are carbon monoxide and hydrogen. The weight ratio of oxygen to steam is thereafter maintained at a value between 0.2 and 3.0. Some thermal cracking of the hydrocarbon material will result in the production of small amounts of low molecular weight hydrocarbons which may be either gaseous or a liquid, but a substantial portion of the solid hydrocarbon material will be converted to carbon monoxide and hydrogen. Carbon monoxide and hydrogen are produced from a spaced apart production well and subjected on the surface to additional treatment as necessary, depending on the use to be made of the produced gaseous materials.

OTHER SEPARATION PROCESSES

Hydraulic Mining Apparatus

D.M. Parkes; U.S. Patent 4,061,398; December 6, 1977; and D.M. Parkes and T.B. Hart; U.S. Patent 4,045,086; August 30, 1977; both assigned to Kaiser Resources Ltd., Canada describe an hydraulic mining apparatus and method wherein the mined aggregate is separated into dry, relatively large aggregate pieces for dry conveyance and wet, relatively small aggregate pieces for wet conveyance.

The method provides for reducing any oversized large aggregate pieces in size so that the large pieces do not exceed a predetermined maximum size. Size reduction is provided by a mechanical breaker and wet, relatively small aggregate is separated out of the mined product prior to the breaking step. The apparatus involves a feeder-breaker mechanism wherein a conveyor running lengthwise of the mechanism first subjects the total mined product to size separation or classification, then directs the larger aggregate pieces through the breaker and, finally, discharges the breaker-treated pieces to a dry conveyor. The separated wet, relatively small aggregate pieces are collected within the mechanism and pumped away.

As shown in Figure 6.14, the feeder-breaker is illustrated within a mine shaft or entry **10**. The roof of the shaft is shown as being supported by arches **12** and the enlarged area of the mine being cut away by the dislodging monitor of the apparatus is designated by the numeral **14**. The floor of the shaft is designated by the numeral **16**. The feeder-breaker apparatus is designated in its entirety by the numeral **18**. The apparatus comprises a chassis **20** in the form of a pan-like structure supported on the floor **16**.

As shown, the chassis comprises a bottom **22**, a forward end **24**, a cutaway rearward end **26** and a top platform **28**. From Figure 6.14d will be appreciated that the top of the chassis is open over the majority of the length thereof, the open portion being designated **30**. Although not illustrated in detail, it should be understood that the chassis is provided with suitable superstructure so that it is selfsupporting and so that the chassis may be moved about without being adversely distorted. Typically, the chassis would be moved into place by either pushing or pulling through means of a suitable traction vehicle, or by winch mounted upon the chassis.

Figure 6.14: Hydraulic Mining Apparatus

a.

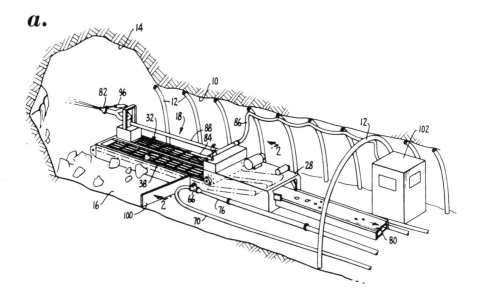

b.

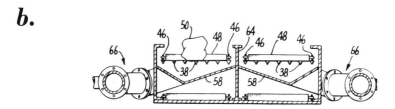

(continued)

Figure 6.14: (continued)

c.

d.

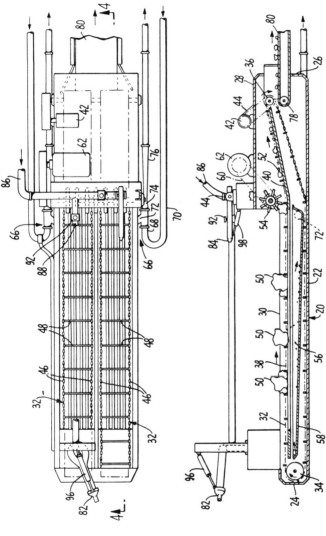

(a) Perspective view of the feeder-breaker as it would appear within a mine
(b) Cross-sectional view through the upstream section of the feeder-breaker taken on the plane
     designated by line 2–2 of Figure 6.14a
(c) Plan view of the feeder-breaker
(d) Cross-sectional elevational view of the feeder-breaker taken on the plane designated by
     line 4–4 in Figure 6.14c

Source: U.S. Patent 4,061,398

A continuous conveyor runs lengthwise of the chassis and comprises: a closed loop perforate chain conveyor 32 trained over sprockets 34 and 36 extending transversely across and supported by the chassis proximate its forward and rearward ends, respectively; a wedge wire grid 38 extending beneath the upstream end of the upper reach of the chain conveyor; and an imperforate plate 40 extending beneath the downstream end of the upper reach of the chain conveyor. The grid 38 and plate 40 are fixedly supported on the chassis 20 and the upper reach of the chain conveyor 32 is disposed to slidably move thereover. The sprockets 34 and 36 are mounted on the chassis for rotation about axes extending generally transversely thereof and drive motor 42 is mounted on the platform 28 and drives the sprocket 36 in a clockwise direction through means of a chain drive 44. The arrow lines in Figure 6.14d indicate the direction of travel of the upper reach of the belt and the direction of rotation of the sprockets 34 and 36.

The chain conveyor 32 is comprised of two sections, each of which extends lengthwise of the feeder-breaker, as may be seen from Figure 6.14c. Each section comprises a pair of chains 46 trained over the sprockets 34 and 36 and a plurality of bars 48 extending transversely between the chains thereof. The bars 48 function to drag aggregate pieces being processed over the upper surfaces of the grid 38 and plate 40. Such pieces are exemplified in Figure 6.14d and designated by the numeral 50 at the upstream portion of the apparatus and the numeral 52 at the downstream portion of the apparatus.

The difference in size between the pieces 50 and 52 is explained by the fact that a rotary breaker 54 is provided intermediate the upstream and downstream sections of the conveyor to reduce the size of the aggregate pieces which pass to the downstream section. The numeral 56, in Figure 6.14d, depicts aggregate pieces which have fallen through the grid 38. These pieces are of relatively small size and collect within a collection sump 58 supported by the chassis 20 intermediate the upper and lower reaches of the chain conveyor 32 and beneath the grid 28.

The rotary breaker 54 may be of the same general construction as that described in Application Ser. No. 597,985. It is supported on the chassis 22 for rotation about an axis extending transversely of the chassis and is driven through a chain drive 60 by a motor 62 supported on the platform 28.

As can best be seen from Figure 6.14d, the sump 58 is of elongated pan-like configuration and slopes downwardly from the forward end (left end, as viewed in Figure 6.14d) to the rearward end of the apparatus. Although referred to in the singular sense, it will be appreciated from Figure 6.14b that the sump actually comprises a pair of trough-like pans or trays and that a partition 64 separates the respective trough-like trays. The lowermost end of each tray of the sump 58 communicates with a jet pump 66 whereby fluid and aggregate particles which collect in the lower end of the sump are exhausted therefrom and pumped away.

The jet pumps 66 are of relatively conventional construction and may be of the type such as Hyjector (Babcock Hydro-Pneumatics, England). Each jet pump comprises a nozzle inlet 68 to which water under pressure is supplied by a feed line 70; an inlet 72 for receipt of the material collected within the sump 58; and a throat discharge 74 communicating with a discharge conduit 76 provided to receive and convey away material from the sump by the jet pump. The arrow lines in Figure 6.14c indicate the direction of flow of the fluid in the feed lines 70 and discharge conduits 76.

The chassis **20** also carries a support roller **78** for a conveyor belt **80** disposed to receive the aggregate pieces **52** as they spill over the downstream end of the conveyor belt **32**. Although not illustrated, it should be understood that the belt **80** would be suitably driven in the direction shown by the arrow line in Figure 6.14d and that the downstream end of the belt would be supported on a support roller. The length of the conveyor **80** and the manner in which it discharges or cooperates with other conveyors would depend upon the setup of the mine being worked.

The basic structure of the feeder-breaker apparatus is completed by a principal jet monitor **82** mounted on the forward end of the apparatus and a secondary jet monitor **84** mounted on the apparatus at a location generally above the breaker **54**. The monitors are provided with high-pressure water through a main supply conduit **86**. The conduit **86** branches to a supply conduit **88** for the monitor **82** and supply conduit for monitor **84**. Control valve **92** is provided in conduit **88**, and another, not shown, controls the conduit for **84**.

The monitor **82** is the principal working monitor of the breaker-feeder and is provided for the purpose of dislodging material from the mine being worked. The enlarged area **14** is intended to depict an area which has been so worked. A cylinder **96** is provided for selectively controlling the direction of the monitor. The monitor **84** is provided for the purpose of breaking up large aggregate pieces once they have been dislodged and have collected either on the floor of the mine or the forward portion of the feeder-breaker. A cylinder **98** is provided to control the direction of the monitor **84**. Because of its more limited function, the angle through which the monitor **84** may be swung is considerably more limited than that of the monitor **82**.

The supporting structure for the feeder-breaker apparatus also includes barriers disposed between the apparatus and the sides of the mine shaft, one such barrier being seen in Figure 6.14a and designated by the numeral **100**. The apparatus is also provided with a control station **102**, generally located somewhat to the rear and one side, as illustrated in Figure 6.14a. An operator is located within the control station and from there remotely controls the operation of the various parts of the feeder-breaker mechanism.

The process thus provides a method and apparatus wherein the mined material is selectively separated into constituents ideally suited for conveyance by pumping or dry conveyor and wherein the constituents for dry conveyance may be reduced in size to obtain optimum operation.

Mechanical Separation

F.A. Gray and J.A. Gray; U.S. Patent 3,891,550; June 24, 1975 describe a process for the mechanical separation of sand from mined bituminous sand deposits in which a mass of mined mixture sufficiently compacted is directed against an oleophilic surface displaceable generally transversely to the direction of the mass in a manner such that a portion of the mass is continuously applied to such surface in the form of a thin layer with the surface being driven at a rate of displacement sufficient to dislodge the sand from the applied layer and recovering the bitumen-enriched residue adhered to the oleophilic surface at a point remote from the region of application and after dislodgment of the sand. It is also a feature to provide a block, preferably of a resilient nature, to bear against the applied thin layer of mixture immediately following its application of the oleophilic surface which enhances the tendency of the bitumen-enriched residue to adhere to the oleophilic surface and increases the tendency of the sand to separate from the mixture under the influence of centrifugal forces thereby improving the efficiency.

Abrading Technique

A process described by *D.J. Harding; U.S. Patent 4,110,195; August 29, 1978; assigned to Magna International Inc., Canada* relates to an apparatus and process for extracting bitumen from mineral particles such as sand. The process avoids many of the problems of the conventional hot water or solvent extraction processes by using an abrading process to remove the bitumen or oil from sand particles, using cool water and little solvent.

The abrading process involves agitating a pulp of tar sand and water, preferably with some small amount of diluent, and then moving this around an annular space at a speed low enough to allow settling of clean sand to form a sand bed in contact with the moving pulp, the speed being high enough to prevent settling of bitumen-coated sand particles, so that the bitumen is abraded from the sand particles and rises in the pulp. Fines and clay which are removed with the water and bitumen can be separated from the water, after removal of the bitumen, to give a sludge suitable for mixing with the clean sand prior to disposal.

Electric Flotation Cell

A process described by *F.E. Vermeulen and F.S. Chute; U.S. Patent 4,136,014; January 23, 1979; assigned to Canadian Patents & Development Limited, Canada* involves an apparatus for the separation of bitumen from tar sands using an electric flotation cell formed of a container in which is placed a charge of unseparated tar sand to a first level and which is then filled with water to a second level and electrodes positioned in the cell in relation to the tar sand such that on application of a voltage to the electrodes an electric current flows through the tar sand and water. It has been found that, after application of the electrical energy to the tar sands, agitation and then separation takes place with the bitumen being floated to the upper surface.

Reduction of Solids Content of Sludge

F.A. Bain and J.O.L. Roberts; U.S. Patent 4,018,664; April 19, 1977; assigned to Great Canadian Oil Sands Limited, Canada describe a process for treating retention pond sludge containing at least 20% solids and associated with the hot water extraction of bitumen from tar sands. More specifically, the process comprises withdrawing a sludge material containing at least 20 wt % solids from a retention pond and agitating the sludge material with additional water containing less than 6% solids to provide a diluted sludge final composition having 6 to 18 wt % dispersed solids therein. The diluted sludge is thereafter settled to provide a lower layer containing a concentration of solids greater than that of the undiluted sludge; a middle layer containing a lower quantity of solids than the diluted sludge; and an upper layer comprised of bituminous froth. The lower layer from this settling step can thereafter be withdrawn and treated to remove the mineral matter and other solids from the water by procedures such as by evaporation and consolidation and other similar means. The bitumen floating on the upper layer of the settling zone can be recovered for use in the production of synthetic crude. Finally, the aqueous middle layer of this settling zone can be stored in a separate storage zone or can optionally be returned to a retention pond such as the pond from which it was originally withdrawn for further settling to provide a supernatant layer of reduced solids suitable for use in the hot water extraction of bitumen from tar sands.

As an example, a typical retention pond associated with the hot water extraction process suitable for processing approximately 140,000 to 150,000 tons of tar sands a day could provide enough sludge material to operate the process at the rate of about 9,000 to 15,000 IGPM (Imperial gallons per minute) on a continuous basis. In processing this quantity of sludge, feed rates could be maintained at about 3,000 to 5,000 IGPM of high solids sludge combined with about 6,000 to 10,000 IGPM of low solids pond water.

By this sludge treating process, it is possible to remove dispersed solids from the pond in the form of sludge at about the same rate as the sludge layer is being formed in the pond. Also, this method provides a means for recovering bitumen from sludge which provides an additional economic incentive to the process.

F.A. Bain and J.O.L. Roberts; U.S. Patent 4,008,146; February 15, 1977; assigned to Great Canadian Oil Sands Limited, Canada describe a process for reducing the quantity of sludge and, in particular, clay dispersed in a wastewater retention pond associated with the hot water process for extracting bitumen from tar sands.

In the process, sludge from a hot water extraction retention pond is mixed with an effluent discharge stream from a hot water extraction process containing at least 20% sand and thereafter settled to form a lower sludge-sand layer and an upper aqueous layer. The lower layer is dispersed over an inclined sand pile zone to form additional sand layers on the sand pile having sludge in the interstices. By this procedure, the sand settled in the sand pile zone contains substantially more clay than sand settled from a hot water extraction process wastewater stream. The upper layer from the settling zone can be transferred to a storage zone, as for example, the retention pond for subsequent settling and use of water released in the hot water extraction process.

Sludge Accumulation and Compaction

R.A. Baillie and J.V.D. Fear; U.S. Patent 3,931,006; January 6, 1976; assigned to Great Canadian Oil Sands Limited, Canada describe a process for treating a retention pond containing the effluent discharge normally provided when bitumen is recovered from tar sands by way of hot water extraction techniques. Most particularly, the process provides a means whereby the sludge layer of the pond is reduced in volume to provide a pond having a lower volume of sludge and, therefore, an overall reduction in colloidally dispersed mineral matter.

The method essentially comprises discharging the effluent from the hot water extraction procedure in a manner so that it is widely dispersed over the surface of the retention pond. This method of adding effluent discharge to the pond allows the sand particles in the effluent to rain down on the pond and thereby rain down through the sludge layer at the bottom of the pond. By this procedure, a part of the dispersed silt and clay in this sludge layer is included in the interstitial volume between sand grains so as to provide a pond containing a substantially smaller sludge layer volume. As a result of the method of the process, more of the water in the pond is suitable for recycle to the hot water extraction technique thereby incorporating efficiencies of water usage in separation of bitumen from tar sands.

Example: As a typical example of utilization of the process, an effluent from the hot water extraction of bitumen from tar sands having approximately 48% water by weight, 40% by weight sand, 2% by weight silt, 9% by weight clay and 1% by weight bitumen was collected from the hot water extraction as an effluent discharge and is sprayed over the surface in an arc of about 100 ft in diameter of a settling pond of approximately 380 acres in surface area. The sand in the effluent is provided at the rate of about 180 tons per day per acre. The pond has an average depth of about 40 ft.

For any noticeable effect to be realized the effluent sprayed on the pond should be applied to provide from about 50 tons per day per acre of pond to about 500 tons per day per acre of pond. The means of applying the effluent discharge to the pond can include a floating barge with a flexible line which permits continuous change in the area of application of the effluent discharge stream.

Freeze-Thaw Method for Reducing Clay Content of Wash Water

J.S. Boyer; U.S. Patent 4,018,682; April 19, 1977; assigned to Sunoco Energy Development Co. describes a method for reducing the clay content of a colloidal clay-water mixture which comprises combining the mixture with air at superatmospheric pressure and expelling the mixture in the form of small droplets at atmospheric pressure at a temperature below 32°F to form synthetic snow. Thereafter, synthetic snow can be melted to recover water containing reduced mineral content. The process is particularly applicable to sludge associated with hot water extraction method for recovering bitumen from tar sands.

As one mode of the process, the following example is provided. An aqueous sludge, having a temperature of about 60°F, is withdrawn from a retention pond which stores wastewater associated with the hot water extraction of bitumen from tar sands. The sludge is characterized as containing 4.3% hydrocarbons, 0.9% sand, 15.8% silt, 7.1% clay and 71.3% water.

The sludge is passed through a heat-exchanging means and recovered at a temperature of about 33°F. The sludge is fed at a rate of 100 gpm at a pressure of 150 psig to a snow gun approximately 4 ft long and 4 inches in diameter having a nozzle on the outlet end 2.5 inches long and a 1.25 inch diameter opening. The snow gun contains an inlet means on one end for the addition of sludge. Air is also added to the sludge in the gun at 150 psig and about 700 ft³ per minute. The ambient temperature of the air is at about –6°F. Artificial snow is formed from the sludge by the rapid expansion of the sludge-air mixture being expelled from the nozzle of the gun. Upon melting, the artificial snow produces water substantially reduced in mineral content.

Clarification of Clay-Containing Water

A process described by *G.A. Specken; U.S. Patent 4,069,152; January 17, 1978* relates to the clarification of clay-containing water of the kind which is obtained from the processing of oil or bituminous sands or from oil and gas well drilling sites. According to the process, it has been found that such clay-containing water can be clarified to a suitable extent by the use of an alkali permanganate, such as potassium permanganate. The permanganate is preferably supplied to the water at a concentration in the range of from about 0.5 to 500 ppm by weight, the actual amount required depending upon the clay concentration in the water which will most likely be in the range of from about 500 to 100,000 ppm.

In general, a concentration of permanganate in the range from about 20 to 100 ppm will be sufficiently effective. The actual amount of permanganate required for any specific clay-containing water of the kind concerned can be determined by routine trial and experiment. In any particular case, it is desirable to use as little permanganate as possible so as to reduce the cost of the clarification process.

It has been found that water of the kind concerned can be adequately clarified by the use of the permanganate alone without requiring additional steps, such as aeration or pH adjustment or the use of some other coagulant. By adequate clarification is meant substantial reduction in the clay concentration, down to perhaps as low as 100 ppm. The reason for the success of the permanganate treatment with clay-containing water of the kind concerned is not clear, but it is thought that the permanganate somehow affects the absorption of hydrocarbons by the clay particles with the result that the clay particles are not kept apart but proceed to coagulate.

In some cases, the use of permanganate alone may result in the clarification process taking rather longer than is desired in commercial practice. It has been found that the clarification process can be expedited by the addition of a water-soluble anionic and/or nonionic polyelectrolyte either before or after the addition of the permanganate. The polyelectrolyte acts as a flocculant. An anionic polyelectrolyte is preferred.

The clarification of the clay-containing water depends on the rate of collision of the suspended clay particles, the permanganate promoting the agglomeration of the clay particles upon collision. This increase in the rate of clarification when the permanganate treatment is preceded or followed by addition of a polyelectrolyte of the kind described above is thought to be due to an effective increase in the rate of collision, the increase perhaps being due, at least in part, to the attractive forces between the charged clay particles and the polyelectrolyte molecules. It has been found that the polyelectrolyte is most effective in increasing the rate of clarification if it is added to the clay-containing water immediately after addition of the permanganate.

COMPANY INDEX

INVENTOR INDEX

U.S. PATENT NUMBER INDEX

4,007,788 - 272	4,043,897 - 37	4,082,145 - 200
4,007,963 - 189	4,045,085 - 129	4,082,146 - 211
4,008,145 - 240	4,045,086 - 413	4,082,645 - 71
4,008,146 - 419	4,046,195 - 313	4,082,646 - 410
4,008,761 - 331	4,046,668 - 377	4,083,404 - 317
4,008,762 - 331	4,046,669 - 389	4,083,604 - 158
4,008,764 - 291	4,047,760 - 163	4,083,770 - 69
4,008,765 - 262	4,048,053 - 256	4,084,637 - 330
4,010,092 - 31	4,052,293 - 105	4,084,640 - 179
4,014,575 - 194	4,054,492 - 364	4,085,030 - 80
4,016,239 - 111	4,054,505 - 398	4,085,972 - 229
4,017,119 - 157	4,054,506 - 398	4,086,962 - 211
4,017,377 - 373	4,056,461 - 97	4,086,963 - 211
4,018,280 - 183	4,057,485 - 389	4,087,347 - 96
4,018,572 - 257	4,057,486 - 401	4,088,562 - 97
4,018,664 - 418	4,057,490 - 240	4,089,375 - 188
4,018,665 - 358	4,058,164 - 268	4,090,945 - 45
4,018,682 - 420	4,058,205 - 86	4,090,951 - 251
4,019,575 - 262	4,058,905 - 55	4,091,869 - 158
4,019,578 - 268	4,059,152 - 313	4,092,237 - 52
4,020,901 - 268	4,059,308 - 177	4,093,027 - 274
4,022,277 - 302	4,060,479 - 39	4,094,767 - 412
4,022,280 - 268	4,061,190 - 180	4,094,768 - 369
4,022,511 - 205	4,061,398 - 413	4,094,769 - 55
4,024,915 - 313	4,063,780 - 168	4,094,781 - 390
4,025,115 - 129	4,064,018 - 72	4,096,057 - 378
4,025,416 - 63	4,065,183 - 176	4,096,912 - 167
4,026,357 - 413	4,065,361 - 101	4,097,360 - 90
4,026,358 - 287	4,066,127 - 275	4,098,648 - 380
4,026,359 - 227	4,066,529 - 52	4,098,674 - 364
4,026,360 - 230	4,067,390 - 232	4,099,783 - 260
4,027,731 - 297	4,067,391 - 305	4,101,172 - 273
4,027,917 - 171	4,067,616 - 298	4,101,412 - 75
4,028,222 - 98	4,067,796 - 378	4,102,773 - 80
4,029,360 - 206	4,068,716 - 286	4,105,072 - 200
4,029,568 - 389	4,068,717 - 274	4,105,502 - 75
4,033,412 - 289	4,069,107 - 95	4,105,536 - 239
4,033,853 - 359	4,069,132 - 65	4,105,537 - 369
4,034,812 - 289	4,069,133 - 65	4,105,664 - 158
4,035,282 - 361	4,069,152 - 421	4,106,814 - 142
4,036,299 - 189	4,070,250 - 75	4,107,029 - 367
4,036,732 - 396	4,071,432 - 70	4,108,760 - 375
4,037,657 - 168	4,071,433 - 407	4,109,715 - 282
4,037,658 - 262	4,071,434 - 407	4,109,718 - 202
4,039,427 - 44	4,071,435 - 252	4,109,720 - 294
4,042,027 - 294	4,071,458 - 286	4,110,193 - 91
4,042,485 - 37	4,072,350 - 172	4,110,194 - 395
4,043,595 - 131	4,075,081 - 238	4,110,195 - 418
4,043,596 - 130	4,075,083 - 38	4,114,687 - 278
4,043,597 - 132	4,076,311 - 283	4,114,690 - 309
4,043,598 - 132	4,076,312 - 202	4,114,691 - 278
4,043,881 - 115	4,079,784 - 320	4,116,180 - 45
4,043,884 - 254	4,080,285 - 240	4,117,886 - 209

NOTICE

Nothing contained in this Review shall be construed to constitute a permission or recommendation to practice any invention covered by any patent without a license from the patent owners. Further, neither the author nor the publisher assumes any liability with respect to the use of, or for damages resulting from the use of, any information, apparatus, method or process described in this Review.

OFFSHORE OIL TECHNOLOGY

Recent Developments 1979

by M.William Ranney

Energy Technology Review No. 38
Ocean Technology Review No. 8

From the time the first submersible drilling structure was used in the Gulf of Mexico in the late 1940s, technology for offshore drilling developed rapidly to service the needs originated with this new era in oil and gas exploitation.

Today engineers are continuing to design new apparatus and systems to improve the world's supply of these resources. This text keeps the reader abreast of these latest developments.

The first chapter reviews the activity in offshore drilling to date, discussing the mobile and fixed structures and equipment employed. Subsequent chapters detail approximately 170 recent processes, many of which are even now being implemented throughout the industry. These processes include the key areas of platform erection, drilling operations, wellhead construction, and storage facilities. Over 80 figures and illustrations accompany the process descriptions.

The partial, condensed table of contents presented below with chapter headings and some subtitles demonstrates the comprehensive range of this text. The numbers in parentheses signify the total number of processes covered in each chapter.

ISBN 0-8155-0741-0

399 pages

CRUDE OIL DRILLING FLUIDS
1979

by Maurice William Ranney

Chemical Technology Review No. 121
Energy Technology Review No. 35

The drilling of oil wells into subterranean reservoirs presents many problems concerning the choice of a drilling fluid. Rotary drilling rigs are used nowadays almost universally throughout the world's oil regions. Perhaps the greatest advantages of rotary drilling over other methods is that the well bore is kept full of liquid during drilling. A weighted fluid (also called drilling mud) in the bore hole serves two important purposes: by its hydrostatic pressure it blocks the entry of formation fluids into the well, thus preventing blowouts and gushers. In addition, the drilling mud carries the crushed rock to the surface, so that the drilling is continuous until the bit wears out.

This apparent simplicity of the process is complicated by many factors, such as sealing the productive formation with a casing, which must have openings to allow the oil to enter the well under controlled conditions.

Many new, potentially oil-producing areas are being explored under oceans, and in arctic and desert regions. Increasing emphasis is also placed on secondary recovery techniques. Research and development activity therefore centers on improvements in drilling fluids, stimulation methods and secondary recovery processes involving water and polymer flooding techniques.

This book, focusing on the U.S. patent literature since 1974, encompasses over 250 processes. A partial and condensed table of contents follows here. Chapter headings and important subtitles are given. Numbers in parentheses indicate the number of processes per topic.

Note: These recent processes provide hundreds of formulations, techniques and new developments which will be used to efficiently recover crude oil from subterranean oil reservoirs in the coming years.

ISBN 0-8155-0732-1

348 pages

BOILER FUEL ADDITIVES FOR POLLUTION REDUCTION AND ENERGY SAVING 1978

Edited by R.C. Eliot

Energy Technology Review No. 33
Pollution Technology Review No. 53
Chemical Technology Review No. 120

Problems of incomplete combustion, soot deposition, and sludge formation are common to a greater or lesser degree with all hydrocarbon fuel oils, especially those sold for use in heavy duty installations, e.g., furnaces and boilers in power plants, large office buildings, hospitals, etc. The problem of particulate emissions is particularly acute, as these carbonaceous contaminants are currently a violation of local anti-pollution laws in many communities.

This book reflects the findings of investigations conducted for the U.S. Environmental Protection Agency and the Federal Energy Administration with the purpose of determining the effectiveness of chemical additives not only in reducing smoke and particulate emissions, but also as a means of increasing overall boiler efficiency, and thus conserving fuel. A survey of the recent patent literature is included.

Various kinds of compounds have shown merit as combustion improvers, including surfactants, organometallics, and low-molecular-weight polymers. Alkaline-earth and transition metal additives in concentrations of 20 ppm to 50 ppm of metal in the fuel oil were effective in reducing particulate emissions. For added versatility the organo-metallic compound is usually blended with dispersants and other ingredients to make a multipurpose product. Judicious application of these "combustion catalysts" should enable the user to cut fuel costs, while lowering air pollution at the same time. A partial table of contents follows here:

ISBN 0-8155-0729-1

230 pages

THE PETROLEUM REFINING INDUSTRY
ENERGY SAVING AND ENVIRONMENTAL CONTROL
1978

by Marshall Sittig

Energy Technology Review No. 24
Pollution Technology Review No. 39

With hardly any new oil refining facilities being built in the United States, this book is especially timely, because existing refineries must necessarily undertake much restructuring and retrofitting to conform to changing technology and product demand.

Some process changes, particularly upgrading of gasoline fractions, due to the elimination of tetraethyl lead, demand more energy; yet savings are possible by switching large process heaters and boilers from gas to liquid fuels. Raising the octane numbers by stricter catalytic reforming produces less gasoline and more sulfur-containing waste oil.

New techniques call for hydrosulfurization units using hydrogen. Hydrogen is dissolved in the liquid product and mixed with purge gas. This is applicable to crudes and wastes. Up to 85% sulfur in the catalytic cracker feed can be removed, and 90% removal of the sulfur in the residuum is realized in an environmentally acceptable manner.

This book demonstrates several processing strategies for wastewater and sulfur emissions. The high amounts of H_2S and NH_3 present in wastewater from Mid-East crudes often makes recovery of these chemicals economically attractive and avoids the effluence of pollutants.

Many other approaches to saving energy and avoiding pollution at profit level in existing and projected refining units are presented in this volume, which is based on various technological studies and U.S. patents. A partial, condensed table of contents follows here.

ISBN 0-8155-0694-5

374 pages

ENHANCED OIL RECOVERY

Secondary and Tertiary Methods 1978

Edited by M. M. Schumacher

Chemical Technology Review No. 103
Energy Technology Review No. 22

This is a book about greater oil recovery by succeeding methods; the possible techniques and their present or future capabilities for extracting more petroleum from oil fields after primary production.

Those methods are also applicable to fields which were abandoned in previous decades when there was a plentiful supply of energy. Sometimes less than one-third of the crude oil in place was recovered, when only the original reservoir pressure was allowed to drive the oil into the producing well.

The concept of enhanced oil recovery applies to a whole collection of methods which are becoming increasingly profitable as energy becomes more expensive and the price of oil goes up. Each method appears to have its own claimed unique capability to extract the most oil from a particular reservoir.

After a decline in pressure has caused the oil recovery to become uneconomic, oil production can be increased by immiscible gas injection and waterflooding. These traditional "secondary" methods are now being supplemented by "tertiary" recovery methods including miscible fluid displacement, microemulsion (micellar) flooding, cyclic steam injection, controlled *in situ* combustion (fireflood) and other related techniques which are either thermal or miscible methods, thereby reducing the surface tension between oil and driving fluid.

Most of the data in this book are based on federally funded studies—a partial and condensed list of contents follows here:

1. DEMAND & SUPPLY
Primary Production
Enhanced Oil Recovery (EOR)
Promise & Potential of EOR
GURC Forecast
Oil Prices vs. EOR Development

2. SECONDARY METHODS
Formation Energy
Pressure Maintenance
Waterflooding
Treatment of Injection Waters
Immiscible Gas Injection

3. TERTIARY RECOVERY—MISCIBLE AGENTS
HC-Miscible Flooding
CO_2-Miscible Flooding
Polymer-Augmented Waterflooding
Micellar Flooding

Performance & Problems
Costs vs. Performance

4. TERTIARY RECOVERY—THERMAL TECHNIQUES
Cyclic Steam Injection
Limitations & Economics
Steam Drive
in situ Combustion
Necessity for Materials Research
Future Projects

5. VARIOUS METHODS
Oil Recovery by Nuclear
   Explosions
Nuclear Stimulation
Seismic & Pollutant Effects
Underground Reservoir Construction

6. SELECTION OF APPROPRIATE TECHNIQUES
Screening Methods
Potentials & Profits

7. MATERIALS NEEDED
Chemicals Used
Water Supplies
Energy Requirements
Research Needs

8. ENVIRONMENTAL ASPECTS
Chemical Hazards
Effects on Groundwater
Emission of
   Steam & Gases

9. STATE OF THE ART
Field Tests Made
Field Test Activity in Texas
Project Developments
Classification by
   Location & Methods

10. EOR PROJECTS FOR RECOVERY OF VISCOUS OILS
The "Heavy Oil" Problem
Solvent Stimulation
   in California
Solvents & Explosives
   to Recover Heavy Oil
   in Kansas
Thermal Recovery of
   Viscous Oils

11. THE FUTURE OF EOR
Constraints to Development
Necessity for Federal
   Participation
Industry's Choices

ISBN 0-8155-0692-9

207 pages